The
Fairy–Faith
in
Celtic Countries

The Fairy-Faith
in
Celtic Countries

W. Y. Evans-Wentz

DOVER PUBLICATIONS, INC.
Mineola, New York

Bibliographical Note

This Dover edition, first published in 2002, is an unabridged republication of the work originally published in 1911 by Henry Frowde, London.

Library of Congress Cataloging-in-Publication Data

Evans-Wentz, W. Y. (Walter Yeeling), 1878-1965.
 The fairy-faith in Celtic countries / W.Y. Evans-Wentz.
  p. cm.
 Originally published: London ; New York : H. Froude, 1911.
 Includes index.
 ISBN-13: 978-0-486-42522-1
 ISBN-10: 0-486-42522-3
  1. Celts—Folklore. 2. Fairies. 3. Celts—Religion I. Title.

GR137 .E9 2002
398'.089'916—dc21

2002074183

Manufactured in the United States by LSC Communications
42522308   2022
www.doverpublications.com

THIS BOOK

DEPENDS CHIEFLY UPON THE ORAL AND WRITTEN TESTIMONY
SO FREELY CONTRIBUTED BY ITS MANY CELTIC AUTHORS,—
THE PEASANT AND THE SCHOLAR, THE PRIEST AND THE SCIENTIST,
THE POET AND THE BUSINESS MAN, THE SEER AND THE NON-SEER,—
AND IN HONOUR OF THEM

I DEDICATE

IT TO

TWO OF THEIR BRETHREN IN IRELAND:

A. E.,

WHOSE UNWAVERING LOYALTY TO THE FAIRY-FAITH
HAS INSPIRED MUCH THAT I HAVE HEREIN WRITTEN,
WHOSE FRIENDLY GUIDANCE IN MY STUDY OF IRISH MYSTICISM
I MOST GRATEFULLY ACKNOWLEDGE ;

AND

WILLIAM BUTLER YEATS,

WHO BROUGHT TO ME AT MY OWN ALMA MATER IN CALIFORNIA
THE FIRST MESSAGE FROM FAIRYLAND,
AND WHO AFTERWARDS IN HIS OWN COUNTRY
LED ME THROUGH THE HAUNTS OF FAIRY KINGS AND QUEENS.

OXFORD
November 1911.

'It remains for ever true that the proper study of mankind is man; and even early man is not beneath contempt, especially when he proves to have had within him the makings of a great race, with its highest notions of duty and right, and all else that is noblest in the human soul.'

The Right Hon. SIR JOHN RHŶS.

CONTENTS

PREFACE

DURING the years 1907–9 this study first took shape, being then based mainly on literary sources; and during the latter year it was successfully presented to the Faculty of Letters of the University of Rennes, Brittany, for the Degree of *Docteur-ès-Lettres*. Since then I have re-investigated the whole problem of the Celtic belief in Fairies, and have collected very much fresh material. Two years ago the scope of my original research was limited to the four chief Celtic countries, but now it includes all of the Celtic countries.

In the present study, which has profited greatly by criticisms of the first passed by scholars in Britain and in France, the original literary point of view is combined with the broader point of view of anthropology. This study, the final and more comprehensive form of my views about the 'Fairy-Faith', would never have been possible had I not enjoyed during many months the kindly advice and constant encouragement of Mr. R. R. Marett, Reader in Social Anthropology in the University of Oxford, and Fellow of Exeter College.

During May 1910 the substance of this essay in its pan-Celtic form was submitted to the Board of the Faculty of Natural Science of Oxford University for the Research Degree of Bachelor of Science, which was duly granted. But the present work contains considerable material not contained in the essay presented to the Oxford examiners, the Right Hon. Sir John Rhŷs and Mr. Andrew Lang; and, therefore, I alone assume entire responsibility for all its possible shortcomings, and in particular for some of its more speculative theories, which to some minds may appear to be in conflict with orthodox views, whether of the theologian or of the man of science. These theories, however venturesome they may appear, are put forth in almost every

case with the full approval of some reliable, scholarly Celt;
and as such they are chiefly intended to make the exposition
of the belief in fairies as completely and as truly Celtic
as possible, without much regard for non-Celtic opinion,
whether this be in harmony with Celtic opinion or not.

As the new manuscript of the ' Fairy-Faith ' lies before
me revised and finished, I realize even more fully than I did
two years ago with respect to the original study, how little
right I have to call it mine. Those to whom the credit for
it really belongs are my many kind friends and helpers in
Ireland, Scotland, Isle of Man, Wales, Cornwall, and Brittany,
and many others who are not Celts, in the three great nations
—happily so intimately united now by unbreakable bonds
of goodwill and international brotherhood—Britain, France,
and the United States of America ; for without the aid of
all these Celtic and non-Celtic friends the work could never
have been accomplished. They have given me their best
and rarest thoughts as so many golden threads ; I have
only furnished the mental loom, and woven these golden
threads together in my own way according to what I take
to be the psychological pattern of the Fairy-Faith.

I am under a special obligation to the following six dis-
tinguished Celtic scholars who have contributed, for my
second chapter, the six introductions to the fairy-lore
collected by me in their respective countries :—Dr. Douglas
Hyde (Ireland) ; Dr. Alexander Carmichael (Scotland);
Miss Sophia Morrison (Isle of Man) ; the Right Hon.
Sir John Rhŷs (Wales) ; Mr. Henry Jenner (Cornwall);
Professor Anatole Le Braz (Brittany).

I am also greatly indebted to the Rev. J. Estlin Carpenter,
Principal of Manchester College, for having aided me with
the parts of this book touching Christian theology; to
Mr. R. I. Best, M.R.I.A., Assistant Librarian, National
Library, Dublin, for having aided me with the parts de-
voted to Irish mythology and literature; and to Mr. William
McDougall, Wilde Reader in Mental Philosophy in the
University of Oxford, for a similar service with respect to
Section IV, entitled ' Science and Fairies '. And to these

and to all the other scholars whose names appear in this preface, my heartiest thanks are due for the assistance which they have so kindly rendered in reading different parts of the *Fairy-Faith* when in proof.

With the deep spirit of reverence which a student feels towards his preceptors, I acknowledge a still greater debt to those among my friends and helpers who have been my Celtic guides and teachers. Here in Oxford University I have run up a long account with the Right Hon. Sir John Rhŷs, the Professor of Celtic, who has introduced me to the study of Modern Irish, and of Arthurian romance and mythology, and has guided me both during the year 1907–8 and ever since in Celtic folk-lore generally. To Mr. Andrew Lang, I am likewise a debtor, more especially in view of the important suggestions which he has given me during the past two years with respect to anthropology and to psychical research. In my relation to the Faculty of Letters of the University of Rennes, I shall always remember the friendly individual assistance offered to me there during the year 1908–9 by Professor Joseph Loth, then Dean in that University, but now of the College of France, in Paris, particularly with respect to Brythonic mythology, philology, and archaeology ; by Professor Georges Dottin, particularly with respect to Gaelic matters ; and by Professor Anatole Le Braz, whose continual good wishes towards my work have been a constant source of inspiration since our first meeting during March 1908, especially in my investigation of *La Légende de la Mort*, and of the related traditions and living folk-beliefs in Brittany—Brittany with its haunted ground of Carnac, home of the ancient Brythonic Mysteries.

W. Y. E. W.

JESUS COLLEGE, OXFORD.
All Saints' Day, 1911.

' There, neither turmoil nor silence. . . .

' Though fair the sight of Erin's plains, hardly will they seem so after you have known the Great Plain. . . .

' A wonder of a land the land of which I speak ; no youth there grows to old age. . . .

' We behold and are not beheld.'—The God Midir, in *Tochmarc Etaine*.

INTRODUCTION

'I have told what I have seen, what I have thought, and what I have learned by inquiry.'—HERODOTUS.

I. THE RELIGIOUS NATURE OF THE FAIRY-FAITH

THERE is probably no other place in Celtic lands more congenial, or more inspiring for the writing down of one's deeper intuitions about the Fairy-Faith, than Carnac, under the shadow of the pagan tumulus and mount of the sacred fire, now dedicated by triumphant Christianity to the Archangel Michael. The very name of Carnac is significant ; [1] and in two continents, Africa and Europe—to follow the certain evidence of archaeology alone [2]—there seem to have been no greater centres for ancient religion than Karnak in Egypt and Carnac in Brittany. On the banks of the Nile the Children of Isis and Osiris erected temples as perfect as human art can make them ; on the shores of the Morbihan the mighty men who were, as it seems, the teachers of our own Celtic forefathers, erected temples of unhewn stone. The wonderful temples in Yucatan, the temple-caves of prehistoric India, Stonehenge in England, the Parthenon, the Acropolis, St. Peter's at Rome, Westminster Abbey, or Notre-Dame, and the Pyramids and temples of Egypt, equally with the Alignements of Carnac, each in their own way record more or less perfectly man's attempt to express materially what he feels spiritually. Perfected art can beautify and make more attractive to the eye and mind, but it cannot enhance in any degree the innate spiritual

---

[1] Quite appropriately it means *place of cairns* or *tumuli*—those prehistoric monuments religious and funereal in their purposes. *Carnac* seems to be a Gallo-Roman form. According to Professor J. Loth, the Breton (Celtic) forms would be : old Celtic, *Carnáco-s* ; old Breton (ninth-eleventh century), *Carnoc* ; Middle Breton (eleventh-sixteenth century), *Carneuc* ; Modern Breton, *Carnec*.

[2] For we cannot offer any proof of what at first sight appears like a philological relation or identity between *Carnac* and *Karnak*.

ideals which men in all ages have held ; and thus it is that
we read amid the rough stone menhirs and dolmens in
Brittany, as amid the polished granite monoliths and
magnificent temples in Egypt, the same silent message from
the past to the present, from the dead to the living. This
message, we think, is fundamentally important in understanding the Celtic Fairy-Faith ; for in our opinion the
belief in fairies has the same origin as all religions and
mythologies.

And there seems never to have been an uncivilized tribe,
a race, or nation of civilized men who have not had some
form of belief in an unseen world, peopled by unseen beings.
In religions, mythologies, and the Fairy-Faith, too, we
behold the attempts which have been made by different
peoples in different ages to explain in terms of human experience this unseen world, its inhabitants, its laws, and
man's relation to it. The Ancients called its inhabitants
gods, genii, daemons, and shades ; Christianity knows them
as angels, saints, demons, and souls of the dead ; to uncivilized tribes they are gods, demons, and spirits of ancestors ; and the Celts think of them as gods, and as fairies of
many kinds.

II THE INTERPRETATION OF THE FAIRY-FAITH

By the Celtic Fairy-Faith we mean that specialized form
of belief in a spiritual realm inhabited by spiritual beings
which has existed from prehistoric times until now in
Ireland, Scotland, Isle of Man, Wales, Cornwall, Brittany,
or other parts of the ancient empire of the Celts. In studying this belief, we are concerned directly with living Celtic
folk-traditions, and with past Celtic folk-traditions as recorded in literature. And if fairies actually exist as invisible
beings or intelligences, and our investigations lead us to the
tentative hypothesis that they do, they are natural and not
supernatural, for nothing which exists can be supernatural ;
and, therefore, it is our duty to examine the Celtic Fairy
Races just as we examine any fact in the visible realm

wherein we now live, whether it be a fact of chemistry, of physics, or of biology. However, as we proceed to make such an examination, we shall have to remember constantly that there is a new set of ideas to work with, entirely different from what we find in natural sciences, and often no adequate vocabulary based on common human experiences. An American who has travelled in Asia and an Englishman who has travelled in Australia may meet in Paris and exchange travelling experiences with mutual understanding, because both of them have experienced travel ; and they will have an adequate vocabulary to describe each experience, because most men have also experienced travel. But a saint who has known the spiritual condition called ecstasy cannot explain ecstasy to a man who has never known it, and if he should try to do so would discover at once that no modern language is suitable for the purpose. His experience is rare and not universal, and men have developed no complete vocabulary to describe experiences not common to the majority of mankind, and this is especially true of psychical experiences. It is the same in dealing with fairies, as these are hypothetically conceived, for only a few men and women can assert that they have seen fairies, and hence there is no adequate vocabulary to describe fairies. Among the Ancients, who dealt so largely with psychical sciences, there seems to have been a common language which could be used to explain the invisible world and its inhabitants ; but we of this age have not yet developed such a language. Consequently, men who deny human immortality, as well as men with religious faith who have not through personal psychical experiences transformed that faith into a fact, nowadays when they happen to read what Plato, Iamblichus, or any of the Neo-Platonists have written, or even what moderns have written in attempting to explain psychic facts, call it all mysticism. And to the great majority of Europeans and Americans, mysticism is a most convenient noun, applicable to anything which may seem reasonable yet wholly untranslatable in terms of their own individual experience ; and mysticism usually means something quite the reverse of scientific simply because we have by usage unwisely limited the meaning of the word *science* to a knowledge of things material and visible, whereas it really means a knowing or a knowledge of everything which exists. We have tried to deal with the rare psychical experiences of Irish, Scotch, Manx, Welsh, or Breton seers, and psychics generally, in the clearest language possible ; but if now and then we are charged with being mystical, this is our defence.

III THE METHOD OF STUDYING THE FAIRY-FAITH

In this study, which is first of all a folk-lore study, we pursue principally an anthropo-psychological method of interpreting the Celtic belief in fairies, though we do not hesitate now and then to call in the aid of philology ; and we make good use of the evidence offered by mythologies, religions, metaphysics, and physical sciences. Folk-lore, a century ago was considered beneath the serious consideration of scholars ; but there has come about a complete reversal of scholarly opinion, for now it is seen that the beliefs of the people, their legends, and their songs are the source of nearly all literatures, and that their institutions and customs are the origin of those of modern times. And, to-day, to the new science of folk-lore,—which, as Mr. Andrew Lang says, must be taken to include psychical research or psychical sciences,—archaeology, anthropology, and comparative mythology and religion are indispensable. Thus folk-lore offers the scientific means of studying man in the sense meant by the poet who declared that the proper study of mankind is man.

IV DIVISIONS OF THE STUDY

This study is divided into four sections or parts. The first one deals with the living Fairy-Faith among the Celts themselves ; the second, with the recorded and ancient Fairy-Faith as we find it in Celtic literature and mythology ; the third, with the Fairy-Faith in its religious aspects ; and in the fourth section an attempt has been made to suggest how the theories of our newest science, psychical research, explain the belief in fairies.

I have set forth in the first section in detail and as clearly as possible the testimony communicated to me by living Celts who either believe in fairies, or else say that they have seen fairies; and throughout other sections I have preferred to draw as much as possible of the material from men and women rather than from books. Books too often are written out of other books, and too seldom from the life of man; and in a scientific study of the Fairy-Faith, such as we have undertaken, the Celt himself is by far the best, in fact the only authority. For us it is much less important to know what scholars think of fairies than to know what the Celtic people think of fairies. This is especially true in considering the Fairy-Faith as it exists now.

V   THE COLLECTING OF MATERIAL

In June, 1908, after a year's preparatory work in things Celtic under the direction of the Oxford Professor of Celtic, Sir John Rhŷs, I began to travel in Wales, Ireland, Scotland, and Brittany, and to collect material there at first hand from the people who have shaped and who still keep alive the Fairy-Faith; and during the year 1909–10 fresh folklore expeditions were made into Brittany, Ireland, and Wales, and then, finally, the study of the Fairy-Faith was made pan-Celtic by similar expeditions throughout the Isle of Man, and into Cornwall. Many of the most remote parts of these lands were visited; and often there was no other plan to adopt, or any method better, or more natural, than to walk day after day from one straw-thatched cottage to another, living on the simple wholesome food of the peasants. Sometimes there was the picturesque mountain-road to climb, sometimes the route lay through marshy peat-lands, or across a rolling grass-covered country; and with each change of landscape came some new thought and some new impression of the Celtic life, or perhaps some new description of a fairy.

This immersion in the most striking natural and social environment of the Celtic race, gave me an insight into the mind, the religion, the mysticism, and the very heart of the Celt himself, such as no mere study in libraries ever could do. I tried to see the world as he does ; I participated in his innermost thoughts about the great problem of life and death, with which he of all peoples is most deeply concerned ; and thus he revealed to me the source of his highest ideals and inspirations. I daily felt the deep and innate serious-ness of his ancestral nature ; and, living as he lives, I tried in all ways to be like him. I was particularly qualified for such an undertaking : partly Celtic myself by blood and perhaps largely so by temperament, I found it easy to sympathize with the Celt and with his environments. Further, being by birth an American, I was in many places privileged to enter where an Englishman, or a non-Celt of Europe would not be ; and my education under the free ideals of a new-world democracy always made it possible for me to view economic, political, religious, and racial questions in Celtic lands apart from the European point of view, and without the European prejudices which are so numerous and so greatly to be regretted. But without any doubt, during my sojourn, extending over three years, among the Celts, these various environments shaped my thoughts about fairies and Fairyland—as they ought to have done if truth is ever to be reached by research.

These experiences of mine lead me to believe that the natural aspects of Celtic countries, much more than those of most non-Celtic countries, impress man and awaken in him some unfamiliar part of himself—call it the Subconscious Self, the Subliminal Self, the Ego, or what you will—which gives him an unusual power to know and to feel invisible, or psychical, influences. What is there, for example, in London, or Paris, or Berlin, or New York to awaken the intuitive power of man, that subconsciousness deep-hidden in him, equal to the solitude of those magical environments of Nature which the Celts enjoy and love ?

In my travels, when the weather was too wild to venture

out by day, or when the more favourable hours of the night had arrived, with fires and candles lit, or even during a road-side chat amid the day's journey, there was gathered together little by little, from one country and another, the mass of testimony which chapter ii contains. And with all this my opinions began to take shape ; for when I set out from Oxford in June, I had no certain or clear ideas as to what fairies are, nor why there should be belief in them. In less than a year afterwards I found myself committed to the Psychological Theory, which I am herein setting forth.

VI Theories of the Fairy-Faith

We make continual reference throughout our study to this Psychological Theory of the Nature and Origin of the Celtic Fairy-Faith, and it is one of our purposes to demonstrate that this is the root theory which includes or absorbs the four theories already advanced to account for the belief in fairies. To guide the reader in his own conclusions, we shall here briefly outline these four theories.

The first of them may be called the Naturalistic Theory, which is, that in ancient and in modern times man's belief in gods, spirits, or fairies has been the direct result of his attempts to explain or to rationalize natural phenomena. Of this theory we accept as true that the belief in fairies often anthropomorphically reflects the natural environment as well as the social condition of the people who hold the belief. For example, amid the beautiful low-lying green hills and gentle dells of Connemara (Ireland), the ' good people ' are just as beautiful, just as gentle, and just as happy as their environment ; while amid the dark-rising mountains and in the mysterious cloud-shadowed lakes of the Scotch Highlands there are fiercer kinds of fairies and terrible water-kelpies, and in the Western Hebrides there is the much-dreaded ' spirit-host ' moving through the air at night.

The Naturalistic Theory shows accurately enough that natural phenomena and environment have given direction to the anthropomorphosing of gods, spirits, or fairies, but after explaining this external aspect of the Fairy-Faith it cannot logically go any further. Or if illogically it does attempt to explain the belief in gods, spirits, or fairies as due entirely to material causes, it becomes, in our opinion, like the psychology of fifty years ago, obsolete ; for now the new psychology or psychical research has been forced to admit—if only as a working hypothesis—the possibility of invisible intelligences or entities able to influence man and nature. We seem even to be approaching a scientific proof of the doctrines of such ancient philosophical scientists as Pythagoras and Plato,—that all external nature, animated throughout and controlled in its phenomena by daemons acting by the will of gods, is to men nothing more than the visible effects of an unseen world of causes.

In the internal aspects of the Fairy-Faith the fundamental fact seems clearly to be that there must have been in the minds of prehistoric men, as there is now in the minds of modern men, a germ idea of a fairy for environment to act upon and shape. Without an object to act upon, environment can accomplish nothing. This is evident. The Naturalistic Theory examines only the environment and its effects, and forgets altogether the germ idea of a fairy to be acted upon ; but the Psychological Theory remembers and attempts to explain the germ idea of a fairy and the effect of nature upon it.

The second theory may be called the Pygmy Theory, which Mr. David MacRitchie, who is definitely committed to it, has so clearly set forth in his well-known work, entitled *The Testimony of Tradition*. This theory is that the whole fairy-belief has grown up out of a folk-memory of an actual Pygmy race. This race is supposed to have been a very early, prehistoric, probably Mongolian race, which inhabited the British Islands and many parts of Continental Europe. When the Celtic nations appeared, these pygmies were driven into mountain fastnesses and into the most inaccessible places, where a few of them may have survived until comparatively historical times.

Over against the champions of the Pygmy Theory may be set two of its opponents, Dr. Bertram C. A. Windle and Mr. Andrew Lang.[1] Dr. Windle, in his Introduction to Tyson's *Philological Essay concerning the Pygmies of the Ancients*, makes these six most destructive criticisms or points against the theory : (1) So far as our present knowledge teaches us, there never was a really Pygmy race inhabiting the northern parts of Scotland ; (2) the mounds with which the tales of little people are associated have not, in many cases, been habitations, but were natural or sepulchral in their nature ; (3) little people are not by any means associated entirely with mounds ; (4) the association of giants and dwarfs in traditions confuses the theory ; (5) there are fairies where no pygmies ever were, as, for example, in North America ; (6) even Eskimos and Lapps have fairy beliefs, and could not have been the original fairies of more modern fairy-lore. Altogether, as we think our study will show, the evidence of the Fairy-Faith itself gives only a slender and superficial support to the Pygmy Theory. We maintain that the theory, so far as it is provable, and this is evidently not very far, is only one strand, contributed by ethnology and social psychology, in the complex fabric of the Fairy-Faith, and is, as such, woven round a psychical central pattern—the fundamental pattern of the Fairy-Faith. Therefore, from our point of view, the Pygmy Theory is altogether inadequate, because it overlooks or misinterprets the most essential and prominent elements in the belief which the Celtic peoples hold concerning fairies and Fairyland.

The Druid Theory to account for fairies is less widespread. It is that the folk-memory of the Druids and their magical practices is alone responsible for the Fairy-Faith. The first suggestion of this theory seems to have been made by the Rev. Dr. Cririe, in his *Scottish Scenery*, published in 1803.[2] Three years later, the Rev. Dr. Graham published

---

[1] Andrew Lang, Kirk's *Secret Commonwealth* (London, 1893), p. xviii; and *History of Scotland* (Edinburgh, 1900–07).

[2] Cf. David MacRitchie's published criticisms of our Psychological Theory

an identical hypothesis in his *Sketches Descriptive of Picturesque Scenery on the Southern Confines of Perthshire.* Mr. MacRitchie suggests, with all reason, that the two writers probably had discussed together the theory, and hence both put it forth. Alfred Maury, in *Les Fées du Moyen-Age,* published in 1843 at Paris, appears to have made liberal use of Patrick Graham's suggestions in propounding his theory that the *fées* or fairy women of the Middle Ages are due to a folk-memory of Druidesses. Maury seems to have forgotten that throughout pagan Britain and Ireland, both much more important for the study of fairies than Celtic Europe during the Middle Ages, Druids rather than Druidesses had the chief influence on the people, and that yet, despite this fact, Irish and Welsh mythology is full of stories about fairy women coming from the Otherworld ; nor is there any proof, or even good ground for argument, that the Irish fairy women are a folk-memory of Druidesses, for if there ever were Druidesses in Ireland they played a subordinate and very insignificant rôle. As in the case of the Pygmy Theory, we maintain that the Druid Theory, also, is inadequate. It discovers a real anthropomorphic influence at work on the outward aspects of the Fairy-Faith, and illogically takes that to be the origin of the Fairy-Faith.

The fourth theory, the Mythological Theory, is of very great importance. It is that fairies are the diminished figures of the old pagan divinities of the early Celts ; and many modern authorities on Celtic mythology and folk-lore hold it. To us the theory is acceptable so far as it goes. But it is not adequate in itself nor is it the root theory, because a belief in gods and goddesses must in turn be explained ; and in making this explanation we arrive at the Psychological Theory, which this study—perhaps the first one of its kind—attempts to set forth.

in *The Celtic Review* (January 1910), entitled *Druids and Mound-Dwellers* ; also his first part of these criticisms, ib. (October 1909), entitled *A New Solution of the Fairy Problem.*

VII. The Importance of Studying the Fairy-Faith

I have made a very careful personal investigation of the surviving Celtic Fairy-Faith by living for many months with and among the people who preserve it ; I have compared fairy phenomena and the phenomena said to be caused by gods, genii, daemons, or spirits of different kinds and recorded in the writings of ancient, mediaeval, and modern metaphysical philosophers, Christian and pagan saints, mystics, and seers, and now more or less clearly substantiated by from thirty to forty years of experimentation in psychical sciences by eminent scientists of our own times, such as Sir William Crookes and Sir Oliver Lodge in England, and M. Camille Flammarion in France. As a result, I am convinced of the very great value of a serious study of the Fairy-Faith. The Fairy-Faith as the folk-religion of the Celts ought, like all religions, to be studied sympathetically as well as scientifically. To those who take a materialistic view of life, and consequently deny the existence of spirits or invisible intelligences such as fairies are said to be, we should say as my honoured American teacher in psychology, the late Dr. William James, of Harvard, used to say in his lectures at Stanford University, ' Materialism considered as a system of philosophy never tries to explain the *Why* of things.' But in our study of the Fairy-Faith we shall attempt to deal with this *Why* of things ; and, then, perhaps the value of studying fairies and Fairyland will be more apparent, even to materialists.

The great majority of men in cities are apt to pride themselves on their own exemption from ' superstition ', and to smile pityingly at the poor countrymen and countrywomen who believe in fairies. But when they do so they forget that, with all their own admirable progress in material invention, with all the far-reaching data of their acquired science, with all the vast extent of their commercial and economic conquests, they themselves have ceased to be natural. Wherever under modern conditions great multitudes of men and women are herded together there is bound to be an unhealthy psychical

atmosphere never found in the country—an atmosphere
which inevitably tends to develop in the average man who
is not psychically strong enough to resist it, lower at the
expense of higher forces or qualities, and thus to inhibit any
normal attempts of the Subliminal Self (a well-accredited
psychological entity) to manifest itself in consciousness. In
this connexion it is highly significant to note that, as far as
can be determined, almost all professed materialists of the
uncritical type, and even most of those who are thinking and
philosophizing sceptics about the existence of a supersensuous
realm or state of conscious being, are or have been city-
dwellers—usually so by birth and breeding. And even where
we find materialists of either type dwelling in the country,
we generally find them so completely under the hypnotic
sway of city influences and mould of thought in matters of
education and culture, and in matters touching religion, that
they have lost all sympathetic and responsive contact with
Nature, because unconsciously they have thus permitted
conventionality and unnaturalness to insulate them from it.
The Celtic peasant, who may be their tenant or neighbour,
is—if still uncorrupted by them—in direct contrast uncon-
ventional and natural. He is normally always responsive to
psychical influences—as much so as an Australian Arunta
or an American Red Man, who also, like him, are fortunate
enough to have escaped being corrupted by what we egotisti-
cally, to distinguish ourselves from them, call ' civilization '.
If our Celtic peasant has psychical experiences, or if he
sees an apparition which he calls one of the ' good people ',
that is to say a fairy, it is useless to try to persuade him that
he is under a delusion : unlike his materialistically-minded
lord, he would not attempt nor even desire to make himself
believe that what he has seen he has not seen. Not only has
he the will to believe, but he has the right to believe ; because
his belief is not a matter of being educated and reasoning
logically, nor a matter of faith and theology—it is a fact of his
own individual experiences, as he will tell you. Such peasant
seers have frequently argued with me to the effect that ' One
does not have to be educated in order to see fairies '.

Unlike the natural mind of the uncorrupted Celt, Arunta, or American Red Man, which is ever open to unusual psychical impressions, the mind of the business man in our great cities tends to be obsessed with business affairs both during his waking and during his dream states, the politician's with politics similarly, the society-leader's with society; and the unwholesome excitement felt by day in the city is apt to be heightened at night through a satisfying of the feeling which it morbidly creates for relaxation and change of stimuli. In the slums, humanity is divorced from Nature under even worse conditions, and becomes wholly decadent. But in slum and in palace alike there is continually a feverish nerve-tension induced by unrest and worry ; there is impure and smoke-impregnated air, a lack of sunshine, a substitution of artificial objects for natural objects, and in place of solitude the eternal din of traffic. Instead of Nature, men in cities (and paradoxically some conventionalized men in the country) have ' civilization '—and ' culture '.

Are city-dwellers like these, Nature's unnatural children, who grind out their lives in an unceasing struggle for wealth and power, social position, and even for bread, fit to judge Nature's natural children who believe in fairies ? Are they right in not believing in an invisible world which they cannot conceive, which, if it exists, they—even though they be scientists—are through environment and temperament alike incapable of knowing ? Or is the country-dwelling, the sometimes ' unpractical ' and ' unsuccessful ', the dreaming, and ' uncivilized' peasant right ? These questions ought to arouse in the minds of anthropologists very serious reflection, world-wide in its scope.

At all events, and equally for the unbeliever and for the believer, the study of the Fairy-Faith is of vast importance historically, philosophically, religiously, and scientifically. In it lie the germs of much of our European religions and philosophies, customs, and institutions. And it is one of the chief keys to unlock the mysteries of Celtic mythology. We believe that a greater age is coming soon, when all the ancient mythologies will be carefully studied and interpreted, and when the mythology of the Celts will be held in very high esteem. But already an age has come when things purely Celtic have begun to be studied; and the close observer can see the awakening genius of the modern Celt manifesting itself in the realm of scholarship, of literature, and even of art—throughout Continental Europe, especially France and Germany, throughout Great Britain and Ireland, and throughout the new Celtic world of America, as far west as San Francisco on the great calm ocean of the future facing Japan and China. In truth the Celtic empire is greater than it ever was before Caesar destroyed its political unity; and its citizens have not forgotten the ancient faith of their ancestors in a world invisible.

W. Y. E. W.

The Fairy–Faith
in
Celtic Countries

SECTION I
THE LIVING FAIRY-FAITH

CHAPTER I
ENVIRONMENT

'In the Beauty of the World lies the ultimate redemption of our mortality. When we shall become at one with nature in a sense profounder even than the poetic imaginings of most of us, we shall understand what now we fail to discern.'—FIONA MACLEOD.

Psychical interpretation—The mysticism of Erin and Armorica—In Ireland —In Scotland—In the Isle of Man—In Wales—In Cornwall—In Brittany.

As a preliminary to our study it is important, as we shall see later, to give some attention to the influences and purely natural environment under which the Fairy-Faith has grown up. And in doing so it will be apparent to what extent there is truth in the Naturalistic Theory ; though from the first our interpretation of Environment is fundamentally psychical. In this first chapter, then, in so far as they can be recorded, we shall record a few impressions, which will, in a way, serve as introductory to the more definite and detailed consideration of the Fairy-Faith itself.

Ireland and Brittany, the two extremes of the modern Celtic world, are for us the most important points from which to take our initial bearings. Both washed by the waters of the Ocean of Atlantis, the one an island, the other a peninsula, they have best preserved their old racial life in its simplicity and beauty, with its high ideals, its mystical traditions, and its strong spirituality. And, curious though the statement may appear to some, this preservation of older manners and traditions does not seem to be due so much to geographical isolation as to subtle forces so strange and mysterious that to know them they must be felt ; and their nature can only be suggested, for it cannot be described.

Over Erin and Armorica, as over Egypt, there hovers a halo
of romance, of strangeness, of mysticism real and positive ;
and, if we mistake not the language of others, these phrases
of ours but echo opinions common to many Celts native of
the two countries—they who have the first right to testify ;
and not only are there poets and seers among them, but
men of the practical world as well, and men of high rank in
scholarship, in literature, in art, and even in science.

In Ireland

If anyone would know Ireland and test these influences—
influences which have been so fundamental in giving to the
Fairy-Faith of the past something more than mere beauty
of romance and attractive form, and something which even
to-day, as in the heroic ages, is ever-living and ever-present
in the centres where men of the second-sight say that they
see fairies in that strange state of subjectivity which the
peasant calls Fairyland—let him stand on the Hill of Tara
silently and alone at sunset, in the noonday, in the mist
of a dark day. Let him likewise silently and alone follow
the course of the Boyne. Let him enter the silence of New
Grange and of Dowth. Let him muse over the hieroglyphics of Lough Crew. Let him feel the mystic beauty of
Killarney, the peacefulness of Glendalough, of Monaster-
boise, of Clonmacnois, and the isolation of Aranmore. Let
him dare to enter the rings of fairies, to tempt the ' good
folk ' at their *raths* and *forts*. Let him rest on the ancient
cairn above the mountain-palace of Finvara and look out
across the battlefields of Moytura. Let him wander amid
the fairy dells of gentle Connemara. Let him behold the
Irish Sea from the Heights of Howth, as Fionn Mac Cumhail
used to do. Let him listen to the ocean-winds amid Dun
Aengus. Let him view the stronghold of Cuchulainn and the
Red Branch Knights. Let him linger beside that mysterious
lake which lies embosomed between two prehistoric cairns
on the summit of enchanted Slieve Gullion, where yet dwells
invisible the mountain's Guardian, a fairy woman. Let
him then try to interpret the mysticism of an ancient Irish

myth, in order to understand why men have been told that in the plain beneath this magic mountain of Ireland mighty warfare was once waged on account of a Bull, by the hosts of Queen Meave against those of Cuchulainn the hero of Ulster. Let him be lost in the mists on the top of Ben Bulbin. Let him know the haunts of fairy kings and queens in Roscommon. Let him follow in the footsteps of Patrick and Bridgit and Columba. When there are dark days and stormy nights, let him sit beside a blazing fire of fragrant peat in a peasant's straw-thatched cottage listening to tales of Ireland's golden age—tales of gods, of heroes, of ghosts, and of fairy-folk. If he will do these things, he will know Ireland, and why its people believe in fairies.

As yet, little has been said concerning the effects of clouds, of natural scenery, of weird and sudden transformations in earth and sky and air, which play their part in shaping the complete Fairy-Faith of the Irish ; but what we are about to say concerning Scotland will suggest the same things for Ireland, because the nature of the landscape and the atmospheric changes are much the same in the two countries, both inland and on their rock-bound and storm-swept shores.

In Scotland

In the moorlands between Trossachs and Aberfoyle, a region made famous by Scott's *Rob Roy*, I have seen atmospheric changes so sudden and so contrasted as to appear marvellous. What shifting of vapours and clouds, what flashes of bright sun-gleams, then twilight at midday! Across the landscape, shadows of black dense fog-banks rush like shadows of flocks of great birds which darken all the earth. Palpitating fog-banks wrap themselves around the mountain-tops and then come down like living things to move across the valleys, sometimes only a few yards above the traveller's head. And in that country live terrible water-kelpies. When black clouds discharge their watery burden it is in wind-driven vertical water-sheets through which the world appears as through an ice-filmed window-pane. Perhaps in a single day there may be the bluest of heavens and the clearest air, the densest clouds and the darkest shadows, the calm of the morning and the wind of the tempest. At night in Aberfoyle after such a day, I witnessed a clear sunset and a fair evening sky; in the morning when I arose, the lowlands along the river were inundated and a thousand cascades, large and small, were leaping down the mountain-highlands, and rain was falling in heavy masses. Within an hour afterwards, as I travelled on towards Stirling, the rain and wind ceased, and there settled down over all the land cloud-masses so inky-black that they seemed like the fancies of some horrible dream. Then like massed armies they began to move to their mountain-strongholds, and stood there; while from the east came perfect weather and a flood of brilliant sunshine.

And in the Highlands from Stirling to Inverness what magic, what changing colours and shadows there were on the age-worn treeless hills, and in the valleys with their clear, pure streams receiving tribute from unnumbered little rills and springs, some dropping water drop by drop as though it were fairy-distilled; and everywhere the heather giving to the mountain-landscape a hue of rich purplish-brown, and to the air an odour of aromatic fragrance.

On to the north-west beyond Inverness there is the same kind of a treeless highland country; and then after a few hours of travel one looks out across the water from Kyle and beholds Skye, where Cuchulainn is by some believed to have passed his young manhood learning feats of arms from fairy women,—Skye, dark, mountainous, majestic, with its waterfalls turning to white spray as they tumble from cliff to cliff into the sound, from out the clouds that hide their mountain-summit sources.

In the Outer Hebrides, as in the Aranmore Islands off West Ireland, influences are at work on the Celtic imagination quite different from those in Skye and its neighbouring islands. Mountainous billows which have travelled from afar out of the mysterious watery waste find their first impediment on the west of these isolated Hebridean isles, and they fling themselves like mad things in full fury against the wild rocky islets fringing the coast. White spray flashes in unearthly forms over the highest cliff, and the unrestrained hurricane whirls it far inland. Ocean's eternally murmuring sounds set up a responsive vibration in the soul of the peasant, as he in solitude drives home his flocks amid the weird gloaming at the end of a December day ; and, later, when he sits brooding in his humble cottage at night, in the fitful flickering of a peat fire, he has a mystic consciousness that deep down in his being there is a more divine music compared with which that of external nature is but a symbol and an echo ; and, as he stirs the glowing peat-embers, phantoms from an irretrievable past seem to be sitting with him on the edge of the half-circle of dying light. Maybe there are skin-clad huntsmen of the sea and land, with spears and knives of bone and flint and shaggy sleeping dogs, or fearless sea-rovers resting wearily on shields of brilliant bronze, or maybe Celtic warriors fierce and bold ; and then he understands that his past and his present are one.

Commonly there is the thickest day-darkness when the driving storms come in from the Atlantic, or when dense fog covers sea and land ; and, again, there are melancholy sea-winds moaning across from shore to shore, bending the bushes of the purple heather. At other times there is a sparkle of the brightest sunshine on the ocean waves, a fierceness foreign to the more peaceful Highlands ; and then again a dead silence prevails at sunrise and at sunset if one be on the mountains, or, if on the shore, no sound is heard save the rhythmical beat of the waves, and now and then the hoarse cry of a sea-bird. All these contrasted conditions may be seen in one day, or each may endure for a day ; and the dark days last nearly all the winter. And then it is, during the long winter, that the crofters and fisher-folk congregate night after night in a different neighbour's house to tell about fairies and ghosts, and to repeat all those old legends so dear to the heart of the Celt. Perhaps every one present has heard the same story or legend a hundred times, yet it is always listened to and told as though it were the

latest bulletin of some great world-stirring event. Over
those little islands, so far away to the north, out on the edge
of the world, in winter-time darkness settles down at four
o'clock or even earlier ; and the islanders hurry through
with their dinner of fish and oat-bread so as not to miss
hearing the first story. When the company has gathered from
far and near, pipes are re-filled and lit and the peat is heaped
up, for the story-telling is not likely to end before midnight.
' The house is roomy and clean, if homely, with its bright
peat fire in the middle of the floor. There are many present
—men and women, boys and girls. All the women are
seated, and most of the men. Girls are crouched between
the knees of fathers or brothers or friends, while boys are
perched wherever—boy-like—they can climb. The house-
man is twisting twigs of heather into ropes to hold
down thatch, a neighbour crofter is twining quicken root
into cords to tie cows, while another is plaiting bent grass
into baskets to hold meal. The housewife is spinning,
a daughter is carding, another daughter is teazing, while
a third daughter, supposed to be working, is away in
the background conversing in low whispers with the son
of a neighbouring crofter. Neighbour wives and neighbour daughters are knitting, sewing, or embroidering.' [1]
Then when the bad weather for fishing has been fully discussed by the men, and the latest gossip by the women,
and the foolish talk of the youths and maidens in the corners
is finished, the one who occupies the chair of honour in the
midst of the ceilidh [2] looks around to be sure that everybody
is comfortable and ready ; and, as his first story begins, even
the babes by instinct cease their noise and crying, and young
and old bend forward eagerly to hear every word. It does

---

[1] Alexander Carmichael, *Carmina Gadelica* (Edinburgh, 1900), i, p. xix.
[2] The *ceilidh* of the Western Hebrides corresponds to the *veillée* of Lower
Brittany (see pp. 221 ff.), and to similar story-telling festivals which
formerly flourished among all the Celtic peoples. ' The *ceilidh* is a literary
entertainment where stories and tales, poems, and ballads, are rehearsed
and recited, and songs are sung, conundrums are put, proverbs are quoted,
and many other literary matters are related and discussed.'—Alexander
Carmichael, *Carmina Gadelica*, i, p. xviii.

not matter if some of the boys and girls do topple over asleep, or even some of the older folk as the hour gets late ; the tales meet no interruption in their even, unbroken flow. And here we have the most Celtic and the most natural environments which the Fairy-Faith enjoys in Scotland. There are still the Southern Highlands in the country around Oban, and the islands near them ; and of all these isles none is so picturesque in history as the one Columba loved so well. Though Iona enjoys less of the wildness of the Hebrides furthest west, it has their storm-winds and fogs and dark days, and their strangeness of isolation. On it, as Adamnan tells us, the holy man fought with black demons who came to invade his monastery, and saw angelic hosts ; and when the angels took his soul at midnight in that little chapel by the sea-shore there was a mystic light which illuminated all the altar like the brightest sunshine. But nowadays, where the saint saw demons and angels the Islanders see ghosts and ' good people ', and when one of these islanders is taken in death it is not by angels—it is by fairies.

In the Isle of Man

In the midst of the Irish Sea, almost equidistant from Ireland, Scotland, and Wales, and concentrating in itself the psychical and magnetic influences from these three Celtic lands, and from Celto-Saxon England too, lies the beautiful kingdom of the great Tuatha De Danann god, Manannan Mac Lir, or, as his loyal Manx subjects prefer to call him, Mannanan-Beg-Mac-y-Leir. In no other land of the Celt does Nature show so many moods and contrasts, such perfect repose at one time and at another time the mightiness of its unloosed powers, when the baffled sea throws itself angrily against a high rock-bound coast, as wild and almost as weather-worn as the western coasts of Ireland and the Hebrides.

But it is Nature's calmer moods which have greater effect upon the Manx people : on the summit of his ancient strong-hold, South Barrule Mountain, the god Manannan yet dwells invisible to mortal eyes, and whenever on a warm day he throws off his magic mist-blanket with which he is wont to cover the whole island, the golden gorse or purple heather blossoms become musical with the hum of bees, and sway gently on breezes made balmy by the tropical warmth of an ocean stream flowing from the far distant Mexican shores of a New World. Then in many a moist and sweet-smelling glen, pure and verdant, land-birds in rejoicing bands add to the harmony of sound, as they gather on the newly-ploughed field or dip themselves in the clear water of the tinkling brook; and from the cliffs and rocky islets on the coast comes the echo of the multitudinous chorus of sea-birds. At sunset, on such a day, as evening calmness settles down, weird mountain shadows begin to move across the dimly-lighted glens; and when darkness has fallen, there is a mystic stillness, broken only by the ceaseless throbbing of the sea-waves, the flow of brooks, and the voices of the night.

In the moorland solitudes, even by day, there sometimes broods a deeper silence, which is yet more potent and full of meaning for the peasant, as under its spell he beholds the peaceful vision, happy and sunlit, of sea and land, of gentle mountains falling away in land-waves into well-tilled plains and fertile valleys; and he comes to feel instinctively the old Druidic Fires relit within his heart, and perhaps unconsciously he worships there in Nature's Temple. The natural beauty without awakens the divine beauty within, and for a second of time he, out of his subconsciousness, is conscious that in Nature there are beings and inaudible voices which have no existence for the flippant pleasure-seeking crowds who come and go. To the multitude, his ancestral beliefs are foolishness, his fairies but the creatures of a fervid Celtic imagination which readily responds to unusual phenomena and environments. They will not believe with him that all beauty and harmony in the world are but symbolic, and that behind these stand unseen sustaining forces and powers which are conscious and eternal; and though by instinct they willingly personify Nature they do not know the secret of why they do so: for them the outer is reality, the inner non-existent.

From the Age of Stone to the civilized era of to-day, the Isle of Man has been, in succession, the home of every known race and people who have flourished in Western Europe ; and though subject, in turn, to the Irish Gael and to the Welsh Brython, to Northmen and to Danes, to Scots and to English, and the scene of sweeping transformations in religion, as pagan cults succeeded one another, to give way to the teaching of St. Patrick and his disciples St. German and St. Maughold, and this finally to the Protestant form of Christianity, the island alone of Celtic lands has been strangely empowered to maintain in almost primitive purity its ancient constitution and freedom, and though geographically at the very centre of the United Kingdom, is not a part of it. The archaeologist may still read in mysterious symbols of stone and earth, as they lie strewn over the island's surface, the history of this age-long panoramic procession of human evolution ; while through these same symbols the Manx seer reads a deeper meaning ; and sometimes in the superhuman realm of radiant light, to which since long ago they have oft come and oft returned, he meets face to face the gods and heroes whose early tombs stand solitary on the wind-swept mountain-top and moorland, or hidden away in the embrace of wild flowers and verdure amid valleys ; and in the darker mid-world he sees innumerable ghosts of many of these races which have perished.

IN WALES

Less can be said of Wales than of Ireland, or of Scotland as a whole. It has, it is true, its own peculiar psychic atmosphere, different, no doubt, because its people are Brythonic Celts rather than Gaelic Celts. But Wales, with conditions more modernized than is the case in Ireland or in the Western Hebrides of Scotland, does not now exhibit in a vigorous or flourishing state those Celtic influences which, when they were active, did so much to create the precious Romances of Arthur and his Brotherhood, and to lay the foundations for the Welsh belief in the *Tylwyth Teg*, a fairy race still surviving in a few favoured localities.

Wales, like all Celtic countries, is a land of long sea-coasts, though there seems to be, save in the mountains of the north, less of mist and darkness and cloud effects than in Ireland and Scotland. In the south, perhaps the most curious influences are to be felt at St. David's Head, and in St. David's itself—once the goal for thousands of pilgrims from many countries of mediaeval Europe, and, probably, in pagan times the seat of an oracle. And a place of like character is the peninsula of Gower, south of Swansea. Caerphilly Castle, where the Green Lady reigns now amid its ruined acres, is a strange place; and so is the hill near Carmarthen, where Merlin is asleep in a cave with the fairy-woman Vivian. But in none of these places to-day is there a strong living faith in fairies as there is, for example, in West Ireland. The one region where I found a real Celtic atmosphere—and it is a region where everybody speaks Welsh—is a mountainous country rarely visited by travellers, save archaeologists, a few miles from Newport; and its centre is the Pentre Evan Cromlech, the finest cromlech in Wales if not in Britain. By this prehistoric monument and in the country round the old Nevern Church, three miles away, there is an active belief in the 'fair-folk', in ghosts, in death-warnings, in death-candles and phantom-funerals, and in witchcraft and black magic. Thence on to Newcastle-Emlyn and its valley, where many of the Mabinogion stories took form, or at least from where they drew rich material in the way of folk-lore,[1] are environments purely Welsh and as yet little disturbed by the commercial materialism of the age.

There remain now to be mentioned three other places in Wales to me very impressive psychically. These are: ancient Harlech, so famous in recorded Welsh fairy-romance —Harlech with its strange stone-circles, and old castle from which the Snowdon Range is seen to loom majestically and clear, and with its sun-kissed bay; Mount Snowdon, with its memories of Arthur and Welsh heroes; and sacred Anglesey or Mona, strewn with tumuli, and dolmens, and pillar-stones—Mona, where the Druids made their last stand

---

[1] I am indebted for this information to the late Mr. Davies, the competent scholar and antiquarian of Newcastle-Emlyn, where for many years he has been vicar.

against the Roman eagles—and its little island called Holyhead, facing Ireland.

However, when all is said, modern Wales is poorer in its fairy atmosphere than modern Ireland or modern Brittany. Certainly there is a good deal of this fairy atmosphere yet, though it has become less vital than the similar fairy atmosphere in the great centres of Erin and Armorica. But the purely social environment under which the Fairy-Faith of Wales survives is a potent force which promises to preserve underneath the surface of Welsh national life, where the commercialism of the age has compelled it to retire in a state of temporary latency, the ancestral idealism of the ancient Brythonic race. In Wales, as in Lower Brittany and in parts of Ireland and the Hebrides, one may still hear in common daily use a language which has been continuously spoken since unknown centuries before the rise of the Roman empire. And the strong hold which the Druidic *Eisteddfod* (an annual national congress of bards and literati) continues to have upon the Welsh people, in spite of their commercialism, is, again, a sign that their hearts remain uncorrupted, that when the more favourable hour strikes they will sweep aside the deadening influences which now hold them in spiritual bondage, and become, as they were in the past, true children of Arthur.

In Cornwall

Strikingly like Brittany in physical aspects, Southern and Western Cornwall is a land of the sea, of rolling plains and moorlands rather than of high hills and mountains, a land of golden-yellow furze-bloom, where noisy crowds of black crows and white sea-gulls mingle together over the freshly-turned or new-sown fields, and where in the spring-time the call of the cuckoo is heard with the song of the skylark. Like the Isle of Man, from the earliest ages Cornwall has been a meeting-place and a battle-ground for contending races. The primitive dark Iberian peoples gave way before Aryan-Celtic invaders, and these to Roman and then to Germanic invaders.

Nature has been kind to the whole of Cornwall, but chiefly upon the peninsula whose ancient capital is Penzance (which possibly means ' the Holy Headland '), and upon the land immediately eastward and northward of it, she has bestowed her rarest gifts. Holding this territory embosomed in the pure waters of Ocean, and breathing over it the pure air of the Atlantic in spring and in summer calm, when the warm vapours from the Gulf Stream sweep over it freely, and make it a land of flowers and of singing-birds, Nature preserves eternally its beauty and its sanctity. There are there ruined British villages whose builders are long forgotten, strange prehistoric circular sun-temples like fortresses crowning the hill-tops, mysterious underground passage-ways, and crosses probably pre-Christian. Everywhere are the records of the mighty past of this thrice-holy Druid land of sunset. There are weird legends of the lost kingdom of Fair Lyonesse, which seers sometimes see beneath the clear salt waves, with all its ancient towns and flowery fields ; legends of Phoenicians and Oriental merchants who came for tin ; legends of gods and of giants, of pixies and of fairies, of King Arthur in his castle at Tintagel, of angels and of saints, of witches and of wizards.

On *Dinsul*, ' Hill dedicated to the Sun,' pagan priests and priestesses kept kindled the Eternal Fire, and daily watched eastward for the rising of the God of Light and Life, to greet his coming with paeans of thanksgiving and praise. Then after the sixth century the new religion had come proclaiming a more mystic Light of the World in the Son of God, and to the pious half-pagan monks who succeeded the Druids the Archangel St. Michael appeared in vision on the Sacred Mount.[1] And before St. Augustine came to Britain the Celts of Cornwall had already combined in their own mystical way the spiritual message of primitive Christianity with the pure nature-worship of their ancestors ; and their

---

[1] In the Gnosis, St. Michael symbolizes the sun, and thus very appropriately at St. Michael's Mount, Cornwall, at Mont St. Michel, Carnac, and also at Mont St. Michel on the coast of Normandy, replaced the Great God of Light and Life, held in supreme honour among the ancient Celts.

land was then, as it most likely had been in pagan days, a centre of pilgrimages for their Celtic kinsmen from Ireland, from Wales, from England, and from Brittany. When in later times new theological doctrines were superimposed on this mysticism of Celtic Christianity, the Sacred Fires were buried in ashes, and the Light and Beauty of the pagan world obscured with sackcloth.

But there in that most southern and western corner of the Isle of Britain, the Sacred Fires themselves still burn on the divine hill-tops, though smothered in the hearts of its children. The Cornishman's vision is no longer clear. He looks upon cromlech and dolmen, upon ancient caves of initiation, and upon the graves of his prehistoric ancestors, and vaguely feels, but does not know, why his land is so holy, is so permeated by an indefinable magic; for he has lost his ancestral mystic touch with the unseen—he is ' educated ' and ' civilized '. The hand of the conqueror has fallen more heavily upon the people of Cornwall than upon any other Celtic people, and now for a time, but let us hope happily only for this dark period of transition, they sleep—until Arthur comes to break the spell and set them free.

In Brittany

As was pointed out at the beginning of this chapter, Ireland and Brittany are to be regarded as the two poles of the modern Celtic world, but it is believed by Celtic mystics that they are much more than this, that they are two of its psychic centres, with Tara and Carnac as two respective points of focus from which the Celtic influence of each country radiates.[1] With such a psychical point of view, it makes no difference at all whether one scholar argues Carnac to be Celtic and another pre-Celtic, for if pre-Celtic, as it most likely is, it has certainly been bequeathed to the people who were and are Celtic, and its influence has been an unbroken thing from times altogether beyond the horizon of

[1] In this connexion we may think of the North and South Magnetic Poles of the earth as centres of definite yet invisible forces which can be detected, and to some extent measured scientifically.

history. According to this theory (and in following it we are merely trying to put on record unique material transmitted to us by the most learned of contemporary Celtic mystics and seers) there seem to be certain favoured places on the earth where its magnetic and even more subtle forces are most powerful and most easily felt by persons susceptible to such things ; and Carnac appears to be one of the greatest of such places in Europe, and for this reason, as has been thought, was probably selected by its ancient priest-builders as the great centre for religious practices, for the celebration of pagan mysteries, for tribal assemblies, for astronomical observations, and very likely for establishing schools in which to educate neophytes for the priesthood. Tara, with its tributary Boyne valley, is a similar place in Ireland, so selected and so used, as, in our study of the cult of fairies and the cult of the dead, manuscript evidence will later indicate. And thus to such psychical and magnetic, or, according perhaps to others, religious or traditional influences as focus themselves at Tara and Carnac, though in other parts of the two countries as well, may be due in a great, even in an essential measure, the vigorous and ever-living Fairy-Faith of Ireland, and the innate and ever-conscious belief of the Breton people in the Legend of the Dead and in a world invisible. For fairies and souls of the dead, though, strictly speaking, not confused, are believed to be beings of the subjective world existing to-day, and influencing mortals, as they have always existed and influenced them according to ancient and modern traditions, and as they appear now in the eyes even of science through the work of a few pioneer scientists in psychical research. And it seems probable that subjective beings of this kind, granting their existence, were made use of by the ancient Druids, and even by Patrick when the old and new religions met to do battle on the Hill of Tara. The control of Tara, as a psychical centre, meant the psychical control of all Ireland. To-day on the Hill of Tara the statue of St. Patrick dwarfs the Liath Stone beside it ; at Carnac the Christian Cross overshadows dolmens and menhirs.

A learned priest of the Roman Church told me, when I met him in Galway, that in his opinion those places in Ireland where ancient sacrifices were performed to pagan or Druid gods are still, unless they have been regularly exorcized, under the control of demons (daemons). And what the Druids were at Tara and throughout Erin and most probably at Carnac as well, the priests were in Egypt, and the pythonesses in Greece. That is to say, Druids, Egyptian priests, priestesses in charge of Greek oracles, are said to have foretold the future, interpreted omens, worked all miracles and wonders of magic by the aid of daemons, who were regarded as an order of invisible beings, intermediary between gods and men, and as sometimes including the shades from Hades.

I should say as before, if he who knowing Ireland, the Land of Faerie, would know in the same manner Brittany, the Land of the Dead, let him silently and alone walk many times—in sun, in wind, in storm, in thick mist—through the long, broad avenues of stone of the Alignements at Carnac. Let him watch from among them the course of the sun from east to west. Let him stand on St. Michael's Mount on the day of the winter solstice, or on the day of the summer solstice. Let him enter the silence of its ancient underground chamber, so dark and so mysterious. Let him sit for hours musing amid cromlechs and dolmens, and beside menhirs, and at holy wells. Let him marvel at the mightiest of menhirs now broken and prostrate at Locmariaquer, and then let him ponder over the subterranean places near it. Let him try to read the symbolic inscriptions on the rocks in Gavrinis. Let him stand on the Île de Sein at sunrise and at sunset. Let him penetrate the solitudes of the Forest of Brocéliande, and walk through the Val-Sans-Retour (Vale-Without-Return). And then let him wander in footpaths with the Breton peasant through fields where good dames sit on the sunny side of a bush or wall, knitting stockings, where there are long hedges of furze, golden-yellow with bloom—even in January—and listen to stories about *corrigans*, and about the dead who mingle here with the

living. Let him enter the peasant's cottage when there is
fog over the land and the sea-winds are blowing across the
shifting sand-dunes, and hear what he can tell him. Let
him, even as he enjoys the picturesque customs and dress of
the Breton folk and looks on at their joyous *ronde* (perhaps
the relic of a long-forgotten sun-dance), observe the depth
of their nature, their almost ever-present sense of the serious-
ness of human life and effort, their beautiful characters as
their mystic land has shaped them without the artificiality
of books and schools, their dreaminess as they look out
across the ocean, their often perfect physique and fine
profiles and rosy cheeks, and yet withal their brooding
innate melancholy. And let him know that there is with
them always an overshadowing consciousness of an invisible
world, not in some distant realm of space, but here and now,
blending itself with this world; its inhabitants, their dead
ancestors and friends, mingling with them daily, and awaiting the hour when the *Ankou* (a King of the Dead) shall call
each to join their invisible company.

SECTION I

THE LIVING FAIRY-FAITH

CHAPTER II

THE TAKING OF EVIDENCE

' During all these centuries the Celt has kept in his heart some affinity
with the mighty beings ruling in the Unseen, once so evident to the heroic
races who preceded him. His legends and faery tales have connected his
soul with the inner lives of air and water and earth, and they in turn have
kept his heart sweet with hidden influence.'—A. E.

Method of presentation—The logical verdict—Trustworthiness of legends
—The Fairy-Faith held by the highly educated Celt as well as by the
Celtic peasant—The evidence is complete and adequate—Its analysis—
The Fairy-Tribes dealt with—Witnesses and their testimony : from
Ireland, with introduction by Dr. Douglas Hyde ; from Scotland,
with introduction by Dr. Alexander Carmichael ; from the Isle of
Man, with introduction by Miss Sophia Morrison ; from Wales, with
introduction by the Right Hon. Sir John Rhŷs ; from Cornwall, with
introduction by Mr. Henry Jenner ; and from Brittany, with introduction by Professor Anatole Le Braz.

I   GENERAL INTRODUCTION

VARIOUS possible plans have presented themselves for
setting forth the living Fairy-Faith as I have found it during
my travels in the six Celtic countries among the people
who hold it.   To take a bit here and a bit there from a miscellaneous group of psychological experiences, fairy legends
and stories which are linked together almost inseparably in
the mind of the one who tells them, does not seem at all
satisfactory, nor even just, in trying to arrive at a correct
result.   Classification under various headings, such, for
example, as Fairy Abductions, Changelings, or Appearances
of Fairies, seems equally unsatisfactory ; for as soon as the
details of folk-lore such as I am presenting are isolated from
one another—even though brought together in related
groups—they must be rudely torn out of their true and
natural environment, and divorced from the psychological

atmosphere amidst which they were first presented by the narrator. The same objection applies to any plan of dividing the evidence into (1) that which is purely legendary ; (2) that which is second-hand or third-hand evidence from people who claim to have seen fairies, or to have been in Fairyland or under fairy influences; and (3) that which is first-hand evidence from actual percipients : these three classes of evidence are so self-evident that every reader will be able to distinguish each class for himself as it occurs, and a mechanical classification by us is unnecessary. So no plan seems so good as the plan I have adopted of permitting all witnesses to give their own testimony in their own way and in its native setting, and then of classifying and weighing such testimony according to the methods of comparative religion and the anthropological sciences.

In most cases, as examination will show, the evidence is so clear that little or no comment is necessary. Most of the evidence also points so much in one direction that the only verdict which seems reasonable is that the Fairy-Faith belongs to a doctrine of souls ; that is to say, that Fairyland is a state or condition, realm or place, very much like, if not the same as, that wherein civilized and uncivilized men alike place the souls of the dead, in company with other invisible beings such as gods, daemons, and all sorts of good and bad spirits. Not only do both educated and uneducated Celtic seers so conceive Fairyland, but they go much further, and say that Fairyland actually exists as an invisible world within which the visible world is immersed like an island in an unexplored ocean, and that it is peopled by more species of living beings than this world, because incomparably more vast and varied in its possibilities.

We should be prepared in hearing the evidence to meet with some contradictions and a good deal of confusion, for many of the people who believe in such a strange world as we have just described, and who think they sometimes have entered it or have seen some of its inhabitants, have often had no training at all in schools or colleges. But when we hear legendary tales which have never been recorded save in the minds of unnumbered generations of men, we ought not on that account to undervalue them ; for often they are better authorities and more trustworthy than many an ancient and carefully inscribed manuscript in the British Museum ; and they are probably far older than the oldest book in the world. Let us, then, for a time, forget that there are such things as libraries and universities, and betake ourselves to the Celtic peasant for instruction, living close to nature as he lives, and thinking the things which he thinks.

But the peasant will not be our only teacher, for we shall also hear much of first importance from city folk of the highest intellectual training. It has become, perhaps always has been in modern times, a widespread opinion, even among some scholars, that the belief in fairies is the property solely of simple, uneducated country-folk, and that people who have had ' a touch of education and a little common sense knocked into their heads ', to use the ordinary language, ' wouldn't be caught believing in such nonsense.' This same class of critics used to make similar remarks about people who said there were ghosts, until the truth of another ' stupid superstition ' was discovered by psychical research. So in this chapter we hope to correct this erroneous opinion about the Fairy-Faith, an opinion chiefly entertained by scholars and others who know not the first real fact about fairies, because they have never lived amongst the people who believe in fairies, but derive all their information from books and hearsay. In due order the proper sort of witnesses will substantiate this position, but before coming to their testimony we may now say that there are men and women in Dublin, in other parts of Ireland, in Scotland, in the Isle of Man, and in Brythonic lands too, whom all the world knows as educated leaders in their respective fields of activity, who not only declare their belief that fairies were, but that fairies are ; and some of these men and women say that they have the power to see fairies as real spiritual beings.

In the evidence about to be presented there has been no selecting in favour of any one theory ; it is presented as discovered. The only liberty taken with some of the evidence has been to put it into better grammatical form, and sometimes to recast an ambiguous statement when I, as collector, had in my own mind no doubt as to its meaning. Translations have been made as literal as possible ; though sometimes it has been found better to offer the meaning rather than what in English would be an obscure colloquialism or idiomatic expression. The method pursued in seeking the evidence has been to penetrate as deeply and in as natural a way as possible the thoughts of the people who believe in fairies and like beings, by living among them and observing their customs and ways of thought, and recording what seemed relevant to the subject under investigation—chance expressions, and legends told under various ordinary conditions—rather than to collect long legends or literary fairy-stories. For these last the reader is referred to the many excellent works on Celtic folk-lore. We have sought to bring together, as perhaps has not been done before, the philosophy of the belief in fairies, rather than the mere fairy-lore itself, though the two cannot be separated. In giving the evidence concerning fairies, we sometimes give evidence which, though akin to it and thus worthy of record, is not strictly fairy-lore. All that we have omitted from the materials in the form first taken down are stories and accounts of things not sufficiently related to the world of Faerie to be of value here.

In no case has testimony been admitted from a person who was known to be unreliable, nor even from a person who was thought to be unreliable. Accordingly, the evidence we are to examine ought to be considered good evidence so far as it goes ; and since it represents almost all known elements of the Fairy-Faith and contains almost all the essential elements upon which the advocates of the Naturalistic Theory, of the Pygmy Theory, of the Druid Theory, of the Mythological Theory, as well as of our own Psychological Theory, must base their arguments, we consider it very adequate evidence. Nearly every witness is a Celt who has been made acquainted with the belief in fairies through direct contact with people who believe in them, or through having heard fairy-traditions among his own kindred, or through personal psychological experiences. And it is exceedingly fortunate for us that an unusually large proportion of these Celtic witnesses are actual percipients and natural seers, because the eliminations from the Fairy-Faith to be brought about in chapter iii by means of an anthropological analysis of evidence will be so extensive that, scientifically and strictly speaking, there will remain as a residual or unknown quantity, upon which our final conclusion must depend, solely the testimony of reliable seer-witnesses. That is to say, no method of anthropological dissection of the evidence can force aside consideration of the ultimate truth which may or may not reside in the testimony of sane and thoroughly reliable seer-witnesses.

Old and young, educated and uneducated, peasant and city-bred, testify to the actual existence of the Celtic Fairy-Faith ; and the evidence from Roman Catholics stands beside that from Protestants, the evidence of priests supports that of scholars and scientists, peasant seers have testified to the same kind of visions as highly educated seers ; and what poets have said agrees with what is told by business men, engineers, and lawyers. But the best of witnesses, like ourselves, are only human, and subject to the shortcomings of the ordinary man, and therefore no claim can be made in any case to infallibility of evidence : all the world over men interpret visions pragmatically and sociologically, or hold beliefs in accord with their own personal experiences ; and are for ever unconsciously immersed in a sea of psychological influences which sometimes may be explainable through the methods of sociological inquiry, sometimes may be supernormal in origin and nature, and hence to be explained most adequately, if at all, through psychical research. Our study is a study of human nature itself, and, moreover, often of human nature in its most subtle aspects, which are called psychical ; and the most difficult problem of all is for human nature to interpret and understand its own ultimate essence and psychological instincts. Our whole aim is to discover what reasonableness may or may not stand behind a belief so vast, so ancient, so common (contrary to popular non-Celtic opinion) to all classes of Celts, and so fundamental a shaping force in European history, religion, and social institutions.

When we state our conviction that the Fairy-Faith is common to all classes of Celts, we do not state that it is common to all Celts. The materialization of the age has affected the Fairy-Faith as it has affected all religious beliefs the world over. This has been pointed out by Dr. Hyde, by Dr. Carmichael, and by Mr. Jenner in their respective introductions for Ireland, Scotland, and Cornwall. Nevertheless, the Fairy-Faith as the folk-religion of the Celtic peoples is still able to count its adherents by hundreds of thousands. Even in many cases where Christian theology has been partially or wholly discarded by educated Celts, in the country or in the city, as being to them in too many details out of harmony with accepted scientific truths, the belief in fairies has been jealously retained, and will, so it would seem, be retained in the future.

We are now prepared to hear about the *Daoine Maithe*, the ' Good People ', as the Irish call their *Sidhe* race ; about the ' People of Peace ', the ' Still-Folk ' or the ' Silent Moving Folk ', as the Scotch call their *Sith* who live in green knolls and in the mountain fastnesses of the Highlands ; about various Manx fairies ; about the *Tylwyth Teg*, the ' Fair-Family ' or ' Fair-Folk ', as the Welsh people call their fairies ; about Cornish Pixies ; and about *Fées* (fairies), *Corrigans*, and the Phantoms of the Dead in Brittany. And along with these, for they are very much akin, let us hear about ghosts—sometimes about ghosts who discover hidden treasure, as in our story of the *Golden Image*—about goblins, about various sorts of death-warnings generally coming from apparitions of the dead, or from banshees, about death-candles and phantom-funerals, about leprechauns, about hosts of the air, and all kinds of elementals and spirits— in short, about all the orders of beings who mingle together in that invisible realm called Fairyland.

II   IN IRELAND

Introduction by DOUGLAS HYDE, LL.D., D. Litt., M.R.I.A.
(*An Craoibhín Aoibhinn*), President of the Gaelic League ;
author of *A Literary History of Ireland*, &c.

Whatever may be thought of the conclusions drawn by
Mr. Wentz from his explorations into the Irish spirit-world,
there can be no doubt as to the accuracy of the data from
which he draws them. I have myself been for nearly a
quarter of a century collecting, off and on, the folk-lore of
Western Ireland, not indeed in the shape in which Mr. Wentz
has collected it, but rather with an eye (partly for linguistic
and literary purposes) to its songs, sayings, ballads, proverbs,
and *sgéalta*, which last are generally the equivalent of the
German Märchen, but sometimes have a touch of the saga
nature about them. In making a collection of these things
I have naturally come across a very large amount of folk-
belief conversationally expressed, with regard to the ' good
people ' and other supernatural manifestations, so that
I can bear witness to the fidelity with which Mr. Wentz
has done his work on Irish soil, for to a great number of
the beliefs which he records I have myself heard parallels,
sometimes I have heard near variants of the stories, sometimes the identical stories. So we may, I think, unhesitat-
ingly accept his subject-matter, whatever, as I said, be the
conclusions we may deduce from them.

The folk-tale (*sean-sgéal*) or Märchen, which I have spent
so much time in collecting, must not be confounded with
the folk-belief which forms the basis of Mr. Wentz's studies.
The *sgéal* or story is something much more intricate, complicated, and thought-out than the belief. One can quite
easily distinguish between the two. One (the belief) is short,
conversational, chiefly relating to real people, and contains
no great sequence of incidents, while the other (the folk-tale)
is long, complicated, more or less conventional, and above
all has its interest grouped around a single central figure,
that of the hero or heroine. I may make this plainer by an
example. Let us go into a cottage on the mountain-side, as

Mr. Wentz and I have done so often, and ask the old man
of the house if he ever heard of such things as fairies, and
he will tell you that ' there is fairies in it surely. Didn't
his own father see the " forth " [1] beyond full of them, and he
passing by of a moonlight night and a little piper among
them, and he playing music that mortal man never heard
the like ? ' or he'll tell you that ' he himself wouldn't say
agin fairies for it 's often he heard their music at the old bush
behind the house '. Ask what the fairies are like, and he
will tell you—well, pretty much what Mr. Wentz tells us.
From this and the like accounts we form our ideas of fairies
and fairy music, of ghosts, mermaids, *púcas*, and so on, but
there is no sequence of incidents, no hero, no heroine, no
story.

Again, ask the old man if he knows e'er a *sean-sgéal* (story
or Märchen), and he will ask you at once, ' Did you ever
hear the Speckled Bull ; did you ever hear the Well at the
end of the world ; did you ever hear the Tailor and the
Three Beasts ; did you ever hear the Hornless Cow ? '
Ask him to relate one of these, and if you get him in the
right vein, which may be perhaps one time in ten, or if you
induce the right vein, which you may do perhaps nine times
out of ten, you will find him begin with a certain gravity
and solemnity at the very beginning, thus, ' There was once,
in old times and in old times it was, a king in Ireland '; or
perhaps ' a man who married a second wife ' ; or perhaps
' a widow woman with only one son ' : and the tale proceeds
to recount the life and adventures of the heroes or heroines,
whose biographies told in Irish in a sort of stereotyped
form may take from ten minutes to half an hour to get
through. Some stories would burn out a dip candle in the
telling, or even last the whole night. But these stories have
little or nothing to say to the questions raised in this book.

The problem we have to deal with is a startling one, as
thus put before us by Mr. Wentz. Are these beings of the
spirit world real beings, having a veritable existence of their
own, in a world of their own, or are they only the creation

---

[1] Anglo-Irish for *rath*, a circular earthen fort.

of the imagination of his informants, and the tradition of bygone centuries ? The newspaper, the ' National ' School, and the *Zeitgeist* have answered to their own entire satisfaction that these things are imagination pure and simple. Yet this off-hand condemnation does not always carry with it a perfect conviction. We do not doubt the existence of tree-martins or kingfishers, although nine hundred and ninety-nine people out of every thousand pass their entire lives without being vouchsafed a glimpse of them in their live state ; and may it not be the same with the creatures of the spirit world, may not they also exist, though to only one in a thousand it be vouchsafed to behold them ? The spirit creatures cannot be stuffed and put into museums, like rare animals and birds, whose existence we might doubt of if we had not seen them there ; yet they may exist just as such animals and birds do, though we cannot see them. I, at least, have often been tempted to think so. But the following considerations, partly drawn from comparative folk-lore, have made me hesitate about definitely accepting any theory.

In the first place, then, viewing the Irish spirit-world as a whole, we find that it contains, even on Mr. Wentz's showing, quite a number of different orders of beings, of varying shapes, appearances, size, and functions. Are we to believe that all those beings equally exist, and, on the principle that there can be no smoke without a fire, are we to hold that there would be no popular conception of the banshee, the leprechaun, or the *Maighdean-mhara* (sea-maiden, mermaid), and consequently no tales told about them, if such beings did not exist, and from time to time allow themselves to be seen like the wood-martin and the kingfisher ? This question is, moreover, further complicated by the belief in the appearance of things that are or appear to be inanimate objects, not living beings, such as the deaf coach or the phantom ship in full sail, the appearance of which Mr. Yeats has immortalized in one of his earliest and finest poems.

Again, although the *bean-sidhe* (banshee), leprechaun, *púca*, and the like are the most commonly known and usually seen creatures of the spirit world, yet great quantities of other appearances are believed to have been also sporadically met with. I very well remember sitting one night some four or five years ago in an hotel in Indianapolis, U.S.A., and talking to four Irishmen, one or two of them very wealthy, and all prosperous citizens of the United States. The talk happened to turn upon spirits—the only time during my entire American experiences in which such a thing happened—and each man of the four had a story of his own to tell, in which he was a convinced believer, of ghostly manifestations seen by him in Ireland. Two of these manifestations were of beings that would fall into no known category ; a monstrous rabbit as big as an ass, which plunged into the sea (rabbits can swim), and a white heifer which ascended to heaven, were two of them. I myself, when a boy of ten or eleven, was perfectly convinced that on a fine early dewy morning in summer when people were still in bed, I saw a strange horse run round a seven-acre field of ours and change into a woman, who ran even swifter than the horse, and after a couple of courses round the field disappeared into our haggard. I am sure, whatever I may believe to-day, no earthly persuasion would, at the time, have convinced me that I did not see this. Yet I never saw it again, and never heard of any one else seeing the same.

My object in mentioning these things is to show that if we concede the real objective existence of, let us say, the apparently well-authenticated banshee (*Bean-sidhe*, ' woman-fairy '), where are we to stop ? for any number of beings, more or less well authenticated, come crowding on her heels, so many indeed that they would point to a far more extensive world of different shapes than is usually suspected, not to speak of inanimate objects like the coach and the ship. Of course there is nothing inherently impossible in all these shapes existing any more than in one of them existing, but they all seem to me to rest upon the same kind of testimony, stronger in the case of some, less strong in the case of others, and it is as well to point out this clearly.

My own experience is that beliefs in the *Sidhe* (pronounced

Shee) folk, and in other denizens of the invisible world is, in many places, rapidly dying. In reading folk-lore collections like those of Mr. Wentz and others, one is naturally inclined to exaggerate the extent and depth of these traditions. They certainly still exist, and can be found if you go to search for them ; but they often exist almost as it were by sufferance, only in spots, and are ceasing to be any longer a power. Near my home in a western county (County Roscommon) rises gently a slope, which, owing to the flatness of the surrounding regions, almost becomes a hill, and is a conspicuous object for many miles upon every side. The old people called it in Irish *Mullach na Sidhe*. This name is now practically lost, and it is called Fairymount. So extinct have the traditions of the *Sidhe*-folk, who lived within the hill, become, that a high ecclesiastic recently driving by asked his driver was there an Irish name for the hill, and what was it, and his driver did not know. There took place a few years ago a much talked of bog-slide in the neighbouring townland of Cloon-Sheever (*Sidhbhair* or *Siabhra*), ' the Meadow of the Fairies,' and many newspaper correspondents came to view it. One of the natives told a sympathetic newspaper reporter, ' Sure we always knew it was going to move, that 's why the place is named Cloon-Sheever, the bog was always in a " shiver " ! ' I have never been able to hear of any legends attached to what must have at one time been held to be the head-quarters of the *Sidhe* for a score of miles round it.

Of all the beings in the Irish mythological world the *Sidhe* are, however, apparently the oldest and the most distinctive. Beside them in literature and general renown all other beings sink into insignificance. A belief in them formerly dominated the whole of Irish life. The *Sidhe* or Tuatha De Danann were a people like ourselves who inhabited the hills —not as a rule the highest and most salient eminences, but I think more usually the pleasant undulating slopes or gentle hill-sides—and who lived there a life of their own, marrying or giving in marriage, banqueting or making war, and leading there just as real a life as is our own. All Irish

literature, particularly perhaps the 'Colloquy of the Ancients' (*Agallamh na Senórach*) abounds with reference to
them. To inquire how the Irish originally came by their
belief in these beings, the *Sidhe* or Tuatha De Danann, is to
raise a question which cannot be answered, any more than
one can answer the question, Where did the Romans obtain
their belief in Bacchus and the fauns, or the Greeks their
own belief in the beings of Olympus?

But granting such belief to have been indigenous to the
Irish, as it certainly seems to have been, then the tall,
handsome fairies of Ben Bulbin and the Sligo district, about
whom Mr. Wentz tells us so much interesting matter, might
be accounted for as being a continuation of the tradition
of the ancient Gaels, or *a piece of heredity inherent in the
folk-imagination*. I mean, in other words, that the tradition
about these handsome dwellers within the hill-sides having
been handed down for ages, and having been perhaps ex-
ceptionally well preserved in those districts, people saw just
what they had always been told existed, or, if I may so put
it, they saw what they expected to see.

Fin Bheara, the King of the Connacht Fairies in Cnoc
Meadha (or Castlehacket) in the County Galway, his Queen
Nuala, and all the beautiful forms seen by Mr. Wentz's seer-
witness (pp. 60 ff.), all the banshees and all the human figures,
white women, and so forth, who are seen in raths and moats
and on hill-sides, are the direct descendants, so to speak, of
the Tuatha De Danann or the *Sidhe*. Of this, I think, there
can be no doubt whatever.

But then how are we to account for the little red-dressed
men and women and the leprechauns? Yet, are they any
more wonderful than the pygmies of classic tradition? Is
not the Mermaid to be found in Greece, and is not the
Lorelei as Germanic as the Kelpy is Caledonian. If we grant
that all these are creatures of primitive folk-belief, then
how they come to be so ceases to be a Celtic problem, it
becomes a world problem. But granted, as I say, that they
were all creatures of primitive folk-belief, then their occasional appearances, or the belief in such, may be accounted

for in exactly the same way as I have suggested to be possible in the case of the Ben Bulbin fairies.

As for the belief in ghosts or *revenants* (in Irish *tais* or *taidhbhse*), it seems to me that this may possibly rest to some extent upon a different footing altogether. Here we are not confronted by a different order of beings of different shapes and attributes from our own, but only with the appearances, amongst the living, of men who were believed or known to be dead or far away from the scene of their appearances. Even those who may be most sceptical about the *Sidhe*-folk and the leprechauns are likely to be convinced (on the mere evidence) that the existence of ' astral bodies ' or ' doubles ', or whatever we may call them, and the appearances of people, especially in the hour of their death, to other people who were perhaps hundreds of miles away at the time, is amply proven. Yet whatever may have been the case originally when man was young, I do not think that this had in later times any more direct bearing upon the belief in the *Sidhe*, the leprechauns, the mermaid, and similar beings than upon the belief in the Greek Pantheon, the naiads, the dryads, or the fauns ; all of which beliefs, probably arising originally from an animistic source, must have differentiated themselves at a very early period. Of course every real apparition, every ' ghost ' apparition, tends now, and must have tended at all times, to strengthen every spirit belief. For do not ghost apparitions belong, in a way, to the same realm as all the others we have spoken of, that is, to a realm equally outside our normal experience ?

Another very interesting point, and one hitherto generally overlooked, is this, that different parts of the Irish soil cherish different bodies of supernatural beings. The North of Ireland believes in beings unknown in the South, and North-East Leinster has spirits unknown to the West. Some places seem to be almost given up to special beliefs. Any outsider, for instance, who may have read that powerful and grisly book, *La Légende de la Mort*, by M. Anatole Le Braz, in two large volumes, all about the awful appearances of *Ankou* (Death), who simply dominates the folk-lore of

Brittany, will probably be very much astonished to know that, though I have been collecting Irish folk-lore all my life, I have never met Death figuring as a personality in more than two or three tales, and these mostly of a trivial or humorous description, though the Deaf Coach (*Cóiste Bodhar*), the belief in which is pretty general, does seem a kind of parallel to the creaking cart in which *Ankou* rides.

I would suggest, then, that the restriction of certain forms of spirits, if I may so call them, to certain localities, may be due to race intermixture. I would imagine that where the people of a primitive tribe settled down most strongly, they also most strongly preserved the memory of those super-natural beings who were peculiarly their own. The *Sidhe*-folk appear to be pre-eminently and distinctively Milesian, but the *geancanach* (name of some little spirit in Meath and portion of Ulster) may have been believed in by a race entirely different from that which believed in the *clúracaun* (a Munster sprite). Some of these beliefs may be Aryan, but many are probably pre-Celtic.

Is it not strange that while the names and exploits of the great semi-mythological heroes of the various Saga cycles of Ireland, Cuchulainn, Conor mac Nessa, Finn, Osgar, Oisin, and the rest, are at present the inheritance of all Ireland, and are known in every part of it, there should still be, as I have said, supernatural beings believed in which are unknown outside of their own districts, and of which the rest of Ireland has never heard? If the inhabitants of the limited districts in which these are seen still think they see them, my suggestion is that the earlier race handed down an account of the primitive beings believed in by their own tribe, and later generations, if they saw anything, saw just what they were told existed.

Whilst far from questioning the actual existence of certain spiritual forms and apparitions, I venture to throw out these considerations for what they may be worth, and I desire again to thank Mr. Wentz for all the valuable data he has collected for throwing light upon so interesting a question.

RATRA, FRENCHPARK,
  COUNTY ROSCOMMON, IRELAND,
    September 1910.

THE FAIRY FOLK OF TARA

On the ancient Hill of Tara, from whose heights the High Kings once ruled all Ireland, from where the sacred fires in pagan days announced the annual resurrection of the sun, the Easter Tide, where the magic of Patrick prevailed over the magic of the Druids, and where the hosts of the Tuatha De Danann were wont to appear at the great Feast of *Samain*, to-day the fairy-folk of modern times hold undisputed sovereignty. And from no point better than Tara, which thus was once the magical and political centre of the Sacred Island, could we begin our study of the Irish Fairy-Faith. Though the Hill has lain unploughed and deserted since the curses of Christian priests fell upon it, on the calm air of summer evenings, at the twilight hour, wondrous music still sounds over its slopes, and at night long, weird processions of silent spirits march round its grass-grown *raths* and *forts*.[1] It is only men who fear the curse of the Christians ; the fairy-folk regard it not.

The Rev. Father Peter Kenney, of Kilmessan, had directed me to John Graham, an old man over seventy years of age, who has lived near Tara most of his life ; and after I had found John, and he had led me from *rath* to *rath* and then right through the length of the site where once stood the banquet hall of kings and heroes and Druids, as he earnestly described the past glories of Tara to which these ancient monuments bear silent testimony, we sat down in the thick sweet grass on the Sacred Hill and began talking of the olden times in Ireland, and then of the ' good people ' :—

The ' Good People's ' Music.—' As sure as you are sitting down I heard the pipes there in that wood (pointing to

[1] Throughout Ireland there are many ancient, often prehistoric, earthworks or tumuli, which are popularly called *forts*, *raths*, or *dúns*, and in folk-belief these are considered fairy hills or the abodes of various orders of fairies. In this belief we see at work a definite anthropomorphism which attributes dwellings here on earth to an invisible spirit-race, as though this race were actually the spirits of the ancient Irish who built the *forts*. As we proceed, we shall see how important and varied a part these earthworks play in the Irish Fairy-Faith (cf. chapter viii, on Archaeology).

a wood on the north-west slope of the Hill, and west of the banquet hall). I heard the music another time on a hot summer evening at the Rath of Ringlestown, in a field where all the grass had been burned off; and I often heard it in the wood of Tara. Whenever the *good people* play, you hear their music all through the field as plain as can be; and it is the grandest kind of music. It may last half the night, but once day comes, it ends.'

Who the ' Good People ' are.—I now asked John what sort of a race the 'good people' are, and where they came from, and this is his reply :—' People killed and murdered in war stay on earth till their time is up, and they are among the *good people*. The souls on this earth are as thick as the grass (running his walking-stick through a thick clump), and you can't see them; and evil spirits are just as thick, too, and people don't know it. Because there are so many spirits knocking (going) about they must appear to some people. The old folk saw the *good people* here on the Hill a hundred times, and they'd always be talking about them. The *good people* can see everything, and you dare not meddle with them. They live in *raths*, and their houses are in them. The opinion always was that they are a race of spirits, for they can go into different forms, and can appear big as well as little.'

EVIDENCE FROM KILMESSAN, NEAR TARA

John Boylin, born in County Meath about sixty years ago, will be our witness from Kilmessan, a village about two miles from Tara; and he, being one of the men of the vicinity best informed about its folk-lore, is able to offer testimony of very great value :—

The Fairy Tribes.—' There is said to be a whole tribe of little red men living in Glen Odder, between Ringlestown and Tara; and on long evenings in June they have been heard. There are other breeds or castes of fairies; and it seems to me, when I recall our ancient traditions, that some of these fairies are of the Fir Bolgs, some of the Tuatha De Danann, and some of the Milesians. All of them have been

seen serenading round the western slope of Tara, dressed in
ancient Irish costumes. Unlike the little red men, these
fairy races are warlike and given to making invasions. Long
processions of them have been seen going round the King's
Chair (an earthwork on which the Kings of Tara are said
to have been crowned) ; and they then would appear like
soldiers of ancient Ireland in review.'

The Fairy Procession.—' We were told as children, that, as
soon as night fell, the fairies from Rath Ringlestown would
form in a procession, across Tara road, pass round certain
bushes which have not been disturbed for ages, and join the
gangkena (?) or host of industrious folk, the red fairies. We
were afraid, and our nurses always brought us home before
the advent of the fairy procession. One of the passes used
by this procession happened to be between two mud-wall
houses ; and it is said that a man went out of one of these
houses at the wrong time, for when found he was dead:
the fairies had *taken* him because he interfered with their
procession.' [1]

Death through Cutting Fairy-Bushes.—' A man named
Caffney cut as fuel to boil his pot of potatoes some of these
undisturbed bushes round which the fairies pass. When
he put the wood under the pot, though it spat fire, and fire-
sparkles would come out of it, it would not burn. The man
pined away gradually. In six months after cutting the fairy-
bushes, he was dead. Just before he died, he told his
experiences with the wood to his brother, and his brother
told me.'

The Fairies are the Dead.—' According to the local belief,
fairies are the spirits of the departed. Tradition says
that Hugh O'Neil in the sixteenth century, after his march
to the south, encamped his army on the *Rath* or *Fort* of
Ringlestown, to be assisted by the spirits of the mighty
dead who dwelt within this *rath*. And it is believed that

---

[1] An Irish mystic, and seer of great power, with whom I have often
discussed the Fairy-Faith in its details, regards ' fairy paths ' or ' fairy
passes ' as actual magnetic arteries, so to speak, through which circulates
the earth's magnetism.

Gerald Fitzgerald has been seen coming out of the Hill of Mollyellen, down in County Louth, leading his horse and dressed in the old Irish costume, with breastplate, spear, and war outfit.'

Fairy Possession.—' Rose Carroll was possessed by a fairy-spirit. It is known that her father held communion with evil spirits, and it appears that they often assisted him. The Carrolls' house was built at the end of a fairy *fort*, and part of it was scooped out of this *fort*. Rose grew so peculiar that her folks locked her up. After two years she was able to shake off the fairy possession by being taken to Father Robinson's sisters, and then to an old witch-woman in Drogheda.'

In the Valley of the Boyne

In walking along the River Boyne, from Slane to Knowth and New Grange, I stopped at the cottage of Owen Morgan, at Ross-na-Righ, or ' the Wood of the Kings ', though the ancient wood has long since disappeared ; and as we sat looking out over the sunlit beauty of Ireland's classic river, and in full view of the first of the famous *moats*, this is what Owen Morgan told me :—

How the Shoemaker's Daughter became the Queen of Tara.— ' In olden times there lived a shoemaker and his wife up there near Moat Knowth, and their first child was taken by the queen of the fairies who lived inside the moat, and a little leprechaun left in its place. The same exchange was made when the second child was born. At the birth of the third child the fairy queen came again and ordered one of her three servants to take the child ; but the child could not be moved because of a great beam of iron, too heavy to lift, which lay across the baby's breast. The second servant and then the third failed like the first, and the queen herself could not move the child. The mother being short of pins had used a needle to fasten the child's clothes, and that was what appeared to the fairies as a beam of iron, for there was virtue in steel in those days.

' So the fairy queen decided to bestow gifts upon the

child ; and advised each of the three servants to give, in turn, a different gift. The first one said, " May she be the grandest lady in the world " ; the second one said, " May she be the greatest singer in the world " ; and the third one said, " May she be the best mantle-maker in the world." Then the fairy queen said, " Your gifts are all very good, but I will give a gift of my own better than any of them : the first time she happens to go out of the house let her come back into it under the form of a rat." The mother heard all that the fairy women said, and so she never permitted her daughter to leave the house.

' When the girl reached the age of eighteen, it happened that the young prince of Tara, in riding by on a hunt, heard her singing, and so entranced was he with the music that he stopped to listen ; and, the song ended, he entered the house, and upon seeing the wonderful beauty of the singer asked her to marry him. The mother said that could not be, and taking the daughter out of the house for the first time brought her back into it in an apron under the form of a rat, that the prince might understand the refusal.

' This enchantment, however, did not change the prince's love for the beautiful singer ; and he explained how there was a day mentioned with his father, the king, for all the great ladies of Ireland to assemble in the Halls of Tara, and that the grandest lady and the greatest singer and the best mantle-maker would be chosen as his wife. When he added that each lady must come in a chariot, the rat spoke to him and said that he must send to her home, on the day named, four piebald cats and a pack of cards, and that she would make her appearance, provided that at the time her chariot came to the Halls of Tara no one save the prince should be allowed near it ; and, she finally said to the prince, " Until the day mentioned with your father, you must carry me as a rat in your pocket."

' But before the great day arrived, the rat had made everything known to one of the fairy women, and so when the four piebald cats and the pack of cards reached the girl's home, the fairies at once turned the cats into the four most

splendid horses in the world, and the pack of cards into
the most wonderful chariot in the world ; and, as the
chariot was setting out from the Moat for Tara, the fairy
queen clapped her hands and laughed, and the enchantment over the girl was broken, so that she became, as
before, the prettiest lady in the world, and she sitting in the
chariot.

' When the prince saw the wonderful chariot coming, he
knew whose it was, and went out alone to meet it ; but
he could not believe his eyes on seeing the lady inside.
And then she told him about the witches and fairies, and
explained everything.

' Hundreds of ladies had come to the Halls of Tara from
all Ireland, and every one as grand as could be. The contest
began with the singing, and ended with the mantle-making,
and the young girl was the last to appear ; but to the amazement of all the company the king had to give in (admit)
that the strange woman was the grandest lady, the greatest
singer, and the best mantle-maker in Ireland ; and when
the old king died she became the Queen of Tara.'

After this ancient legend, which Owen Morgan heard from
the old folks when he was a boy, he told me many anecdotes
about the ' good people ' of the Boyne, who are little men
usually dressed in red.

The ' Good People ' at New Grange.—Between Knowth and
New Grange I met Maggie Timmons carrying a pail of
butter-milk to her calves; and when we stopped on the road to
talk, I asked her, in due time, if any of the ' good people ' ever
appeared in the region, or about New Grange, which we
could see in the field, and she replied, in reference to New
Grange :—' I am sure the neighbours used to see the *good
people* come out of it at night and in the morning. The
good people inherited the *fort.*'

Then I asked her what the ' good people ' are, and she
said :—' When they disappear they go like fog ; they must
be something like spirits, or how could they disappear in that
way ? I knew of people,' she added, ' who would milk in
the fields about here and spill milk on the ground for the

good people; and pots of potatoes would be put out for the *good people* at night.' (See chap. viii for additional New Grange folk-lore.)

THE TESTIMONY OF AN IRISH PRIEST

We now pass directly to West Ireland, in many ways our most important field, and where of all places in the Celtic world the Fairy-Faith is vigorously alive; and it seems very fitting to offer the first opportunity to testify in behalf of that district to a scholarly priest of the Roman Church, for what he tells us is almost wholly the result of his own memories and experiences as an Irish boy in Connemara, supplemented in a valuable way by his wider and more mature knowledge of the fairy-belief as he sees it now among his own parishioners :—

Knock Ma Fairies.—' Knock Ma, which you see over there, is said to contain excavated passages and a palace where the fairies live, and with them the people they have *taken*. And from the inside of the hill there is believed to be an entrance to an underground world. It is a common opinion that after consumptives die they are there with the fairies in good health. The wasted body is not taken into the hill, for it is usually regarded as not the body of the deceased but rather as that of a changeling, the general belief being that the real body and the soul are carried off together, and those of an old person from Fairyland substituted. The old person left soon declines and dies.'

Safeguards against Fairies.—' It was proper when having finished milking a cow to put one's thumb in the pail of milk, and with the wet thumb to make the sign of the cross on the thigh of the cow on the side milked, to be safe against fairies. And I have seen them when churning put a live coal about an inch square under the churn, because it was an old custom connected with fairies.'

Milk and Butter for Fairies.—' Whatever milk falls on the ground in milking a cow is taken by the fairies, for fairies need a little milk. Also, after churning, the knife which is run through the butter in drying it must not be scraped

clean, for what sticks to it belongs to the fairies. Out of
three pounds of butter, for example, an ounce or two would
be left for the fairies. I have seen this several times.'

Crossing a Stream, and Fairies.—' When out on a dark
night, if pursued by fairies or ghosts one is considered quite
safe if one can get over some stream. I remember coming
home on a dark night with a boy companion and hearing
a noise, and then after we had run to a stream and crossed
it feeling quite safe.'

Fairy Preserves.—' A heap of stones in a field should not be
disturbed, though needed for building—especially if they are
part of an ancient tumulus. The fairies are said to live inside
the pile, and to move the stones would be most unfortunate.
If a house happens to be built on a fairy preserve, or in
a fairy track, the occupants will have no luck. Everything
will go wrong. Their animals will die, their children fall
sick, and no end of trouble will come on them. When the
house happens to have been built in a fairy track, the doors
on the front and back, or the windows if they are in the
line of the track, cannot be kept closed at night, for the
fairies must march through. Near Ballinrobe there is an
old *fort* which is still the preserve of the fairies, and the
land round it. The soil is very fine, and yet no one would
dare to till it. Some time ago in laying out a new road
the engineers determined to run it through the *fort*, but
the people rose almost in rebellion, and the course had to
be changed. The farmers wouldn't cut down a tree or bush
growing on the hill or preserve for anything.'

Fairy Control over Crops.—' Fairies are believed to control
crops and their ripening. A field of turnips may promise
well, and its owner will count on so many tons to the acre,
but if when the crop is gathered it is found to be far short
of the estimate, the explanation is that the fairies have
extracted so much substance from it. The same thing is
the case with corn.'

November Eve and Fairies.—' On November Eve it is not
right to gather or eat blackberries or sloes, nor after that
time as long as they last. On November Eve the fairies

pass over all such things and make them unfit to eat. If one dares to eat them afterwards one will have serious illness. We firmly believed this as boys, and I laugh now when I think how we used to gorge ourselves with berries on the last day of October, and then for weeks after pass by bushes full of the most luscious fruit, and with mouths watering for it couldn't eat it.'

Fairies as Flies.—' There is an old abbey on the river, in County Mayo, and people say the fairies had a great battle near it, and that the slaughter was tremendous. At the time, the fairies appeared as swarms of flies coming from every direction to that spot. Some came from Knock Ma, and some from South Ireland, the opinion being that fairies can assume any form they like. The battle lasted a day and a night, and when it was over one could have filled baskets with the dead flies which floated down the river.'

Those who Return from Faerie.—' Persons in a short trance-state of two or three days' duration are said to be away with the fairies enjoying a festival. The festival may be very material in its nature, or it may be purely spiritual. Sometimes one may thus go to Faerie for an hour or two ; or one may remain there for seven, fourteen, or twenty-one years. The mind of a person coming out of Fairyland is usually a blank as to what has been seen and done there. Another idea is that the person knows well enough all about Fairyland, but is prevented from communicating the knowledge. A certain woman of whom I knew said she had forgotten all about her experiences in Faerie, but a friend who heard her objected, and said she did remember, and wouldn't tell. A man may remain awake at night to watch one who has been to Fairyland to see if that one holds communication with the fairies. Others say in such a case that the fairies know you are on the alert, and will not be discovered.'

THE TESTIMONY OF A GALWAY PIPER

Fairies = Sidheóga.—According to our next witness, Steven Ruan, a piper of Galway, with whom I have often talked, there is one class of fairies ' who are nobody else than the

spirits of men and women who once lived on earth '; and
the banshee is a dead friend, relative, or ancestor who
appears to give a warning. ' The fairies ', he says, ' never
care about old folks. They only *take* babies, and young men
and young women. If a young wife dies, she is said to have
been *taken* by *them*, and ever afterwards to live in Fairyland.
The same things are said about a young man or a child who
dies. Fairyland is a place of delights, where music, and
singing, and dancing, and feasting are continually enjoyed ;
and its inhabitants are all about us, as numerous as the
blades of grass.'

A Fairy Dog.—In the course of another conversation,
Steven pointed to a rocky knoll in a field not far from his
home, and said :—' I saw a dog with a white ring around
his neck by that hill there, and the oldest men round Galway
have seen him, too, for he has been here for one hundred
years or more. He is a dog of the *good people*, and only
appears at certain hours of the night.'

An Old Piper in Fairyland.—And before we had done
talking, the subject of fairy-music came up, and the following little story coming from one of the last of the old Irish
pipers himself, about a brother piper, is of more than ordinary
value :—' There used to be an old piper called Flannery who
lived in Oranmore, County Galway. I imagine he was one
of the old generation. And one time the *good people* took
him to Fairyland to learn his profession. He studied music
with them for a long time, and when he returned he was as
great a piper as any in Ireland. But he died young, for the
good people wanted him to play for them.'

THE TESTIMONY OF ' OLD PATSY ' OF ARANMORE

Our next witness is an old man, familiarly called ' Old
Patsy ', who is a native of the Island of Aranmore, off the
coast from Galway, and he lives on the island amid a little
group of straw-thatched fishermen's homes called Oak
Quarter. As ' Old Patsy ' stood beside a rude stone cross
near Oak Quarter, in one of those curious places on Aranmore, where each passing funeral stops long enough to erect

a little memorial pile of stones on the smooth rocky surface of the roadside enclosure, he told me many anecdotes about the mysteries of his native island.

Aranmore Fairies.—Twenty years or so ago round the *Bedd* of Dermot and Grania, just above us on the hill, there were seen many fairies, ' crowds of them,' said ' Old Patsy ', and a single deer. They began to chase the deer, and followed it right over the island. At another time similar little people chased a horse. ' The rocks were full of them, and they were small fellows.'

A Fairy Beating—in a Dream.—' In the South Island,' he continued, ' as night was coming on, a man was giving his cow water at a well, and, as he looked on the other side of a wall, he saw many strange people playing hurley. When they noticed him looking at them, one came up and struck the cow a hard blow, and turning on the man cut his face and body very badly. The man might not have been so badly off, but he returned to the well after the first encounter and got five times as bad a beating ; and when he reached home he couldn't speak at all, until the cock crew. Then he told about his adventures, and slept a little. When he woke up in the daylight he was none the worse for his beating, for the fairies had rubbed something on his face.' Patsy says he knew the man, who if still alive is now in America, where he went several years ago.

Where Fairies Live.—When I asked Patsy where the fairies live, he turned half around, and pointing in the direction of Dun Aengus, which was in full view on the sharp sky-line of Aranmore, said that there, in a large tumulus on the hillside below it, they had one of their favourite abodes. But, he added, ' The rocks are full of them, and they are small fellows.' Just across the road from where we were standing, in a spot near Oak Quarter, another place was pointed out where the fairies are often seen dancing. The name of it is *Moneen an Damhsa*, ' the Little Bog of the Dance.' Other sorts of fairies live in the sea ; and some of them who live on Aranmore (probably in conjunction with those in the sea) go out over the water and cause storms and wind.

The Testimony of a Roman Catholic Theologian

The following evidence, by the Rev. Father ——, came out during a discussion concerning spirits and fairies as regarded by Roman Catholic theology, which he and I enjoyed when we met as fellow travellers in Galway Town :—

Of Magic and Place-spirits.—' Magic, according to Catholic theology, is nothing else than the solicitation of spiritual powers to help us. If evil spirits are evoked by certain irrational practices it is unholy magic, and this is altogether forbidden by our Church. All charms, spells, divination, necromancy, or geomancy are unholy magic. Holy magic is practised by carrying the Cross in Christ. Now evil magic has been practised here in Ireland : butter has been *taken* so that none came from the churning ; cows have been made to die of maladies ; and fields made unproductive. A cow was bought from an old woman in Connemara, and no butter was ever had from the cow until exorcism with holy water was performed. This is reported to me as a fact.' And in another relation the Rev. Father —— said what for us is highly significant :—' My private opinion is that in certain places here in Ireland where pagan sacrifices were practised, evil spirits through receiving homage gained control, and still hold control, unless driven out by exorcisms.'

The Testimony of the Town Clerk of Tuam

To the town clerk of Tuam, Mr. John Glynn, who since his boyhood has taken a keen interest in the traditions of his native county, I am indebted for the following valuable summary of the fairy creed in that part of North Galway where Finvara rules :—

Fairies of the Tuam Country.—' The whole of Knock Ma (*Cnoc Meadha* [1]), which probably means Hill of the Plain, is said to be the palace of Finvara, king of the Connaught

---

[1] ' Irish scholars differ as to the signification of *Meadha*. Some say that it is the genitive case of *Meadh*, the name of some ancient chieftain who was buried in the hill. *Knock Magh* is the spelling often used by writers who hold that the name means " Hill of the Plain ".'—John Glynn.

fairies. There are a good many legends about Finvara, but very few about Queen Meave in this region.'

Famine of 1846–7 caused by Fairies.—' During 1846–7 the potato crop in Ireland was a failure, and very much suffering resulted. At the time, the country people in these parts attributed the famine to disturbed conditions in the fairy world. Old Thady Steed once told me about the conditions then prevailing, " Sure, we couldn't be any other way ; and I saw the *good people* and hundreds besides me saw them fighting in the sky over Knock Ma and on towards Galway." And I heard others say they saw the fighting also.'

Fairyland ; and the Seeress.—' Fairies are said to be immortal, and the fairy world is always described as an immaterial place, though I do not think it is the same as the world of the dead. Sick persons, however, are often said to be with the fairies, and when cured, to have come back. A woman who died here about thirty years ago was commonly believed to have been with the fairies during her seven years' sickness when she was a maiden. She married after coming back, and had children ; and she was always able to see the *good people* and to talk with them, for she had the second-sight. And it is said that she used to travel with the fairies at night. After her marriage she lived in Tuam, and though her people were six or seven miles out from Tuam in the country, she could always tell all that was taking place with them there, and she at her own home at the time.'

Fairies on May Day.—' On May Day the *good people* can steal butter if the chance is given them. If a person enters a house then, and churning is going on, he must take a hand in it, or else there will be no butter. And if fire is given away on May Day nothing will go right for the whole year.'

The Three Fairy Drops.—' Even yet certain things are due the fairies ; for example, two years ago, in the Court Room here in Tuam, a woman was on trial for watering milk, and to the surprise of us all who were conducting the proceedings, and, it can be added, to the great amusement of

the onlookers, she swore that she had only added " the three
fairy drops ".'

Food of Fairies.—' Food, after it has been put out at night
for the fairies, is not allowed to be eaten afterwards by man
or beast, not even by pigs. Such food is said to have no real
substance left in it, and to let anything eat it wouldn't
be thought of. The underlying idea seems to be that the
fairies extract the spiritual essence from food offered to
them, leaving behind the grosser elements.'

Fairy Warfare.—' When the fairy tribes under the various
kings and queens have a battle, one side manages to have
a living man among them, and he by knocking the fairies
about turns the battle in case the side he is on is losing. It
is always usual for the Munster fairy king to challenge
Finvara, the Connaught fairy king.'

County Sligo, and the Testimony of a Peasant Seer [1]

The Ben Bulbin country in County Sligo is one of those
rare places in Ireland where fairies are thought to be visible,
and our first witness from there claims to be able to see
the fairies or ' gentry ' and to talk with them. This mortal
so favoured lives in the same townland where his fathers
have lived during four hundred years, directly beneath the
shadows of Ben Bulbin, on whose sides Dermot is said to
have been killed while hunting the wild-boar. And this
famous old mountain, honeycombed with curious grottoes
ages ago when the sea beat against its perpendicular flanks,

[1] On September 8, 1909, about a year after this testimony was given,
Mr. ——, our seer-witness, at his own home near Grange, told to me again
the same essential facts concerning his psychical experiences as during
my first interview with him, and even repeated word for word the expressions the ' gentry ' used in communicating with him. Therefore I feel that
he is thoroughly sincere in his beliefs and descriptions, whatever various
readers may think of them. As his neighbours said to me about him—
and I interviewed a good many of them—' Some give in to him and some
do not ' ; but they always spoke of him with respect, though a few naturally consider him eccentric. At the time of our second meeting (which
gave me a chance to revise the evidence as first taken down) Mr. ——
made this additional statement :—' The *gentry* do not tell all their secrets,
and I do not understand many things about them, nor can I be sure that
everything I tell concerning them is exact.'

is the very place where the 'gentry' have their chief abode. Even on its broad level summit, for it is a high square table-land like a mighty cube of rock set down upon the earth by some antediluvian god, there are treacherous holes, wherein more than one hunter may have been lost for ever, penetrating to unknown depths; and by listening one can hear the tides from the ocean three or four miles away surging in and out through ancient subterranean channels, connected with these holes. In the neighbouring mountains there are long caverns which no man has dared to penetrate to the end, and even dogs, it is said, have been put in them never to emerge, or else to come out miles away.

One day when the heavy white fog-banks hung over Ben Bulbin and its neighbours, and there was a weird almost-twilight at midday over the purple heather bog-lands at their base, and the rain was falling, I sat with my friend before a comfortable fire of fragrant turf in his cottage and heard about the 'gentry' :—

Encounters with the 'Gentry'.—'When I was a young man I often used to go out in the mountains over there (pointing out of the window in their direction) to fish for trout, or to hunt ; and it was in January on a cold, dry day while carrying my gun that I and a friend with me, as we were walking around Ben Bulbin, saw one of the *gentry* for the first time. I knew who it was, for I had heard the *gentry* described ever since I could remember ; and this one was dressed in blue with a head-dress adorned with what seemed to be frills.[1] When he came up to us, he said to me in a sweet and silvery voice, " The seldomer you come to this mountain the better. A young lady here wants to take you away." Then he told us not to fire off our guns, because the *gentry* dislike being disturbed by the noise. And he seemed to be like a soldier of the *gentry* on guard. As we were leaving the mountains, he told us not to look back, and we didn't. Another time I was alone trout-fishing in nearly the same region when I heard a voice say, " It is —— bare-

---

[1] A learned and more careful Irish seer thinks this head-dress should really be described as an aura.

footed and fishing." Then there came a whistle like music and a noise like the beating of a drum, and soon one of the *gentry* came and talked with me for half an hour. He said, " Your mother will die in eleven months, and do not let her die unanointed." And she did die within eleven months. As he was going away he warned me, " You must be in the house before sunset. Do not delay ! Do not delay ! They can do nothing to you until I get back in the castle." As I found out afterwards, he was going to *take* me, but hesitated because he did not want to leave my mother alone. After these warnings I was always afraid to go to the mountains, but lately I have been told I could go if I took a friend with me.'

' *Gentry* ' *Protection*.—' The *gentry* have always befriended and protected me. I was drowned twice but for them. Once I was going to Durnish Island, a mile off the coast. The channel is very deep, and at the time there was a rough sea, with the tide running out, and I was almost lost. I shrieked and shouted, and finally got safe to the mainland. The day I talked with one of the *gentry* at the foot of the mountain when he was for *taking* me, he mentioned this, and said they were the ones who saved me from drowning then.'

' *Gentry* ' *Stations*.—' Especially in Ireland, the *gentry* live inside the mountains in beautiful castles ; and there are a good many branches of them in other countries. Like armies, they have various stations and move from one to another. Some live in the Wicklow Mountains near Dublin.'

' *Gentry* ' *Control Over Human Affairs*.—' The *gentry* take a great interest in the affairs of men, and they always stand for justice and right. Any side they favour in our wars, that side wins. They favoured the Boers, and the Boers did get their rights. They told me they favoured the Japanese and not the Russians, because the Russians are tyrants. Sometimes they fight among themselves. One of them once said, " I'd fight for a friend, or I'd fight for Ireland." '

The ' Gentry ' Described.—In response to my wish, this description of the ' gentry ' was given :—' The folk are the grandest I have ever seen. They are far superior to us, and that is why they are called the *gentry*. They are not a working class, but a military-aristocratic class, tall and noble-appearing. They are a distinct race between our own and that of spirits, as they have told me. Their qualifications are tremendous. " We could cut off half the human race, but would not," they said, " for we are expecting salvation." And I knew a man three or four years ago whom they struck down with paralysis. Their sight is so penetrating that I think they could see through the earth. They have a silvery voice, quick and sweet. The music they play is most beautiful. They *take* the whole body and soul of young and intellectual people who are interesting, transmuting the body to a body like their own. I asked them once if they ever died, and they said, " No ; we are always kept young." Once they take you and you taste food in their palace you cannot come back. You are changed to one of them, and live with them for ever. They are able to appear in different forms. One once appeared to me, and seemed only four feet high, and stoutly built. He said, " I am bigger than I appear to you now. We can make the old young, the big small, the small big." One of their women told all the secrets of my family. She said that my brother in Australia would travel much and suffer hardships, all of which came true ; and foretold that my nephew, then about two years old, would become a great clergyman in America, and that is what he is now. Besides the *gentry*, who are a distinct class, there are bad spirits and ghosts, which are nothing like them. My mother once saw a leprechaun beside a bush hammering. He disappeared before she could get to him, but he also was unlike one of the *gentry*.' [1]

---

[1] I have been told by a friend in California, who is a student of psychical sciences, that there exist in certain parts of that state, notably in the Yosemite Valley, as the Red Men seem to have known, according to their traditions, invisible races exactly comparable to the ' gentry ' of this Ben Bulbin country such as our seer-witness describes them and as other seers in Ireland have described them, and quite like the ' people of peace ' as described by Kirk, the seventh son, in his *Secret Commonwealth* (see this study, p. 85 n.). These California races are said to exist now, as the Irish and Scotch invisible races are said to exist now, by seers who can behold them ; and, like the latter races, are described as a distinct order of beings who

EVIDENCE FROM GRANGE

Our next witness, who lives about three miles from our last witness, is Hugh Currid, the oldest man in Grange ; and so old is he that now he does little more than sit in the chimney-corner smoking, and, as he looks at the red glow of the peat, dreaming of the olden times. Hugh knows English very imperfectly, and so what he narrated was in the ancient Gaelic which his fathers spoke. When Father Hines took me to Hugh's cottage, Hugh was in his usual silent pose before the fire. At first he rather resented having his thoughts disturbed, but in a few minutes he was as talkative as could be, for there is nothing like the mention of Ireland to get him started. The Father left us then ; and with the help of Hugh's sister as an interpreter I took down what he said :—

The Flax-Seller's Return from Faerie.—' An old woman near Lough More, where Father Patrick was drowned,[1] who used to make her living by selling flax at the market, was *taken* by the *gentry*, and often came back afterwards to her three children to comb their hair. One time she told a neighbour that the money she saved from her dealings in flax would be found near a big rock on the lake-shore, which she indicated, and that she wanted the three children to have it.'

A Wife Recovered from the ' Gentry '.—' A man's young wife died in confinement while he was absent on some business at Ballingshaun, and one of the *gentry* came to him and

have never been in physical embodiments. If we follow the traditions of the Red Men, the Yosemite invisible tribes are probably but a few of many such tribes scattered throughout the North American continent ; and equally with their Celtic relatives they are described as a warlike race with more than human powers over physical nature, and as able to subject or destroy men.

[1] This refers to a tale told by Hugh Currid, in August, 1908, about Father Patrick and Father Dominick, which is here omitted because re-investigation during my second visit to Grange, in September, 1909, showed the tale to have been incorrectly reported. The same story, however, based upon facts, according to several reliable witnesses, was more accurately told by Patrick Waters at the time of my re-investigation, and appears on page 51.

said she had been *taken*. The husband hurried home, and that night he sat with the body of his wife all alone. He left the door open a little, and it wasn't long before his wife's spirit came in and went to the cradle where her child was sleeping. As she did so, the husband threw at her a charm of hen's dung which he had ready, and this held her until he could call the neighbours. And while they were coming, she went back into her body, and lived a long time afterwards. The body was stiff and cold when the husband arrived home, though it hadn't been washed or dressed.'

A Tailor's Testimony

Our next witness is Patrick Waters, by trade a tailor, living in Cloontipruckilish, a cross-road hamlet less than two miles from Hugh Currid's home. His first story is a parallel to one told about the minister of Aberfoyle who was *taken* by the ' good people' (pp. 89 ff.) :—

The Lost Bride.—' A girl in this region died on her wedding-night while dancing. Soon after her death she appeared to her husband, and said to him, " I'm not dead at all, but I am put from you now for a time. It may be a long time, or a short time, I cannot tell. I am not badly off. If you want to get me back you must stand at the gap near the house and catch me as I go by, for I live near there, and see you, and you do not see me." He was anxious enough to get her back, and didn't waste any time in getting to the gap. When he came to the place, a party of strangers were just coming out, and his wife soon appeared as plain as could be, but he couldn't stir a hand or foot to save her. Then there was a scream and she was gone. The man firmly believed this, and would not marry again.'

The Invisible Island.—' There is an enchanted island which is an invisible island between Innishmurray and the mainland opposite. It is only seen once in seven years. I saw it myself, and so did four or five others with me. A boatman from Sligo named Carr took two strange men with him towards Innishmurray, and they disappeared at the spot where the island is, and he thought they had fallen overboard and been drowned. Carr saw one of the same men in Connelly (County Donegal), some six months or so after, and with great surprise said to him, " Will you tell me the wonders of the world ? Is it you I saw drowned near Innishmurray ? " " Yes," he said ; and then asked, " Do you see me ? " " Yes," answered Carr. " But," said the man again, " you do not see me with both eyes ? " Then Carr closed one eye to be sure, and found that he saw him with one eye only. And he told the man which one it was. At this information the fairy man blew on Carr's face, and Carr never saw him again.'

A Dream.—' My father dreamt he saw two armies coming in from the sea, walking on the water. Reaching the strand, they lined up and commenced a battle, and my father was in great terror. The fighting was long and bloody, and when it was over every fighter vanished, the wounded and dead as well as the survivors. The next morning an old woman who had the reputation of talking with the fairies came in the house to my father, who, though greatly disturbed over the dream, had told us nothing of it, and asked him, " Have you anything to tell ? I couldn't but laugh at you," she added, and before my father could reply, continued, " Well, Jimmy, you won't tell the news, so I will." And then she began to tell about the battle. " Ketty ! " exclaimed my father at this, " can it be true ? And who were the men beside me ? " When Ketty told him, they turned out to be some of his dead friends. She received her information from a drowned man whom she met on the spot where the *gentry* armies had come ashore ; and, in the place where they fought, the sand was all burnt red, as from fire.'

As the narrator reflected on this dream story, he remarked about dreams generally :—' The reason our dreams appear different from what they are is because while in them we can't touch the body and transform it. People believe themselves to be with the dead in dreams.'

During September 1909, when I had several fresh interviews with Patrick Waters, I verified all of his 1908 testimony such as it appears above ; and among unimportant anecdotes I have omitted from the matter taken down in 1908 one anecdote about our seer-witness from County Sligo, because it proved to be capable of opposite interpretations. Patrick Waters, however, like many of his neighbours, thoroughly supports Hugh Currid's opinion that our seer-witness ' surely sees something, and it must be the *gentry* '; and of Hugh Currid himself, Patrick Waters said, ' Hugh Currid did surely see the *gentry* ; he saw them passing this way like a blast of wind.' Patrick's fresh testimony now follows, the story about Father Patrick and Father Dominick coming first :—

Father Patrick and Father Dominick.—' Father Patrick Noan while bathing in the harbour at Carns (about three miles north-west of Grange) was drowned. His body was soon brought ashore, and his brother, Father Dominick Noan, was sent for. When Father Dominick arrived, one of the men who had collected around the body said to him, " Why don't you do something for your brother Patrick ? " " Why don't somebody ask me ? " he replied, " for I must be asked in the name of God." So Jimmy McGowan went on his knees and asked for the honour of God that Father Dominick should bring Father Patrick back to life ; and, at this, Father Dominick took out his breviary and began to read. After a time he whistled, and began to read again. He whistled a second time, and returned to the reading. Upon his whistling the third time, Father Patrick's spirit appeared in the doorway.

' " Where were you when I whistled the first time ? " Father Dominick asked. " I was at a hurling match with the *gentry* on Mulloughmore strand." " And where were you at the second whistle ? " " I was coming over Corrick Fadda ; and when you whistled the third time I was here at the door." Father Patrick's spirit had gone back into the body, and Father Patrick lived round here as a priest for a long time afterwards.

' There was no such thing as artificial respiration known hereabouts when this happened some fifty or sixty years ago. I heard this story, which I know is true, from many persons who saw Father Dominick restore his brother to life.'

A Druid Enchantment.—After this strange psychical narrative, there followed the most weird legend I have heard in Celtic lands about Druids and magic. One afternoon Patrick Waters pointed out to me the field, near the sea-coast opposite Innishmurray, in which the ancient menhir containing the ' enchantment ' used to stand ; and, at another time, he said that a bronze wand covered with curious marks (or else interlaced designs) was found not far from the ruined dolmen and *allée couverte* on the farm of Patrick Bruan, about two miles southward. This last statement, like the story itself, I have been unable to verify in any way.

' In times before Christ there were Druids here who enchanted one another with Druid rods made of brass, and metamorphosed one another into stone and lumps of oak. The question is, Where are the spirits of these Druids now ? Their spirits are wafted through the air, and the man or beast they meet is smitten, while their own bodies are still under enchantment. I had such a Druid enchantment in my hand ; it wasn't stone, nor marble, nor flint, and had human shape. It was found in the centre of a big rock on Innis-na-Gore ; and round this rock light used to appear at night. The man who owned the stone decided to blast it up, and he found at its centre the enchantment—just like a man, with head and legs and arms.[1] Father Healy took the enchantment away, when he was here on a visit, and said that it was a Druid enchanted, and that to get out of the rock was one part of the releasement, and that there would be a second and complete releasement of the Druid.'

The Fairy Tribes Classified.—Finally I asked Patrick to classify, as far as he could, all the fairy tribes he had ever heard about, and he said :—' The leprechaun is a red-capped fellow who stays round pure springs, generally shoemaking

---

[1] It happened that I had in my pocket a fossil, picked out of the neighbouring sea-cliff rocks, which are very rich in fossils. I showed this to Pat to ascertain if what he had had in his hand looked anything like it, and he at once said ' No '.

for the rest of the fairy tribes. The lunantishees are the tribes that guard the blackthorn trees or sloes ; they let you cut no stick on the eleventh of November (the original November Day), or on the eleventh of May (the original May Day). If at such a time you cut a blackthorn, some misfortune will come to you. Pookas are black-featured fellows mounted on good horses ; and are horse-dealers. They visit racecourses, but usually are invisible. The *gentry* are the most noble tribe of all ; and they are a big race who came from the planets—according to my idea ; they usually appear white. The *Daoine Maithe* (though there is some doubt, the same or almost the same as the *gentry*) were next to Heaven at the Fall, but did not fall ; they are a people expecting salvation.'

BRIDGET O'CONNER'S TESTIMONY

Our next witness is Bridget O'Conner, a near neighbour to Patrick Waters, in Cloontipruckilish. When I approached her neat little cottage she was cutting sweet-pea blossoms with a pair of scissors, and as I stopped to tell her how pretty a garden she had, she searched out the finest white bloom she could find and gave it to me. After we had talked a little while about America and Ireland, she said I must come in and rest a few minutes, and so I did ; and it was not long before we were talking about fairies :—

The Irish Legend of the Dead.—' Old Peggy Gillin, dead these thirty years, who lived a mile beyond Grange, used to cure people with a secret herb shown to her by her brother, dead of a fairy-stroke. He was drowned and *taken* by the fairies, in the big drowning here during the herring season. She would pull the herb herself and prepare it by mixing spring water with it. Peggy could always talk with her dead relatives and friends, and continually with her brother, and she would tell everybody that they were with the fairies. Her daughter, Mary Short, who inherited some of her mother's power, died here about three or four years ago.

' I remember, too, about Mary Leonard and her daughter, Nancy Waters. Both of them are dead now. The daughter was the first to die, as it happened, and in child-birth. When she was gone, her mother used to wail and cry in an awful manner ; and one day the daughter appeared to her in the garden, and said, " The more you wail for me, the more I am in torment. Pray for me, but do not wail." '

A Midwife Story.—' A country nurse was requested by a strange man on horseback to go with him to exercise her profession ; and she went with him to a castle she didn't know. When the baby was born, every woman in the place where the event happened put her finger in a basin of water and rubbed her eyes, and so the nurse put her finger in and rubbed it on one of her eyes. She went home and thought no more about it. But one day she was at the fair in Grange and saw some of the same women who were in the castle when the baby was born ; though, as she noticed, she only could see them with the one eye she had wet with the water from the basin. The nurse spoke to the women, and they wanted to know how she recognized them ; and she, in reply, said it was with the one eye, and asked, " How is the baby ? " " Well," said one of the fairy women; " and what eye do you see us with ? " " With the left eye," answered the nurse. Then the fairy woman blew her breath against the nurse's left eye, and said, " You'll never see me again." And the nurse was always blind in the left eye after that.'

THE SPIRIT WORLD AT CARNS

The Carns or Mount Temple country, about three miles from Grange, County Sligo, has already been mentioned by witnesses as a ' gentry ' haunt, and so now we shall hear what one of its oldest and most intelligent native inhabitants says of it. John McCann had been referred to, by Patrick Waters, as one who knows much about the ' gentry ' at first hand, and we can be sure that what he offers us is thoroughly reliable evidence. For many years, John McCann, born in 1830, by profession a carpenter and boat-builder, has been official mail-carrier to Innishmurray ; and he knows quite as much about the strange little island and the mainland opposite it

as any man living. His neat little cottage is on the shore
of the bay opposite the beautiful fairy-haunted Darnish
Island ; and, as we sat within it beside a brilliant peat fire,
and surrounded by all the family, this is what was told
me :—

A ' Gentry ' Medium.—' Ketty Rourk (or Queenan) could
tell all that would happen—funerals, weddings, and so forth.
Sure some spirits were coming to her. She said they were
the *gentry* ; that the *gentry* are everywhere ; and that my
drowned uncles and grandfather and other dead are among
them. A drowned man named Pat Nicholson was her
adviser. He used to live just a mile from here ; and she
knew him before he was drowned.'

Here we have, clearly enough, a case of ' mediumship ', or
of communication with the dead, as in modern Spiritualism.
And the following story, which like this last has numerous
Irish parallels, illustrates an ancient and world-wide animistic
belief, that in sickness—as in dreams—the soul goes out of
the body as at death, and meets the dead in their own
fairy world.

The Clairvoyance of Mike Farrell.—' Mike Farrell, too,
could tell all about the *gentry*, as he lay sick a long time.
And he told about Father Brannan's youth, and even the
house in Roscommon in which the Father was born ; and
Father Brannan never said anything more against Mike
after that. Mike surely saw the *gentry* ; and he was with
them during his illness for twelve months. He said they
live in *forts* and at Alt Darby (" the Big Rock "). After
he got well, he went to America, at the time of the famine.'

The ' Gentry ' Army.—' The *gentry* were believed to live
up on this hill (Hill of the Brocket Stones, *Cluach-a-brac*),
and from it they would come out like an army and march
along the road to the strand. Very few persons could see
them. They were thought to be like living people, but in
different dress. They seemed like soldiers, yet it was known
they were not living beings such as we are.'

The Seership of Dan Quinn.—' On Connor's Island (about
two miles southward from Carns by the mainland) my uncle,

Dan Quinn, often used to see big crowds of the *gentry* come
into his house and play music and dance. The house would
be full of them, but they caused him no fear. Once on such
an occasion, one of them came up to him as he lay in bed,
and giving him a green leaf told him to put it in his mouth.
When he did this, instantly he could not see the *gentry*, but
could still hear their music. Uncle Dan always believed he
recognized in some of the *gentry* his drowned friends. Only
when he was alone would the *gentry* visit him. He was a
silent old man, and so never talked much; but I know that
this story is as true as can be, and that the *gentry* always
took an interest in him.'

Under the Shadow of Ben Bulbin and Ben Waskin

I was driving along the Ben Bulbin road, on the ocean
side, with Michael Oates, who was on his way from his
mountain-side home to the lowlands to cut hay ; and as we
looked up at the ancient mountain, so mysterious and silent
in the shadows and fog of a calm early morning of summer,
he told me about its invisible inhabitants :—

The ' Gentry ' Huntsmen.—' I knew a man who saw the
gentry hunting on the other side of the mountain. He saw
hounds and horsemen cross the road and jump the hedge in
front of him, and it was one o'clock at night. The next day
he passèd the place again, and looked for the tracks of the
huntsmen, but saw not a trace of tracks at all.'

The ' Taking ' of the Turf-Cutter.—After I had heard àbout
two boys who were drowned opposite Innishmurray, and
who afterwards appeared as apparitions, for the *gentry* had
them, this curious story was related :—' A man was cutting
turf out on the side of Ben Bulbin when a strange man came
to him and said, " You have cut enough turf for to-day.
You had better stop and go home." The turf-cutter looked
around in surprise, and in two seconds the strange man had
disappeared ; but he decided to go home. And as soon as he
was home, such a feeling came over him that he could not
tell whether he was alive or dead. Then he took to his bed
and never rose again.'

Hearing the ' Gentry ' Music.—At this Michael said to his companion in the cart with us, William Barber, ' You tell how you heard the music ' ; and this followed :—' One dark night, about one o'clock, myself and another young man were passing along the road up there round Ben Bulbin, when we heard the finest kind of music. All sorts of music seemed to be playing. We could see nothing at all, though we thought we heard voices like children's. It was the music of the *gentry* we heard.'

My next friend to testify is Pat Ruddy, eighty years old, one of the most intelligent and prosperous farmers living beside Ben Bulbin. He greeted me in the true Irish way, but before we could come to talk about fairies his good wife induced me to enter another room where she had secretly prepared a great feast spread out on a fresh white cloth, while Pat and myself had been exchanging opinions about America and Ireland. When I returned to the kitchen the whole family were assembled round the blazing turf fire, and Pat was soon talking about the ' gentry ' :—

Seeing the ' Gentry ' Army.—' Old people used to say the *gentry* were in the mountains ; that is certain, but I never could be quite sure of it myself. One night, however, near midnight, I did have a sight : I set out from Bantrillick to come home, and near Ben Bulbin there was the greatest army you ever saw, five or six thousand of them in armour shining in the moonlight. A strange man rose out of the hedge and stopped me, for a minute, in the middle of the road. He looked into my face, and then let me go.'

An Ossianic Fragment.—' A man went away with the *good people* (or *gentry*), and returned to find the townland all in ruins. As he came back riding on a horse of the *good people*, he saw some men in a quarry trying to move a big stone. He helped them with it, but his saddle-girth broke, and he fell to the ground. The horse ran away, and he was left there, an old man ' [1] (cf. pp. 346–7).

---

[1] After this Ossianic fragment, which has been handed down orally, I asked Pat if he had ever heard the old people talk about Dermot and Grania, and he replied :—' To be sure I have. Dermot and Grania used to

A Schoolmaster's Testimony

A schoolmaster, who is a native of the Ben Bulbin country, offers this testimony :—' There is implicit belief here in the *gentry*, especially among the old people. They consider them the spirits of their departed relations and friends, who visit them in joy and in sorrow. On the death of a member of a family, they believe the spirits of their near relatives are present ; they do not see them, but feel their presence. They even have a strong belief that the spirits show them the future in dreams ; and say that cases of affliction are always foreshown in a dream.

' The belief in changelings is not now generally prevalent ; but in olden times a mother used to place a pair of iron tongs over the cradle before leaving the child alone, in order that the fairies should not change the child for a weakly one of their own. It was another custom to take a wisp of straw, and, lighting one end of it, make a fiery sign of the cross over a cradle before a babe could be placed in it.'

With the Irish Mystics in the *Sidhe* World

Let us now turn to the Rosses Point country, which, as we have already said, is one of the very famous places for seeing the ' gentry ', or, as educated Irish seers who make pilgrimages thither call them, the *Sidhe*. I have been told by more than one such seer that there on the hills and Greenlands (a great stretch of open country, treeless and grass-grown), and on the strand at Lower Rosses Point—called Wren Point by the country-folk—these beings can be seen and their wonderful music heard ; and a well-known Irish artist has shown me many drawings, and paintings in oil, of these *Sidhe* people as he has often beheld them at those

live in these parts. Dermot stole Finn MacCoul's sister, and had to flee away. He took with him a bag of sand and a bunch of heather ; and when he was in the mountains he would put the bag of sand under his head at night, and then tell everybody he met that he had slept on the sand (the sea-shore); and when on the sand he would use the bunch of heather for a pillow, and say he had slept on the heather (the mountains). And so nobody ever caught him at all.'

places and elsewhere in Ireland. They are described as a race of majestic appearance and marvellous beauty, in form human, yet in nature divine. The highest order of them seems to be a race of beings evolved to a superhuman plane of existence, such as the ancients called gods ; and with this opinion, strange as it may seem in this age, all the educated Irish seers with whom I have been privileged to talk agree, though they go further, and say that these highest *Sidhe* races still inhabiting Ireland are the ever-young, immortal divine race known to the ancient men of Erin as the Tuatha De Danann.

Of all European lands I venture to say that Ireland is the most mystical, and, in the eyes of true Irishmen, as much the Magic Island of Gods and Initiates now as it was when the Sacred Fires flashed from its purple, heather-covered mountain-tops and mysterious round towers, and the Greater Mysteries drew to its hallowed shrines neophytes from the West as well as from the East, from India and Egypt as well as from Atlantis ; [1] and Erin's mystic-seeing sons still watch and wait for the relighting of the Fires and the restoration of the old Druidic Mysteries. Herein I but imperfectly echo the mystic message Ireland's seers gave me, a pilgrim to their Sacred Isle. And until this mystic message is interpreted, men cannot discover the secret of Gaelic myth and song in olden or in modern times, they cannot drink at the ever-flowing fountain of Gaelic genius, the perennial source of inspiration which lies behind the new revival of literature and art in Ireland, nor understand the seeming reality of the fairy races.

An Irish Mystic's Testimony

Through the kindness of an Irish mystic, who is a seer, I am enabled to present here, in the form of a dialogue, very rare and very important evidence, which will serve to illustrate and to confirm what has just been said above about the mysticism of Ireland. To anthropologists this evidence may be of more than ordinary value when they know that

[1] As to probable proof that there was an Atlantis, see p. 333 n.

it comes from one who is not only a cultured seer but who is also a man conspicuously successful in the practical life of a great city :—

Visions.—

Q.—Are all visions which you have had of the same character ?

A.—' I have always made a distinction between pictures seen in the memory of nature and visions of actual beings now existing in the inner world. We can make the same distinction in our world : I may close my eyes and see you as a vivid picture in memory, or I may look at you with my physical eyes and see your actual image. In seeing these beings of which I speak, the physical eyes may be open or closed : mystical beings in their own world and nature are never seen with the physical eyes.'

Otherworlds.—

Q.—By the inner world do you mean the Celtic Otherworld?

A.—' Yes ; though there are many Otherworlds. The *Tir-na-nog* of the ancient Irish, in which the races of the *Sidhe* exist, may be described as a radiant archetype of this world, though this definition does not at all express its psychic nature. In *Tir-na-nog* one sees nothing save harmony and beautiful forms. There are other worlds in which we can see horrible shapes.'

Classification of the ' Sidhe '.—

Q.—Do you in any way classify the *Sidhe* races to which you refer ?

A.—' The beings whom I call the *Sidhe*, I divide, as I have seen them, into two great classes : those which are shining, and those which are opalescent and seem lit up by a light within themselves. The shining beings appear to be lower in the hierarchies ; the opalescent beings are more rarely seen, and appear to hold the positions of great chiefs or princes among the tribes of Dana.'

Conditions of Seership.—

Q.—Under what state or condition and where have you seen such beings ?

A.—' I have seen them most frequently after being away from a city or town for a few days. The whole west coast of Ireland from Donegal to Kerry seems charged with a magical power, and I find it easiest to see while I am there. I have always found it comparatively easy to see visions while at ancient monuments like New Grange and Dowth, because I think such places are naturally charged with psychical forces, and were for that reason made use of long ago as sacred places. I usually find it possible to throw myself into the mood of seeing ; but sometimes visions have forced themselves upon me.'

The Shining Beings.—

Q.—Can you describe the shining beings ?

A.—' It is very difficult to give any intelligible description of them. The first time I saw them with great vividness I was lying on a hill-side alone in the west of Ireland, in County Sligo : I had been listening to music in the air, and to what seemed to be the sound of bells, and was trying to understand these aerial clashings in which wind seemed to break upon wind in an ever-changing musical silvery sound. Then the space before me grew luminous, and I began to see one beautiful being after another.'

The Opalescent Beings.—

Q.—Can you describe one of the opalescent beings ?

A.—' The first of these I saw I remember very clearly, and the manner of its appearance : there was at first a dazzle of light, and then I saw that this came from the heart of a tall figure with a body apparently shaped out of half-transparent or opalescent air, and throughout the body ran a radiant, electrical fire, to which the heart seemed the centre. Around the head of this being and through its waving luminous hair, which was blown all about the body like living strands of gold, there appeared flaming wing-like auras. From the being itself light seemed to stream outwards in every direction ; and the effect left on me after the vision was one of extraordinary lightness, joyousness, or ecstasy.

' At about this same period of my life I saw many of these

great beings, and I then thought that I had visions of
Aengus, Manannan, Lug, and other famous kings or princes
among the Tuatha De Danann ; but since then I have seen
so many beings of a similar character that I now no longer
would attribute to any one of them personal identity with
particular beings of legend ; though I believe that they
correspond in a general way to the Tuatha De Danann or
ancient Irish gods.'

Stature of the ' Sidhe '.—

Q.—You speak of the opalescent beings as great beings ;
what stature do you assign to them, and to the shining
beings ?

A.—' The opalescent beings seem to be about fourteen
feet in stature, though I do not know why I attribute to
them such definite height, since I had nothing to compare
them with ; but I have always considered them as much
taller than our race. The shining beings seem to be about
our own stature or just a little taller. Peasant and other
Irish seers do not usually speak of the *Sidhe* as being little,
but as being tall : an old schoolmaster in the West of
Ireland described them to me from his own visions as tall
beautiful people, and he used some Gaelic words, which
I took as meaning that they were shining with every
colour.'

The worlds of the ' Sidhe.'—

Q.—Do the two orders of *Sidhe* beings inhabit the same
world ?

A.—' The shining beings belong to the mid-world ; while
the opalescent beings belong to the heaven-world. There
are three great worlds which we can see while we are
still in the body : the earth-world, mid-world, and heaven-
world.'

Nature of the ' Sidhe.'—

Q.—Do you consider the life and state of these *Sidhe*
beings superior to the life and state of men ?

A.—' I could never decide. One can say that they themselves are certainly more beautiful than men are, and that their worlds seem more beautiful than our world.

' Among the shining orders there does not seem to be any individualized life : thus if one of them raises his hands all raise their hands, and if one drinks from a fire-fountain all do ; they seem to move and to have their real existence in a being higher than themselves, to which they are a kind of body. Theirs is, I think, a collective life, so unindividualized and so calm that I might have more varied thoughts in five hours than they would have in five years ; and yet one feels an extraordinary purity and exaltation about their life. Beauty of form with them has never been broken up by the passions which arise in the developed egotism of human beings. A hive of bees has been described as a single organism with disconnected cells ; and some of these tribes of shining beings seem to be little more than one being manifesting itself in many beautiful forms. I speak this with reference to the shining beings only : I think that among the opalescent or *Sidhe* beings, in the heaven-world, there is an even closer spiritual unity, but also a greater individuality.'

Influence of the ' Sidhe ' on Men.—

Q.—Do you consider any of these *Sidhe* beings inimical to humanity ?

A.—' Certain kinds of the shining beings, whom I call wood beings, have never affected me with any evil influences I could recognize. But the water beings, also of the shining tribes, I always dread, because I felt whenever I came into contact with them a great drowsiness of mind and, I often thought, an actual drawing away of vitality.'

Water Beings Described.—

Q.—Can you describe one of these water beings ?

A.—' In the world under the waters—under a lake in the West of Ireland in this case—I saw a blue and orange coloured king seated on a throne ; and there seemed to be some fountain of mystical fire rising from under his throne, and he breathed this fire into himself as though it were his life. As I looked, I saw groups of pale beings, almost grey in colour, coming down one side of the throne by the fire-fountain. They placed their head and lips near the heart of the elemental king, and, then, as they touched him, they shot upwards, plumed and radiant, and passed on the other side, as though they had received a new life from this chief of their world.'

Wood Beings Described.—

Q.—Can you describe one of the wood beings ?

A.—' The wood beings I have seen most often are of a shining silvery colour with a tinge of blue or pale violet, and with dark purple-coloured hair.'

Reproduction and Immortality of the ' Sidhe '.—

Q.—Do you consider the races of the *Sidhe* able to reproduce their kind ; and are they immortal ?

A.—' The higher kinds seem capable of breathing forth beings out of themselves, but I do not understand how they do so. I have seen some of them who contain elemental beings within themselves, and these they could send out and receive back within themselves again.

' The immortality ascribed to them by the ancient Irish is only a relative immortality, their space of life being much greater than ours. In time, however, I believe that they grow old and then pass into new bodies just as men do, but whether by birth or by the growth of a new body I cannot say, since I have no certain knowledge about this.'

Sex among the ' Sidhe '.—

Q.—Does sexual differentiation seem to prevail among the Sidhe races ?

A.—' I have seen forms both male and female, and forms which did not suggest sex at all.'

' Sidhe ' and Human Life.—

Q.—(1) Is it possible, as the ancient Irish thought, that certain of the higher *Sidhe* beings have entered or could enter our plane of life by submitting to human birth ? (2) On the other hand, do you consider it possible for men in trance or at death to enter the *Sidhe* world ?

A.—(1) ' I cannot say.' (2) ' Yes ; both in trance and after death. I think any one who thought much of the *Sidhe* during his life and who saw them frequently and brooded on them would likely go to their world after death.'

Social Organization of the ' Sidhe '.—

Q.—You refer to chieftain-like or prince-like beings, and to a king among water beings; is there therefore definite social organization among the various *Sidhe* orders and races, and if so, what is its nature ?

A.—' I cannot say about a definite social organization. I have seen beings who seemed to command others, and who were held in reverence. This implies an organization, but whether it is instinctive like that of a hive of bees, or consciously organized like human society, I cannot say.'

Lower ' Sidhe ' as Nature Elementals.—

Q.—You speak of the water-being king as an elemental king ; do you suggest thereby a resemblance between lower *Sidhe* orders and what mediaeval mystics called elementals ?

A.—' The lower orders of the *Sidhe* are, I think, the nature elementals of the mediaeval mystics.'

Nourishment of the Higher ' Sidhe '.—

Q.—The water beings as you have described them seem to be nourished and kept alive by something akin to electrical fluids ; do the higher orders of the *Sidhe* seem to be similarly nourished ?

A.—' They seemed to me to draw their life out of the Soul of the World.'

Collective Visions of ' Sidhe ' Beings.—

Q.—Have you had visions of the various *Sidhe* beings in company with other persons ?

A.—' I have had such visions on several occasions.'

And this statement has been confirmed to me by three participants in such collective visions, who separately at different times have seen in company with our witness the same vision at the same moment. On another occasion, on the Greenlands at Rosses Point, County Sligo, the same

Sidhe being was seen by our present witness and a friend
with him, also possessing the faculty of seership, at a time
when the two percipients were some little distance apart,
and they hurried to each other to describe the being, not
knowing that the explanation was mutually unnecessary.
I have talked with both percipients so much, and know
them so intimately that I am fully able to state that as
percipients they fulfil all necessary pathological conditions
required by psychologists in order to make their evidence
acceptable.

PARALLEL EVIDENCE AS TO THE *SIDHE* RACES

In general, the rare evidence above recorded from the
Irish seer could be paralleled by similar evidence from at
least two other reliable Irish people, with whom also I have
been privileged to discuss the Fairy-Faith. One is a member
of the Royal Irish Academy, the other is the wife of a well-
known Irish historian ; and both of them testify to having
likewise had collective visions of *Sidhe* beings in Ireland.

This is what Mr. William B. Yeats wrote to me, while this
study was in progress, concerning the Celtic Fairy Kingdom :—' I am certain that it exists, and will some day be
studied as it was studied by Kirk.' [1]

INDEPENDENT EVIDENCE FROM THE *SIDHE* WORLD

One of the most remarkable discoveries of our Celtic
researches has been that the native population of the Rosses
Point country, or, as we have called it, the *Sidhe* world, in
most essentials, and, what is most important, by independent folk-testimony, substantiate the opinions and statements of the educated Irish mystics to whom we have
just referred, as follows :—

John Conway's Vision of the ' Gentry '.—In Upper Rosses
Point, Mrs. J. Conway told me this about the ' gentry ' :—
' John Conway, my husband, who was a pilot by profession,

---

[1] This refers to Robert Kirk, minister of Aberfoyle, who wrote *The Secret
Commonwealth* (see this study, p. 85 n.).

in watching for in-coming ships used to go up on the high hill among the Fairy Hills ; and there he often saw the *gentry* going down the hill to the strand. One night in particular he recognized them as men and women of the *gentry ;* and they were as big as any living people. It was late at night about forty years ago.'

Ghosts and Fairies.—When first I introduced myself to Owen Conway, in his bachelor quarters, a cosy cottage at Upper Rosses Point, he said that Mr. W. B. Yeats and other men famous in Irish literature had visited him to hear about the fairies, and that though he knew very little about the fairies he nevertheless always likes to talk of them. Then Owen began to tell me about a man's ghost which both he and Bran Reggan had seen at different times on the road to Sligo, then about a woman's ghost which he and other people had often seen near where we were, and then about the exorcizing of a haunted house in Sligo some sixty years ago by Father McGowan, who as a result died soon afterwards, apparently having been killed by the exorcized spirits. Finally, I heard from him the following anecdotes about the fairies :—

A Stone Wall overthrown by ' Fairy ' Agency.—' Nothing is more certain than that there are fairies. The old folks always thought them the fallen angels. At the back of this house the fairies had their pass. My neighbour started to build a cow-shed, and one wall abutting on the pass was thrown down twice, and nothing but the fairies ever did it. The third time the wall was built it stood.'

Fairies passing through Stone Walls.—' Where MacEwen's house stands was a noted fairy place. Men in building the house saw fairies on horses coming across the spot, and the stone walls did not stop them at all.'

Seeing the ' Gentry '.—' A cousin of mine, who was a pilot, once went to the watch-house up there on the Point to take his brother's place ; and he saw ladies coming towards him as he crossed the Greenlands. At first he thought they were coming from a dance, but there was no dance going then, and, if there had been, no human beings dressed like them

and moving as they were could have come from any part of
the globe, and in so great a party, at that hour of the night.
Then when they passed him and he saw how beautiful they
were, he knew them for the *gentry* women.'

'Michael Reddy (our next witness) saw the *gentry* down
on the Greenlands in regimentals like an army, and in daylight. He was a young man at the time, and had been sent
out to see if any cattle were astray.'

And this is what Michael Reddy, of Rosses Point, now
a sailor on the ship *Tartar*, sailing from Sligo to neighbouring ports on the Irish coast, asserts in confirmation of Owen
Conway's statement about him :—' I saw the *gentry* on the
strand (at Lower Rosses Point) about forty years ago. It
was afternoon. I first saw one of them like an officer pointing at me what seemed a sword ; and when I got on the
Greenlands I saw a great company of *gentry*, like soldiers,
in red, laughing and shouting. Their leader was a big man,
and they were ordinary human size. As a result [of this
vision] I took to my bed and lay there for weeks. Upon
another occasion, late at night, I was with my mother
milking cows, and we heard the *gentry* all round us talking,
but could not see them.'

Going to the 'Gentry' through Death, Dreams, or Trance.—
John O'Conway, one of the most reliable citizens of Upper
Rosses Point, offers the following testimony concerning the
'gentry' :—' In olden times the *gentry* were very numerous
about *forts* and here on the Greenlands, but rarely seen.
They appeared to be the same as any living men. When
people died it was said the *gentry* took them, for they would
afterwards appear among the *gentry*.'

'We had a ploughman of good habits who came in one
day too late for his morning's work, and he in excuse very
seriously said, "May be if you had travelled all night as
much as I have you wouldn't talk. I was away with the
gentry, and save for a lady I couldn't have been back now.
I saw a long hall full of many people. Some of them I knew
and some I did not know. The lady saved me by telling
me to eat no food there, however enticing it might be." '

'A young man at Drumcliffe was *taken* [in a trance state], and was with the *Daoine Maithe* some time, and then got back. Another man, whom I knew well, was haunted by the *gentry* for a long time, and he often went off with *them*' (apparently in a dream or trance state).

'*Sidhe*' *Music.*—The story which now follows substantiates the testimony of cultured Irish seers that at Lower Rosses Point the music of the *Sidhe* can be heard :—' Three women were gathering shell-fish, in the month of March, on the lowest point of the strand (Lower Rosses or Wren Point) when they heard the most beautiful music. They set to work to dance with it, and danced themselves sick. They then thanked the invisible musician and went home.'

THE TESTIMONY OF A COLLEGE PROFESSOR

Our next witness is the Rev. Father ——, a professor in a Catholic college in West Ireland, and most of his statements are based on events which happened among his own acquaintances and relatives, and his deductions are the result of careful investigation :—

Apparitions from Fairyland.—' Some twenty to thirty years ago, on the borders of County Roscommon near County Sligo, according to the firm belief of one of my own relatives, a sister of his was *taken* by the fairies on her wedding-night, and she appeared to her mother afterwards as an apparition. She seemed to want to speak, but her mother, who was in bed at the time, was thoroughly frightened, and turned her face to the wall. The mother is convinced that she saw this apparition of her daughter, and my relative thinks she might have saved her.

' This same relative who gives it as his opinion that his sister was *taken* by the fairies, at a different time saw the apparition of another relative of mine who also, according to similar belief, had been *taken* by the fairies when only five years old. The child-apparition appeared beside its living sister one day while the sister was going from the yard into the house, and it followed her in. It is said the child was *taken* because she was such a good girl.'

Nature of the Belief in Fairies.—'As children we were always afraid of fairies, and were taught to say " God bless *them* ! God bless *them* ! " whenever we heard them mentioned.

' In our family we always made it a point to have clean water in the house at night for the fairies.

' If anything like dirty water was thrown out of doors after dark it was necessary to say " *Hugga, hugga salach !* " as a warning to the fairies not to get their clothes wet.

' Untasted food, like milk, used to be left on the table at night for the fairies. If you were eating and food fell from you, it was not right to take it back, for the fairies wanted it. Many families are very serious about this even now. The luckiest thing to do in such cases is to pick up the food and eat just a speck of it and then throw the rest away to the fairies.

' Ghosts and apparitions are commonly said to live in isolated thorn-bushes, or thorn-trees. Many lonely bushes of this kind have their ghosts. For example, there is Fanny's Bush, Sally's Bush, and another I know of in County Sligo near Boyle.'

Personal Opinions.—' The fairies of any one race are the people of the preceding race—the Fomors for the Fir Bolgs, the Fir Bolgs for the Dananns, and the Dananns for us. The old races died. Where did they go ? They became spirits—and fairies. Second-sight gave our race power to see the inner world. When Christianity came to Ireland the people had no *definite* heaven. Before, their ideas about the other world were vague. But the older ideas of a spirit world remained side by side with the Christian ones, and being preserved in a subconscious way gave rise to the fairy world.'

EVIDENCE FROM COUNTY ROSCOMMON

Our next place for investigation will be the ancient province of the great fairy-queen Meave, who made herself famous by leading against Cuchulainn the united armies of four of the five provinces of Ireland, and all on account of a bull which she coveted. And there could be no better part of it to visit than Roscommon, which Dr. Douglas Hyde has made popular in Irish folk-lore.

Dr. Hyde and the Leprechaun.—One day while I was privileged to be at Ratra, Dr. Hyde invited me to walk with him in the country. After we had visited an old *fort* which belongs to the ' good people ', and had noticed some other of their haunts in that part of Queen Meave's realm, we entered a straw-thatched cottage on the roadside and found the good house-wife and her fine-looking daughter both at home. In response to Dr. Hyde's inquiries, the mother stated that one day, in her girlhood, near a hedge from which she was gathering wild berries, she saw a leprechaun in a hole under a stone :—' He wasn't much larger than a doll, and he was most perfectly formed, with a little mouth and eyes.' Nothing was told about the little fellow having a money-bag, although the woman said people told her afterwards that she would have been rich if she had only had sense enough to catch him when she had so good a chance.[1]

The Death Coach.—The next tale the mother told was about the death coach which used to pass by the very house we were in. Every night until after her daughter was born she used to rise up on her elbow in bed to listen to the death coach passing by. It passed about midnight, and she could hear the rushing, the tramping of the horses, and most beautiful singing, just like fairy music, but she could not understand the words. Once or twice she was brave enough to open the door and look out as the coach passed, but she could never see a thing, though there was

[1] In going from East Ireland to Galway, during the summer of 1908, I passed through the country near Mullingar, where there was then great excitement over a leprechaun which had been appearing to school-children and to many of the country-folk. I talked with some of the people as I walked through part of County Meath about this leprechaun, and most of them were certain that there could be such a creature showing itself; and I noticed, too, that they were all quite anxious to have a chance at the money-bag, if they could only see the little fellow with it. I told one good-natured old Irishman at Ballywillan—where I stopped over night—as we sat round his peat fire and pot of boiling potatoes, that the leprechaun was reported as captured by the police in Mullingar. ' Now that couldn't be, at all,' he said instantly, ' for everybody knows the leprechaun is a spirit and can't be caught by any blessed policeman, though it is likely one might get his gold if they got him cornered so he had no chance to run away. But the minute you wink or take your eyes off the little devil, sure enough he is gone.'.

the noise and singing. One time a man had to wait on the roadside to let the fairy horses go by, and he could hear their passing very clearly, and couldn't see one of them.

When we got home, Dr. Hyde told me that the fairies of the region are rarely seen. The people usually say that they hear or feel them only.

The 'Good People' and Mr. Gilleran.—After the mother had testified, the daughter, who is quite of the younger generation, gave her own opinion. She said that the 'good people' live in the *forts* and often take men and women or youths who pass by the *forts* after sunset ; that Mr. Gilleran, who died not long ago, once saw certain dead friends and recognized among them those who were believed to have been *taken* and those who died naturally, and that he saw them again when he was on his death-bed.

We have here, as in so many other accounts, a clear connexion between the realm of the dead and Fairyland.

The Testimony of a Lough Derg Seer

Neil Colton, seventy-three years old, who lives in Tamlach Townland, on the shores of Lough Derg, County Donegal, has a local reputation for having seen the 'gentle folk', and so I called upon him. As we sat round his blazing turf fire, and in the midst of his family of three sturdy boys—for he married late in life—this is what he related :—

A Girl Recovered from Faerie.—' One day, just before sunset in midsummer, and I a boy then, my brother and cousin and myself were gathering bilberries (whortleberries) up by the rocks at the back of here, when all at once we heard music. We hurried round the rocks, and there we were within a few hundred feet of six or eight of the *gentle folk*, and they dancing. When they saw us, a little woman dressed all in red came running out from them towards us, and she struck my cousin across the face with what seemed to be a green rush. We ran for home as hard as we could, and when my cousin reached the house she fell dead. Father saddled a horse and went for Father Ryan. When Father Ryan arrived, he put a stole about his neck and began praying over my cousin and reading psalms and striking her with the stole ; and in that way brought her back. He said if she had not caught hold of my brother, she would have been *taken* for ever.'

The ' Gentle Folk '.—' The *gentle folk* are not earthly people ; they are a people with a nature of their own. Even in the water there are men and women of the same character. Others have caves in the rocks, and in them rooms and apartments. These races were terribly plentiful a hundred years ago, and they'll come back again. My father lived two miles from here, where there were plenty of the *gentle folk*. In olden times they used to take young folks and keep them and draw all the life out of their bodies. Nobody could ever tell their nature exactly.'

EVIDENCE FROM COUNTY FERMANAGH

From James Summerville, eighty-eight years old, who lives in the country near Irvinestown, I heard much about the 'wee people' and about banshees, and then the following remarkable story concerning the ' good people ' :—

Travelling Clairvoyance through ' Fairy ' Agency.—' From near Ederney, County Fermanagh, about seventy years ago, a man whom I knew well was taken to America on Hallow Eve Night ; and *they* (the *good people*) made him look down a chimney to see his own daughter cooking at a kitchen fire. Then *they* took him to another place in America, where he saw a friend he knew. The next morning he was at his own home here in Ireland.

' This man wrote a letter to his daughter to know if she was at the place and at the work on Hallow Eve Night, and she wrote back that she was. He was sure that it was the *good people* who had taken him to America and back in one night.'

EVIDENCE FROM COUNTY ANTRIM

At the request of Major R. G. Berry, M.R.I.A., of Richill Castle, Armagh, Mr. H. Higginson, of Glenavy, County Antrim, collected all the material he could find concerning the fairy-tradition in his part of County Antrim, and sent

to me the results, from which I have selected the very interesting, and, in some respects, unique tales which follow :—

The Fairies and the Weaver.—' Ned Judge, of Sophys
Bridge, was a weaver. Every night after he went to bed
the weaving started of itself, and when he arose in the morning he would find the dressing which had been made ready
for weaving so broken and entangled that it took him hours
to put it right. Yet with all this drawback he got no poorer,
because the fairies left him plenty of household necessaries,
and whenever he sold a web [of cloth] he always received
treble the amount bargained for.'

Meeting Two Regiments of ' Them '.—' William Megarry,
of Ballinderry, as his daughter who is married to James
Megarry, J.P., told me, was one night going to Crumlin on
horseback for a doctor, when after passing through Glenavy
he met just opposite the Vicarage two regiments of *them*
(the fairies) coming along the road towards Glenavy. One
regiment was dressed in red and one in blue or green uniform.
They were playing music, but when they opened out to let
him pass through the middle of *them* the music ceased until
he had passed by.'

IN CUCHULAINN'S COUNTRY : A CIVIL ENGINEER'S TESTIMONY

In the heroic days of pagan Ireland, as tradition tells, the
ancient earthworks, now called the Navan Rings, just outside Armagh, were the stronghold of Cuchulainn and the
Red Branch Knights ; and, later, under Patrick, Armagh
itself, one of the old mystic centres of Erin, became the
ecclesiastical capital of the Gaels. And from this romantic
country, one of its best informed native sons, a graduate
civil engineer of Dublin University, offers the following
important evidence :—

The Fairies are the Dead.—' When I was a youngster near
Armagh, I was kept good by being told that the fairies
could take bad boys away. The sane belief about the fairies,
however, is different, as I discovered when I grew up. The
old people in County Armagh seriously believe that the

fairies are the spirits of the dead ; and they say that if you have many friends deceased you have many friendly fairies, or if you have many enemies deceased you have many fairies looking out to do you harm.'

Food-Offerings to Place-Fairies.—' It was very usual formerly, and the practice is not yet given up, to place a bed, some other furniture, and plenty of food in a newly-constructed dwelling the night before the time fixed for moving into it ; and if the food is not consumed, and the crumbs swept up by the door in the morning, the house cannot safely be occupied. I know of two houses now that have never been occupied, because the fairies did not show their willingness and goodwill by taking food so offered to them.'

On the Slopes of Slieve Gullion

In climbing to the summit of Cuchulainn's mountain, which overlooks parts of the territory made famous by the ' Cattle Raid of Cooley ', I met John O'Hare, sixty-eight years old, of Longfield Townland, leading his horse to pasture, and I stopped to talk with him about the ' good people '.

' The *good people* in this mountain,' he said, ' are the people who have died and been *taken*; the mountain is enchanted.'

The ' Fairy' Overflowing of the Meal-Chest.—' An old woman came to the wife of Steven Callaghan and told her not to let Steven cut a certain hedge. " It is where we shelter at night," the old woman added ; and Mrs. Callaghan recognized the old woman as one who had been *taken* in confinement. A few nights later the same old woman appeared to Mrs. Callaghan and asked for charity ; and she was offered some meal, which she did not take. Then she asked for lodgings, but did not stop. When Mrs. Callaghan saw the meal-chest next morning it was overflowing with meal : it was the old woman's gift for the hedge.'

The Testimony of two Dromintee Percipients

After my friend, the Rev. Father L. Donnellan, C.C., of Dromintee, County Armagh, had introduced me to Alice Cunningham, of his parish, and she had told much about the 'gentle folk', she emphatically declared that they do exist —and this in the presence of Father Donnellan—because she has often seen them on Carrickbroad Mountain, near where she lives. And she then reported as follows concerning enchanted Slieve Gullion :—

The ' Sidhe' Guardian of Slieve Gullion.—' The top of Slieve Gullion is a very *gentle* place. A fairy has her house there by the lake, but she is invisible. She interferes with nobody. I hear of no *gentler* places about here than Carrickbroad and Slieve Gullion.'

Father Donnellan and I called next upon Thomas McCrink and his wife at Carrifamayan, because Mrs. McCrink claims to have seen some of the ' good people ', and this is her testimony :—

Nature of the ' Good People '.—' I've heard and felt the *good people* coming on the wind ; and I once saw them down in the middle field on my father's place playing football. They are still on earth. Among them are the spirits of our ancestors ; and these rejoice whenever good fortune comes our way, for I saw them before my mother won her land [after a long legal contest] in the field rejoicing.

' Some of the *good people* I have thought were fallen angels, though these may be dead people whose time is not up. We are only like shadows in this world : my mother died in England, and she came to me in the spirit. I saw her plainly. I ran to catch her, but my hands ran through her form as if it were mere mist. Then there was a crack, and she was gone.' And, finally, after a moment, our percipient said :—' The fairies once passed down this lane here on a Christmas morning ; and I took them to be suffering souls out of Purgatory, going to mass.'

THE TESTIMONY OF A DROMINTEE SEERESS

Father Donnellan, the following day, took me to talk with almost the oldest woman in his parish, Mrs. Biddy Grant, eighty-six years old, of Upper Toughal, beside Slieve Gullion. Mrs. Grant is a fine specimen of an Irishwoman, with white hair, clear complexion, and an expression of great natural intelligence, though now somewhat feeble from age. Her

mind is yet clear, however; and her testimony is substantiated by this statement from her own daughter, who
lives with her:—' My mother has the power of seeing
things. It is a fact with her that spirits exist. She has
seen much, even in her old age ; and what she is always
telling me scares me half to death.'

The following is Mrs. Grant's direct testimony given at
her own home, on September 20, 1909, in answer to our
question if she knew anything about the ' good people ' :—

Seeing the ' Good People ' as the Dead.—' I saw *them* once
as plain as can be—big, little, old, and young. I was in bed
at the time, and a boy whom I had reared since he was born
was lying ill beside me. Two of *them* came and looked at
him ; then came in three of *them*. One of *them* seemed to
have something like a book, and he put his hand to the boy's
mouth; then he went away, while others appeared, opening
the back window to make an avenue through the house;
and through this avenue came great crowds. At this I shook
the boy, and said to him, " Do you see anything ? " " No,"
he said ; but as I made him look a second time he said,
" I do." After that he got well.

' These *good people* were the spirits of our dead friends,
but I could not recognize them. I have often seen them
that way while in my bed. Many women are among them.
I once touched a boy of theirs, and he was just like feathers
in my hand ; there was no substance in him, and I knew
he wasn't a living being. I don't know where they live ;
I've heard they live in the *Carrige* (rocks). Many a time I've
heard of their *taking* people or leading them astray. They
can't live far away when they come to me in such a rush.
They are as big as we are. I think these fairy people are all
through this country and in the mountains.'

An Apparition of a ' Sidhe ' Woman ?—' At a wake I went
out of doors at midnight and saw a woman running up and
down the field with a strange light in her hand. I called out
my daughter, but she saw nothing, though all the time the
woman dressed in white was in the field, shaking the light
and running back and forth as fast as you could wink.

I thought the woman might be the spirit of Nancy Frink, but I was not sure.' (Cf. pp. 60 ff., 83, 155, 215.)

EVIDENCE FROM LOUGH GUR, COUNTY LIMERICK

One of the most interesting parts of Ireland for the archaeologist and for the folk-lorist alike is the territory immediately surrounding Lough Gur, County Limerick. Shut in for the most part from the outer world by a circle of low-lying hills on whose summits fairy goddesses yet dwell invisibly, this region, famous for its numerous and well-preserved cromlechs, dolmens, menhirs, and tumuli, and for the rare folk-traditions current among its peasantry, has long been popularly regarded as a sort of Otherworld preserve haunted by fairy beings, who dwell both in its waters and on its land.

There seems to be no reasonable doubt that in pre-Christian times the Lough Gur country was a very sacred spot, a mystic centre for pilgrimages and for the celebration of Celtic religious rites, including those of initiation. The Lough is still enchanted, but once in seven years the spell passes off it, and it then appears like dry land to any one that is fortunate enough to behold it. At such a time of disenchantment a Tree is seen growing up through the lake-bottom—a Tree like the strange World-Tree of Scandinavian myth. The Tree is covered with a Green Cloth, and under it sits the lake's guardian, a woman knitting.[1] The peasantry about Lough Gur still believe that beneath its waters there is one of the chief entrances in Ireland to *Tir-na-nog*, the 'Land of Youth', the Fairy Realm. And when a child is stolen by the Munster fairies, ' Lough Gur is conjectured to be the place of its unearthly transmutation from the human to the fairy state.'[1]

---

[1] Cf. David Fitzgerald, *Popular Tales of Ireland*, in *Rev. Celt.*, iv. 185–92 ; and *All the Year Round*, New Series, iii. ' This woman guardian of the lake is called Toice Bhrean, "untidy " or "lazy wench ". According to a local legend, she is said to have been originally the guardian of the sacred well, from which, owing to her neglect, Lough Gur issued ; and in this rôle she corresponds to Liban, daughter of Eochaidh Finn, the guardian of the sacred well from which issued Lough Neagh, according to the *Dinnshenchas* and the tale of Eochaidh MacMairido.'—J. F. LYNCH.

To my friend, Count John de Salis, of Balliol College, I am indebted for the following legendary material, collected by him on the fairy-haunted Lough Gur estate, his ancestral home, and annotated by the Rev. J. F. Lynch, one of the best-informed antiquarians living in that part of South Ireland :—

The Fairy Goddesses, Aine and Fennel (or Finnen).—' There are two hills near Lough Gur upon whose summits sacrifices and sacred rites used to be celebrated according to living tradition.   One, about three miles south-west of the lake, is called Knock Aine, Aine or Ane being the name of an ancient Irish goddess, derived from *an*, " bright." The other, the highest hill on the lake-shores, is called Knock Fennel or Hill of the Goddess Fennel, from *Finnen* or *Finnine* or *Fininne*, a form of *fin*, " white."   The peasantry of the region call Aine one of the Good People ; [1] and they say that

---

[1] It was on the bank of the little river Camóg, which flows near Lough Gur, that the Earl of Desmond one day saw Aine as she sat there combing her hair.   Overcome with love for the fairy-goddess, he gained control over her through seizing her cloak, and made her his wife.   From this union was born the enchanted son Geróid Iarla, even as Galahad was born to Lancelot by the Lady of the Lake.   When Geróid had grown into young manhood, in order to surpass a woman he leaped right into a bottle and right out again, and this happened in the midst of a banquet in his father's castle.   His father, the earl, had been put under taboo by Aine never to show surprise at anything her magician son might do, but now the taboo was forgotten, and hence broken, amid so unusual a performance ; and immediately Geróid left the feasting and went to the lake.   As soon as its water touched him he assumed the form of a goose, and he went swimming over the surface of the Lough, and disappeared on Garrod Island.

According to one legend, Aine, like the Breton *Morgan*, may sometimes be seen combing her hair, only half her body appearing above the lake. And in times of calmness and clear water, according to another legend, one may behold beneath Aine's lake the lost enchanted castle of her son Geróid, close to Garrod Island—so named from Geróid or ' Gerald '.

Geróid lives there in the under-lake world to this day, awaiting the time of his normal return to the world of men (see our chapter on re-birth, p. 386).   But once in every seven years, on clear moonlight nights, he emerges temporarily, when the Lough Gur peasantry see him as a phantom mounted on a phantom white horse, leading a phantom or fairy cavalcade across the lake and land.   A well-attested case of such an apparitional appearance of the earl has been recorded by Miss Anne Baily, the percipient having been Teigue O'Neill, an old blacksmith whom she knew (see *All the Year Round*, New Series, iii. 495-6, London, 1870).   And Moll

Fennel (apparently her sister goddess or a variant of herself)
lived on the top of Knock Fennel' (termed Finnen in a
State Paper dated 1200).

The Fairy Boat-Race.—' Different old peasants have told
me that on clear calm moonlight nights in summer, fairy
boats appear racing across Lough Gur. The boats come
from the eastern side of the lake, and when they have arrived
at Garrod Island, where the Desmond Castle lies in ruins,
they vanish behind Knock Adoon. There are four of these
phantom boats, and in each there are two men rowing and
a woman steering. No sound is heard, though the seer can
see the weird silvery splash of the oars and the churning of
the water at the bows of the boats as they shoot along. It
is evident that they are racing, because one boat gets ahead
of the others, and all the rowers can be seen straining at the
oars. Boats and occupants seem to be transparent, and you

Riall, a young woman also known to Miss Baily, saw the phantom earl by
himself, under very weird circumstances, by day, as she stood at the margin
of the lake washing clothes (ib., p. 496).

Some say that Aine's true dwelling-place is in her hill; upon which on
every St. John's Night the peasantry used to gather from all the immediate
neighbourhood to view the moon (for Aine seems to have been a moon goddess, like Diana), and then with torches (*cliars*) made of bunches of straw
and hay tied on poles used to march in procession from the hill and afterwards run through cultivated fields and amongst the cattle. The underlying
purpose of this latter ceremony probably was—as is the case in the Isle of
Man and in Brittany (see pp. 124 n., 273), where corresponding fire-ceremonies
surviving from an ancient agricultural cult are still celebrated—to exorcise
the land from all evil spirits and witches in order that there may be good
harvests and rich increase of flocks. Sometimes on such occasions the
goddess herself has been seen leading the sacred procession (cf. the Bacchus
cult among the ancient Greeks, who believed that the god himself led his
worshippers in their sacred torch-light procession at night, he being like
Aine in this respect, more or less connected with fertility in nature). One
night some girls staying on the hill late were made to look through a magic
ring by Aine, and lo the hill was crowded with the folk of the fairy goddess
who before had been invisible. The peasants always said that Aine is
' the best-hearted woman that ever lived ' (cf. David Fitzgerald, *Popular
Tales of Ireland*, in *Rev. Celt.*, iv. 185–92).

In *Silva Gadelica* (ii. 347–8), Aine is a daughter of Eogabal, a king of
the Tuatha De Danann, and her abode is within the *sidh*, named on her
account '*Aine cliach*, now Cnoc Aine, or Knockany'. In another passage
we read that Manannan took Aine as his wife (ib., ii. 197). Also see in
Silva Gadelica, ii, pp. 225, 576.

cannot see exactly what their nature is. One old peasant told me that it is the shining brightness of the clothes on the phantom rowers and on the women who steer which makes them visible.

' Another man, who is about forty years of age, and as far as I know of good habits, assures me that he also has seen this fairy boat-race, and that it can still be seen at the proper season.'

The Bean-Tighe.[1]—'The *Bean-tighe*, the fairy housekeeper of the enchanted submerged castle of the Earl of Desmond, is supposed to appear sitting on an ancient earthen monument shaped like a great chair and hence called *Suidheachan*, the " Housekeeper's Little Seat," on Knock Adoon (Hill of the Fort), which juts out into the Lough. The *Bean-tighe*, as I have heard an old peasant tell the tale, was once asleep on her Seat, when the *Buachailleen*[2] or " Little Herd Boy "

---

[1] ' In some local tales the *Bean-tighe*, or *Bean a'tighe* is termed *Bean-sidhe* (Banshee), and *Bean Chaointe*, or "wailing woman ", and is identified with Aine. In an elegy by Ferriter on one of the Fitzgeralds, we read :—

> Aine from her closely hid nest did awake,
> The woman of wailing from Gur's voicy lake.

' Thomas O'Connellan, the great minstrel bard, some of whose compositions are given by Hardiman, died at Lough Gur Castle about 1700, and was buried at New Church beside the lake. It is locally believed that Aine stood on a rock of Knock Adoon and " keened " O'Connellan whilst the funeral procession was passing from the castle to the place of burial.'— J. F. LYNCH.

A Banshee was traditionally attached to the Baily family of Lough Gur ; and one night at dead of night, when Miss Kitty Baily was dying of consumption, her two sisters, Miss Anne Baily and Miss Susan Baily, who were sitting in the death chamber, ' heard such sweet and melancholy music as they had never heard before. It seemed to them like distant cathedral music. . . . The music was not in the house. . . . It seemed to come through the windows of the old castle, high in the air.' But when Miss Anne, who went downstairs with a lighted candle to investigate the weird phenomenon, had approached the ruined castle she thought the music came from above the house ; ' and thus perplexed, and at last frightened, she returned.' Both sisters are on record as having distinctly heard the fairy music, and for a long time (*All the Year Round*, New Series, iii. 496–7 ; London, 1870).

[2] ' The *Buachailleen* is most likely one of the many forms assumed by the shape-shifting Fer Fi, the Lough Gur Dwarf, who at Tara, according to the *Dinnshenchas* of Tuag Inbir (see *Folk-Lore*, iii ; and A. Nutt, *Voyage of Bran*, i. 195 ff.), took the shape of a woman ; and we may trace the tales

stole her golden comb. When the *Bean-tighe* awoke and saw
what had happened, she cast a curse upon the cattle of the
Buachailleen, and soon all of them were dead, and then
the " Little Herd Boy " himself died, but before his death
he ordered the golden comb to be cast into the Lough.' [1]

Lough Gur Fairies in General.—' The peasantry in the
Lough Gur region commonly speak of the *Good People* or of
the *Kind People* or of the *Little People*, their names for the
fairies. The leprechaun indicates the place where hidden
treasure is to be found. If the person to whom he reveals
such a secret makes it known to a second person, the first
person dies, or else no money is found : in some cases the
money is changed into ivy leaves or into furze blossoms.

' I am convinced that some of the older peasants still
believe in fairies. I used to go out on the lake occasionally
on moonlight nights, and an old woman supposed to be
a " wise woman " (a seeress), hearing about my doing this,
told me that under no circumstances should I continue the
practice, for fear of " Them People " (the fairies). One
evening in particular I was warned by her not to venture on
the lake. She solemnly asserted that the " Powers of Darkness " were then abroad, and that it would be misfortune
for me to be in their path.[2]

' Under ordinary circumstances, as a very close observer
of the Lough Gur peasantry informs me, the old people will

of Geróid Iarla to Fer Fi, who, and not Geróid, is believed by the oldest of
the Lough Gur peasantry to be the owner of the lake. Fer Fi is the son
of Eogabal of Sídh Eogabail, and hence brother to Aine. He is also foster-
son of Manannan Mac Lir, and a Druid of the Tuatha De Danann (cf.
Silva Gadelica, ii. 225 ; also *Dinnshenchas* of Tuag Inbir). At Lough Gur
various tales are told by the peasants concerning the Dwarf, and he is
still stated by them to be the brother of Aine. For the sake of experiment I once spoke very disrespectfully of the Dwarf to John Punch, an
old man, and he said to me in a frightened whisper : " Whisht ! he'll
hear you." Edward Fitzgerald and other old men were very much afraid
of the Dwarf.'—J. F. LYNCH.

[1] ' Compare the tale of Excalibur, the Sword of King Arthur, which
King Arthur before his death ordered Sir Bedivere to cast into the lake
whence it had come.'—J. F. LYNCH.

[2] ' It is commonly believed by young and old at Lough Gur that a human
being is drowned in the Lake once every seven years, and that it is the
Bean Fhionn, or " White Lady " who thus *takes* the person.'—J. F. LYNCH.

pray to the Saints, but if by any chance such prayers remain unanswered they then invoke other powers, the fairies, the goddesses Aine and Fennel, or other pagan deities, whom they seem to remember in a vague subconscious manner through tradition.'

TESTIMONY FROM A COUNTY KERRY SEER

To another of my fellow students in Oxford, a native Irishman of County Kerry, I am indebted for the following evidence :—

A Collective Vision of Spiritual Beings.—' Some few weeks before Christmas, 1910, at midnight on a very dark night, I and another young man (who like myself was then about twenty-three years of age) were on horseback on our way home from Limerick. When near Listowel, we noticed a light about half a mile ahead. At first it seemed to be no more than a light in some house ; but as we came nearer to it and it was passing out of our direct line of vision we saw that it was moving up and down, to and fro, diminishing to a spark, then expanding into a yellow luminous flame. Before we came to Listowel we noticed two lights, about one hundred yards to our right, resembling the light seen first. Suddenly each of these lights expanded into the same sort of yellow luminous flame, about six feet high by four feet broad. In the midst of each flame we saw a radiant being having human form. Presently the lights moved toward one another and made contact, whereupon the two beings in them were seen to be walking side by side. The beings' bodies were formed of a pure dazzling radiance, white like the radiance of the sun, and much brighter than the yellow light or aura surrounding them. So dazzling was the radiance, like a halo, round their heads that we could not distinguish the countenances of the beings ; we could only distinguish the general shape of their bodies ; though their heads were very clearly outlined because this halo-like radiance, which was the brightest light about them, seemed to radiate from or rest upon the head of each being. As we travelled on, a house intervened between us and the lights, and we saw no more of them. It was the first time we had ever seen such phenomena, and in our hurry to get home we were not wise enough to stop and make further examination. But ever since that night I have frequently seen, both in Ireland and in England, similar lights with spiritual beings in them.' (Cf. pp. 60 ff., 77, 133, 155, 215, 483.)

Reality of the Spiritual World.—' Like my companion, who saw all that I saw of the first three lights, I formerly had always been a sceptic as to the existence of spirits ; now I know that there is a spiritual world. My brother, a physician, had been equally sceptical until he saw, near our home at Listowel, similar lights containing spiritual beings and was obliged to admit the genuineness of the phenomena.

' In whatever country we may be, I believe that we are for ever immersed in the spiritual world ; but most of us cannot perceive it on account of the unrefined nature of our physical bodies. Through meditation and psychical training one can come to see the spiritual world and its beings. We pass into the spirit realm at death and come back into the human world at birth ; and we continue to reincarnate until we have overcome all earthly desires and mortal appetites. Then the higher life is open to our consciousness and we cease to be human ; we become divine beings.' (Recorded in Oxford, England, August 12, 1911.)

III   IN SCOTLAND

Introduction by ALEXANDER CARMICHAEL, Hon. LL.D. of the University of Edinburgh ; author of *Carmina Gadelica.*

The belief in fairies was once common throughout Scotland—Highland and Lowland. It is now much less prevalent even in the Highlands and Islands, where such beliefs linger longer than they do in the Lowlands. But it still lives among the old people, and is privately entertained here and there even among younger people ; and some who hold the belief declare that they themselves have seen fairies. Various theories have been advanced as to the origin of

fairies and as to the belief in them. The most concrete form
in which the belief has been urged has been by the Rev.
Robert Kirk, minister of Aberfoyle, in Perthshire.[1] Another
theory of the origin of fairies I took down in the island of
Miunghlaidh (Minglay); and, though I have given it in
Carmina Gadelica, it is sufficiently interesting to be quoted
here. During October 1871, Roderick Macneill, known as
' Ruaraidh mac Dhomhuil, then ninety-two years of age,
told it in Gaelic to the late J. F. Campbell of Islay and the
writer, when they were storm-stayed in the precipitous
island of Miunghlaidh, Barra :—

' The Proud Angel fomented a rebellion among the angels
of heaven, where he had been a leading light. He declared
that he would go and found a kingdom for himself. When
going out at the door of heaven the Proud Angel brought
prickly lightning and biting lightning out of the doorstep
with his heels. Many angels followed him—so many that at
last the Son called out, " Father ! Father ! the city is being
emptied ! " whereupon the Father ordered that the gates
of heaven and the gates of hell should be closed. This was
instantly done. And those who were in were in, and those
who were out were out ; while the hosts who had left
heaven and had not reached hell flew into the holes of the
earth, like the stormy petrels. These are the Fairy Folk—ever
since doomed to live under the ground, and only allowed to
emerge where and when the King permits. They are never
allowed abroad on Thursday, that being Columba's Day ;
nor on Friday, that being the Son's Day ; nor on Saturday,
that being Mary's Day ; nor on Sunday, that being the
Lord's Day.

> God be between me and every fairy,
> Every ill wish and every druidry ;
> To-day is Thursday on sea and land,
> I trust in the King that they do not hear me.

---

[1] It was the belief of the Rev. Robert Kirk, as expressed by him in his
Secret Commonwealth of Elves, Fauns, and Fairies, that the fairy tribes are
a distinct order of created beings possessing human-like intelligence and
supernormal powers, who live and move about in this world invisible to
all save men and women of the second-sight (see this study, pp. 89, 91 n).

On certain nights when their *bruthain* (bowers) are open
and their lamps are lit, and the song and the dance are
moving merrily, the fairies may be heard singing light-
heartedly :—

> Not of the seed of Adam are we,
> Nor is Abraham our father ;
> But of the seed of the Proud Angel,
> Driven forth from Heaven.'

The fairies entered largely into the lives and into the
folk-lore of the Highland people, and the following examples
of things named after the fairies indicate the manner in
which the fairies dominated the minds of the people of
Gaeldom :—*teine sith*, ' fairy fire ' (*ignis fatuus*) ; *breaca
sith*, ' fairy marks,' livid spots appearing on the faces of
the dead or dying ; *marcachd shith*, ' fairy riding,' paralysis
of the spine in animals, alleged to be brought on by the
fairy mouse riding across the backs of animals while they
are lying down ; *piob shith*, ' fairy pipe ' or ' elfin pipe ',
generally found in ancient underground houses ; *miaran na
mna sithe*, ' the thimble of the fairy woman,' the fox-glove ;
lion na mna sithe, ' lint of the fairy woman,' fairy flax, said
to be beneficial in certain illnesses ; and *curachan na mna
sithe*, ' coracle of the fairy woman,' the shell of the blue
valilla. In place-names *sith*, ' fairy,' is common. Glenshee,
in Perthshire, is said to have been full of fairies, but the
screech of the steam-whistle frightened them underground.
There is scarcely a district of the Highlands without its
fairy knoll, generally the greenest hillock in the place.
' The black chanter of Clan Chattan ' is said to have been
given to a famous Macpherson piper by a fairy woman who
loved him ; and the Mackays have a flag said to have been
given to a Mackay by a fairy sweetheart. The well-known
fairy flag of Dunvegan is said to have been given to a Macleod
of Macleod by a fairy woman ; and the Macrimmons of
Bororaig, pipers to the Macleods of Macleod, had a chanter
called ' *Sionnsair airgid na mna sithe*', ' the silver chanter of
the fairy woman.' A family in North Uist is known as
Dubh-sith, ' Black fairy,' from a tradition that the family

had been familiar with the fairies in their secret flights and nightly migrations.

Donald Macalastair, seventy-nine years of age, crofter, Druim-a-ghinnir, Arran, told me, in the year 1895, the following story in Gaelic :—' The fairies were dwelling in the knoll, and they had a near neighbour who used to visit them in their home. The man used to observe the ways of the fairies and to do as they did. The fairies took a journey upon them to go to Ireland, and the man took upon him to go with them. Every single fairy of them caught a ragwort and went astride it, and they were pell-mell, every knee of them across the Irish Ocean in an instant, and across the Irish Ocean was the man after them, astride a ragwort like one of themselves. A little wee tiny fairy shouted and asked were they all ready, and all the others replied that they were, and the little fairy called out :—

> My king at my head,
> Going across in my haste,
> On the crests of the waves,
> To Ireland.

" Follow me," said the king of the fairies, and away they went across the Irish Ocean, every mother's son of them astride his ragwort. Macuga (Cook) did not know on earth how he would return to his native land, but he leapt upon the ragwort as he saw the fairies do, and he called as he heard them call, and in an instant he was back in Arran. But he had got enough of the fairies on this trip itself, and he never went with them again.'

The fairies were wont to take away infants and their mothers, and many precautions were taken to safeguard them till purification and baptism took place, when the fairy power became ineffective. Placing iron about the bed, burning leather in the room, giving mother and child the milk of a cow which had eaten of the *mothan*, pearl-wort (*Pinguicula vulgaris*), a plant of virtue, and similar means were taken to ensure their safety. If the watching-women neglected these precautions, the mother or child or both were spirited away to the fairy bower. Many stories are current on this subject.

Sometimes the fairies helped human beings with their work, coming in at night to finish the spinning or the housework, or to thresh the farmer's corn or fan his grain. On such occasions they must not be molested nor interfered with, even in gratitude. If presented with a garment they will go away and work no more. This method of getting rid of them is often resorted to, as it is not easy always to find work for them to do.

Bean chaol a chot uaine 's na gruaige buidhe, ' the slender woman of the green kirtle and of the yellow hair,' is wise of head and deft of hand. She can convert the white water of the rill into rich red wine and the threads of the spiders into a tartan plaid. From the stalk of the fairy reed she can bring the music of the lull of the peace and of the repose, however active the brain and lithe the limb; and she can rouse to mirth and merriment, and to the dance, men and women, however dolorous their condition. From the bower could be heard the pipe and the song and the voice of laughter as the fairies ' sett ' and reeled in the mazes of the dance. Sometimes a man hearing the merry music and seeing the wonderful light within would be tempted to go in and join them, but woe to him if he omitted to leave a piece of iron at the door of the bower on entering, for the cunning fairies would close the door and the man would find no egress. There he would dance for years—but to him the years were as one day—while his wife and family mourned him as dead.

The flint arrow-heads so much prized by antiquarians are called in the Highlands *Saighead sith,* fairy arrows. They are said to have been thrown by the fairies at the sons and daughters of men. The writer possesses one which was thrown at his own maid-servant one night when she went to the peatstack for peats. She was aware of something whizzing through the silent air, passing through her hair, grazing her ear and falling at her feet. Stooping in the bright moonlight the girl picked up a fairy arrow !

' But faith is dead—such things do not happen now,' said a courteous informant. If not quite dead it is almost dead, hastened by the shifting of population, the establishment of means of communication, the influx of tourists, and the scorn of the more materialistic of the incomers and of the people themselves.

EDINBURGH,
  October 1910.

ABERFOYLE, THE COUNTRY OF ROBERT KIRK

My first hunt for fairies in Scotland began at Aberfoyle, where the Highlands and the Lowlands meet, and in the very place where Robert Kirk, the minister of Aberfoyle, was *taken* by them, in the year 1692. The minister spent a large part of his time studying the ways of the 'good people', and he must have been able to see them, for he was a seventh son. Mrs. J. MacGregor, who keeps the key to the old churchyard where there is a tomb to Kirk, though many say there is nothing in it but a coffin filled with stones, told me that Kirk was taken into the Fairy Knoll, which she pointed to just across a little valley in front of us, and is there yet, for the hill is full of caverns, and in them the ' good people ' have their homes. And she added that Kirk appeared to a relative of his after he was *taken*, and said that he was in the power of the ' good people ', and couldn't get away. ' But,' says he, ' I can be set free if you will have my cousin do what I tell him when I appear again at the christening of my child in the parsonage.' According to Mr. Andrew Lang; who reports the same tradition in more detail in his admirable Introduction to *The Secret Commonwealth*, the cousin was Grahame of Duchray, and the thing he was to do was to throw a dagger over Kirk's head. Grahame was at hand at the christening of the posthumous child, but was so astonished to see Kirk appear as Kirk said he would, that he did not throw the dagger, and so Kirk became a perpetual prisoner of the ' good people '.

After having visited Kirk's tomb, I called on the Rev. William M. Taylor, the present successor of Kirk, and, as we sat together in the very room where Kirk must have written his *Secret Commonwealth*, he told me that tradition reports Kirk as having been *taken* by the fairies while he was walking on their hill, which is but a short way from the parsonage. ' At the time of his disappearance, people said he was *taken* because the fairies were displeased with him for prying into their secrets. At all events, it seems likely that Kirk was taken ill very suddenly with something like apoplexy while on the Fairy Knoll, and died there. I have searched the presbytery books, and find no record of how Kirk's death really took place ; but of course there is not the least doubt of his body being in the grave.' So thus, according to Mr. Taylor, we are to conclude that if the fairies carried off anything, it must have been the spirit or soul of Kirk. I talked with others round Aberfoyle about Kirk, and some would have it that his body and soul were both *taken*, and that what was buried was no corpse at all. Mrs. Margaret MacGregor, one of the few Gaelic speakers of the old school left in Aberfoyle, holds another opinion, for she said to me, ' Nothing could be surer than that the *good people* took Kirk's spirit only.'

In the Aberfoyle country, the Fairy-Faith, save for the stories about Kirk, which will probably persist for a long time yet, is rapidly passing. In fact it is almost forgotten now. Up to thirty years ago, as Mr. Taylor explained, before the railway reached Aberfoyle, belief in fairies was much more common. Nowadays, he says, there is no real fairy-lore among the peasants ; fifty to sixty years ago there was. And in his opinion, ' the fairy people of three hundred years ago in Scotland were a distinct race by themselves. They had never been human beings. The belief in them was a survival of paganism, and not at all an outgrowth of Christian belief in angelic hosts.'

A Scotch Minister's Testimony

A Protestant minister of Scotland will be our next witness. He is a native of Ross-shire, though he draws many of his stories from the Western Hebrides, where his calling has placed him. Because he speaks from personal knowledge of the living Fairy-Faith as it was in his boyhood and is now, and chiefly because he has had the rare privilege of conscious contact with the fairy world, his testimony is of the highest value.

Reality of Fairies.—' When I was a boy I was a firm believer in fairies ; and now as a Christian minister I believe in the possibility and also the reality of these spiritual orders, but I wish only to know those orders which belong to the realm of grace. It is very certain that they exist. I have been in a state of ecstasy, and have seen spiritual beings which form these orders.[1]

' I believe in the actuality of evil spirits ; but people in the Highlands having put aside paganism, evil spirits are not seen now.'

This explanation was offered of how fairies may exist and yet be invisible :—' Our Saviour became invisible though in the body ; and, as the Scriptures suggest, I suppose we are obliged to concede a similar power of invisibility to spirits as well, good and evil ones alike.'

Precautions against Fairies.—' I remember how an old woman pulled me out of a fairy ring to save me from being *taken*.

' If a mother takes some bindweed and places it burnt at the ends over her babe's cradle, the fairies have no power over the child. The bindweed is a common roadside convolvulus.

' As a boy, I saw two old women passing a babe over red-hot coals, and then drop some of the cinders in a cup of water and give the water to the babe to drink, in order to cure it of a fairy stroke.'

Fairy Fights on Halloween.—' It is a common belief now that on Halloween the fairies, or the fairy hosts, have fights.

---

[1] The Rev. Robert Kirk, in his *Secret Commonwealth*, defines the second-sight, which enabled him to see the 'good people', as 'a rapture, transport, and sort of death '. He and our present witness came into the world with this abnormal faculty ; but there is the remarkable case to record of the late Father Allen Macdonald, who during a residence of twenty years on the tiny and isolated Isle of Erisgey, Western Hebrides, acquired the second-sight, and was able some years before he died there (in 1905) to exercise it as freely as though he had been a natural-born seer.

Lichens on rocks after there has been a frost get yellowish-red, and then when they thaw and the moisture spreads out from them the rocks are a bright red ; and this bright red is said to be the blood of the fairies after one of their battles.'

Fairies and the Hump-back.—The following story by the present witness is curious, for it is the same story of a hump-back which is so widespread. The fact that in Scotland the hump is removed or added by fairies as it is in Ireland, in Cornwall by pixies, and in Brittany by *corrigans*, goes far to prove the essential identity of these three orders of beings. The story comes from one of the remote Western Hebrides, Benbecula :—' A man who was a hump-back once met the fairies dancing, and danced with their queen ; and he sang with them, " Monday, Tuesday, Wednesday," so well that they took off his hump, and he returned home a straight-bodied man. Then a tailor went past the same place, and was also admitted by the fairies to their dance. He caught the fairy queen by the waist, and she resented his familiarity. And in singing he added " Thursday " to their song and spoilt it. To pay the tailor for his rudeness and ill manners, the dancers took up the hump they had just removed from the first man and clapped it on his back, and the conceited fellow went home a hump-back.'

Libations to Fairies.—' An elder in my church knew a woman who was accustomed, in milking her cows, to offer libations to the fairies.[1] The woman was later converted to Christ and gave up the practice, and as a result one of her cows was *taken* by the fairies. Then she revived the practice.

' The fairy queen who watches over cows is called *Gruagach* in the Islands, and she is often seen. In pouring libations to her and her fairies various kinds of stones, usually with hollows in them, are used.[2]

---

[1] In his note to *Le Chant des Trépassés (Barzaz Breiz*, p. 507), Villemarqué reports that in some localities in Lower Brittany on All Saints Night libations of milk are poured over the tombs of the dead. This is proof that the nature of fairies in Scotland and of the dead in Brittany is thought to be the same.

[2] ' In many parts of the Highlands, where the same deity is known, the stone into which women poured the libation of milk is called *Leac na*

' In Lewis libations are poured to the goddess [or god] of the sea, called *Shoney*,[1] in order to bring in seaweed. Until modern times in Iona similar libations were poured to a god corresponding to Neptune.'

IN THE HIGHLANDS

I had the pleasure as well as the great privilege of setting out from Inverness on a bright crisp September morning in company with Dr. Alexander Carmichael, the well-known folk-lorist of Scotland, to study the Fairy-Faith as it exists now in the Highlands round Tomatin, a small country village about twenty miles distant. We departed by an early train ; and soon reaching the Tomatin country began our search—Dr. Carmichael for evidence regarding rare and curious Scotch beliefs connected with folk-magic, such as blood-stopping at a distance and removing motes in the eye at a distance, and I for Highland ghosts and fairies.

Our first experience was with an old man whom we met on the road between the railway station and the post office, who could speak only Gaelic. Dr. Carmichael talked with him awhile, and then asked him about fairies, and he said there were some living in a cave some way off, but as the distance was rather too far we decided not to call on them. Then we went on to see the postmaster, Mr. John Mac-Dougall, and he told us that in his boyhood the country-folk

Gruagaich, "Flag-stone of the Gruagach." If the libation was omitted in the evening, the best cow in the fold would be found dead in the morning.'
—ALEXANDER CARMICHAEL.

[1] Dr. George Henderson, in *The Norse Influence on Celtic Scotland* (Glasgow, 1901), p. 101, says :—' *Shony* was a sea-god in Lewis, where ale was sacrificed to him at Hallowtide. After coming to the church of St. Mulvay at night a man was sent to wade into the sea, saying : "Shony, I give you this cup of ale hoping that you will be so kind as to give us plenty of sea-ware for enriching our ground the ensuing year." As *δ* from Norse would become *o*, and *fn* becomes *nn*, one thinks of *Sjöfn*, one of the goddesses in the Edda. In any case the word is Norse.' It seems, therefore, that the Celtic stock in Lewis have adopted the name *Shony* or *Shoney*, and possibly also the god it designates, through contact with Norsemen ; but, at all events, they have assimilated him to their own fairy pantheon, as we can see in their celebrating special libations to him on the ancient Celtic feast of the dead and fairies, Halloween.

round Tomatin believed thoroughly in fairies. He said they thought of them as a race of spirits capable of making themselves visible to mortals, as living in underground places, as *taking* fine healthy babes and leaving changelings in their place. These changelings would waste away and die in a short time after being left. So firmly did the old people believe in fairies then that they would ridicule a person for not believing. And now quite the reverse state has come about.[1]

THE TESTIMONY OF JOHN DUNBAR OF INVEREEN

We talked with other Highlanders in the country round Tomatin, and heard only echoes, mostly fragmentary, of what their forefathers used to believe about fairies. But at Invereen we discovered John Dunbar, a Highlander, who really knows the Fairy-Faith and is not ashamed to explain it. Speaking partly from experience and partly from what he has heard his parents relate concerning the ' good people ', he said :—

The Sheep and the Fairy-Hunting.—' I believe people saw fairies, but I think one reason no one sees them now is because every place in this parish where they used to appear has been put into sheep, and deer, and grouse, and shooting. According to tradition, Coig na Fearn is the place where the last fairy was seen in this country. Before the big sheep came, the fairies are supposed to have had a premonition that their domains were to be violated by them. A story is told of a fight between the sheep and fairies, or else of the fairies hunting the sheep :—James MacQueen, who could traffic with the fairies, whom he regarded as ghosts or spirits, one night on his old place, which now is in sheep, was lying down all alone and heard a small and big barking of dogs, and a small and big bleating of sheep, though no sheep were there then. It was the fairy-hunting he heard. " I put an

---

[1] This, as Dr. Carmichael told me, I believe very justly represents the present state of folk-lore in many parts of the Highlands. There are, it is true, old men and women here and there who know much about fairies, but they, fearing the ridicule of a younger and ' educated ' generation, are generally unwilling to admit any belief in fairies.

axe under my head and I had no fear therefore," he always repeated when telling the story. I believe the man saw and heard something. And MacQueen used to aid the fairies, and on that account, as he was in the habit of saying, he always found more meal in his chest than he thought he had.'

Fairies.—' My grandmother believed firmly in fairies, and I have heard her tell a good many stories about them. They were a small people dressed in green, and had dwellings underground in dry spots. Fairies were often heard in the hills over there (pointing), and I believe something was there. They were awful for music, and used to be heard very often playing the bagpipes. A woman wouldn't go out in the dark after giving birth to a child before the child was christened, so as not to give the fairies power over her or the child. And I have heard people say that if fairies were refused milk and meat they would *take* a horse or a cow ; and that if well treated they would repay all gifts.'

Time in Fairyland.—' People would be twenty years in Fairyland and it wouldn't seem more than a night. A bride-groom who was *taken* on his wedding-day was in Fairyland for many generations, and, coming back, thought it was next morning. He asked where all the wedding-guests were, and found only one old woman who remembered the wedding.'

Highland Legend of the Dead.—As I have found to be the case in all Celtic countries equally, fairy stories nearly always, in accordance with the law of psychology known as ' the association of ideas ', give place to or are blended with legends of the dead. This is an important factor for the Psychological Theory. And what follows proves the same ideas to be present to the mind of Mr. Dunbar :—

' Some people after death are seen in their old haunts ; no mistake about it. A bailiff had false corn and meal measures, and so after he died he came back to his daughter and told her he could have no peace until the measures were burned. She complied with her father's wish, and his spirit was never seen again. I have known also of phantom funerals of people who died soon afterwards being seen on the road at night.'

To the Western Hebrides

From Inverness I began my journey to the Western Hebrides. While I waited for the steamer to take me from Kyle to the Isle of Skye, an old man with whom I talked on the docks said this about Neill Mackintosh, of Black Island:—
' You can't argue with the old man that he hasn't seen fairies. He can tell you all about them.'

Evidence from the Isle of Skye

Miss Frances Tolmie, who was born at Uignish, Isle of Skye, and has lived many years in the isle in close touch with some of its oldest folk, contributes, from Edinburgh, the evidence which follows. The first two tales were told in the parish of Minginish a number of years ago by Mary Macdonald, a goat-herd, and have their setting in the region of the Koolian [1] range of mountains on the west side of Skye.

The Fatal Peat Ember.—' An aged nurse who had fallen fast asleep as she sat by the fire, was holding on her knees a newly-born babe. The mother, who lay in bed gazing dreamily, was astonished to see three strange little women enter the dwelling. They approached the unconscious child, and she who seemed to be their leader was on the point of lifting it off the nurse's lap, when the third exclaimed :—
" Oh! let us leave this one with her as we have already taken so many!" "So be it," replied the senior of the party in a tone of displeasure, " but when that peat now burning on the hearth shall be consumed, her life will surely come to an end." Then the three little figures passed out. The good wife, recognizing them to be fairies, sprang from her bed and poured over the fire all the water she could find, and extinguished the half-burnt ember. This she wrapped

---

[1] The following note by Miss Tolmie is of great interest and value, especially when one bears in mind Cuchulainn's traditional relation with Skye (see p. 4) :—' The Koolian range should never be written *Cu-chullin*. The name is written here with a K, to ensure its being correctly uttered and written. It is probably a Norse word ; but, as yet, a satisfactory explanation of its origin and meaning has not been published. In Gaelic the range is always alluded to (in the masculine singular) as the Koolian.

carefully in a piece of cloth and deposited at the very bottom of a large chest, which afterwards she always kept locked.

' Years passed, and the babe grew into a beautiful young woman. In the course of time she was betrothed ; and, according to custom, not appearing in public at church on the Sunday preceding the day appointed for her marriage, remained at home alone. To amuse herself, she began to search the contents of all the keeping-places in the house, and came at last to the chest containing the peat ember. In her haste, the good mother had that day forgotten the key of the chest, which was now in the lock. At the bottom of the chest the girl found a curious packet containing nothing but a morsel of peat, and this apparently useless thing she tossed away into the fire. When the peat was well kindled the young girl began to feel very ill, and when her mother returned was dying. The open chest and the blazing peat explained the cause of the calamity. The fairy's prediction was fulfilled.'

Results of Refusing Fairy Hospitality.—' Two women were walking toward the Point when one of them, hearing churning going on under a hillock, expressed aloud a wish for some buttermilk. No sooner had she spoken than a very small figure of a woman came out with a bowlful and offered it to her, but the thirsty woman, ignorant of fairy customs and the penalty attending their infringement, declined the kind offer of refreshment, and immediately found herself a prisoner in the hillock. She was led to an apartment containing a chest full of meal and a great bag of wool, and was told by the fairy that when she had eaten all the meal and spun all the wool she would be free to return to her home. The prisoner at once set herself to eating and spinning assiduously, but without apparent result, and despairing of completing the task consulted an old man of very sad countenance who had long been a captive in the hillock. He willingly gave her his advice, which was to wet her left eye with saliva each morning before she settled down to her task. She followed this advice, and gradually the wool and the meal were exhausted. Then the fairy granted her freedom, but in doing so cursed

the old man, and said that she had it in her power to keep
him in the hillock for ever.'

The Fairies' ' Waulking' (Fulling).—'At Ebost, in Braca-
dale, an old woman was living in a little hut, with no companion save a wise cat. As we talked, she expressed her
wonder that no fairies are ever seen or heard nowadays. She
could remember hearing her father tell how he, when a herd-
boy, had heard the fairies singing a "waulking" song in
Dun-Osdale, an ancient and ruined round tower in the
parish of Dùirinish, and not far from Heléval *mhor* (great)
and Heléval *bheag* (less)—two hills occasionally alluded to
as "Macleod's Tables". The youth was lying on the grass-
grown summit of the ruin, and heard them distinctly. As
if with exultation, one voice took the verse and then the
whole company joined in the following chorus : " *Ho !
fir-e ! fair-e, foirm ! Ho ! Fair-eag-an an clò !* (Ho ! well
done ! Grand ! Ho ! bravo the web [of homespun] ! " '

Crodh Chailean.—' This tale was related by Mr. Neil
Macleod, the bard of Skye :—" Colin was a gentleman of
Clan Campbell in Perthshire, who was married to a beautiful
maiden whom the fairies carried off on her marriage-day, and
on whom they cast a spell which rendered her invisible for a
day and a year. She came regularly every day to milk the cows
of her sorrowing husband, and sang sweetly to them while she
milked, but he never once had the pleasure of beholding her,
though he could hear perfectly what she sang. At the expiry
of the year she was, to his great joy, restored to him." ' [1]

---

[1] Dr. Alexander Carmichael found that the scene of this widespread tale
is variously laid, in Argyll, in Perth, in Inverness, and in other counties
of the Highlands. From his own collection of folk-songs he contributes
the following verses to illustrate the song (existing in numerous versions),
which the maiden while invisible used to sing to the cows of Colin :—

> Crodh Chailean ! crodh Chailean !
> Crodh Chailean mo ghaoil,
> Crodh Chailean mo chridhe,
>   Air lighe cheare fraoish.

> (Cows of Colin ! cows of Colin !
> Cows of Colin of my love,
> Cows of Colin of my heart,
>   In colour of the heather-hen.)

In one of Dr. Carmichael's versions, ' Colin's wife and her infant child had
been lifted away by the fairies to a fairy bower in the glen between the

Fairy Legend of the Macleod Family.—' There is a legend told of the Macleod family :—Soon after the heir of the Macleods was born, a beautiful woman in wonderful raiment, who was a fairy woman or banshee (there were joyous as well as mourning banshees) appeared at the castle, and went directly to the babe's cradle. She took up the babe and chanted over it a series of verses, and each verse had its own melody. The verses foretold the future manhood of the young child, and acted as a protective charm over its life. Then she put the babe back into its cradle, and, going out, disappeared across the moorlands.

' For many generations it was a custom in the Macleod family that whoever was the nurse of the heir must sing those verses as the fairy woman had sung them. After a time the song was forgotten, but at a later period it was partially recovered, and to-day it is one of the proud folk-lore heritages of the Macleod family.' [1]

Origin and Nature of the Fairy-Faith.—Finally, with respect to the origin and nature of the Scotch Fairy-Faith, Miss Tolmie states :—' As a child I was not permitted to hear about fairies. At twenty I was seeking and trying to understand the beliefs of my fathers in the light of modern ideas. I was very determined not to lose the past.

' The fairy-lore originated in a cultured class in very ancient times. The peasants inherited it ; they did not invent it. With the loss of Gaelic in our times came the loss of folk-ideals. The classical and English influences combined had a killing effect ; so that the instinctive religious feeling which used to be among our people when they kept alive the fairy-traditions is dead. We have intellectually-constructed creeds and doctrines which take its place.

' We always thought of fairies as mysterious little beings

hills.' There she was kept nursing the babes which the fairies had stolen, until ' upon Hallow Eve, when all the bowers were open ', Colin by placing a steel tinder above the lintel of the door to the fairy bower was enabled to enter the bower and in safety lead forth his wife and child.

[1] In this beautiful fairy legend we recognize the fairy woman as one of the Tuatha De Danann-like fairies—one of the women of the *Sidhe*, as Irish seers call them.

living in hills. They were capricious and irritable, but not wicked. They could do a good turn as well as a bad one. They were not aerial, but had bodies which they could make invisible ; and they could make human bodies invisible in the same way. Besides their hollow knolls and mounds there seemed to be a subterranean world in which they also lived, where things are like what they are in this world.'

THE ISLE OF BARRA,[1] WESTERN HEBRIDES

We pass from Cuchulainn's beautiful island to what is now the most Celtic part of Scotland—the Western Hebrides, where the ancient life is lived yet, and where the people have more than a faith in spirits and fairies. And no one of the Western Hebrides, perhaps excepting the tiny island of Erisgey, has changed less during the last five hundred years than Barra.

Our Barra guide and interpreter, Michael Buchanan, a native and a life-long resident of Barra, is seventy years old, yet as strong and active as a city man at fifty. He knows intimately every old man on the island, and as he was able to draw them out on the subject of the ' good people ' as no stranger could do, I was quite willing, as well as obliged on account of the Scotch Gaelic, to let him act

---

[1] It is interesting to know that the present inhabitants of Barra, or at least most of them, are the descendants of Irish colonists who belonged to the clan Eoichidh of County Cork, and who emigrated from there to Barra in A. D. 917. They brought with them their old customs and beliefs, and in their isolation their children have kept these things alive in almost their primitive Celtic purity. For example, besides their belief in fairies, May Day, Baaltine, and November Eve are still rigorously observed in the pagan way, and so is Easter—for it, too, before being claimed by Christianity, was a sun festival. And how beautiful it is in this age to see the youths and maidens and some of the elders of these simple-hearted Christian fisher-folk climb to the rocky heights of their little island-home on Easter morn to salute the sun as it rises out of the mountains to the east, and to hear them say that the sun dances with joy that morning because the Christ is risen. In a similar way they salute the new moon, making as they do so the sign of the cross. Finn Barr is said to have been a County Cork man of great sanctity ; and he probably came to Barra with the colony, for he is the patron saint of the island, and hence its name. (To my friend, Mr. Michael Buchanan, of Barra, I am indebted for this history and these traditions of his native isle.)

on my behalf in all my collecting on Barra. Mr. Buchanan is the author of a little book called *The MacNeils of Barra Genealogy*, published in the year 1902. He was the official interpreter before the Commission of Inquiry which was appointed by the British Parliament in 1883 to search into the oppression of landlordism in the Highlands and Islands, and he acted in the same capacity before the Crofters' Commission and the Deer-Forest Commission. We therefore feel perfectly safe in allowing him to present, before our jury trying the Fairy-Faith, the evidence of the Gaelic-speaking witnesses from Barra.

JOHN MACNEIL'S TESTIMONY

We met the first of the Barra witnesses on the top of a rocky hill, where the road from Castlebay passes. He was carrying on his back a sack of sand heavy enough for a college athlete, and he an old man between seventy and eighty years of age. Michael Buchanan has known John MacNeil all his life, for they were boys together on the island ; and there is not much difference between them in age, our interpreter being the younger. Then the three of us sat down on a grassy knoll, all the world like a fairy knoll, though it was not ; and when pipes were lit and the weather had been discussed, there was introduced the subject of the ' good people '—all in Gaelic, for our witness now about to testify knows no English—and what John MacNeil said is thus interpreted by Michael Buchanan :—

A Fairy's Visit.—' Yes, I have ' (in answer to a question if he had heard of people being *taken* by the ' good people ' or fairies). ' A fairy woman visited the house of a young wife here in Barra, and the young wife had her baby on her breast at the time. The first words uttered by the fairy woman were, " Heavy is your child ; " and the wife answered, " Light is everybody who lives the longest." " Were it not that you have answered my question," said the fairy woman, " and understood my meaning, you should have been less your child." And then the fairy woman departed.'

Fairy-Singing.—' My mother, and two other women well

known here in Barra, went to a hill one day to look after their sheep, and, a thick fog coming on, they had to rest awhile. They then sat down upon a knoll and began to sing a *walking* (cloth-working) song, as follows :—" It is early to-day that I have risen ; " and, as they sang, a fairy woman in the rocks responded to their song with one of her own.'

Nature of Fairies.—Then the question was asked if fairies were men or spirits, and this is the reply :—' I never saw any myself, and so cannot tell, but they must be spirits from all that the old people tell about them, or else how could they appear and disappear so suddenly ? The old people said they didn't know if fairies were flesh and blood, or spirits. They saw them as men of more diminutive stature than our race. I heard my father say that fairies used to come and speak to natural people, and then vanish while one was looking at them. Fairy women used to go into houses and talk and then vanish. The general belief was that the fairies were spirits who could make themselves seen or not seen at will. And when they *took* people they *took* body and soul together.'

THE TESTIMONY OF JOHN CAMPBELL, NINETY-FOUR YEARS OLD

Our next witness from Barra is John Campbell, who is ninety-four years old, yet clear-headed. He was born on Barra at Sgalary, and lives near there now at Breuvaig. We were on our way to call at his home, when we met him coming on the road, with a cane in each hand and a small sack hanging from one of them. Michael saluted him as an old acquaintance, and then we all sat down on a big boulder in the warm sunshine beside the road to talk. The first thing John wanted was tobacco, and when this was supplied we gradually led from one subject to another until he was talking about fairies. And this is what he said about them :—

The Fairy and the Fountain.—' I had a companion by the name of James Galbraith, who was drowned about forty years ago, and one time he was crossing from the west side of the island to the east side, to the township called Sgalary, and feeling thirsty took a drink out of a spring well on the mountain-side. After he had taken a drink, he looked about him and saw a woman clad in green, and imagined that no woman would be clad in such a colour except a fairy woman. He went on his way, and when he hadn't gone far, looked back, and, as he looked, saw the woman vanish out of his sight. He afterwards reported the incident at his father's house in Sgalary, and his father said he also had seen a woman clad in clothes of green at the same place some nights before.'

A Step-son Pitied by the Fairies.—' I heard my father say that a neighbour of his father, that is of my grandfather, was married twice, and had three children from the first marriage, and when married for the second time, a son and daughter. His second wife did not seem to be kind enough to the children of the first wife, neglecting their food and clothing and keeping them constantly at hard work in the fields and at herding.

' One morning when the man and his second wife were returning from mass they passed the pasture where their cows were grazing and heard the enjoyable *skirrels* of the bagpipes. The father said, " What may this be ? " and going off the road found the eldest son of the first wife playing the bagpipes to his heart's pleasure ; and asked him earnestly, " How did you come to play the bagpipes so suddenly, or where did you get this splendid pair of bagpipes ? " The boy replied, " An old man came to me while I was in the action of roasting pots in a pit-fire and said, ' Your step-mother is bad to you and in ill-will towards you.' I told the old man I was sensible that that was the case, and then he said to me, ' If I give you a trade will you be inclined to follow it ? ' I said yes, and the old man then continued, ' How would you like to be a piper by trade ? ' ' I would gladly become a piper,' says I, ' but what am I to do without the bagpipes and the tunes to play ? ' ' I'll supply the bagpipes,' he said, ' and as long as you have

them you'll never want for the most delightful tunes.' ''
The male descendants of the boy in question were all famous
pipers thereafter, and the last of them was a piper to the
late Cluny MacPherson of Cluny.'

Nature of Fairies.—At this point, Michael turned the
trend of John's thoughts to the nature of fairies, with the
following result :—' The general belief of the people here
during my father's lifetime was that the fairies were more of
the nature of spirits than of men made of flesh and blood,
but that they so appeared to the naked eye that no difference
could be marked in their forms from that of any human
being, except that they were more diminutive. I have heard
my father say it was the case that fairy women used to take
away children from their cradles and leave different children
in their places, and that these children who were left would
turn out to be old men.

' At Barra Head, a fairy woman used to come to a man's
window almost every night as though looking to see if the
family was home. The man grew suspicious, and decided
the fairy woman was watching her chance to steal his wife,
so he proposed a plan. It was then and still is the custom
after thatching a house to rope it across with heather-spun
ropes, and, at the time, the man was busy spinning some of
them ; and he told his wife to take his place that night to
spin the heather-rope, and said he would take her spinning-
wheel. They were thus placed when the fairy woman made
the usual look in at the window, and she seeing that her
intention was understood, said to the man, " You are yourself at the spinning-wheel and your wife is spinning the
heather-rope."

'I have heard it said that the fairies live in knolls on
a higher level than that of the ground in general, and that
fairy songs are heard from the faces of high rocks. The
fairies of the air (the fairy or spirit hosts) are different from
those in the rocks. A man whom I've seen, Roderick Mac-
Neil, was lifted by the hosts and left three miles from where
he was taken up. The hosts went at about midnight. A
man awake at midnight is in danger. Cows and horses are

sometimes shot in place of men ' (and why, will be explained
by later witnesses).

Father MacDonald's Opinions.—We then asked about the
late Rev. Donald MacDonald, who had the reputation of
knowing all about fairies and spirits when he lived here in
these islands, and John said :—' I have heard my wife say
that she questioned Father MacDonald, who was then a
parish priest here in Barra, and for whom she was a housekeeper, if it was possible that such beings or spirits as fairies
were in existence. He said " Yes ", and that they were those
who left Heaven after the fallen angels ; and that those
going out after the fallen angels had gone out were so
numerous and kept going so long that St. Michael notified
Christ that the throne was fast emptying, and when Christ
saw the state of affairs he ordered the doors of Heaven to be
closed at once, saying as he gave the order, " Who is out is
out and who is in is in." And the fairies are as numerous
now as ever they were before the beginning of the world.'
(Cf. pp. 47, 53, 67, 76, 85, 109, 113, 116, 129, 154, 205, 212.)

Here we left John, and he, continuing on his way up the
mountain road in an opposite direction from us and round
a turn, disappeared almost as a fairy might.

AN AGED PIPER'S TESTIMONY

We introduce now as a witness Donald McKinnon, ninety-
six years old, a piper by profession ; and not only is he the
oldest man on Barra, but also the oldest man among all our
witnesses. He was born on the Island of South Uist, one of
the Western Hebrides north of Barra, and came to Barra in
1836, where he has lived ever since. In spite of being four
years less than a hundred in age, he greeted us very heartily,
and as he did not wish us to sit inside, for his chimney
happened not to be drawing very well, and was filling the
straw-thatched cottage with peat smoke, we sat down outside on the grass and began talking ; and as we came to
fairies this is what he said :—

Nature of Fairies.—' I believe that fairies exist as a tribe
of spirits, and appear to us in the form of men and women.

People who saw fairies can yet describe them as they appeared dressed in green. No doubt there are fairies in other countries as well as here.

' In my experience there was always a good deal of difference between the fairies and the hosts. The fairies were supposed to be living without material food, whereas the hosts were supposed to be living upon their own booty. Generally, the hosts were evil and the fairies good, though I have heard that the fairies used to *take* cattle and leave their old men rolled up in the hides. One night an old witch was heard to say to the fairies outside the fold, " We cannot get anything to-night." The old men who were left behind in the hides of the animals *taken*, usually disappeared very suddenly. I saw two men who used to be lifted by the hosts. They would be carried from South Uist as far south as Barra Head, and as far north as Harris. Sometimes when these men were ordered by the hosts to kill men on the road they would kill instead either a horse or a cow; for in that way, so long as an animal was killed, the injunction of the hosts was fulfilled.' To illustrate at this point the idea of fairies, Donald repeated the same legend told by our former witness, John Campbell, about the emptying of Heaven and the doors being closed to keep the remainder of its population in. Then he told the following story about fairies :—

The Fairy-Belt.—' I heard of an apprentice to carpentry who was working with his master at the building of a boat, a little distance from his house, and near the sea. He went to work one morning and forgot a certain tool which he needed in the boat-building. He returned to his carpenter-shed to get it, and found the shed filled with fairy men and women. On seeing him they ran away so greatly confused that one of the women forgot her gird (belt), and he picked it up. In a little while she came back for the gird, and asked him to give it her, but he refused to do so. Thereupon she promised him that he should be made master of his trade wherever his lot should fall without serving further apprenticeship. On that condition he gave her the gird; and rising early next morning he went to the yard where the boat was a-building and put in two planks so perfectly that when the master arrived and saw them, he said to him, " Are you aware of anybody being in the building-yard last night, for I see by the work done that I am more likely to be an apprentice than the person who put in those two planks, whoever he is. Was it you that did it ? " The reply was in the affirmative, and the apprentice told his master the circumstances under which he gained the rapid mastership of his trade.'

Across the Mountains

It was nearing sunset now, and a long mountain-climb was ahead of us, and one more visit that evening, before we should begin our return to Castlebay, and so after this story we said a hearty good-bye to Donald, with regret at leaving him. When we reached the mountain-side, one of the rarest of Barra's sights greeted us. To the north and south in the golden glow of a September twilight we saw the long line of the Outer Hebrides like the rocky backbone of some submerged continent. The scene and colours on the land and ocean and in the sky seemed more like some magic vision, reflected from Faerie by the ' good people ' for our delight, than a thing of our own world. Never was air clearer or sea calmer, nor could there be air sweeter than that in the mystic mountain-stillness holding the perfume of millions of tiny blossoms of purple and white heather ; and as the last honey-bees were leaving the beautiful blossoms their humming came to our ears like low, strange music from Fairyland.

Marian MacLean of Barra, and her Testimony

Our next witness to testify is a direct descendant of the ancient MacNeils of Barra. Her name now is Marian Mac-Lean ; and she lives in the mountainous centre of Barra at Upper Borve. She is many years younger than the men who have testified, and one of the most industrious women on the island. It was already dark and past dinner-time when we entered her cottage, and so, as we sat down before a blazing peat-fire, she at once offered us some hot milk and biscuits, which we were only too glad to accept. And, as we ate, we talked first about our hard climb in the darkness across the mountains, and through the thick heather-bushes, and then about the big rock which has a key-hole in it, for it contains a secret entrance to a fairy palace. We had examined it in the twilight as we came through the mountain pass which it guards, and my guide Michael had assured me that more than one islander, crossing at the hour we were, had seen some of the fairies near it. We waited in front of the big rock in hopes one might appear for our benefit, but, in spite of our strong belief that there are fairies there, not a single one would come out. Perhaps they came and we couldn't see them ; who knows ?

Fairies and Fairy Hosts ('*Sluagh*').[1]—'O yes,' Marian said, as she heard Michael and myself talking over our hot milk, 'there are fairies there, for I was told that the Pass was a notable fairy haunt.' Then I said through Michael, 'Can you tell us something about what these fairies are?' And from that time, save for a few interruptions natural in conversation, we listened and Marian talked, and told stories as follows :—

'Generally, the fairies are to be seen after or about sunset, and walk on the ground as we do, whereas the hosts travel in the air above places inhabited by people. The hosts used to go after the fall of night, and more particularly about midnight. You'd hear them going in fine weather against a wind like a covey of birds. And they were in the habit of lifting men in South Uist, for the hosts need men to help in shooting their javelins from their bows against women in the action of milking cows, or against any person working at night in a house over which they pass. And I have heard of good sensible men whom the hosts took, shooting a horse or cow in place of the person ordered to be shot.

[1] '*Sluagh*, "hosts," the spirit-world. The "hosts" are the spirits of mortals who have died. . . . According to one informant, the spirits fly about in great clouds, up and down the face of the world like the starlings, and come back to the scenes of their earthly transgressions. No soul of them is without the clouds of earth, dimming the brightness of the works of God, nor can any win heaven till satisfaction is made for the sins of earth.'—ALEXANDER CARMICHAEL, *Carmina Gadelica*, ii. 330.

' There was a man who had only one cow and one daughter. The daughter was milking the cow at night when the hosts were passing, and that human being whom the hosts had lifted with them was her father's neighbour. And this neighbour was ordered by the hosts to shoot the daughter as she was milking, but, knowing the father and daughter, he shot the cow instead. The next morning he went where the father was and said to him, " You are missing the cow." " Yes," said the father, " I am." And the man who had shot the cow said, " Are you not glad your cow and not your daughter was *taken* ? For I was ordered to shoot your daughter and I shot your cow, in order to show blood on my arrow." " I am very glad of what you have done if that was the case," the father replied. " It was the case," the neighbour said.

' My father and grandfather knew a man who was carried by the hosts from South Uist here to Barra. I understand when the hosts take away earthly men they require another man to help them. But the hosts must be spirits. My opinion is that they are both spirits of the dead and other spirits not the dead. A child was taken by the hosts and returned after one night and one day, and found at the back of the house with the palms of its hands in the holes in the wall, and with no life in its body. It was dead in the spirit. It is believed that when people are dropped from a great height by the hosts they are killed by the fall. As to fairies, my firm opinion is that they are spirits who appear in the shape of human beings.'

The question was now asked whether the fairies were anything like the dead, and Marian hesitated about answering. She thought they were like the dead, but not to be identified with them. The fallen-angel idea concerning fairies was an obstacle she could not pass, for she said, ' When the fallen angels were cast out of Heaven God commanded them thus :—" You will go to take up your abodes in crevices, under the earth, in mounds, or soil, or rocks." And according to this command they have been condemned to inhabit the places named for a certain period of time, and when it is expired before the consummation of the world, they will be seen as numerous as ever.'

Now we heard two good stories, the first about fairy women spinning for a mortal, the second about a wonderful changeling who was a magic musician :—

Fairy-Women Spinners.—' I have heard my father, Alexander MacNeil, who was well known to Mr. [Alexander] Carmichael and to Mr. J. F. Campbell of Islay, say that his father knew a woman in the neighbourhood who was in a hurry to have her stock of wool spun and made into cloth, and one night this woman secretly wished to have some women to help her. So the following morning there appeared at her house six or seven fairy women in long green robes, all alike chanting, " A wool-card, and a spinning-wheel." And when they were supplied with the instruments they were so very desirous to get, they all set to work, and by midday of that morning the cloth was going through the process of the hand-loom. But they were not satisfied with finishing the work the woman had set before them, but asked for new employment. The woman had no more spinning or weaving to be done, and began to wonder how she was to get the women out of the house. So she went into her neighbour's house and informed him of her position in regard to the fairy women. The old man asked what they were saying. " They are earnestly petitioning for some work to do, and I have no more to give them," the woman replied. " Go you in," he said to her, " and tell them to spin the sand, and if then they do not move from your house, go out again and yell in at the door that Dun Borve is in fire ! " The first plan had no effect, but immediately on hearing the cry, " Dun Borve is in fire ! " the fairy women disappeared invisibly. And as they went, the woman heard the melancholy wail, " Dun Borve is in fire ! Dun Borve is in fire ! And what will become of our hammers and anvil ? "—for there was a smithy in the fairy-dwelling.'

The Tailor and the Changeling.—' There was a young wife of a young man who lived in the township of Allasdale, and the pair had just had their first child. One day the mother left her baby in its cradle to go out and do some shearing, and when she returned the child was crying in a most unusual fashion. She fed him as usual on porridge and milk, but he wasn't satisfied with what seemed to her enough for any one of his age, yet every suspicion escaped her attention. As it happened, at the time there was a web of home-made cloth in the house waiting for the tailor. The tailor came and began to work up the cloth. As the woman was going out to her customary shearing operation, she warned the tailor if he heard the child continually crying not to pay much attention to it, adding she would attend to it when she came home, for she feared the child would delay him in his work.

' All went well till about noon, when the tailor observed the child rising up on its elbow and stretching its hand to a sort of shelf above the cradle and taking down from it a yellow chanter [of a bagpipe]. And then the child began to play. Immediately after the child began to play the chanter, the house filled with young fairy women all clad in long green robes, who began to dance, and the tailor had to dance with them. About two o'clock that same afternoon the women disappeared unknown to the tailor, and the chanter disappeared from the hands of the child also unknown to the tailor ; and the child was in the cradle crying as usual.

' The wife came home to make the dinner, and observed that the tailor was not so far advanced with his work as he ought to be in that space of time. However, when the fairy women disappeared, the child had enjoined upon the tailor never to tell what he had seen. The tailor promised to be faithful to the child's injunctions, and so he said nothing to the mother.

' The second day the wife left for her occupation as usual, and told the tailor to be more attentive to his work than the day before. A second time at the same hour of the day the child in the cradle, appearing more like an old man than a child, took the chanter and began to play. The same fairy women filled the house again, and repeated their dance, and the tailor had to join them.

' Naturally the tailor was as far behind with his work the second day as the first day, and it was very noticeable to the woman of the house when she returned. She thereupon requested him to tell her what the matter might be. Then he said to her, " I urge upon you after going to bed to-night not to fondle that child, because he is not your child, nor is he a child : he is an old fairy man. And to-morrow, at dead tide, go down to the shore and wrap him in your plaid and put him upon a rock and begin to pick that shell-fish which is called limpet, and for your life do not leave the shore until such a time as the tide will flow so high that you will scarcely be able to wade in to the main shore." The woman complied with the tailor's advice, and when she had waded to the main shore and stood there looking at the child on the rock, it cried to her, " You had a great need to do what you have done. Otherwise you'd have seen another ending of your turn ; but blessing be to you and curses on your adviser." When the wife arrived home her own natural child was in the cradle.'

THE TESTIMONY OF MURDOCH MACLEAN

The husband of Marian MacLean had entered while the last stories were being told, and when they were ended the spirit was on him, and wishing to give his testimony he began :—

Lachlann's Fairy Mistress.—' My grandmother, Catherine MacInnis, used to tell about a man named Lachlann, whom she knew, being in love with a fairy woman. The fairy woman made it a point to see Lachlann every night, and he being worn out with her began to fear her. Things got so bad at last that he decided to go to America to escape the fairy woman. As soon as the plan was fixed, and he was about to emigrate, women who were milking at sunset out in the meadows heard very audibly the fairy woman singing this song :—

What will the brown-haired woman do
When Lachlann is on the billows ?

'Lachlann emigrated to Cape Breton, landing in Nova Scotia; and in his first letter home to his friends he stated that the same fairy woman was haunting him there in America.'[1]

Abduction of a Bridegroom.—'I have heard it from old people that a couple, newly married, were on their way to the home of the bride's father, and for some unknown reason the groom fell behind the procession, and seeing a fairy-dwelling open along the road was taken into it. No one could ever find the least trace of where he went, and all hope of seeing him again was given up. The man remained with the fairies so long that when he returned two generations had disappeared during the lapse of time. The township in which his bride's house used to be was depopulated and in ruins for upwards of twenty years, but to him the time had seemed only a few hours; and he was just as fresh and youthful as when he went in the fairy-dwelling.'

Nature of Fairies.—Previous to his story-telling Murdoch had heard us discussing the nature and powers of fairies, and at the end of this account he volunteered, without our asking for it, an opinion of his own :—'This (the story just told by him) leads me to believe that the spirit and body [of a mortal] are somehow mystically combined by fairy enchantment, for the fairies had a mighty power of enchanting natural people, and could transform the physical body in some way. It cannot be but that the fairies are spirits. According to my thinking and belief they cannot be anything but spirits. My firm belief, however, is that they are not the spirits of dead men, but are the fallen angels.'

Then his wife Marian had one more story to add, and she at once, when she could, began :—

The Messenger and the Fairies.—'Yes, I have heard the

---

[1] This curious tale suggests that certain of the fairy women who entice mortals to their love in modern times are much the same, if not the same, as the *succubi* of Middle-Age mystics. But it is not intended by this observation to confuse the higher orders of the *Sidhe* and all the fairy folk like the fays who come from Avalon with *succubi*; though *succubi* and fairy women in general were often confused and improperly identified the one with the other. It need not be urged in this example of a 'fairy woman' that we have to do not with a being of flesh and blood, whatever various readers may think of her.

following incident took place here on the Island of Barra about
one hundred years ago :—A young woman taken ill suddenly
sent a messenger in all haste to the doctor for medicine. On
his return, the day being hot and there being five miles to
walk, he sat down at the foot of a knoll and fell asleep ; and
was awakened by hearing a song to the following air : " Ho,
ho, ho, hi, ho, ho. Ill it becomes a messenger on an important message to sleep on the ground in the open air." '

And with this, for the hour was late and dark, and we
were several miles from Castlebay, we bade our good friends
adieu, and began to hunt for a road out of the little mountain
valley where Murdoch and Marian guard their cows and
sheep. And all the way to the hotel Michael and I discussed
the nature of fairies. Just before midnight we saw the
welcome lights in Castlebay across the heather-covered hills,
and we both entered the hotel to talk. There was a blazing
fire ready for us and something to eat. Before I took my
final leave of my friend and guide, I asked him to dictate
for me his private opinions about fairies, what they are and
how they appear to men, and he was glad to meet my
request. Here is what he said about the famous folk-lorist,
the late Mr. J. F. Campbell, with whom he often worked in
Barra, and for himself :—

MICHAEL BUCHANAN'S DEPOSITION CONCERNING FAIRIES

' I was with the late Mr. J. F. Campbell during his first
and second tour of the Island of Barra in search of legendary
lore strictly connected with fairies, and I know from daily
conversing with him about fairies that he held them to be
spirits appearing to the naked eye of the spectator as any
of the present or former generations of men and women,
except that they were smaller in stature. And I know
equally that he, holding them to be spirits, thought they
could appear or disappear at will. My own firm belief is that
the fairies were or are only spirits which were or are seen in
the shape of human beings, but smaller as regards stature.
I also firmly believe in the existence of fairies as such ; and
accept the modern and ancient traditions respecting the

ways and customs of various fairy tribes, such as John
Mackinnon, the old piper, and John Campbell, and the
MacLeans told us. And I therefore have no hesitation in
agreeing with the views held by the late Mr. J. F. Campbell
regarding fairies.'

THE RECITERS' LAMENT, AND THEIR STORY

The following material, so truly Celtic in its word-colour
and in the profound note of sadness and lamentation dominat-
ing it, may very appropriately conclude our examination of
the Fairy-Faith of Scotland, by giving us some insight into
the mind of the Scotch peasants of two generations ago, and
into the then prevailing happy social environment under
which their belief in fairies flourished. For our special use
Dr. Alexander Carmichael has rendered it out of the original
Gaelic, as this was taken down by him in various versions
in the Western Hebrides. One version was recited by Ann
Macneill, of Barra, in the year 1865, another by Angus
Macleod, of Harris, in 1877. In relation to their belief in
fairies the anti-clerical bias of the reciters is worth noting as
a curious phenomenon :—

' That is as I heard when a hairy little fellow upon the
knee of my mother. My mother was full of stories and
songs of music and chanting. My two ears never heard
musical fingers more preferable for me to hear than the
chanting of my mother. If there were quarrels among
children, as there were, and as there will be, my beloved
mother would set us to dance there and then. She herself
or one of the other crofter women of the townland would
sing to us the mouth-music. We would dance there till we
were seven times tired. A stream of sweat would be falling
from us before we stopped—hairful little lassies and stumpy
little fellows. These are scattered to-day ! scattered to-day
over the wide world ! The people of those times were full
of music and dancing stories and traditions. The clerics
have extinguished these. May ill befall them ! And what
have the clerics put in their place ? Beliefs about creeds,

and disputations about denominations and churches ! May
lateness be their lot ! It is they who have put the cross
round the heads and the entanglements round the feet
of the people. The people of the Gaeldom of to-day are
anear perishing for lack of the famous feats of their fathers.
The black clerics have suppressed every noble custom among
the people of the Gaeldom—precious customs that will
never return, no never again return.' (Now follows what
the Reciters heard upon the knee of their mother) :—

'"I have never seen a man fairy nor a woman fairy, but
my mother saw a troop of them. She herself and the other
maidens of the townland were once out upon the summer
sheiling (grazing). They were milking the cows, in the evening gloaming, when they observed a flock of fairies reeling
and setting upon the green plain in front of the knoll. And,
oh King ! but it was they the fairies themselves that had
the right to the dancing, and not the children of men !
Bell-helmets of blue silk covered their heads, and garments
of green satin covered their bodies, and sandals of yellow
membrane covered their feet. Their heavy brown hair was
streaming down their waist, and its lustre was of the fair
golden sun of summer. Their skin was as white as the swan of
the wave, and their voice was as melodious as the mavis of the
wood, and they themselves were as beauteous of feature and
as lithe of form as a picture, while their step was as light and
stately and their minds as sportive as the little red hind of the
hill. The damsel children of the *sheiling*-fold never saw sight
but them, no never sight but them, never aught so beautiful.

'"There is not a wave of prosperity upon the fairies of
the knoll, no, not a wave. There is no growth nor increase,
no death nor withering upon the fairies. Seed unfortunate
they ! They went away from the Paradise with the One of
the Great Pride. When the Father commanded the doors
closed down and up, the intermediate fairies had no alter-
native but to leap into the holes of the earth, where they
are, and where they will be."

' This is what I heard upon the knee of my beloved mother.
Blessings be with her ever evermore ! '

IV   IN THE ISLE OF MAN

Introduction by SOPHIA MORRISON, Hon. Secretary of the Manx Language Society.

The Manx hierarchy of fairy beings people hills and glens, caves and rivers, mounds and roads ; and their name is legion.   Apparently there is not a place in the island but has its fairy legend.   Sir Walter Scott said that the ' Isle of Man, beyond all other places in Britain, was a peculiar depository of the fairy-traditions, which, on the Island being conquered by the Norse, became in all probability chequered with those of Scandinavia, from a source peculiar and more direct than that by which they reached Scotland and Ireland '.

A good Manxman, however, does not speak of fairies— the word *ferish*, a corruption of the English, did not exist in the island one hundred and fifty years ago.   He talks of ' The Little People ' (*Mooinjer veggey*), or, in a more familiar mood, of ' Themselves ', and of ' Little Boys ' (*Guillyn veggey*), or ' Little Fellas '.   In contradistinction to mortals he calls them ' Middle World Men ', for they are believed to dwell in a world of their own, being neither good enough for Heaven nor bad enough for Hell.

At the present moment almost all the older Manx peasants hold to this belief in fairies quite firmly, but with a certain dread of them ; and, to my knowledge, two old ladies of the better class yet leave out cakes and water for the fairies every night.   The following story, illustrative of the belief, was told to me by Bill Clarke :—

' Once while I was fishing from a ledge of rocks that runs out into the sea at Lag-ny-Keilley, a dense grey mist began to approach the land, and I thought I had best make for home while the footpath above the rocks was visible.   When getting my things together I heard what sounded like a lot of children coming out of school.   I lifted my head, and behold ye, there was a fleet of fairy boats each side of the rock.   Their riding-lights were shining like little stars, and I heard one of the *Little Fellas* shout, " *Hraaghyn boght as*

*earish broigh, skeddan dy liooar ec yn mooinjer seihll shoh,
cha nel veg ain*" (Poor times and dirty weather, and herring
enough at the people of this world, nothing at us). Then
they dropped off and went agate o' the flitters.'

'Willy-the-Fairy,' as he is called, who lives at Rhenass,
says he often hears the fairies singing and playing up the
Glen o' nights. I have heard him sing airs which he said
he had thus learned from the *Little People.*[1]

Again, there is a belief that at Keeill Moirrey (Mary's
Church), near Glen Meay, a little old woman in a red cloak
is sometimes seen coming over the mountain towards the
keeill, ringing a bell, just about the hour when church
service begins. Keeill Moirrey is one of the early little
Celtic cells, probably of the sixth century, of which nothing
remains but the foundations.

And the following prayer, surviving to our own epoch, is
most interesting. It shows, in fact, pure paganism ; and
we may judge from it that the ancient Manx people regarded
Manannan, the great Tuatha De Danann god, in his true
nature, as a spiritual being, a Lord of the Sea, and as belonging to the complex fairy hierarchy. This prayer was given
to me by a Manxwoman nearly one hundred years old, who
is still living. She said it had been used by her grandfather,
and that her father prayed the same prayer—substituting
St. Patrick's name for Manannan's :—

*Manannan beg mac y Leirr, fer vannee yn Ellan,
Bannee shin as nyn maatey, mie goll magh
As cheet stiagh ny share lesh bio as marroo " sy vaatey ".*

(Little Manannan son of Leirr, who blest our Island,
Bless us and our boat, well going out
And better coming in with living and dead [fish] in the
       boat).

.   .   .   .

It seems to me that no one of the various theories so far
advanced accounts in itself for the Fairy-Faith. There is

---

[1] ' " Willy-the-Fairy," otherwise known as William Cain, is the musician
referred to by the late Mr. John Nelson (p. 131). The latter's statement
that William Cain played one of these fairy tunes at one of our Manx
entertainments in Peel is perfectly correct.'—SOPHIA MORRISON.

always a missing factor, an unknown quantity which has yet to be discovered. No doubt the Pygmy Theory explains a good deal. In some countries a tradition has been handed down of the times when there were races of diminutive men in existence—beings so small that their tiny hands could have used the flint arrow-heads and scrapers which are like toys to us. No such tradition exists at the present day in the Isle of Man, but one might have filtered down from the far-off ages and become innate in the folk-memory, and now, unknown to the Manx peasant, may possibly suggest to his mind the troops of *Little People* in the shadowy glen or on the lonely mountain-side. Again, the rustling of the leaves or the sough of the wind may be heard by the peasant as strange and mysterious voices, or the trembling shadow of a bush may appear to him as an unearthly being. Natural facts, explainable by modern science, may easily remain dark mysteries to those who live quiet lives close to Nature, far from sophisticated towns, and whose few years of schooling have left the depths of their being undisturbed, only, as it were, ruffling the shallows.

But this is not enough. Even let it be granted that nine out of every ten cases of experiences with fairies can be analysed and explained away—there remains the tenth. In this tenth case one is obliged to admit that there is something at work which we do not understand, some force in play which, as yet, we know not. In spite of ourselves we feel ' There's Powers that's in '. These Powers are not necessarily what the superstitious call ' supernatural '. We realize now that there is nothing supernatural—that what used to be so called is simply something that we do not understand at present. Our forefathers would have thought the telephone, the X-rays, and wireless telegraphy things ' supernatural '. It is more than possible that our descendants may make discoveries equally marvellous in the realms both of mind and matter, and that many things, which nowadays seem to the materialistically-minded the creations of credulous fancy, may in the future be understood and recognized as part of the one great scheme of things.

Some persons are certainly more susceptible than others to these unknown forces. Most people know reliable instances of telepathy and presentiment amongst their acquaintances. It seems not at all contrary to reason that both matter and mind, in knowledge of which we have not gone so very far after all, may exist in forms as yet entirely unknown to us. After all, beings with bodies and personalities different from our own may well inhabit the unseen world around us : the Fairy Hound, white as driven snow, may show himself at times among his mundane companions ; *Fenodyree* may do the farm-work for those whom he favours ; the *Little People* may sing and dance o' nights in Colby Glen. Let us not say it is ' impossible '.

PEEL, ISLE OF MAN,
September 1910.

ON THE SLOPES OF SOUTH BARRULE

I was introduced to the ways and nature of Manx fairies in what is probably the most fairy-haunted part of the isle—the southern slopes of South Barrule, the mountain on whose summit Manannan is said to have had his stronghold, and whence he worked his magic, hiding the kingdom in dense fog whenever he beheld in the distance the coming of an enemy's ship or fleet. And from a representative of the older generation, Mrs. Samuel Leece, who lives at Ballamodda, a pleasant village under the shadow of South Barrule, I heard the first story :—

Baby and Table Moved by Fairies.—' I have been told of *their* (the fairies') taking babies, though I can't be sure it is true. But this did happen to my own mother in this parish of Kirk Patrick about eighty years since : She was in bed with her baby, but wide awake, when she felt the baby pulled off her arm and heard the rush of *them*. Then she mentioned the Almighty's name, and, as *they* were hurrying away, a little table alongside the bed went round about the floor twenty times. Nobody was in the room with my mother, and she always allowed it was the *little fellows*.'

Manx Tales in a Snow-bound Farm-house

When our interesting conversation was over, Mrs. Leece directed me to her son's farm-house, where her husband, Mr. Samuel Leece, then happened to be ; and going there through the snow-drifts, I found him with his son and the family within. The day was just the right sort to stir Manx memories, and it was not long before the best of stories about the 'little people' were being told in the most natural way, and to the great delight of the children. The grand-father, who is eighty-six years of age, sat by the open fire smoking ; and he prepared the way for the stories (three of which we record) by telling about a ghost seen by himself and his father, and by the announcement that ' the fairies are thought to be spirits '.

Under 'Fairy' Control.—' About fifty years ago,' said Mr. T. Leece, the son, ' Paul Taggart, my wife's uncle, a tailor by trade, had for an apprentice, Humphrey Keggan, a young man eighteen or nineteen years of age ; and it often happened that while the two of them would be returning home at nightfall, the apprentice would suddenly disappear from the side of the tailor, and even in the midst of a con-versation, as soon as they had crossed the burn in the field down there (indicating an adjoining field). And Taggart could not see nor hear Humphrey go. The next morning Humphrey would come back, but so worn out that he could not work, and he always declared that *little men* had come to him in crowds, and used him as a horse, and that with them he had travelled all night across fields and over hedges.' The wife of the narrator substantiated this strange psychological story by adding :—' This is true, because I know my Uncle Paul too well to doubt what he says.' And she then related the two following stories :—

Heifer Killed by Fairy Woman's Touch.—' Aunt Jane was coming down the road on the other side of South Barrule when she saw a strange woman' (who Mr. T. Leece suggested was a witch) 'appear in the middle of the gorse and walk right over the gorse and heather in a place where

no person could walk. Then she observed the woman go
up to a heifer and put her hand on it ; and within a few
days that heifer was dead.'

The Fairy Dog.—' This used to happen about one hundred
years ago, as my mother has told me :—Where my grandfather John Watterson was reared, just over near Kerroo
Kiel (Narrow Quarter), all the family were sometimes sitting
in the house of a cold winter night, and my great grandmother and her daughters at their wheels spinning, when
a little white dog would suddenly appear in the room. Then
every one there would have to drop their work and prepare
for *the company* to come in : they would put down a fire and
leave fresh water for *them*, and hurry off upstairs to bed.
They could hear *them* come, but could never see them, only
the dog. The dog was a fairy dog, and a sure sign of their
coming.'

TESTIMONY OF A HERB-DOCTOR AND SEER

At Ballasalla I was fortunate enough to meet one of the
most interesting of its older inhabitants, John Davies, a
Celtic medicine-man, who can cure most obstinate maladies
in men or animals with secret herbs, and who knows very
much about witchcraft and the charms against it. ' Witches
are as common as ducks walking barefooted,' he said, using
the duck simile, which is a popular Manx one ; and he cited
two particular instances from his own experience. But for
us it is more important to know that John Davies is also an
able seer. The son of a weaver, he was born in County Down,
Ireland, seventy-eight years ago ; but in earliest boyhood
he came with his people to the Isle of Man, and grew up in
the country near Ramsay, and so thoroughly has he identified
himself with the island and its lore, and even with its ancient
language, that for our purposes he may well be considered a
Manxman. His testimony about Manx fairies is as follows :—

Actual Fairies Described.—' I am only a poor ignorant
man ; when I was married I couldn't say the word " matri-
mony " in the right way. But one does not have to be
educated to see fairies, and I have seen them many a time.

I have seen them with the naked eye as numerous as I have seen scholars coming out of Ballasalla school ; and I have been seeing them since I was eighteen to twenty years of age. The last one I saw was in Kirk Michael. Before education came into the island more people could see the fairies ; now very few people can see them. But *they* (the fairies) are as thick on the Isle of Man as ever *they* were. *They* throng the air, and darken Heaven, and rule this lower world. It is only twenty-one miles from this world up to the first heaven.[1] There are as many kinds of fairies as populations in our world. I have seen some who were about two and a half feet high ; and some who were as big as we are. I think very many such fairies as these last are the lost souls of the people who died before the Flood. At the Flood all the world was drowned ; but the Spirit which God breathed into Adam will never be drowned, or burned, and it is as much in the sea as on the land. Others of the fairies are evil spirits : our Saviour drove a legion of devils into a herd of swine ; the swine were choked, but not the devils. You can't drown devils ; it is spirits they are, and just like a shadow on the wall.' I here asked about the personal aspects of most fairies of human size, and my friend said :—
' *They* appear to me in the same dress as in the days when they lived here on earth ; the spirit itself is only what God blew into Adam as the breath of life.'

It seems to me that, on the whole, John Davies has had genuine visions, but that whatever he may have seen has been very much coloured in interpretation by his devout knowledge of the Christian Bible, and by his social environment, as is self-evident.

TESTIMONY OF A BALLASALLA MANXWOMAN

A well-informed Manxwoman, of Ballasalla, who lives in the ancient stone house wherein she was born, and in which before her lived her grandparents, offers this testimony :—

Concerning Fairies.—' I've heard a good deal of talk

---

[1] This is the Mid-world of Irish seers, who would be inclined to follow the Manx custom and call the fairies ' the People of the Middle World '.

about fairies, but never believed in them myself ; the old
people thought them the ghosts of the dead or some such
things. They were like people who had gone before (that is,
dead). If there came a strange sudden knock or noises, or
if a tree took a sudden shaking when there was no wind,
people used to make out it was caused by the fairies. On
the 11th of May[1] we used to gather mountain-ash (*Cuirn*)
with red berries on it, and make crosses out of its sprigs, and
put them over the doors, so that the fairies would not come
in. My father always saw that this was done ; he said we
could have no luck during the year if we forgot to do it.'

TESTIMONY GIVEN IN A JOINER'S SHOP

George Gelling, of Ballasalla, a joiner, has a local reputation for knowing much about the fairies, and so I called on
him at his workshop. This is what he told me :—

Seeing the Fairies.—' I was making a coffin here in the
shop, and, after tea, my apprentice was late returning ; he
was out by the hedge just over there looking at a crowd of
little people kicking and dancing. One of them came up and
asked him what he was looking at ; and this made him run
back to the shop. When he described what he had seen,
I told him they were nothing but fairies.'

Hearing Fairy Music.—' Up by the abbey on two different
occasions I have heard the fairies. They were playing tunes
not of this world, and on each occasion I listened for nearly
an hour.'

Mickleby and the Fairy Woman.—' A man named Mickleby
was coming from Derbyhaven at night, when by a certain

[1] 'May 11=in Manx *Oie Voaldyn*, "May-day Eve." On this evening the
fairies were supposed to be peculiarly active. To propitiate them and to
ward off the influence of evil spirits, and witches, who were also active at
this time, green leaves or boughs and *sumark* or primrose flowers were
strewn on the threshold, and branches of the *cuirn* or mountain ash made
into small crosses without the aid of a knife, which was on no account to
be used (steel or iron in any form being taboo to fairies and spirits), and
stuck over the doors of the dwelling-houses and cow-houses. Cows were
further protected from the same influences by having the *Bollan-feaill-
Eoin* (John's feast wort) placed in their stalls. This was also one of the
occasions on which no one would give fire away, and on which fires were
and are still lit on the hills to drive away the fairies.'—SOPHIA MORRISON.

stream he met two ladies. He saluted them, and then walked along with them to Ballahick Farm. There he saw a house lit up, and they took him into it to a dance. As he danced, he happened to wipe away his sweat with a part of the dress of one of the two strange women who was his partner. After this adventure, whenever Mickleby was lying abed at night, the woman with whom he danced would appear standing beside his bed. And the only way to drive her away was to throw over her head and Mickleby a linen sheet which had never been bleached.'

Nature of Fairies.—' The fairies are spirits. I think they are in this country yet : A man below here forgot his cow, and at a late hour went to look for her, and saw that crowds of fairies like little boys were with him. [St.] Paul said that spirits are thick in the air, if only we could see them ; and we call spirits fairies. I think the old people here in the island thought of fairies in the same way.'

The Fairies' Revenge.—William Oates now happened to come into the workshop, and being as much interested in the subject under discussion as ourselves, offered various stories, of which the following is a type :—' A man named Watterson, who used often to see the fairies in his house at Colby playing in the moonlight, on one occasion heard them coming just as he was going to bed. So he went out to the spring to get fresh water for them ; and coming into the house put the can down on the floor, saying, " Now, little beggars, drink away." And at that (an insult to the fairies) the water was suddenly thrown upon him.'

A VICAR'S TESTIMONY

When I called on the Rev. J. M. Spicer, vicar of Malew parish, at his home near Castletown, he told me this very curious story :—

The Taking of Mrs. K——.—' The belief in fairies is quite a living thing here yet. For example, old Mrs. K——, about a year ago, told me that on one occasion, when her daughter had been in Castletown during the day, she went out to the road at nightfall to see if her daughter was yet

in sight, whereupon a whole crowd of fairies suddenly surrounded her, and began taking her off toward South Barrule
Mountain ; and, she added, " I couldn't get away from *them*
until I had called my son." '

A CANON'S TESTIMONY

I am greatly indebted to the Rev. Canon Kewley, of
Arbory, for the valuable testimony which follows, and
especially for his kindness in allowing me to record what is
one of the clearest examples of a collective hallucination
I have heard about as occurring in the fairy-haunted regions
of Celtic countries :—

A Collective Hallucination.—' A good many things can be
explained as natural phenomena, but there are some things
which I think cannot be. For example, my sister and myself
and our coachman, and apparently the horse, saw the same
phenomenon at the same moment : one evening we were
driving along an avenue in this parish when the avenue
seemed to be blocked by a great crowd of people, like a
funeral procession ; and the crowd was so dense that we
could not see through it. The throng was about thirty to
forty yards away. When we approached, it melted away,
and no person was anywhere in sight.'

The Manx Fairy-Faith.—' Among the old people of this
parish there is still a belief in fairies. About eighteen years
ago, I buried a man, a staunch Methodist, who said he once
saw the road full of fairies in the form of little black pigs,
and that when he addressed them, " In the name of God
what are ye ? " they immediately vanished. He was certain
they were the fairies. Other old people speak of the fairies
as the *little folk*. The tradition is that the fairies once inhabited this island, but were banished for evil-doing. The
elder-tree, in Manx *tramman*, is supposed to be inhabited by
fairies. Through accident, one night a woman ran into such
a tree, and was immediately stricken with a terrible swelling
which her neighbours declared came from disturbing the
fairies in the tree. This was on the borders of Arbory
parish.'

The Canon favours the hypothesis that in much of the folk-belief concerning fairies and Fairyland there is present an instinct, as seen among all peoples, for communion with the other world, and that this instinct shows itself in another form in the Christian doctrine of the Communion of Saints.

FAIRY TALES ON CHRISTMAS DAY

The next morning, Christmas morning, I called at the picturesque roadside home of Mrs. Dinah Moore a Manx-woman living near Glen Meay ; and she contributed the best single collection of Manx folk-legends I discovered on the island. The day was bright and frosty, and much snow still remained in the shaded nooks and hollows, so that a seat before the cheerful fire in Mrs. Moore's cottage was very comfortable ; and with most work suspended for the ancient day of festivities in honour of the Sun, re-born after its death at the hands of the Powers of Darkness, all conditions were favourable for hearing about fairies, and this may explain why such important results were obtained.

Fairy Deceit.—' I heard of a man and wife who had no children. One night the man was out on horseback and heard a little baby crying beside the road. He got off his horse to get the baby, and, taking it home, went to give it to his wife, and it was only a block of wood. And then the old fairies were outside yelling at the man : " *Eash un oie, s'cheap t'ou mollit !* " (Age one night, how easily thou art deceived !).'

A Midwife's Strange Experience.—' A strange man took a nurse to a place where a baby boy was born. After the birth, the man set out on a table two cakes, one of them broken and the other one whole, and said to the nurse : " Eat, eat ; but don't eat of the cake which is broken nor of the cake which is whole." And the nurse said : " What in the name of the Lord am I going to eat ? " At that all the fairies in the house disappeared ; and the nurse was left out on a mountain-side alone.'

A Fairy-Baking.—' At night the fairies came into a house in Glen Rushen to bake. The family had put no water out for them ; and a beggar-man who had been left lodging on the sofa downstairs heard the fairies say, " We have no water, so we'll take blood out of the toe of the servant who forgot our water." And from the girl's blood they mixed their dough. Then they baked their cakes, ate most of them, and poked pieces up under the thatched roof. The next day the servant-girl fell ill, and was ill until the old beggar-man returned to the house and cured her with a bit of the cake which he took from under the thatch.'

A Changeling Musician.—' A family at Dalby had a poor idiot baby, and when it was twenty years old it still sat by the fire just like a child. A tailor came to the house to work on a day when all the folks were out cutting corn, and the idiot was left with him. The tailor began to whistle as he sat on the table sewing, and the little idiot sitting by the fire said to him : " If you'll not tell anybody when they come in, I'll dance that tune for you." So the little fellow began to dance, and he could step it out splendidly. Then he said to the tailor : " If you'll not tell anybody when they come in, I'll play the fiddle for you." And the tailor and the idiot spent a very enjoyable afternoon together. But before the family came in from the fields, the poor idiot, as usual, was sitting in a chair by the fire, a big baby who couldn't hardly talk. When the mother came in she happened to say to the tailor, " You've a fine chap here," referring to the idiot. " Yes, indeed," said the tailor, " we've had a very fine afternoon together ; but I think we had better make a good fire and put him on it." " Oh ! " cried the mother, " the poor child could never even walk." " Ah, but he can dance and play the fiddle, too," replied the tailor. And the fire was made ; but when the idiot saw that they were for putting him on it he pulled from his pocket a ball, and this ball went rolling on ahead of him, and he, going after it, was never seen again.' After this strange story was finished I asked Mrs. Moore where she had heard it, and she said :—
' I have heard this story ever since I was a girl. I knew the house and family, and so did my mother. The family's name was Cubbon.'

The Fenodyree's (or ' Phynnodderee's ') Disgust.—' During snowy weather, like this, the Fenodyree would gather in the sheep at night ; and during the harvest season would do the threshing when all the family were abed. One time, however, just over here at Gordon Farm, the farmer saw him, and he was naked ; and so the farmer put out a new suit of clothes for him. The Fenodyree came at night, and looking at the clothes with great disgust at the idea of wearing such things, said :—

> *Bayrn* da'n chione, doogh da'n chione,
> Cooat da'n dreeym, doogh da'n dreeym,
> Breechyn da'n toin, doogh da'n toin,
> Agh my she lhiat Gordon mooar,
> Cha nee lhiat Glion reagh Rushen.

> (Cap for the head, alas ! poor head,
> Coat for the back, alas ! poor back,
> Breeches for the breech, alas ! poor breech,
> But if big Gordon [farm] is thine,
> Thine is not the merry Glen of Rushen.) [1]

And off he went to Glen Rushen for good.'

TESTIMONY FROM THE KEEPER OF PEEL CASTLE

From Mrs. Moore's house I walked on to Peel, where I was fortunate in meeting, in his own home, Mr. William Cashen, the well-known keeper of the famous old Peel Castle, within whose yet solid battlements stands the one true round tower outside of Ireland. I heard first of all about the fairy dog—the *Moddey Doo* (Manx for Black Dog)—which haunts the castle ; and then Mr. Cashen related to me the following anecdotes and tales about Manx fairies :—

Prayer against the Fairies.—' My father's and grandfather's idea was that the fairies tumbled out of the battlements of Heaven, falling earthward for three days and three nights as thick as hail ; and that one third of them fell into

---

[1] I am wholly indebted to Miss Morrison for these Manx verses and their translation, which I have substituted for Mrs. Moore's English rendering. Miss Morrison, after my return to Oxford, saw Mrs. Moore and took them down from her, a task I was not well fitted to do when the tale was told.

the sea, one third on the land, and one third remained in
the air, in which places they will remain till the Day of
Judgement. The old Manx people always believed that this
fall of the fairies was due to the first sin, pride ; and here is
their prayer against the fairies :—" *Jee saue mee voish cloan
ny moyrn*" (God preserve me from the children of pride [or
ambition]).'

A Man's Two Wives.—' A Ballaleece woman was captured
by the fairies ; and, soon afterwards, her husband took a new
wife, thinking the first one gone for ever. But not long after
the marriage, one night the first wife appeared to her former
husband and said to him, and the second wife overheard
her : " You'll sweep the barn clean, and mind there is not
one straw left on the floor. Then stand by the door, and at
a certain hour a company of people on horseback will ride
in, and you lay hold of that bridle of the horse I am on, and
don't let it go." He followed the directions carefully, but
was unable to hold the horse : the second wife had put some
straw on the barn floor under a bushel.'

Sounds of Infinity.—' On Dalby Mountain, this side of
Cronk-yn-Irree-Laa the old Manx people used to put their
ears to the earth to hear the Sounds of Infinity (*Sheean-ny-
Feaynid*), which were sounds like murmurs. They thought
these sounds came from beings in space ; for in their belief
all space is filled with invisible beings.' [1]

To the Memory of a Manx Scholar

Since the following testimony was written down, its
author, the late Mr. John Nelson, of Ramsey, has passed
out of our realm of life into the realm invisible. He was
one of the few Manxmen who knew the Manx language
really well, and the ancient traditions which it has preserved

---

[1] It has been suggested, and no doubt correctly, that these murmuring
sounds heard on Dalby Mountain are due to the action of sea-waves, close
at hand, washing over shifting masses of pebbles on the rock-bound shore.
Though this be the true explanation of the phenomenon itself, it only
proves the attribution of cause to be wrong, and not the underlying
animistic conception of spiritual beings.

both orally and in books. In his kindly manner and with fervent loyalty toward all things Celtic, he gave me leave, during December 1909, to publish for the first time the interesting matter which follows ; and, with reverence, we here place it on record to his memory :—

A Blinding by Fairies.—' My grandfather, William Nelson, was coming home from the herring fishing late at night, on the road near Jurby, when he saw in a pea-field, across a hedge, a great crowd of *little fellows* in red coats dancing and making music. And as he looked, an old woman from among them came up to him and spat in his eyes, saying : " You'll never see us again " ; and I am told that he was blind afterwards till the day of his death. He was certainly blind for fourteen years before his death, for I often had to lead him around ; but, of course, I am unable to say of my own knowledge that he became blind immediately after his strange experience, or if not until later in life ; but as a young man he certainly had good sight, and it was believed that the fairies destroyed it.'

The Fairy Tune.—' William Cain, of Glen Helen (formerly Rhenass), was going home in the evening across the mountains near Brook's Park, when he heard music down below in a glen, and saw there a great glass house like a palace, all lit up. He stopped to listen, and when he had the new tune he went home to practise it on his fiddle ; and recently he played the same fairy tune at Miss Sophia Morrison's Manx entertainment in Peel.'

Manannan the Magician.—Mr. Nelson told a story about a *Buggane* or *Fenodyree*, such as we already have, and explained the *Glashtin* as a water-bull, supposed to be a goblin half cow and half horse, and then offered this tradition about Manannan :—' It is said that Manannan was a great magician, and that he used to place on the sea pea-shells, held open with sticks and with sticks for masts standing up in them, and then so magnify them that enemies beheld them as a strong fleet, and would not approach the island. Another tradition is that Manannan on his three legs (the Manx coat of arms) could travel from one end to

the other of his isle with wonderful swiftness, moving like
a wheel.' [1]

Testimony of a Farmer and Fisherman

From the north of the island I returned to Peel, where
I had arranged to meet new witnesses, and the first one of
these is James Caugherty, a farmer and fisherman, born in
Kirk Patrick fifty-eight years ago, who testified (in part) as
follows :—

Churn Worked by Fairies.—' Close by Glen Cam (Winding
Glen), when I was a boy, our family often used to hear the
empty churn working in the churn-house, when no person
was near it, and they would say, "Oh, it 's the *little fellows*." '

A Remarkable Changeling Story.—' Forty to fifty years
ago, between St. John's and Foxdale, a boy, with whom
I often played, came to our house at nightfall to borrow
some candles, and while he was on his way home across the
hills he suddenly saw a little boy and a little woman coming
after him. If he ran, they ran, and all the time they gained
on him. Upon reaching home he was speechless, his hands
were altered (turned awry), and his feet also, and his finger-
nails had grown long in a minute. He remained that way
a week. My father went to the boy's mother and told her it
wasn't Robby at all that she saw ; and when my father was
for taking the tongs and burning the boy with a piece of
glowing turf [as a changeling test], the boy screamed awfully.
Then my father persuaded the mother to send a messenger
to a doctor in the north near Ramsey " doing charms ", to see
if she couldn't get Robby back. As the messenger was returning, the mother stepped out of the house to relieve him,
and when she went into the house again her own Robby was
there. As soon as Robby came to himself all right, he said
a little woman and a little boy had followed him, and that

---

[1] In this mythological rôle, Manannan is apparently a sun god or else
the sun itself ; and the Manx coat of arms, which is connected with him,
being a sun symbol, suggests to us now ages long prior to history, when
the Isle of Man was a Sacred Isle dedicated to the cult of the Supreme God
of Light and Life, and when all who dwelt thereon were regarded as the
Children of the Sun.

just as he got home he was conscious of being taken away by them, but he didn't know where they came from nor where they took him. He was unable to tell more than this. Robby is alive yet, so far as I know ; he is Robert Christian, of Douglas.'

EVIDENCE FROM A MEMBER OF THE HOUSE OF KEYS

Mr. T. C. Kermode, of Peel, member of the House of Keys, the Lower House of the Manx Parliament, very kindly dictated for my use the following statement concerning fairies which he himself has seen :—

Reality of Fairies.—' There is much belief here in the island that there actually are fairies ; and I consider such belief based on an actual fact in nature, because of my own strange experience. About forty years ago, one October night, I and another young man were going to a kind of Manx harvest-home at Cronk-a-Voddy. On the Glen Helen road, just at the Beary Farm, as we walked along talking, my friend happened to look across the river (a small brook), and said : " Oh look, there are the fairies. Did you ever see them ? " I looked across the river and saw a circle of supernatural light, which I have now come to regard as the " astral light " or the light of Nature, as it is called by mystics, and in which spirits become visible. The spot where the light appeared was a flat space surrounded on the sides away from the river by banks formed by low hills ; and into this space and the circle of light, from the surrounding sides apparently, I saw come in twos and threes a great crowd of little beings smaller than Tom Thumb and his wife. All of them, who appeared like soldiers, were dressed in red. They moved back and forth amid the circle of light, as they formed into order like troops drilling. I advised getting nearer to them, but my friend said, " No, I'm going to the party." Then after we had looked at them a few minutes my friend struck the roadside wall with a stick and shouted, and we lost the vision and the light vanished.'

The Manx Fairy-Faith.—' I have much evidence from old Manx people, who are entirely reliable and God-fearing, that they have seen the fairies hunting with hounds and horses, and on the sea in ships, and under other conditions, and that they have heard their music. They consider the fairies a complete nation or world in themselves, distinct from our world, but having habits and instincts like ours. Social organization among them is said to be similar to that among men, and they have their soldiers and commanders. Where the fairies actually exist the old people cannot tell, but they certainly believe that they can be seen here on earth.'

Testimony from a Past Provincial Grand Master

Mr. J. H. Kelly, Past Provincial Grand Master of the Isle of Man District of Oddfellows, a resident of Douglas, offers the following account of a curious psychical experience of his own, and attributes it to fairies :—

A Strange Experience with Fairies.—' Twelve to thirteen years ago, on a clear moonlight night, about twelve o'clock, I left Laxey ; and when about five miles from Douglas, at Ballagawne School, I heard talking, and was suddenly conscious of being in the midst of an invisible throng. As this strange feeling came over me, I saw coming up the road four figures as real to look upon as human beings, and of medium size, though I am certain they were not human. When these four, who seemed to be connected with the invisible throng, came out of the Garwick road into the main road, I passed into a by-road leading down to a very peaceful glen called Garwick Glen ; and I still had the same feeling that invisible beings were with me, and this continued for a mile. There was no fear or emotion or excitement, but perfect calm on my part. I followed the by-road ; and when I began to mount a hill there was a sudden and strange quietness, and a sense of isolation came over me, as though the joy and peace of my life had departed with the invisible throng. From different personal experiences like this one, I am firmly of the opinion and belief that the fairies exist. One cannot say that they are wholly physical or wholly spiritual, but the impression left upon my mind is that they are an absolutely real order of beings not human.'

Invoking Little Manannan, son of Leirr, to give us safe passage across his watery domain, we now go southward to the nearest Brythonic country, the Land of Arthur, WALES.

V IN WALES

Introduction by The Right Hon. SIR JOHN RHŶS, M.A., D.Litt., F.B.A., Hon. LL.D. of the University of Edinburgh ; Professor of Celtic in the University of Oxford ; Principal of Jesus College ; author of *Celtic Folklore, Welsh and Manx*, &c.

The folk-lore of Wales in as far as it concerns the Fairies consists of a very few typical tales, such as :—

(1) The Fairy Dance and the usual entrapping of a youth, who dances with the Little People for a long time, while he supposes it only a few minutes, and who if not rescued is taken by them.

(2) There are other ways in which recruits may be led into Fairyland and induced to marry fairy maidens, and any one so led away is practically lost to his kith and kin, for even if he be allowed to visit them, the visit is mostly cut short in one way or another.

(3) A man catches a fairy woman and marries her. She proves to be an excellent housewife, but usually she has had put into the marriage-contract certain conditions which, if broken, inevitably release her from the union, and when so released she hurries away instantly, never to return, unless it be now and then to visit her children. One of the conditions, especially in North Wales, is that the husband should never touch her with iron. But in the story of the Lady of Llyn y Fan Fach, in Carmarthenshire, the condition is that he must not strike the wife without a cause three times, the striking being interpreted to include any slight tapping, say, on the shoulder. This story is one of the most remarkable on record in Wales, and it recalls the famous tale of Undine, published in German many years ago by

De La Motte Fouqué. It is not known where he found it, or whether the people among whom it was current were pure Germans or of Celtic extraction.

(4) The Fairies were fond of stealing nice healthy babies and of leaving in their place their own sallow offspring. The stories of how the right child might be recovered take numerous forms ; and some of these stories suggest how weak and sickly children became the objects of systematic cruelty at the hands of even their own parents. The changeling was usually an old man, and many were the efforts made to get him to betray his identity.

(5) There is a widespread story of the fairy husband procuring for his wife the attendance of a human midwife. The latter was given a certain ointment to apply to the baby's eyes when she dressed it. She was not to touch either of her own eyes with it, but owing to an unfailing accident she does, and with the eye so touched she is enabled to see the fairies in their proper shape and form. This has consequences: The fairy husband pays the midwife well, and discharges her. She goes to a fair or market one day and observes her old master stealing goods from a stall, and makes herself known to him. He asks her with which eye she sees him. She tells him, and the eye to which he objects he instantly blinds.

(6) Many are the stories about the fairies coming into houses at night to wash and dress their children after everybody is gone to bed. A servant-maid who knows her business leaves a vessel full of water for them, and takes care that the house is neat and tidy, and she then probably finds in the morning some fairy gift left her, whereas if the house be untidy and the water dirty, they will pinch her in her sleep, and leave her black and blue.

(7) The fairies were not strong in their household arrangements, so it was not at all unusual for them to come to the farm-houses to borrow what was wanting to them.

In the neighbourhood of Snowdon the fairies were believed to live beneath the lakes, from which they sometimes came forth, especially on misty days, and children used to be warned not to stray away from their homes in that sort of weather, lest they should be kidnapped by them. These fairies were not Christians, and they were great thieves. They were fond of bright colours. They were sharp of hearing, and no word that reached the wind would escape them. If a fairy's proper name was discovered, the fairy to whom it belonged felt baffled.[1]

Some characteristics of the fairies seem to argue an ancient race, while other characteristics betray their origin in the workshop of the imagination ; but generally speaking, the fairies are heterogeneous, consisting partly of the divinities of glens and forests and mountains, and partly of an early race of men more or less caricatured and equipped by fable with impossible attributes.[2]

JESUS COLLEGE, OXFORD,
    October 1910.

Our field of research in the Land of Arthur includes all the coast counties save Cardiganshire, from Anglesey on the north to Glamorganshire on the south. At the very beginning of our investigation of the belief in the *Tylwyth Teg*,

[1] Sir John Rhŷs tells me that this Snowdon fairy-lore was contributed by the late Lady Rhŷs, who as a girl lived in the neighbourhood of Snowdon and heard very much from the old people there, most of whom believed in the fairies ; and she herself then used to be warned, in the manner mentioned, against being carried away into the under-lake Fairyland.

[2] Cf. *Celtic Folklore, Welsh and Manx*, pp. 683-4 n., where Sir John Rhŷs says of his friend, Professor A. C. Haddon :—' I find also that he, among others, has anticipated me in my theory as to the origins of the fairies : witness the following extract from the syllabus of a lecture delivered by him at Cardiff in 1894 on *Fairy Tales*:—" What are the fairies ?—Legendary origin of the fairies. It is evident from fairy literature that there is a mixture of the possible and the impossible, of fact and fancy. Part of fairy-dom refers to (1) spirits that never were embodied : other fairies are (2) spirits of environment, nature or local spirits, and household or domestic spirits ; (3) spirits of the organic world, spirits of plants, and spirits of animals ; (4) spirits of men, or ghosts ; and (5) witches and wizards, or men possessed with other spirits. All these, and possibly other elements, enter into the fanciful aspects of Fairyland, but there is a large residuum of real occurrences ; these point to a clash of races, and we may regard many of these fairy sagas as stories told by men of the Iron Age of events which happened to men of the Bronze Age in their conflicts with men of the Neolithic Age, and possibly these, too, handed on traditions of the Paleolithic Age." '

or ' Fair Folk ' in the Isle of Anglesey or Mona, the ancient stronghold of the Druids, we shall see clearly that the testimony offered by thoroughly reliable and prominent native witnesses is surprisingly uniform, and essentially animistic in its nature ; and in passing southward to the end of Wales we shall find the Welsh Fairy-Faith with this same uniformity and exhibiting the same animistic background everywhere we go.

TESTIMONY OF AN ANGLESEY BARD

Mr. John Louis Jones, of Gaerwen, Anglesey, a native bard who has taken prizes in various Eisteddfods, testifies as follows :—

Tylwyth Teg's Visits.—' When I was a boy here on the island, the *Tylwyth Teg* were described as a race of little beings no larger than children six or seven years old, who visited farm-houses at night after all the family were abed. No matter how securely closed a house might be, the *Tylwyth Teg* had no trouble to get in. I remember how the old folk used to make the house comfortable and put fresh coals on the fire, saying, " Perhaps the *Tylwyth Teg* will come to-night." Then the *Tylwyth Teg*, when they did come, would look round the room and say, " What a clean beautiful place this is ! " And all the while the old folk in bed were listening. Before departing from such a clean house the *Tylwyth Teg* always left a valuable present for the family.'

Fairy Wife and Iron Taboo.—' A young man once caught one of the *Tylwyth Teg* women, and she agreed to live with him on condition that he should never touch her with iron. One day she went to a field with him to catch a horse, but in catching the horse he threw the bridle in such a way that the bit touched the *Tylwyth Teg* woman, and all at once she was gone. As this story indicates, the *Tylwyth Teg* could make themselves invisible. I think they could be seen by some people and not by other people. The old folk thought them a kind of spirit race from a spirit world.'

EVIDENCE FROM CENTRAL ANGLESEY

Owing to the very kindly assistance of Mr. E. H. Thomas, of Llangefni, who introduced me to the oldest inhabitants of his town, in their own homes and elsewhere, and then acted as interpreter whenever Welsh alone was spoken, I gleaned very clear evidence from that part of Central Anglesey. Seven witnesses, two of whom were women, ranging in age from seventy-two to eighty-nine years, were thus interviewed, and each of them stated that in their childhood the belief in the *Tylwyth Teg* as a non-human race of good little people—by one witness compared to singing angels—was general. Mr. John Jones, the oldest of the seven, among much else, said in Welsh :—' I believe personally that the *Tylwyth Teg* are still existing ; but people can't see them. I have heard of two or three persons being together and one only having been able to see the *Tylwyth Teg*.'

TESTIMONY FROM TWO ANGLESEY CENTENARIANS

Perhaps nowhere else in Celtic lands could there be found as witnesses two sisters equal in age to Miss Mary Owen and Mrs. Betsy Thomas, in their hundred and third and hundredth year respectively (in 1909). They live a quiet life on their mountain-side farm overlooking the sea, in the beautiful country near Pentraeth, quite away from the rush and noise of the great world of commercial activity ; and they speak only the tongue which their prehistoric Kimric ancestors spoke before Roman, or Saxon, or Norman came to Britain. Mr. W. Jones, of Plas Tinon, their neighbour, who knows English and Welsh well, acted as interpreter. The elder sister testified first :—

' *Tylwyth Teg's* ' *Nature.*—' There were many of the *Tylwyth Teg* on the Llwydiarth Mountain above here, and round the Llwydiarth Lake where they used to dance ; and whenever the prices at the Llangefni market were to be high they would chatter very much at night. They appeared only after dark ; and all the good they ever did was singing and dancing. Ann Jones, whom I knew very well, used often to see the *Tylwyth Teg* dancing and singing, but if she then went up to them they would disappear. She told me they are an invisible people, and very small. Many others besides Ann Jones have seen the *Tylwyth Teg* in these mountains, and have heard their music and song. The ordinary opinion was that the *Tylwyth Teg* are a race of spirits. I believe in them as an invisible race of good little people.'

Fairy Midwife and Magic Oil.—' The *Tylwyth Teg* had a kind of magic oil, and I remember this story about it :— A farmer went to Llangefni to fetch a woman to nurse his wife about to become a mother, and he found one of the *Tylwyth Teg*, who came with him on the back of his horse. Arrived at the farm-house, the fairy woman looked at the wife, and giving the farmer some oil told him to wash the baby in it as soon as it was born. Then the fairy woman disappeared. The farmer followed the advice, and what did he do in washing the baby but get some oil on one of his own eyes. Suddenly he could see the *Tylwyth Teg*, for the oil had given him the second-sight. Some time later the farmer was in Llangefni again, and saw the same fairy woman who had given him the oil. " How is your wife getting on ? " she asked him. " She is getting on very well," he replied. Then the fairy woman added, " Tell me with which eye you see me best." " With this one," he said, pointing to the eye he had rubbed with the oil. And the fairy woman put her stick in that eye, and the farmer never saw with it again.' [1]

[1] This is the one tale I have found in North Wales about a midwife and fairies—a type of tale common to West Ireland, Isle of Man, Cornwall, and Brittany, but in a reverse version, the midwife there being (as she is sometimes in Welsh versions) one of the human race called in by fairies. If evidence of the oneness of the Celtic mind were needed we should find it here (cf. pp. 50, 54, 127, 175, 182, 205). There are in this type of fairy-tale, as the advocates of the Pygmy Theory may well hold, certain elements most likely traceable to a folk-memory of some early race, or special class of some early race, who knew the secrets of midwifery and the use of medicines when such knowledge was considered magical. But in each example of this midwife story there is the germ idea—no matter what other ideas cluster round it—that fairies, like spirits, are only to be seen by an extra-human vision, or, as psychical researchers might say, by clairvoyance.

Seeing '*Tylwyth Teg*'.—The younger sister's testimony
is as follows:—'I saw one of the *Tylwyth Teg* about sixty
years ago, near the Tynymyndd Farm, as I was passing by
at night. He was like a little man. When I approached
him he disappeared suddenly. I have heard about the
dancing and singing of the *Tylwyth Teg*, but never have
heard the music myself. The old people said the *Tylwyth
Teg* could appear and disappear when they liked; and
I think as the old people did, that they are some sort of
spirits.'

TESTIMONY FROM AN ANGLESEY SEERESS

At Pentraeth, Mr. Gwilyn Jones said to me:—'It always
was and still is the opinion that the *Tylwyth Teg* are a race
of spirits. Some people think them small in size, but the
one my mother saw was ordinary human size.' At this,
I immediately asked Mr. Jones if his mother was still living,
and he replying that she was, gave me her address in Llanfair. So I went directly to interview Mr. Jones's mother,
Mrs. Catherine Jones, and this is the story about the one of
the *Tylwyth Teg* she saw:—

'*Tylwyth Teg*' *Apparition*.—'I was coming home at
about half-past ten at night from Cemaes, on the path to
Simdda Wen, where I was in service, when there appeared
just before me a very pretty young lady of ordinary size.
I had no fear, and when I came up to her put out my
hand to touch her, but my hand and arm went right through
her form. I could not understand this, and so tried to
touch her repeatedly with the same result; there was no
solid substance in the body, yet it remained beside me,
and was as beautiful a young lady as I ever saw. When
I reached the door of the house where I was to stop, she
was still with me. Then I said "Good night" to her. No
response being made, I asked, "Why do you not speak?"
And at this she disappeared. Nothing happened afterwards,
and I always put this beautiful young lady down as one
of the *Tylwyth Teg*. There was much talk about my experience when I reported it, and the neighbours, like myself,

thought I had seen one of the *Tylwyth Teg.* I was about twenty-four years old at the time of this incident.' [1]

TESTIMONY FROM A PROFESSOR OF WELSH

Just before crossing the Menai Straits I had the good fortune to meet, at his home in Llanfair, Mr. J. Morris Jones, M.A. (Oxon.), Professor of Welsh in the University College at Bangor, and he, speaking of the fairy-belief in Anglesey as he remembers it from boyhood days, said :—

' *Tylwyth Teg.'*—' In most of the tales I heard repeated when I was a boy, I am quite certain the implication was that the *Tylwyth Teg* were a kind of spirit race having human characteristics, who could at will suddenly appear and suddenly disappear. They were generally supposed to live underground, and to come forth on moonlight nights, dressed in gaudy colours (chiefly in red), to dance in circles in grassy fields. I cannot remember having heard changeling stories here in the Island : I think the *Tylwyth Teg* were generally looked upon as kind and good-natured, though revengeful if not well treated. And they were believed to have plenty of money at their command, which they could bestow on people whom they liked.'

EVIDENCE FROM NORTH CARNARVONSHIRE

Upon leaving Anglesey I undertook some investigation of the Welsh fairy-belief in the country between Bangor and Carnarvon. From the oldest Welsh people of Treborth

---

[1] After this remarkable story, Mrs. Jones told me about another very rare psychical experience of her own, which is here recorded because it illustrates the working of the psychological law of the association of ideas : —' My husband, Price Jones, was drowned some forty years ago, within four miles of Arms Head, near Bangor, on Friday at midday ; and that night at about one o'clock he appeared to me in our bedroom and laid his head on my breast. I tried to ask him where he came from, but before I could get my breath he was gone. I believed at the time that he was out at sea perfectly safe and well. But next day, Saturday, at about noon, a message came announcing his death. I was as fully awake as one can be when I thus saw the spirit of my husband. He returned to me a second time about six months later.' Had this happened in West Ireland, it is almost certain that public opinion would have declared that Price Jones had been *taken* by the ' gentry ' or ' good people '.

I heard the same sort of folk-lore as we have recorded from Anglesey, except that prominence was given to a flourishing belief in *Bwganod*, goblins or bogies. But from Mr. T. T. Davis Evans, of Port Dinorwic, I heard the following very unusual story based on facts, as he recalled it first hand :—

Jones's Vision.—William Jones, who some sixty years ago declared he had seen the *Tylwyth Teg* in the Aberglaslyn Pass near Beddgelert, was publicly questioned about them in Bethel Chapel by Mr. Griffiths, the minister ; and he explained before the congregation that the Lord had given him a special vision which enabled him to see the *Tylwyth Teg*, and that, therefore, he had seen them time after time as little men playing along the river in the Pass. The minister induced Jones to repeat the story many times, because it seemed to please the congregation very much ; and the folks present looked upon Jones's vision as a most wonderful thing.'

EVIDENCE FROM SOUTH CARNARVONSHIRE

To Mr. E. D. Rowlands, head master of the schools at Afonwen, I am indebted for a summary of the fairy-belief in South Carnarvonshire :—

' *Tylwyth Teg.*'—' According to the belief in South Carnarvonshire, the *Tylwyth Teg* were a small, very pretty people always dressed in white, and much given to dancing and singing in rings where grass grew. As a rule, they were visible only at night ; though in the day-time, if a mother while hay-making was so unwise as to leave her babe alone in the field, the *Tylwyth Teg* might take it and leave in its place a hunchback, or some deformed object like a child. At night, the *Tylwyth Teg* would entice travellers to join their dance and then play all sorts of tricks on them.' [1]

Fairy Cows and Fairy Lake-Women.—' Some of the

---

[1] Here we find the *Tylwyth Teg* showing quite the same characteristics as Welsh elves in general, as Cornish pixies, and as Breton *corrigans*, or *lutins* ; that is, given to dancing at night, to stealing children, and to deceiving travellers.

Tylwyth Teg lived in caves ; others of them lived in lake-bottoms. There is a lake called Llyn y Morwynion, or " Lake of the Maidens ", near Festiniog, where, as the story goes, a farmer one morning found in his field a number of very fine cows such as he had never seen before. Not knowing where they came from, he kept them a long time, when, as it happened, he committed some dishonest act and, as a result, women of the *Tylwyth Teg* made their appearance in the pasture and, calling the cows by name, led the whole herd into the lake, and with them disappeared beneath its waters. The old people never could explain the nature of the *Tylwyth Teg*, but they always regarded them as a very mysterious race, and, according to this story of the cattle, as a supernatural race.'

EVIDENCE FROM MERIONETHSHIRE

Mr. Louis Foster Edwards, of Harlech, recalling the memories of many years ago, offers the following evidence :—

Scythe-Blades and Fairies.—' In an old inn on the other side of Harlech there was to be an entertainment, and, as usual on such occasions, the dancing would not cease until morning. I noticed, before the guests had all arrived, that the landlady was putting scythe-blades edge upwards up into the large chimney, and, wondering why it was, asked her. She told me that the fairies might come before the entertainment was over, and that if the blades were turned edge upwards it would prevent the fairies from troubling the party, for they would be unable to pass the blades without being cut.'

' *Tylwyth Teg* ' *and their World.*—' There was an idea that the *Tylwyth Teg* lived by plundering at night. It was thought, too, that if anything went wrong with cows or horses the *Tylwyth Teg* were to blame. As a race, the *Tylwyth Teg* were described as having the power of invisibility ; and it was believed they could disappear like a spirit while one happened to be observing them. The world in which they lived was a world quite unlike ours, and mortals taken to it by them were changed in nature.

The way a mortal might be taken by the *Tylwyth Teg* was by being attracted into their dance. If they thus took you away, it would be according to our time for twelve months, though to you the time would seem no more than a night.'

FAIRY TRIBES IN MONTGOMERYSHIRE

From Mr. D. Davies-Williams, who outlined for me the Montgomeryshire belief in the *Tylwyth Teg* as he has known it intimately, I learned that this is essentially the same as elsewhere in North and Central Wales. He summed up the matter by saying :—

Belief in Tylwyth Teg.—' It was the opinion that the *Tylwyth Teg* were a real race of invisible or spiritual beings living in an invisible world of their own. The belief in the *Tylwyth Teg* was quite general fifty or sixty years ago, and as sincere as any religious belief is now.'

Our next witness is the Rev. Josiah Jones, minister of the Congregational Church of Machynlleth ; and, after a lifetime's experience in Montgomeryshire, he gives this testimony :—

A Deacon's Vision.—' A deacon in my church, John Evans, declared that he had seen the *Tylwyth Teg* dancing in the day-time, within two miles from here, and he pointed out the very spot where they appeared. This was some twenty years ago. I think, however, that he saw only certain reflections and shadows, because it was a hot and brilliant day.'

Folk-Beliefs in General.—' As I recall the belief, the old people considered the *Tylwyth Teg* as living beings half-way between something material and spiritual, who were rarely seen. When I was a boy there was very much said, too, about corpse-candles and phantom funerals, and especially about the *Bwganod*, plural of *Bwgan*, meaning a sprite, ghost, hobgoblin, or spectre. The *Bwganod* were supposed to appear at dusk, in various forms, animal and human ; and grown-up people as well as children had great fear of them.'

A Minister's Opinion.—' Ultimately there is a substance of truth in the fairy-belief, but it is wrongly accounted for in the folk-lore : I once asked Samuel Roberts, of Llan-brynmair, who was quite a noted Welsh scholar, what he thought of the *Tylwyth Teg*, of hobgoblins, spirits, and so forth ; and he said that he believed such things existed, and that God allowed them to appear in times of great ignorance to convince people of the existence of an invisible world.'

IN CARDIGANSHIRE ; AND A FOLK-LORIST'S TESTIMONY

No one of our witnesses from Central Wales is more intimately acquainted with the living folk-beliefs than Mr. J. Ceredig Davies, of Llanilar, a village about six miles from Aberystwyth ; for Mr. Davies has spent many years in collecting folk-lore in Central and South Wales. He has interviewed the oldest and most intelligent of the old people, and while I write this he has in the press a work entitled *The Folk-Lore of Mid and West Wales*. Mr. Davies very kindly gave me the following outline of the most prominent traits in the Welsh fairy-belief according to his own investigations :—

' *Tylwyth Teg* '.—' The *Tylwyth Teg* were considered a very small people, fond of dancing, especially on moonlight nights. They often came to houses after the family were abed ; and if milk was left for them, they would leave money in return ; but if not treated kindly they were revengeful. The changeling idea was common : the mother coming home would find an ugly changeling in the cradle. Sometimes the mother would consult the *Dynion Hysbys*, or " Wise Men " as to how to get her babe back. As a rule, treating the fairy babe roughly and then throwing it into a river would cause the fairy who made the change to appear and restore the real child in return for the changeling.'

' *Tylwyth Teg* ' *Marriage Contracts.*—' Occasionally a young man would see the *Tylwyth Teg* dancing, and, being drawn into the dance, would be taken by them and married to one of their women. There is usually some condition in the marriage contract which becomes broken, and, as a result, the fairy wife disappears—usually into a lake. The marriage contract specifies either that the husband must never touch his fairy wife with iron, or else never beat or strike her three times. Sometimes when fairy wives thus disappear, they take with them into the lake their fairy cattle and all their household property.'

'*Tylwyth Teg*' *Habitations.*—' The *Tylwyth Teg* were generally looked upon as an immortal race. In Cardiganshire they lived underground ; in Carmarthenshire in lakes ; and in Pembrokeshire along the sea-coast on enchanted islands amid the Irish Sea. I have heard of sailors upon seeing such islands trying to reach them ; but when approached, the islands always disappeared. From a certain spot in Pembrokeshire, it is said that by standing on a turf taken from the yard of St. David's Cathedral, one may see the enchanted islands.' [1]

'*Tylwyth Teg*' *as Spirits of Druids.*—' By many of the old people the *Tylwyth Teg* were classed with spirits. They were not looked upon as mortal at all. Many of the Welsh looked upon the *Tylwyth Teg* or fairies as the spirits of Druids dead before the time of Christ, who being too good to be cast into Hell were allowed to wander freely about on earth.'

TESTIMONY FROM A WELSHMAN NINETY-FOUR YEARS OLD

At Pontrhydfendigaid, a village about two miles from the railway-station called Strata Florida, I had the good fortune to meet Mr. John Jones, ninety-four years old, yet of strong physique, and able to write his name without eye-glasses. Both Mr. J. H. Davies, Registrar of the University College of Aberystwyth, and Mr. J. Ceredig Davies, the eminent folk-lorist of Llanilar, referred me to Mr. John Jones as one of the most remarkable of living Welshmen who could tell about the olden times from first-hand knowledge.

---

[1] This folk-belief partially sustains the view put forth in our chapter on Environment, that St. David's during pagan times was already a sacred spot and perhaps then the seat of a druidic oracle.

Mr. John Jones speaks very little English, and Mr. John Rees, of the Council School, acted as our interpreter. This is the testimony :—

Pygmy-sized ' Tylwyth Teg '.—' I was born and bred where there was tradition that the *Tylwyth Teg* lived in holes in the hills, and that none of these *Tylwyth Teg* was taller than three to four feet. It was a common idea that many of the *Tylwyth Teg*, forming in a ring, would dance and sing out on the mountain-sides, or on the plain, and that if children should meet with them at such a time they would lose their way and never get out of the ring. If the *Tylwyth Teg* fancied any particular child they would always keep that child, taking off its clothes and putting them on one of their own children, which was then left in its place. They took only boys, never girls.'

Human-sized ' Tylwyth Teg '.—' A special sort of *Tylwyth Teg* used to come out of lakes and dance, and their fine looks enticed young men to follow them back into the lakes, and there marry one of them. If the husband wished to leave the lake he had to go without his fairy wife. This sort of *Tylwyth Teg* were as big as ordinary people ; and they were often seen riding out of the lakes and back again on horses.'

' Tylwyth Teg' as Spirits of Prehistoric Race.—' My grandfather told me that he was once in a certain field and heard singing in the air, and thought it spirits singing. Soon afterwards he and his brother in digging dikes in that field dug into a big hole, which they entered and followed to the end. There they found a place full of human bones and urns, and naturally decided on account of the singing that the bones and urns were of the *Tylwyth Teg*.' [1]

A Boy's Visit to the ' Tylwyth Teg's ' King.—' About

---

[1] Here we have an example of the *Tylwyth Teg* being identified with a prehistoric race, quite in accordance with the argument of the Pygmy Theory. We have, however, as the essential idea, that the *Tylwyth Teg* heard singing were the spirits of this prehistoric race. Thus our contention that ancestral spirits play a leading part in the fairy-belief is sustained, and the Pygmy Theory appears quite at its true relative value—as able to explain one subordinate ethnological strand in the complex fabric of the belief.

eighty years ago, at Tynylone, my grandfather told me this story : " A boy ten years old was often whipped and cruelly treated by his schoolmaster because he could not say his lessons very well. So one day he ran away from school and went to a river-side, where some little folk came to him and asked why he was crying. He told them the master had punished him ; and on hearing this they said, ' Oh ! if you will stay with us it will not be necessary for you to go to school. We will keep you as long as you like.' Then they took him under the water and over the water into a cave underground, which opened into a great palace where the *Tylwyth Teg* were playing games with golden balls, in rings like those in which they dance and sing. The boy had been taken to the king's family, and he began to play with the king's sons. After he had been there in the palace in the full enjoyment of all its pleasures he wished very much to return to his mother and show her the golden ball which the *Tylwyth Teg* gave him. And so he took the ball in his pocket and hurried through the cave the way he had come ; but at the end of it and by the river two of the *Tylwyth Teg* met him, and taking the ball away from him they pushed him into the water, and through the water he found his way home. He told his mother how he had been away for a fortnight, as he thought, but she told him it had been for two years. Though the boy often tried to find the way back to the *Tylwyth Teg* he never could. Finally, he went back to school, and became a most wonderful scholar and parson." [1]

In Merlin's Country ; and a Vicar's Testimony

The Rev. T. M. Morgan, vicar of Newchurch parish, two miles from Carmarthen, has made a very careful study of the folk-traditions in his own parish and in other regions

[1] This story is much like the one recorded by Giraldus Cambrensis about a boy going to Fairyland and returning to his mother (see this study, p. 324). The possibility that it may be an independent version of the folk-tale told to Cambrensis which has continued to live on among the people makes it highly interesting.

Mr. Jones gives further evidence on the re-birth doctrine in Wales (pp. 388-9), and concerning Merlin and sacrifice to appease place-spirits (pp. 436-7).

of Carmarthenshire, and is able to offer us evidence of the
highest value, as follows :—[1]

'*Tylwyth Teg*' *Power over Children.*—' The *Tylwyth Teg*
were thought to be able to take children. " You mind, or
the *Tylwyth Teg* will take you away," parents would say to
keep their children in the house after dark. It was an
opinion, too, that the *Tylwyth Teg* could transform good
children into kings and queens, and bad children into
wicked spirits, after such children had been *taken*—perhaps
in death. The *Tylwyth Teg* were believed to live in some
invisible world to which children on dying might go to be
rewarded or punished, according to their behaviour on this
earth. Even in this life the *Tylwyth Teg* had power over
children for good or evil. The belief, as these ideas show,
was that the *Tylwyth Teg* were spirits.'

'*Tylwyth Teg*' *as Evil Spirits.*—A few days after my
return to Oxford, the Rev. T. M. Morgan, through his son,
Mr. Basil I. Morgan, of Jesus College, placed in my hands
additional folk-lore evidence from his own parish, as follows :
—' After Mr. Wentz visited me on Thursday, September 30,
1909, I went to see Mr. Shem Morgan, the occupier of
Cwmcastellfach farm, an old man about seventy years old.
He told me that in his childhood days a great dread of the
fairies occupied the heart of every child. They were considered to be evil spirits who visited our world at night,
and dangerous to come in contact with ; there were no good
spirits among them. He related to me three narratives
touching the fairies' :—

'*Tylwyth Teg's*' *Path.*—The first narrative illustrates that
the *Tylwyth Teg* have paths (precisely like those reserved
for the Irish *good people* or for the Breton dead), and that
it is death to a mortal while walking in one of these paths
to meet the *Tylwyth Teg*.

'*Tylwyth Teg*' *Divination.*—The second narrative I quote :
—' A farmer of this neighbourhood having lost his cattle,

---

[1] As a result of his researches, the Rev. T. M. Morgan has just published
a new work, entitled *The History and Antiquities of the Parish of Newchurch*
(Carmarthen, 1910).

went to consult *y dyn hysbys* (a diviner), in Cardiganshire, who was friendly with the fairies. Whenever the fairies visited the diviner they foretold future events, secrets, and the whereabouts of lost property. After the farmer reached the diviner's house the diviner showed him the fairies, and then when the diviner had consulted them he told the farmer to go home as soon as he could and that he would find the cattle in such and such a place. The farmer did as he was directed, and found the cattle in the very place where the *dyn hysbys* told him they would be.' And the third narrative asserts that a man in the parish of Trelech who was fraudulently excluded by means of a false will from inheriting the estate of his deceased father, discovered the defrauder and recovered the estate, solely through having followed the advice given by the *Tylwyth Teg*, when (again as in the above account) they were called up as spirits by a *dyn hysbys*, a Mr. Harries, of Cwrt y Cadno, a place near Aberystwyth.[1]

TESTIMONY FROM A JUSTICE OF THE PEACE

Mr. David Williams, J.P., who is a member of the Cymmrodorion Society of Carmarthen, and who has sat on the judicial bench for ten years, offers us the very valuable evidence which follows :—

'*Tylwyth Teg*' *and their King and Queen.*—' The general idea, as I remember it, was that the *Tylwyth Teg* were only visitors to this world, and had no terrestrial habitations. They were as small in stature as dwarfs, and always appeared in white. Often at night they danced in rings amid green fields. Most of them were females, though they had a king; and, as their name suggests, they were very beautiful in appearance. The king of the *Tylwyth Teg* was called *Gwydion*

---

[1] In these last two anecdotes, as in modern ' Spiritualism ', we observe a popular practice of necromancy or the calling up of spirits, so-called ' materialization ' of spirits, and spirit communication through a human ' medium ', who is the *dyn hysbys*, as well as divination, the revealing of things hidden and the foretelling of future events. This is direct evidence that Welsh fairies or the *Tylwyth Teg* were formerly the same to Welshmen as spirits are to Spiritualists now. We seem, therefore, to have proof of our Psychological Theory (see chap. xi).

ab Don, Gwyd referring to a temperament in man's nature. His residence was among the stars, and called *Caer Gwydion.* His queen was *Gwenhidw.* I have heard my mother call the small fleece-like clouds which appear in fine weather the *Sheep of Gwenhidw.'* [1]

'Tylwyth Teg' as Aerial Beings.—Mr. Williams's testimony continues, and leads us directly to the Psychological or Psychical Theory :—' As aerial beings the *Tylwyth Teg* could fly and move about in the air at will. They were a special order of creation. I never heard that they grew old ; and whether they multiplied or not I cannot tell. In character they were almost always good.'

Ghosts and Apparitions.—Our conversation finally drifted towards ghosts and apparitions, as usual, and to Druids. In the chapter dealing with Re-birth (pp. 390–1) we shall record what Mr. Williams said about Druids, and here what he said about ghosts and apparitions :—' Sixty years ago there was hardly an individual who did not believe in apparitions ; and in olden times Welsh families would collect round the fire at night and each in turn give a story about the *Tylwyth Teg* and ghosts.'

Conferring Vision of a Phantom Funeral.—' There used to be an old man at Newchurch named David Davis (who lived about 1780–1840), of Abernant, noted for seeing

---

[1] Here we have a combination of many distinct elements and influences. As among mortals, so among the *Tylwyth Teg* there is a king ; and this conception may have arisen directly from anthropomorphic influences on the ancient Brythonic religion, or it may have come directly from druidic teachings. The locating of *Gwydion ab Don,* like a god, in a heaven-world, rather than like his counterpart, *Gwynn ab Nudd,* in a hades-world, is probably due to a peculiar admixture of Druidism and Christianity : at first, both gods were probably druidic or pagan, and the same, but *Gwynn ab Nudd* became a demon or evil god under Christian influences, while *Gwydion ab Don* seems to have curiously retained his original good reputation in spite of Christianity (cf. p. 320). The name *Gwenhidw* reminds us at once of Arthur's queen *Gwenhwyvar* or ' White Apparition ' ; and the sheep of *Gwenhidw* can properly be explained by the Naturalistic Theory. It seems, however, that analogy was imaginatively suggested between the Queen *Gwenhidw* as resembling the Welsh White Lady or a ghost-like being, and her sheep, the clouds, also of a necessarily ghost-like character. All this is an admirable illustration of the great complexity of the Fairy-Faith.

phantom funerals. One appeared to him once when he was with a friend. " Do you see it ? Do you see it ? " the old man excitedly asked. " No," said his friend. Then the old man placed his foot on his friend's foot, and said, " Do you see it now ? " And the friend replied that he did.' [1]

Magic and Witchcraft.—Finally, we shall hear from Mr. Williams about Welsh magic and witchcraft, which cannot scientifically be divorced from the belief in fairies and apparitions :—' There used to be much witchcraft in this country ; and it was fully believed that some men, if advanced scholars, had the power to injure or to bewitch their neighbours by magic. The more advanced the scholar the better he could carry on his craft.'

ADDITIONAL EVIDENCE FROM CARMARTHENSHIRE

My friend, and fellow student at Jesus College, Mr. Percival V. Davies, of Carmarthen, contributes, as supplementary to what has been recorded above, the following evidence, from his great-aunt, Mrs. Spurrell, also of Carmarthen, a native Welshwoman who has seen a *canwyll gorff* (corpse-candle) :—

Bendith y Mamau.—' In the Carmarthenshire country, fairies (*Tylwyth Teg*) are often called *Bendith y Mamau*, the " Mothers' Blessing." '

How Ten Children Became Fairies.—' Our Lord, in the days when He walked the earth, chanced one day to approach a cottage in which lived a woman with twenty children. Feeling ashamed of the size of her family, she hid half of them from the sight of her divine visitor. On His departure she sought for the hidden children in vain ; they had become fairies and had disappeared.'

IN PEMBROKESHIRE ; AT THE PENTRE EVAN CROMLECH

Our Pembrokeshire witness is a maiden Welshwoman, sixty years old, who speaks no English, but a university graduate, her nephew, will act as our interpreter. She was

---

[1] The parallel between this Welsh method of conferring vision and the Breton method is very striking (cf. p. 215).

born and has lived all her life within sight of the famous
Pentre Evan Cromlech, in the home of her ancestors, which
is so ancient that after six centuries of its known existence
further record of it is lost.   In spite of her sixty years, our
witness is as active as many a city woman of forty or forty-
five.   Since her girlhood she has heard curious legends and
stories, and, with a more than ordinary interest in the lore
of her native country, has treasured them all in her clear
and well-trained memory.   The first night, while this well-
stored memory of hers gave forth some of its treasures, we
sat in her own home, I and my friend, her nephew, on one
side in a chimney-seat, and she and her niece on the other
side in another, exposed to the cheerful glow and warmth
of the fire.   When we had finished that first night it was two
o'clock, and there had been no interruption to the even flow
of marvels and pretty legends.   A second night we spent
likewise.   What follows now is the result, so far as we are
concerned with it :—

Fairies and Spirits.—' Spirits and fairies exist all round
us, invisible.   Fairies have no solid bodily substance.   Their
forms are of matter like ghostly bodies, and on this account
they cannot be caught.   In the twilight they are often seen,
and on moonlight nights in summer.   Only certain people
can see fairies, and such people hold communication with
them and have dealings with them, but it is difficult to get
them to talk about fairies.   I think the spirits about us are
the fallen angels, for when old Doctor Harris died his books
on witchcraft had to be burned in order to free the place
where he lived from evil spirits.   The fairies, too, are sometimes called the fallen angels.   They will do good to those
who befriend them, and harm to others.   I think there must
be an intermediate state between life on earth and heavenly
life, and it may be in this that spirits and fairies live.   There
are two distinct types of spirits : one is good and the other
is bad.   I have heard of people going to the fairies and
finding that years passed as days, but I do not believe in
changelings, though there are stories enough about them.
That there are fairies and other spirits like them, both good

and bad, I firmly believe. My mother used to tell about seeing the " fair-folk " dancing in the fields near Cardigan ; and other people have seen them round the cromlech up there on the hill (the Pentre Evan Cromlech). They appeared as little children in clothes like soldiers' clothes, and with red caps, according to some accounts.

Death-Candles Described.—' I have seen more than one death-candle. I saw one death-candle right here in this room where we are sitting and talking.' I was told by the nephew and niece of our present witness that this particular death-candle took an untrodden course from the house across the fields to the grave-yard, and that when the death of one of the family occurred soon afterwards, their aunt insisted that the corpse should be carried by exactly the same route ; so the road was abandoned and the funeral went through the ploughed fields. Here is the description of the death-candle as the aunt gave it in response to our request :—' The death-candle appears like a patch of bright light ; and no matter how dark the room or place is, everything in it is as clear as day. The candle is not a flame, but a luminous mass, lightish blue in colour, which dances as though borne by an invisible agency, and sometimes it rolls over and over. If you go up to the light it is nothing, for it is a spirit. Near here a light as big as a pot was seen, and rays shot out from it in all directions. The man you saw here in the house to-day, one night as he was going along the road near Nevern, saw the death-light of old Dr. Harris, and says it was lightish green.'

Gors Goch Fairies.—Now we began to hear more about fairies :—' One night there came a strange rapping at the door of the ancient manor on the Gors Goch farm over in Cardiganshire, and the father of the family asked what was wanted. Thin, silvery voices said they wanted a warm place in which to dress their children and to tidy them up. The door opened then, and in came a dozen or more little beings, who at once set themselves to hunting for a basin and water, and to cleaning themselves. At daybreak they departed, leaving a pretty gift in return for the kindness.

In this same house at another time, whether by the same
party of little beings or by another could not be told,
a healthy child of the family was *changed* because he was
unbaptized, and a frightful-looking child left in his place.
The mother finally died of grief, and the other children died
because of the loss of their mother, and the father was left
alone. Then some time after this, the same little folks who
came the first time returned to clean up, and when they departed, in place of their former gifts of silver, left a gift of gold.
It was not long before the father became heir to a rich farm
in North Wales, and going to live on it became a magician,
for the little people, still befriending him, revealed themselves
in their true nature and taught him all their secrets.'

Levi Salmon's Control of Spirits.—' Levi Salmon, who
lived about thirty years ago, between here and Newport,
was a magician, and could call up good and bad spirits ; but
was afraid to call up the bad ones unless another person
was with him, for it was a dangerous and terrible ordeal.
After consulting certain books which he had, he would draw
a circle on the floor, and in a little while spirits like bulls
and serpents and other animals would appear in it, and all
sorts of spirits would speak. It was not safe to go near
them ; and to control them Levi held a whip in his hand.
He would never let them cross the circle. And when he
wanted them to go away he always had to throw something
to the chief spirit.'

The Haunted Manor and the Golden Image.—I offer now,
in my own language, the following remarkable story :—
The ancient manor-house on the Trewern Farm (less than
a mile from the Pentre Evan Cromlech) had been haunted
as long as anybody could remember. Strange noises were
often heard in it, dishes would dance about of their own
accord, and sometimes a lady dressed in silk appeared.
Many attempts were made to lay the ghosts, but none
succeeded. Finally things got so bad that nobody wanted
to live there. About eighty years ago the sole occupants of
the haunted house were Mr. —— and his two servants. At
the time, it was well known in the neighbourhood that all

at once Mr. —— became very wealthy, and his servants seemed able to buy whatever they wanted. Everybody wondered, but no one could tell where the money came from; for at first he was a poor man, and he couldn't have made much off the farm. The secret only leaked out through one of the servants after Mr. —— was dead. The servant declared to certain friends that one of the ghosts, or, as he thought, the Devil, appeared to Mr. —— and told him there was an image of great value walled up in the room over the main entrance to the manor. A search was made, and, sure enough, a large image of solid gold was found in the very place indicated, built into a recess in the wall. Mr. —— bound the servants to secrecy, and began to turn the image into money. He would cut off small pieces of the image, one at a time, and take them to London and sell them. In this way he sold the whole image, and nobody was the wiser. After the image was found and disposed of, ghosts were no longer seen in the house, nor were unusual noises heard in it at night. The one thing which beyond all doubt is true is that when Mr. —— died he left his son an estate worth about £50,000 (an amount probably greatly in excess of the true one); and people have always wondered ever since where it came from, if not in part from the golden image.[1]

[1] This is the substance of the story as it was told to me by a gentleman who lives within sight of the farm where the image is said to have been found. And one day he took me to the house and showed me the room and the place in the wall where the find was made. The old manor is one of the solidest and most picturesque of its kind in Wales, and, in spite of its extreme age, well preserved. He, being as a native Welshman of the locality well acquainted with its archaeology, thinks it safe to place an age of six to eight hundred years on the manor. What is interesting about this matter of age arises from the query, Was the image one of the Virgin or of some Christian saint, or was it a Druid idol? Both opinions are current in the neighbourhood, but there is a good deal in favour of the second. The region, the little valley on whose side stands the Pentre Evan Cromlech, the finest in Britain, is believed to have been a favourite place with the ancient Druids; and in the oak groves which still exist there tradition says there was once a flourishing pagan school for neophytes, and that the cromlech instead of being a place for interments or for sacrifices was in those days completely enclosed, forming like other cromlechs a darkened chamber in which novices when initiated were placed for a certain number of days—the interior being called the ' Womb or Court of Ceridwen '.

Hundreds of parallel stories in which, instead of ghosts, fairies and demons are said to have revealed hidden treasure could be cited.

IN THE GOWER PENINSULA, GLAMORGANSHIRE

Our investigations in Glamorganshire cover the most interesting part, the peninsula of Gower, where there are peculiar folk-lore conditions, due to its present population being by ancestry English and Flemish as well as Cornish and Welsh. Despite this race admixture, Brythonic beliefs have generally survived in Gower even among the non-Celts ; and because of the Cornish element there are pixies, as shown by the following story related to me in Swansea by Mr. ——, a well-known mining engineer :—

Pixies.—' At Newton, near the Mumbles (in Gower), an old woman, some twenty years ago, assured me that she had seen the pixies. Her father's grey mare was standing in the trap before the house ready to take some produce to the Swansea market, and when the time for departure arrived the pixies had come, but no one save the old woman could see them. She described them to me as like tiny men dancing on the mare's back and climbing up along the mare's mane. She thought the pixies some kind of spirits who made their appearance in early morning ; and all mishaps to cows she attributed to them.'

TESTIMONY FROM AN ARCHAEOLOGIST

The Rev. John David Davis, rector of Llanmadoc and Cheriton parishes, and a member of the Cambrian Archaeological Society, has passed many years in studying the antiquities and folk-lore of Gower, being the author of various antiquarian works ; and he is without doubt the oldest and best living authority to aid us. The Rector very willingly offers this testimony :—

Pixies and 'Verry Volk'.—'In this part of Gower, the name *Tylwyth Teg* is never used to describe fairies ; *Verry Volk* is used instead. Some sixty years ago, as I can remember, there was belief in such fairies here in Gower, but now there is almost none. Belief in apparitions still exists to some extent. One may also hear of a person being pixy-led ; the pixies may cause a traveller to lose his way at night if he crosses a field where they happen to be. To take your coat off and turn it inside out will break the pixy spell.[1] The *Verry Volk* were always little people dressed in scarlet and green ; and they generally showed themselves dancing on moonlight nights. I never heard of their making changelings, though they had the power of doing good or evil acts, and it was a very risky thing to offend them. By nature they were benevolent.'

A 'Verry Volk' Feast.—' I heard the following story many years ago :—The tenant on the Eynonsford Farm here in Gower had a dream one night, and in it thought he heard soft sweet music and the patter of dancing feet. Waking up, he beheld his cow-shed, which opened off his bedroom, filled with a multitude of little beings, about one foot high, swarming all over his fat ox, and they were preparing to slaughter the ox. He was so surprised that he could not move. In a short time the *Verry Volk* had killed, dressed, and eaten the animal. The feast being over, they collected the hide and bones, except one very small leg-bone which they could not find, placed them in position, then stretched the hide over them ; and, as the farmer looked, the ox appeared as sound and fat as ever, but when he let it out to pasture in the morning he observed that it had a slight lameness in the leg lacking the missing bone.' [2]

---

[1] The same remedy is prescribed in Brittany when mischievous *lutins* or *corrigans* lead a traveller astray, in Ireland when the *good people* lead a traveller astray ; and at Rollright, Oxfordshire, England, an old woman told me that it is efficacious against being led astray through witchcraft. Obviously the fairy and witch spell are alike.

[2] The same sort of a story as this is told in Lower Brittany, where the *corrigans* or *lutins* slaughter a farmer's fat cow or ox and invite the farmer to partake of the feast it provides. If he does so with good grace and humour, he finds his cow or ox perfectly whole in the morning, but if he refuses to join the feast or joins it unwillingly, in the morning he is likely to find his cow or ox actually dead and eaten.

Fairies Among Gower English Folk

The population of the Llanmadoc region of Gower are generally English by ancestry and speech ; and not until reaching Llanmorlais, beyond Llanridian, did I find anything like an original Celtic and Welsh-speaking people, and these may have come into that part within comparatively recent times ; and yet, as the above place-names tend to prove, in early days all these regions must have been Welsh. It may be argued, however, that this English-speaking population may be more Celtic than Saxon, even though emigrants from England. In any case, we can see with interest how this so-called English population now echo Brythonic beliefs which they appear to have adopted in Gower, possibly sympathetically through race kinship ; and the following testimony offered by Miss Sarah Jenkins, postmistress of Llanmadoc, will enable us to do so :—

Dancing with Fairies.—‘ A man, whose Christian name was William, was enticed by the fairy folk to enter their dance, as he was on his way to the Swansea market in the early morning. They kept him dancing some time, and then said to him before they let him go, “ Will dance well ; the last going to market and the first that shall sell.” And though he arrived at the market very late, he was the first to sell anything.’

Fairy Money.—‘ An old woman, whom I knew, used to find money left by the fairies every time they visited her house. For a long time she observed their request, and told no one about the money ; but at last she told, and so never found money afterwards.

Nature of Fairies.—‘ The fairies (*verry volk*) were believed to have plenty of music and dancing. Sometimes they appeared dressed in bright red. They could appear and disappear suddenly, and no one could tell how or where.’

Conclusion

Much more might easily be said about Welsh goblins, about Welsh fairies who live in caves, or about Welsh fairy women who come out of lakes and rivers, or who are the presiding spirits of sacred wells and fountains,[1] but these will have some consideration later, in Section III. For the purposes of the present inquiry enough evidence has been offered to show the fundamental character of Brythonic fairy-folk as we have found them. And we can very appropriately close this inquiry by allowing our Welsh-speaking witness from the Pentre Evan country, Pembrokeshire, to tell us one of the prettiest and most interesting fairy-tales in all Wales. The name of Taliessin appearing in it leads us to suspect that it may be the remnant of an ancient bardic tale which has been handed down orally for centuries. It will serve to illustrate the marked difference between the short conversational stories of the living Fairy-Faith and the longer, more polished ones of the traditional Fairy-Faith; and we shall see in it how a literary effect is gained at the expense of the real character of the fairies themselves, for it transforms them into mortals :—

Einion and Olwen.—' My mother told the story as she used to sit by the fire in the twilight knitting stockings :—" One day when it was cloudy and misty, a shepherd boy going to the mountains lost his way and walked about for hours. At last he came to a hollow place surrounded by rushes where he saw a number of round rings. He recognized the place as one he had often heard of as dangerous for shepherds, because of the rings. He tried to get away from there, but he could not. Then an old, merry, blue-eyed man appeared. The boy, thinking to find his way home, followed the old man, and the old man said to him, ' Do not speak a word till I tell you.' In a little while they came to a *menhir* (long stone). The old man tapped it three times, and then lifted it up. A narrow path with steps descending was revealed, and from it emerged a bluish-white light. ' Follow me,' said the old man, ' no harm will come to you.' The boy did so, and it was not long before he saw a fine, wooded, fertile country with a beautiful palace, and rivers and mountains. He reached the palace and was enchanted by the

---

[1] See Sir John Rhŷs, *Celtic Folk-Lore : Welsh and Manx* (Oxford, 1901), *passim.*

singing of birds. Music of all sorts was in the palace, but
he saw no people. At meals dishes came and disappeared of
their own accord. He could hear voices all about him, but
saw no person except the old man—who said that now he
could speak. When he tried to speak he found that he could
not move his tongue. Soon an old lady with smiles came to
him leading three beautiful maidens, and when the maidens
saw the shepherd boy they smiled and spoke, but he could
not reply. Then one of the girls kissed him; and all at once
he began to converse freely and most wittily. In the full
enjoyment of the marvellous country he lived with the
maidens in the palace a day and a year, not thinking it
more than a day, for there was no reckoning of time in that
land. When the day and the year were up, a longing to see
his old acquaintances came on him ; and thanking the old
man for his kindness, he asked if he could return home. The
old man said to him, 'Wait a little while'; and so he waited.
The maiden who had kissed him was unwilling to have him
go ; but when he promised her to return, she sent him off
loaded with riches.

' " At home not one of his people or old friends knew him.
Everybody believed that he had been killed by another
shepherd. And this shepherd had been accused of the
murder and had fled to America.

' " On the first day of the new moon the boy remembered
his promise, and returned to the other country ; and there
was great rejoicing in the beautiful palace when he arrived.
Einion, for that was the boy's name, and Olwen, for that was
the girl's name, now wanted to marry ; but they had to go
about it quietly and half secretly, for the *fair-folk* dislike
ceremony and noise. When the marriage was over, Einion
wished to go back with Olwen to the upper world. So two
snow-white ponies were given them, and they were allowed
to depart.

' " They reached the upper world safely ; and, being
possessed of unlimited wealth, lived most handsomely on
a great estate which came into their possession. A son was
born to them, and he was called Taliessin. People soon

began to ask for Olwen's pedigree, and as none was given it was taken for granted that she was one of the *fair-folk*. ' Yes, indeed,' said Einion, ' there is no doubt that she is one of the *fair-folk*, there is no doubt that she is one of the very *fair-folk*, for she has two sisters as pretty as she is, and if you saw them all together you would admit that the name is a suitable one.' And this is the origin of the term *fair-folk (Tylwyth Teg)*." '

From Wales we go to the nearest Brythonic country, Cornwall, to study the fairy-folk there.

VI   IN CORNWALL

Introduction by HENRY JENNER, Member of the Gorsedd of the Bards of Brittany; Fellow and Local Secretary for Cornwall of the Society of Antiquaries ; author of *A Handbook of the Cornish Language*, &c.

In Cornwall the legends of giants, of saints, or of Arthur and his knights, the observances and superstitions connected with the prehistoric stone monuments, holy wells, mines, and the like, the stories of submerged or buried cities, and the fragments of what would seem to be pre-Christian faiths, have no doubt occasional points of contact with Cornish fairy legends, but they do not help to explain the fairies very much. Yet certain it is that not only in Cornwall and other Celtic lands, but throughout most of the world, a belief in fairies exists or has existed, and so widespread a belief must have a reason for it, though not necessarily a good one. That which with unconscious humour men generally call ' education ' has in these days caused those lower classes, to whom the deposit of this faith was entrusted, to be ashamed of it, and to despise and endeavour to forget it. And so now in Cornwall, as elsewhere at that earlier outbreak of Philistinism, the Reformation,

> From haunted spring and grassy ring
>   Troop goblin, elf and fairy,
> And the kelpie must flit from the black bog-pit,
>   And the brownie must not tarry.

But, in spite of Protestantism, school-boards, and education committees, ' pisky-pows ' are still placed on the ridge-tiles of West Cornish cottages, to propitiate the piskies and give them a dancing-place, lest they should turn the milk sour, and St. Just and Morvah folk are still ' pisky-led ' on the Gump (*an Ûn Gumpas*, the Level Down, between Chûn Castle and Carn Kenidjack), and more rarely St. Columb and Roche folk on Goss Moor. It will not do to say that it is only another form of ' whisky-led '. That is an evidently modern explanation, invented since the substitution of strange Scottish and Irish drinks for the good ' Nantes ' and wholesome ' Plymouth ' of old time, and it does not fit in with the phenomena. It was only last winter, in a cottage not a hundred yards from where I am writing, that milk was set at night for piskies, who had been knocking on walls and generally making nuisances of themselves. Apparently the piskies only drank the ' astral ' part of the milk (whatever that may be) and then the neighbouring cats drank what was left, and it disagreed with them. I cannot vouch for the truth of the part about the piskies and the ' astral ' milk— I give it as it was told to me by the occupant of the cottage, who was not unacquainted with ' occult ' terminology—but I do know that the milk was consumed, and that the cats, one of which was my own, were with one accord unwell all over the place. But for the present purpose it does not matter whether these things really happened or not. The point is that people thought they happened.

Robert Hunt, in his *Popular Romances of the West of England*, divided the fairies of Cornish folk-lore into five classes : (1) the Small People ; (2) the Spriggans ; (3) the Piskies ; (4) the Buccas, Bockles, or Knockers ; (5) the Brownies. This is an incorrect classification. The *Pobel Vean* or Small People, the Spriggans, and the Piskies are not really distinguishable from one another. Bucca, who properly is but one, is a deity not a fairy, and it is said that at Newlyn, the great seat of his worship, offerings of fish are still left on the beach for him. His name is the Welsh *pwca*, which is probably ' Puck ', though Shakespeare's Puck was just a pisky, and it may be connected with the general Slavonic word *Bog*, God; so that if, as some say, *buccaboo* is really meant for *Bucca-du*, Black Bucca, this may be an equivalent of *Czernobog*, the Black God, who was the Ahriman of Slavonic dualism, and *Bucca-widn* (White Bucca), which is rarer, though the expression does come into a St. Levan story, may be the corresponding *Bielobog*. *Bockle*, which personally I have never heard used, suggests the Scottish *bogle*, and both may be diminutives of *bucca*, *bog*, *bogie*, or *bug*, the last in the sense in which one English version translates the *timor nocturnus* of Psalm xc. 5, not in that of *cimex lectularius*. But *bockle* and *brownie* are probably both foreign importations borrowed from books, though a 'brownie' *eo nomine* has been reported from Sennen within the last twenty years.

The Knockers or Knackers are mine-spirits, quite unconnected with Bucca or bogles. The story, as I have always heard it, is that they are the spirits of Jews who were sent by the Romans to work in the tin mines, some say for being concerned in the Crucifixion of our Lord, which sounds improbable.* They are benevolent spirits, and warn miners of danger.

But the only true Cornish fairy is the Pisky, of the race which is the *Pobel Vean* or Little People, and the Spriggan is only one of his aspects. The Pisky would seem to be the 'Brownie' of the Lowland Scot, the *Duine Sith* of the Highlander, and, if we may judge from an interesting note in Scott's *The Pirate*, the 'Peght' of the Orkneys. If *Daoine Sith* really means 'The Folk of the Mounds' (barrows), not 'The People of Peace', it is possible that there is something in the theory that Brownie, *Duine Sith*, and 'Peght', which is Pict, are only in their origin ways of expressing the little dark-complexioned aboriginal folk who were supposed to inhabit the barrows, cromlechs, and *allées couvertes*, and whose cunning, their only effective weapon against the mere strength of the Aryan invader, earned them a reputation for magical powers. Now *Pisky* or *Pisgy* is really *Pixy*. Though as a patriotic Cornishman I ought not to admit it,

I cannot deny, especially as it suits my argument better, that the Devon form is the correct one. But after all there has been always a strong Cornish element in Devon, even since the time when Athelstan drove the Britons out of Exeter and set the Tamar for their boundary, and I think the original word is really Cornish. The transposition of consonants, especially when *s* is one of them, is not uncommon in modern Cornish English. *Hosged* for *hogshead*, and *haps* for *hasp* are well-known instances. If we take the root of *Pixy*, *Pix*, and divide the double letter *x* into its component parts, we get *Piks* or *Pics*, and if we remember that a final *s* or *z* in Cornish almost always represents a *t* or *d* of Welsh and Breton (cf. *tas* for *tad*, *nans* for *nant*, *bos* for *bod*), we may not unreasonably, though without absolute certainty, conjecture that *Pixy* is *Picty* in a Cornish form.[1]

Without begging any question concerning the origin, ethnology, or homogeneity of those who are called ' Picts ' in history, from the times of Ammianus Marcellinus and Claudian until Kenneth MacAlpine united the Pictish kingdom with the Scottish, we can nevertheless accept the fact that the name ' Pict ' has been popularly applied to some pre-Celtic race or races, to whom certain ancient structures, such as ' vitrified forts ' and ' Picts' houses ' have been attributed.   In Cornwall there are instances of prehistoric structures being called ' Piskies' Halls ' (there is an *allée couverte* so called at Bosahan in Constantine), and ' Piskies' Crows ' (*Crow* or *Craw*, Breton *Krao*, is a shed or hovel ; ' pegs' craw' is still used for ' pig-sty ') ; and there are three genuine examples of what would in Scotland be called ' Picts' Houses ' just outside St. Ives in the direction of Zennor, though only modern antiquaries have applied that name to them.   In the district in which they are, the fringe of coast from St. Ives round by Zennor, Morvah, Pendeen, and St. Just nearly to Sennen, are found to this day a strange

---

[1] The *New English Dictionary*, s.v. *Pixy*, gives rather vaguely a Swedish dialect word, *pysg*, a small fairy. It also mentions *pix* as a Devon imprecation, ' a pix take him.' I suspect the last is only an *umlaut* form of a common Shakespearean imprecation. If not, it is interesting, and reminds one of the fate of Margery Dawe, ' Piskies came and carr'd her away.'

and separate people of Mongol type, like the Bigaudens of
Pont l'Abbé and Penmarc'h in the Breton Cornouailles, one
of those ' fragments of forgotten peoples ' of the ' sunset
bound of Lyonesse ' of whom Tennyson tells. They are
a little ' stuggy ' dark folk, and until comparatively modern
times were recognized as different from their Celtic neighbours, and were commonly believed to be largely wizards
and witches. One of Mr. Wentz's informants seems to
attribute to Zennor a particularly virulent brand of pisky,
and Zennor is the most primitive part of that district.
Possibly the more completely unmixed ancestors of this race
were ' more so ' than the present representatives; but, be
this as it may, if *Pixy* is really *Picty*, it would seem that,
like the inhabitants of the extreme north of the British Isles,
the south-western Britons eventually applied the fairly
general popular name of the mysterious, half dreaded, half
despised aboriginal to a race of preternatural beings in
whose existence they believed, and, with the name, transferred some of the qualities, attributes, and legends, thus
producing a mixed mental conception, now known as ' pisky '
or ' pixy '.

There seems to have been always and everywhere (or
nearly so) a belief in a race, neither divine nor human, but
very like to human beings, who existed on a ' plane ' different
from that of humans, though occupying the same space.
This has been called the ' astral ' or the ' fourth-dimensional '
plane. Why ' astral ' ? why ' fourth-dimensional ' ? why
' plane ' ? are questions the answers to which do not matter,
and I do not attempt to defend the terms, but you must call
it something. This is the belief to which Scott refers in the
introduction to *The Monastery*, as the ' beautiful but almost
forgotten theory of astral spirits or creatures of the elements,
surpassing human beings in knowledge and power, but
inferior to them as being subject, after a certain space of
years, to a death which is to them annihilation '. The sub-
divisions and elaborations of the subject by Paracelsus, the
Rosicrucians, and the modern theosophists are no doubt
amplifications of that popular belief, which, though rather

undefined, resembles the theory of these mystics in its main outlines, and was probably what suggested it to them.

These beings are held to be normally imperceptible to human senses, but conditions may arise in which the ' astral ' plane ' of the elementals and that part of the ' physical plane ' in which, if one may so express it, some human being happens to be, may be in such a relation to one another that these and other spirits may be seen and heard. Some such condition is perhaps described in the story of Balaam the soothsayer, in that incident when ' the Lord opened the eyes of the young man and he saw, and behold, the mountain was full of horses and chariots of fire round about Elisha ', and possibly also in the mysterious ' sound of a going in the tops of the mulberry trees ' which David heard ; but no doubt in these cases it was angels and not elementals. It may also be allowable to suggest, without irreverence, that the Gospel stories of the Transfiguration and Ascension are connected with the same idea, though the latter is expressed in the form of the geocentric theory of the universe.

The Cornish pisky stories are largely made up of instances of contact between the two ' planes ', sometimes accidental, sometimes deliberately induced by incantations or magic eye-salve, yet with these stories are often mingled incidents that are not preternatural at all. How, when, and why this belief arose, I do not pretend even to conjecture ; but there it is, and though of course the holders of it do not talk about ' planes ', that is very much the notion which they appear to have.

I do not think that the piskies were ever definitely held to be the spirits of the dead, and while a certain confusion has arisen, as some of Mr. Wentz's informants show, I think it belongs to the confused eschatology of modern Protestants. To a pre-Reformation Cornishman, or indeed to any other Catholic, the idea was unthinkable. ' Justorum animae in manu Dei sunt, et non tanget illos tormentum malitiae : visi sunt oculis insipientium mori : illi autem sunt in pace,' and the transmigration of the souls of the faithful departed into another order of beings, not disembodied because never embodied, was to them impossible. Such a notion is on a par with the quaint but very usual hope of the modern ' Evangelical ' Christian, so beautifully expressed in one of Hans Andersen's stories, that his departed friends are promoted to be ' angels '. There may be, perhaps, an idea, as there certainly is in the Breton Death-Faith, that the spirits of the faithful dead are all round us, and are not rapt away into a *distant* Paradise or Purgatory. This may be of pre-Christian origin, but does not contradict any article of the Christian faith. The warnings, apparitions, and hauntings, the ' calling of the dead ' at sea, and other details of Cornish Death-Legends, seem to point to a conception of a ' plane ' of the dead, similar to but not necessarily identical with that of the elementals. Under some quite undefined conditions contact may occur with the ' physical plane ', whence the alleged incidents ; but this Cornish Death-Faith, though sometimes, as commonly in Brittany, presenting similar phenomena, has in itself nothing to do with piskies, and as for the unfaithful departed, their destination was also well understood, and it was not Fairyland. There are possible connecting links in the not very common idea that piskies are the souls of unbaptized children, and in the more common notion that the *Pobel Vean* are, not the disembodied spirits, but the living souls and bodies of the old Pagans, who, refusing Christianity, are miraculously preserved alive, but are condemned to decrease in size until they vanish altogether. Some authorities hold that it is the race and not the individual which dwindles from generation to generation.

This last idea, as well as the name ' pixy ', gives some probability to the conclusion that, as applied to Cornwall, Mr. MacRitchie's theory represents a part of the truth, and that on to an already existing belief in elementals have been grafted exaggerated traditions of a dark pre-Celtic people. These were not necessarily pygmies, but smaller than Celts, and may have survived for a long time in forests and hill countries, sometimes friendly to the taller race, whence come the stories of piskies working for farmers, sometimes hostile, which may account for the legends of changelings and other mischievous tricks. This is how it appears to one who knows his Cornwall in all its aspects fairly well, but does not profess to be an expert in folk-lore.

BOSPOWES, HAYLE, CORNWALL,
July 1910.

Our investigation of the Fairy-Faith in Cornwall covers the region between Falmouth and the Land's End, which is now the most Celtic ; and the Tintagel country on the north coast. It is generally believed that ancient Cornish legends, like the Cornish language, are things of the past only, but I am now no longer of that opinion. Undoubtedly Cornwall is the most anglicized of all Celtic lands we are studying, and its folk-lore is therefore far from being as virile as the Irish folk-lore ; nevertheless, through its people, racially mixed though they are, there still flows the blood and the inspiration of a prehistoric native ancestry, and among the oldest Cornish men and women of many an isolated village, or farm, there yet remains some belief in fairies and pixies. Moreover, throughout all of Old Cornwall there is a very living faith in the Legend of the Dead ; and that this Cornish Legend of the Dead, with its peculiar Brythonic character, should be parallel as it is to the Breton Legend of the Dead, has heretofore, so far as I am aware, not been pointed out. I am giving, however, only a very few of the Cornish death-legends collected, because in essence most of them are alike.

A CORNISH HISTORIAN'S TESTIMONY

I was privileged to make my first call in rural Cornwall at the pretty country home of Miss Susan E. Gay, of Crill, about three miles from Falmouth ; and Miss Gay, who has written a well-known history of Falmouth (*Old Falmouth*, London, 1903), very willingly accorded me an interview on the subject of my inquiry, and finally dictated for my use the following matter :—

Pixies as 'Astral Plane' Beings.—' The pixies and fairies are little beings in the human form existing on the ' astral plane ', who may be in the process of evolution ; and, as such, I believe people have seen them. The ' astral plane ' is not known to us now because our psychic faculty of perception has faded out by non-use, and this condition has been brought about by an almost exclusive development of the physical brain ; but it is likely that the psychic faculty will develop again in its turn.'

Psychical Interpretation of Folk-Lore.—' It is my point of view that there is a basis of truth in the folk-lore. With its remnants of occult learning, magic, charms, and the like, folk-lore seems to be the remains of forgotten psychical facts, rather than history, as it is often called.'

PEASANT EVIDENCE FROM THE CRILL COUNTRY

Miss Gay kindly gave me the names of certain peasants in the Crill region, and from one of them, Mrs. Harriett Christopher, I gleaned the following material :—

A Pisky Changeling.—' A woman who lived near Breage Church had a fine girl baby, and she thought the piskies came and took it and put a withered child in its place. The withered child lived to be twenty years old, and was no larger when it died than when the piskies brought it. It was fretful and peevish and frightfully shrivelled. The parents believed that the piskies often used to come and look over a certain wall by the house to see the child. And I heard my grandmother say that the family once put the child out of doors at night to see if the piskies would take it back again.'

Nature of Piskies.—' The piskies are said to be very small. You could never see them by day. I used to hear my grandmother, who has been dead fifty years, say that the piskies used to hold a fair in the fields near Breage, and that people saw them there dancing. I also remember her saying that it was customary to set out food for the piskies at night. My grandmother's great belief was in piskies and in spirits ; and she considered piskies spirits. She used to tell so many stories about spirits [of the dead] coming back and such things that I would be afraid to go to bed.'

EVIDENCE FROM CONSTANTINE

Our witnesses from the ancient and picturesque village of Constantine are John Wilmet, seventy-eight years old, and his good wife, two most excellent and well-preserved types of the passing generation of true Cornish stock. John began by telling me the following tale about an *allée couverte*— a tale which in one version or another is apt to be told of most Cornish megaliths :—

A Pisky-House.—' William Murphy, who married my sister, once went to the pisky-house at Bosahan with a surveyor, and the two of them heard such unearthly noises in it that they came running home in great excitement, saying they had heard the piskies.'

The Pisky Thrasher.—' On a farm near here, a pisky used to come at night to thrash the farmer's corn. The farmer in payment once put down a new suit for him. When the pisky came and saw it, he put it on, and said :—

> Pisky fine and pisky gay,
> Pisky now will fly away.

And they say he never returned.'

Nature of Piskies.—' I always understood the piskies to be little people. A great deal was said about ghosts in this place. Whether or not piskies are the same as ghosts I cannot tell, but I fancy the old folks thought they were.'

Exorcism.—' A farmer who lived two miles from here, near the Gweek River, called Parson Jago to his house to have him quiet the ghosts or spirits regularly haunting it, for Parson Jago could always put such things to rest. The clergyman went to the farmer's house, and with his whip formed a circle on the floor and then commanded the spirit, which made its appearance on the table, to come down into the circle. While on the table the spirit had been visible to all the family, but as soon as it got into the ring it disappeared ; and the house was never haunted afterwards.'

AT ST. MICHAEL'S MOUNT, MARAZION

Our next place for an investigation of the surviving Cornish Fairy-Faith is Marazion, the very ancient British town opposite the isle called St. Michael's Mount. (From Constantine I walked through the country to this point, talking with as many old people as possible, but none of them knew very much about ancient Cornish beliefs.) It is believed, though the matter is very doubtful, that Marazion was the chief mart for the tin trade of Celtic Britain, and that the Mount—sacred to the Sun and to the Pagan Mysteries long before Caesar crossed the Channel from Gaul—sheltered the brilliantly-coloured sailing-ships of the Phoenicians.[1] In such a romantic town, where Oriental merchants and Celtic pilgrims probably once mingled together, one might expect some survival of olden beliefs and customs.

Piskies.—To Mr. Thomas G. Jago, of Marazion, with a memory extending backwards more than seventy years, he being eighty years old, I am indebted for this statement about the pisky creed in that locality :—' I imagine that one hundred and fifty years ago the belief in piskies and spirits was general. In my boyhood days, piskies were often called " the mites " (little people) : they were regarded as little spirits. The word *piskies* is the old Cornish brogue for pixies. In certain grass fields, mushrooms growing in a circle might be seen of a morning, and the old folks pointing to the mushrooms would say to the children, " Oh, the piskies have been dancing there last night." '

Two more of the oldest natives of Marazion, among others with whom I talked, are William Rowe, eighty-two years old, and his married sister seventy-eight years old. About the piskies Mr. Rowe said this :—' People would go out at night and lose their way and then declare that they had been pisky-led. I think they meant by this that they fell under some spiritual influence—that some spirit led them astray. The piskies were said to be small, and they were

---

[1] ' Some say that the Phoenicians never came to Cornwall at all, and that their Ictis was Vectis (the Isle of Wight) or even Thanet.'—HENRY JENNER.

thought of as spirits.'[1] Mr. Rowe's sister added :—' If we
as children did anything wrong, the old folks would say
to us, " The piskies will carry you away if you do that
again." '

Witch-Doctors.—I heard the following witch-story from
a lawyer, a native of the district, who lives in the country
just beyond Marazion :—' Jimmy Thomas, of Wendron
parish, who died within the last twenty-five years, was
the last witch-doctor I know about in West Cornwall. He
was supposed to have great power over evil spirits. His
immediate predecessor was a woman, called the " Witch of
Wendron ", and she did a big business. My father once
visited her in company with a friend whose father had lost
some horses. This was about seventy to eighty years ago.
The witch when consulted on this occasion turned her back
to my father's companion, and began talking to herself in
Cornish. Then she gave him some herbs. His father used
the herbs, and no more horses died : the herbs were supposed to have driven all evil spirits out of the stable.'

IN PENZANCE : AN ARCHITECT'S TESTIMONY

Penzance from earliest times has undoubtedly been, as it
is now, the capital of the Land's End district, the Sacred
Land of Britain. And in Penzance I had the good fortune
to meet those among its leading citizens who still cherish
and keep alive the poetry and the mystic lore of Old Cornwall ; and to no one of them am I more indebted than to
Mr. Henry Maddern, F.I.A.S. Mr. Maddern tells me that
he was initiated into the mysteries of the Cornish folk-lore
of this region when a boy in Newlyn, where he was born, by
his old nurse Betty Grancan, a native Zennor woman, of
stock probably the most primitive and pure in the British
Islands. At his home in Penzance, Mr. Maddern dictated
to me the very valuable evidence which follows :—

Two Kinds of Pixies.—' In this region there are two kinds
of pixies, one purely a land-dwelling pixy and the other
a pixy which dwells on the sea-strand between high and low

---

[1] 'This is, I think, the usual Cornish belief.'—HENRY JENNER.

water mark.[1] The land-dwelling pixy was usually thought
to be full of mischievous fun, but it did no harm. There was
a very prevalent belief, when I was a boy, that this sea-
strand pixy, called *Bucca*,[2] had to be propitiated by a *cast*
(three) of fish, to ensure the fishermen having a good *shot*
(catch) of fish. The land pixy was supposed to be able to
render its devotees invisible, if they only anointed their eyes
with a certain green salve made of secret herbs gathered
from Kerris-moor.[3] In the invisible condition thus induced,
people were able to join the pixy revels, during which,
according to the old tradition, time slipped away very, very
rapidly, though people returned from the pixies no older
than when they went with them.'

The Nurse and the Ointment.—' I used to hear about a
Zennor girl who came to Newlyn as nurse to the child of
a gentleman living at Zimmerman-Cot. The gentleman
warned her never to touch a box of ointment which he
guarded in a special room, nor even to enter that room ; but
one day in his absence she entered the room and took some
of the ointment. Suspecting the qualities of the ointment,
she put it on her eyes with the wish that she might see where
her master was. She immediately found herself in the
higher part of the orchard amongst the pixies, where they
were having much *junketing* (festivity and dancing) ; and
there saw the gentleman whose child she had nursed. For
a time she managed to evade him, but before the *junketing*
was at an end he discovered her and requested her to go

---

[1] 'About Porth Curnow and the Logan Rock there are little spots of
earth in the face of the granite cliffs where sea-daisies (thrift) and other
wild flowers grow. These are referred to the sea pisky, and are known as
"piskies' gardens." '—HENRY JENNER.

[2] I was told by another Cornishman that, in a spirit of municipal rivalry
and fun, the Penzance people like to taunt the people of Newlyn (now
almost a suburb of Penzance) by calling them *Buccas*, and that the
Newlyn townsmen very much resent being so designated. Thus what no
doubt was originally an ancient cult to some local sea-divinity called
Bucca, has survived as folk-humour. (See Mr. Jenner's Introduction,
p. 164.)

[3] 'Another version, which is more usual, is that the pisky anointed the
person's eyes and so rendered itself visible.'—HENRY JENNER.

home; and then, to her intense astonishment, she learned that she had been away twenty years, though she was unchanged. The gentleman scolded her for having touched the ointment, paid her wages in full, and sent her back to her people. She always had the one regret, that she had not gone into the forbidden room at first.'

The Tolcarne Troll.—' The fairy of the Newlyn Tolcarne [1] was in some ways like the Puck of the English Midlands. But this fairy, or troll, was supposed to date back to the time of the Phoenicians. He was described as a little old pleasant-faced man dressed in a tight-fitting leathern jerkin, with a hood on his head, who lived invisible in the rock. Whenever he chose to do so he could make himself visible. When I was a boy it was said that he spent his time voyaging from here to Tyre on the galleys which carried the tin ; and, also, that he assisted in the building of Solomon's Temple. Sometimes he was called " the Wandering One ", or " Odin the Wanderer ". My old nurse, Betty Grancan, used to say that you could call up the troll at the Tolcarne if while there you held in your hand three dried leaves, one of the ash, one of the oak, and one of the thorn, and pronounced an incantation or charm. Betty would never tell me the words of the charm, because she said I was too much of a sceptic. The words of such a Cornish charm had to pass from one believer to another, through a woman to a man, and from a man to a woman, and thus alternately.' [2]

Nature of Pixies.—' Pixies were often supposed to be the souls of the prehistoric dwellers of this country. As such, pixies were supposed to be getting smaller and smaller, until finally they are to vanish entirely. The country pixies inhabiting the highlands from above Newlyn on to St. Just were considered a wicked sort. Their great ambition was to

---

[1] This is a natural outcropping of greenstone on a commanding hill just above the vicarage in Newlyn, and concerning it many weird legends survive. In pre-Christian times it was probably one of the Cornish sacred spots for the celebration of ancient rites—probably in honour of the Sun—and for divination.

[2] For more about the Tolcarne Troll see chapter on Celtic Re-birth p. 391.

change their own offspring for human children; and the true child could only be got back by laying a four-leaf clover on the changeling. A *winickey* child—one which was weak, frail, and peevish—was of the nature of a changeling. Miner pixies, called "knockers", would accept a portion of a miner's *croust* (lunch) on good faith, and by knocking lead him to a rich mother-lode, or warn him by knocking if there was danger ahead or a cavern full of water; but if the miner begrudged them the *croust*, he would be left to his own resources to find the lode, and, moreover, the "knockers" would do all they could to lead him away from a good lode. These mine pixies, too, were supposed to be spirits, sometimes spirits of the miners of ancient times.' [1]

Fairies and Pixies.—' In general appearance the fairies were much the same as pixies. They were small men and women, much smaller than dwarfs. The men were swarthy in complexion, and the women had a clear complexion of a peach-like bloom. None ever appeared to be more than five-and-twenty to thirty years old. I have heard my nurse say that she could see scores of them whenever she picked a four-leaf clover and put it in the wisp of straw which she carried on her head as a cushion for the bucket of milk. Her theory was that the richness of the milk was what attracted them. Pixies, like fairies, very much enjoyed milk, and people of miserly nature used to put salt around a cow to keep the pixies away; and then the pixies would lead such mean people astray the very first opportunity that came. According to some country-people, the pixies have been seen in the day-time, but usually they are only seen at night.'

A CORNISH EDITOR'S OPINION

Mr. Herbert Thomas, editor of four Cornish papers, *The Cornishman, The Cornish Telegraph, Post,* and *Evening*

---

[1] Mr. John B. Cornish, solicitor, of Penzance, told me that when he once suggested to an old miner who fully believed in the ' knockers ', that the noises they were supposed to make were due to material causes, the old miner became quite annoyed, and said, ' Well, I guess I have ears to hear.'

Times, and a true Celt himself, has been deeply interested in the folk-lore of Cornwall, and has made excellent use of it in his poetry and other literary productions ; so that his personal opinions, which follow, as to the probable origin of the fairy-belief, are for our study a very important contribution :—

Animistic Origin of Belief in Pixies.—' I should say that the modern belief in pixies, or in fairies, arose from a very ancient Celtic or pre-Celtic belief in spirits. Just as among some savage tribes there is belief in gods and totems, here there was belief in little spirits good and bad, who were able to help or to hinder man. Belief in the supernatural, in my opinion, is the root of it all.'

A CORNISH FOLK-LORIST'S TESTIMONY

In Penzance I had the privilege of also meeting Miss M. A. Courtney, the well-known folk-lorist, who quite agrees with me in believing that there is in Cornwall a widespread Legend of the Dead ; and she cited a few special instances in illustration, as follows :—

Cornish Legend of the Dead.—' Here amongst the fishermen and sailors there is a belief that the dead in the sea will be heard calling if a drowning is about to occur. I know of a woman who went to a clergyman to have him exorcize her of the spirit of her dead sister, which she said appeared in the form of a bee. And I have heard of miners believing that white moths are spirits.' [1]

EVIDENCE FROM NEWLYN

In Newlyn, Mrs. Jane Tregurtha gave the following important testimony :—

The ' Little Folk '.—' The old people thoroughly believed in the *little folk*, and that they gambolled all over the moors on moonlight nights. Some pixies would rain down blessings and others curses ; and to remove the curses people

---

[1] For the Cornish folk-lore already published by Miss M. A. Courtney, the reader is referred to her work, *Cornish Feasts and Folk-Lore* (Penzance, 1890).

would go to the wells blessed by the saints. Whenever anything went wrong in the kitchen at night the pixies were
blamed. After the 31st of October [or after Halloween] the
blackberries are not fit to eat, for the pixies have then been
over them ' (cf. the parallel Irish belief, p. 38).

Fairy Guardian of the Men-an-Tol.[1]—' At the Men-an-Tol
there is supposed to be a guardian fairy or pixy who can
make miraculous cures. And my mother knew of an actual
case in which a changeling was put through the stone in
order to get the real child back. It seems that evil pixies
changed children, and that the pixy at the Men-an-Tol being
good, could, in opposition, undo their work.'

Exorcism.—' A spirit was put to rest on the Green here in
Newlyn. The parson prayed and fasted, and then commanded the spirit to *teeme* (dip dry) the sea with a limpet
shell containing no bottom ; and the spirit is supposed to
be still busy at this task.'

Piskies as Apparitions.—When I talked with her in her
neat cottage at Newlyn, Miss Mary Ann Chirgwin (who was
born on St. Michael's Mount in 1825) told me this :—' The
old people used to say the piskies were apparitions of the
dead come back in the form of little people, but I can't
remember anything more than this about them.'

AN ARTIST'S TESTIMONY

One of the members of the Newlyn Art School was able
to offer a few of his own impressions concerning the pixies
of Devonshire, where he has frequently made sketches of
pixies from descriptions given to him by peasants :—

Devonshire Pixies.—' Throughout all the west of Devonshire, anywhere near the moorlands, the country people are

---

[1] A curious holed stone standing between two low menhirs on the moors
beyond the Lanyon Dolmen, near Madron ; but in Borlase's time (cf. his
Antiquities of Cornwall, ed. 1769, p. 177) the three stones were not as now
in a direct line. The Men-an-Tol has aroused much speculation among
archaeologists as to its probable use or meaning. No doubt it was astronomical and religious in its significance ; and it may have been a calendar
stone with which ancient priests took sun observations (cf. Sir Norman
Lockyer, *Stonehenge and Other Stone Monuments*) ; or it may have been
otherwise related to a sun cult, or to some pagan initiatory rites.

much given to belief in pixies and ghosts. I think they expect to see them about the twilight hour ; though I have not found anybody who has actually seen a pixy—the belief now is largely based on hearsay.'

TESTIMONY FROM THE HISTORIAN OF MOUSEHOLE

To Mr. Richard Harry, the historian of Mousehole, I am indebted for these remarks about the nature and present state of the belief in pixies as he observes it in that region :—

The Pixy Belief.—' The piskies, thought of as little people who appear on moonlight nights, are still somewhat believed in here. If interfered with too much they are said to exhibit almost fiendish powers. In a certain sense they are considered spiritual, but in another sense they are much materialized in the conceptions of the people. Generally speaking, the belief in them has almost died out within the last fifty years.'

A SEAMAN'S TESTIMONY

' Uncle Billy Pender,' as our present witness is familiarly called, is one of the oldest natives of Mousehole, being eighty-five years old ; and most of his life has been passed on the ocean, as a fisherman, seaman, and pilot. After having told me the usual things about piskies, fairies, spirits, ghosts, and the devil, Uncle Billy Pender was very soon talking about the dead :—

Cornish Legend of the Dead.—' I was up in bed, and I suppose asleep, and I dreamt that the boy James came to my bedside and woke me up by saying, " How many lights does Death put up ? " And in the dream there appeared such light as I never saw in my life ; and when I woke up another light like it was in the room. Within three months afterwards we buried two grand-daughters out of this house. This was four years ago.' When this strange tale was finished, Uncle Billy Pender's daughter, who had been listening, added :—' For three mornings, one after another, there was a robin at our cellar door before the deaths, and my husband said he didn't like that.'

Then Uncle Billy told this weird Breton-like tale :—
'"Granny" told about a boat named *Blücher*, going from
Newlyn to Bristol with six thousand mackerel, which put in
at Arbor Cove, close to Padstow, on account of bad weather.
The boat dragged her anchors and was lost. "Granny"
afterwards declared that he saw the crew going up over
the Newlyn Slip ; and the whole of Newlyn and Mousehole
believed him.'

TESTIMONY BY TWO LAND'S END FARMERS

In the Sennen country, within a mile of the end of Britain,
I talked with two farmers who knew something about piskies.
The first one, Charles Hutchen, of Trevescan, told me this
legend :—

A St. Just Pisky.—' Near St. Just, on Christmas Day,
a pisky carried away in his cloak a boy, but the boy got
home. Then the pisky took him a second time, and again
the boy got home. Each time the boy was away for only an
hour ' (probably in a dream or trance state).

Seeing the Pisky-Dance.—Frank Ellis, seventy-eight years
old, of the same village of Trevescan, then gave the following
evidence :—' Up on Sea-View Green there are two rings
where the piskies used to dance and play music on a moonlight night. I've heard that they would come there from
the moors. *Little people* they are called. If you keep quiet
when they are dancing you'll see them, but if you make
any noise they'll disappear.' Frank Ellis's wife, who is
a very aged woman, was in the house listening to the conversation, and added at this point :—' My grandmother,
Nancy Maddern, was down on Sea-View Green by moonlight
and saw the piskies dancing, and passed near them. She
said they were like little children, and had red cloaks.'

TESTIMONY FROM A SENNEN COVE FISHERMAN

John Gilbert Guy, seventy-eight years old, a retired
fisherman of Sennen Cove, offers very valuable testimony,
as follows :—

' *Small People* '.—' Many say they have seen the *small*

people here by the hundreds. In Ireland they call the *small people* the fairies. My mother believes there were such things, and so did the old folks in these parts. My grandmother used to put down a good furze fire for *them* on stormy nights, because, as she said, " *They* are a sort of people wandering about the world with no home or habitation, and ought to be given a little comfort." The most fear of *them* was that they might come at night and change a baby for one that was no good. My mother said that Joan Nicholas believed the fairies had changed her baby, because it was very small and cross-tempered. Up on the hill you'll see a round ring with grass greener than anywhere else, and that is where the *small people* used to dance.'

Danger of Seeing the ' Little People '.—' I heard that a woman set out water to wash her baby in, and that before she had used the water the *small people* came and washed their babies in it. She didn't know about this, and so in washing her baby got some of the water in her eyes, and then all at once she could see crowds of *little people* about her. One of them came to her and asked if she was able to see their crowd, and when she said " Yes," the *little people* wanted to take her eyes out, and she had to clear away from them as fast as she could.'

TESTIMONY FROM A CORNISH MINER

William Shepherd, a retired miner of Pendeen, near St. Just, where he has passed all his life, offers us from his own experiences under the earth the evidence which follows :—

Mine Piskies.—' There are mine-piskies which are not the " knockers ". I've heard old men in the mines say that they have seen them, and they call them the *small people*. It appears that they don't like company, for they are always seen singly. The " knockers " are spirits, too, as one might say. They are said to bring bad luck, while the *small people* may bring good luck.'

TESTIMONY FROM KING ARTHUR'S COUNTRY

Leaving the Land's End district and South Cornwall, we now pass northward to King Arthur's country. Our chief researches there are to be made outside the beaten track of tourists as far as possible, in the country between Camelford and Tintagel. At Delabole, the centre of this district, we find our first witness, Henry Spragg, a retired slate-quarry-man, seventy years old. Mr. Spragg has had excellent opportunities of hearing any folk-lore that might have been living during his lifetime ; and what he offers first is about King Arthur :—

King Arthur.—' We always thought of King Arthur as a great warrior. And many a time I've heard old people say that he used to appear in this country in the form of a nath.'[1] This was all that could be told of King Arthur ; and the conversation finally was directed toward piskies, with the following results :—

Piskies.—' A man named Bottrell, who lived near St. Teath, was pisky-led at West Down, and when he turned his pockets inside out he heard the piskies going away laughing.[2] Often my grandmother used to say when I got home after dark, " You had better mind, or the piskies will carry you away." And I can remember hearing the old people say that the piskies are the spirits of dead-born children.' From pixies the conversation drifted to the spirit-hounds ' often heard at night near certain haunted downs in St. Teath parish ', and then, finally, to ordinary Cornish legends about the dead.

Our next witnesses from Delabole are John Male, eighty-

---

[1] I asked what a nath is, and Mr. Spragg explained :—' A nath is a bird with a beak like that of a parrot, and with black and grey feathers. The naths live on sea-islands in holes like rabbits, and before they start to fly they first run.' The nath, as Mr. Henry Jenner informs me, is the same as the puffin (*Fratercula arctica*), called also in Cornwall a ' sea parrot '.

[2] Sometimes it is necessary to turn your coat inside out. A Zennor man said that to do the same thing with your socks or stockings is as good. In Ireland this strange psychological state of going astray comes from walking over a fairy domain, over a confusing-sod, or getting into a fairy pass.

two years old, one of the very oldest men in King Arthur's country, and his wife ; and all of Mr. Male's ancestors as far back as he can trace them have lived in the same parish.

Piskies in General.—Mr. Male remarked :—' I have heard a good deal about the piskies, but I can't remember any of the old women's tales. I have heard, too, of people saying that they had seen the piskies. It was thought that when the piskies have misled you they show themselves jumping about in front of you ; they are a race of little people who live out in the fields.' Mrs. Male had now joined us at the open fire, and added :—' Piskies always come at night, and in marshy ground there are round places called pisky beds where they play. When I was little, my mother and grandmother would be sitting round the fire of an evening telling fireside stories, and I can remember hearing about a pisky of this part who stole a new coat, and how the family heard him talking to himself about it, and then finally say :—

> Pisky fine and pisky gay,
> Pisky 's got a bright new coat,
> Pisky now will run away.

And I can just remember one bit of another story : A pisky looked into a house and said :—

> All alone, fair maid ?
> No, here am I with a dog and cat,
> And apples to eat and nuts to crack.'

Tintagel Folk-Beliefs.—A retired rural policeman of the Tintagel country, where he was born and reared, and now keeper of the Passmore Edwards Art Gallery at Newlyn, offered this testimony from Tintagel :—' In Tintagel I used to sit round the fire at night and hear old women tell so much about piskies and ghosts that I was then afraid to go out of doors after darkness had fallen. They religiously believed in such things, and when I expressed my doubts I was driven away as a rude boy. They thought if you went to a certain place at a certain hour of the night that you could there see the piskies as little spirits. It was held that the piskies could lead you astray and play tricks on you,

but that they never did you any serious injury.' Of the
Arthurian folk-legend at Tintagel he said :—' The spirit of
King Arthur is supposed to be in the Cornish chough—
a beautiful black bird with red legs and red beak.'

We now leave Great Britain and cross the English Channel
to Little Britain, the third of the Brythonic countries.

VII IN BRITTANY

Introduction by ANATOLE LE BRAZ, Professor of French
Literature, University of Rennes, Brittany ; author of
La Légende de la Mort, Au Pays des Pardons, &c.

MON CHER MONSIEUR WENTZ,

Il me souvient que, lors de votre soutenance de thèse
devant la Faculté des Lettres de l'Université de Rennes, un
de mes collègues, mon ami, le professeur Dottin, vous
demanda :

' Vous croyez, dites-vous, à l'existence des fées ? En avez-
vous vu ? '

Vous répondîtes, avec autant de phlegme que de sin-
cérité :

' Non. J'ai tout fait pour en voir, et je n'en ai jamais vu.
Mais il y a beaucoup de choses que vous n'avez pas vues,
monsieur le professeur, et dont vous ne songeriez cependant
pas à nier l'existence. Ainsi fais-je à l'égard des fées.'

Je suis comme vous, mon cher monsieur Wentz : je n'ai

My dear Mr. Wentz,

I recollect that, at the time of your examination on your thesis before
the Faculty of Letters of the University of Rennes, one of my colleagues,
my friend Professor Dottin, put to you this question :—

' You believe, you assert, in the existence of fairies ? Have you seen
any ? '

You answered, with equal coolness and candour :

' No. I have made every effort to do so, and I have never seen any.
But there are many things which you, sir, have not seen, and of which,
nevertheless, you would not think of denying the existence. That is my
attitude toward fairies.'

I am like you, my dear Mr. Wentz : I have never seen fairies. It is true

jamais vu de fées. J'ai bien une amie très chère que nous avons baptisée de ce nom, mais, malgré tous ses beaux dons magiques, elle n'est qu'une humble mortelle. En revanche, j'ai vécu, tout enfant, parmi des personnes qui avaient avec les fées véritables un commerce quasi journalier. C'était dans une petite bourgade de Basse-Bretagne, peuplée de paysans à moitié marins, et de marins à moitié paysans. Il y avait, non loin du village, une ancienne gentilhommière que ses propriétaires avaient depuis long-temps abandonnée pour on ne savait au juste quel motif. On continuait de l'appeler le ' château ' de Lanascol, quoi-qu'elle ne fût plus guère qu'une ruine. Il est vrai que les avenues par lesquelles on y accédait avaient conservé leur aspect seigneurial, avec leurs quadruples rangées de vieux hêtres dont les vastes frondaisons se miraient dans de magnifiques étangs. Les gens d'alentour se risquaient peu, le soir, dans ces avenues. Elles passaient pour être, à partir du coucher du soleil, le lieu de promenade favori d'une ' dame ' que l'on désignait sous le nom de *Groac'h Lanascol*, — la ' Fée de Lanascol '.

Beaucoup disaient l'avoir rencontrée, et la dépeignaient sous les couleurs, du reste, les plus diverses. Ceux-ci fai-saient d'elle une vieille femme, marchant toute courbée, les

that I have a very dear lady friend whom we have christened by that name [fairy], but, in spite of all her fair supernatural gifts, she is only a humble mortal. On the other hand, I lived, when a mere child, among people who had almost daily intercourse with real fairies. That was in a little township in Lower Brittany, inhabited by peasants who were half sailors, and by sailors who were half peasants. There was, not far from the village, an ancient manor-house long abandoned by its owners, for what reason was not known exactly. It continued to be called the ' Château ' of Lanascol, though it was hardly more than a ruin. It is true that the avenues by which one approached it had retained their feudal aspect, with their fourfold rows of ancient beeches whose huge masses of foliage were reflected in splendid pools. The people of the neighbourhood seldom ventured into these avenues in the evening. They were supposed to be, from sunset onwards, the favourite walking-ground of a ' lady ' who went by the name of *Groac'h Lanascol*, the ' Fairy of Lanascol '.

Many claimed to have met her, and described her in colours which were, however, the most varied. Some represented her as an old woman

deux mains appuyées sur un tronçon de béquille avec lequel,
de temps en temps, elle remuait, à l'automne, les feuilles
mortes. Les feuilles mortes qu'elle retournait ainsi devenaient
soudain brillantes comme de l'or et s'entrechoquaient avec
un bruit clair de métal. Selon d'autres, c'était une jeune
princesse, merveilleusement parée, sur les pas de qui s'em-
pressaient d'étranges petits hommes noirs et silencieux.
Elle s'avançait d'une majestueuse allure de reine. Parfois
elle s'arrêtait devant un arbre, et l'arbre aussitôt s'inclinait
comme pour recevoir ses ordres. Ou bien, elle jetait un
regard sur l'eau d'un étang, et l'étang frissonnait jusqu'en
ses profondeurs, comme agité d'un mouvement de crainte
sous la puissance de son regard.

On racontait sur elle cette curieuse histoire :—

Les propriétaires de Lanascol ayant voulu se défaire d'un
domaine qu'ils n'habitaient plus, le manoir et les terres qui
en dépendaient furent mis en adjudication chez un notaire
de Plouaret. Au jour fixé pour les enchères nombre d'ache-
teurs accoururent. Les prix étaient déjà montés très haut,
et le domaine allait être adjugé, quand, à un dernier appel
du crieur, une voix féminine, très douce et très impérieuse
tout ensemble, s'éleva et dit :

' Mille francs de plus ! '

who walked all bent, her two hands leaning on a stump of a crutch with
which, in autumn, from time to time she stirred the dead leaves. The
dead leaves which she thus stirred became suddenly shining like gold, and
clinked against one another with the clear sound of metal. According to
others, it was a young princess, marvellously adorned, after whom there
hurried curious little black silent men. She advanced with a majestic
and queenly bearing. Sometimes she stopped in front of a tree, and
the tree at once bent down as if to receive her commands. Or again, she
would cast a look on the water of a pool, and the pool trembled to its very
depths, as though stirred by an access of fear beneath the potency of her look.
The following strange story was told about her :—
The owners of Lanascol having desired to get rid of an estate which
they no longer occupied, the manor and lands attached to it were put up
to auction by a notary of Plouaret. On the day fixed for the bidding a
number of purchasers presented themselves. The price had already reached
a large sum, and the estate was on the point of being knocked down,
when, on a last appeal from the auctioneer, a female voice, very gentle
and at the same time very imperious, was raised and said :
' A thousand francs more ! '

Il y eut grande rumeur dans la salle. Tout le monde cherche des yeux la personne qui avait lancé cette sur- enchère, et qui ne pouvait être qu'une femme. Mais il ne se trouva pas une seule femme dans l'assistance. Le notaire demanda :

' Qui a parlé ? '

De nouveau, la même voix se fit entendre.

' Groac'h Lanascol ! ' répondit-elle.

Ce fut une débandade générale. Depuis lors, il ne s'était jamais présenté d'acquéreur, et voilà pourquoi, répétait-on couramment, Lanascol était toujours à vendre.

Si je vous ai entretenu à plaisir de la Fée de Lanascol, mon cher monsieur Wentz, c'est qu'elle est la première qui ait fait impression sur moi, dans mon enfance. Combien d'autres n'en ai-je pas connu, par la suite, à travers les récits de mes compatriotes des grèves, des champs ou des bois ! La Bretagne est restée un royaume de féerie. On n'y peut voyager l'espace d'une lieue sans côtoyer la demeure de quelque fée mâle ou femelle. Ces jours derniers, comme j'accomplissais un pèlerinage d'automne à l'hallucinante forêt de Paimpont, toute hantée encore des grands souvenirs de la légende celtique, je croisai, sous les opulents ombrages

A great commotion arose in the hall. Every one's eyes sought for the person who had made this advance, and who could only be a woman. But there was not a single woman among those present. The notary asked :
' Who spoke ? '
Again the same voice made itself heard.
' The Fairy of Lanascol ! ' it replied.
A general break-up followed. From that time forward no purchaser has ever appeared, and, as the current report ran, that was the reason why Lanascol continued to be for sale.
I have designedly quoted to you the story of the Fairy of Lanascol, my dear Mr. Wentz, because she was the first to make an impression on me in my childhood. How many others have I come to know later on in the course of narratives from those who lived with me on the sandy beaches, in the fields or the woods ! Brittany has always been a kingdom of Faerie. One cannot there travel even a league without brushing past the dwelling of some male or female fairy. Quite lately, in the course of an autumn pilgrimage to the hallucinatory forest of Paimpont (or Brocéliande), still haunted throughout by the great memories of Celtic legend, I encountered beneath the thick foliage of the Pas-du-Houx, a woman gathering faggots,

du Pas-du-Houx, une ramasseuse de bois mort, avec qui je
ne manquai pas, vous pensez bien, de lier conversation. Un
des premiers noms que je prononçai fut naturellement celui
de Viviane.

' Viviane ! ' se récria la vieille pauvresse. ' Ah ! bénie
soit-elle, la bonne Dame ! car elle est aussi bonne que
belle... Sans sa protection, mon homme, qui travaille dans
les coupes, serait tombé, comme un loup, sous les fusils des
gardes...' Et elle se mit à me conter comme quoi son mari,
un tantinet braconnier comme tous les bûcherons de ces
parages, s'étant porté, une nuit, à l'affût du chevreuil, dans
les environs de la Butte-aux-Plaintes, avait été surpris en
flagrant délit par une tournée de gardes. Il voulut fuir : les
gardes tirèrent. Une balle l'atteignit à la cuisse : il tomba,
et il s'apprêtait à se faire tuer sur place, plutôt que de se
rendre, lorsque, entre ses agresseurs et lui, s'interposa
subitement une espèce de brouillard très dense qui voila
tout, — le sol, les arbres, les gardes et le blessé lui-même. Et
il entendit une voix sortie du brouillard, une voix légère
comme un bruit de feuilles, murmurer à son oreille : ' Sauve-
toi, mon fils : l'esprit de Viviane veillera sur toi jusqu'à ce
que tu aies rampé hors de la forêt.'

with whom I did not fail, as you may well imagine, to enter into
conversation. One of the first names I uttered was naturally that of
Vivian.

' Vivian ! ' cried out the poor old woman. ' Ah ! a blessing on her,
the good Lady ! for she is as good as she is beautiful. . . . Without her
protection my good man, who works at woodcutting, would have fallen,
like a wolf, beneath the keepers' guns. . . .' And she began to narrate
to me ' as how ' her husband, something of a poacher like all the wood-
cutters of these districts, had one night gone to watch for a roebuck in
the neighbourhood of the Butte-aux-Plaintes, and had been caught red-
handed by a party of keepers. He sought to fly : the keepers fired.
A bullet hit him in the thigh : he fell, and was making ready to let himself
be killed on the spot, rather than surrender, when there suddenly inter-
posed between him and his assailants a kind of very thick mist which
covered everything—the ground, the trees, the keepers, and the wounded
man himself. And he heard a voice coming out of the mist, a voice gentle
like the rustling of leaves, and murmuring in his ear : ' Save thyself, my
son : the spirit of Vivian will watch over thee till thou hast crawled out
of the forest.'

' Telles furent les propres paroles de la fée,' conclut la
ramasseuse de bois mort.

Et, dévotement, elle se signa, car la religieuse Bretagne —
vous le savez — vénère les fées à l'égal des saintes.

.   .   .   .

J'ignore s'il faut rattacher les lutins au monde des fées,
mais, ce qui est sûr, c'est que cette charmante et malicieuse
engeance a toujours pullulé dans notre pays. Je me suis
laissé dire qu'autrefois chaque maison avait le sien. C'était
quelque chose comme le petit dieu pénate. Tantôt visible,
tantôt invisible, il présidait à tous les actes de la vie do-
mestique. Mieux encore : il y participait, et de la façon la
plus efficace. A l'intérieur du logis, il aidait les servantes,
soufflait le feu dans l'âtre, surveillait la cuisson de la nour-
riture pour les hommes ou pour les bêtes, apaisait les cris
de l'enfant couché dans le bas de l'armoire, empêchait les
vers de se mettre dans les pièces de lard suspendues aux
solives. Il avait pareillement dans son lot le gouvernement
des étables et des écuries : grâce à lui, les vaches donnaient
un lait abondant en beurre, et les chevaux avaient la croupe
ronde, le poil luisant. Il était, en un mot, le bon génie de
la famille, mais c'était à la condition que chacun eût pour
lui les égards auxquels il avait droit. Si peu qu'on lui

' Such were the actual words of the fairy,' concluded the faggot-gatherer.
And she crossed herself devoutly, for pious Brittany, as you know, reveres
fairies as much as saints.

.   .   .   .

I do not know if *lutins* (mischievous spirits) should be included in the
fairy world, but what is certain is that this charming and roguish tribe
has always abounded in our country. I have been told that formerly
every house had its own. It (the *lutin*) was something like the little
Roman household god. Now visible, now invisible, it presided over all
the acts of domestic life. Nay more; it shared in them, and in the most
effective manner. Inside the house it helped the servants, blew up the
fire on the hearth, supervised the cooking of the food for men or beasts,
quieted the crying of the babe lying in the bottom of the cupboard, and
prevented worms from settling in the pieces of bacon hanging from the
beams. Similarly there fell within its sphere the management of the
byres and stables : thanks to it the cows gave milk abounding in butter,
and the horses had round croups and shining coats. It was, in a word,
the good genius of the house, but conditionally on every one paying to
it the respect to which it had the right. If neglected, ever so little,

manquât, sa bonté se changeait en malice et il n'était point
de mauvais tours dont il ne fût capable envers les gens qui
l'avaient offensé, comme de renverser le contenu des mar-
mites sur le foyer, d'embrouiller la laine autour des que-
nouilles, de rendre infumable le tabac des pipes, d'emmêler
inextricablement les crins des chevaux, de dessécher le pis
des vaches ou de faire peler le dos des brebis. Aussi s'effor-
çait-on de ne le point mécontenter. On respectait soigneuse-
ment toutes ses habitudes, toutes ses manies. C'est ainsi
que, chez mes parents, notre vieille bonne Filie n'enlevait
jamais le trépied du feu sans avoir la précaution de l'asperger
d'eau pour le refroidir, avant de le ranger au coin de
l'âtre. Si vous lui demandiez pourquoi ce rite, elle vous
répondait :
  ' Pour que le lutin ne s'y brûle pas, si, tout à l'heure,
il s'asseyait dessus.'

.   .   .   .

Il appartient encore, je suppose, à la catégorie des
hommes-fées, ce *Bugul-Noz*, ce mystérieux ' Berger de la
nuit ' dont les Bretons des campagnes voient se dresser, au
crépuscule, la haute et troublante silhouette, si, d'aventure,
il leur arrive de rentrer tard du labour. On n'a jamais pu me
renseigner exactement sur le genre de troupeau qu'il faisait
paître, ni sur ce que présageait sa rencontre. Le plus souvent,

its kindness changed into spite, and there was no unkind trick of which
it was not capable towards people who had offended it, such as upsetting
the contents of the pots on the hearth, entangling wool round distaffs,
making tobacco unsmokeable, mixing a horse's mane in inextricable confusion, drying up the udders of cows, or stripping the backs of sheep. Therefore care was taken not to annoy it. Careful attention was paid to all its
habits and humours. Thus, in my parents' house, our old maid Filie never
lifted the trivet from the fire without taking the precaution of sprinkling
it with water to cool it, before putting it away at the corner of the hearth.
If you asked her the reason for this ceremony, she would reply to you :
  ' To prevent the *lutin* burning himself there, if, presently, he sat on it.'

.   .   .   .

Further, I suppose there should be included in the class of male fairies
that *Bugul-Noz*, that mysterious Night Shepherd, whose tall and alarming
outline the rural Bretons see rising in the twilight, if, by chance, they
happen to return late from field-work. I have never been able to obtain
exact information about the kind of herd which he fed, nor about what
was foreboded by the meeting with him. Most often such a meeting is

on la redoute. Mais, comme l'observait avec raison une de mes conteuses, Lise Bellec, s'il est préférable d'éviter le *Bugul-Noz*, il ne s'ensuit pas, pour cela, que ce soit un méchant Esprit. D'après elle, il remplirait plutôt une fonction salutaire, en signifiant aux humains, par sa venue, que la nuit n'est pas faite pour s'attarder aux champs ou sur les chemins, mais pour s'enfermer derrière les portes closes et pour dormir. Ce berger des ombres serait donc, somme toute, une manière de bon pasteur. C'est pour assurer notre repos et notre sécurité, c'est pour nous sous-traire aux excès du travail et aux embûches de la nuit qu'il nous force, brebis imprudentes, à regagner prompte-ment le bercail.

Sans doute est-ce un rôle tutélaire à peu près semblable qui, dans la croyance populaire, est dévolu à un autre homme-fée, plus spécialement affecté au rivage de la mer, comme l'indique son nom de *Yann-An-Ôd*. Il n'y a pas, sur tout le littoral maritime de la Bretagne ou, comme on dit, dans tout l'*armor*, une seule région où l'existence de ce ' Jean des Grèves ' ne soit tenue pour un fait certain, dûment constaté, indéniable. On lui prête des formes variables et des aspects différents. C'est tantôt un géant, tantôt un nain. Il porte tantôt un ' suroit ' de toile huilée, tantôt un large chapeau de feutre noir. Parfois, il s'appuie sur une

---

dreaded. Yet, as one of my female informants, Lise Bellec, reasonably pointed out, if it is preferable to avoid the *Bugul-Noz* it does not from that follow that he is a harmful spirit. According to her, he would rather fulfil a beneficial office, in warning human beings, by his coming, that night is not made for lingering in the fields or on the roads, but for shutting oneself in behind closed doors and going to sleep. This shepherd of the shades would then be, take it altogether, a kind of good shepherd. It is to ensure our rest and safety, to withdraw us from excesses of toil and the snares of night, that he compels us, thoughtless sheep, to return quickly to the fold.

No doubt it is an almost similar protecting office which, in popular belief, has fallen to another male fairy, more particularly attached to the seashore, as his name, *Yann-An-Ôd*, indicates. There is not, along all the coast of Brittany or, as it is called, in all the *Armor*, a single district where the existence of this ' John of the Dunes ' is not looked on as a real fact, fully proved and undeniable. Changing forms and different aspects are attributed to him. Sometimes he is a giant, sometimes a dwarf. Some-times he wears a seaman's hat of oiled cloth, sometimes a broad black felt hat. At times he leans on an oar and recalls the enigmatic personage,

rame et fait penser au personnage énigmatique, armé du même attribut, qu'Ulysse doit suivre, dans l'*Odyssée*. Mais, toujours, c'est un héros marin dont la mission est de parcourir les plages, en poussant par intervalles de longs cris stridents, propres à effrayer les pêcheurs qui se seraient laissé surprendre dehors par les ténèbres de la nuit. Il ne fait de mal qu'à ceux qui récalcitrent ; encore ne les frappet-il que dans leur intérêt, pour les contraindre à se mettre à l'abri. Il est, avant tout, un ' avertisseur '. Ses cris ne rappellent pas seulement au logis les gens attardés sur les grèves ; ils signalent aussi le dangereux voisinage de la côte aux marins qui sont en mer et, par là, suppléent à l'insuffisance du mugissement des sirènes ou de la lumière des phares.

Remarquons, à ce propos, qu'on relève un trait analogue dans la légende des vieux saints armoricains, pour la plupart émigrés d'Irlande. Un de leurs exercices coutumiers consistait à déambuler de nuit le long des côtes où ils avaient établi leurs oratoires, en agitant des clochettes de fer battu dont les tintements étaient destinés, comme les cris de *Yann-An-Ôd*, à prévenir les navigateurs que la terre était proche.

Je suis persuadé que le culte des saints, qui est la première et la plus fervente des dévotions bretonnes, conserve bien des traits d'une religion plus ancienne où la croyance

possessed of the same attribute, whom Ulysses has to follow, in the *Odyssey*. But he is always a marine hero whose office it is to traverse the shores, uttering at intervals long piercing cries, calculated to frighten away fishermen who may have allowed themselves to be surprised outside by the darkness of night. He only hurts those who resist ; and even then would only strike them in their own interest, to force them to seek shelter. He is, before all, one who warns. His cries not only call back home people out late on the sands; they also inform sailors at sea of the dangerous proximity of the shore, and, thereby, make up for the insufficiency of the hooting of sirens or of the light of lighthouses.

We may remark, in this connexion, that a parallel feature is observed in the legend of the old Armorican saints, who were mostly emigrants from Ireland. One of their usual exercises consisted in parading throughout the night the coasts where they had set up their oratories, shaking little bells of wrought iron, the ringing of which, like the cries of *Yann-An-Ôd*, was intended to warn voyagers that land was near.

I am persuaded that the worship of saints, which is the first and most fervent of Breton religious observances, preserves many of the features

aux fées jouait le principal rôle. Et il en va de même, j'en suis convaincu, pour ces mythes funéraires que j'ai recueillis sous le titre de *La Légende de la Mort* chez les Bretons armoricains. A vrai dire, dans la conception bretonne, les morts ne sont pas morts ; ils vivent d'une vie mystérieuse en marge de la vie réelle, mais leur monde reste, en définitive, tout mêlé au nôtre et, sitôt que la nuit tombe, sitôt que les vivants proprement dits s'abandonnent à la mort momentanée du sommeil, les soi-disant morts redeviennent les habitants de la terre qu'ils n'ont jamais quittée. Ils reprennent leur place à leur foyer d'autrefois, ils vaquent à leurs anciens travaux, ils s'intéressent au logis, aux champs, à la barque ; ils se comportent, en un mot, comme ce peuple des hommes et des femmes-fées qui formait jadis une espèce d'humanité plus fine et plus délicate au milieu de la véritable humanité.

.   .   .   .

J'aurais encore, mon cher monsieur Wentz, bien d'autres types à évoquer, dans cet intermonde de la féerie bretonne qui, chez mes compatriotes, ne se confond ni avec ce monde-ci, ni avec l'autre, mais participe à la fois de tous les deux, par un singulier mélange de naturel et de surnaturel. Je n'ai voulu, en ces lignes rapides, que montrer la richesse de la matière à laquelle vous avez, avec tant de conscience et

of a more ancient religion in which a belief in fairies held the chief place. The same, I feel sure, applies to those death-myths which I have collected under the name of the Legend of the Dead among the Armorican Bretons. In truth, in the Breton mind, the dead are not dead ; they live a mysterious life on the edge of real life, but their world remains fully mingled with ours, and as soon as night falls, as soon as the living, properly so called, give themselves up to the temporary sleep of death, the so-called dead again become the inhabitants of the earth which they have never left. They resume their place at their former hearth, devote themselves to their old work, take an interest in the home, the fields, the boat ; they behave, in a word, like the race of male and female fairies which once formed a more refined and delicate species of humanity in the midst of ordinary humanity.

.   .   .   .

I might, my dear Mr. Wentz, evoke many other types from this intermediate world of Breton Faerie, which, in my countrymen's mind, is not identical with this world nor with the other, but shares at once in both, through a curious mixture of the natural and supernatural. I have only intended in these hasty lines to show the wealth of material to which you have

de ferveur, appliqué votre effort. Et maintenant, que les fées vous soient douces, mon cher ami ! Elles ne seront que justes en favorisant de toute leur tendresse le jeune et brillant écrivain qui vient de restaurer leur culte en rénovant leur gloire.

RENNES,
ce 1ᵉʳ *novembre* 1910.

BRETON FAIRIES OR *FÉES*

In Lower Brittany, which is the genuinely Celtic part of Armorica, instead of finding a widespread folk-belief in fairies of the kind existing in Wales, Ireland, and Scotland, we find a widespread folk-belief in the existence of the dead, and to a less extent in that of the *corrigan* tribes. For our Psychological Theory this is very significant. It seems to indicate that among the Bretons—who are one of the most conservative Celtic peoples—the Fairy-Faith finds its chief expression in a belief that men live after death in an invisible world, just as in Ireland the dead and fairies live in Fairyland. This opinion was first suggested to me by Professor Anatole Le Braz, author of *La Légende de la Mort*, and by Professor Georges Dottin, both of the University of Rennes. But before evidence to sustain and to illustrate this opinion is offered, it will be well to consider the less important Breton *fées* or beings like them, and then *corrigans* and *nains* (dwarfs).

The ' Grac'hed Coz'.—F. M. Luzel, who collected so many of the popular stories in Brittany, found that what few *fées* or fairies there are almost always appear in folk-lore as little old women, or as the Breton story-teller usually calls them, *Grac'hed coz*. I have selected and abridged

with so much conscientiousness and ardour devoted your efforts. And now may the fairies be propitious to you, my dear friend ! They will do nothing but justice in favouring with all their goodwill the young and brilliant writer who has but now revived their cult by renewing their glory.

RENNES,
November 1, 1910.

the following legendary tale from his works to illustrate the nature of these Breton fairy-folk :—

In ancient times, as we read in *La Princesse Blondine*, a rich nobleman had three sons ; the oldest was called Cado, the second, Méliau, and the youngest, Yvon. One day, as they were together in a forest with their bows and arrows, they met a little old woman whom they had never seen before, and she was carrying on her head a jar of water. ' Are you able, lads,' Cado asked his two brothers, ' to break with an arrow the jar of the little old woman without touching her ? ' ' We do not wish to try it,' they said, fearing to injure the good woman. ' All right, I'll do it then, watch me.' And Cado took his bow and let fly an arrow. The arrow went straight to its mark and split the jar without touching the little old woman ; but the water wet her to the skin, and, in anger, she said to the skilful archer : ' You have failed, Cado, and I will be revenged on you for this. From now until you have found the Princess Blondine all the members of your body will tremble as leaves on a tree tremble when the north wind blows.' And instantly Cado was seized by a trembling malady in all his body. The three brothers returned home and told their father what had happened ; and the father, turning to Cado, said : ' Alas, my unfortunate son, you have failed. It is now necessary for you to travel until you find the Princess Blondine, as the *fée* said, for that little old woman was a *fée*, and no doctor in the world can cure the malady she has put upon you.' [1]

' *Fées* ' *of Lower Brittany.*—Throughout the Morbihan and Finistère, I found that stories about *fées* are much less common than about *corrigans*, and in some localities extremely rare ; but the ones I have been fortunate enough to collect are much the same in character as those gathered in the Côtes-du-Nord by Luzel, and elsewhere by other collectors. Those I here record were told to me at Carnac during the summer of 1909 ; the first one by M. Yvonne Daniel,

---

[1] Cf. F. M. Luzel, *Contes populaires de Basse-Bretagne* (Paris, 1887), i. 177–97 ; following the account of Ann Drann, a servant at Coat-Fual, Plouguernevel (Côtes-du-Nord), November 1855.

a native of the Île de Croix (off the coast north-west of
Carnac) ; and the others by M. Goulven Le Scour.[1]
' The little Île de Croix was especially famous for its old
fées ; and the following legend is still believed by its oldest
inhabitants :—" An aged man who had suffered long from
leprosy was certain to die within a short time, when a woman
bent double with age entered his house. She asked from
what malady he suffered, and on being informed began to
say prayers. Then she breathed upon the sores of the
leper, and almost suddenly disappeared : the *fée* had cured
him." '
' It is certain that about fifty years ago the people in
Finistère still believed in *fées*. It was thought that the *fées*
were spirits who came to predict some unexpected event in
the family. They came especially to console orphans who
had very unkind step-mothers. In their youth, Tanguy du
Chatel and his sister Eudes were protected by a *fée* against
the misfortune which pursued them ; the history of Brittany
says so. In Léon it is said that the *fées* served to guide
unfortunate people, consoling them with the promise of
a happy and victorious future. In the Cornouailles, on the
contrary, it is said that the *fées* were very evilly disposed,
that they were demons.
' My grandmother, Marie Le Bras, had related to me that
one evening an old *fée* arrived in my village, Kerouledic
(Finistère), and asked for hospitality. It was about the year
1830. The *fée* was received ; and before going to bed she
predicted that the little daughter whom the mother was
dressing in night-clothes would be found dead in the cradle
the next day. This prediction was only laughed at ; but in
the morning the little one was dead in her cradle, her eyes
raised toward Heaven. The *fée*, who had slept in the stable,
was gone.'

[1] My Breton friend, M. Goulven Le Scour, was born November 20,
1851, at Kerouledic in Plouneventer, Finistère. He is an antiquarian,
a poet, and, as we shall see, a folk-lorist of no mean ability. In 1902, at
the *Congrès d'Auray* of Breton poets and singers, he won two prizes for
poetry, and, in 1901, a prize at the *Congrès de Quimperlé* or *Concours de
Recueils poétiques*.

In these last three accounts, by M. Le Scour, we observe three quite different ideas concerning the Breton fairies or *fées* : in Finistère and in Léon the *fées* are regarded as good protecting spirits, almost like ancestral spirits, which originally they may have been ; in the Cornouailles they are evil spirits ; while in the third account, about the old *fée*—and in the legend of the leper cured by a *fée*—the *fées* are rationalized, as in Luzel's tale quoted above, into sorceresses or *Grac'hed Coz*.

Children Changed by ' Fées '.—M. Goulven Le Scour, at my request, wrote down in French the following account of actual changelings in Finistère :—' I remember very well that there was a woman of the village of Kergoff, in Plouneventer, who was called ——,[1] the mother of a family. When she had her first child, a very strong and very pretty boy, she noticed one morning that he had been changed during the night ; there was no longer the fine baby she had put to bed in the evening ; there was, instead, an infant hideous to look at, greatly deformed, hunchbacked, and crooked, and of a black colour. The poor woman knew that a *fée* had entered the house during the night and had changed her child.

' This changed infant still lives, and to-day he is about seventy years old. He has all the possible vices ; and he has tried many times to kill his mother. He is a veritable demon ; he often predicts the future, and has a habit of running abroad during the night. They call him the " Little *Corrigan* ", and everybody flees from him. Being poor and infirm now, he has been obliged to beg, and people give him alms because they have great fear of him. His nick-name is Olier.

' This woman had a second, then a third child, both of whom were seen by everybody to have been born with no infirmity ; and, in turn, each of these two was stolen by a *fée* and replaced by a little hunchback. The second child was a most beautiful daughter. She was *taken* during the

---

[1] This story concerns persons still living, and, at M. Le Scour's suggestion, I have omitted their names.

night and replaced by a little girl babe, so deformed that it resembled a ball. If her brother Olier was bad, she was even worse ; she was the terror of the village, and they called her Anniac. The third child met the same luck, but was not so bad as the first and second.

' The poor mother, greatly worried at seeing what had happened, related her troubles to another woman. This woman said to her, " If you have another child, place with it in the cradle a little sprig of box-wood which has been blessed (by a priest), and the *fée* will no longer have the power of stealing your children." And when a fourth child was born to the unfortunate woman it was not stolen, for she placed in the cradle a sprig of box-wood which had been blessed on Palm Sunday (*Dimanche des Rameaux*).[1]

' The first three children I knew very well, and they were certainly hunchbacked : it is pretended in the country that the *fées* who come at night to make changelings always leave in exchange hunchbacked infants. It is equally pretended that a mother who has had her child so changed need do nothing more than leave the little hunchback out of doors crying during entire hours, and that the *fée* hearing it will come and put the true child in its place. Unfortunately, Yvonna —— did not know what she should have done in order to have her own children again.'

Transformation Power of ' Fées '.—At Kerallan, near Carnac, this is what Madame Louise Le Rouzic said about the transformation power of *fées* :—' It is said that the *fées* of the region when insulted sometimes changed men into beasts or into stones.'[2]

Other Breton Fairies.—Besides the various types of *fées* already described, we find in Luzel's collected stories a few

---

[1] By a Carnac family I was afterwards given a sprig of such blessed box-wood, and was assured that its exorcizing power is still recognized by all old Breton families, most of whom seem to possess branches of it.

[2] This idea seems related to the one in the popular Morbihan legend of how St. Cornely, the patron saint of the country and the saint who presides over the Alignements and domestic horned animals, changed into upright stones the pagan forces opposing him when he arrived near Carnac ; and these stones are now the famous Alignements of Carnac.

other types of fairy-like beings : in *Les Compagnons* (The Companions),[1] the *fée* is a magpie in a forest near Rennes—just as in other Celtic lands, fairies likewise often appear as birds (see our study, pp. 302 ff.) ; in *La Princesse de l'Étoile Brillante* (The Princess of the Brilliant Star),[1] a princess under the form of a duck plays the part of a fairy (cf. how fairy women took the form of water-fowls in the tale entitled the *Sick Bed of Cuchulainn* (see our study, p. 345) ; in *Pipi Menou et les Femmes Volantes* (Pipi Menou and the Flying Women),[1] there are fairy women as swan-maidens ; and then there are yet to be mentioned *Les Morgans de l'île d'Ouessant* (The *Morgans* of the Isle of Ushant), who live under the sea in rare palaces where mortals whom they love and marry are able to exist with them.   In some legends of the *Morgans*, like one recorded by Luzel, the men and women of this water-fairy race, or the *Morgans* and *Morganezed*, seem like anthropomorphosed survivals of ancient sea-divinities, such, for example, as the sea-god called *Shony*, to whom the people of Lewis, Western Hebrides, still pour libations that he may send in sea-weed, and the sea-god to whom anciently the people of Iona poured libations.[2]

The ' Morgan '.—To M. J. Cuillandre (Glanmor), President of the *Fédération des Étudiants Bretons*, I am indebted for the following weird legend of the *Morgan*, as it is told among the Breton fisher-folk on the Île Molène, Finistère :—
' Following a legend which I have collected on the Île Molène, the *Morgan* is a fairy eternally young, a virgin seductress whose passion, never satisfied, drives her to despair. Her place of abode is beneath the sea ; there she possesses marvellous palaces where gold and diamonds glimmer. Accompanied by other fairies, of whom she is in some respects the queen, she rises to the surface of the waters in the splendour of her unveiled beauty. By day she slumbers amid the coolness of grottoes, and woe to him who troubles her sleep. By night she lets herself be lulled by the waves in the neighbourhood of the rocks. The sea-foam crystallizes at her

---

[1] Luzel, op. cit., iii. 226-311 ; i. 128-218 ; ii. 349-54.
[2] Ib., ii. 269 ; cf. our study, p. 93.

touch into precious stones, of whiteness as dazzling as that of her body. By moonlight she moans as she combs her fair hair with a comb of fine gold, and she sings in a harmonious voice a plaintive melody whose charm is irresistible. The sailor who listens to it feels himself drawn toward her, without power to break the charm which drags him onward to his destruction ; the bark is broken upon the reefs : the man is in the sea, and the *Morgan* utters a cry of joy. But the arms of the fairy clasp only a corpse ; for at her touch men die, and it is this which causes the despair of the amorous and inviolate *Morgan*. She being pagan, it suffices to have been touched by her in order to suffer the saddest fate which can be reserved to a Christian. The unfortunate one whom she had clasped is condemned to wander for ever in the trough of the waters, his eyes wide open, the mark of baptism effaced from his forehead. Never will his poor remains know the sweetness of reposing in holy ground, never will he have a tomb where his kindred might come to pray and to weep.'

Origin of the ' Morgan '.—The following legendary origin is attributed to the *Morgan* by M. Goulven Le Scour, our Carnac witness :—' Following the old people and the Breton legends, the *Morgan* (*Mari Morgan* in Breton) was Dahut, the daughter of King Gradlon, who was ruler of the city of Is. Legend records that when Dahut had entered at night the bedchamber of her father and had cut from around his neck the cord which held the key of the sea-dike flood-gates, and had given this key to the Black Prince, under whose evil love she had fallen, and who, according to belief, was no other than the Devil, St. Guenolé soon afterwards began to cry aloud, " Great King, arise ! The flood-gates are open, and the sea is no longer restrained ! "[1] Suddenly the old King Gradlon arose, and, leaping on his horse, was fleeing from the city with St. Guenolé, when he encountered his

---

[1] According to the annotations to a legend recorded by Villemarqué, in his *Barzaz Breiz*, pp. 39–44, and entitled the *Submersion de la Ville d'Is*, St. Guenolé was traditionally the founder of the first monastery raised in Armorica ; and Dahut the princess stole the key from her sleeping father in order fittingly to crown a banquet and midnight debaucheries which were being held in honour of her lover, the Black Prince.

own daughter amid the waves. She piteously begged aid of
her father, and he took her up behind him on the horse ;
but St. Guenolé, seeing that the waters were gaining on
them, said to the king, " Throw into the sea the demon you
have behind you, and we shall be saved ! " Thereupon
Gradlon flung his daughter into the abyss, and he and
St. Guenolé were saved. Since that time, the fishermen
declare that they have seen, in times of rough sea and clear
moonlight, Dahut, daughter of King Gradlon, sitting on the
rocks combing her fair hair and singing, in the place where
her father flung her. And to-day there is recognized under
the Breton name *Marie Morgan*, the daughter who sings
amid the sea.'

Breton Fairyland Legends.—In a legend concerning Mona
and the king of the *Morgans*, much like the Christabel story
of English poets, we have a picture of a fairyland not under
ground, but under sea ; and this legend of Mona and her
Morgan lover is one of the most beautiful of all the fairy-
tales of Brittany.[1] Another one of Luzel's legends, concerning a maiden who married a dead man, shows us Fairyland
as a world of the dead. It is a very strange legend, and one
directly bearing on the Psychological Theory ; for this dead
man, who is a dead priest, has a palace in a realm of enchantment, and to enter his country one must have a white fairy-
wand with which to strike ' in the form of a cross ' two blows
upon the rock concealing the entrance.[1] M. Paul Sébillot
records from Upper Brittany a tradition that beneath the
sea-waves there one can see a subterranean world containing fields and villages and beautiful castles ; and it is so
pleasant a world that mortals going there find years no
longer than days.[2]

Fairies of Upper Brittany.[3]—Principally in Upper Brittany,
M. Sébillot found rich folk-lore concerning *fées*, though

[1] Luzel, op. cit., ii. 257–68 ; i. 3–13.
[2] P. Sébillot, *Traditions et superstitions de la Haute-Bretagne* (Paris,
1882), i. 100.
[3] General references : Sébillot, ib. ; and his *Folk-Lore de France* (Paris,
1905).

some of his material is drawn from peasants and fishermen who are not so purely Celtic as those in Lower Brittany ; and he very concisely summarizes the various names there given to the fairy-folk as follows :—' They are generally called *Fées* (Fairies), sometimes *Fêtes* (Fates), a name nearer than *fées* to the Latin *Fata* ; *Fête* (fem.) and *Fête* (mas.) are both used, and from *Fête* is probably derived *Faito* or *Faitaud*, which is the name borne by the fathers, the husbands, or the children of the *fées* (Saint-Cast). Near Saint-Briac (Ille-et-Vilaine) they are sometimes called *Fions* ; this term, which is applied to both sexes, seems also to designate the mischievous *lutins* (sprites). Round the Mené, in the cantons of Collinée and of Moncontour, they are called *Margot la Fée*, or *ma Commère* (my Godmother) *Margot*, or even the *Bonne Femme* (Good Woman) *Margot*. On the coast they are often enough called by the name of *Bonnes Dames* (Good Ladies), or of *nos Bonnes Mères les Fées* (our Good Mothers the Fairies) ; usually they are spoken of with a certain respect.' [1] As the same authority suggests, probably the most characteristic *Fées* in Upper Brittany are the *Fées des Houles* (Fairies of the Billows) ; and traditions say that they lived in natural caverns or grottoes in the sea-cliffs. They form a distinct class of sea-fairies unknown elsewhere in France or Europe.[2] M. Sébillot regards them as sea-divinities greatly rationalized. Associated with them are the *fions*, a race of dwarfs having swords no bigger than pins.[2] A pretty legend about magic buckwheat cakes, which in different forms is widespread throughout all Brittany, is told of these little cave-dwelling fairies :—

Like the larger *fées* the *fions* kept cattle ; and one day a black cow belonging to the *fions* of Pont-aux-Hommes-Nées ate the buckwheat in the field of a woman of that neighbourhood. The woman went to the *fions* to complain, and in reply to her a voice said : ' Hold your tongue ; you will be paid for your buckwheat ! ' Thereupon the *fions* gave the woman a cupful of buckwheat, and promised her

[1] Sébillot, *Traditions et superstitions de la Haute-Bretagne*, i. 73-4.
[2] Ib., i. 102, 103-4.

that it would never diminish so long as none should be given away. That year buckwheat was very scarce, but no matter how many buckwheat cakes the woman and her family ate there was never diminution in the amount of the fairy buckwheat. At last, however, the unfortunate hour came. A rag-gatherer arrived and asked for food. Thoughtlessly the woman gave him one of her buckwheat cakes, and suddenly, as though by magic, all the rest of the buckwheat disappeared for ever.

Along the Rance the inhabitants tell about *fées* who appear during storms. These storm-fairies are dressed in the colours of the rainbow, and pass along following a most beautiful *fee* who is mounted in a boat made from a nautilus of the southern seas. And the boat is drawn by two sea-crabs. In no other place in Brittany are similar *fées* said to exist.[1] In Upper Brittany, as in Lower Brittany, the *fées* generally had their abodes in tumuli, in dolmens, in forests, in waste lands where there are great rocks, or about menhirs ; and many other kinds of spirits lived in the sea and troubled sailors and fisher-folk. Like all fairy-folk of Celtic countries, those of Upper Brittany were given to stealing children. Thus at Dinard not long ago there was a woman more than thirty years old who was no bigger than a girl of ten, and it was said she was a fairy changeling.[2] In Lower Brittany the *taking* of children was often attributed to dwarfs rather than to *fées*, though the method of making the changeling speak is the same as in Upper Brittany, namely, to place in such a manner before an open fire a number of eggshells filled with water that they appear to the changeling—who is placed where he can well observe all the proceedings—like so many small pots of cooking food ; whereupon, being greatly astonished at the unusual sight, he forgets himself and speaks for the first time, thus betraying his demon nature.

The following midwife story, as told by J. M. Comault, of Gouray, in 1881, is quite a parallel to the one we have recorded (on p. 54) as coming from Grange, Ireland :—

[1] Sébillot, *Traditions et superstitions de la Haute-Bretagne*, i. 83.
[2] Ib., i. 90-1.

A midwife who delivered a *Margot la fée* carelessly allowed some of the fairy ointment to get on one of her own eyes. The eye at once became clairvoyant, so that she beheld the *fées* in their true nature. And, quite like a midwife in a similar story about the *fées des houles*, this midwife happened to see a *fée* in the act of stealing, and spoke to her. Thereupon the *fée* asked the midwife with which eye she beheld her, and when the midwife indicated which one it was, the *fée* pulled it out.[1]

Generally, like their relatives in insular Celtdom, the fairies of Upper Brittany could assume various forms, and could even transform the human body ; and they were given to playing tricks on mortals, and always to taking revenge on them if ill-treated. In most ways they were like other races of fairies, Celtic and non-Celtic, though very much anthropomorphosed in their nature by the peasant and mariner.

As a rule, the *fées* of Upper Brittany are described in legend as young and very beautiful. Some, however, appear to be centuries old, with teeth as long as a human hand, and with backs covered with seaweeds, and mussels, or other marine growths, as an indication of their great age.[2] At Saint-Cast they are said to be dressed (like the *corrigans* at Carnac, see p. 208) in *toile*, a kind of heavy linen cloth.[2]

On the sea-coast of Upper Brittany the popular opinion is that the *fées* are a fallen race condemned to an earthly exile for a certain period. In the region of the Mené, canton of Collinée, the old folk say that, after the angels revolted, those left in paradise were divided into two parts : those who fought on the side of God and those who remained neutral. These last, already half-fallen, were sent to the earth for a time, and became the *fées*.[2]

The general belief in the interior of Brittany is that the *fées* once existed, but that they disappeared as their country was changed by modern conditions. In the region of the Mené and of Ercé (Ille-et-Vilaine) it is said that for more than a century there have been no *fées* ; and on the sea-coast,

---

[1] Cf. ib., i. 109.   [2] Cf. ib., i. 74-5, &c.

where it is still firmly believed that the *fées* used to live in
the billows or amid certain grottoes in the cliffs against
which the billows broke, the opinion is that they disappeared
at the beginning of the last century. The oldest Bretons
say that their parents or grandparents often spoke about
having seen *fées*, but very rarely do they say that they
themselves have seen *fées*. M. Sébillot found only two who
had. One was an old needle-woman of Saint-Cast, who had
such fear of *fées* that if she was on her way to do some
sewing in the country, and it was night, she always took
a long circuitous route to avoid passing near a field known
as the *Couvent des Fées*. The other was Marie Chéhu,
a woman eighty-eight years old.[1]

THE *CORRIGAN* RACE [2]

It is the *corrigan* race, however, which, more than *fées* or
fairies, forms a large part of the invisible inhabitants of
Brittany ; and this race of *corrigans* and *nains* (dwarfs)
may be made to include many kinds of *lutins*, or as they are
often called by the peasant, *follets* or *esprits follets* (playful
elves). Though the peasants both in Upper and in Lower
Brittany may have no strong faith in *fées*, most of them say
that *corrigans*, or *nains*, and mischievous house-haunting
spirits still exist. But in a few localities, as M. Sébillot
discovered, there is an opinion that the *lutins* departed with
the *fées*, and with them will return in this century, because
during each century with an odd number like 1900, the fairy
tribes of all kinds are said to be visible or to reappear among
men, and to become invisible or to disappear during each
century with an even number like 1800. So this is the visible
century.

Corrigans and *follets* only show themselves at night, or in
the twilight. No one knows where they pass the day-time.

---

[1] Cf. Sébillot, *Traditions et superstitions de la Haute-Bretagne*, i, 74–5, &c.
[2] In Lower Brittany the *corrigan* tribes collectively are commonly called
Corrikêt, masculine plural of *Corrik*, diminutive of *Corr*, meaning ' Dwarf ' ;
or *Corriganed*, feminine plural of *Corrigan*, meaning ' Little Dwarf '.
Many other forms are in use. (Cf. R. F. Le Men, *Trad. et supers. de la
Basse-Bretagne*, in *Rev. Celt.*, i. 226–7.)

Some *lutins* or *follets*, after the manner of Scotch kelpies, live solitary lives in lakes or ponds (whereas *corrigans* are socially united in groups or families), and amuse themselves by playing tricks on travellers passing by after dark. Souvestre records a story showing how the *lutins* can assume any animal form, but that their natural form is that of a little man dressed in green ; and that the *corrigans* have declared war on them for being too friendly to men.[1] From what follows about *lutins*, by M. Goulven Le Scour, they show affinity with Pucks and such shape-shifting hobgoblins as are found in Wales :—' The *lutins* were little dwarfs who generally appeared at cross-roads to attack belated travellers. And it is related in Breton legends that these *lutins* sometimes transformed themselves into black horses or into goats ; and whoever then had the misfortune to encounter them sometimes found his life in danger, and was always seized with great terror.' But generally, what the Breton peasant tells about *corrigans* he is apt to tell at another time about *lutins*. And both tribes of beings, so far as they can be distinguished, are the same as the elfish peoples—pixies in Cornwall, Robin Good-fellows in England, goblins in Wales, or brownies in Scotland. Both *corrigans* and *lutins* are supposed to guard hidden treasure ; some trouble horses at night ; some, like their English cousins, may help in the house-work after all the family are asleep ; some cause nightmare ; some carry a torch like a Welsh death-candle ; some trouble men and women like obsessing spirits ; and nearly all of them are mischievous. In an article in the *Revue des Traditions Populaires* (v. 101), M. Sébillot has classified more than fifty names given to *lutins* and *corrigans* in Lower Brittany, according to the form under which these spirits appear, their peculiar traits, dwelling-places, and the country they inhabit.

Like the fairies in Britain and Ireland, the *corrigans* and the Cornish pixies find their favourite amusement in the circular dance. When the moon is clear and bright they gather for their frolic near menhirs, and dolmens, and

---

[1] Cf. *Foyer breton*, i. 199.

tumuli, and at cross-roads, or even in the open country ;
and they never miss an opportunity of enticing a mortal
passing by to join them. If he happens to be a good-natured
man and enters their sport heartily, they treat him quite as
a companion, and may even do him some good turn ; but if
he is not agreeable they will make him dance until he falls
down exhausted, and should he commit some act thoroughly
displeasing to them he will meet their certain revenge. According to a story reported from Lorient (Morbihan) [1] it is taboo
for the *corrigans* to make a complete enumeration of the
days of the week :—

The ' Corrigan ' Taboo.—' At night, the *corrigans* dance,
singing, "Monday, Tuesday, Wednesday, Thursday, Friday";
they are prohibited from completing the enumeration of the
days of the week. A *corrigan* having had the misfortune to
permit himself to be tempted to add " Saturday ", immediately became hunchbacked. His comrades, stupefied and
distressed, attempted in vain to knock in his hump with
blows of their fists.'

' *Corrigans* ' *at Carnac.*—How the tradition of the dancing
corrigans and their weekday song still lives, appears from
the following accounts which I found at and near Carnac,
the first account having been given during January 1909
by Madame Marie Ezanno, of Carnac, then sixty-six years
old :—' The *corrigans* are little dwarfs who formerly, by
moonlight, used to dance in a circle on the prairies. They
sang a song the couplet of which was not understood, but
only the refrain, translated in Breton : " *Di Lun* (Monday),
Di Merh (Tuesday), *Di Merhier* (Wednesday)."

' They whistled in order to assemble. Where they danced
mushrooms grew ; and it was necessary to maintain silence
so as not to interrupt them in their dance. They were often
very brutal towards a man who fell under their power, and
if they had a grudge against him they would make him
submit to the greatest tortures. The peasants believed
strongly in the *corrigans*, because they thus saw them and
heard them. The *corrigans* dressed in very coarse white

---

[1] By ' E. R.', in *Mélusine* (Paris), i. 114.

linen cloth. They were mischievous spirits (*esprits follets*), who lived under dolmens.'

One morning, M. Lemort and myself called upon Madame Louise Le Rouzic in her neat home at Kerallan, a little group of thatched cottages about a mile from Carnac. As we entered, Madame Le Rouzic herself was sitting on a long wooden bench by the window knitting, and her daughter was watching the savoury-smelling dinner as it boiled in great iron pots hanging from chains over a brilliant fire on the hearth. Large gleaming brass basins were ranged on a shelf above the broad open chimney-place wherein the fire burned, and massive bedsteads carved after the Breton style stood on the stone floor. When many things had been talked about, our conversation turned to *corrigans*, and then the good woman of the house told us these tales :—

'*Corrigans*' *at Church.*—' In former times a young girl having taken the keys of the church (presumably at Carnac) and having entered it, found the *corrigans* about to dance ; and the *corrigans* were singing, "*Lundi, Mardi*" (Monday, Tuesday). On seeing the young girl, they stopped, surrounded her, and invited her to dance with them. She accepted, and, in singing, added to their song "*Mercredi*" (Wednesday). In amazement, the *corrigans* cried joyfully, " She has added something to our song ; what shall we give her as recompense ? " And they gave her a bracelet. A friend of hers meeting her, asked where the fine bracelet came from ; and the young girl told what had happened. The second girl hurried to the church, and found the *corrigans* still dancing the *rond*. She joined their dance, and, in singing, added " *Jeudi* " (Thursday) to their song ; but that broke the cadence ; and the *corrigans* in fury, instead of recompensing her wished to punish her. " What shall we do to her ? " one of them cried. " Let the day be as night to her ! " the others replied. And by day, wherever she went, she saw only the night.'

The ' Corrigans' ' *Sabbath.*—' Where my grandfather lived,' continued Madame Le Rouzic, ' there was a young girl who went to the sabbath of the *corrigans* ; and when she returned

and was asked where she had been, said, " I have travelled
over water, wood, and hedges." And she related all she had
seen and heard. Then one night, afterwards, the *corrigans*
came into the house, beat her, and dragged her from bed.
Upon hearing the uproar, my grandfather arose and found
the girl lying flat on the stone floor. " Never question me
again," she said to him, " or they will kill me." ' [1]

' *Corrigans* ' *as Fairies.*—Some Breton legends give *corrigans* the chief characteristics of fairies in Celtic Britain and
Ireland ; and Villemarqué in his *Barzaz Breiz* (pp. 25–30)
makes the Breton word *corrigan* synonymous with *fée* or
fairy, thus :—' *Le Seigneur Nann et la Fée* (*Aotrou Nann hag
ar Corrigan*).' In this legend the *corrigan* seems clearly
enough to be a water-fairy : ' The *Korrigan* was seated at
the edge of her fountain, and she was combing her long fair
hair.' But unlike most water-fairies, the *Fée* lives in a grotto,
which, according to Villemarqué, is one of those ancient
monuments called in Breton *dolmen*, or *ti ar corrigan* ; in
French, *Table de pierres*, or *Grotte aux Fées*—like the famous
one near Rennes. The fountain where the *Fée* was seated
seems to be one of those sacred fountains, which, as Villemarqué says, are often found near a *Grotte aux Fées*, and
called *Fontaine de la Fée*, or in Breton, *Feunteun ar corrigan*.

' In another of Villemarqué's legends, *L'Enfant Supposé*,
after the egg-shell test has been used and the little *corrigan*-
changeling is replaced by the real child, the latter, as though all
the while it had been in an unconscious trance-state—which

---

[1] This account about *corrigans*, more rational than any preceding it,
may possibly refer to a dream or trance-like state of mind on the part of
the young girl ; and if it does, we can then compare the presence of a mortal
at this *corrigan* sabbath, or even at the ordinary witches' sabbath, to the
presence of a mortal in Fairyland. And according to popular Breton belief,
as reliable peasants assure me, during dreams, trance, or ecstasy, the soul
is supposed to depart from the body and actually see spirits of all kinds
in another world, and to be then under their influence. While many details
in the more conventional *corrigan* stories appear to reflect a folk-memory
of religious dances and songs, and racial, social, and traditional usages of
the ancient Bretons, the animistic background of them could conceivably
have originated from psychical experiences such as this girl is supposed to
have had.

has a curious bearing on our Psychological Theory—stretches forth its arms and awakening exclaims, ' Ah ! mother, what a long time I have been asleep.' [1] And in *Les Nains* we see the little *Duz* or dwarfs inhabiting a cave and guarding treasures.[1]

In his introduction to the *Barzaz Breiz*, Villemarqué describes *les korrigan*, whom he equates with *les fées*, as very similar to ordinary fairies. They can foretell the future, they know the art of war—quite like the Irish ' gentry ' or Tuatha De Danann—they can assume any animal form, and are able to travel from one end of the world to another in the twinkling of an eye. They love feasting and music—like all Celtic fairy-folk ; and dance in a circle holding hands, but at the least noise disappear. Their favourite haunts are near fountains and dolmens. They are little beings not more than two feet high, and beautifully proportioned, with bodies as aerial and transparent as those of wasps. And like all fairy, or elvish races, and like the Breton *Morgans* or water-spirits, they are given to stealing the children of mortals. Professor J. Loth has called my attention to an unpublished Breton legend of his collection, in which there are fairy-like beings comparable to these described by Villemarqué ; and he tells me, too, that throughout Brittany one finds to-day the counterpart of the Welsh *Tylwyth Teg* or ' Fair Family ', and that both in Wales and Brittany the *Tylwyth Teg* are popularly described as little women, or maidens, like fairies no larger than children.

Fairies and Dwarfs.—Where Villemarqué draws a clear distinction is between these *korrigan* and *fées* on the one hand, and the *nains* or dwarfs on the other. These last are what we have found associated or identified with *corrigans* in the Morbihan. Villemarqué describes the *nains* as a hideous race of beings with dark or even black hairy bodies, with voices like old men, and with little sparkling black eyes. They are fond of playing tricks on mortals who fall into their power ; and are given to singing in a circular dance the week-day song. Very often *corrigans* regarded as *nains*, equally with all kinds of *lutins*, are believed to be evil spirits or

[1] Villemarqué, *Barzaz Breiz* (Paris, 1867), pp. 33, 35.

demons condemned to live here on earth in a penitential state
for an indefinite time ; and sometimes they seem not much
different from what Irish Celts, when talking of fairies, call
fallen angels. *Le Nain de Kerhuiton*, translated from Breton
by Professor J. Loth, in part illustrates this :—Upon seeing
water boiling in a number of egg-shells ranged before an open
fire, a *polpegan*-changeling is so greatly astonished that he
unwittingly speaks for the first time, and says, ' Here I
am almost one hundred years old, and never such a thing
have I yet seen ! ' ' Ah ! son of Satan ! ' then cries out the
mother, as she comes from her place of hiding and beats the
polpegan—who thus by means of the egg-shell test has been
tricked into revealing his demon nature.[1]   In a parallel
story, reported by Villemarqué in his *Barzaz Breiz* (p. 33 n.),
a *nain*-changeling is equally astonished to see a similar row
of egg-shells boiling before an open fire like so many pots of
food, and gives himself away through the following remark :
—' I have seen the acorn before the oak ; I have seen the
egg before the white chicken : I have never seen the equal
to this.'

Nature of the ' Corrigans '.—As to the general ideas about
the *corrigans*, M. Le Scour says :—' Formerly the *corrigans*
were the terror of the country-folk, especially in Finistère, in the Morbihan, and throughout the Côtes-du-Nord.
They were believed to be souls in pain, condemned to wander
at night in waste lands and marshes. Sometimes they were
seen as dwarfs ; and often they were not seen at all, but
were heard in houses making an infernal noise.   Unlike the
lavandières de nuits (phantom washerwomen of the night),
they were heard only in summer, never in winter.'

THE BRETON LEGEND OF THE DEAD

We come now to the Breton Legend of the Dead, common
generally to all parts of Armorica, though probably even
more widespread in Lower Brittany than in Upper Brittany ;
and this we call the Armorican Fairy-Faith. Even where
the peasants have no faith in *fées* or fairies, and where their

[1] J. Loth, in *Annales de Bretagne* (Rennes), x. 78-81.

faith in *corrigans* is weak or almost gone, there is a strong conviction among them that the souls of the dead can show themselves to the living, a vigorous belief in apparitions, phantom-funerals, and various death-warnings. As Professor Anatole Le Braz has so well said in his introduction to *La Légende de la Mort*, ' the whole conscience of these people is fundamentally directed toward that which concerns death. And the ideas which they form of it, in spite of the strong Christian imprint which they have received, do not seem much different from those which we have pointed out among their pagan ancestors. For them, as for the primitive Celts, death is less a change of condition than a journey, a departure for another world.' And thus it seems that this most popular of the Breton folk-beliefs is genuinely Celtic and extremely ancient. As Renan has said, the Celtic people are ' a race mysterious, having knowledge of the future and the secret of death '.[1] And whereas in Ireland unusual happenings or strange accidents and death are attributed to fairy interference, in Brittany they are attributed to the influence of the dead.

The Breton Celt makes no distinction between the living and the dead. All alike inhabit this world, the one being visible, the other invisible. Though seers can at all times behold the dead, on November Eve (*La Toussaint*) and on Christmas Eve they are most numerous and most easily seen ; and no peasant would think of questioning their existence. In Ireland and Scotland the country-folk fear to speak of fairies save through an euphemism, and the Bretons speak of the dead indirectly, and even then with fear and trembling.

The following legend, which I found at Carnac, will serve to illustrate both the profundity of the belief in the power of the dead over the living in Lower Brittany, and how deeply the people can be stirred by the predictions of one who can see the dead ; and the legend is quite typical of those so common in Armorica :—

Fortelling Deaths.—' Formerly there was a woman whom

[1] E. Renan, *Essais de morale et de critique* (Paris, 1859), p. 451.

spirits impelled to rise from her bed, it made no difference at what hour of the night, in order to behold funerals in the future. She predicted who should die, who should carry the corpse, who the cross, and who should follow the *cortège.* Her predictions frightened every one, and made her such a terror to the country that the mayor had threatened to take legal proceedings against her if she continued her practice ; but she was compelled to tell the things which the spirits showed her. It is about ten years since this woman died in the hospital at Auray.'

Testimony of a Breton Seeress.—There lives in the little hamlet of Kerlois, less than a mile from Carnac, a Breton seeress, a woman who since eight years of age has been privileged to behold the world invisible and its inhabitants, quite like the woman who died at Auray. She is Madame Eugénie Le Port, now forty-two years old, and what she tells of things seen in this invisible world which surrounds her, might easily be taken for Irish legends about fairies. Knowing very little French, because she is thoroughly Breton, Madame Le Port described her visions in her own native tongue, and her eldest daughter acted as interpreter. I had known the good woman since the previous winter, and so we were able to converse familiarly ; and as I sat in her own little cottage, in company with her husband and daughters, and with M. Lemort, who acted as recording secretary, this is what she said in her clear earnest manner in answer to my questions :—

' We believe that the spirits of our ancestors surround us and live with us. One day on a road from Carnac I encountered a woman of Kergoellec who had been dead eight days. I asked her to move to one side so that I could pass, and she vanished. This was eleven o'clock in the morning. I saw her at another time in the Marsh of Breno ; I spoke, but she did not reply. On the route from Plouharnel (near Carnac) I saw in the day-time the funeral of a woman who did not die until fifteen days afterwards. I recognized perfectly all the people who took part in it ; but the person with me saw nothing. Another time, near three o'clock in the afternoon, and eight days before her death, I saw upon the same route the funeral of a woman who was drowned. And I have seen a phantom horse going to the sabbath, and as if forced along against its will, for it reared and pawed the earth. When Pierre Rouzic of Kerlois died, I saw a light of all colours between heaven and earth, the very night of his death. I have seen a woman asleep whose spirit must have been free, for I saw it hovering outside her body. She was not awakened [at the time] for fear that the spirit would not find its body again.' In answer to my question as to how long these various visions usually lasted, Madame Le Port said :—' They lasted about a quarter of an hour, or less, and all of them disappeared instantaneously.' As Madame Le Port now seemed unable to recall more of her visions, I finally asked her what she thought about *corrigans*, and she replied :—' I believe they exist as some special kind of spirits, though I have never seen any.'

Proof that the Dead Exist.—This is what M. Jean Couton, an old Breton, told me at Carnac :—' I am only an old peasant, without instruction, without any education, but let me tell you what I think concerning the dead. Following my own idea, I believe that after death the soul always exists and travels among us. I repeat to you that I have belief that the dead are seen ; I am now going to prove this to you in the following story :—

' One winter evening I was returning home from a funeral. I had as companion a kinswoman of the man just buried. We took the train and soon alighted in the station of Plouharnel. We still had three kilometres to go before reaching home, and as it was winter, and at that epoch there was no stage-coach, we were obliged to travel afoot. As we were going along, suddenly there appeared to my companion her dead relative whom we had buried that day. She asked me if I saw anything, and since I replied to her negatively she said to me, " Touch me, and you will see without doubt." I touched her, and I saw the same as she did, the person just dead, whom I clearly recognized.' [1]

[1] In Ireland it is commonly held that a seer beholding a fairy can make

Phantom Washerwomen.—Concerning a very popular Breton belief in phantom washerwomen (*les lavandières de nuits* ; or in Breton, *cannered noz*), M. Goulven Le Scour offers the following summary :—' The *lavandières de nuits* were heard less often than the *corrigans*, but were much more feared. It was usually towards midnight that they were heard beating their linen in front of different washing-places, always some way from the villages. According to the old folk of the past generation, when the phantom washerwomen would ask a certain passer-by to help them to wring sheets, he could not refuse, under pain of being stopped and wrung like a sheet himself. And it was necessary for those who aided in wringing the sheets to turn in the same direction as the washerwomen ; for if by misfortune the assistant turned in an opposite direction, he had his arms wrung in an instant. It is believed that these phantom washerwomen are women condemned to wash their mortuary sheets during whole centuries ; but that when they find some mortal to wring in an opposite direction, they are delivered.' [1]

Breton Animistic Beliefs.—M. Z. Le Rouzic, a Breton Celt who has spent most of his life studying the archaeology and folk-lore of the Morbihan, and who is at present Keeper of the Miln Museum at Carnac, summarizes for us the state of popular beliefs as he finds them existing in the Carnac country now :—' There are few traditions concerning the *fées* in the region of Carnac ; but the belief in spirits, good and bad—which seems to me to be the same as the belief in *fées*—is general and profound, as well as the belief in the incarnation of spirits. And I am convinced that these beliefs are the reminiscences of ancient Celtic beliefs held by the Druids and conserved by Christianity.'

In Finistère, as purely Breton as the Morbihan, I found the Legend of the Dead just as widespread, and the belief

a non-seer see it also by coming into bodily *rapport* with the non-seer (cf. p. 152).

[1] It is sometimes believed that phantom washerwomen are undergoing penance for having wilfully brought on an abortion by their work, or else for having strangled their babe.

in spirits and the apparitional return of the dead quite as profound ; but nothing worth recording concerning fairies. The stories which follow were told to me by M. Pierre Vichon, a pure Breton Celt, born at Lescoff, near the Pointe du Raz, Finistère, in 1842. Peter is a genuine old ' sea-dog ', having made the tour of the globe, and yet he has not lost the innate faith of his ancient ancestors in a world invisible ; for though he says he cannot believe all that the people in his part of Finistère tell about spirits and ghosts, he must have a belief that the dead as spirits exist and influence the living, because of his own personal experience—one of the most remarkable of its kind. Peter speaks Breton, French, and English fluently, and since he had an opportunity for the first time in seventeen months of using English, he told me the stories in my own native language :—

Pierre Vichon's Strange Experience.—' Some forty years ago a strange thing happened in my life. A relative of mine had taken service in the Austrian army, for by profession he was a soldier, though at first he had begun to study for the priesthood. During the progress of the war I had no news from him ; and, then one day while I was on the deck of a Norwegian ship just off Dover (England), my fellow sailors heard a noise as though of a gun being discharged, and the whirr of a shot. At the same moment I fell down on the deck as though mortally wounded, and lay in an unconscious state for two hours. When the news came, it was ascertained that at the very moment I fell and the gun-report was heard, my relative in Austria had been shot in the head and fell down dead. And he had been seen to throw his hands up to his head to grasp it just as I did.'

An Apparition of the Dead.—' I had another relative who died in a hospital near Christiania, Norway ; and on the day he died a sister of mine, then a little girl, saw his spirit appear here in Lescoff, and she easily recognized it ; but none of her girl companions with her at the time saw the spirit. After a few days we had the news of the death, and the time of it and the time of my sister's seeing the spirit coincided exactly.'

In all the peninsula of which the famous and dangerous
Pointe du Raz is the terminus, similar stories are current.
And among the fisher-folk with whom I lived on the strange
and historic Île de Sein, the Legend of the Dead is even more
common.

The Dead and Fairies Compared.—Without setting down
here in detail numerous other death-legends which we have
collected, we may now note how much the same are the
powers and nature of the dead and spirits in Brittany, and
the power and nature of the fairy races in Celtic Britain
and Ireland. Thus the Breton dead strike down the living
just as fairies are said to do ; the *Ankou*,[1] who is a king of
the dead, and his subjects, like a fairy king and fairies, have
their own particular paths or roads over which they travel
in great sacred processions ;[2] and exactly as fairies, the
hosts of the dead are in possession of the earth on November
Eve, and the living are expected to prepare a feast and
entertainment for them of curded-milk, hot pancakes, and
cider, served on the family table covered with a fresh white
table-cloth, and to supply music. The Breton dead come to
enjoy this hospitality of their friends ; and as they take
their places at the table the stools are heard to move, and
sometimes the plates ; and the musicians who help to entertain them think that at times they feel the cold breath of the
invisible visitors. Concerning this same feast of the dead
(*La Toussaint*) Villemarqué in his *Barzaz Breiz* (p. 507)
records that in many parts of Brittany libations of milk

---

[1] Every parish in the uncorrupted parts of Brittany has its own *Ankou*,
who is the last man to die in the parish during the year. Each King of the
Dead, therefore, never holds office for more than twelve months, since
during that period he is certain to have a successor. Sometimes the *Ankou*
is Death itself personified. In the Morbihan, the *Ankou* occasionally may
be seen as an apparition entering a house where a death is about to occur ;
though more commonly he is never seen, his knocking only is heard, which
is the rule in Finistère. In Welsh mythology, Gwynn ab Nudd, king of
the world of the dead, is represented as playing a rôle parallel to that
of the Breton *Ankou*, when he goes forth with his fierce hades-hounds hunting
the souls of the dying. (Cf. Rhŷs, *Arth. Leg.*, p. 155.)

[2] Cf. A. Le Braz, *La Légende de la Mort* ; Introduction by L. Marillier
(Paris, 1893), pp. 31, 40.

are poured over or near ancestral tombs—just as in Ireland and Scotland libations of milk are poured to fairies. And the people of Armorica at other times than November Eve remember the dead very appropriately, as in Ireland the Irish remember fairies. The Breton peasant thinks of the dead as frequently as the Irishman thinks of fairies. One day while I was walking toward Carnac there was told to me in the most ordinary manner a story about a dead man who used to be seen going along the very road I was on. He quite often went to the church in Carnac seeking prayers for his soul. And almost every man or woman one meets in rural Lower Brittany can tell many similar stories. If a mortal should happen to meet one of the dead in Brittany and be induced to eat food which the dead sometimes offer, he will never be able to return among the living,[1] for the effect would be the same as eating fairy-food. Like ghosts and fairies in Ireland, Scotland, and Wales, in Brittany the dead guard hidden treasure. It is after sunset that the dead have most power to strike down the living,[1] and to *take* them just as fairies do. A natural phenomenon, a malady, a death, or a tempest may be the work of a spirit in Brittany,[1] and in Ireland the work of a fairy. The Breton dead, like the Scotch fairies described in Kirk's *Secret Commonwealth*, are capable of making themselves visible or invisible to mortals, at will.[1] Their bodies—for they have bodies—are material,[1] being composed of matter in a state unknown to us ; and the bodies of daemons as described by the Ancients are made of congealed air. The dead in Brittany have forms more slender and smaller in stature than those of the living ;[1] and herein we find one of the factors which supporters of the Pygmy Theory would emphasize, but it is thoroughly psychical. Old Breton farmers after death return to their farms, as though come from Fairyland ; and sometimes they even take a turn at the ploughing.[1] As in Ireland, so in Brittany, the day belongs to the living, and the night, when a mortal is safer indoors than out, to spirits and the dead.[1] The Bretons

[1] Cf. Le Braz, *La Légende de la Mort* ; Introduction by Marillier, pp. 47, 46, 7-8, 40, 45, 46.

take great care not to counterfeit the dead nor to speak
slightingly of them,[1] for, like fairies, they know all that is
done by mortals, and can hear all that is said about them,
and can take revenge. Just as in the case of all fairies and
goblins, the dead disappear at first cock-crow.[2] The world
of the dead, like the land of Faerie or the Otherworld, may be
underground, in the air, in a hill or mountain like a fairy
palace, under a river or sea, and even on an island out amid
the ocean.[2] As other Celts do against evil spirits and fairies,
the Breton peasants use magic against evil souls of the
dead,[3] and the priests use exorcisms. The Breton realm of
the dead equally with the Irish Fairyland is an invisible
world peopled by other kinds of spirits besides disembodied
mortals and fairies.[4] The dead haunt houses just as Robin
Good-fellows and brownies, or pixies and goblins, generally
do. The dead are fond of frequenting cross-roads, and so
are all sorts of fairies. In Brittany one must always guard
against the evil dead, in Cornwall against pixies, in other
Celtic lands against different kinds of fairies. In Ireland
and Scotland there is the banshee, in Wales the death-
candle, in Brittany the *Ankou* or king of the dead, to foretell
a death. And as the banshee wails before the ancestral
mansion, so the *Ankou* sounds its doleful cry before the door
of the one it calls.[4] There seems not to be a family in the
Carnac region of the Morbihan without some tradition of
a warning coming before the death of one of its members.
In Ireland only certain families have a banshee, but in
Brittany all families. Professor Le Braz has devoted a large
part of his work on *La Légende de la Mort* to these Breton
death-warnings or *intersignes*. They may be shades of the
dead under many aspects—ghostly hands, or ghosts of
inanimate objects. They may come by the fall of objects
without known cause ; by a magpie resting on a roof—just
as in Ireland ; by the crowing of cocks, and the howling of

---

[1] Cf. Le Braz, *La Légende de la Mort*; Introduction by Marillier, p. 43.
[2] Ib. ; Notes by G. Dottin (Paris, 1902), p. 44.
[3] Ib. ; Introduction by Marillier, pp. 19, 23, 68.
[4] Cf. ib. ; Introduction by Marillier, pp. 53 ff., 68.

dogs at night. They may be death-candles or torches, dreams, peculiar bodily sensations, images in water, phantom funerals, and death-chariots or death-coaches as in Wales.

The Bretons may be said to have a Death-Faith, whereas the other Celts have a Fairy-Faith, and both are a real folk-religion innate in the Celtic nature, and thus quite as influential as Christianity. Should Christianity in some way suddenly be swept away from the Celt he would still be religious, for it is his nature to be so. And as Professor Le Braz has suggested to me, Carnac with its strange monuments of an unknown people and time, and wrapped in its air of mystery and silence, is a veritable Land of the Dead. I, too, have felt that there are strange, vague, indefinable influences at work at Carnac at all times of the day and night, very similar to those which I have felt in the most fairy-haunted regions of Ireland. We might say that all of Brittany is a Land of the Dead, and ancient Carnac its Centre, just as Ireland is Fairyland, with its Centre at ancient Tara.

CONCLUSION

We can very appropriately conclude our inquiry about Brittany with a very beautiful description of a *Veillée* in Lower Brittany, written down in French for our special use by the Breton poet, M. Le Scour, of Carnac, and here translated. M. Le Scour draws the whole picture from life, and from his own intimate experience. It will serve to give us some insight into the natural literary ability of the Breton Celts, to illustrate their love of tales dealing with the marvellous and the supernormal, and is especially valuable for showing the social environment amidst which the Fairy-Faith of Lower Brittany lives and flourishes, isolated from foreign interference :—

A ' *Veillée* ' [1] in Lower Brittany.—' The wind was blowing

---

[1] A Breton night's entertainment held in a peasant's cottage, stable, or other warm outhouse. In parts of the Morbihan and of Finistère where the old Celtic life has escaped modern influences, almost every winter night the Breton Celts, like their cousins in very isolated parts of West

from the east, and in the intermittent moonlight the roof of
the thatched cottage already gleamed with a thin covering
of snow which had fallen since sunset. Each comer reached
on the run the comfortable bakehouse, wherein Alain Corre
was at work kneading his batch of barley bread; and the
father Le Scour was never the last to arrive, because he
liked to get the best seat in front of the bake-oven.

' Victor had promised us for that night a pretty story
which no person had ever heard before. I was not more
than fourteen years old then, but like all the neighbours
I hurried to get a place in order to hear Victor. My mother
was already there, making her distaff whirr between her two
fingers as she sat in the light of a rosin candle, and my
brother Yvon was finishing a wooden butter-spoon. Every
few minutes I and my little cousin went out to see if it was
still snowing, and if Victor had arrived.

' At last Victor entered, and everybody applauded, the
young girls lengthening out their distaffs to do him reverence. Then when silence was restored, after some of the
older men had several times shouted out, " Let us com-
mence; hold your tongues," Victor began his story as
follows :—

' " Formerly, in the village of Kastel-Laer, Plouneventer
(Finistère), there were two neighbours; the one was Paol
al Ludu and the other Yon Rustik. Paol al Ludu was
a good-for-nothing sort of fellow; he gained his living
easily, by cheating everybody and by robbing his neighbours; and being always well dressed he was much envied
by his poorer acquaintances. Yon Rustik, on the contrary,
was a poor, infirm, and honest man, always seeking to do
good, but not being able to work, had to beg.

' " One evening our two men were disputing. Paol al Ludu
treated Yon shamefully, telling him that it would be absurd
to think an old lame man such as he was could ever get to
Paris; ' But I,' added Paol, ' am going to see the capital
and amuse myself like a rich *bourgeois*. At this, Yon offered

Ireland and in the Western Hebrides, find their chief enjoyment in story-
telling festivals, some of which I have been privileged to attend.

to bet with Paol that in spite of infirmities he would also go to Paris ; and being an honest man he placed his trust in God. The wager was mutually agreed to, and our two men set out for Paris by different routes.

' " Paol al Ludu, who had no infirmities, arrived at Paris within three weeks. He followed the career of a thief, and deceived everybody ; and as he was well dressed, people had confidence in him. The poor Yon Rustik, on the contrary, did not travel rapidly. He was obliged to beg his way, and being meanly dressed was compelled to sleep outdoors when he could not find a stable. At the end of a month he arrived in a big forest in the region of Versailles, and having no other shelter for the night chose a great oak tree which was hollowed by the centuries and lined with fungi within. In front of this ancient oak there was a fountain which must have been miraculous, for it flowed from east to west, and Yon had closely observed it.

' " Towards midnight Yon was awakened by a terrible uproar ; there were a hundred *corrigans* dancing round the fountain. He overheard one of them say to the others : ' I have news to report to you ; I have cast an evil spell upon the daughter of the King, and no mortal will ever be able to cure her, and yet in order to cure her nothing more would be needed than a drop of water from this fountain.' The *corrigan* who thus spoke was upon two sticks [1] (crippled), and commanded all the others. The beggar having understood the conversation, awaited impatiently the departure of the *corrigans*. When they were gone, he took a little water from the fountain in a bottle, and hurried on to Paris, where he arrived one fine morning.

' " In the house where Yon stopped to eat his crust of dry bread he heard it reported that the daughter of the King was very ill, and that the wisest doctors in France had been sent for. Three days later, Yon Rustik presented himself at the palace, and asked audience with the King, but as he was so shabbily dressed the attendants did not wish to let him

---

[1] The word in the MS. is *boiteux*, and in relation to a devil or demon this seems to be the proper rendering.

enter. When he strongly insisted, they finally prevailed upon the King to receive him ; and then Yon told the King that he had come to cure the princess. Thereupon the King caused Yon to be fittingly dressed and presented before the sick-bed ; and Yon drew forth his bottle of water, and, at his request, the princess drank it to the last drop. Suddenly she began to laugh with joy, and throwing her arms about the neck of the beggar thanked him : she was radically cured. At once the King gave orders that his golden coach of state be made ready ; and placing the princess and the beggar on one seat, made a tour throughout all the most beautiful streets of Paris. Never before were such crowds seen in Paris, for the proclamation had gone forth that the one who had made the miraculous cure was a beggar.

' " Paol al Ludu, who was still in Paris, pressed forward to see the royal coach pass, and when he saw who sat next to the princess he was beside himself with rage. But before the day was over he discovered Yon in the great hotel of the city, and asked him how it was that he had been able to effect the cure ; and Yon replied to his old rival that it was with the water of a miraculous fountain, and relating everything which had passed, explained to him in what place the hollow oak and the fountain were to be found.

' " Paol did not wait even that night, but set off at once to find the miraculous fountain. When he finally found it the hour was almost midnight, and so he hid himself in the hollow of the oak, hoping to overhear some mysterious revelation. Midnight had hardly come when a frightful uproar commenced : this time the crippled *corrigan* chief was swearing like a demon, and he cried to the others, ' The daughter of the King has been cured by a beggar ! He must have overheard us by hiding in the hollow of that d—d old oak. Quick ! let fire be put in it, for it has brought us misfortune.'

' " In less than a minute, the trunk of the oak was in flames ; and there were heard the cries of anguish of Paol al Ludu and the gnashing of his teeth, as he fought against death. Thus the evil and dishonest man ended his life, while Yon Rustik received a pension of twenty thousand francs, and was able to live happy for many years, and to give alms to the poor." '

Here M. Le Scour ends his narrative, leaving the reader to imagine the enthusiastic applause and fond embraces bestowed upon Victor for this most marvellous story, by the happy gathering of country-folk in that cosy warm bakehouse in Lower Brittany, while without the cold east wind of winter was whirling into every nook and corner the falling flakes of snow.

The evidence from Ireland, Scotland, Isle of Man, Wales, Cornwall, and Brittany, which the living Celtic Fairy-Faith offers, has now been heard ; and, as was stated at the beginning of the inquiry, apparently most of it can only be interpreted as belonging to a world-wide doctrine of souls. But before this decision can be arrived at safely, all the evidence should be carefully estimated according to anthropological and psychological methods ; and this we shall proceed to do in the following chapter, before passing to Section II of our study.

SECTION I
THE LIVING FAIRY-FAITH

CHAPTER III

AN ANTHROPOLOGICAL EXAMINATION OF THE EVIDENCE

Anthropology is concerned with man and what is in man—*humani nihil a se alienum putat.*—ANDREW LANG.

The Celtic Fairy-Faith as part of a World-wide Animism—Shaping Influence of Social Psychology—Smallness of Elvish Spirits and Fairies, according to Ethnology, Animism, and Occult Sciences—The Changeling Belief and its explanation according to the Kidnap, Human-Sacrifice, Soul-Wandering, and Demon-Possession Theory—Ancient and Modern Magic and Witchcraft shown to be based on definite psychological laws— Exorcisms—Taboos, of Name, Food, Iron, Place—Taboos among Ancient Celts—Food-Sacrifice—Legend of the Dead—Conclusion : The background of the modern belief in Fairies is animistic.

THE CELTIC FAIRY-FAITH AS PART OF A WORLD-WIDE ANIMISM

THE modern belief in fairies, with which until now we have been specifically concerned, is Celtic only in so far as it reflects Celtic traditions and customs, Celtic myth and religion, and Celtic social and environmental conditions. Otherwise, as will be shown throughout this and succeeding chapters, it is in essence a part of a world-wide animism, which forms the background of all religions in whatever stage of culture religions exist or to which they have attained by evolution, from the barbarism of the Congo black man to the civilization of the Archbishop of Canterbury ; and as far back as we can go into human origins there is some corresponding belief in a fairy or spirit realm, as there is to-day among contemporary civilized and uncivilized races of all countries. We may therefore very profitably begin our examination of the living Fairy-Faith of the Celts by comparing it with a few examples, taken almost at random, from the animistic beliefs current among non-Celtic peoples.

To the Arunta tribes of Central Australia, furthest removed in space from the Celts and hence least likely to have been influenced by them, let us go first, in order to examine their doctrine of ancestral *Alcheringa* beings and of the *Iruntarinia*, which offers an almost complete parallel to the Celtic belief in fairies. These *Alcheringa* beings and *Iruntarinia*—to ignore the secondary differences between the two—are a spirit race inhabiting an invisible or fairy world. Only certain persons, medicine-men and seers, can see them ; and these describe them as thin and shadowy, and, like the Irish *Sidhe*, as always youthful in appearance. Precisely like their Celtic counterparts in general, these Australian spirits are believed to haunt inanimate objects such as stones and trees ; or to frequent totem centres, as in Ireland demons (daemons) are believed to frequent certain places known to have been anciently dedicated to the religious rites of the pre-Christian Celts ; and, quite after the manner of the Breton dead and of most fairies, they are said to control human affairs and natural phenomena. All the Arunta invariably regard themselves as incarnations or reincarnations of these ancestral spirit-beings ; and, in accordance with evidence to be set forth in our seventh chapter, ancient and modern Celts have likewise regarded themselves as incarnations or reincarnations of ancestors and of fairy beings. Also the Arunta think of the *Alcheringa* beings exactly as Celts think of fairies : as real invisible entities who must be propitiated if men wish to secure their goodwill ; and as beneficent and protecting beings when not offended, who may attach themselves to individuals as guardian spirits.[1]

Among the Melanesian peoples there is an equally firm faith in spiritual beings, which they call *Vui* and *Wui*, and

[1] B. Spencer and F. T. Gillen, *Nat. Tribes of Cent. Aust.* (London, 1899), chapters xi, xv.

these beings have very many of the chief attributes of the *Alcheringa* beings.[1]

In Africa, the *Amatongo*, or *Abapansi* of Amazulu belief, have essentially the same motives for action toward men and women, and exhibit the same powers, as the Scotch and Irish peasants assign to the 'good people'. They *take* the living through death ; and people so *taken* appear afterwards as apparitions, having become *Amatongo*.[2]

In the New World, we find in the North American Red Men a race as much given as the Celts are to a belief in various spirits like fairies. They believe that there are spirits in lakes, in rivers and in waterfalls, in rocks and trees, in the earth and in the air ; and that these beings produce storms, droughts, good and bad harvests, abundance and scarcity of game, disease, and the varying fortunes of men. Mr. Leland, who has carefully studied these American beliefs, says that the *Un à games-suk*, or little spirits inhabiting rocks and streams, play a much more influential part in the social and religious life of the North American Red Men than elves or fairies ever did among the Aryans.[3]

In Asia there is the well-known and elaborate animistic creed of the Chinese and of the Japanese, to be in part illustrated in subsequent sections. In popular Indian belief, as found in the Panjab, there is no essential difference between various orders of beings endowed with immortality, such as ghosts and spirits on the one hand, and gods, demigods, and warriors on the other; for whether in bodies in this world or out of bodies in the invisible world, they equally live and act—quite as fairies do.[4] Throughout the Malay Peninsula, belief in many orders of good and bad spirits, in demon-possession, in exorcism, and in the power of black magicians is very common.[5] But in the *Phi* races of Siam

[1] R. H. Codrington, *Journ. Anthrop. Inst.* x. 261 ; *The Melanesians* (Oxford, 1891), pp. 123, 151, &c. ; also cf. F. W. Christian, *The Caroline Islands* (London, 1899), pp. 281 ff., &c.

[2] H. Callaway, *The Religious System of the Amazulu* (London, 1868), pp. 226-7.   [3] C. G. Leland, *Memoirs* (London, 1893), i. 34.

[4] R. C. Temple, *Legends of the Panjab*, in *Folk-Lore*, x. 395.

[5] W. W. Skeat, *Malay Magic* (London, 1900), *passim*.

we discover what is probably the most important and complete parallel to the Celtic Fairy-Faith existing in Asia.

According to the Siamese folk-belief, all the stars and various planets, as well as the ethereal spaces, are the dwelling-places of the *Thévadas*, gods and goddesses of the old pre-Buddhist mythology, who correspond pretty closely to the Tuatha De Danann of Irish mythology ; and this world itself is peopled by legions of minor deities called *Phi*, who include all the various orders of good and bad spirits continually influencing mankind. Some of these *Phi* live in forests, in trees, in open spaces ; and watercourses are full of them. Others inhabit mountains and high places. A particular order who haunt the sacred trees surrounding the Buddhist temples are known as *Phi nang mai* ; and since *nang* is the word for female, and *mai* for tree, they are comparable to tree-dwelling fairies, or Greek wood-nymphs. Still another order called *Chao phum phi* (gods of the earth) are like house-frequenting brownies, fairies, and pixies, or like certain orders of *corrigans* who haunt barns, stables, and dwellings ; and in many curious details these *Chao phum phi* correspond to the Penates of ancient Rome. Not only is the worship of this order of *Phi* widespread in Siam, but to every other order of *Phi* altars are erected and propitiatory offerings made by all classes of the Siamese people.[1]

Before passing westwards to Europe, in completion of our rapid folk-lore tour of the world, we may observe that the Persians, even those who are well educated, have a firm belief in *jinns* and *afreets*, different orders of good and bad spirits with all the chief characteristics of fairies.[2] And modern Arabs and Egyptians and Egyptian Turks hold similar animistic beliefs.[3]

[1] Hardouin, *Traditions et superstitions siamoises*, in *Rev. Trad. Pop.*, v. 257–67.

[2] Ella G. Sykes, *Persian Folklore*, in *Folk-Lore*, xii. 263.

[3] I am directly indebted for this information to a friend who is a member of Lincoln College, Oxford,' Mr. Mohammed Said Loutfy, of Barkein, Lower Egypt. Mr. Loutfy has come into frequent and very intimate contact with these animistic beliefs in his country, and he tells me that they are common to all classes of almost all races in modern Egypt. The common Egyptian spellings are *afreet*, in the singular, and *afaareet* in the

In Europe, the Greek peasant as firmly believes in nymphs
or nereids as the Celtic peasant believes in fairies; and
nymphs, nereids, and fairies alike are often the survivals
of an ancient mythology. Mr. J. C. Lawson, who has very
carefully investigated the folk-lore of modern Greece, says:
' The nereids are conceived as women half-divine yet not
immortal, always young, always beautiful, capricious at best,
and at their worst cruel. Their presence is suspected everywhere. I myself had a nereid pointed out to me by my
guide, and there certainly was the semblance of a female
figure draped in white, and tall beyond human stature,
flitting in the dusk between the gnarled and twisted boles
of an old olive-yard. What the apparition was, I had no
leisure to investigate; for my guide with many signs of the
cross and muttered invocations of the Virgin urged my
mule to perilous haste along the rough mountain path.'
Like Celtic fairies, these Greek nereids have their queens;
they dance all night, disappearing at cock-crow; they can
cast spells on animals or maladies on men and women; they
can shift their shape; they *take* children in death and make
changelings; and they fall in love with young men.[1]

Among the Roumain peoples the widespread belief in the
Iele shows in other ways equally marked parallels with the
Fairy-Faith of the Celts. These *Iele* wait at cross-roads and
near dwellings, or at village fountains or in fields and woods,
where they can best cast on men and women various maladies.
Sometimes they fall in love with beautiful young men and
women, and have on such occasions even been controlled by
their mortal lovers. They are extremely fond of music and
dancing, and many a shepherd with his pipes has been
favoured by them, though they have their own music and
songs too. The Albanian peoples have evil fairies, no taller
than children twelve years old, called in Modern Greek τὰ

plural, for spiritual beings, who are usually described by percipients as of
pygmy stature, but as being able to assume various sizes and shapes. The
djinns, on the contrary, are described as tall spiritual beings possessing
great power.
    [1] J. C. Lawson, *Modern Greek Folk-Lore* (Cambridge, 1910), pp. 131-7,
139-46, 163.

ἐξωτικά, ' those without,' who correspond to the *Iele*. Young people who have been enticed to enter their round dance afterwards waste away and die, apparently becoming one of ' those without '. These Albanian spirits, like the ' good people ' and the Breton dead, have their own particular paths and retreats, and whoever violates these is struck and falls ill.[1] These parallels from Roumain lands are probably due to the close Aryan relationship between the Roumains, the Greeks, and the Celts. The *Iele* seem nothing more than the nymphs and nereids of classical antiquity transformed under Christian influence into beings who contradict their original good character, as in Celtic lands the fairy-folk have likewise come to be fallen angels and evil spirits.

There is an even closer relationship between the Italian and Celtic fairies. For example, among the Etruscan-Roman people there are now flourishing animistic beliefs almost identical in all details with the Fairy-Faith of the Celts.[2] In a very valuable study on the Neo-Latin Fay, Mr. H. C. Coote writes :—' Who were the Fays—the *fate* of later Italy, the *fées* of mediaeval France ? For it is perfectly clear that the *fatua*, *fata*, and *fée* are all one and the same word.' And he proceeds to show that the race of immortal damsels whom the old natives of Italy called *Fatuae* gave origin to all the family of *fées* as these appear in Latin countries, and that the Italians recognized in the Greek nymphs their own *Fatuae*.[3]

It is quite evident that we have here discovered in Italy, as we discovered in Greece and Roumain lands, fairies very Celtic in character ; and should further examination be made of modern European folk-lore yet other similar fairies would be found, such, for example, as the elves of Germany and of Scandinavia, or as the *servans* of the Swiss peasant. And in all cases, whether the beliefs examined be Celtic or

---

[1] L. Sainéan, *Les Fées méchantes d'après les croyances du peuple roumain*, in *Mélusine*, x. 217-26, 243-54.

[2] Cf. C. G. Leland, *Etruscan Roman Remains in Pop. Trad.* (London, 1892), pp. 162, 165, 223, &c.

[3] H. C. Coote, *The Neo-Latin Fay*, in *Folk-Lore Record*, ii. 1-18.

non-Celtic, Aryan or non-Aryan, from Australia, Polynesia,
Africa, America, Asia, or Europe, they are in essence animistically the same, as later sections in this chapter will
make clear. But while the parallelism of these beliefs is
indicated it is, of course, not meant for a moment that in
all of the cases or in any one of the cases the specific differences are not considerable. The ground of comparison consists simply in those generic characteristics which these
fairy-faiths, as they may be called, invariably display—
characteristics which we have good precedent for summing
up in the single adjective animistic.

Shaping Influence of Social Psychology

For the term animism we have to thank Dr. E. B. Tylor,
whose *Primitive Culture*, in which the animistic theory is
developed, may almost be said to mark the beginning of
scientific anthropology. In this work, however, there is
a decided tendency (which indeed displays itself in most of
the leading anthropological works, as, for example, in those
by Dr. Frazer) to regard men, or at any rate primitive men,
as having a mind absolutely homogeneous, and therefore as
thinking, feeling, and acting in the same way under all conditions alike. But a decided change is beginning to manifest
itself in the interpretation of the customs and beliefs of the
ruder races. It is assumed as a working principle that each
ethnic group has or tends to have an individuality of its
own, and, moreover, that the members of such a group
think, feel, and act primarily as the representatives, so to
speak, of that ethnic individuality in which they live, move,
and have their being. That is to say, a social as contrasted
with an individual psychology must, it is held, pronounce
both the first and last word regarding all matters of mythology, religion, and art in its numerous forms. The reason is
that these are social products, and as such are to be understood only in the light of the laws governing the workings of
the collective mind of any particular ethnic group. Such a
method is, for instance, employed in Mr. William McDougall's
Social Psychology, in Mr. R. R. Marett's *Threshold of Religion*,

and in many anthropological articles to be found in *L'Année Sociologique.*

If, therefore, we hold by this new and fruitful method of social psychology we must be prepared to treat the Fairy-Faith of the Celtic peoples also in and for itself, as expressive of an individuality more or less unique. It might, indeed, be objected that these peoples are not a single social group, but rather a number of such groups, and this is, in a way, true. Nevertheless their folk-lore displays such remarkable homogeneity, from whatever quarter of the Celtic world it be derived, that it seems the soundest method to treat them as one people for all the purposes of the student of sociology, mythology, and religion. Granting, then, such a unity in the beliefs of the pan-Celtic race, we are finally obliged to distinguish as it were two aspects thereof.

On the one hand there is shown, even in the mere handful of non-Celtic parallels, which for reasons of space we have been content to cite, as well as in their Celtic equivalents, a generic element common to all peoples living under primitive conditions of society. It is emphatically a social element, but at the same time one which any primitive society is bound to display. On the other hand, in a second aspect, the Celtic beliefs show of themselves a character which is wholly Celtic : in the Fairy-Faith, which is generically animistic, we find reflected all sorts of specific characteristics of the Celtic peoples—their patriotism, their peculiar type of imagination, their costumes, amusements, household life, and social and religious customs generally. With this fact in mind, we may proceed to examine certain of the more specialized aspects of the Fairy-Faith, as manifested both among Celts and elsewhere.

The Smallness of Elvish Spirits and Fairies

Ethnological or Pygmy Theory

In any anthropological estimate of the Fairy-Faith, the pygmy stature so commonly attributed to various orders of Celtic and of non-Celtic fairies should be considered.

Various scholarly champions of the Pygmy Theory have attempted to explain this smallness of fairies by means of the hypothesis that the belief in such fairies is due *wholly* to a folk-memory of small-statured pre-Celtic races ; [1] and

---

[1] We cannot here attempt to present, even in outline, all the complex ethnological arguments for and against the existence in prehistoric times of European pygmy races. Attention ought, however, to be called to the remarkable finds recently made in the *Grotte des Enfants*, at Mentone, France. A certain number of well-preserved skeletons of probably the earliest men who dwelt on the present land surface of Europe, which were found there, suggest that different racial stocks, possibly in succession, have preceded the Aryan stock. The first race, as indicated by two small negroid-looking skeletons of a woman, 1,580 mm. (62·21 inches), and of a boy 1,540 mm. (60·63 inches) in height, found in the lowest part of the *Grotte*, was probably Ethiopian. The succeeding race was probably Mongolian, judging from other remains found in another part of the same *Grotte*, and especially from the Chancelade skeleton with its distinctly Eskimo appearance, only 1,500 mm. (59·06 inches) high, discovered near Perigneux, France. The race succeeding this one was possibly the one out of which our own Aryan race evolved. In relation to the Pygmy Theory these recent finds are of the utmost significance. They confirm Dr. Windle's earlier conclusion, that, contrary to the argument advanced to support the Pygmy Theory, the neolithic races of Central Europe were not true pygmies—a people whose average stature does not exceed four feet nine inches (cf. B. C. A. Windle, *Tyson's Pygmies of the Ancients*, London, 1894, Intro-duction). And, furthermore, these finds show, as far as any available ethnological data can, that there are no good reasons for believing that European and, therefore, Celtic lands were once dominated by pygmies even in epochs so remote that we can only calculate them in tens of thou-sands of years. Nevertheless, it is very highly probable that a folk-memory of Lappish, Pictish, or other small but not true pygmy races, has super-ficially coloured the modern fairy traditions of Northern Scotland, of the Western Hebrides (where what may prove to have been Lapps' or Picts' houses undoubtedly remain), of Northern Ireland, of the Isle of Man, and slightly, if indeed at all, the fairy traditions of other parts of the Celtic world (cf. David MacRitchie, *The Testimony of Tradition*, London, 1890 ; and his criticism of our own Psychological Theory, in the *Celtic Review*, October 1909 and January 1910, entitled respectively, *A New Solution of the Fairy Problem*, and *Druids and Mound-Dwellers*).

Again, the very small flint implements frequently found in Celtic lands and elsewhere have perhaps very reasonably been attributed to a long-forgotten pygmy race ; though we must bear in mind in this connexion that it would be very unwise to conclude definitely that no race save a small-statured race could have made and used such implements : American Red Men were, when discovered by Europeans, and still are, making and using the tiniest of arrow-heads, precisely the same in size and design as those found in Celtic lands and attributed to pygmies. The use of small flint implements for special purposes, e. g. arrows for shooting small game

they add that these races, having dwelt in caverns like the prehistoric Cave Men, and in underground houses like those of Lapps or Eskimos, gave rise to the belief in a fairy world existing in caverns and under hills or mountains. When analysed, our evidence shows that in the majority of cases witnesses have regarded fairies either as non-human nature-spirits or else as spirits of the dead ; that in a comparatively limited number of cases they have regarded them as the souls of prehistoric races ; and that occasionally they have regarded the belief in them as due to a folk-memory of such races. It follows, then, from such an analysis of evidence, that the Pygmy Theory probably does explain some ethno-logical elements which have come to be almost inseparably interwoven with the essentially animistic fabric of the primitive Fairy-Faith. But though the theory may so account for such ethnological elements, it disregards the animism that has made such interweaving possible ; and, on the whole, we are inclined to accept Mr. Jenner's view of the theory (see p. 169). Since the Pygmy Theory thus fails entirely to provide a basis for what is by far the most important part of the Fairy-Faith, a more adequate theory is required.

Animistic Theory

The testimony of Celtic literature goes to show that leprechauns and similar dwarfish beings are not due to a folk-memory of a real pygmy race, that they are spirits like elves, and that the folk-memory of a Lappish-like people (who may have been Picts) evidently was confused with them, so as to result in their being anthropomorphosed. Thus, in *Fionn's Ransom*, there is reference to an under-sized apparently Lappish-like man, who may be a Pict ; and as Campbell, who records the ancient tale, has observed, there are many similar traditional Highland tales about little men or even about true dwarfs who are good bowmen ; [1]

like birds, for spearing fish, and for use in warfare as poisoned arrows, seems to have been common to most primitive peoples of normal stature. Contemporary pygmy races, far removed from Celtic lands, are also using them, and no doubt their prehistoric ancestors used them likewise.

[1] J. G. Campbell, *The Fians* (London, 1891), p. 239. An Irish dwarf

but it is very certain that such tales have often blended with
other tales, in which supernatural figures like fairies play
a rôle ; and, apparently, the former kind of tales are much
more historical and modern in their origin, while the latter
are more mythological and extremely archaic. This blending of the natural or ethnological and the supernatural—in
quite the same manner as in the modern Fairy-Faith—is
clearly seen in another of Campbell's collected tales, *The
Lad with the Skin Coverings*,[1] which in essence is an otherworld tale : ' a little thickset man in a russet coat,' who is
a magician, but who otherwise seems to be a genuine Lapp
dressed in furs, is introduced into a story where real fairy-
like beings play the chief parts. Again, in Irish literature,
we read of a *loch luchra* or ' lake of the pygmies '.[2] Light
is thrown upon this reference by what is recorded about the
leprechauns and Fergus :—While asleep on the seashore one
day, Fergus was about to be carried off by the *luchorpáin* ;
' whereat he awoke and caught three of them, to wit, one
in each of his two hands, and one on his breast. " Life for
life " (i. e. protection), say they. " Let my three wishes
(i. e. choices) be given," says Fergus. " Thou shalt have,"
says the dwarf, " save that which is impossible for us."
Fergus requested of him knowledge of passing under loughs
and linns and seas. " Thou shalt have," says the dwarf,
" save one which I forbid to thee : thou shalt not go under
Lough Rudraide [which] is in thine own country." Thereafter the *luchuirp* (little bodies) put herbs into his ears, and
he used to go with them under seas. Others say the dwarf
gave his cloak to him, and that Fergus used to put it on
his head and thus go under seas.'[3] In an etymological
comment on this passage, Sir John Rhŷs says :—' The words
luchuirp and *luchorpáin* [Anglo-Irish leprechaun] appear to
mean literally " small bodies ", and the word here rendered

is minutely described in *Silva Gadelica* (ii. 116), O'Grady's translation.
Again, in Malory's *Morte D'Arthur* (B. XII. cc. i-ii) a dwarf is mentioned.
   [1] Campbell, *The Fians*, p. 265.
   [2] S. H. O'Grady, *Silva Gadelica* (London, 1892), ii. 199.
   [3] Commentary on the *Senchas Már*, i. 70-1, Stokes's translation, in *Rev.
Celt.*, i. 256-7.

dwarf is in the Irish *abac*, the etymological equivalent of the Welsh *avanc*, the name by which certain water inhabitants of a mythic nature went in Welsh. . . .'[1]

Besides what we find in the recorded Fairy-Faith, there are very many parallel traditions, both Celtic and non-Celtic, about various classes of spirits, like leprechauns or other small elvish beings, which Dr. Tylor has called nature-spirits;[2] and apparently all of these can best be accounted for by means of the animistic hypothesis. For example, in North America (as in Celtic lands) there is no proof of there ever having been an actual dwarf race, but Lewis and Clark, in their *Travels to the Source of the Missouri River*, found among the Sioux a tradition that a hill near the Whitestone River, which the Red Men called the ' Mountain of Little People ' or ' Little Spirits ', was inhabited by pygmy demons in human form, about eighteen inches tall, armed with sharp arrows, and ever on the alert to kill mortals who should dare to invade their domain. So afraid were all the tribes of Red Men who lived near the mountain of these little spirits that no one of them could be induced to visit it.[3] And we may compare this American spirit-haunted hill with similar natural hills in Scotland said to be fairy knolls : one near the turning of a road from Reay Wick to Safester, Isle of Unst ;[4] one the well-known fairy-haunted Tomnahurich, near Inverness ;[4] and a third, the hill at Aberfoyle on which the ' people of peace ' took the Rev. Robert Kirk when he profaned it by walking on it ; or we may equate the American hill with the fairy-haunted Slieve Gullion and Ben Bulbin in Ireland.

The Iroquois had a belief that they could summon dwarfs, who were similar nature-spirits, by knocking on a certain

---

[1] Sir John Rhŷs, *Hibbert Lectures* (London, 1888), p. 592. Dwarfs supernatural in character also appear in the *Mabinogion*, and one of them is an attendant on King Arthur. In Béroul's *Tristan*, Frocin, a dwarf, is skilled in astrology and magic, and in the version by Thomas we find a similar reference.

[2] Tylor, *Prim. Cult.*,[4] i. 385.

[3] Cf. Windle, op. cit., Intro., p. 57.

[4] Hunt, *Anthrop. Mems.*, ii. 294 ; cf. Windle, op. cit., Intro., p. 57.

large stone.[1] Likewise the Polong, a Malay familiar spirit, is ' an exceedingly diminutive female figure or mannikin '.[2] East Indian nature-spirits, too, are pygmies in stature.[3] In Polynesia, entirely independent of the common legends about wild races of pygmy stature, are myths about the spirits called *wui* or *vui*, who correspond to European dwarfs and trolls. These little spirits seem to occupy the same position toward the Melanesian gods or culture heroes, Qat of the Banks Islands and Tagaro of the New Hebrides, as daemons toward Greek gods, or as good angels toward the Christian Trinity, or as fairy tribes toward the Brythonic Arthur and toward the Gaelic hero Cuchulainn.[4] Similarly in Hindu mythology pygmies hold an important place, being sculptured on most temples in company with the gods; e. g. Siva is accompanied by a bodyguard of dwarfs, and one of them, the three-legged Bhringi, is a good dancer [5]—like all *corrigans*, pixies, and most fairies.

Beyond the borders of Celtic lands—in Southern Asia with its islands, in Melanesia with New Guinea, and in Central Africa—pygmy races, generally called Negritos, exist at the present day ; but they themselves have a fairy-faith, just as their normal-sized primitive neighbours have, and it would hardly be reasonable to argue that either of the two fairy-faiths is due to a folk-memory of small-statured peoples. Ancient and thoroughly reliable manuscript records testify to the existence of pygmies in China during the twenty-third century B.C.;[6] yet no one has ever tried to explain the well-known animistic beliefs of modern China-men in ghosts, demons, and in little nature-spirits like fairies, by saying that these are a folk-memory of this ancient pygmy race. In Yezo and the Kurile Islands of Japan still survive a few of the hairy Ainu, a Caucasian-

---

[1] Smith, *Myths of the Iroquois*, in *Amer. Bur. Eth.*, ii. 65.

[2] Skeat, *Malay Magic*, p. 329.

[3] Monier-Williams, *Brāhminism and Hindūism* (London, 1887), p. 236.

[4] Codrington, *The Melanesians*, p. 152.

[5] *Dwarfs in the East*, in *Folk-Lore*, iv. 401-2.

[6] Lacouperie, *Babylonian and Oriental Record*, v ; cf. Windle, op. cit., Intro., pp. 21-2.

like, under-sized race ; and their immediate predecessors, whom they exterminated, were a Negrito race, who, according to some traditions, were two to three feet in stature, and, according to other traditions, only one inch in stature.[1] Both pygmy races, the surviving and the exterminated race, seem independently to have evolved a belief in ghosts and spirits, so that here again it need not be argued that the present pre-Buddhist animism of the Japanese is due to a folk-memory of either Ainus or Negritos.

Further examination of the animistic hypothesis designed to explain the smallness of elvish spirits leads away from mere mythology into psychology, and sets us the task of finding out if, after all, primitive ideas about the disembodied human soul may not have originated or at least have helped to shape the Celtic folk conception of fairies as small-statured beings. Mr. A. E. Crawley, in his *Idea of the Soul* (pp. 200-1, 206), shows by carefully selected evidence from ancient and modern psychologies that ' first among the attributes of the soul in its primary form may be placed its size ', and that ' in the majority of cases it is a miniature replica of the person, described often as a mannikin, or homunculus, of a few inches in height '. Sometimes the soul is described as only about three inches in stature. Dr. Frazer shows, likewise, that by practically all contemporary primitive peoples the soul is commonly regarded as a dwarf.[2]

The same opinions regarding the human soul prevailed among ancient peoples highly civilized, i.e. the Egyptians and Greeks, and may have thence directly influenced Celtic tradition. Thus, in bas-relief on the Egyptian temple of *Dêr el Bahri*, Queen Hatshepsû Rāmaka is making offerings of perfume to the gods, while just behind her stands her *Ka* (soul) as a pygmy so little that the crown of its head is just on a level with her waist.[3] The *Ka* is usually represented as about half the size of an ordinary man. In the *Book of*

---

[1] A. H. S. Landor, *Alone with the Hairy Ainu* (London, 1893), p. 251 ; also Windle, op. cit., Intro., pp. 22-4.

[2] J. G. Frazer, *Golden Bough*[2] (London, 1900), i. 248 ff.

[3] Cf. A. Wiedemann, *Ancient Egyptian Doctrine Immortality* (London, 1895), p. 12.

the Dead, the *Ba*, which like the *Ka* is one of the many separable parts of the soul, is represented as a very little man with wings and bird-like body.

On Greek vases the human soul is depicted as a pygmy issuing from the body through the mouth ; and this conception existed among Romans and Teutons.[1] Like their predecessors the Egyptians, the Greeks also often represented the soul as a small winged human figure, and Romans, in turn, imagined the soul as a pygmy with butterfly wings. These ideas reappear in mediaeval reliefs and pictures wherein the soul is shown as a child or little naked man going out of the dying person's mouth ;[2] and, according to Cædmon, who was educated by Celtic teachers, angels are small and beautiful [3]—quite like good fairies.

Alchemical and Mystical Theory

In the positive doctrines of mediaeval alchemists and mystics, e. g. Paracelsus and the Rosicrucians, as well as their modern followers, the ancient metaphysical ideas of Egypt, Greece, and Rome find a new expression ; and these doctrines raise the final problem—if there are any scientific grounds for believing in such pygmy nature-spirits as these remarkable thinkers of the Middle Ages claim to have studied as beings actually existing in nature. To some extent this interesting problem will be examined in our chapter entitled *Science and Fairies*; here we shall simply outline the metaphysical theory, adding the testimony of some of its living advocates to explain the smallness of elvish spirits and fairies.

These mediaeval metaphysicians, inheritors of pre-Platonic, Platonic, and neo-Platonic teachings, purposely obscured their doctrines under a covering of alchemical terms, so as to safeguard themselves against persecution, open discussion of occultism not being safe during the

---

[1] Cf. A. E. Crawley, *Idea of the Soul* (London, 1909), p. 186.

[2] Examples are in Orcagna's fresco of ' The Triumph of Death ', in the Campo Santo of Pisa (cf. A. Wiedemann, *Anc. Egy. Doct. Immort.*, p. 34 ff.) ; and over the porch of the Cathedral Church of St. Trophimus, at Arles.

[3] Cf. Crawley, op. cit., p. 187.

Middle Ages, as it was among the ancients and happily is now again in our own generation. But they were quite scientific in their methods, for they divided all invisible beings into four distinct classes : the Angels, who in character and function are parallel to the gods of the ancients, and equal to the Tuatha De Danann of the Irish, are the highest ; below them are the Devils or Demons, who correspond to the fallen angels of Christianity ; the third class includes all Elementals, sub-human Nature-Spirits, who are generally regarded as having pygmy stature, like the Greek daemons ; and the fourth division comprises the Souls of the Dead, and the shades or ghosts of the dead.

For us, the third class, which includes spirits of pygmy-like form, is the most important in this present discussion. All its members are of four kinds, according as they inhabit one of the four chief elements of nature.[1] Those inhabiting the earth are called Gnomes. They are definitely of pygmy stature, and friendly to man, and in fairy-lore ordinarily correspond to mine-haunting fairies or goblins, to pixies, *corrigans*, leprechauns, and to such elves as live in rocks, caverns, or earth—an important consideration entirely overlooked by champions of the Pygmy Theory. Those inhabiting the air are called Sylphs. These Sylphs, commonly described as little spirits like pygmies in form, correspond to most of the fairies who are not of the Tuatha De Danann or ' gentry ' type, and who as a race are beautiful and graceful. They are quite like the fairies in Shakespeare's *Midsummer-Night's Dream* ; and especially like the aerials in *The Tempest*, which, according to Mr. Morton Luce, a commentator on the drama, seem to have been shaped by Shakespeare from his knowledge of Rosicrucian occultism, in which such spirits hold an important place. Those inhabiting the water are called Undines, and correspond exactly to the fairies who live in sacred fountains, lakes, or rivers. And the fourth kind, those inhabiting the fire, are

---

[1] General references : Eliphas Levi, *Dogme et Rituel de la Haute Magie* (Paris) ; Paracelsus ; A. E. Waite, *The Occult Sciences* (London, 1891).

called Salamanders, and seldom appear in the Celtic Fairy-Faith : they are supreme in the elementary hierarchies. All these Elementals, who procreate after the manner of men, are said to have bodies of an elastic half-material essence, which is sufficiently ethereal not to be visible to the physical sight, and probably comparable to matter in the form of invisible gases. Mr. W. B. Yeats has given this explanation :—' Many poets, and all mystic and occult writers, in all ages and countries, have declared that behind the visible are chains on chains of conscious beings, who are not of heaven but of the earth, who have no inherent form, but change according to their whim, or the mind that sees them. You cannot lift your hand without influencing and being influenced by hordes. The visible world is merely their skin. In dreams we go amongst them, and play with them, and combat with them. They are, perhaps, human souls in the crucible—these creatures of whim.' [1] And bringing this into relation with ordinary fairies, he says :—' Do not think the fairies are always little. Everything is capricious about them, even their size. They seem to take what size or shape pleases them.' [1] In *The Celtic Twilight* Mr. Yeats makes the statement that the ' fairies in Ireland are sometimes as big as we are, sometimes bigger, and sometimes, as I have been told, about three feet high.' [2]

Mrs. X, a cultured Irishwoman now living in County Dublin, who as a percipient fulfils all the exacting requirements which psychologists and pathologists would demand, tells me that very frequently she has had visions of fairy beings in Ireland, and her own classification and description of these fairy beings, chiefly according to their stature, are as follows :—' Among the usually invisible races which I have seen in Ireland, I distinguish five classes. (1) There are the Gnomes, who are earth-spirits, and who seem to be a sorrowful race. I once saw some of them distinctly on the side of Ben Bulbin. They had rather round heads and dark thick-set bodies, and in stature were about two and

---

[1] W. B. Yeats, *Irish Fairy and Folk-Tales* (London), p. 2.
[2] W. B. Yeats, *The Celtic Twilight* (London, 1902), p. 92 n.

one-half feet. (2) The Leprechauns are different, being full of mischief, though they, too, are small. I followed a leprechaun from the town of Wicklow out to the *Carraig Sidhe,* " Rock of the Fairies," a distance of half a mile or more, where he disappeared. He had a very merry face, and beckoned to me with his finger. (3) A third class are the Little People, who, unlike the Gnomes and Leprechauns, are quite good-looking ; and they are very small. (4) The Good People are tall beautiful beings, as tall as ourselves, to judge by those I saw at the *rath* in Rosses Point. They direct the magnetic currents of the earth. (5) The Gods are really the Tuatha De Danann, and they are much taller than our race. There may be many other classes of invisible beings which I do not know.' (Recorded on October 16, 1910.)

And independently of the Celtic peoples there is available very much testimony of the most reliable character from modern disciples of the mediaeval occultists, e. g. the Rosicrucians, and the Theosophists, that there exist in nature invisible spiritual beings of pygmy stature and of various forms and characters, comparable in all respects to the little people of Celtic folk-lore. How all this is parallel to the Celtic Fairy-Faith is perfectly evident, and no comment of ours is necessary.[1]

This point of view, presented by mediaeval and modern occult sciences and confirmed by Celtic and non-Celtic percipients, when considered in relation to its non-Celtic sources and then at once contrasted with ancient and modern Celtic beliefs of the same character which constitute it—to be seen in the above Gaelic and Brythonic manuscript and other evidence, and in Cædmon's theory that angels are small beings—plunges us into the very complex and extremely difficult problem how far fairies as pygmy spirits may be purely Celtic, and how far they may reflect beliefs not Celtic. The problem, however, is far too complicated to be discussed here ; and one may briefly say that there seems to have been a time in the evolution of

[1] In this connexion should be read Mr. Jenner's Introduction, pp. 167 ff.

animism when the ancient Celts of Britain, of Ireland, and of Continental Europe too, held, in common with the ancient Greeks, Romans, and Teutons, an original Aryan doctrine. This doctrine, after these four stocks separated in possession of it, began to evolve its four specialized aspects which we now can study ; and in the Irish Universities of the early Christian centuries, when Ireland was the centre of European learning, the classical and Celtic aspects of it met for the first time since their prehistoric divorcement. There, as is clearly seen later among the mediaeval alchemists and occultists, a new influence—from Christian theology—was superadded to the ancient animistic beliefs of Europe as they had evolved up to that time.

Conclusion

The ethnological argument, after allowing for all its short-comings, suggests that small-statured races like Lapps and Eskimos (though not necessarily true pygmy races, of whose existence in Europe there is no proof available) did once inhabit lands where there are Celts, and that a Celtic folk-memory of these could conceivably have originated a belief in certain kinds of fairies, and thus have been a shaping influence in the animistic traditions about other fairies. The animistic argument shows that pygmies described in Celtic literature and in Celtic and non-Celtic mythologies are nearly always to be thought of as non-human spirits ; and that there is now and was in past ages a world-wide belief that the human soul is in stature a pygmy. The philosophical argument of alchemists and mystics, in a way, draws to itself the animistic argument, and sets up the hypothesis that the smallness of elves and fairies is due to their own nature, because they actually exist as invisible tribes of non-human beings of pygmy size and form.

THE CHANGELING BELIEF

The smallness of fairies, which has just been considered, and the belief in changelings are the two most prominent characteristics of the Fairy-Faith, according to our evidence in chapter ii; and we are now to consider the second. The prevalent and apparently the only important theories which are current to explain this belief in changelings may be designated as the Kidnap Theory and the Human-Sacrifice Theory. These we shall proceed to estimate, after which there will be introduced newer and seemingly more adequate theories.

Kidnap Theory

Some writers have argued that the changeling belief merely reflects a time when the aboriginal pre-Celtic peoples held in subjection by the Celts, and forced to live in mountain caverns and in secret retreats underground, occasionally kidnapped the children of their conquerors, and that such kidnapped children sometimes escaped and told to their Celtic kinsmen highly romantic tales about having been in an underground fairy-world with fairies. Frequently this argument has taken a slightly different form : that instead of unfriendly pre-Celtic peoples it was magic-working Druids who—either through their own choice or else, having been driven to bay by the spread of Christianity, through force of circumstances—dwelt in secret in chambered mounds or souterrains, or in dense forests, and then stole young people for recruits, sometimes permitting them, years afterwards, when too old to be of further use, to return home under an inviolable vow of secrecy.[1] And Mr. David MacRitchie in supporting his own Pygmy Theory has made interesting modern elaborations of these two slightly different theories concerning changelings.[2]

As already pointed out, there are definite ethnological elements blended in the other parts of the complex Fairy-Faith; and so in this part of it, the changeling belief, there are conceivably more of such elements which lend some sup-

[1] Cf. Cririe, *Scottish Scenery* (London, 1803), pp. 347–8 ; P. Graham, *Sketches Descriptive of Picturesque Scenery on the Southern Confines of Perthshire* (Edinburgh, 1812), pp. 248–50, 253 ; Mahé, *Essai sur les Antiquités du Départ. du Morbihan* (Vannes, 1825) ; Maury, *Les Fées du Moyen-Age* (Paris, 1843).

[2] David MacRitchie, *Druids and Mound Dwellers*, in *Celtic Review* (January 1910) ; and his *Testimony of Tradition*.

port to the Kidnap Theory. In itself, however, as we hope to show conclusively, the Theory, failing to grasp the essential and underlying character of this belief, does not adequately explain it.

Human-Sacrifice Theory

Alfred Nutt advanced a theory, which anticipated one part of our own, that ' the changeling story is found to be connected with the antique conception of life and sacrifice '. And he wrote :—' It is at least possible that the sickly and ailing would be rejected when the time came for each family to supply its quota of victims, and this might easily translate itself in the folk-memory into the statement that the fairies had carried off the healthy ' (alone acceptable as sacrifice) ' and left in exchange the sickly.' [1] Though our evidence will not permit us to accept the theory (why it will not will be clear as we proceed) that some such sacrificial customs among the ancient Celts entirely account for the changeling story, yet we consider it highly probable that the theory helps to explain particular aspects of the complex tradition, and that the underlying philosophy of sacrifice extended in an animistic way, as we shall try to extend it, probably offers more complete explanation.

Thus, the Mexicans believed that the souls of all sacrificed children went to live with the god Tlaloc in his heaven-world.[2] Among the Greeks, a sacrificed victim appears to have been sent as a messenger, bearing a message repeated to him before death to some god.[3] On the funeral pile of Patroclus were laid Trojan captives, together with horses and hounds, a practice corresponding to that of American Red Men ; the idea being that the sacrificed Trojans and the horses and hounds as well, were thus sent to serve the slain warriors in the otherworld. Among ourselves in Europe and in America it is not uncommon to read in the daily newspaper about a suicide as resulting from the belief that

---

[1] K. Meyer and A. Nutt, *Voyage of Bran* (London, 1895-7), ii. 231-2.
[2] Cf. Tylor, *Prim. Cult.*,⁴ ii. 61.
[3] Lawson, *Modern Greek Folklore*, pp. 356, 359.

death alone can bring union with a deceased sweetheart or loved one. These examples, and very many parallel ones to be found the world over, seem to furnish the key to the theory of sacrifice : namely, that by extinguishing life in this world it is transmitted to the world of the gods, spirits, and the dead.

Both Sir John Rhŷs and D'Arbois de Jubainville have shown that the Irish were wont to sacrifice the first-born of children and of flocks.[1] O'Curry points out a clear case of human sacrifice at an ancient Irish funeral [2] :—' Fiachra then brought fifty hostages with him from Munster ' ; and, when he died, ' the hostages which he brought from the south were buried alive around the *Fert* (burial mound) of Fiachra.' More commonly the ancient Celts seem to have made sacrifices to appease place-spirits before the erection of a new building, by sending to them through death the soul of a youth (see p. 436).

It is in such animistic beliefs as these, which underlie sacrifice, that we find a partial solution of the problem of changeling belief. But the sacrifice theory is also inadequate ; for, though changelings may in some cases in ancient times have conceivably been the sickly children discarded by priests as unfit for sending to the gods or fairies, how can we explain actual changelings to be met with to-day in all Celtic lands ? Some other hypothesis is evidently necessary.

Soul-Wandering Theory

Comparative study shows that non-Celtic changeling beliefs parallel to those of the Celts exist almost everywhere, that they centre round the primitive idea that the human soul can be abstracted from the body by disembodied spirits and by magicians, and that they do not depend upon the sacrifice theory, though animistically closely related to it. For example, according to the Lepers' Islanders, ghosts steal men—as fairies do—' to add them to their company ;

---

[1] Rhŷs, *Hib. Lect.*, p. 201 ; Jubainville, *Cyc. Myth. Irl.*, pp. 106–8.
[2] E. O'Curry, *Manners and Customs* (Dublin, 1873), I. cccxx ; from *Book of Ballymote*, fol. 145, b. b.

and if a man has left children when he died, one of whom sickens afterwards, it is said that the dead father takes it.'[1] In Banks Island, Polynesia, the ghost of a woman who has died in childbirth is greatly dreaded : as long as her child is on earth she cannot proceed to Panoi, the otherworld ; and the relatives take her child to another house, ' because they know that the mother will come back to take its soul.'[2] When a Motlav child sneezes, the mother will cry, ' Let him come back into the world ! let him remain.' Under similar circumstances in Mota, the cry is, ' Live ; roll back to us ! ' ' The notion is that a ghost is drawing a child's soul away.' If the child falls ill the attempt has succeeded, and a wizard throws himself into a trance and goes to the ghost-world to bring the child's soul back.[3] In the islands of Kei and Kisar a belief prevails that the spirits of the dead can take to themselves the souls of the living who go near the graves.[4] Sometimes a Polynesian mother insists on being buried with her dead child ; or a surviving wife with her dead husband, so that there will be no separation.[5] These last practices help to illustrate the Celtic theory behind the belief that fairies can abduct adults.

Throughout Melanesia sickness is generally attributed to the soul's absence from the body, and this state of disembodiment is believed to be due to some ghost's or spirit's interference,[6] just as among Celts sickness is often thought to be due to fairies having taken the soul to Fairyland. An old Irish piper who came up to Lady Gregory's home at Coole Park told us that a certain relative of his, a woman, had lain in a semi-conscious state of illness for months, and that when she recovered full consciousness she declared she had been with the ' good people '.

Folk-beliefs like all the above, which more adequately explain the changeling idea than the Human-Sacrifice Theory, are world-wide, being at once Celtic and non-Celtic.[7]

---

[1] Codrington, *The Melanesians*, p. 286.   [2] Ib., p. 275.
[3] Ib., pp. 226, 208-9.   [4] Crawley, *Idea of the Soul*, p. 114.
[5] Codrington, *The Melanesians*, p. 289.   [6] Ib., p. 194.
[7] Cf. Crawley, *Idea of the Soul*, chap. iv.

Demon-Possession Theory

There has been among many peoples, primitive and civilized, a complementary belief to the one that evil spirits or ghosts may steal a soul and so cause in the vacated body illness if the abduction is temporary, and death if it is permanent : namely, a belief that demons, who sometimes may be souls of the dead, can possess a human body while the soul is out of it during sleep, or else can expel the soul and occupy its place.[1] When complete possession of this character takes place there is—as in ' mediumship '—a change of personality, and the manner, thoughts, actions, language, and the whole nature of the possessed person are radically changed. Sometimes a foreign tongue, of which the subject is ignorant, is fluently spoken. When the possession is an evil one, as Dr. Nevius has observed in China, where the phenomena are common, the change of character is in the direction of immorality, frequently in strong contrast with the character of the subject under normal conditions, and is often accompanied by paroxysms and contortions of the body, as I have often been solemnly assured by Celts is the case in a changeling. (See M. Le Scour's account on page 198, of three changelings that he saw in one family in Finistère ; and compare what is said about fairy changelings in Ireland, Scotland, Isle of Man, Wales, and Cornwall.)

A conception like that among the Chinese, of how an evil spirit may dispossess the soul inhabiting a child's or adult's body, seems to be the basis and original conception behind the fairy-changeling belief in all Celtic and other countries. When a child has been changed by fairies, and an old fairy left in its place, the child has been, according to this theory, dispossessed of its body by an evil fairy, which a Chinaman calls a demon, while the leaving behind of the old fairy accounts for the changed personality and changed facial expression of the demon-possessed infant. The Chinese demon enters into

---

[1] For a thorough and scientific discussion of this matter, see J. L. Nevius, *Demon Possession* (London, 1897).

and takes complete possession of the child's body while the child's soul is out of it during sleep—and all fairies make changelings when a babe is asleep in its cradle at night, or during the day when it is left alone for a short time. The Chinese child-soul is then unable to return into its body until some kind of magical ceremony or exorcism expels the possessing demon ; and through precisely similar methods, often aided by Christian priests, Celts cure changelings made by fairies, pixies, and *corrigans*. In the following account, therefore, apparently lies the root explanation of the puzzling beliefs concerning fairy changelings so commonly met with in the Celtic Fairy-Faith :—' To avert the calamity of nursing a demon, dried banana-skin is burnt to ashes, which are then mixed with water. Into this the mother dips her finger and paints a cross upon the sleeping babe's forehead. In a short time the demon soul returns—for the soul wanders from the body during sleep and is free—but, failing to recognize the body thus disguised, flies off. The true soul, which has been waiting for an opportunity, now approaches the dormant body, and, if the mark has been washed off in time, takes possession of it ; but if not, it, like the demon, failing to recognize the body, departs, and the child dies in its sleep.' [1]

In relation to this Demon-Possession Theory, the writer has had the opportunity of observing carefully some living changelings among the Celts, and is convinced that in many such cases there is an undoubted belief expressed by the parents and friends that fairy-possession has taken place. This belief often translates itself naturally into the folk-theory that the body of the child has also been changed, when examination proves only a change of personality as recognized by psychologists ; or, in a distinct type of changelings, those who exhibit great precocity in childhood

---

[1] N. G. Mitchell-Innes, *Birth, Marriage, and Death Rites of the Chinese*, in *Folk-Lore Journ.*, v. 225. Very curiously, the pagan Chinese mother uses the sign of the cross against the demon as Celtic mothers use it against fairies ; and no exorcism by Catholic or Protestant to cure a fairy change-ling or to drive out possessing demons is ever performed without this world-wide and pre-Christian sign of the cross (see pp. 270–1).

combined with an old and wizened countenance, there is neither a changed personality nor demon-possession, but simply some abnormal physical or mental condition, in the nature of cretinism, atrophy, marasmus, or arrested development. One of the most striking examples of a changeling exists at Plouharnel-Carnac, Brittany, where there is now living a dwarf Breton whom I have photographed and talked with, and who may possibly combine in himself both the abnormal psychical and the abnormal pathological conditions. He is no taller than a normal child ten years old, but being over thirty years old he is thick-set, though not deformed. All the peasants who know him call him ' the Little *Corrigan* ', and his own mother declares that he is not the child she gave birth to. He once said to me with a kind of pathetic protest, ' Did M.—— tell you that I am a demon ? '

Conclusion

The Kidnap Theory, resting entirely upon the ethnological and social or psychological elements which we have elsewhere pointed out as existing in the superficial aspects of the essentially animistic Fairy-Faith as a whole, is accordingly limited in its explanation of this specialized part of the Fairy-Faith, the changeling belief, to these same elements which may exist in the changeling belief. And, on the showing of anthropology, the other theories undoubtedly offer a more adequate explanation.

By means of sacrifice, according to its underlying philosophy, man is able to transmit souls from this world to the world where dwell the gods and fairy-folk both good and evil. Thus, had Abraham sacrificed Isaac, the soul of Isaac would have been taken to heaven by Jehovah as fairies take souls to Fairyland through death. But the difference is that in human sacrifice men do voluntarily and for specific religious ends what various kinds of fairies or spirits would do without human intervention and often maliciously, as our review of ancient and modern theories of sacrifice has shown. Gods and fairies are spiritual beings ; hence only the spiritual part of man can be delivered over to them.

Melanesians and other peoples whose changeling beliefs have now been examined, regard all illness and death as the result of spirit interference ; while, Celts regard strange maladies in children and in adults as the result of fairy interference. And to no Celt is death in early life a natural thing : if it comes to a child or to a beautiful youth in any way whatsoever, the fairies have taken what they coveted. In all mythologies gods have always enjoyed the companionship of beautiful maidens, and goddesses the love of heroic youths ; and they have often taken them to their world as the Tuatha De Danann took the great heroes of the ancient Celts to the Otherworld or Avalon, and as they still in the character of modern fairies abduct brides and young mothers, and bridegrooms or other attractive young men whom they wish to have with them in Fairyland (see our chapters iv–vi).

Where sacrifice or death has not brought about such complete transfer or abduction of the soul to the fairy world, there is only a temporary absence from human society ; and, meanwhile, the vacated body is under a fairy spell and lies ill, or unconscious if there is a trance state. If the body is an infant's, a fairy may possess it, as in the Chinese theory of demon-possession. In such cases the Celts often think that the living body is that of another child once *taken* but since grown too old for Fairyland ; though the rational explanation frequently is purely pathological. Looked at philosophically, a fairy exchange of this kind is fair and evenly balanced, and there has been no true robbery. And in this aspect of the changeling creed—an aspect of it purely Celtic—there seems to be still another influence apart from human sacrifice, soul-abductions, demon or fairy-possession, and disease ; namely, a greatly corrupted folk-memory of an ancient re-birth doctrine : the living are taken to the dead or the fairies and then sent back again, after the manner of Socrates' argument that the living come from the dead and the dead from the living (cf. our chapter vii). In all such exchanges, the economy of Nature demands that the balance between the two worlds be maintained : hence there arose the theories of human sacrifice, of soul abduction, of

demon or fairy-possession ; and in all these collectively is
to be found the complete psychological explanation of the
fairy-changeling and fairy-abduction beliefs among ancient
and modern Celts as these show themselves in the Fairy-
Faith. All remaining classes of changelings, which fall outside the scope of this clearly defined psychological theory,
are to be explained pathologically.

MAGIC AND WITCHCRAFT

The evidence from each Celtic country shows very clearly
that magic and witchcraft are inseparably blended in the
Fairy-Faith, and that human beings, i.e. ' charmers,' *dynion
hysbys*, and other magicians, and sorceresses, are often
enabled through the aid of fairies to perform the same
magical acts as fairies ; or, again, like Christian priests who
use exorcisms, they are able, acting independently, to
counteract fairy power, thereby preventing changelings or
curing them, saving churnings, healing man or beast of
' fairy-strokes ', and, in short, nullifying all undesirable
influences emanating from the fairy world. A correct
interpretation of these magical elements so prominent in the
Fairy-Faith is of fundamental importance, because if made
it will set us on one of the main psychical highways which
traverse the vast territory of our anthropological inquiry.
Let us, then, undertake such an interpretation, first setting
up, as we must, some sort of working hypothesis as to what
magic is, witchcraft being assumed to be a part of magic.

Theories of Modern Anthropologists

We may define magic, as understood by ancients and
moderns, civilized or non-civilized, apart from conjuring,
which is mere jugglery and deception of the senses, as the art
of controlling for particular ends various kinds of invisible
forces, often, and, as we hold, generally thought of as intelligent spirits.   This is somewhat opposed to Mr. Marett's
point of view, which emphasizes ' pre-animistic influences ',
i.e. ' powers to which the animistic form is very vaguely
attributed if at all.'   And, in dealing with the anthro-

pological aspects of spell-casting in magical operations, Mr. Marett conceives such a magical act to be in relation to the magician ' generically, a projection of imperative will, and specifically one that moves on a supernormal plane ', and the victim's position towards this invisible projected force to be ' a position compatible with *rapport* '.[1] He also thinks it probable that the essence of the magician's supernormal power lies in what Melanesians call *mana*.[1] In our opinion *mana* may be equated with what William James, writing of his attitude toward psychical phenomena, called a universally diffused ' soul-stuff ' leaking through, so to speak, and expressing itself in the human individual.[2] On this view, Mr. Marett's theory would amount to saying that magicians are able to produce magical effects because they are able to control this ' soul-stuff ' ; and our evidence would regard all spirits and fairies as portions of such universally diffused *mana*, ' soul-stuff ', or, as Fechner might call it, the ' Soul of the World '. Moreover, in essence, such an idea of magic coincides, when carefully examined, with what ancient thinkers like Plato, Iamblichus, the Neo-Platonists generally, and mediaeval magicians like Paracelsus and Eliphas Levi, called magic ; and agrees with ancient Celtic magic—judging from what Roman historians have recorded concerning it, and from Celtic manuscripts themselves.

Other modern anthropologists have set up far less satisfactory definitions of magic. According to Dr. Frazer, for example, magic assumes, as natural science does, that ' one event follows another necessarily and invariably without the intervention of any spiritual or personal agency '.[3] Such a theory is not supported by the facts of anthropology ; and does not even apply to those specialized and often superficial kinds of magic classed under it by Dr. Frazer as ' sympathetic and imitative magic ', i.e. that through which like produces like, or part produces whole. To our

[1] R. R. Marett, *The Threshold of Religion* (London, 1909), p. 58, &c. ; p. 67.

[2] W. James, *Confidences of a ' Psychical Researcher '*, in *American Magazine* (October 1909).

[3] Frazer, *The Golden Bough* [3] (London, 1911), i. 220.

mind, sympathetic and imitative magic (to leave out of
account many fallacious and irrational ritualistic practices,
which Dr. Frazer includes under these loose terms), *when
genuine*, in their varied aspects are directly dependent upon
hypnotic states, upon telepathy, mind-reading, mental suggestion, association of ideas, and similar processes ; in short,
are due to the operation of mind on mind and will on will,
and, moreover, are recognized by primitive races to have
this fundamental character. Or, according to the Fairy-
Faith, they are caused by a fairy or disembodied spirit
acting upon an embodied one, a man or woman ; and not,
as Dr. Frazer holds, through ' mistaken applications of one
or other of two great fundamental laws of thought, namely,
the association of ideas by similarity and the association of
ideas by contiguity in space or time '.[1]

The mechanical causation theory of magic, as thus set
forth in *The Golden Bough*, does not imply *mana* or will-
power, as Mr. Marett's more adequate theory does in part :
Dr. Frazer wishes us to regard animistic religious practices
as distinct from magic.[2] Nevertheless, in direct opposition
to Dr. Frazer's view, the weight of the evidence from the
past and from the present, which we are about to offer, is
decidedly favourable to our regarding magic and religion as
complementary to one another and, for all ordinary purposes of the anthropologist, as in principle the same. The
testimony touching magicians in all ages, Celtic magic and
witchcraft as well, besides that resulting from modern
psychical research, tends to establish an almost exclusively
animistic hypothesis to account for fairy magical phenomena and like phenomena among human beings ; and with
these phenomena we are solely concerned.

Among the Ancients [3]

Among the more cultured Greeks and Romans—and the
same can be said of most great nations of antiquity—it was

---

[1] Frazer, *The Golden Bough*,[2] i. 221-2.

[2] Ib., chap. iv.

[3] See Apuleius, *De Deo Socratis* ; Cicero, *De Natura Deorum* (lib. i);
Iamblichus, *De Mysteriis Aegypt., Chaldaeor., Assyrior.* ; Plato, *Timaeus*,

an unquestioned belief that innumerable gods, placed in hierarchies, form part of an unbroken spiritual chain at the lowest end of which stands man, and at the highest the incomprehensible Supreme Deity. These gods, having their abodes throughout the Universe, act as the agents of the Unknown God, directing the operation of His cosmic laws and animating every star and planet. Inferior to these gods, and to man also, the ancients believed there to be innumerable hosts of invisible beings, called by them daemons, who, acting as the servants of the gods, control, and thus in a secondary sense create, all the minor phenomena of inanimate and animate nature, such as tempests, atmospheric disturbances generally, the failure of crops or their abundance, maladies and their cure, good and evil passions in men, wars and peace, and all the blessings and curses which affect the purely human life.

Man, being of the god-race and thus superior to these lower, servile entities, could, like the gods, control them if adept in the magical sciences ; for ancient Magic, about which so much has been written and about which so little has been understood by most people in ancient, mediaeval, and modern times, is according to the wisest ancients nothing more than the controlling of daemons, shades, and all sorts of secondary spirits or elementals by men specially trained for that purpose. Sufficient records are extant to make it evident that the fundamental training of Egyptian, Indian, Assyrian, Greek, Roman, and Druid priests was in the magical or occult sciences. Pliny, in his *Natural History*, says :—' And to-day Britain practises the art [of magic] with religious awe and with so many ceremonies that it might seem to have made the art known to the Persians.' [1] Herein, then, is direct evidence that the Celtic Fairy-Faith, considered in its true psychic nature, has been immediately shaped by the ancient Celtic religion ; and, as our witness

---

Symposium, Politicus, Republic, ii. iii. x ; Plutarch, *De Defectu Oraculorum, The Daemon of Socrates, Isis and Osiris* ; Proclus, *Commentarius in Platonis Alcibiadem.*

[1] Pliny, *Natural History*, xxx. 14.

from the Isle of Skye so clearly set forth, that it originated among a cultured class of the Celts more than among the peasants. And, in accordance with this evidence, Professor Georges Dottin, who has made a special study of the historical records concerning Druidism, writes :—' The Druids of Ireland appear to us above all as magicians and prophets. They foretell the future, they interpret the secret will of the *fées* (fairies), they cast lots.' [1] Thus, in spite of the popular and Christian reshaping which the belief in fairies has had to endure, its origin is easily enough discerned even in its modern form, covered over though this is with accretions foreign to its primal character.

Magic was the supreme science because it raised its adepts out of the ordinary levels of humanity to a close relationship with the gods and creative powers. Nor was it a science to be had for the asking, ' for many were the wand-bearers and few the chosen.' Roman writers tell us that neophytes for the druidic priesthood often spent twenty years in severe study and training before being deemed fit to be called Druids. We need not, however, in this study enter into an exposition of the ordeals and trials of candidates seeking magical training, or else initiation into the Mysteries. There were always two schools to which they could apply, directly opposed in their government and policy—the school of white magic and the school of black magic ; the former being a school in which magical powers were used in religious rites and always for good ends, the latter a school in which all magical powers were used for wholly selfish and evil ends. In both schools the preliminary training was the same ; that is to say, the first thing taught to the neophyte was self-control. When he proved himself absolutely his own master, when his teachers were certain that he could not be dominated by another will or by any outside or psychic influence, then for the first time he was permitted to exercise his own iron will in controlling daemons, ghosts, and all the elemental hosts of the air—either as a white magician or as a black magician. [2]

[1] Cf. G. Dottin, *La Religion des Celtes* (Paris, 1904), p. 44.
[2] The neo-Platonists generally, including Porphyry, Julian, Iamblichus,

The magical sciences taught (an idea which still holds its ground, as one can discover in modern India) that by formulas of invocation, by chants, by magic sounds, by music, these invisible beings can be made to obey the will of the magician even as they obey the will of the gods. The calling up of the dead and talking with them is called necromancy ; the foretelling through spiritual agency and otherwise of coming events or things hidden, like the outcome of a battle, is called divination ; the employment of charms against children so as to prevent their growing is known as fascination ; to cause any ill fortune or death to fall upon another person by magic is sorcery ; to excite the sexual passions of man or woman, magical mixtures called philtres are used. Almost all these definitions apply to the practices of black magic. But the great schools known as the Mysteries were of white magic, in so far as they practised the art ; and such men as Pythagoras, Plato, and Aeschylus, who are supposed to have been initiated into them, always held them in the highest reverence, though prohibited from directly communicating anything of their esoteric teachings concerning the origin and destiny of man, the nature of the gods, and the constitution of the universe and its laws.

In Plato's *Banquet* the power or function of the daemonic element in nature is explained. Socrates asks of the prophetess Diotima what is the power of the daemonic element (personified as Love for the purposes of the argument), and she replies :—' He interprets between gods and men, conveying and taking across to the gods the prayers and sacrifices

and Maximus, being persuaded of man's power to call up and control spirits, called white magic *theurgy*, or the invoking of good spirits, and the reverse *goëty*, or the calling up and controlling of evil spirits for criminal purposes. Cf. F. Lélut, *Du Démon de Socrate* (Paris, 1836).

If white magic be correlated with religion as religion is popularly conceived, namely the cult of supernatural powers friendly to man, and black magic be correlated with magic as magic tends to be popularly conceived, namely witchcraft and devil-worship, we have a satisfactory historical and logical basis for making a distinction between religion and magic ; religion (including white magic) is a social good, magic (black magic) is a social evil. Such a distinction as Dr. Frazer makes is untenable within the field of true magic.

of men, and to men the commands and replies of the gods ; he is the mediator who spans the chasm which divides them, and therefore in him all is bound together, and through him the arts of the prophets and priests, their sacrifices and mysteries and charms, and all prophecy and incantation find their way. For God mingles not with man ; but through the daemonic element (or Love) all the intercourse and converse of God with man, whether awake or asleep, is carried on. The wisdom which understands this is spiritual.' [1]

Among the Ancient Celts

If we turn now directly to Celtic magic in ancient times, we discover that the testimony of Pliny is curiously confirmed by Celtic manuscripts, chiefly Irish ones, and that then, as now, witchcraft and fairy powers over men and women are indistinguishable in their general character. Thus, in the *Echtra Condla*, ' the Adventures of Connla,' the fairy woman says of Druidism and magic :—' Druidism is not loved, little has it progressed to honour on the Great Strand. When his law shall come it will scatter the charms of Druids *from journeying on the lips of black, lying demons* '—so characterized by the Christian transcribers.[2] In *How Fionn Found his Missing Men*, an ancient tale preserved by oral tradition until recorded by Campbell, it is said that ' Fionn then went out with Bran (his fairy dog). There were millions of people (apparitions) out before him, called up by some sleight of hand '.[3] In the *Leabhar na h-Uidre*, or ' Book of the Dun Cow ' (p. 43 a), compiled from older manuscripts about A.D. 1100, there is a clear example of Irish fetishism based on belief in the power of demons :—' . . . for their swords used to turn against them (the Ulstermen) when they made a false trophy. Reasonable [was] this ; for demons used to speak to them from their arms, so that hence their arms were safeguards.' [4]

Shape-shifting quite after the fairy fashion is very

---

[1] Cf. B. Jowett, *Dialogues of Plato* (Oxford, 1892), i. 573.
[2] Cf. Meyer and Nutt, *Voyage of Bran* (London, 1895-7), i. 146.
[3] Campbell, *The Fians*, p. 195.
[4] Cf. Stokes's trans. in *Rev. Celt.*, i. 261.

frequently met with in old Celtic literature. Thus, in the Rennes *Dinnshenchas* there is this passage showing that spirits or fairies were regarded as necessary for the employment of magic :—' Folks were envious of them (Faifne the poet and his sister Aige) : so they loosed elves at them who transformed Aige into a fawn ' (the form assumed by the fairy mother of Oisin, see p. 299 n.), ' and sent her on a circuit all round Ireland, and the fians of Meilge son of Cobthach, king of Ireland, killed her.' [1] A fact which ought to be noted in this connexion is that kings or great heroes, rather than ordinary men and women, are very commonly described as being able to shift their own shape, or that of other people ; e. g. ' Mongan took on himself the shape of Tibraide, and gave Mac an Daimh the shape of the cleric, with a large tonsure on his head.' [2] And when this fact is coupled with another, namely the ancient belief that such kings and great heroes were incarnations and reincarnations of the Tuatha De Danann, who form the supreme fairy hierarchy, we realize that, having such an origin, they were simply exercising in human bodies powers which their divine race exercise over men from the fairy world (see our chapter iv).

In Brythonic literature and mythology, magic and witchcraft with the same animistic character play as great or even a greater rôle than in Gaelic literature and mythology. This is especially true with respect to the Arthurian Legend, and to the *Mabinogion*, some of which tales are regarded by scholars as versions of Irish ones. Sir John Rhŷs and Professor J. Loth, who have been the chief translators of the *Mabinogion*, consider their chief literary machinery to be magic (see our chapter v).

So far it ought to be clear that Celtic magic contains much animism in its composition, and that these few illustrations of it, selected from numerous illustrations in the ancient Fairy-Faith, confirm Pliny's independent testimony that in his age the Britons seemed capable of instructing even the Persians themselves in the magical arts.

[1] Cf. Stokes's trans. in *Rev. Celt.*, xv. 307.
[2] From the *Conception of Mongán*, cf. Meyer, *Voyage of Bran*, i. 77.

European and American Witchcraft

In a general way, the history of witchcraft in Europe and in the American colonies is supplementary to what has already been said, seeing that it is an offshoot of mediaeval magic, which in turn is an offshoot of ancient magic. Witchcraft in the West, in probably a majority of cases, is a mere fabric of absurd superstitions and practices—as it is shown to be by the evidence brought out in so many of the horrible legal and ecclesiastical processes conducted against helpless and eccentric old people, and other men and women, including the young, often for the sake of private revenge, and generally on no better foundation than hearsay and false accusations. In the remaining instances it undoubtedly arose, as ancient witchcraft (black magic) seems to have arisen, through the infiltration of occult knowledge into uneducated and often criminally inclined minds, so that what had formerly been secretly guarded among the learned, and generally used for legitimate ends, degenerated in the hands of the unfit into black magic. In our own age, a parallel development, which adequately illustrates our subject of inquiry, has taken place in the United States : fragments of magical lore bequeathed by Mesmer and his immediate predecessors, the alchemists, were practically and honestly applied to the practice of magnetic healing and healing through mental suggestion by a small group of practitioners in Massachusetts, and then with much ingenuity and real genius were applied by Mary Baker Eddy to the interpretation of miraculous healing by Jesus Christ. Hence arose a new religion called Christian Science. But this religious movement did not stop at mental healing : according to published reports, during the years 1908–9 the leader of the New York First Church of Christ, Scientist, was deposed, and, with certain of her close associates, was charged with having projected daily against the late Mrs. Eddy's adjutant a current of 'malicious animal magnetism' from New York to Boston, in order to bring about his death. The process is said to have been for the deposed

leader and her friends to sit together in a darkened room
with their eyes closed. ' Then one of them would say :
" You all know Mr. ——. You all know that his place is
in the darkness whence he came. If his place is six feet
under ground, that is where he should be." Then all present
would concentrate their minds on the one thought—Mr. ——
and six feet under ground.' And this practice is supposed
to have been kept up for days. Mrs. ——, who gives this
testimony, is a friend of the victim, and she asserts that these
evil thought-waves slowly but surely began his effacement,
and that had the black magicians down in New York not
been discovered in time, Mr. —— could not have withstood
the forces.[1] Perhaps so enlightened a country as the United
States may in time see history repeat itself, and add a
new chapter to witchcraft ; for the true witches were not
the kind who are popularly supposed to ride on broom-
sticks and to keep a house full of black cats, and the sooner
this is recognized the better.

According to this aspect of Christian Science, ' malicious
animal magnetism ' (or black magic), an embodied spirit,
i. e. a man or woman, possesses and can employ the same
magical powers as a disembodied spirit—or, as the Celts
would say, the same magical powers as a fairy—casting
spells, and producing disease and death in the victim. And
this view coincides with ordinary witchcraft theories ; for
witches have been variously defined as embodied spirits
who have ability to act in conjunction with disembodied
spirits through the employment of various occult forces, e.g.
forces comparable to Mesmer's odic forces, to the Melanesian
mana, or to the ' soul-stuff ' postulated by William James,
or, as Celts think, to forces focused in fairies themselves.
So, also, according to Mr. Marett's view, there is a state of
rapport between the victim and the magician or witch ;
and where such a state of *rapport* exists there is some *mana*-
like force passing between the two poles of the magical

---

[1] Quoted and summarized from *Projectors of ' Malicious Animal Magnetism '*, in *Literary Digest*, xxxix. No. 17, pp. 676-7 (New York and
London, October 23, 1909).

circuit, whether it be only unconscious mental or electrical force emanating from the operator, or an extraneous force brought under control and concentrated in some such conscious unit as we designate by the term ' spirit ', ' devil ', or ' fairy '.

In conformity with this psychical or animistic view of witchcraft, in the Capital Code of Connecticut (A.D. 1642) a witch is defined as one who ' hath or consorteth with a familiar spirit '.[1] European codes, as illustrated by the sixth chapter of Lord Coke's *Third Institute*, have parallels to this definition :—' A witch is a person which hath conference with the devil ; to consult with him to do some act.' [1] And upon these theories, not upon the broomstick and black-cat conception, were based the trials for witchcraft during the seventeenth century.

The Bible, then so frequently the last court of appeal in such matters, was found to sustain such theories about witches in the classical example of the Witch of Endor and Saul ; and the idea of witchcraft in Europe and America came to be based—as it probably always had been in pagan times—on the theory that living persons could control or be controlled by disembodied spirits for evil ends. Hence all black magicians, and what are now known as ' spirit mediums ', were made liable by law to the death penalty.[2]

In mediaeval Europe the great difficulty always was, as is shown in the trials of Jeanne d'Arc, to decide whether the invisible agent in magical processes, such as was imputed to the accused, was an angel or a demon. If an angel, then the accused was a saint, and might become a candidate for canonization ; but if a demon, the accused was a witch, and liable to a death-sentence. The wisest old doctors of the University of Paris, who sat in judgement (or were consulted) in one of Jeanne's trials, could not fully decide this knotty problem, nor, apparently, the learned churchmen who also tried her ; but evidently they all agreed that it

---

[1] Cf. Nevius, *Demon Possession*, pp. 300-1.

[2] For a fuller discussion of the history of witchcraft see *The Superstitions of Witchcraft*, by Howard Williams, London, 1865.

was better to waive the question. And, finally, an innocent peasant girl who had heard Divine Voices, and who had thereby miraculously saved her king and her country, was burned at the stake, under the joint direction of English civil and ecclesiastical authorities, and, if not technically, at least practically, with the full approval of the corresponding French authorities, at Rouen, France, May 30, A.D. 1431.[1] In April, A.D. 1909, almost five centuries afterwards, it has been decided with tardy justice that Jeanne's Voices were those of angels and not of demons, and she has been made a saint.

How the case of Jeanne d'Arc bears directly upon the Fairy-Faith is self-evident : One of the first questions asked by Jeanne's inquisitors was ' if she had any knowledge of those who went to the Sabbath with the fairies ? or if she had not assisted at the assemblies held at the fountain of the fairies, near Domremy, around which dance malignant spirits ? ' And another question exactly as recorded was this :—' *Interroguée s'elle croiet point au devant de aujourduy, que les fées feussent maulvais esperis : respond qu'elle n'en sçavoit rien.*'[2]

Conclusion

Finally, we may say that what medicine-men are to American Indians, to Polynesians, Australians, Africans, Eskimos, and many other contemporary races, or what the mightier magicians of modern India are to their people, the ' fairy-doctors ' and ' charmers ' of Ireland, Scotland, and Man are to the Gaels, and the '*Dynion Hysbys*' or ' Wise Men ' of Wales, the witches of Cornwall, and the seers, sorceresses, and exorcists of Brittany are to the Brythons. These Gaelic and Brythonic magicians and witches, and ' fairy mediums ', almost invariably claim to derive their power from their ability to see and to communicate with fairies, spirits, and the dead ; and they generally say that they are enabled through such spiritual agencies to reveal the past, to foretell the future, to locate

---

[1] Cf. J. Quicherat, *Procès* (Paris, 1845), *passim*.
[2] Ib., i. 178.

lost property, to cast spells upon human beings and upon animals, to remove such spells, to cure fairy strokes and changelings, to perform exorcisms, and to bring people back from Fairyland.

We arrive at the following conclusion :—If, as eminent psychical researchers now postulate (and as many of them believe), there are active and intelligent disembodied beings able to act psychically upon embodied men in much the same way that embodied men are known ordinarily to act psychically upon one another, then there is every logical and common-sense reason for extending this psychical hypothesis so as to include the ancient, mediaeval, and modern theory of magic and witchcraft, namely, that what embodied men and women can do in magical ways, as for example in hypnotism, disembodied men and women can do. Further, if fairies, in accord with reliable testimony from educated and critical percipients, hypothetically exist (whatever their nature may be), they may be possessed of magical powers of the same sort, and so can cast spells upon or possess living human beings as Celts believe and assert. And this hypothesis coincides in most essentials with the one we used as a basis for this discussion, that, in accordance with the Melanesian doctrine of control of ghosts and spirits with their inherent *mana*, magical acts are possible.[1] This in turn applied to the Celts amounts to a hypothetical confirmation of the ancient druidical doctrine that through control of fairies or demons (daemons) Druids or magicians could control the weather and natural phenomena connected with vegetable and animal processes, could cast spells, could divine the future, could execute all magical acts.

Exorcisms

According to the testimony of anthropology, exorcism as a religious practice has always flourished wherever animistic beliefs have furnished it with the necessary environment ; and not only has exorcism been a fundamental part of religious practices in past ages, but it is so at the present

[1] Codrington, *The Melanesians*, pp. 127, 200, 202-3 ff.

day.   Among Christians, Celtic and non-Celtic, among
followers of all the great historical religions, and especially
among East Indians, Chinese, American Red Men, Polynesians, and most Africans, the expelling of demons from
men and women, from animals, from inanimate objects, and
from places, is sanctioned by well-established rituals.   Exorcism as applied to the human race is thus defined in the
Dictionnaire de Théologie (Roman Catholic) by L'Abbé
Bergier :—' *Exorcism*—conjuration, prayer to God, and command given to the demon to depart from the body of persons
possessed.'   The same authority thus logically defends its
practice by the Church :—' Far from condemning the opinion
of the Jews, who attributed to the demon certain maladies,
that divine Master confirmed it.' [1]   And whenever exorcism
of this character has been or is now generally practised, the
professional exorcist appears as a personage just as necessary
to society as the modern doctor, since nearly all diseases
were and to some extent are still, both among Christians
and non-Christians, very often thought to be the result of
demon-possession.

When we come to the dawn of the Christian period in
Ireland and in Scotland, we see Patrick and Columba, the
first and greatest of the Gaelic missionaries, very extensively
practising exorcism ; and there is every reason to believe
(though the data available on this point are somewhat unsatisfactory) that their wide practice of exorcism was quite
as much a Christian adaptation of pre-Christian Celtic
exorcism, such as the Druids practised, as it was a continuation of New Testament tradition.   We may now present
certain of the data which tend to verify this supposition,
and by means of them we shall be led to realize how fundamentally such an animistic practice as exorcism must have
shaped the Fairy-Faith of the Celts, both before and after
the coming of Christianity.

' Once upon a time,' so the tale runs about Patrick, ' his
foster-mother went to milk the cow.   He also went with her
to drink a draught of new milk.   Then the cow goes mad in

---

[1] Bergier, *Dict. de Théol.* (Paris, 1848), ii. 541-2, &c.

the byre and killed five other kine : a demon, namely, entered her. There was great sadness on his foster-mother, and she told him to bring the kine back to life. Then he brought the kine to life, so that they were whole, and he cured the mad one. So God's name and Patrick's were magnified thereby.'[1] On another occasion, when demons came to Ireland in the form of black birds, quite after the manner of the Irish belief that fairies assume the form of crows (see pp. 302–5), the Celtic ire of Patrick was so aroused in trying to exorcize them out of the country that he threw his bell at them with such violence that it was cracked, and then he wept :—' Now at the end of those forty days and forty nights' [of Patrick's long fast on the summit of Crua-chan Aigle or Croagh Patrick, Ireland's Holy Mountain] ' the mountain was filled with black birds, so that he knew not heaven or earth. He sang maledictive psalms at them. They left him not because of this. Then his anger grew against them. He strikes his bell at them, so that the men of Ireland heard its voice, and he flung it at them, so that a gap broke out of it, and that [bell] is " Brigit's Gapling ". Then Patrick weeps till his face and his chasuble in front of him were wet. No demon came to the land of Erin after that till the end of seven years and seven months and seven days and seven nights. Then the angel went to console Patrick and cleansed the chasuble, and brought white birds round the Rick, and they used to sing sweet melodies for him.'[1] In Adamnan's *Life of S.Columba* it is said that 'accord-ing to custom ', which in all probability was established in pagan times by the Druids and then maintained by their Christian descendants, it was usual to exorcize even a milk vessel before milking, and the milk in it afterwards.[2] Thus Adamnan tells us that one day a youth, Columban by name, when he had finished milking, went to the door of St. Columba's cell carrying the pail full of new milk that, *according to*

---

[1] W. Stokes, *Tripartite Life* (London, 1887), pp. 13, 115.
[2] I am personally indebted to Dr. W. J. Watson, of Edinburgh, for having directed my attention to this curious passage, and for having pointed out its probable significance in relation to druidical practices.

custom, the saint might exorcize it. When the holy man had
made the sign of the cross in the air, the air ' was greatly
agitated, and the bar of the lid, driven through its two holes,
was shot away to some distance ; the lid fell to the ground,
and most of the milk was spilled on the soil.' Then the
saint chided the youth, saying :—' Thou hast done carelessly in thy work to-day ; for thou hast not cast out the
demon that was lurking in the bottom of the empty pail, by
tracing on it, before pouring in the milk, the sign of the
Lord's cross ; and now not enduring, thou seest, the virtue
of the sign, he has quickly fled away in terror, while at the
same time the whole of the vessel has been violently shaken,
and the milk spilled. Bring then the pail nearer to me, that
I may bless it.' When the half-empty pail was blessed, in
the same moment it was refilled with milk. At another time,
the saint, to destroy the practice of sorcery, commanded
Silnan, a peasant sorcerer, to draw a vessel full of milk
from a bull ; and by his diabolical art Silnan drew the milk.
Then Columba took it and said :—' Now it shall be proved
that this, which is supposed to be true milk, is not so, but
is blood deprived of its colour by the fraud of demons to
deceive men ; and straightway the milky colour was turned
into its own proper quality, that is, into blood.' And it is
added that ' The bull also, which for the space of one hour
was at death's door, wasting and worn by a horrible emacia-
tion, in being sprinkled with water blessed by the Saint,
was cured with wonderful rapidity.' [1]

And to-day, as in the times of Patrick and Columba,
exorcism is practised in Ireland and in the Western Hebrides
of Scotland by the clergy of the Roman Church against
fairies, demons, or evil spirits, when a person is possessed by
them—that is to say, ' fairy-struck,' or when they have
entered into some house or place ; and on the Scotch mainland individual Protestants have been known to practise
it. A haunted house at Balechan, Perthshire, in which
certain members of the Psychical Research Society had
taken up summer quarters to ' investigate ', was exorcized

[1] Adamnan, *Life of S. Columba*, B. II, cc. xvi, xvii.

by the late Archbishop of Edinburgh, assisted by a priest
from the Outer Isles.[1]

Among the nine orders of the Irish ecclesiastical organization of Patrick's time, one was composed of exorcists.[2]
The official ceremony for the ordination of an exorcist in
the Latin Church was established by the Fourth Council of
Carthage, and is indicated in nearly all the ancient rituals.
It consists in the bishop giving to the candidate the book of
exorcisms and saying as he does so :—' Receive and understand this book, and have the power of laying hands upon
demoniacs, whether they be baptized, or whether they be
catechumens.' [3] By a decree of the Church Council of
Orange, making men possessed of a demon ineligible to
enter the priesthood, it would seem that the number of
demoniacs must have been very great.[3] As to the efficacy
of exorcisms, the church Fathers during the first four centuries, when the Platonic philosophy was most influential in
Christianity, are agreed.[3]

In estimating the shaping influences, designated by us
as fundamental, which undoubtedly were exerted upon the
Fairy-Faith through the practice of exorcism, it is necessary
to realize that this animistic practice holds a very important
position in the Christian religion which for centuries the
Celtic peoples have professed. One of the two chief sacra-
ments of Christianity, that of Baptism, is preceded by
a definitely recognized exorcism, as shown in the Roman
Ritual, where we can best study it. In the Exhortation
preceding the rite the infant is called a slave of the demon,
and by baptism is to be set free. The salt which is placed
in the mouth of the infant by the priest during the ceremony
has first been exorcized by special rites. Then there follows
before the entrance to the baptismal font a regular exorcism
pronounced over the child : the priest taking some of his
own saliva on the thumb of his right hand, touches the child's

---

[1] For this fact I am personally indebted to Mrs. W. J. Watson, of Edinburgh.

[2] Stokes, *Tripartite Life*, pp. clxxx, 303, 305 ; from *Book of Armagh*,
fo. 9, A 2, and fo. 9, B 2.

[3] Bergier, *Dict. de Théol.*, ii. 545, 431, 233.

ears and nostrils, and commands the demon to depart out of the child. After this part of the ceremony is finished, the priest makes on the child's forehead a sign of the cross with holy oil. Finally, in due order, comes the actual baptism.[1] And even after baptismal rites have expelled all possessing demons, precautions are necessary against a repossession : St. Augustine has said that exorcisms of precaution ought to be performed over every Christian daily ; and it appears that faithful Roman Catholics who each day employ holy water in making the sign of the cross, and all Protestants who pray ' lead us not into temptation, but deliver us from evil ', are employing such exorcisms :[2] St. Gregory of Nazianzus writes, ' Arm yourself with the sign of the cross which the demons fear, and before which they take their flight '[3] ; and by the same sign, said St. Athanasius, ' All the illusions of the demon are dissipated and all his snares destroyed.'[4] An eminent Catholic theologian asserts that saints who, since the time of Jesus Christ, have been endowed with the power of working miracles, have always made use of the sign of the cross in driving out demons, in curing maladies, and in raising the dead. In the *Instruction sur le Rituel*,[5] it is said that water which has been blessed is particularly designed to be used against demons ; in the *Apostolic Constitutions*, formulated near the end of the fourth century, holy water is designated as a means of purification from sin and of putting the demon to flight.[6] And nowadays when the priest passes through his congregation casting over them holy water, it is as an exorcism of precaution ; or when as in France each mourner

---

[1] See *Instruction sur le Rituel*, par l'Évêque de Toulon, iii. 1–16. ' In the Greek rite (of baptism), the priest breathes thrice on the catechumen's mouth, forehead, and breast, praying that every unclean spirit may be expelled.'—W. Bright, *Canons of First Four General Councils* (Oxford, 1892), p. 122.

[2] Cf. Godescard, *Vies des Saints* (Paris, 1835), xiii. 254–66.

[3] *De Incarnatione Verbi* (ed. Ben.), i. 88 ; cf. Godescard, op. cit., xiii. 254–66.

[4] Godescard, *Vies des Saints*, xiii. 263–4.

[5] Par Joly de Choin, Évêque de Toulon, i. 639.

[6] Bergier, *Dict. de Théol.*, ii. 335.

at a grave casts holy water over the corpse, it is undoubtedly
—whether done consciously as such or not—to protect the
soul of the deceased from demons who are held to have as
great power over the dead as over the living. Other forms
of exorcism, too, are employed. For example, in the *Lebar
Brecc*, it is said of the Holy Scripture that ' By it the snares
of devils and vices are expelled from every faithful one in
the Church '.[1] And from all this direct testimony it seems
to be clear that many of the chief practices of Christians
are exorcisms, so that, like the religion of Zoroaster, the religion founded by Jesus has come to rest, at least in part,
upon the basic recognition of an eternal warfare between
good and bad spirits for the control of Man.

The curing of diseases through Christian exorcism is by
no means rare now, and it was common a few centuries ago.
Thus in the eighteenth century, beginning with 1752 and
till his death, Gassner, a Roman priest of Closterle, diocese
of Coire, Switzerland, devoted his life to curing people
of possessions, declaring that one third of all maladies are
so caused, and fixed his head-quarters at Elwangen, and
later at Ratisbon. His fame spread over many countries
of Europe, and he is said to have made ten thousand cures
solely by exorcism.[2] And not only are human ills overcome
by exorcism, but also the maladies of beasts : at Carnac, on
September 13, there continues to be celebrated an annual fête
in honour of St. Cornely, the patron saint of the country and
the saint who (as his name seems to suggest) presides over
domestic *horned* animals ; and if there is a cow, or even a sheep
suffering from some ailment which will not yield to medicine,
its owner leads it to the church door beneath the saint's
statue, and the priest blesses it, and, as he does so, casts
over it the exorcizing holy water. The Church Ritual designates two forms of Benediction for such animals, one form
for those who are ordinarily diseased, and another for those
suffering from some contagious malady. In each ceremony
there comes first the sprinkling of the animal with holy

[1] Stokes, *Tripartite Life*, Intro., p. 162.
[2] J. E. Mirville, *Des Esprits* (Paris, 1853), i. 475.

water as it stands before the priest at the church door ; and
then there follows in Latin a direct invocation to God to
bless the animal, ' to extinguish in it all diabolical powers,'
to defend its life, and to restore it to health.[1]

In 1868, according to Dr. Evans, an old cow-house in
North Wales was torn down, and in its walls was found
a tin box containing an exorcist's formula. The box and
its enclosed manuscript had been hidden there some years
previously to ward off all evil spirits and witchcraft, for
evidently the cattle had been dying of some strange malady
which no doctors could cure. Because of its unique nature,
and as an illustration of what Welsh exorcisms must have
been like, we quote the contents of the manuscripts both as
to spelling and punctuation as checked by Sir John Rhŷs
with the original, except the undecipherable symbols which
come after the archangels' names :—

' ✠ Lignum sanctae crusis defendat me a malis presentibus
preateritus & futuris ; interioribus & exterioribus ✠✠
Daniel Evans ✠✠ Omnes spiritus laudet Dominum : Mosen
habent & prophetas. Exergat Deus & disipenture inimi-
ciessus ✠ . ✠ O Lord Jesus Christ I beseech thee to preserve
me Daniel Evans ; and all that I possess from the power
of all evil men, women ; spirits, or wizards, or hardness of
heart, and this I will trust thou will do by the same power
as thou didst cause the blind to see the lame to walk and
they that were possesed with unclean spirits to be in their
own minds Amen Amen ✠✠✠✠ pater pater pater Noster
Noster Noster aia aia aia Jesus ✠ Christus ✠ Messyas ✠
Emmanuel ✠ Soter ✠ Sabaoth ✠ Elohim ✠ on ✠ Adonay
✠ Tetragrammaton ✠ Ag ꞉ ꞉ ✠ Panthon ✠ . . . reaton
✠ Agios ✠ Jasper ✠ Melchor ✠ Balthasar Amen ✠✠✠
✳ ♃ ✳ ♀ ✳ ☿ △ ♄ △ ♃ △ ☾ . ☉ ✳ ♃ ✳ ☾ ✠✠ And by
the power of our Lord Jesus Christ and His Hevenly Angels
Gabriel [*symbols*   ]   being our Redeemer and Saviour from
Michail [*symbols*   ]   all witchcraft and from assaults of the
                           Devil Amen ✠ O Lord Jesus Christ
I beseech thee to preserve me and all that I possess from

[1] *Instructions sur le Rituel*, par Joly de Choin, iii. 276-7.

the power of all evil men ; women ; spirits ; or wizards past. present, or to come inward and outward Amen ✠ ✠.'[1]

From India Mr. W. Crooke reports similar exorcisms and charms to cure and to protect cattle.[2] Thus there is employed in Northern India the *Ajaypâl jantra*, i. e. 'the charm of the Invincible Protector,' one of Vishnu's titles, in his character as the earth-god Bhûmiya—in Scotland it would be the charm of the Invincible Fairy who presides over the flocks and to whom libations are poured—in order to exorcize diseased cattle or else to prevent cattle from becoming diseased. This *Ajaypâl jantra* is a rope of twisted straw, in which chips of wood are inserted. ' In the centre of the rope is suspended an earthen platter, inside which an incantation is inscribed with charcoal, and beside it is hung a bag containing seven kinds of grain.' The rope is stretched between two poles at the entrance of a village, and under it the cattle pass to and fro from pasture. The following is the incantation found on one of the earthen saucers :—' O Lord of the Earth on which this cattle-pen stands, protect the cattle from death and disease ! I know of none, save thee, who can deliver them.' In the Morbihan, Lower Brittany, we seem to see the same folk-custom, somewhat changed to be sure ; for on St. John's Day, the christianized pagan sun-festival in honour of the summer solstice, in which fairies and spirits play so prominent a part in all Celtic countries, just outside a country village a great fire is lit in the centre of the main road and covered over with green branches, in order to produce plenty of smoke, and then on either side of this fire and through the exorcizing smoke are made to pass all the domestic animals in the district as a protection against disease and evil spirits, to secure their fruitful increase, and, in the case of cows, abundant milk supply. Mr. Milne, while making excavations in the Carnac country, discovered the image of a small bronze cow, now in the Carnac Museum, and this would seem to indicate that before Christian times there was in the Morbihan a cult of cattle,

---

[1] G. Evans, *Exorcism in Wales*, in *Folk-Lore*, iii. 274-7.
[2] W. Crooke, in *Folk-Lore*, xiii. 189-90.

preserved even until now, no doubt, in the Christian fête of St. Cornely, just as in St. Cornely's Fountain there is preserved a pagan holy well.

It ought now to be clear that both pre-Christian and Christian exorcisms among Celts have shaped the Fairy-Faith in a very fundamental manner. And anthropologically the whole subject of exorcism falls in line with the Psychological Theory of the nature and origin of the belief in fairies in Celtic countries.

TABOOS

We find that taboos, or prohibitions of a religious and social character, are as common in the living Fairy-Faith as exorcisms. The chief one is the taboo against naming the fairies, which inevitably results in the use of euphemisms, such as ' good people ', ' gentry ', ' people of peace ', *Tylwyth Teg* (' Fair Folk '), or *bonnes dames* (' good ladies '). A like sort of taboo, with its accompanying use of euphemisms, existed among the Ancients, e.g. among the Egyptians and Babylonians, and early Celts as well, in a highly developed form ; and it exists now among the native peoples of Australia, Polynesia, Central Africa, America, in Indian systems of Yoga, among modern Greeks, and, in fact, almost everywhere where there are vestiges of a primitive culture.[1] And almost always such a taboo is bound up with animistic and magical elements, which seem to form its background, just as it is in our own evidence.

To discuss name taboo in all its aspects would lead us more deeply into magic and comparative folk-lore than we have yet gone, and such discussion is unnecessary here. We may therefore briefly state that the root of the matter would seem to be that the name and the dread power named are so closely associated in the very concrete thought of the primitive culture that the one virtually is the other : just as one inevitably calls up the other for the modern thinker,

[1] For ancient usages see F. Lenormant, *Chaldean Magic* (London, 1877), pp. 103–4 ; Iamblichus and other Neo-Platonists ; and for modern usages see Marett, *Threshold of Religion*, chap. iii.

so it is that, in the world of objective fact, for the primitive philosopher the one is equivalent to the other. The primitive man, in short, has projected his subjective associations into reality. As regards euphemisms, the process of development possibly is that first you employ any substitute name, and that secondly you go on to employ such a substitute name as will at the same time be conciliatory. In the latter case, a certain anthropomorphosing of the power behind the taboo would seem to be involved.[1]

Next in prominence comes the food taboo ; and to this, also, there are non-Celtic parallels all the world over, now and in ancient times. We may take notice of three very striking modern parallels :—A woman visited her dead brother in Panoi, the Polynesian Otherworld, and ' he cautioned her to eat nothing there, and she returned '.[2] A Red Man, Ahaktah, after an apparent death of two days' duration, revived, and declared that he had been to a beautiful land of tall trees and singing-birds, where he met the spirits of his forefathers and uncle. While there, he felt hunger, and seeing in a bark dish some wild rice, wished to eat of it, but his uncle would allow him none. In telling about this psychical adventure, Ahak-tah said :—' Had I eaten of the food of spirits, I never should have returned to earth.' [3] Also a New Zealand woman visited the Otherworld in a trance, and her dead father whom she met there ordered her to eat no food in that land, so that she could return to this world to take care of her child.[4]

All such parallels, like their equivalents in Celtic belief, seem to rest on this psychological and physiological conception in the folk-mind. Human food is what keeps life going in a human body ; fairy food is what keeps life going in a fairy body ; and since what a man eats makes him what he is physically, so eating the food of Fairyland or of the land of the dead will make the eater partake of the bodily

[1] Cf. Marett, *Is Taboo a Negative Magic ?* in *The Threshold of Religion*, pp. 85–114.

[2] Codrington, *The Melanesians*, p. 277.

[3] Eastman, *Dacotah*, p. 177 ; cf. Tylor, *Prim. Cult.*,[4] ii. 52 n.

[4] Shortland, *Trad. of New Zeal.*, p. 150 ; cf. Tylor, op. cit., ii. 51-2.

nature of the beings it nourishes. Hence when a man or woman has once entered into such relation or communion with the Otherworld of the dead, or of fairies, by eating their food, his or her physical body [1] by a subtle transformation adjusts itself to the new kind of nourishment, and becomes spiritual like a spirit's or fairy's body, so that the eater cannot re-enter the world of the living. A study of food taboos confirms this conclusion.[2]

A third prominent taboo, the iron taboo, has been explained by exponents of the Pygmy Theory as pointing to a prehistoric race in Celtic lands who did not know iron familiarly, and hence venerated it so that in time it came to be religiously regarded as very efficacious against spirits and fairies. Undoubtedly there may be much reason in this explanation, which gives some ethnological support to the Pygmy Theory. Apparently, however, it is only a partial explanation of iron taboo in general, because, in many cases, iron in ancient religious rites certainly had magical properties attributed to it, which to us are quite unexplainable from this ethnological point of view ; [3] and in Melanesia and in Africa, where iron is venerated now, the same explanation through ethnology seems far-fetched. But at present there seem to be no available data to explain adequately this iron taboo, though we have strong reasons for thinking that the philosophy underlying it is based on mystical conceptions of virtues attributed—reasonably or unreasonably—to various metals and precious stones, and that a careful examination of alchemical sciences would probably arrive at an explanation wholly psychological.

Besides many other miscellaneous taboos noticeable in

---

[1] Precisely like Celtic peasants, primitive peoples often fail to take into account the fact that the physical body is in reality left behind upon entering the trance state of consciousness known to them as the world of the departed and of fairies, because there they seem still to have a body, the ghost body, which to their minds, in such a state, is undistinguishable from the physical body. Therefore they ordinarily believe that the body and soul both are taken.

[2] Frazer, *Golden Bough*,[2] *passim.*

[3] Cf. ib., i. 344 ff., 348 ; iii. 390.

the evidence, there is a place taboo which is prominent.
Thus, if an Irishman cuts a thorn tree growing on a spot
sacred to the fairies, or if he violates a fairy preserve of any
sort, such as a fairy path, or by accident interferes with
a fairy procession, illness and possibly death will come to his
cattle or even to himself. In the same way, in Melanesia,
violations of sacred spots bring like penalties : ' A man
planted in the bush near Olevuga some coco-nut and almond
trees, and not long after died,' the place being a spirit preserve ; [1] and a man in the Lepers' Island lost his senses,
because, as the natives believed, he had unwittingly trodden
on ground sacred to Tagaro, and ' the ghost of the man
who lately sacrificed there was angry with him'.[1] In this
case the wizards were called in and cured the man by
exorcisms,[1] as Irishmen, or their cows, are cured by the
exorcisms of ' fairy-doctors ' when ' fairy-struck ' for some
similar violation. The animistic background of place taboos
in the Fairy-Faith is in these cases apparent.

Among Ancient Celts

In the evidence soon to be examined from the recorded
Fairy-Faith, we shall find taboos of various kinds often more
prominent than in the living Fairy-Faith.[2] So essential are
they to the character of much of the literary and mythological matter with which we shall have to deal in the following chapters, that at this point some suggestions ought to be
made concerning their correct anthropological interpretation.

Almost every ancient Irish taboo is connected with a king
or with a great hero like Cuchulainn ; and, in Ireland
especially, all such kings and heroes were considered of
divine origin, and as direct incarnations, or reincarnations
of the Tuatha De Danann, the true Fairies, originally inhabitants of the Otherworld. (See our chapter vii.) As
Dr. Frazer points out to have been the case among non-
Celts, with whom the same theory of incarnated divinities
has prevailed, royal taboos are to isolate the king from all

---

[1] Codrington, *The Melanesians*, pp. 177, 218-9.
[2] Cf. Eleanor Hull, *Old Irish Tabus or Geasa*, in *Folk-Lore*, xii. 41 ff.

sources of danger, especially from all magic and witchcraft, and they act in many cases ' so to say, as electrical insulators' to preserve him or heroes who are equally divine.[1]

The early Celts recognized an intimate relationship between man and nature : unperceived by man, unseen forces—not dissimilar to what Melanesians call *Mana*—(looked on as animate and intelligent and frequently individual entities) guided every act of human life. It was the special duty of Druids to act as intermediaries between the world of men and the world of the Tuatha De Danann ; and, as old Irish literature indicates clearly, it was through the exercise of powers of divination on the part of Druids that these declared what was taboo or what was unfavourable, and also what it was favourable for the divine king or hero to perform. As long as man kept himself in harmony with this unseen fairy-world in the background of nature, all was well ; but as soon as a taboo was broken, disharmony in the relationship—which was focused in a king or hero—was set up ; and when, as in the case of Cuchulainn, many taboos were violated, death was inevitable and not even the Tuatha De Danann could intercede.

Breaking of a royal or hero taboo not only affects the violator, but his subjects or followers as well : in some cases the king seems to suffer vicariously for his people. Almost every great Gaelic hero—a god or Great Fairy Being incarnate—is overshadowed with an impending fate, which only the strictest observance of taboo can avoid.[2]

Irish taboo, and inferentially all Celtic taboo, dates back to an unknown pagan antiquity. It is imposed at or before birth, or again during life, usually at some critical period, and when broken brings disaster and death to the breaker. Its whole background appears to rest on a supernatural relationship between divine men and the Otherworld of the Tuatha De Danann ; and it is very certain that this ancient relationship survives in the living Fairy-Faith as one between

---

[1] Cf. Frazer, *Golden Bough*,[2] i. 233 ff., 343.
[2] Cf. E. J. Gwynn, *On the Idea of Fate in Irish Literature*, in *Journ. Ivernian Society* (Cork), April 1910.

ordinary men and the fairy-world. Therefore, almost all taboos surviving among Celts ought to be interpreted psychologically or even psychically, and not as ordinary social regulations.

FOOD-SACRIFICE

Food-sacrifice plays a very important rôle in the modern Fairy-Faith, being still practised, as our evidence shows, in each one of the Celtic countries. Without any doubt it is a survival from pagan times, when, as we shall observe later (in chapter iv. 291, and elsewhere), propitiatory offerings were regularly made to the Tuatha De Danann as gods of the earth, and, apparently, to other orders of spiritual beings. The anthropological significance of such food-sacrifice is unmistakable.

With the same propitiatory ends in view as modern Celts now have in offering food to fairies, ancient peoples, e.g. the Greeks and Romans, maintained a state ritual of sacrifices to the gods, genii, daemons, and to the dead. And such sacrifices, so essential a part of most ancient religions, were based on the belief, as stated by Porphyry in his *Treatise Concerning Abstinence*, that all the various orders of gods, genii or daemons, enjoy as nourishment the odour of burnt offerings. And like the Fairy-Folk, the daemons of the air live not on the gross substance of food, but on its finer invisible essences, conveyed to them most easily on the altar-fire.[1] Socrates, Plato, Xenophon, and other leading Greeks, as well as the Romans of a like metaphysical school, unite in declaring the fundamental importance to the welfare of the State of regular sacrifices to the gods and to the daemons who control all natural phenomena, since they caused, if not neglected, abundant harvests and national prosperity. For unto the gods is due by right a part of all things which they give to man for his happiness.

[1] Cf. our evidence, pp. 38, 44 ; also Kirk's *Secret Commonwealth* (c. i), where it is said of the ' good people ' or fairies that their bodies are so ' plyable thorough the Subtilty of the Spirits that agitate them, that they can make them appear or disappear att Pleasure. Some have Bodies or Vehicles so spungious, thin, and delecat, that they are fed by only sucking into some fine spirituous Liquors, that pierce lyke pure Air and Oyl '.

The relation which the worship of ancestors held to that of the gods above, who are the Olympian Gods, the great Gods, and to the Gods below, who are the Gods of the Dead, and also to the daemons, and heroes or divine ancestors, is thus set forth by Plato in his *Laws* :—' In the first place, we affirm that next after the Olympian Gods, and the Gods of the State, honour should be given to the Gods below. . . . Next to these Gods, a wise man will do service to the daemons or spirits, and then to the heroes, and after them will follow the sacred places of private and ancestral Gods, having their ritual according to law. Next comes the honour of living parents.' [1]

It is evident from this direct testimony that the same sort of philosophy underlies food-sacrifice among the Celts and other peoples as we discovered underlying human-sacrifice, in our study of the Changeling Belief ; and that the Tuatha De Danann in their true mythological nature, and fairies, their modern counterpart, correspond in all essentials to Greek and Roman gods, genii, and daemons, and are often confused with the dead.

THE CELTIC LEGEND OF THE DEAD

The animistic character of the Celtic Legend of the Dead is apparent ; and the striking likenesses constantly appearing in our evidence between the ordinary apparitional fairies and the ghosts of the dead show that there is often no essential and sometimes no distinguishable difference between these two orders of beings, nor between the world of the dead and fairyland. We reserve for our chapter on *Science and Fairies* the scientific consideration of the psychology of this relationship, and of the probability that fairies as souls of the dead and as ghosts of the dead actually exist and influence the living.

GENERAL CONCLUSION

The chief anthropological problems connected with the modern Fairy-Faith, as our evidence presents it, have now

[1] *Laws*, iv ; cf. Jowett, *Dialogues of Plato*, v. 282–90.

been examined, at sufficient length, we trust, to explain
their essential significance ; and problems, to some extent
parallel, connected with the ancient Fairy-Faith have likewise been examined. There remain, however, very many
minor anthropological problems not yet touched upon ; but
several of the most important of these, e. g. various cults
of gods, spirits, fairies, and the dead, and folk-festivals
thereto related (see Section III) ; the circular fairy-dance
(see pp. 405–6) ; or the fairy world as the Otherworld (see
chap. vi), or as Purgatory (see chap. x), will receive consideration in following chapters, and so will certain very
definite psychological problems connected with dreams, and
trance-like states, with supernormal lapse of time, and with
seership.   We may now sum up the results so far attained.

Whether we examine the Fairy-Faith as a whole or whether
we examine specialized parts of it like those relating to the
smallness of fairies, to changelings, to witchcraft and magic,
to exorcisms, to taboos, and to food-sacrifice, in all cases
comparative folk-lore shows that the beliefs composing
it find their parallels the world over, and that fairy-like
beings are objects of belief now not only in Celtic countries,
but in Central Australia, throughout Polynesia, in Africa,
among American Red Men, in Asia generally, in Southern,
Western, and Northern Europe, and, in fact, wherever
civilized and primitive men hold religious beliefs.   From
a rationalist point of view anthropologists would be inclined
to regard the bulk of this widespread belief in spiritual
beings as being purely mythical, but for us to do so and
stop there would lead to no satisfactory solution : the origin
of myth itself needs to be explained, and one of the chief
objects of our study throughout the remainder of this book
is to make an attempt at such an explanation, especially of
Celtic myth.

Again, if we examine all fairy-like beings from a certain
superficial point of view, or even from the mythological point
of view, it is easy to discern that they are universally credited
with precisely the same characters, attributes, actions, or
powers as the particular peoples possess who have faith in

them ; and then the further fact emerges that this anthropomorphosing is due directly to the more immediate social
environment : we see merely an anthropomorphically
coloured picture of the whole of an age-long social evolution of the tribe, race, or nation who have fostered the
particular aspect of this one world-wide folk-religion. But
if we look still deeper, we discover as background to the
myths and the social psychology a profound animism. This
animism appears in its own environment in the shading away
of the different fairy-like beings into spirits and ghosts of
the departed. Going deeper yet, we find that such animistic
beliefs as concern themselves exclusively with the realm of
the dead are in many cases apparently so well founded on
definite provable psychical experiences on the part of living
men and women that the aid of science itself must be called
in to explain them, and this will be done in our chapter
entitled *Science and Fairies.*

So far it ought to be clear that already our evidence
points to a very respectable residue in the experiences of
percipients, which cannot be explained away—as can the
larger mass of the evidence—as due to ethnological, anthropomorphic, naturalistic, or sociological influences on the Celtic
mind ; and for the present this must be designated as the
x or unknown quantity in the Fairy-Faith. In chapter xi
this *x* quantity, augmented by whatever else is to be elicited
from further evidence, will be specifically discussed.

These points of view derived from our anthropological
examination of the chief parts of the evidence presented
by the living Fairy-Faith will be kept constantly before us
as we proceed further ; and what has been demonstrated
anthropologically in this chapter will serve to interpret what
is to follow until chapter xi is reached. With this tentative
position we pass to Section II of this study, and shall there
begin to examine, as we have just done with their modern
Fairy-Faith, the ancient Fairy-Faith of the Celts.

SECTION II
THE RECORDED FAIRY-FAITH

CHAPTER IV

THE PEOPLE OF THE GODDESS DANA (*TUATHA DÉ DANANN*) OR THE *SIDHE* (PRONOUNCED *SHEE*) [1]

' So firm was the hold which the ethnic gods of Ireland had taken upon the imagination and spiritual sensibilities of our ancestors that even the monks and christianized bards never thought of denying them. They doubtless forbade the people to worship them, but to root out the belief in their existence was so impossible that they could not even dispossess their own minds of the conviction that the gods were real supernatural beings.'—STANDISH O'GRADY.

The Goddess Dana and the modern cult of St. Brigit—The Tuatha De Danann or *Sidhe* conquered by the Sons of Mil—But Irish seers still see the *Sidhe*—Old Irish MSS. faithfully represent the Tuatha De Danann—The *Sidhe* as a spirit race—*Sidhe* palaces—The ' Taking ' of mortals—Hill visions of *Sidhe* women—*Sidhe* minstrels and musicians —Social organization and warfare among the *Sidhe*—The *Sidhe* war-goddesses, the *Badb*—The *Sidhe* at the Battle of Clontarf, A. D. 1014—Conclusion.

THE People of the Goddess Dana, or, according to D'Arbois de Jubainville, the People of the god whose mother was

[1] Chief general references : *Le Cycle Mythologique Irlandais* (Paris, 1884) and *L'Épopée celtique en Irlande* (Paris, 1892)—both by H. D'Arbois de Jubainville. Chief sources : The *Book of Armagh*, a collection of ecclesiastical MSS. probably written at Armagh, and finished in A. D. 807 by the learned scribe Ferdomnach of Armagh ; the *Leabhar na h-Uidhre* or ' Book of the Dun Cow ', the most ancient of the great collections of MSS. containing the old Irish romances, compiled about A. D. 1100 in the monastery of Clonmacnoise ; the *Book of Leinster*, a twelfth-century MS. compiled by Finn Mac Gorman, Bishop of Kildare ; the *Yellow Book of Lecan* (fifteenth century) ; and the *Book of Lismore*, an old Irish MS. found in 1814 by workmen while making repairs in the castle of Lismore, and thought to be of the fifteenth century. The *Book of Lismore* contains the *Agallamh na senórach* or ' Colloquy of the Ancients ', which has been edited by S. H. O'Grady in his *Silva Gadelica* (London, 1892), and by Whitley Stokes, *Ir. Texte*, iv. 1. For additional texts and editions of texts see Notes by R. I. Best to his translations of *Le Cycle Mythologique Irlandais* (Dublin, 1903).

called Dana,[1] are the Tuatha De Danann of the ancient mythology of Ireland. The Goddess Dana, called in the genitive Danand, in middle Irish times was named Brigit.[1] And this goddess Brigit of the pagan Celts has been supplanted by the Christian St. Brigit [1]; and, in exactly the same way as the pagan cult once bestowed on the spirits in wells and fountains has been transferred to Christian saints, to whom the wells and fountains have been re-dedicated, so to St. Brigit as a national saint has been transferred the pagan cult rendered to her predecessor. Thus even yet, as in the case of the minor divinities of their sacred fountains, the Irish people through their veneration for the good St. Brigit, render homage to the divine mother of the People who bear her name Dana,—who are the ever-living invisible Fairy-People of modern Ireland. For when the Sons of Mil, the ancestors of the Irish people, came to Ireland they found the Tuatha De Danann in full possession of the country. The Tuatha De Danann then retired before the invaders, without, however, giving up their sacred Island. Assuming invisibility, with the power of at any time reappearing in a human-like form before the children of the Sons of Mil, the People of the Goddess Dana became and are the Fairy-Folk, the *Sidhe* of Irish mythology and romance.[2] Therefore it is that to-day Ireland contains two races,—a race visible which we call Celts, and a race invisible which we call Fairies. Between these two races there is constant intercourse even now ; for Irish seers say that they can behold the majestic, beautiful *Sidhe*, and according to them the *Sidhe* are a race quite distinct from our own, just as living and possibly more powerful. These *Sidhe* (who are the ' gentry ' of the Ben Bulbin country and have kindred elsewhere in Ireland, Scotland,

---

[1] Cf. *Le Cycle Myth. Irl.*, pp. 144–5.

[2] Cf. *Le Cycle Myth. Irl.*, pp. 266–7. From the way they are described in many of the old Irish manuscripts, we may possibly regard the Tuatha De Danann as reflecting to some extent the characteristics of an early human population in Ireland. In other words, on an already flourishing belief in spiritual beings, known as the *Sidhe*, was superimposed, through anthropomorphism, an Irish folk-memory about a conquered pre-Celtic race of men who claimed descent from a mother goddess called Dana.

and probably in most other countries as well, such as the invisible races of the Yosemite Valley) have been described more or less accurately by our peasant seer-witnesses from County Sligo and from North and East Ireland. But there are other and probably more reliable seers in Ireland, men of greater education and greater psychical experience, who know and describe the *Sidhe* races as they really are, and who even sketch their likenesses. And to such seer Celts as these, Death is a passport to the world of the *Sidhe*, a world where there is eternal youth and never-ending joy, as we shall learn when we study it as the Celtic Otherworld.

The recorded mythology and literature of ancient Ireland have, very faithfully for the most part, preserved to us clear pictures of the Tuatha De Danann; so that disregarding some Christian influence in the texts of certain manuscripts, much rationalization, and a good deal of poetical colouring and romantic imagination in the pictures, we can easily describe the People of the Goddess Dana as they appeared in pagan days, when they were more frequently seen by mortals than now. Perhaps the Irish folk of the olden times were even more clairvoyant and spiritual-minded than the Irish folk of to-day. So by drawing upon these written records let us try to understand what sort of beings the *Sidhe* were and are.

NATURE OF THE *SIDHE*

In the *Book of Leinster*[1] the poem of *Eochaid* records that the Tuatha De Danann, the conquerors of the Fir-Bolgs, were hosts of *siabra*; and *siabra* is an Old Irish word meaning fairies, sprites, or ghosts. The word fairies is appropriate if restricted to mean fairies like the modern ' gentry '; but the word *ghosts* is inappropriate, because our evidence shows that the only relation the *Sidhe* or real Fairies hold to ghosts is a superficial one, the *Sidhe* and ghosts being alike only in respect to invisibility. In the two chief Irish MSS., the *Book of the Dun Cow* and the *Book of Leinster*, the Tuatha De Danann are described as ' gods

[1] Page 10, col. 2, ll. 6–8 ; cf. *Le Cycle Myth. Irl.*, p. 143.

and not-gods ' ; and Sir John Rhŷs considers this an ancient formula comparable with the Sanskrit *deva* and *adeva*, but not with ' poets (*dée*) and husbandmen (*an dée*) ' as the author of *Cóir Anmann* learnedly guessed.[1] It is also said, in the *Book of the Dun Cow*, that wise men do not know the origin of the Tuatha De Danann, but that ' it seems likely to them that they came from heaven, on account of their intelligence and for the excellence of their know-ledge '.[2] The hold of the Tuatha De Danann on the Irish mind and spirit was so strong that even Christian tran-scribers of texts could not deny their existence as a non-human race of intelligent beings inhabiting Ireland, even though they frequently misrepresented them by placing them on the level of evil demons,[3] as the ending of the story of the *Sick-Bed of Cuchulainn* illustrates :—' So that this was a vision to Cuchulainn of being stricken by the people of the *Sid* : for the demoniac power was great before the faith ; and such was its greatness that the demons used to fight bodily against mortals, and they used to show them delights and secrets of how they would be in immortality. It was thus they used to be believed in. So it is to such phantoms the ignorant apply the names of *Side* and *Aes Side*.' [4]   A passage in the *Silva Gadelica* (ii. 202–3) not only tends to confirm this last statement, but it also shows that the Irish people made a clear distinction between the god-race and our own :—In *The Colloquy with the Ancients*, as St. Patrick and Caeilte are talking with one another, ' a lone woman robed in mantle of green, a smock of soft silk being next her skin, and on her forehead a glittering plate of yellow gold,' came to them ; and when Patrick asked from whence she came, she replied : ' Out of *uaimh Chruachna*, or " the cave of Cruachan ".' Caeilte then asked : ' Woman, my soul, who art thou ? ' ' I am *Scothniamh* or " Flower-lustre ", daughter of the Daghda's son Bodhb derg.' Caeilte proceeded : ' And what started thee hither ? ' ' To

---

[1] Rhŷs, *Hib. Lect.*, p. 581 n. ; and *Cóir Anmann*, in *Ir. Texte*, III, ii. 355.
[2] Kuno Meyer's trans. in *Voy. of Bran*, ii. 300.
[3] Cf. Standish O'Grady, *Early Bardic Literature* (London, 1879), pp. 65–6.
[4] L. U. ; cf. A. Nutt, *Voy. of Bran*, i. 157–8.

require of thee my marriage-gift, because once upon a time thou promisedst me such.' And as they parleyed Patrick broke in with : ' It is a wonder to us how we see you two : the girl young and invested with all comeliness ; but thou Caeilte, a withered ancient, bent in the back and dingily grown grey.' ' Which is no wonder at all,' said Caeilte, ' for no people of one generation or of one time are we : *she is of the Tuatha Dé Danann, who are unfading and whose duration is perennial ; I am of the sons of Milesius, that are perishable and fade away.*' The exact distinction is between Caeilte, a withered old ancient—in most ways to be regarded as a ghost called up that Patrick may question him about the past history of Ireland—and a fairy-woman who is one of the *Sidhe* or Tuatha De Danann.[1]

In two of the more ancient Irish texts, the *Echtra Nerai* [2] or ' Expedition of Nera ', a preliminary tale in the introduction to the *Táin bó Cuailnge* or ' Theft of the Cattle of Cuailnge ' ; and a passage from the *Togail Bruidne dâ Derga*, or ' Destruction of Da Derga's Hostel ', [3] there seems

---

[1] Before Caeilte appears, Patrick is chanting Mass and pronouncing benediction ' on the rath in which Finn Mac Cumall (the slain leader of the Fianna) has been: the rath of Drumderg '. This chanting and benediction act magically as a means of calling up the ghosts of the other Fianna, for, as the text continues, thereupon ' the clerics saw Caeilte and his band draw near them ; and fear fell on them before the tall men with their huge wolf-dogs that accompanied them, *for they were not people of one epoch or of one time with the clergy.* Then Heaven's distinguished one, that pillar of dignity and angel on earth, Calpurn's son Patrick, apostle of the Gael, rose and took the aspergillum to sprinkle holy water on the great men ; floating over whom until that day there had been [and were now] a thousand legions of demons. Into the hills and " skalps ", into the outer borders of the region and of the country, the demons forthwith departed in all directions ; after which the enormous men sat down ' (*Silva Gadelica*, ii. 103). Here, undoubtedly, we observe a literary method of rationalizing the ghosts of the Fianna ; and their sudden and mysterious coming and personal aspects can be compared with the sudden and mysterious coming and personal aspects of the Tuatha De Danann as recorded in certain Irish manuscripts.

[2] Kuno Meyer's trans. in *Rev. Celt.*, x. 214–27. This tale is probably as old as the ninth or tenth century, so far as its present form is concerned, though representing very ancient traditions (Nutt, *Voy. of Bran*, i. 209).

[3] Stokes's trans. in *Rev. Celt.* xxii. 36–40. This text is one of the earliest with references to fairy beings, and may go back to the eighth

no reasonable doubt whatever about the Tuatha De Danann or *Sidhe* being a race like what we call spirits. The first text describes how Ailill and Medb in their palace of Cruachan celebrated the feast of *Samain* (November Eve, a feast of the dead even in pre-Christian times). Two culprits had been executed on the day before, and their bodies, according to the ancient Irish custom, were left hanging from a tree until the night of *Samain* should have passed ; for on that night it was dangerous to touch the bodies of the dead while demons and the people of the *Sidhe* were at large throughout all Ireland, and mortals found near dead bodies at such a time were in great danger of being *taken* by these spirit hosts of the Tuatha De Danann. And so on this very night, when thick darkness had settled down, Ailill desired to test the courage of his warriors, and offered his own gold-hilted sword to any young man who would go out and tie a coil of twisted twigs around the leg of one of the bodies suspended from the tree. After many had made the attempt and failed, because unable to brave the legions of demons and fairies, Nera alone succeeded ; but his success cost him dear, for he finally fell under the power both of the dead man, round whose legs he had tied the coil, and of an elfin host : with the dead man's body on his back, Nera was obliged to go to a strange house that the thirst of the dead man might be assuaged therein ; and the dead man in drinking scattered ' the last sip from his lips at the faces of the people that were in the house, so that they all died '. Nera carried back the body; and on returning to Cruachan he saw the fairy hosts going into the cave, ' for the fairy-mounds of Erinn are always opened about Halloween.' Nera followed after them until he came to their king in a palace of the Tuatha De Danann, seemingly in the cavern or elsewhere underground ; where he remained and was married to one of the fairy women. She it was who revealed to Nera the secret hiding-place, in a mysterious well, of the king's golden crown, and then betrayed her

or ninth century as a literary composition, though it too represents much older traditions.

whole people by reporting to Nera the plan they had for attacking Ailill's court on the Halloween to come. Moreover, Nera was permitted by his fairy wife to depart from the *sid* ; and he in taking leave of her asked : ' How will it be believed of me that I have gone into the *sid* ? ' ' Take fruits of summer with thee,' said the woman. ' Then he took wild garlic with him and primrose and golden fern.' And on the following November Eve when the *sid* of Cruachan was again open, ' the men of Connaught and the black hosts of exile ' under Ailill and Medb plundered it, taking away from it the crown of Briun out of the well. But ' Nera was left with his people in the *sid*, and has not come out until now, nor will he come till Doom.'

All of this matter is definitely enough in line with the living Fairy-Faith : there is the same belief expressed as now about November Eve being the time of all times when ghosts, demons, spirits, and fairies are free, and when fairies *take* mortals and marry them to fairy women ; also the beliefs that fairies are living in secret places in hills, in caverns, or under ground—palaces full of treasure and open only on November Eve. In so far as the real fairies, the *Sidhe*, are concerned, they appear as the rulers of the Feast of the Dead or *Samain*, as the controllers of all spirits who are then at large ; and, allowing for some poetical imagination and much social psychology and anthropomorphism, elements as common in this as in most literary descriptions concerning the Tuatha De Danann, they are faithfully enough presented.

The second text describes how King Conaire, in riding along a road toward Tara, saw in front of him three strange horsemen, three men of the *Sidhe* :—' Three red frocks had they, and three red mantles : three red steeds they bestrode, and three red heads of hair were on them. Red were they all, both body and hair and raiment, both steeds and men.' ' Who is it that fares before us ? ' asked Conaire. ' It was a taboo of mine for those Three to go before me—the three Reds to the house of Red. Who will follow them and tell them to come towards me in my track ? ' ' I will follow

them,' says Lé fri flaith, Conaire's son. ' He goes after
them, lashing his horse, and overtook them not. There was
the length of a spearcast between them : but they did not
gain upon him and he did not gain upon them.' All attempts
to come up with the red horsemen failed. But at last,
before they disappeared, one of the Three said to the king's
son riding so furiously behind them, ' Lo, my son, great the
news. Weary are the steeds we ride. We ride the steeds of
Donn Tetscorach (?) from the elfmounds. Though we are
alive we are dead. Great are the signs : destruction of life :
sating of ravens : feeding of crows, strife of slaughter :
wetting of sword-edge, shields with broken bosses in hours
after sundown. Lo, my son ! ' Then they disappear.
When Conaire and his followers heard the message, fear fell
upon them, and the king said : ' All my taboos have seized
me to-night, since those Three [Reds] [are the] banished
folks (?).' In this passage we behold three horsemen of the
Sidhe banished from their elfmound because guilty of falsehood. Visible for a time, they precede the king and so
violate one of his taboos ; and then delivering their fearful
prophecy they vanish. These three of the Tuatha De
Danann, majestic and powerful and weird in their mystic red,
are like the warriors of the ' gentry ' seen by contemporary
seers in West Ireland. Though dead, that is in an invisible
world like the dead, yet they are living. It seems that in
all three of the textual examples already cited, the scribe
has emphasized a different element in the unique nature of
the Tuatha De Danann. In the *Colloquy* it is their eternal
youth and beauty, in the *Echtra Nerai* it is their supremacy
over ghosts and demons on *Samain* and their power to steal
mortals away at such a time, and in this last their respect
for honesty. And in each case their portrayal corresponds
to that of the ' gentry ' and *Sidhe* by modern Irishmen ; so
that the old Fairy-Faith and the new combine to prove the
People of the God whose mother was Dana to have been
and to be a race of beings who are like mortals, but not
mortals, who to the objective world are as though dead,
yet to the subjective world are fully living and conscious.

O'Curry says :—' The term (*sidh*, pron. *shee*), as far as we know it, is always applied in old writings to the palaces, courts, halls, or residences of those beings which in ancient Gaedhelic mythology held the place which ghosts, phantoms, and fairies hold in the superstitions of the present day.' [1] In modern Irish tradition, ' the People of the *Sidhe*,' or simply the *Sidhe*, refer to the beings themselves rather than to their places of habitation.   Partly perhaps on account of this popular opinion that the *Sidhe* are a subterranean race, they are sometimes described as gods of the earth or *dei terreni*, as in the *Book of Armagh*; and since it was believed that they, like the modern fairies, control the ripening of crops and the milk-giving of cows, the ancient Irish rendered to them regular worship and sacrifice, just as the Irish of to-day do by setting out food at night for the fairy-folk to eat.

Thus after their conquest, these *Sidhe* or Tuatha De Danann in retaliation, and perhaps to show their power as agricultural gods, destroyed the wheat and milk of their conquerors, the Sons of Mil, as fairies to-day can do ; and the Sons of Mil were constrained to make a treaty with their supreme king, Dagda, who, in *Cóir Anmann* (§ 150), is himself called an earth-god.   Then when the treaty was made the Sons of Mil were once more able to gather wheat in their fields and to drink the milk of their cows ; [2] and we can suppose that ever since that time their descendants, who are the people of Ireland, remembering that treaty, have continued to reverence the People of the Goddess Dana by pouring libations of milk to them and by making them offerings of the fruits of the earth.

THE PALACES OF THE *SIDHE*

The marvellous palaces to which the Tuatha De Danann retired when conquered by the race of Mil were hidden in

---

[1] E. O'Curry, *Lectures on Manuscript Materials* (Dublin, 1861), p. 504.
[2] In the *Book of Leinster*, pp. 245–6 ; cf. *Le Cycle Myth. Irl.*, p. 269.

the depths of the earth, in hills, or under ridges more or
less elevated.[1] At the time of their conquest, Dagda their
high king made a distribution of all such palaces in his
kingdom. He gave one *sid* to Lug, son of Ethne, another
to Ogme ; and for himself retained two—one called *Brug
na Boinne*, or Castle of the Boyne, because it was situated
on or near the River Boyne near Tara, and the other called
Sid or *Brug Maic ind Oc*, which means Enchanted Palace or
Castle of the Son of the Young. And this Mac ind Oc was
Dagda's own son by the queen Boann, according to some
accounts, so that as the name (Son of the Young) signifies,
Dagda and Boann, both immortals, both Tuatha De Danann,
were necessarily always young, never knowing the touch of
disease, or decay, or old age. Not until Christianity gained
its psychic triumph at Tara, through the magic of Patrick
prevailing against the magic of the Druids—who seem to
have stood at that time as mediators between the People
of the Goddess Dana and the pagan Irish—did the Tuatha
De Danann lose their immortal youthfulness in the eyes of
mortals and become subject to death. In the most ancient
manuscripts of Ireland the pre-Christian doctrine of the
immortality of the divine race ' persisted intact and without
restraint ' ;[2] but in the *Senchus na relec* or ' History of
the Cemeteries ', from the *Leabhar na h-Uidhre*, and in the
Lebar gabala or ' Book of the Conquests ', from the *Book
of Leinster*, it was completely changed by the Christian
scribes.[2]

When Dagda thus distributed the underground palaces,
Mac ind Oc, or as he was otherwise called Oengus, was absent
and hence forgotten. So when he returned, naturally he
complained to his father, and the *Brug na Boinne*, the king's
own residence, was ceded to him for a night and a day, but
Oengus maintained that it was for ever. This palace was
a most marvellous one : it contained three trees which
always bore fruit, a vessel full of excellent drink, and two
pigs—one alive and the other nicely cooked ready to eat

---

[1] Cf. *Mesca Ulad*, Hennessy's ed., in *Todd Lectures*, Ser. 1 (Dublin, 1889),
p. 2.   [2] Cf. *Le Cycle Myth. Irl.*, pp. 273-6.

at any time ; and in this palace no one ever died.[1] In the *Colloquy*, Caeilte tells of a mountain containing a fairy palace which no man save Finn and six companions, Caeilte being one of these, ever entered. The Fenians, while hunting, were led thither by a fairy woman who had changed her shape to that of a fawn in order to allure them ; and the night being wild and snowy they were glad to take shelter therein. Beautiful damsels and their lovers were the inhabitants of the palace ; in it there was music and abundance of food and drink ; and on its floor stood a chair of crystal.[2] In another fairy palace, the enchanted cave of Keshcorran, Conaran, son of Imidel, a chief of the Tuatha De Danann, had sway ; ' and so soon as he perceived that the hounds' cry now sounded deviously, he bade his three daughters (that were full of sorcery) to go and take vengeance on Finn for his hunting '[3]—just as nowadays the ' good people' take vengeance on one of our race if a fairy domain is violated. Frequently the fairy palace is under a lake, as in the christianized story of the *Disappearance of Caenchomrac* :—Once when ' the cleric chanted his psalms, he saw [come] towards him a tall man that emerged out of the loch : from the bottom of the water that is to say.' This tall man informed the cleric that he came from an underwater monastery, and explained ' that there should be subaqueous inhabiting by men is with God no harder than that they should dwell in any other place '.[4] In all these ancient literary accounts of the *Sidhe*-palaces we easily recognize the same sort of palaces as those described to-day by Gaelic peasants as the habitations of the ' gentry ', or ' good people ', or ' people of peace.' Such habitations are in mountain caverns like those of Ben Bulbin or Knock Ma, or in fairy hills or knolls like the Fairy-Hill at Aberfoyle on which Robert Kirk is believed to have been *taken*, or beneath lakes. This brings us directly to the way in which the *Sidhe* or Tuatha De Danann of the olden times *took* fine-looking young men and maidens.

[1] Cf. *Le Cycle Myth. Irl.*; pp. 273-6.   [2] Cf. *Silva Gadelica*, ii. 222-3.
[3] Ib., ii. 343-7.   [4] Ib., ii. 94-6.

How the *Sidhe* ' took ' Mortals

Perhaps one of the earliest and most famous literary
accounts of such a *taking* is that concerning Aedh, son of
Eochaid Lethderg son of the King of Leinster, who is
represented as contemporary with Patrick.[1] While Aedh
was enjoying a game of hurley with his boy companions near
the *sidh* of Liamhain Softsmock, two of the *sidh*-women,
who loved the young prince, very suddenly appeared, and as
suddenly took him away with them into a fairy palace and
kept him there three years. It happened, however, that he
escaped at the end of that time, and, knowing the magical
powers of Patrick, went to where the holy man was, and
thus explained himself :—' Against the youths my opponents I (i. e. my side) took seven goals ; but at the last one
that I took, here come up to me two women clad in green
mantles : two daughters of *Bodhb derg mac an Daghda*, and
their names *Slad* and *Mumain*. Either of them took me by
a hand, and they led me off to a garish *brugh* ; whereby for
now three years my people mourn after me, the *sidh*-folk
caring for me ever since, and until last night I got a chance
opening to escape from the *brugh*, when to the number of
fifty lads we emerged out of the *sidh* and forth upon the
green. Then it was that I considered the magnitude of that
strait in which they of the *sidh* had had me, and away from
the *brugh* I came running to seek thee, holy Patrick.' ' That,'
said the saint, ' shall be to thee a safeguard, so that neither
their power nor their dominion shall any more prevail
against thee.' And so when Patrick had thus made Aedh
proof against the power of the fairy-folk, he kept him with
him under the disguise of a travelling minstrel until, arriving
in Leinster, he restored him to his father the king and to his
inheritance : Aedh enters the palace in his minstrel disguise ;
and in the presence of the royal assembly Patrick commands
him : ' Doff now once for all thy dark capacious hood, and
well mayest thou wear thy father's spear ! ' When the lad
removed his hood, and none there but recognized him, great

[1] *Silva Gadelica*, ii. 204-20.

was the surprise. He seemed like one come back from the
dead, for long had his heirless father and people mourned
for him. ' By our word,' exclaimed the assembly in their
joyous excitement, ' it is a good cleric's gift ! ' And the
king said : ' Holy Patrick, seeing that till this day thou hast
nourished him and nurtured, let not the Tuatha De Danann's
power any more prevail against the lad.' And Patrick
answered : ' That death which the King of Heaven and
Earth hath ordained is the one that he will have.' This
ancient legend shows clearly that the Tuatha De Danann,
or *Sidhe*, in the time when the scribe wrote the *Colloquy*
were thought of in the same way as now, as able to *take*
beautiful mortals whom they loved, and able to confer upon
them fairy immortality which prevented ' that death which
the King of Heaven and Earth hath ordained '.

Mortals, did they will it, could live in the world of the
Sidhe for ever, and we shall see this more fully in our study
of the Otherworld. But here it will be interesting to learn
that, unlike Aedh, whom some perhaps would call a foolish
youth, Laeghaire, also a prince, for he was the son of the
king of Connaught, entered a *dún* of the *Sidhe*, taking fifty
other warriors with him ; and he and his followers found
life in Fairyland so pleasant that they all decided to enjoy
it eternally. Accordingly, when they had been there a
year, they planned to return to Connaught in order to bid
the king and his people a final farewell. They announced
their plan, and Fiachna of the *Sidhe* told them how to
accomplish it safely :—' If ye would come back take with
you horses, but by no means dismount from off them ' ; ' So
it was done : they went their way and came upon a general
assembly in which Connaught, as at the year expired,
mourned for the aforesaid warrior-band, whom now all at
once they perceived above them (i. e. on higher ground).
Connaught sprang to meet them, but Laeghaire cried :
" Approach us not [to touch us] : 'tis to bid you farewell
that we are here ! " " Leave me not ! " Crimthann, his
father, said : " Connaught's royal power be thine ; their
silver and their gold, their horses with their bridles, and their

noble women be at thy discretion, only leave me not!'' But Laeghaire turned from them and so entered again into the *sídh*, where with Fiachna he exerciseṣ joint kingly rule ; nor is he as yet come out of it.' [1]

HILL VISIONS OF *SIDHE* WOMEN

There are many recorded traditions which represent certain hills as mystical places whereon men are favoured with visions of fairy women. Thus, one day King Muir-

---

[1] *Silva Gadelica*, ii. 290–1. In many old texts mortals are not forcibly *taken* ; but go to the fairy world through love for a fairy woman ; or else to accomplish there some mission.

No doubt the most curious elements in this text are those which represent the prince and his warrior companions, fresh come from Fairyland, as in some mysterious way so changed that they must neither dismount from their horses and thus come in contact with the earth, nor allow any mortal to touch them ; for to his father the king who came forward in joy to embrace him after having mourned him as dead, Laeghaire cried, ' Approach us not to touch us!' Some unknown magical bodily transmutation seems to have come about from their sojourn among the Tuatha De Danann, who are eternally young and unfading—a transmutation apparently quite the same as that which the 'gentry' are said to bring about now when one of our race is taken to live with them. And in all fairy stories no mortal ever returns from Fairyland a day older than on entering it, no matter how many years may have elapsed. The idea reminds us of the dreams of mediaeval alchemists who thought there exists, if one could only discover it, some magic potion which will so transmute every atom of the human body that death can never affect it. Probably the Christian scribe in writing down these strange words had in mind what Jesus said to Mary Magdalene when she beheld him after the Resurrection :—' Touch me not ; for I am not yet ascended unto the Father.' The parallel would be a striking and exact one in any case, for it is recorded that Jesus after he had arisen from the dead—had come out of Hades or the invisible realm of subjectivity which, too, is Fairyland—appeared to some and not to others—some being able to recognize him and others not; and concerning the nature of Jesus's body at the Ascension not all theologians are agreed. Some believe it to have been a physical body so purified and transmuted as to be like, or the same as, a spiritual body, and thus capable of invisibility and of entrance into the Realm of Spirit. The Scotch minister and seer used this same parallel in describing the nature and power of fairies and spirits (p. 91) ; hence it would seem to follow, if we admit the influence in the Irish text to be Christian, that early, like modern Christians, have, in accordance with Christianity, described the nature of the *Sidhe* so as to correspond with what we know it to be in the Fairy-Faith itself, both anciently and at the present day.

chertach came forth to hunt on the border of the Brugh (near Stackallan Bridge, County Meath), and his companions left him alone on his hunting-mound. ' He had not been there long when he saw a solitary damsel beautifully formed, fair-haired, bright-skinned, with a green mantle about her sitting near him on the turfen mound ; and it seemed to him that of womankind he had never beheld her equal in beauty and refinement.' [1]   In the Mabinogion of *Pwyll, Prince of Dyvet*, which seems to be only a Brythonic treatment of an original Gaelic tale, Pwyll seating himself on a mound where any mortal sitting might see a prodigy, saw a fairy woman ride past on a white horse, and she clad in a garment of shining gold. Though he tried to have his servitor on the swiftest horse capture her, ' There was some magic about the lady that kept her always the same distance ahead, though she appeared to be riding slowly.' When on the second day Pwyll returned to the mound the fairy woman came riding by as before, and the servitor again gave unsuccessful chase. Pwyll saw her in the same manner on the third day. He thereupon gave chase himself, and when he exclaimed to her, ' For the sake of the man whom you love, wait for me ! ' she stopped ; and by mutual arrangement the two agreed to meet and to marry at the end of a year.[2]

THE MINSTRELS OR MUSICIANS OF THE *SIDHE*

Not only did the fairy-folk of more ancient times enjoy wonderful palaces full of beauty and riches, and a life of eternal youth, but they also had, even as now, minstrelsy and rare music—music to which that of our own world could not be compared at all ; for even Patrick himself said that it would equal the very music of heaven if it were not for ' a twang of the fairy spell that infests it '.[3]   And this is how it was that Patrick heard the fairy music :—As he was travelling through Ireland he once sat down on a grassy

[1] *Death of Muirchertach*, Stokes's trans., in *Rev. Celt.*, xxiii. 397.
[2] Cf. J. Loth, *Les Mabinogion* (Paris, 1889), i. 38–52.
[3] *Silva Gadelica*, ii. 187–92.

knoll, as he often did in the good old Irish way, with Ulidia's king and nobles and Caeilte also : ' Nor were they long there before they saw draw near them a *scológ* or " non-warrior " that wore a fair green mantle having in it a fibula of silver ; a shirt of yellow silk next his skin, over and outside that again a tunic of soft satin, and with a *timpán* (a sort of harp) of the best slung on his back. " Whence comest thou, *scológ*? " asked the king. " Out of the *sídh* of the Daghda's son Bodhb Derg, out of Ireland's southern part." " What moved thee out of the south, and who art thou thyself ? " " I am Cascorach, son of Cainchinn that is *ollave* to the Tuatha De Danann, and am myself the makings of an *ollave* (i. e. an aspirant to the grade). What started me was the design to acquire knowledge, and information, and lore for recital, and the Fianna's mighty deeds of valour, from Caeilte son of Ronan." Then he took his *timpán* and made for them music and minstrelsy, so that he sent them slumbering off to sleep.' And Cascorach's music was pleasing to Patrick, who said of it : ' Good indeed it were, but for a twang of the fairy spell that infests it ; barring which nothing could more nearly than it resemble Heaven's harmony.' [1] And that very night which followed the day on which the *ollave* to the Tuatha De Danann came to them was the Eve of *Samain*. There was also another of these fairy *timpán*-players called ' the wondrous elfin man ', ' Aillén mac Midhna of the Tuatha De Danann, that out of *sídh* Finnachaidh to the northward used to come to Tara : the manner of his coming being with a musical *timpán* in his hand, the which whenever any heard he would at once sleep. Then, all being lulled thus, out of his mouth Aillén would emit a blast of fire. It was on the solemn *Samain*-Day (November Day) he came in every year, played his *timpán*, and to the fairy music that he made all hands would fall asleep. With his breath he used to blow up the flame and so, during a three-and-twenty years' spell, yearly burnt up Tara with all her gear.' And it is said that Finn, finally overcoming the magic of Aillén, slew him.[1]

[1] *Silva Gadelica*, ii. 142–4.

Perhaps in the first musician, Cascorach, though he is
described as the son of a Tuatha De Danann minstrel, we
behold a mortal like one of the many Irish pipers and
musicians who used to go, or even go yet, to the fairy-folk
to be educated in the musical profession, and then come back
as the most marvellous players that ever were in Ireland ;
though if Cascorach were once a mortal it seems that he has
been quite transformed in bodily nature so as to be really
one of the Tuatha De Danann himself. But Aillén mac
Midhna is undoubtedly one of the mighty ' gentry ' who
could—as we heard from County Sligo—destroy half the
human race if they wished. Aillén visits Tara, the old
psychic centre both for Ireland's high-kings and its Druids.
He comes as it were against the conquerors of his race, who
in their neglectfulness no longer render due worship and
sacrifice on the Feast of *Samain* to the Tuatha De Danann,
the gods of the dead, at that time supreme ; and then it is
that he works his magic against the royal palaces of the
kings and Druids on the ancient Hill. And to overcome the
magic of Aillén and slay him, that is, make it impossible for
him to repeat his annual visits to Tara, it required the might
of the great hero Finn, who himself was related to the same
Sidhe race, for by a woman of the Tuatha De Danann he
had his famous son Ossian (Oisin).[1]

In *Gilla dé*, who is Manannan mac Lir, the greatest
magician of the Tuatha De Danann, disguised as a being
who can disappear in the twinkling of an eye whenever he
wishes, and reappear unexpectedly as a ' kern that wore
garb of yellow stripes ', we meet with another fairy musician.
And to him O'Donnell says :—' By Heaven's grace again,
since first I heard the fame of them that within the hills and
under the earth beneath us make the fairy music, . . . music
sweeter than thy strains I have never heard ; thou art in
sooth a most melodious rogue ! ' [2] And again it is said of

---

[1] Campbell, *The Fians*, pp. 79–80. In *Silva Gadelica*, ii. 522, it is stated
that the mother of Ossian bore him whilst in the shape of a doe. The
mother of Ossian in animal shape may be an example of an ancient Celtic
totemistic survival.

[2] *Silva Gadelica*, ii. 311–24.

him :—' Then the *gilla decair* taking a harp played music
so sweet . . . and the king after a momentary glance at his
own musicians never knew which way he went from him.' [1]

SOCIAL ORGANIZATION AND WARFARE AMONG THE *SIDHE*

So far, we have seen only the happy side of the life of
the *Sidhe*-folk—their palaces and pleasures and music ; but
there was a more human (or anthropomorphic) side to their
nature in which they wage war on one another, and have
their matrimonial troubles even as we moderns. And we
turn now to examine this other side of their life, to behold
the *Sidhe* as a warlike race ; and as we do so let us remember
that the 'gentry' in the Ben Bulbin country and in all
Ireland, and the people of Finvara in Knock Ma, and also
the invisible races of California, are likewise described as
given to war and mighty feats of arms.

The invisible Irish races have always had a very distinct
social organization, so distinct in fact that Ireland can be
divided according to its fairy kings and fairy queens and
their territories even now ; [2] and no doubt we see in this
how the ancient Irish anthropomorphically projected into
an animistic belief their own social conditions and racial
characteristics. And this social organization and territorial
division ought to be understood before we discuss the social
troubles and consequent wars of the *Sidhe*-folk. For example in Munster Bodb was king and his enchanted
palace was called the *Sid* of the Men of Femen ; [3] and we
already know about the over-king Dagda and his Boyne
palace near Tara. In more modern times, especially in
popular fairy-traditions, Eevil or Eevinn (*Aoibhill* or *Aoibhinn*) of the *Craig Liath* or Grey Rock is a queen of the
Munster fairies ; [4] and Finvara is king of the Connaught
fairies (see p. 42). There are also the Irish fairy-queens

[1] *Silva Gadelica*, ii. 311–24.
[2] For an enumeration of the Tuatha De Danann chieftains and their
respective territories see *Silva Gadelica*, ii. 225.
[3] Cf. *Le Cycle Myth. Irl.*, p. 285.
[4] I am personally indebted for these names to Dr. Douglas Hyde.

Cleeona (*Cliodhna*, or in an earlier form *Clidna* [cf. p. 356]) and Aine (see p. 79 above).

We are now prepared to see the Tuatha De Danann in their domestic troubles and wars; and the following story is as interesting as any, for in it Dagda himself is the chief actor. Once when his own son Oengus fell sick of a love malady, King Dagda, who ruled all the *Sidhe*-folk in Ireland, joined forces with Ailill and Medb in order to compel Ethal Anbual to deliver up his beautiful daughter Caer whom Oengus loved. When Ethal Anbual's palace had been stormed and Ethal Anbual reduced to submission, he declared he had no power over his daughter Caer, for on the first of November each year, he said, she changed to a swan, or from a swan to a maiden again. 'The first of November next,' he added, 'my daughter will be under the form of a swan, near the Loch bel Draccon. Marvellous birds will be seen there : my daughter will be surrounded by a hundred and fifty other swans.' When the November Day arrived, Oengus went to the lake, and, seeing the swans and recognizing Caer, plunged into the water and instantly became a swan with her. While under the form of swans, Oengus and Caer went together to the Boyne palace of the king Dagda, his father, and remained there ; and their singing was so sweet that all who heard it slept three days and three nights.[1] In this story, new elements in the nature of the *Sidhe* appear, though like modern ones : the *Sidhe* are able to assume other forms than their own, are subject to enchantments like mortals ; and when under the form of swans are in some perhaps superficial aspects like the swan-maidens in stories which are world-wide, and their swan-song has the same sweetness and magical effect as in other countries.[2]

In the Rennes *Dinnshenchas* there is a tale about a war among the 'men of the Elfmounds' over 'two lovable maidens who dwelt in the elfmound', and when they delivered the battle 'they all shaped themselves into the

---

Cf. *Le Cycle Myth. Irl.*, pp. 284-9 ; cf. *Rev. Celt.*, iii. 347.
[2] Cf. E. S. Hartland, *Science of Fairy Tales* (London, 1891), cc. x-xi.

shapes of deer '.[1] Midir's sons under Donn mac Midir, in rebellion against the Daghda's son Bodh Derg, fled away to an obscure *sidh*, where in yearly battle they met the hosts of the other Tuatha De Danann under Bodh Derg ; and it was into this *sidh* or fairy palace on the very eve before the annual contest that Finn and his six companions were enticed by the fairy woman in the form of a fawn, to secure their aid.[2] And in another tale, Laeghaire, son of the king of Connaught, with fifty warriors, plunged into a lake to the fairy world beneath it, in order to assist the fairy man, who came thence to them, to recover his wife stolen by a rival.[2]

THE *SIDHE* AS WAR-GODDESSES OR THE *BADB*

It is in the form of birds that certain of the Tuatha De Danann appear as war-goddesses and directors of battle,[3]— and we learn from one of our witnesses (p. 46) that the ' gentry ' or modern *Sidhe*-folk take sides even now in a great war, like that between Japan and Russia. It is in their relation to the hero Cuchulainn that one can best study the People of the Goddess Dana in their rôle as controllers of human war. In the greatest of the Irish epics, the *Tain Bó Cuailnge*, where Cuchulainn is under their influence, these war-goddesses are called *Badb*[4] (or *Bodb*) which here seems to be a collective term for *Neman, Macha*, and *Morrigu* (or *Morrigan*)[5]—each of whom exercises a particular supernatural power. *Neman* appears as the confounder of armies, so that friendly bands, bereft of their senses by her, slaughter one another; *Macha* is a fury that riots and revels among

---

[1] Stokes's trans. in *Rev. Celt.*, xvi. 274–5.

[2] *Silva Gadelica*, ii. 222 ff.; ii. 290. In another version of the second tale, referred to above (on page 295), Laeghaire and his fifty companions enter the fairy world through a *dún*.

[3] Sometimes, as in *Da Choca's Hostel* (*Rev. Celt.*, xxi. 157, 315), the *Badb* appears as a weird woman uttering prophecies. In this case the *Badb* watches over Cormac as his doom comes. She is described as standing on one foot, and with one eye closed (apparently in a bird's posture), as she chanted to Cormac this prophecy :—' I wash the harness of a king who will perish.'

[4] Synonymous names are *Badb-catha, Fea, Ana*. Cf. *Rev. Celt.*, i. 35–7.

[5] Cf. Hennessy, *Ancient Irish Goddess of War*, in *Rev. Celt.*, i. 32–55.

the slain ; while *Morrigu*, the greatest of the three, by her presence infuses superhuman valour into Cuchulainn, nerves him for the cast, and guides the course of his unerring spear. And the Tuatha De Danann in infusing this valour into the great hero show themselves—as we already know them to be on *Samain* Eve—the rulers of all sorts of demons of the air and awful spirits :—In the *Book of Leinster* (fol. 57, B 2) it is recorded that ' the satyrs, and sprites, and maniacs of the valleys, and demons of the air, shouted about him, for the Tuatha De Danann were wont to impart their valour to him, in order that he might be more feared, more dreaded, more terrible, in every battle and battle-field, in every combat and conflict, into which he went.'

The Battles of Moytura seem in most ways to be nothing more than the traditional record of a long warfare to determine the future spiritual control of Ireland, carried on between two diametrically opposed orders of invisible beings, the Tuatha De Danann representing the gods of light and good and the Fomorians representing the gods of darkness and evil. It is said that after the second of these battles ' The *Morrigu*, daughter of Ernmas (the Irish war-goddess), proceeded to proclaim that battle and the mighty victory which had taken place, to the royal heights of Ireland and to its fairy host and its chief waters and its river-mouths '.[1] For good had prevailed over evil, and it was settled that all Ireland should for ever afterwards be a sacred country ruled over by the People of the Goddess Dana and the Sons of Mil jointly. So that here we see the Tuatha De Danann with their war-goddess fighting their own battles in which human beings play no part.

It is interesting to observe that this Irish war-goddess, the *bodb* or *badb*, considered of old to be one of the Tuatha De Danann, has survived to our own day in the fairy-lore of the chief Celtic countries. In Ireland the survival is best seen in the popular and still almost general belief among the peasantry that the fairies often exercise their magical powers under the form of royston-crows ; and for this

---

[1] Stokes, *Second Battle of Moytura*, in *Rev. Celt.*, xii. 109–11.

reason these birds are always greatly dreaded and avoided.
The resting of one of them on a peasant's cottage may
signify many things, but often it means the death of one of
the family or some great misfortune, the bird in such a case
playing the part of a *bean-sidhe* (banshee). And this folk-
belief finds its echo in the recorded tales of Wales, Scotland,
and Brittany. In the *Mabinogi*, ' Dream of Rhonabwy,'
Owain, prince of Rheged and a contemporary of Arthur,
has a wonderful crow which always secures him victory in
battle by the aid of three hundred other crows under its
leadership. In Campbell's *Popular Tales of the West Highlands* the fairies very often exercise their power in the form
of the common hoody crow ; and in Brittany there is a folk-
tale entitled ' *Les Compagnons* '[1] in which the chief actor is
a fairy under the form of a magpie who lives in a royal
forest just outside Rennes.[2]

W. M. Hennessy has shown that the word *bodb* or *badb*,
aspirated *bodhbh* or *badhbh* (pronounced *bov* or *bav*), originally signified rage, fury, or violence, and ultimately implied
a witch, fairy, or goddess ; and that as the memory of this
Irish goddess of war survives in folk-lore, her emblem is the
well-known scald-crow, or royston-crow.[3] By referring to
Peter O'Connell's *Irish Dictionary* we are able to confirm
this popular belief which identifies the battle-fairies with

---

[1] Luzel, *Contes populaires de Basse Bretagne*, iii. 296–311.

[2] The Celtic examples recall non-Celtic ones : the raven was sacred
among the ancient Scandinavians and Germans, being looked upon as
the emblem of Odin ; in ancient Egypt and Rome commonly, and to a less
extent in ancient Greece, gods often declared their will through birds or
even took the form of birds ; in Christian scriptures the Spirit of God or
the Holy Ghost descended upon Jesus at his baptism in the semblance of
a dove ; and it is almost a world-wide custom to symbolize the human
soul under the form of a bird or butterfly. Possibly such beliefs as these
are relics of a totemistic creed which in times long previous to history was
as definitely held by the ancestors of the nations of antiquity, including
the ancient Celts, as any totemistic creed to be found now among native
Australians or North American Red Men. At all events, in the story of a
bird ancestry of Conaire we seem to have a perfectly clear example of
a Celtic totemistic survival—even though Dr. Frazer may not admit it
as such (cf. *Rev. Celt.*, xxii. 20, 24 ; xii. 242–3).

[3] Hennessy, *The Ancient Irish Goddess of War*, in *Rev. Celt.*, i. 32–57.

the royston-crow, and to discover that there is a definite relationship or even identification between the *Badb* and the *Bean-sidhe* or banshee, as there is in modern Irish folk-lore between the royston-crow and the fairy who announces a death. *Badb-catha* is made to equal ' Fionog, a royston-crow, a squall crow ' ; *Badb* is defined as a ' *bean-sidhe*, a female fairy, phantom, or spectre, supposed to be attached to certain families, and to appear sometimes in the form of squall-crows, or royston-crows ' ; and the *Badb* in the three-fold aspect is thus explained : ' *Macha*, i. e. a royston-crow ; *Morrighain*, i. e. the great fairy ; *Neamhan*, i. e. *Badb catha no feannog; a badb catha*, or royston-crow.' Similar explanations are given by other glossarists, and thus the evidence of etymological scholarship as well as that of folk-lore support the Psychological Theory.

THE *SIDHE* IN THE BATTLE OF CLONTARF, A.D. 1014

The People of the Goddess Dana played an important part in human warfare even so late as the Battle of Clontarf, fought near Dublin, April 23, 1014 ; and at that time fairy women and phantom-hosts were to the Irish unquestionable existences, as real as ordinary men and women. It is recorded in the manuscript story of the battle, of which numerous copies exist, that the fairy woman Aoibheall [1] came to Dunlang O'Hartigan before the battle and begged him not to fight, promising him life and happiness for two hundred years if he would put off fighting for a single day ; but the patriotic Irishman expressed his decision to fight for Ireland, and then the fairy woman foretold how he and his friend Murrough, and Brian and Conaing and all the nobles of Erin and even his own son Turlough, were fated to fall in the conflict.

On the eve of the battle, Dunlang comes to his friend Murrough directly from the fairy woman ; and Murrough

---

[1] *Aoibheall*, who came to tell Brian Borumha of his death at Clontarf, was the family banshee of the royal house of Munster. Cf. J. H. Todd, *War of the Gaedhil with the Gaill* (London, 1867), p. 201.

upon seeing him reproaches him for his absence in these words :—'Great must be the love and attachment of some woman for thee which has induced thee to abandon me.' 'Alas O King,' answered Dunlang, ' the delight which I have abandoned for thee is greater, if thou didst but know it, namely, life without death, without cold, without thirst, without hunger, without decay, beyond any delight of the delights of the earth to me, until the judgement, and heaven after the judgement ; and if I had not pledged my word to thee I would not have come here ; and, moreover, it is fated for me to die on the day that thou shalt die.' When Murrough has heard this terrible message, the prophecy of his own death in the battle, despondency seizes him ; and then it is that he declares that he for Ireland like Dunlang for honour has also sacrificed the opportunity of entering and living in that wonderful Land of Eternal Youth :—' Often was I offered in hills, and in fairy mansions, this world (the fairy world) and these gifts, but I never abandoned for one night my country nor mine inheritance for them.' [1]

And thus is described the meeting of the two armies at Clontarf, and the demons of the air and the phantoms, and all the hosts of the invisible world who were assembled to scatter confusion and to revel in the bloodshed, and how above them in supremacy rose the *Badb* :—' It will be one of the wonders of the day of judgement to relate the description of this tremendous onset. There arose a wild, impetuous, precipitate, mad, inexorable, furious, dark, lacerating, merciless, combative, contentious *badb*, which was shrieking and fluttering over their heads. And there arose also the satyrs, and sprites, and the maniacs of the valleys, and the witches, and goblins, and owls, and destroying demons of the air and firmament, and the demoniac phantom host ; and they were inciting and sustaining valour and battle with them.' [2] It is said of Murrough (*Murchadh*) as he entered the thick of the fight and prepared to assail the

---

[1] Hyde, *Literary History of Ireland*, p. 440.

[2] Cf. Hennessy, in *Rev. Celt.*, i. 39–40. In place of *badb*, Dr. Hyde (*Lit. Hist. Irl.*, p. 440) uses the word *vulture*.

foreign invaders, the Danes, when they had repulsed the Dal-Cais, that ' he was seized with a boiling terrible anger, an excessive elevation and greatness of spirit and mind. A bird of valour and championship rose in him, and fluttered over his head and on his breath '.[1]

CONCLUSION

The recorded or manuscript Fairy-Faith of the Gaels corresponds in all essentials with the living Gaelic Fairy-Faith : the Tuatha De Danann or *Sidhe*, the ' Gentry ', the ' Good People ', and the ' People of Peace ' are described as a race of invisible divine beings eternally young and unfading. They inhabit fairy palaces, enjoy rare feasts and love-making, and have their own music and minstrelsy. They are essentially majestic in their nature ; they wage war in their own invisible realm against other of its inhabitants like the ancient Fomorians ; they frequently direct human warfare or nerve the arm of a great hero like Cuchulainn ; and demons of the air, spirit hosts, and awful unseen creatures obey them. Mythologically they are gods of light and good, able to control natural phenomena so as to make harvests come forth abundantly or not at all. But they are not such mythological beings as we read about in scholarly dissertations on mythology, dissertations so learned in their curious and unreasonable and often unintelligible hypotheses about the workings of the mind among primitive men. The way in which social psychology has deeply affected all such animistic beliefs was pointed out above in chapter iii. In chapter xi, entitled *Science and Fairies*, our position with respect to the essential nature of the fairy races will be made clear.

---

[1] Hennessy, in *Rev. Celt.*, i. 52.

SECTION II
THE RECORDED FAIRY-FAITH

CHAPTER V

BRYTHONIC DIVINITIES AND THE BRYTHONIC FAIRY-FAITH [1]

'On the one hand we have the man Arthur, whose position we have tried to define, and on the other a greater Arthur, a more colossal figure, of which we have, so to speak, but a *torso* rescued from the wreck of the Celtic pantheon.'—The Right Hon. Sir JOHN RHŶS.

The god Arthur and the hero Arthur—Sevenfold evidence to show Arthur as an incarnate fairy king—Lancelot the foster-son of a fairy woman —Galahad the offspring of Lancelot and the fairy woman Elayne— Arthur as a fairy king in *Kulhwch and Olwen*—Gwynn ab Nudd— Arthur like Dagda, and like Osiris—Brythonic fairy-romances : their evolution and antiquity—Arthur in Nennius, Geoffrey, Wace, and in Layamon—Cambrensis' Otherworld tale—Norman-French writers of twelfth and thirteenth centuries—*Romans d'Aventure* and *Romans Bretons*—Origins of the 'Matter of Britain'—Fairy-romance episodes in Welsh literature—Brythonic origins.

ARTHUR AND ARTHURIAN MYTHOLOGY

As we have just considered the Gaelic Divinities in their character as the Fairy-Folk of popular Gaelic tradition, so now we proceed to consider the Brythonic Divinities in the same way, beginning with the greatest of them all, Arthur. Even a superficial acquaintance with the Arthurian Legend

---

[1] Chief general reference : Sir John Rhŷs, *Arthurian Legend* (Oxford, 1891). Chief sources : Nennius, *Historia Britonum* (circa 800); Geoffrey of Monmouth, *Historia Regum Britanniae* (circa 1136) ; Wace, *Le Roman de Brut* (circa 1155); Layamon's *Brut* (circa 1200) ; Marie de France, *Lais* (twelfth-thirteenth century) ; *The Four Ancient Books of Wales* twelfth-fifteenth century), edited by W. F. Skene ; *The Mabinogion* (based on the *Red Book of Hergest*, a fourteenth-century manuscript), edited by Lady Charlotte Guest, Sir John Rhŷs and J. G. Evans, and Professor J. Loth ; Malory, *Le Morte D'Arthur* (1470) ; *The Myvyrian Archaiology of Wales*, collected out of ancient manuscripts (Denbigh, 1870); *Iolo Manuscripts*, a selection of ancient Welsh manuscripts (Llandovery, 1848).

shows how impossible it is to place upon it any one interpretation to the exclusion of other interpretations, for in one aspect Arthur is a Brythonic divinity and in another a sixth-century Brythonic chieftain.   But the explanation of this double aspect seems easy enough when we regard the historical Arthur as a great hero, who, exactly as in so many parallel cases of national hero-worship, came—within a comparatively short time—to be enshrined in the imagination of the patriotic Brythons with all the attributes anciently belonging to a great Celtic god called Arthur.[1]   The hero and the god were first confused, and then identified,[2] and hence arose that wonderful body of romance which we call Arthurian, and which has become the glory of English literature.

Arthur in the character of a culture hero,[3] with god-like powers to instruct mortals in wisdom, and, also, as a being in some way related to the sun—as a sun-god perhaps—can well be considered the human-divine institutor of the mystic brotherhood known as the Round Table. We ought, probably, to consider Arthur, like Cuchulainn, as a god incarnate in a human body for the purpose of educating the race of men ; and thus, while living as a man, related definitely and, apparently, consciously to the invisible gods or fairy-folk. Among the Aztecs and Peruvians in the New World, there was a widespread belief that great heroes who had once been men have now their celestial abode in the sun, and from time to time reincarnate to become teachers of

[1] In a Welsh poem of the twelfth century (see W. F. Skene, *Four Ancient Books*, Edinburgh, 1868, ii. 37, 38) wherein the war feats of Prince Geraint are described, his men, who lived and fought a long time after the period assigned to Arthur, are called the men of Arthur ; and, as Sir John Rhŷs thinks, this is good evidence that the genuine Arthur was a mythical figure, one might almost be permitted to say a god, who overshadows and directs his warrior votaries, but who, never descending into the battle, is in this respect comparable with the Irish war-goddess the *Badb* (cf. Rhŷs, *Celtic Britain*, London, 1904, p. 236.

[2] Cf. Rhŷs, *Arth. Leg.*, chap. 1.

[3] Cf. Rhŷs, *Arth. Leg.*, pp. 24, 48. Sir John Rhŷs sees good reasons for regarding Arthur as a culture hero, because of Arthur's traditional relation with agriculture, which most culture heroes, like Osiris, have taught their people (ib., pp. 41–3).

their less developed brethren of our own race; and a
belief of the same character existed among the Egyptians
and other peoples of the Old World, including the Celts.
It will be further shown, in our study of the Celtic Doctrine
of Re-birth, that anciently among the Gaels and Brythons
such heroes as Cuchulainn and Arthur were also considered
reincarnate sun-divinities. As a being related to the sun,
as a sun-god, Arthur is like Osiris, the Great Being, who
with his brotherhood of great heroes and god-companions
enters daily the underworld or Hades to battle against the
demons and forces of evil,[1] even as the Tuatha De Danann
battled against the Fomors. And the most important things
in the traditions of the great Brythonic hero connect him
directly with this strange world of subjectivity. First of all,
his own father, Uthr Bendragon,[2] was a king of Hades, so
that Arthur himself, being his child, is a direct descendant
of this Otherworld. Second, the Arthurian Legend traces
the origin of the Round Table back to Arthur's father,
Hades being ' the realm whence all culture was fabled to
have been derived '.[3] Third, the name of Arthur's wife,
Gwenhwyvar, resolves itself into White Phantom or White
Apparition, in harmony with Arthur's line of descent from
the region of phantoms and apparitions and fairy-folk.
Thus:—*Gwenhwyvar* or *Gwenhwyfar* equals *Gwen* or *Gwenn*,
a Brythonic word meaning white, and *hwyvar*, a word not
found in the Brythonic dialects, but undoubtedly cognate
with the Irish word *siabhradh*, a fairy, equal to *siabhra*,
siabrae, *siabur*, a fairy, or ghost, the Welsh and the Irish
word going back to the form **seibaro*.[4] Hence the name
of Arthur's wife means the *white ghost* or *white phantom*,
quite in keeping with the nature of the Tuatha De Danann
and that of the fairy-folk of Wales or *Tylwyth Teg*—the
' Fair Family '.

Fourth, as a link in the chain of evidence connecting

---

[1] Cf. G. Maspero, *Contes populaires de l'Égypte Ancienne*[3] (Paris, 1906),
Intro., p. 57.

[2] Sommer's Malory's *Morte D'Arthur*, iii. 1.

[3] Rhŷs, *Arth. Leg.*, p. 9.

[4] I am indebted to Professor J. Loth for help with this etymology.

Arthur with the invisible world where the Fairy-People live, his own sister is called *Morgan le Fay* in the romances,[1] and is thus definitely one of the fairy women who, according to tradition, are inhabitants of the Celtic Otherworld sometimes known as Avalon. Fifth, in the Welsh Triads,[2] Llacheu, the son of Arthur and Gwenhwyvar, is credited with clairvoyant vision, like the fairy-folk, so that he understands the secret nature of all solid and material things ; and ' the story of his death as given in the second part of the Welsh version of the Grail, makes him hardly human at all.'[3] Sixth, the name of Melwas, the abductor of Arthur's wife, is shown by Sir John Rhŷs to mean a prince-youth or a princely youth, and the same authority considers it probable that, as such, Melwas or Maelwas was a being endowed with eternal youth,—even as Midir, the King of the Tuatha De Danann, who though a thousand years old appeared handsome and youthful. So it seems that the abduction of Gwenhwyfar was really a fairy abduction, such as we read about in the domestic troubles of the Irish fairy-folk, on a level with the abduction of Etain by her Otherworld husband Midir.[4] And in keeping with this superhuman character of the abductor of the White Phantom or Fairy, Chrétien de Troyes, in his metrical romance *Le Conte de la Charrette*, describes the realm of which Melwas was lord as a place whence no traveller returns.[5] As further proof that the realm of Melwas was meant by Chrétien to be the subjective world, where the god-like Tuatha De Danann, the *Tylwyth Teg*, and the shades of the dead equally exist, it is said that access to it was by two narrow bridges ; ' one called *li Ponz Evages* or the Water Bridge, because it was a narrow passage a foot and a half wide and as much in height, with water above and below it as well as on both sides ' ; the other

---

[1] Cf. Rhŷs, *Arth Leg.*, p. 22.

[2] i. 10 ; ii. 21[b] ; iii. 70 ; cf. Rhys, *Arth. Leg.*, p. 60.

[3] See Williams' *Seint Greal*, pp. 278, 304, 341, 617, 634, 658, 671 ; Rhŷs, *Arth. Leg.*, p. 61.

[4] Cf. Rhŷs, *Arth. Leg.*, pp. 51, 35 ; and see our study, pp. 374–6.

[5] *Chevalier de la Charrette* (ed. by Tarbé), p. 22 ; *Romania*, xii. 467, 515 ; cf. Rhŷs, *Arth. Leg.*, p. 54.

li Ponz de l'Espée or the Sword Bridge, because it consisted of the edge of a sword two lances in length.[1] The first bridge, considered less perilous than the other, was chosen by Gauvain (Gwalchmei), when with Lancelot he was seeking to rescue Gwenhwyfar ; but he failed to cross it. Lancelot with great trouble crossed the second. In many mythologies and in world-wide folk-tales there is a narrow bridge or bridges leading to the realm of the dead. Even Mohammed in the *Koran* declares it necessary to cross a bridge as thin as a hair, if one would enter Paradise. And in living folk-lore in Celtic countries, as we found among the Irish peasantry, the crossing of a bridge or stream of water when pursued by fairies or phantoms is a guarantee of protection. There is always the mystic water between the realm of the living and the realm of subjectivity.[2] In ancient Egypt there was always the last voyage begun on the sacred Nile ; and in all classical literature Pluto's realm is entered by crossing a dark, deep river,—the river of forgetfulness between physical consciousness and spiritual consciousness. Burns has expressed this belief in its popular form in his *Tam O'Shanter*. And in our Arthurian parallel there is a clear enough relation between the beings inhabiting the invisible realm and the Brythonic heroes and gods. How striking, too, as Gaston Paris has pointed out, is the similarity between Melwas' capturing Gwenhwyvar as she was in the woods a-maying, and the rape of Proserpine by Pluto, the god of Hades, while she was collecting flowers in the fields.[3]

A curious matter in connexion with this episode of Gwenhwyvar's abduction should claim our attention. Malory relates[4] that when Queen Guenever advised her knights of the Table Round that on the morrow (May Day, when fairies have special powers) she would go on maying, she warned them all to be well-horsed and *dressed in green*. This was the colour that nearly all the fairy-folk of Britain and

---

[1] *Romania*, xii. 467-8, 473-4; cf. Rhŷs, *Arth. Leg.*, p. 55.
[2] Cf. Tylor, *Prim. Cult.*,⁴ ii. 93-4.
[3] *Romania*, xii. 508 ;. cf. Rhŷs, *Arth. Leg.*, p. 54.   [4] Book XIX, c. i.

Ireland wear. It symbolizes, as many ancient mystical writings declare, eternal youth, and resurrection or re-birth, as in nature during the springtime, when all vegetation after its death-sleep of winter springs into new life.[1] In the *Myvyrian Archaiology*,[2] Arthur when he has reached the realm of Melwas speaks with Gwenhwyvar,[3] he being

[1] In the *Lebar Brecc* there is a tract describing eight Eucharistic Colours and their mystical or hidden meaning ; and green is so described that we recognize in its Celtic-Christian symbolism the same essential significance as in the writings of both pagan and non-Celtic Christian mystics, thus :—
' This is what the Green denotes, when he (the priest) looks at it : that his heart and his mind be filled with great faintness and exceeding sorrow : for what is understood by it is his burial at the end of life under mould of earth ; for green is the original colour of every earth, and therefore the colour of the robe of Offering is likened unto green ' (Stokes, *Tripartite Life*, Intro., p. 189). During the ceremonies of initiation into the Ancient Mysteries, it is supposed that the neophyte left the physical body in a trance state, and in full consciousness, which he retained afterwards, entered the subjective world and beheld all its wonders and inhabitants ; and that coming out of that world he was clothed in a robe of sacred green to sym-bolize his own spiritual resurrection and re-birth into real life—for he had penetrated the Mystery of Death and was now an initiate. Even yet there seems to be an echo of the ancient Egyptian Mysteries in the Festival of Al-Khidr celebrated in the middle of the wheat harvest in Lower Egypt. Al-Khidr is a holy personage who, according to the belief of the people, was the Vizier of Dhu'l-Karnen, a contemporary of Abraham, and who, never having died, is still living and will continue to live until the Day of Judgement. And he is always represented ' clad in green garments, whence probably the name ' he bears. Green is thus associated with a hero or god who is immortal and unchanging, like the Tuatha De Danann and fairy races (see Sir Norman Lockyer's *Stonehenge and Other Stone Monuments*, London, 1909, p. 29). In modern Masonry, which preserves many of the ancient mystic rites, and to some extent those of initiation as anciently performed, green is the symbol of life, immutable nature, of truth, and victory. In the evergreen the Master Mason finds the emblem of hope and immortality. And the masonic authority who gives this information suggests that in all the Ancient Mysteries this symbolism was carried out —green symbolizing the birth of the world and the moral creation or resurrection of the initiate (*General History, Cyclopedia, and Dictionary of Freemasonry*, by Robert Macoy, 33°, New York, 1869).

[2] *Myv. Arch.*, i. 175. The text itself in this work is said to be copied from the *Green Book*—now unknown. Cf. Rhŷs, *Arth. Leg.* p. 56 n.

[3] In this text, the Gwenhwyvar who is in the power of Melwas is referred to as Arthur's second wife Gwenhwyvar, for according to the Welsh Triads (i. 59 ; ii. 16 ; iii. 109) there are three wives of Arthur all named Gwen-hwyvar. As Sir John Rhŷs observes, no poet has ever availed himself of all three, for the evident reason that they would have spoilt his plot (*Arth. Leg.*, p. 35).

on a black horse and she on a green one :—' Green is my steed of the tint of the leaves.' Arthur's black horse— black perhaps signifying the dead to whose realm he has gone—being proof against all water, may have been, there- fore, proof against the inhabitants of the world of shades and against fairies :—

> Black is my steed and brave beneath me,
> No water will make him fear,
> And no man will make him swerve.

The fairy colour, in different works and among different authors differing both in time and country, continues to attach itself to the abduction episode. Thus, in the four- teenth century the poet D. ab Gwilym alludes to Melwas himself as having a cloak of green :—' The sleep of Melwas beneath (or in) the green cloak.' Sir John Rhŷs, who makes this translation, observes that another reading still of *y glas glog* resolves it into a green bower to which Melwas took Gwenhwyvar.[1] In any case, the reference is significant, and goes far, in combination with the other references, to repre- sent the White Phantom or Fairy and her lover Melwas as beings of a race like the Irish *Sidhe* or People of the Goddess Dana. And though by no means exhausting all examples tending to prove this point, we pass on to the seventh and most important of our links in the sequence of evidence, the carrying of Arthur to Avalon in a fairy ship by fairy women.

From the first, Arthur was under superhuman guidance and protection. Merlin the magician, born of a spirit or daemon, claimed Arthur before birth and became his teacher afterwards. From the mysterious Lady of the Lake, Arthur received his magic sword *Excalibur*,[2] and to her returned it, through Sir Bedivere. During all his time on earth the ' lady

---

[1] D. ab Gwilym's Poetry (London, 1789), poem cxi, line 44. Cf. Rhŷs, *Arth. Leg.*, p. 66.

[2] Malory, Book I, c. xxv. One account of Arthur's sword *Caledvwlch* or *Caleburn* describes it as having been made in the Isle of Avalon (Lady Ch. Guest's *Mabinogion*, ii. 322 n. ; also *Myv. Arch.*, ii. 306).

of the lake that was always friendly to King Arthur '[1] watched over him ; and once when she saw him in great danger, like the Irish *Morrigu* who presided over the career of Cuchulainn, she sought to save him, and with the help of Sir Tristram succeeded.[1] The passing of Arthur to Avalon or Faerie seems to be a return to his own native realm of subjectivity. His own sister was with him in the ship, for she was of the invisible country too.[2] And another of his companions on his voyage from the visible to the invisible was his life-guardian Nimue, the lady of the lake. Merlin could not be of the company, for he was already in Faerie with the Fay Vivian. Behold the passing of Arthur as Malory describes it :—'. . . thus was he led away in a ship wherein were three queens ; that one was King Arthur's sister, Queen Morgan le Fay ; the other was the Queen of Northgalis ; the third was the Queen of the Waste Lands. Also there was Nimue, the chief lady of the lake, that had wedded Pelleas the good knight ; and this lady had done much for King Arthur, for she would never suffer Sir Pelleas to be in no place where he should be in danger of his life.' [3] Concerning the great Arthur's return from Avalon we shall speak in the chapter dealing with Re-birth. And we pass now from Arthur and his Brotherhood of gods and fairy-folk to Lancelot and his son Galahad—the two chief knights in the Arthurian Romance.

According to one of the earliest accounts we have of Lancelot, the German poem by Ulrich von Zatzikhoven, as analysed by Gaston Paris, he was the son of King Pant and Queen Clarine of Genewis.[4] In consequence of the hatred

---

[1] Malory, Book IX, c. xv ; Sir John Rhŷs takes the Lady of the Lake who sends Arthur the sword and the one who aids him afterwards (though, apparently by error, two characters in Malory) as different aspects of the one lake-lady *Morgen* (*Arth. Leg.*, p. 348).

[2] Merlin explained to Arthur that King Loth's wife was Arthur's own sister (Sommer's *Malory*, i. 64–5) ; and King Loth is one of the rulers of the Otherworld.

[3] Book XXI, c. vi.

[4] This poem, according to Gaston Paris, was translated during the late twelfth century from a French original now lost (*Romania*, x. 471). Cf. Rhŷs, *Arth. Leg.*, p. 127.

of their subjects the royal pair were forced to flee when Lancelot was only a year old. During the flight, the king, mortally wounded, died ; and just as the queen was about to be taken captive, a fairy rising in a cloud of mist carried away the infant Lancelot from where his parents had placed him under a tree. The fairy took him to her abode on an island in the midst of the sea, from whence she derived her title of Lady of the Lake, and he, as her adopted son, the name of *Lancelot du Lac* ; and her island-world was called the Land of Maidens. Having lived in that world of Faerie so long, it was only natural that Lancelot should have grown up more like one of its fair-folk than like a mortal. No doubt it was on account of his half-supernatural nature that he fell in love with the White Phantom, Gwenhwyvar, the wife of the king who had power to enter Hades and return again to the land of the living. Who better than Lancelot could have rescued Arthur's queen ? No one else in the court was so well fitted for the task. And it was he who was able to cross one of the magic bridges into the realm of Melwas, the Otherworld, while Gauvain (in the English form, Gawayne) failed.

Malory's narrative records how Lancelot, while suffering from the malady of madness caused by Gwenhwyvar's jealous expulsion of Elayne his fairy-sweetheart,—quite a parallel case to that of Cuchulainn when his wife Emer expelled his fairy-mistress Fand,—fought against a wild boar and was terribly wounded, and how afterwards he was nursed by his own Elayne in Fairyland, and healed and restored to his right mind by the Sangreal. Then Sir Ector and Sir Perceval found him there in the Joyous Isle enjoying the companionship of Elayne, where he had been many years, and from that world of Faerie induced him to return to Arthur's court. And, finally, comes the most important element of all to show how closely related Lancelot is with the fairy world and its people, and how inseparable from that invisible realm another of the fundamental elements in the life of Arthur is—the Quest of the Holy Grail, and the story of Galahad, who of all the knights was pure and good enough to behold the Sacred Vessel, and who was the offspring of the foster-son of the Lady of the Lake and the fairy woman Elayne.[1]

In the strange old Welsh tale of *Kulhwch and Olwen* we find Arthur and his knights even more closely identified with the fairy realm than in Malory and the Norman-French writers ; and this is important, because the ancient tale is, as scholars think, probably much freer from foreign influences and re-working than the better-known romances of Arthur, and therefore more in accord with genuine Celtic beliefs and folk-lore, as we shall quickly see. The court of King Arthur to which the youth Kulhwch goes seeking aid in his enterprise seems in some ways—though the parallel is not complete enough to be emphasized—to be a more artistic, because literary, picture of that fairy court which the Celtic peasant locates under mountains, in caverns, in hills, and in knolls, a court quite comparable to that of the Irish *Sidhe*-folk or Tuatha De Danann. Arthur is represented in the midst of a brilliant life where, as in the fairy palaces, there is much feasting ; and Kulhwch being invited to the feasting says, ' I came not here to consume meat and drink.'

And behold what sort of personages from that court Kulhwch has pledged to him, so that by their supernatural assistance he may obtain Olwen, herself perhaps a fairy held under fairy enchantment [2]: the sons of Gwawrddur Kyrvach,

[1] Malory, Book XII, cc. iii–x ; Rhŷs, *Arth. Leg.*, pp. 145, 164. Galahad, however, does not belong to the more ancient Arthurian romances at all, so far as scholars can determine ; and, therefore, too much emphasis ought not to be placed on this episode in connexion with the character of Arthur.

[2] We should like to direct the reader's attention to the interesting similarity shown between this old story of *Kulhwch and Olwen* and the fairy legend which we found living in South Wales, and now recorded by us on page 161, under the title of *Einion and Olwen*. As we have there suggested, the legend seems to be the remnant of a very ancient bardic tale preserved in the oral traditions of the people ; and the prevalence of such bardic traditions in a part of Wales where some of the *Mabinogion* stories either took shape, or from where they drew folk-lore material, would make it probable that there may even be some close relationship between the Olwen of the story and the Olwen of our folk-tale. If it could be shown that there is, we should be able at once to regard both

whom Arthur had power to call from the confines of hell ; Morvran the son of Tegid, who, because of his ugliness, was thought to be a demon ; Sandde Bryd Angel, who was so beautiful that mortals thought him a ministering angel ; Henbedestyr, with whom no one could keep pace ' either on horseback, or on foot ', and who therefore seems to be a spirit of the air ; Henwas Adeinawg, with whom ' no four-footed beast could run the distance of an acre, much less go beyond it' ; Sgilti Yscawndroed, who must have been another spirit or fairy, for ' when he intended to go on a message for his Lord (Arthur, who is like a Tuatha De Danann king), he never sought to find a path, but knowing whither he was to go, if his way lay through a wood he went along the tops of the trees ', and ' during his whole life, a blade of reed-grass bent not beneath his feet, much less did one ever break, so lightly did he tread ' ; Gwallgoyc, who ' when he came to a town, though there were three hundred houses in it, if he wanted anything, he would not let sleep come to the eyes of any whilst he remained there ' ; Osla Gyllellvawr, who bore a short broad dagger, and ' when Arthur and his hosts came before a torrent, they would seek for a narrow place where they might pass the water, and would lay the sheathed dagger across the torrent, and it would form a bridge sufficient for the armies of the three Islands of Britain, and of the three islands adjacent, with their spoil.' It seems very evident that this is the magic bridge, so often typified by a sword or dagger, which connects the world invisible with our own, and over which all shades and spirits pass freely to and fro. In this case we think Arthur is very clearly a ruler of the spirit realm, for, like the great Tuatha De Danann king Dagda, he can command its fairy-like inhabitants, and his army is an army of spirits or fairies. The unknown author of *Kulhwch*, like Spenser in modern times in his *Faerie Queene*, seems to have made the Island of Britain the realm of Faerie—the Celtic Otherworld—and Arthur its king. But let us take a look at more of the men pledged to

Olwens as ' Fair-Folk ' or of the *Tylwyth Teg*, and the quest of Kulhwch as really a journey to the Otherworld to gain a fairy wife.

Kulhwch from among Arthur's followers : Clust the son of
Clustveinad, who possessed clairaudient faculties of so extraordinary a kind that ' though he were buried seven cubits
beneath the earth, he would hear the ant fifty miles off rise
from her nest in the morning ' ; and the wonderful Kai,
who could live nine days and nine nights under water, for his
breath lasted this long, and he could exist the same length
of time without sleep. ' A wound from Kai's sword no
physician could heal.' And at will he was as tall as the
highest tree in the forest. ' And he had another peculiarity :
so great was the heat of his nature, that, when it rained
hardest, whatever he carried remained dry for a handbreadth above and a handbreadth below his hand ; and
when his companions were coldest, it was to them as fuel
with which to light their fire.'

Yet besides all these strange knights, Arthur commanded
a being who is without any reasonable doubt a god or ruler
of the subjective realm—' Gwynn ab Nudd, whom God has
placed over the brood of devils in Annwn, lest they should
destroy the present race. He will never be spared thence.'
Whatever each one of us may think of this wonderful
assembly of warriors and heroes who recognized in Arthur
their chief, they are certainly not beings of the ordinary
type,—in fact they seem not of this world, but of that
hidden land to which we all shall one day journey.[1] But to
avoid too much conjecture and to speak with a degree of
scientific exactness as to how Arthur and these companions
of his are to be considered, let us undertake a brief investigation into the mythological character and nature of the chief
one of them next to the great hero—Gwynn ab Nudd.
Professor J. Loth has said that ' nothing shows better the
evolution of mythological personages than the history of
Gwynh ' ;[2] and in Irish we have the equivalent form of
Nudd in the name Nuada—famous for having had a hand

---

[1] We may even have in the story of *Kulhwch and Olwen* a symbolical or
mystical account of ancient Brythonic rites of initiation, which have also
directly to do with the spiritual world and its invisible inhabitants.

[2] Cf. J. Loth, *Les Mabinogion* (Paris, 1889), p. 252 n.

of silver ; and Nuada of the Silver Hand was a king of the
Tuatha De Danann. The same authority thus describes
Gwynn, the son of Nudd :—' Gwynn, like his father Nudd,
is an ancient god of the Britons and of the Gaels. Christian
priests have made of him a demon. The people persisted in
regarding him as a powerful and rich king, the sovereign
of supernatural beings.'[1] And referring to Gwynn, Professor Loth in his early edition of *Kulhwch* says :—' Our
author has had an original idea : he has left him in hell, to
which place Christianity had made him descend, but for a
motive which does him the greatest honour : God has given
him the strength of demons to control them and to prevent
them from destroying the present race of men : he is indispensable down there.'[1] Lady Guest calls Gwynn the King
of Faerie,[2] the ruler of the *Tylwyth Teg* or ' Family of Beauty',
who are always joyful and well-disposed toward mortals ;
and also the ruler of the Elves (Welsh *Ellyllon*), a goblin
race who take special delight in misleading travellers and in
playing mischievous tricks on men. It is even said that
Gwynn himself is given to indulging in the same mischievous
amusements as his elvish subjects.

The evidence now set forth seems to suggest clearly and
even definitely that Arthur in his true nature is a god of
the subjective world, a ruler of ghosts, demons, and demon
rulers, and fairies ; that the people of his court are more
like the Irish *Sidhe*-folk than like mortals ; and that as
a great king he is comparable to Dagda the over-king of all
the Tuatha De Danann. Arthur and Osiris, two culture
heroes and sun-gods, as we suggested at first, are strikingly
parallel. Osiris came from the Otherworld to this one,
became the first Divine Ruler and Culture Hero of Egypt,
and then returned to the Otherworld, where he is now a king.
Arthur's father was a ruler in the Otherworld, and Arthur
evidently came from there to be the Supreme Champion of
the Brythons, and then returned to that realm whence he

---

[1] Cf. J. Loth, *Le Mabinogi de Kulhwch et Olwen* (Saint-Brieuc, 1888),
Intro., p. 7.

[2] Lady Ch. Guest's *Mabinogion* (London, 1849), ii. 323 n.

took his origin, a realm which poets called Avalon. The passing of Arthur seems mystically to represent the sunset over the Western Ocean : Arthur disappears beneath the horizon into the Lower World which is also the Halls of Osiris, wherein Osiris journeys between sunset and sunrise, between death and re-birth. Merlin found the infant Arthur floating on the waves : the sun rising across the waters is this birth of Arthur, the birth of Osiris. In the chapter on Re-birth, evidence will be offered to show that as a culture hero Arthur is to be regarded as a sun-god incarnate in a human body to teach the Brythons arts and sciences and hidden things—even as Prometheus and Zeus are said to have come to earth to teach the Greeks ; and that as a sixth-century warrior, Arthur, in accordance with the Celtic Doctrine of Re-birth, is an ancient Brythonic hero reincarnate.

THE LITERARY EVOLUTION AND THE ANTIQUITY OF THE BRYTHONIC FAIRY-ROMANCES

After the Norman Conquest of England in 1066, the ancient fairy-romances of the Brythons began to exercise their remarkable literary influence as we see it now in the evolution of the Arthurian Legend. And in this evolution of the Arthurian Legend we find the proof of the antiquity of the Brythonic Fairy-Faith, just as we find in the old Irish manuscripts the proof of the antiquity of the Gaelic Fairy-Faith.

Long before 1066, Gildas gives the first recorded germs of the Arthurian story in his *De Excidio et Conquestu Britanniae*, though they are hardly distinguishable as such. His failure to mention the name of Arthur, though treating of the whole period when Arthur is supposed to have lived, he himself being contemporary with the period, raises the very difficult question which we have already mentioned, Did the mighty Brythonic hero ever have an actual historical existence ? Almost three hundred years later—a period sufficiently removed from Gildas to have made Arthur the supreme champion of the falling Brythons, granting that he did exist during the sixth century as a Brythonic chieftain—in the

Historia Britonum, completed about the year 800, and attributed to Nennius, Arthur, for the first time in a known manuscript, is mentioned as a character of British history.[1] All that can be definitely said of the narrative of Nennius ' is that it represents more or less inconsistent British traditions of uncertain age '.[1] That it is not always historical, many scholars are agreed. Dr. R. H. Fletcher says, ' There is always the possibility that Arthur never existed at all, and that even Nennius's comparatively modest eulogy has no firmer foundation than the persistent stories of ancient Celtic myth or the patriotic figments of the ardent Celtic imagination.'[2] Sir John Rhys also propounds a similar view.[3] Thus, for example, Nennius states that Arthur in one battle slew single handed more than nine hundred men ; and, again, that the number of Arthur's always-successful battles was twelve, as though Arthur were the sun or a sun-god, and his battles the twelve months of the solar year.[2]

Between Nennius and Geoffrey of Monmouth there is an intermediate stage in the development of the Arthurian Legend, during which the character of Arthur tends to become more romantic ; but for our purpose this period is of slight importance. Thereafter, by means of Geoffrey's famous *Historia Regum Britanniae*, written about 1136, the Arthurian Legend gained popularity throughout Western Europe. In this work Arthur ceases to be purely historical, and appears as a great king enveloped in the mythical atmosphere of a Celtic hero, and with him Merlin and Lear are for the first time definitely enshrined in the literature of Britain.[4] Arthur's career is completely sketched in the *Historia*, from birth to his mysterious departure for the Isle of Avalon after the last fight with Modred, when fairy

---

[1] Cf. R. H. Fletcher, *Arthurian Material in the Chronicles*, in *Harv. Stud. and Notes in Phil. and Lit.*, x. 20–1.

[2] Fletcher, ib., x. 29 ; 26.

[3] Rhŷs, *Arth. Leg.*, p. 7 ; and Rhŷs, *The Welsh People*[2] (London, 1902), p. 105.

[4] Cf. Fletcher, op. cit., x. 43–115 ; from ed. by San-Marte (A. Schulz), *Gottfried's von Monmouth Hist. Reg. Brit.* (Halle, 1854), Eng. trans. by A. Thompson, *The British History*, &c. (1718).

women take him to cure him of his wounds (Book XI, 1-2).
Geoffrey, thus the father of the Arthurian Legend in English
and European literature, was undoubtedly a Welshman
who probably had natural opportunities of knowing the
true character of Arthur from genuine Brythonic sources,
though we know little about his life. His *Historia*, as the
researches of scholars have shown, was the sum total in his
time of all Arthurian history and myth, whether written or
orally transmitted, which he could collect ; just as Malory's
Le Morte d'Arthur was a compendium of Arthurian material
in the time of Edward IV.

There followed many imitations and translations of the
Historia. The most important of these appeared in 1155,
Le Roman de Brut or ' The Story of Brutus ', by the Norman
poet Wace. The *Brut*, though fundamentally a rimed version
of the *Historia*, is much more than a mere translation :
Wace has improved on it ; and he gives a convincing
impression that he had access to Celtic Arthurian stories not
drawn upon by Geoffrey, for he gives new touches about
Gawain, mentions the Britons' expectation of Arthur's
return from Faerie, and the institution of the Round Table.[1]

Somewhere about the year 1200, Layamon, a simple-
hearted Saxon priest, wrote another *Brut*, based upon the
metrical one by Wace ; and in the literature of England,
Layamon's work is the most valuable single production
between the Conquest and Chaucer. The life of Layamon
is very obscure, but it seems reasonably certain that for a
long time he lived on the Welsh marches in North Worcester-
shire, in the midst of living Brythonic traditions, which he
used at first hand ; and, as a result, we find in his *Brut*
legends not recorded in Geoffrey, or Wace, or in any earlier
or contemporary literature. For our purposes the most
interesting of many interesting additions made by Layamon
are the curious passages about the fairy elves at Arthur's
birth, and about the way in which Arthur was taken by
them to their queen Argante in Avalon to be cured of his
wounds :—' The time came that was chosen, then was

[1] Cf. Fletcher, op. cit., pp. 117-44.

Arthur born. So soon as he came on earth elves took him ;
they enchanted the child into magic most strong ; they gave
him might to be the best of all knights ; they gave him
another thing, that he should be a rich king ; they gave
him the third, that he should live long; they gave to him
·the prince virtues most good, so that he was most generous of
all men alive. This the elves gave him, and thus the child
thrived.' [1]

In the last fatal battle Modred is slain and Arthur is
grievously wounded. As Arthur lies wounded, Constantine,
Cador's son, the earl of Cornwall, and a relative of Arthur,
comes to him. Arthur greets him with these words :—
' " Constantine, thou art welcome ; thou wert Cador's son.
I give thee here my kingdom . . . And I will fare to Avalun,
to the fairest of all maidens, to Argante the queen, and elf
most fair, and she shall make my wounds all sound ; make
me all whole with healing draughts. And afterwards I will
come [again] to my kingdom, and dwell with the Britons
with mickle joy." Even with the words, there approached
from the sea that was, a short boat, floating with the waves ;
and two women therein, wondrously formed ; and they took
Arthur anon, and bare him quickly, and laid him softly
down, and forth gan depart. Then it was accomplished that
Merlin whilom said, that mickle care (sorrow) should be of
Arthur's departure. The Britons believe that he is alive,
and dwelleth in Avalun with the fairest of all elves ; and
the Britons even yet expect when Arthur shall return.' [2]

During this same period, Giraldus Cambrensis (1147–1223)
in his *Itinerarium Cambriae* (Book I, c. 8) collected a popular
Otherworld tale. It is about a priest named Elidorus, who
when a boy in Gower, the western district of Glamorganshire, had free passage between this world of ours and an
underground country inhabited by a race of little people
who spoke a language like Greek. This tends to prove that

[1] Sir Frederic Madden, *Layamon's Brut* (London, 1847), ii. 384. Here
the Germanic elves are by Layamon made the same in character and
nature as Brythonic elves or fairies.

[2] Madden, *Layamon's Brut*, ii. 144.

the Fairy-Faith was then flourishing among the people of Wales.

It was chiefly during the twelfth and thirteenth centuries that the Arthurian Legend as a thing of literature began to take definite shape. The old romances of the Brythons were cultivated and revised, and written down by men and women of literary genius. Chrétien de Troyes, who recorded a large number of legendary stories in verse, Marie de France, famous for her *Lais*, Thomas, the author of the chief version of the *Tristan* legend,[1] Béroul, who recorded a less important version of this legend,[2] and Robert de Boron, who did much to develop the legend of the Holy Grail, were among the greatest workers in the French Celtic Revival of this time.

Professor Brown has shown that ' almost every incident in Chrétien's *Iwain* was suggested by an ancient Celtic tale, dealing with the familiar theme of a journey to win a fairy mistress in the Otherworld.'[3] The fay whom Iwain marries is called Laudine ; and, like one of the fairies who live in sacred waters, she has her favourite fountain which the knight guards, as though he were the Black Knight in the old Welsh tale of *The Lady of the Fountain.* Both Gaston Paris and Alfred Nutt have also recognized the tale of *Iwain* as a fairy romance.[4] Professor Loth observes that, ' It is not impossible that Chrétien had known, among fairy legends, Armorican legends, concerning the fairies of waters, whose rôle is identical with that of the Welsh *Tylwyth Teg.*'[5]

In *Lanval*, one of the *Lais*[6] by Marie de France, written during the twelfth century, probably while its author was living in England, we have direct proof that there was then flourishing in Brittany—well known to Marie de France,

[1] J. Bédier's ed., *Société des anciens textes français* (Paris, 1902).

[2] E. Muret's ed., *Société des anciens textes français* (Paris, 1903).

[3] A. C. L. Brown, *The Knight and the Lion* ; also, by same author, *Iwain*, in *Harv. Stud. and Notes in Phil. and Lit.*, vii. 146, &c.

[4] *Celtic Mag.*, xii. 555 ; *Romania* (1888) ; cf. Brown, ib.

[5] J. Loth, *Les Romans arthuriens*, in *Rev. Celt.*, xiii. 497.

[6] *Bibliotheca Normannica*, iii, *Die Lais der Marie de France*, pp. 86–112.

who was French by birth and training—a popular belief in fairy women who lived in the Otherworld, and who could *take* mortals on whom their love fell.   It is probable that the older lay, to which Marie de France refers in the beginning of her *Lanval*, may have been the anonymous one of *Graelent*, sometimes improperly attributed to her.   Zimmer and Foerster place the origin of *Graelent* in Brittany [1] ; and the similarity of the heroes in the two poems seems to be due to a very ancient Brythonic Fairy-Faith.   Dr. Schofield sees in *Graelent* an older form of the more polished *Lanval* ; and remarks that the chief difference in the two *lais* is found in the way the hero meets the fairy women.   In the case of Lanval, when he leaves the court, he goes to rest beside a river where two beautiful maidens come to him ; Graelent is alone in the woods when he sees a hind whiter than snow, and following it comes to a place where fairy damsels are bathing in a fountain.   There seems to be no doubt that in both poems the maidens and damsels are fairies quite like the Tuatha De Danann, with power to cast their spell over beautiful young men whom they wish to have for husbands. In *Guingemor*, another of the old Breton lays, ascribed by Gaston Paris to Marie de France, we find again fairy-romance episodes similar to those in *Lanval* and *Graelent*.[2]   The *Lais* of Marie de France had many imitators in England.   Chaucer, too, has made it clear that he knew a good deal about the old Breton *lais* and their subjects or ' matter ', for in the *Prologue to the Frankeleyn's Tale* he writes :—

> Thise olde gentil Britons in hir dayes
> Of diverse aventures maden layes,
> Rymeyed in hir firste Briton tonge.

We may now briefly examine, in a general way, some of the most noteworthy of the more obscure, but for us important Old French fairy-romances of a kindred Brythonic or Arthurian character, called *Romans d'Aventure* and *Romans*

---

[1] Cf. W. H. Schofield, *The Lays of Graelent and Lanval, and the Story of Wayland*, in Pub. Mod. Lang. Ass. of America, xv. 176.

[2] Cf. Schofield, *The Lay of Guingamor*, in *Harv. Stud. and Notes in Phil. and Lit.*, v. 221–2.

Bretons, wherein *fées* appear or are mentioned : i. e. *Le Bel Inconnu, Blancadin, Brun de la Montaigne, Claris et Laris, Dolopathos, Escanor, Floriant et Florete, Partonopeus, La Vengeance Raguidel, Joufrois*, and *Amada et Ydoine*.[1] In these romances, fairies commonly appear as most beautiful supernormal women who love mortal heroes. They are seen chiefly at night, frequenting forests and fountains, and like all fairies disappear at or before cock-crow. They are skilled in magic and astrology ; like the Greek Fates, some of them spin and weave and have great influence over the lives of mankind. They are represented as relatively immortal, so long is their span of life compared to ours ; but, ultimately, they seem to be subject to a change such as we call death. This indeed is never specifically mentioned, only implied by the statements that they enjoy childhood and then womanhood, being thus created and not eternal beings. Some are very prominent figures, like *Morgain la Fée*, Arthur's sister. In most cases they are beneficent, and frequently act as guardian spirits for their special hero, just as the Lake Lady for Arthur and the *Morrigu* for Cuchulainn. So strong is the faith in these *fées* that a man meeting unusual success is often described as *féed*—that is endowed with fairy power or under fairy protection, as Perceval's adversary, the Knight of the Dragon, states.[2] In *Joufrois*, too, the power of the fairies, or else the special protection of God, is considered the cause of success in arms.[3] In *Brun de la Montaigne, Morgain la Fée* is represented as the cousin of Arthur ; and Butor, the father of Brun, mentions several localities in different lands, which, like the Forest of Brocéliande in Brittany, the chief theatre of this romance, are fairy haunts ; and he names them as being under the

---

[1] For editions, and fuller details of the fairy elements, see De La Warr B. Easter, *A Study of the Magic Elements in the* ROMANS D'AVENTURE *and the* ROMANS BRETONS (Johns Hopkins Univ., Baltimore, 1906). See also Lucy A. Paton, *Studies in the Fairy Mythology of the Arthurian Romance*, Radcliffe College Monograph XIII (New York, 1903).

[2] Perc., vi. 235 ; cf. Easter's Dissertation, p. 42 n.

[3] *Joufrois*, 3179 ff. ; ed. Hofmann und Muncker (Halle, 1880) ; cf. Easter's Diss., pp. 40–2 n.

dominion of Arthur, who is described as a great fairy king.[1]

Such fairy romances as the above (and they are but a few examples selected from among a vast number) often localized in Brittany, raise the perplexing and far-reaching problem concerning the origin of the 'Matter of Britain'. The most reasonable position to take with respect to this problem would seem to be that Celtic traditions flourished wherever there were Gaels and Brythons, that there was much interchange of these traditions between one Celtic country and another—especially between Wales and Ireland and across the channel between Brittany and South England, including Cornwall and Wales, both before and after the Christian era. Further, the Arthurian fairy-romances, based upon such interchanged Celtic traditions, grew up with a Brythonic background, chiefly after the Norman Conquest, both in Armorica and in Britain, and became in the later Middle Ages one of the chief glories of English and of European literature.

In concluding this slight examination of Brythonic fairy-romances, we may very briefly suggest by means of a few selected examples what fairies are like in the *Mabinogion* stories and in the *Four Ancient Books of Wales*. *Kulhwch and Olwen*, the chief literary treasure-house of ancient magical and mystical Otherworld and fairy traditions of the Brythons, which we have already considered in relation to Arthur, 'appears to be built upon Arthurian and other legends of native growth.'[2] Unmistakable Welsh parallels to the Irish fairy-belief appear in the *Mabinogi of Pwyll, Prince of Dyfed*, where the two chief incidents are Pwyll's journey to the Otherworld after he and Arawn its ruler have exchanged shapes and kingdoms for a year, and the marriage of Pwyll to a fairy damsel ; in the *Mabinogi* of *Manawyddan*, which contains much magic and shape-shifting, and the

---

[1] *Brun*, 562 ff., 3237, 3251, 3396, 3599 ff. ; ed. Paul Meyer (Paris,1875) ; cf. ib., pp. 42 n., 44 n.

[2] E. Anwyl, *The Four Branches of the Mabinogi*, in *Zeit. für Celt. Phil.* (London, Paris, 1897), i. 278.

description of a fairy castle belonging to Llwyd ; and in the *Mabinogi* of *Branwen, the Daughter of Llyr,* where there is the episode of the seven-year feast at Harlech over the Head of Bran, during which the Birds of Rhiannon's realm sing so sweetly that time passes abnormally fast. The subject-matter of the four true *Mabinogion* (composed before the eleventh century) is, as Sir John Rhŷs has pointed out, the fortunes of three clans of superhuman beings comparable to the Irish Tuatha De Danann : (1) the Children of Llyr, (2) the Children of Don, (3) and the Family of Pwyll.[1] Herein, then, the ancient Gaelic and Brythonic Fairy-Faiths coincide, and show the unity of the Celtic race which evolved them.

In the *Four Ancient Books of Wales,* which are poetical compositions, whereas the *Mabinogion* tales are prose with extremely little verse, there are certain interesting passages to illustrate the ancient Fairy-Faith of the Brythons from some of its purest sources. The first selected example comes from the *Black Book of Caermarthen.* It is a poem, some-times called the *Avallenau,* from among the poems relating to the Battle of Arderydd ; and it represents *Myrddin* or Merlin, the famous magician of Arthur, quite at the mercy of sprites. The passage is an interesting one as showing that in the region where Merlin is supposed to be under the enchantment of the fairy woman Vivian he was regarded as no longer able to exercise his wonted control over spirits like fairies. As in ancient non-Celtic belief, where the loss of chastity in a magician, that is to say in one able to com-mand certain orders of invisible beings, always leads to his falling under their lawless power, so was it with Merlin when overcome by Vivian. And this is Merlin's lamentation :—

Ten years and forty, as the toy of lawless ones,
Have I been wandering in gloom among sprites.
After wealth in abundance and entertaining minstrels,
I have been [here so long that] it is useless for gloom and
    sprites to lead me astray.[2]

[1] Cf. Nutt, *Voy. of Bran,* ii. 19, 21.
[2] *Black Book of Caermarthen,* xvii, stanza 7, ll. 5–8. This book dates from 1154 to 1189 as a manuscript; cf. Skene, *Four Anc. Books,* i. 3, 372.

In a dialogue between Myrddin and his sister Gwenddydd, contained in the *Red Book of Hergest I*,[1] there is a curious reference to ghosts of the mountain who, just like fairies that live in the mountains, steal away men's reason when they *strike* them,—in death which may appear natural, in sickness, or in accident. And after his death—after he has been *taken* by these ghosts of the mountain—Myrddin returns as a ghost and speaks from the grave a prophecy which ' the ghost of the mountain in Aber Carav '[2] told him. Not only do these passages prove the Celtic belief in ghosts like fairies to have existed anciently in Wales ; but they show also that the recorded Fairy-Faith of the Brythons, like that of the Gaels of Ireland and Scotland, directly attests and confirms our Psychological Theory. Like a record from the official proceedings of the Psychical Research Society itself, they form one of the strongest proofs that fairies, ghosts, and shades were confused, all alike, in the mind of the Welsh poet, mingling together in that realm where mortals see with a new vision, and exist with a body invisible to us.

Our study of the literary evolution of the Brythonic fairy-romances shows that as early as about the year 800 Arthurian traditions were known, though possibly Arthur himself never had historical existence. By about 1136, when Geoffrey's famous *Historia* appeared, these traditions were already highly developed in Britain, and Arthur had become a great Brythonic hero enveloped in a halo of romance and myth, and, as an Otherworld being, was definitely related to Avalon and its fairy inhabitants. This new literary material of Celtic origin opened up to Europe by Geoffrey rapidly began to influence profoundly the form of continental as well as English poetry and prose, chiefly through the writers of the Norman-French period of the twelfth and thirteenth centuries. In itself it was in no wise

[1] Stanzas 19–20. This book took shape as a manuscript from the fourteenth to fifteenth century, according to Skene. Cf. Skene, *Four Anc. Books*, i. 3, 464.
[2] See *A Fugitive Poem of Myrddin in his Grave. Red Book of Hergest*, ii. Skene, ib., i. 478–81, stanza 27.

essentially different from what we find as fairy romances in the old Irish manuscripts written during the same and earlier periods. Welsh literature, however it may be related to Irish, shows a common origin with it. The four true *Mabinogion* as stories are earlier than 1100 ; *Kulhwch and Olwen* in its present form most probably dates from the latter half of the twelfth century ; the *Four Ancient Books of Wales* date from the twelfth to the fifteenth centuries as manuscripts. In both ancient and modern times there was much interchange of material between Irish Gaels and Brythons ; and Brittany as well as Britain and Ireland undoubtedly contributed to the evolution of the complex fairy romances which formed the germ of the Arthurian Legend.

When we stop to consider how long it may have taken the Brythonic Fairy-Faith, as well as that of the Gaels, to become so widespread and popular among the Celtic peoples that it could take such definite shape as it now shows in all the oldest manuscripts in different languages, we can easily wander backward into periods of enlightenment and civilization beyond the horizon of our little fragments of recorded history. Who can tell how many ages ago the Fairy-Faith began its first evolution, or who can say that there was ever a Celt who did not believe in, or know about fairies ?

SECTION II
THE RECORDED FAIRY-FAITH

CHAPTER VI

THE CELTIC OTHERWORLD [1]

In Ireland this world and the world we go to after death are not far apart.'—W. B. YEATS.

' Many go to the Tir-na-nog in sleep, and some are said to have remained there, and only a vacant form is left behind without the light in the eyes which marks the presence of a soul.'—A. E.

General ideas of the Otherworld : its location ; its subjectivity ; its names ; its extent ; Tethra one of its kings—The Silver Branch and the Golden Bough ; and Initiations—The Otherworld the Heaven-World of all religions—Voyage of Bran—Cormac in the Land of Promise—Magic Wands—Cuchulainn's Sick-Bed—Ossian's return from Fairyland—Lanval's going to Avalon—Voyage of Mael-Duin —Voyage of Teigue—Adventures of Art—Cuchulainn's and Arthur's Otherworld Quests—Literary Evolution of idea of Happy Other-world.

GENERAL DESCRIPTION

THE Heaven-World of the ancient Celts, unlike that of the Christians, was not situated in some distant, unknown region of planetary space, but here on our own earth. As it was necessarily a subjective world, poets could only describe it in terms more or less vague ; and its exact geographical location, accordingly, differed widely in the minds of scribes from century to century. Sometimes, as is usual to-day in fairy-lore, it was a subterranean world entered through caverns, or hills, or mountains, and inhabited by many races and orders of invisible beings, such as demons, shades, fairies, or even gods. And the underground world

---

[1] Chief general references : H. D'Arbois de Jubainville, L'Épopée cel-tique en Irlande, Le Cycle Mythologique Irlandais ; Kuno Meyer and Alfred Nutt, The Happy Otherworld and the Celtic Doctrine of Re-birth. Chief sources : the Leabhar na h-Uidhre (A.D. 1100); the Book of Leinster (twelfth century); the Lais of Marie de France (twelfth to thirteenth century) ; the White Book of Rhyderch, Hengwrt Coll. (thirteenth to four-teenth century) ; the Yellow Book of Lecan (fifteenth century); the Book of Lismore (fifteenth century) ; the Book of Fermoy (fifteenth century); the Four Ancient Books of Wales (twelfth to fifteenth century).

of the *Sidhe*-folk, which cannot be separated from it, was divided into districts or kingdoms under different fairy kings and queens, just as the upper world of mortals. We already know how the Tuatha De Danann or *Sidhe*-folk, after their defeat by the Sons of Mil at the Battle of Tailte, retired to this underground world and took possession of its palaces beneath the green hills and vales of Ireland ; and how from there, as gods of the harvest, they still continued to exercise authority over their conquerors, or marshalled their own invisible spirit-hosts in fairy warfare, and sometimes interfered in the wars of men.

More frequently, in the old Irish manuscripts, the Celtic Otherworld was located in the midst of the Western Ocean, as though it were the ' double ' of the lost Atlantis ; [1] and Manannan Mac Lir, the Son of the Sea—perhaps himself the ' double ' of an ancient Atlantean king—was one of the divine rulers of its fairy inhabitants, and his palace, for he was one of the Tuatha De Danann, was there rather than in Ireland ; and when he travelled between the two countries it was in a magic chariot drawn by horses who moved over the sea-waves as on land. And fairy women came from that mid-Atlantic world in magic boats like spirit boats, to charm away such mortal men as in their love they chose, or else to take great Arthur wounded unto death. And in that island world there was neither death nor pain nor

[1] One of the commonest legends among all Celtic peoples is about some lost city like the Breton Is, or some lost land or island (cf. Rhŷs, *Arth. Leg.*, c. xv, and *Celtic Folk-Lore*, c. vii) ; and we can be quite sure that if, as some scientists now begin to think (cf. Batella, *Pruebas geológicas de la existencia de la Atlántida*, in *Congreso internacional de Americanistas*, iv., Madrid, 1882; also Meyers, *Grosses Konversations-Lexikon*, ii. 44, Leipzig und Wien, 1903) Atlantis once existed, its disappearance must have left from a prehistoric epoch a deep impress on folk-memory. But the Otherworld idea being in essence animistic is not to be regarded, save from a superficial point of view, as conceivably having had its origin in a lost Atlantis. The real evolutionary process, granting the disappearance of this island continent, would seem rather to have been one of localizing and anthropomorphosing very primitive Aryan and pre-Aryan beliefs about a heavenworld, such as have been current among almost all races of mankind in all stages of culture, throughout the two Americas and Polynesia as well as throughout Europe, Asia, and Africa. (Cf. Tylor, *Prim. Cult.*,[4] ii. 62, 48, &c.)

scandal, nought save immortal and unfading youth, and endless joy and feasting.

Even yet at rare intervals, like a phantom, Hy Brasil appears far out on the Atlantic. No later than the summer of 1908 it is said to have been seen from West Ireland, just as that strange invisible island near Innishmurray, inhabited by the invisible ' gentry ', is seen—once in seven years. And too many men of intelligence testify to having seen Hy Brasil at the same moment, when they have been together, or separated, as during the summer of 1908, for it to be explained away as an ordinary illusion of the senses. Nor can it be due to a mirage such as we know, because neither its shape nor position seems to conform to any known island or land mass. The Celtic Otherworld is like that hidden realm of subjectivity lying just beyond the horizon of mortal existence, which we cannot behold when we would, save with the mystic vision of the Irish seer. Thus in the legend of Bran's friends, who sat over dinner at Harlech with the Head of Bran for seven years, three curious birds acted as musicians, the Three Birds of Rhiannon, which were said to sing the dead back to life and the living into death ;—but the birds were not in Harlech, they were out over the sea in the atmosphere of Rhiannon's realm in the bosom of Cardigan Bay.[1] And though we might say of that Otherworld, as we learn from these Three Birds of Rhiannon, and as Socrates would say, that its inhabitants are come from the living and the living in our world from the dead there, yet, as has already been set forth in chapter iv, we ought not to think of the *Sidhe*-folk, nor of such great heroes and gods as Arthur and Cuchulainn and Finn, who are also of its invisible company, as in any sense half-conscious shades ; for they are always represented as being in the full enjoyment of an existence and consciousness greater than our own.

In Irish manuscripts, the Otherworld beyond the Ocean bears many names. It is *Tir-na-nog*, ' The Land of Youth'; *Tir-Innambéo*, ' The Land of the Living '; *Tir Tairngire*,

---

[1] *White Book of Rhyderch*, folio 291ᵃ ; cf. Rhŷs, *Arth. Leg.*, pp. 268–9.

'The Land of Promise'; *Tír N-aill*, 'The Other Land (or World)'; *Mag Már*, 'The Great Plain'; and also *Mag Mell*, 'The Plain Agreeable (or Happy).'

But this western Otherworld, if it is what we believe it to be—a poetical picture of the great subjective world—cannot be the realm of any one race of invisible beings to the exclusion of another. In it all alike—gods, Tuatha De Danann, fairies, demons, shades, and every sort of disembodied spirits—find their appropriate abode; for though it seems to surround and interpenetrate this planet even as the X-rays interpenetrate matter, it can have no other limits than those of the Universe itself. And that it is not an exclusive realm is certain from what our old Irish manuscripts record concerning the Fomorian races.[1] These, when they met defeat on the battle-field of Moytura at the hands of the Tuatha De Danann, retired altogether from Ireland, their overthrow being final, and returned to their own invisible country—a mysterious land beyond the Ocean, where the dead find a new existence, and where their god-king Tethra ruled, as he formerly ruled in this world. And the fairy women of Tethra's kingdom, even like those who came from the Tuatha De Danann of Erin, or those of Manannan's ocean-world, enticed mortals to go with them to be heroes under their king, and to behold there the assemblies of ancestors. It was one of them who came to Connla, son of Conn, supreme king of Ireland; and this was her message to him :—'The immortals invite you. You are going to be one of the heroes of the people of Tethra. You will always be seen there, in the assemblies of your ancestors, in the midst of those who know and love you.' And with the fairy spell upon him the young prince entered the glass boat of the fairy woman, and his father the king, in great tribulation and wonder, beheld them disappear across the waters never to return.[1]

[1] From *Echtra Condla*, in the *Leabhar na h-Uidhre*. Cf. *Le Cycle Myth. Irl.*, pp. 192–3.

THE SILVER BRANCH [1] AND THE GOLDEN BOUGH

To enter the Otherworld before the appointed hour marked by death, a passport was often necessary, and this was usually a silver branch of the sacred apple-tree bearing blossoms, or fruit, which the queen of the Land of the Ever-Living and Ever-Young gives to those mortals whom she wishes for as companions ; though sometimes, as we shall see, it was a single apple without its branch. The queen's gifts serve not only as passports, but also as food and drink for mortals who go with her. Often the apple-branch produces music so soothing that mortals who hear it forget all troubles and even cease to grieve for those whom the fairy women *take*. For us there are no episodes more important than those in the ancient epics concerning these apple-tree talismans, because in them we find a certain key which unlocks the secret of that world from which such talismans are brought, and proves it to be the same sort of a place as the Otherworld of the Greeks and Romans. Let us then use the key and make a few comparisons between the Silver Branch of the Celts and the Golden Bough of the Ancients, expecting the two symbols naturally to differ in their functions, though not fundamentally.

It is evident at the outset that the Golden Bough was as much the property of the queen of that underworld called Hades as the Silver Branch was the gift of the Celtic fairy queen, and like the Silver Bough it seems to have been the symbolic bond between that world and this, offered as a tribute to Proserpine by all initiates, who made the mystic voyage in full human consciousness. And, as we suspect, there may be even in the ancient Celtic legends of mortals who make that strange voyage to the Western Otherworld and return to this world again, an echo of initiatory rites—perhaps druidic—similar to those of Proserpine as shown in the journey of Aeneas, which, as Virgil records it, is undoubtedly a poetical rendering of an actual psychic experience of a great initiate.

[1] Cf. Eleanor Hull, *The Silver Bough in Irish Legend*, in *Folk-Lore*, xii.

In Virgil's classic poem the Sibyl commanded the plucking of the sacred bough to be carried by Aeneas when he entered the underworld ; for without such a bough plucked near the entrance to Avernus from the wondrous tree sacred to Infernal Juno (i. e. Proserpine) none could enter Pluto's realm.[1] And when Charon refused to ferry Aeneas across the Stygian lake until the Sibyl-woman drew forth the Golden Bough from her bosom, where she had hidden it, it becomes clearly enough a passport to Hades, just as the Silver Branch borne by the fairy woman is a passport to *Tír N-aill* ; and the Sibyl-woman who guided Aeneas to the Greek and Roman Otherworld takes the place of the fairy woman who leads mortals like Bran to the Celtic Otherworld.[2]

THE OTHERWORLD IDEA LITERALLY INTERPRETED

With this parallel between the Otherworld of the Celts and that of the Ancients seemingly established, we may leave poetical images and seek a literal interpretation for the animistic idea about those realms. The Rites of Proserpine as conducted in the Mysteries of Antiquity furnish us with the means ; and in what Servius has written we have the material ready.[3] Taking the letter Y, which Pythagoras said is like life with its dividing ways of good and evil, as the mystic symbol of the branch which all initiates like Aeneas offered to Proserpine in the subjective world while there out of the physical body, he says of the initiatory rites :—' He (the poet) could not join the Rites of Proserpine without having the branch to hold up. And by " *going to the shades* " he (the poet) *means celebrating the Rites of Proserpine.*'[3] This passage is certainly capable of but one meaning ; and

---

[1] Cf. Eleanor Hull, op. cit., p. 431.

[2] Classical parallels to the Celtic Otherworld journeys exist in the descent of Dionysus to bring back Semele, of Orpheus to recover his beloved Eurydike, of Herakles at the command of his master Eurystheus to fetch up the three-headed Kerberos—as mentioned first in Homer's *Iliad* (cf. Tylor, *Prim. Cult.*,[4] ii. 48); and chiefly in the voyage of Odysseus across the deep-flowing Ocean to the land of the departed (Homer, *Odyss.* xi).

[3] Servius, *ad Aen.*, vi. 136 ff.

we may perhaps assume that the invisible realm of the
Ancients, which is called Hades, is like the Celtic Otherworld located in the Western Ocean, and is also like, or has
its mythological counterpart in, the Elysian Fields to the
West, reserved by the Greeks and Romans for their gods
and heroes, and in the Happy Otherworld of Scandinavian,
Iranian, and Indian mythologies. It must then follow that
all these realms—though placed in different localities by
various nations, epochs, traditions, scribes, and poets (even
as the under-ground world of the Tuatha De Danann in
Ireland differs from that ruled over by one of their own race,
Manannan the Son of the Sea)—are simply various ways
which different Aryan peoples have had of looking at that
one great invisible realm of which we have just spoken,
and which forms the Heavenworld of every religion, Aryan
and non-Aryan, known to man. And if this conclusion is
accepted, and it seems that it must be, merely on the evidence of the literary or recorded Celtic Fairy-Faith, our
Psychological Theory stands proven.

The Rites of Proserpine had many counterparts. Thus,
to pass on to another parallel, in the Mysteries of Eleusis
the disappearance of the Maiden into the under-world, into
Hades, the land of the dead, was continually re-enacted in
a sacred drama, and it no doubt was one of the principal rites
attending initiation. In our study of the Celtic Doctrine of
Re-birth, we shall return to this subject of Celtic Initiation.

The Voyage of Bran, Son of Febal

We are well prepared now to enjoy the best known voyages
which men, heroes, and god-men, are said to have made to
Avalon, or the Land of the Living, through the invitation of
a fairy woman or else of the god Manannan himself ; and
probably the most famous is that of the *Voyage of Bran,
Son of Febal*, as so admirably translated from the original
old Irish saga by Dr. Kuno Meyer.[1] Perhaps in all Celtic

---

[1] *Voy. of Bran*, i, pp. 2 ff. The tale is based on seven manuscripts
ranging in age from the *Leabhar na h-Uidhre* of about A.D. 1100 to six
others belonging to the fourteenth, fifteenth, and sixteenth centuries (cf.
ib., p. xvi).

literature no poem surpasses this in natural and simple beauty.

One day Bran heard strange music behind him as he was alone in the neighbourhood of his stronghold ; and as he listened, so sweet was the sound that it lulled him to sleep. When he awoke, there lay beside him a branch of silver so white with blossoms that it was not easy to distinguish the blossoms from the branch.   Bran took up the branch and carried it to the royal house, and, when the hosts were assembled therein, they saw a woman in strange raiment standing on the floor.   Whence she came and how, no one could tell.   And as they all beheld her, she sang fifty quatrains to Bran :—

> A branch of the apple-tree from Emain
> I bring, like those one knows ;
> Twigs of white silver are on it,
> Crystal brows with blossoms.
>
> There is a distant isle,
> Around which sea-horses glisten :
> A fair course against the white-swelling surge,—
> Four feet uphold it.

.   .   .   .   .   .

When the song was finished, ' the woman went from them while they knew not whither she went.   And she took her branch with her.   The branch sprang from Bran's hand into the hand of the woman, nor was there strength in Bran's hand to hold the branch.'   The next day, with the fairy spell upon him, Bran begins the voyage towards the setting sun.   On the ocean he meets Manannan riding in his magic chariot over the sea-waves ; and the king tells Bran that he is returning to Ireland after long ages.   Parting from the Son of the Sea, Bran goes on, and the first island he and his companions reach is the ' Island of Joy ', where one of the party is set ashore ; the second isle is the ' Land of Women ', where the queen draws Bran and his followers to her realm with a magic clew, and then entertains them for what seems no more than a year, though ' it chanced to be many years '. After a while, home-sickness seizes the adventurers and they

come to a unanimous decision to return to Ireland ; but
they depart under a taboo not to set foot on earth, or
at least not till holy water has been sprinkled on them.
In their coracle they arrive before a gathering at Srub
Brain, probably in West Kerry, and Bran (who may now
possibly be regarded as an apparition temporarily returned
from the Otherworld to bid his people farewell) announces
himself, and this reply is made to him :—' We do not know
such a one, though the Voyage of Bran is in our ancient
stories.' Then one of Bran's party, in his eagerness to land,
broke the taboo ; he ' leaps from them out of the coracle.
As soon as he touched the earth of Ireland, forthwith he
was a heap of ashes, as though he had been in the earth
for many hundred years. . . . Thereupon, to the people of
the gathering, Bran told all his wanderings from the
beginning until that time. And he wrote these quatrains
in Ogam, and then bade them farewell. And from that
hour his wanderings are not known.'

Cormac's Adventure in the Land of Promise [1]

In *Cormac's Adventure in the Land of Promise*, there is
again a magic silver branch with three golden apples on
it :—' One day, at dawn in May-time, Cormac, grandson of
Conn, was alone on Múr Tea in Tara. He saw coming
towards him a sedate (?), grey-headed warrior. . . . A branch
of silver with three golden apples on his shoulder. Delight
and amusement to the full was it to listen to the music of
that branch, for men sore wounded, or women in child-bed,
or folk in sickness, would fall asleep at the melody when that
branch was shaken.' And the warrior tells Cormac that he
has come from a land where only truth is known, where
there is ' neither age nor decay nor gloom nor sadness nor
envy nor jealousy nor hatred nor haughtiness '. On his
promising the unknown warrior any three boons that he
shall ask, Cormac is given the magic branch. The grey-

[1] This tale exists in several manuscripts of the fourteenth and fifteenth
centuries; i. e. *Book of Ballymote*, and *Yellow Book of Lecan*, as edited and
translated by Stokes, in *Irische Texte*, III. i. 183–229 ; cf. *Voy. of Bran*, i.
190 ff. ; cf. *Le Cycle Myth. Irl.*, pp. 326–33.

headed warrior disappears suddenly ; ' and Cormac knew
not whither he had gone.'

' Cormac turned into the palace. The household mar-
velled at the branch. Cormac shook it at them, and cast
them into slumber from that hour to the same time on the
following day. At the end of a year the warrior comes into
his meeting and asked of Cormac the consideration for his
branch. " It shall be given," says Cormac. " I will take
[thy daughter] Ailbe to-day," says the warrior. So he took
the girl with him. The women of Tara utter three loud
cries after the daughter of the king of Erin. But Cormac
shook the branch at them, so that he banished grief from
them all and cast them into sleep. That day month comes
the warrior and takes with him Carpre Lifechair (the son
of Cormac). Weeping and sorrow ceased not in Tara after
the boy, and on that night no one therein ate or slept, and
they were in grief and in exceeding gloom. But Cormac
shook the branch at them, and they parted from [their]
sorrow. The same warrior comes again. " What askest
thou to-day ? " says Cormac. " Thy wife," saith he, " even
Ethne the Longsided, daughter of Dunlang king of Leinster."
Then he takes away the woman with him.' Thereupon
Cormac follows the messenger, and all his people go with
him. But ' a great mist was brought upon them in the midst
of the plain of the wall. Cormac found himself on a great
plain alone '. It is the ' Land of Promise '. Palaces of
bronze, and houses of white silver thatched with white
birds' wings are there. ' Then he sees in the garth a shining
fountain, with five streams flowing out of it, and the hosts
in turn a-drinking its water. Nine hazels of Buan grow over
the well. The purple hazels drop their nuts into the fountain, and the five salmon which are in the fountain sever
them, and send their husks floating down the streams.
Now the sound of the falling of those streams is more melodious than any music that [men] sing.' [1]

---

[1] The fountain is a sacred fountain containing the sacred salmon ; and
the nine hazels are the sacred hazels of inspiration and poetry. These
passages are among the most mystical in Irish literature. Cf. pp. 432-3.

Cormac having entered the fairy palace at the fountain beholds ' the loveliest of the world's women '. After she has been magically bathed, he bathes, and this, apparently, is symbolical of his purification in the Otherworld. Finally, at a feast, the warrior-messenger sings Cormac to sleep ; and when Cormac awakes he sees beside him his wife and children, who had preceded him thither to the Land of Promise. The warrior-messenger who *took* them all is none other than the great god Manannan Mac Lir of the Tuatha De Danann.

There in the Otherworld, Cormac gains a magic cup of gold richly and wondrously wrought, which would break into three pieces if ' three words of falsehood be spoken under it ', and the magic silver branch ; and Manannan, as the god-initiator, says to Ireland's high king :—' Take thy family then, and take the Cup that thou mayest have it for discerning between truth and falsehood. And thou shalt have the Branch for music and delight. And on the day that thou shalt die they all will be taken from thee. I am Manannan, son of Ler, king of the Land of Promise ; *and to see the Land of Promise was the reason I brought* [*thee*] *hither*. . . . The fountain which thou sawest, with the five streams out of it, is the Fountain of Knowledge, and the streams are the five senses through which knowledge is obtained (?). And no one will have knowledge who drinketh not a draught out of the fountain itself and out of the streams. The folk of many arts are those who drink of them both.'

' Now on the morrow morning, when Cormac arose, he found himself on the green of Tara, with his wife and his son and daughter, and having his Branch and his Cup. Now that was afterwards [called] " Cormac's Cup ", and it used to distinguish between truth and falsehood with the Gael. Howbeit, as had been promised him [by Manannan], it remained not after Cormac's death.' [1]

This beautiful tale evidently echoes in an extremely poetical and symbolical manner a very ancient Celtic initiation of a king and his family into the mystic cult of the mighty god Manannan, Son of the Sea. They enter the

[1] Cf. Stokes's trans. in *Irische Texte* (Leipzig, 1891), III. i. 211–16.

Otherworld in a trance state, and on waking are in Erin again, spiritually enriched. The Cup of Truth is probably the symbol of having gained knowledge of the Mystery of Life and Death, and the Branch, that of the Peace and Joy which comes to all who are truly Initiated ; for to have passed from the realm of mortal existence to the Realm of the Dead, of the Fairy-Folk, of the Gods, and back again, with full human consciousness all the while, was equivalent to having gained the Philosopher's Stone, the Elixir of Life, the Cup of Truth, and to having bathed in the Fountain of Eternal Youth which confers triumph over Death and unending happiness. Thus we may have here a Celtic poetical parallel to the initiatory journey of Aeneas to the Land of the Dead or Hades.

The Magic Wand of Gods, Fairies, and Druids

Manannan of the Tuatha De Danann, as a god-messenger from the invisible realm bearing the apple-branch of silver, is in externals, though not in other ways, like Hermes, the god-messenger from the realm of the gods bearing his wand of two intertwined serpents.[1] In modern fairy-lore this divine branch or wand is the magic wand of fairies ; or where messengers like old men guide mortals to an underworld it is a staff or cane with which they strike the rock hiding the secret entrance.

The Irish Druids made their wands of divination from the

---

[1] The Greeks saw in Hermes the symbol of the Logos. Like Manannan, he conducted the souls of men to the Otherworld of the gods, and then brought them back to the human world. Hermes ' holds a rod in his hands, beautiful, golden, wherewith he spellbinds the eyes of men whomsoever he would, and wakes them again from sleep '—in initiations ; while Manannan and the fairy beings lure mortals to the fairy world through sleep produced by the music of the Silver Branch.—Hippolytus on the Naasenes (from the Hebrew *Nachash*, meaning a ' Serpent '), a Gnostic school ; cf. G. R. S. Mead, *Fragments of a Faith Forgotten*, pp. 198, 201. Or again, ' the Caduceus, or Rod of Mercury (Hermes), and the Thyrsus in the Greek Mysteries, which conducted the soul from life to death, and from death to life, figured forth the serpentine power in man, and the path whereby it would carry the " man " aloft to the height, if he would but cause the " Waters of the Jordan " to " flow upwards ".'—G. R. S. Mead. ib., p. 185.

yew-tree ; and, like the ancient priests of Egypt, Greece, and
Rome, are believed to have controlled spirits, fairies, daemons,
elementals, and ghosts while making such divinations. It
will help us to understand how closely the ancient symbols
have affected our own life and age—though we have forgotten their relation with the Otherworld—by offering a few
examples, beginning with the ancient Irish bards who were
associated with the Druids. A wand in the form of a
symbolic branch, like a little spike or crescent with gently
tinkling bells upon it, was borne by them ; and in the piece
called *Mesca Ulad* or ' Inebriety of the Ultonians '[1] it is
said of the chief bard of Ulster, Sencha, that in the midst
of a bloody fray he ' waved the peaceful branch of Sencha,
and all the men of Ulster were silent, quiet '. In *Agallamh
an dá Shuadh* or the ' Dialogue of the two Sages ',[2] the mystic
symbol used by gods, fairies, magicians, and by all initiates
who know the mystery of life and death, is thus described
as a Druid symbol :—' Neidhe ' (a young bard who aspired
to succeed his father as chief poet of Ulster), ' made his
journey with a silver branch over him. The *Anradhs*, or
poets of the second order, carried a silver branch, but the
Ollamhs, or chief poets, carried a branch of gold ; all other
poets bore a branch of bronze.'[3] Modern and ancient
parallels are world-wide, among the most civilized as among
the least civilized peoples, and in civil or religious life among
ourselves. Thus, it was with a magic rod that Moses struck
the rock and pure water gushed forth, and he raised the
same rod and the Red Sea opened ; kings hold their sceptres
no less than Neptune his trident ; popes and bishops have
their croziers ; in the Roman Church there are little wand-
like objects used to perform benedictions ; high civil officials
have their mace of office ; and all the world over there are
the wands of magicians and of medicine-men.

[1] Cf. Hennessy's ed. in *Todd Lectures*, ser. I. i. 9.
[2] Among the early ecclesiastical manuscripts of the so-called *Prophecies.*
See E. O'Curry, *Lectures*, p. 383.
[3] Cf. Eleanor Hull, op. cit., pp. 439–40.

THE SICK-BED OF CUCHULAINN

We turn now to the story of the *Sick-Bed of Cuchulainn*.[1] And this is how the great hero of Ulster was fairy-struck. Manannan Mac Lir, tiring of his wife Fand, had deserted her, and so she, wishing to marry Cuchulainn, went to Ireland with her sister Liban. Taking the form of two birds bound together by a chain of red gold, Fand and Liban rested on a lake in Ulster where Cuchulainn should see them as he was hunting. To capture the two birds, Cuchulainn cast a javelin at them, but they escaped, though injured. Disappointed at a failure like this, which for him was most unusual, Cuchulainn went away to a menhir where he sat down and fell asleep. Then he saw two women, one in a green and one in a crimson cloak ; and the woman in green coming up to him laughed and struck him with a whip-like object. The woman in crimson did likewise, and alternately the two women kept striking him till they left him almost dead. And straightway the mighty hero of the Red Branch Knights took to his bed with a strange malady, which no Druid or doctor in all Ireland could cure.

Till the end of a year Cuchulainn lay on his sick-bed at Emain-Macha without speaking to any one. Then—the day before *Samain* (November Eve)—there came to him an unknown messenger who sang to him a wonderful song, promising to cure him of his malady if he would only accept the invitation of the daughters of Aed Abrat to visit them in the Otherworld. When the song was ended, the messenger departed, ' and they knew not whence he came nor whither he went.' Thereupon Cuchulainn went to the place where the malady had been put on him, and there appeared to him again the woman in the green cloak. She let it be known to Cuchulainn that she was Liban, and that she was longing for him to go with her to the Plain of Delight to

---

[1] Now in three versions based on the *L. U.* MS. Our version is collated from O'Curry's translation in *Atlantis*, i. 362–92, ii. 98–124, as revised by Kuno Meyer, *Voy. of Bran*, i. 152 ff. ; and from Jubainville's translation in *L'Ép. celt. en Irl.*, pp. 170–216.

fight against Labraid's enemies. And she promised Cuchulainn as a reward that he would get Fand to wife. But Cuchulainn would not accept the invitation without knowing to what country he was called. So he sent his charioteer Laeg to bring back from there a report. Laeg went with the fairy woman in a boat of bronze, and returned; and when Cuchulainn heard from him the wonderful glories of that Otherworld of the *Sidhe* he willingly set out for it.

After Cuchulainn had overthrown Labraid's enemies and had been in the Otherworld a month with the fairy woman Fand, he returned to Ireland alone; though afterwards in a place agreed upon, Fand joined him. Emer, the wife of Cuchulainn, was overcome with jealousy and schemed to kill Fand, so that Fand returned to her husband the god Manannan and he received her back again. When she was gone Cuchulainn could not be consoled; but Emer obtained from the Druids a magic drink for Cuchulainn, which made him forget all about the Otherworld and the fairy woman Fand. And another drink the Druids gave to Emer so that she forgot all her jealousy; and then Manannan Mac Lir himself came and shook his mantle between Cuchulainn and Fand to prevent the two ever meeting again. And thus it was that the *Sidhe*-women failed to steal away the great Cuchulainn. The magic of the Druids and the power of the Tuatha De Danann king triumphed; and the Champion of Ulster did not go to the Otherworld until he met a natural death in that last great fight.[1]

OSSIAN'S RETURN FROM FAIRYLAND [2]

Ossian too, like Cuchulainn, was enticed into Fairyland by a fairy woman:—She carries him away on a white horse, across the Western Ocean; and as they are moving

[1] As Alfred Nutt pointed out, ' There is no parallel to the position or to the sentiments of Fand in the post-classic literature of Western Europe until we come to Guinevere and Isolt, Ninian and Orgueilleuse' (*Voy. of Bran*, i. 156 n.).

[2] See poem *Tir na nog* (Land of Youth), by Michael Comyn, composed or collected about the year 1749. Ed. by Bryan O'Looney, in *Trans. Ossianic Soc.*, iv. 234-70.

over the sea-waves they behold a fair maid on a brown horse, and she holding in her right hand a golden apple. After the hero had married his fairy abductress and lived in the Otherworld for three hundred years, an overpowering desire to return to Ireland and join again in the councils of his dearly beloved Fenian Brotherhood took possession of him, and he set out on the same white horse on which he travelled thence with the fairy princess, for such was his wife. And she, as he went, thrice warned him not to lay his ' foot on level ground ', and he heard from her the startling announcement that the Fenians were all gone and Ireland quite changed.

Safe in Ireland, Ossian seeks the Brotherhood, and though he goes from one place to another where his old companions were wont to meet, not one of them can he find. And how changed is all the land ! He realizes at last how long he must have been away. The words of his fairy wife are too sadly true.

While Ossian wanders disconsolately over Ireland, he comes to a multitude of men trying to move an enormous slab of marble, under which some other men are lying. ' Ossian's assistance is asked, and he generously gives it. But in leaning over his horse, to take up the stone with one hand, the girth breaks, and he falls. Straightway the white horse fled away on his way home, and Ossian became aged, decrepit, and blind.' [1]

The Going of Lanval to Avalon

The fairy romances which were recorded during the mediaeval period in continental Europe report a surprisingly large number of heroes who, like Cuchulainn and Ossian, fell under the power of fairy women or *fées*, and followed one of them to the Apple-Land or Avalon. Besides

[1] Laeghaire, who also came back from Fairyland on a fairy horse, and fifty warriors with him each likewise mounted, to say good-bye for ever to the king and people of Connaught, were warned as they set out for this world not to dismount if they wished to return to their fairy wives. The warning was strictly observed, and thus they were able to go back to the *Sidhe*-world (see p. 295).

Arthur, they include Sir Lancelot, Sir Gawayne, Ogier, Guingemor and Lanval (see pp. 325–6). The story of Lanval is told by Marie de France in one of her *Lais*, and is so famous a one that we shall briefly outline it :—

Lanval was a mediaeval knight who lived during the time of King Arthur in Brittany. He was young and very beautiful, so that one of the fairy damsels fell in love with him ; and in the true Irish fashion—himself and his fairy sweetheart mounted on the same fairy horse—the two went riding off to Fairyland :—

> On the horse behind her
> With full rush Lanval jumped.
> With her he goes away into Avalon,
> According to what the Briton tells us,
> Into an isle, which is very beautiful.[1]

THE VOYAGE OF TEIGUE, SON OF CIAN

There is another type of *imram* in which through adventure rather than through invitation from one of the fairy beings, men enter the Otherworld; as illustrated by the *Voyage of Mael-Duin*,[2] and by the still more beautiful *Voyage of Teigue, Son of Cian*. This last old Irish story summarizes many of the Otherworld elements we have so far considered, and (though it shows Christian influences) gives us a very clear picture of the Land of Youth amid the Western Ocean—a land such as Ponce De Leon and so many brave navigators sought in America :—

Teigue, son of Cian, and heir to the kingship of West Munster, with his followers set out from Ireland to recover his wife and brethren who had been stolen by Cathmann and his band of sea-rovers from Fresen, a land near Spain. It was the time of the spring tide, when the sea was rough, and storms coming on the voyagers they lost their way. After about nine weeks they came to a land fairer than any land they had ever beheld—it was the Happy Otherworld. In

---

[1] Cf. *Bibliotheca Normannica*, iii, *Die Lais der Marie de France*, pp. 86–112.

[2] Cf. Stokes's trans., in *Rev. Celt.*, ix. 453–95, x. 50–95. Most of the tale comes fom the *L. U.* MS. ; cf. *L'Ép. celt. en Irl.*, pp. 449–500.

it were many ' red-laden apple-trees, with leafy oaks too
in it, and hazels yellow with nuts in their clusters ' ; and
' a wide smooth plain clad in flowering clover all bedewed
with honey '.   In the midst of this plain Teigue and his
companions descried three hills, and on each of them an
impregnable place of strength.   At the first stronghold,
which had a rampart of white marble, Teigue was welcomed
by ' a white-bodied lady, fairest of the whole world's women ' ;
and she told him that the stronghold is the abode ' of Ireland's kings :   from Heremon son of Milesius to Conn of the
Hundred Battles, who was the last to pass into it '.   Teigue
with his people moved on till they gained the middle *dún*,
the *dún* with a rampart of gold.   There also ' they found
a queen of gracious form, and she draped in vesture of
a golden fabric ', who tells them that they are in the Earth's
fourth paradise.

At the third *dún*, the *dún* with a silver rampart, Teigue
and his party met Connla, the son of Conn of the Hundred
Battles.   ' In his hand he held a fragrant apple having the
hue of gold ; a third part of it he would eat, and still, for all
he consumed, never a whit would it be diminished.'   And
at his side sat a young woman of many charms, who spake
thus to Teigue :—' I had bestowed on him (i. e. felt for him)
true affection's love, and therefore wrought to have him
come to me in this land ; where our delight, both of us, is
to continue in looking at and in perpetual contemplation of
one another :   above and beyond which we pass not, to
commit impurity or fleshly sin whatsoever.'   Both Connla
and his friend were clad in vestments of green—like the
fairy-folk ; and their step was so light that hardly did the
beautiful clover-heads bend beneath it.   And the apple ' it
was that supported the pair of them and, when once they
had partaken of it, nor age nor dimness could affect them '.
When Teigue asked who occupied the *dún* with the silver
rampart the maiden with Connla made this reply :—' In
that one there is not any one.   For behoof of the righteous
kings that after acceptance of the Faith shall rule Ireland
it is that yonder *dún* stands ready ; and we are they who,

until such those virtuous princes shall enter into it, keep the same : in the which, Teigue my soul, thou too shalt have an appointed place.' ' Obliquely across the most capacious palace Teigue looked away ' (as he was observing the beauty of the yet uninhabited *dún*), ' and marked a thickly furnished wide-spreading apple-tree that bare blossoms and ripe fruit both. " What is that apple-tree beyond ? " he asked [of the maiden], and she made answer :—" That apple-tree's fruit it is that for meat shall serve the congregation which is to be in this mansion, *and a single apple of the same it was that brought (coaxed away) Connla to me.*" '

Then the party rested, and there came towards them a whole array of feminine beauty, among which was a lovely damsel of refined form who foretold to Teigue the manner and time of his death, and as a token she gave him ' a fair cup of emerald hue, in which are inherent many virtues : for [among other things] though it were but water poured into it, incontinently it would be wine '. And this was her farewell message to Teigue :—' From that (the cup), let not thine hand part ; but have it for a token : when it shall escape from thee, then in a short time after shalt thou die ; and where thou shalt meet thy death is in the glen that is on Boyne's side : there the earth shall grow into a great hill, and the name that it shall bear will be *croidhe eisse* ; there too (when thou shalt first have been wounded by a roving wild hart, after which Allmarachs will slay thee) I will bury thy body ; but thy soul shall come with me hither, where till the Judgement's Day thou shalt assume a body light and ethereal.'

As the party led by Teigue were going down to the sea-shore to depart, the girl who had been escorting them asked ' how long they had been in the country '. ' In our estimation,' they replied, ' we are in it but one single day.' She, however, said : ' For an entire twelvemonth ye are in it ; during which time ye have had neither meat nor drink, nor, how long soever ye should be here, would cold or thirst or hunger assail you.' And when Teigue and his party had entered their *currach* they looked astern, but ' they saw not the land from which they came, for incontinently an obscuring magic veil was drawn over it '.[1]

THE ADVENTURES OF ART, SON OF CONN

This interesting *imram* combines, in a way, the type of tale wherein a fairy woman comes from the Otherworld to our world—though in this tale she is banished from there— and the type of tale wherein the Otherworld is found through adventure :—

Bécuma Cneisgel, a woman of the Tuatha De Danann, because of a transgression she had committed in the Other- world with Gaidiar, Manannan's son, was banished thence. She came to Conn, high king of Ireland, and she bound him to do her will ; and her judgement was that Art, the son of Conn, should not come to Tara until a year was past. During the year, Conn and Bécuma were together in Tara, ' and there was neither corn nor milk in Ireland during that time.' The Tuatha De Danann sent this dreadful famine ; for they, as agricultural gods, thus showed their displeasure at the unholy life of Ireland's high king with the evil woman whom they had banished. The Druids of all Ireland being called together, declared that to appease the Tuatha De Danann ' the son of a sinless couple should be brought to Ireland and slain before Tara, and his blood mingled with the soil of Tara ' (cf. p. 436). It was Conn himself who set out for the Otherworld and found there the sinless boy, the son of the queen of that world, and he brought him back to Tara. A strange event saves the youth :—' Just then they (the assembly of people and Druids, with Conn, Art, and Finn) heard the lowing of a cow, and a woman wailing continually behind it. And they saw the cow and the woman making for the assembly.' The woman had come from the Otherworld to save Segda ; and the cow was accepted as a sacrifice in place of Segda, owing to the wonders it dis- closed ; for its two bags when opened contained two birds —one with one leg and one with twelve legs, and ' the one-

---

[1] *Silva Gadelica*, ii. 385-401. The MS. text, *Echtra Thaidg mheic Chéin*, or ' The Adventure of Cian's son Teigue ', is found in the *Book of Lismore*.

legged bird prevailed over the bird with twelve legs '. Then rising up and calling Conn aside, the woman declared to him that until he put aside the evil woman Bécuma ' a third of its corn, and its milk, and its mast ' should be lacking to Ireland. ' And she took leave of them then and went off with her son, even Segda. And jewels and treasures were offered to them, but they refused them.'

In the second part of this complex tale, Bécuma and Art are together playing a game. Art finally loses, because ' the men of the *sidh* (like invisible spirits) began to steal the pieces ' with which he and the woman play ; and, as a result, Bécuma put on him this taboo :—' Thou shalt not eat food in Ireland until thou bring with thee Delbchaem, the daughter of Morgan.' ' Where is she ? ' asked Art. ' In an isle amid the sea, and that is all the information that thou wilt get.' ' And he put forth the coracle, and travelled the sea from one isle to another until he came to a fair, strange island,' the Otherworld. The blooming women of that land entertain the prince of Ireland during six weeks, and instruct him in all the dangers he must face and the conquests he must make.

Having successfully met all the ordeals, Art secures Delbchaem, daughter of Morgan the king of the ' Land of Wonders ', and returns to Ireland. ' She had a green cloak of one hue about her, with a gold pin in it over her breast, and long, fair, very golden hair. She had dark-black eyebrows, and flashing grey eyes in her head, and a snowy-white body.' And upon seeing the chaste and noble Delbchaem with Art, Bécuma, the banished woman of the Tuatha De Danann, lamenting, departs from Tara for ever.[1]

OTHERWORLD QUESTS OF CUCHULAINN AND OF ARTHUR

There is yet the distinct class of tales about journeys to a fairy world which is a Hades world beneath the earth, or in some land of death, rather than amid the waves of the Western Ocean. Thus there is a curious poem in the *Book*

---

[1] Summarized and quoted from translation by R. I. Best, in *Ériu*, iii. 150–73. The text is found in the *Book of Fermoy* (pp. 139–45), a fifteenth-century codex in the Royal Irish Academy.

of the Dun Cow describing an expedition led by Cuchulainn
to the stronghold of Scáth in the land of Scáth, or, as the
name means, land of Shades, where the hero gains the
king's cauldron.[1] And the poem suggests why so few who
invaded that Hades world ever returned—perhaps why,
mystically speaking, so few men could escape either through
initiation or re-birth the natural confusion and forgetfulness arising out of death.

In the *Book of Taliessin* a weird poem, *Preiddeu Annwfn*,
or the ' Spoils of Annwn ', describes, in language not always
clear, how the Brythonic Arthur made a similar journey to
the Welsh Hades world named Annwn, where he, like Cuchulainn in Scáth, gained possession of a magic cauldron—
a pagan Celtic type of the Holy Grail—which furnishes
inexhaustible food though ' it will not boil the food of
a coward '. But in stanzas iii and iv of *Preiddeu Annwfn*,
Annwn, or Uffern as it is otherwise called, is not an underground realm, but some world to be reached like the Gaelic
Land of Promise by sea. Annwn is also called Caer Sidi,
which in another poem of the *Book of Taliessin* (No. XIV) is
thought of as an island of immortal youth amid ' the streams
of the ocean ' where there is a food-giving fountain.[2]

LITERARY EVOLUTION OF THE HAPPY OTHERWORLD IDEA

We have now noticed two chief classes of Otherworld
legends. In one there is the beautiful and peaceful *Tír In-
nambéo* or ' Land of the Living' under Manannan's rule across
the seas, and its fairy inhabitants are principally women who
lure away noble men and youths through love for them ;
in the other there is a Hades world—often confused with the
former—in which great heroes go on some mysterious
quest. Sometimes this Hades world is inseparable from the
underground palaces or world of the Tuatha De Danann.
Again, it may be an underlake fairy-realm like that entered
by Laeghaire and his fifty companions (see p. 302) ; or, as in

---

[1] Folios 113-15, trans. O'Beirne Crow, *Journ. Kilkenny Archae. Soc.*
(1870-1), pp. 371-448 ; cf. Rhŷs, *Hib. Lect.*, pp. 260-1.
[2] Cf. Skene, *Four Ancient Books of Wales*, i. 264-6, 276, &c.

Gilla Decair,[1] of late composition, it is an under-well land wherein Dermot has adventures. And, in a similar tale, Murough, on the invitation of a mysterious stranger who comes out of a lake and then disappears ' like the mist of a winter fog or the whiff of a March wind ', dives beneath the lake's waters, and is escorted to the palace of King Under-Wave, wherein he sees the stranger as the water-king himself sitting on a golden throne (cf. pp. 63-4). In continual feasting there Murough passes a day and a year, thinking the time only a few days.[2]

As a rule the Hades world, or underground and under-wave world, is unlike Manannan's peaceful ocean realm, being often described as a place of much strife ; and mortals are usually induced to enter it to aid in settling the troubles of its fairy inhabitants.

All the numerous variations of Otherworld tales now extant in Celtic literature show a common pre-Christian origin, though almost all of them have been coloured by Christian ideas about heaven, hell, and purgatory. From the earliest tales of the over-sea Otherworld type, like those of Bran, Maelduin, and Connla, all of which may go back to the early eighth century as compositions, the christianizing influence is already clearly begun ; and in the *Voyage of Snedgus and of Mac Riagla*, of the late ninth century, this influence predominates.[3] Purely Christian texts of about the same period or later describe the Christian heaven as though it were the pagan Otherworld. Some of these, like the Latin version of the tale of *St. Brandan's Voyage*, greatly influenced European literature, and probably contributed to the discovery of the New World.[3]

The combination of Christian and pagan Celtic ideas is well shown in the *Voyage of the Húi Corra* [4] :—' Thereafter

---

[1] Cf. *Silva Gadelica*, ii. 301 ff., from Additional MS. 34119, dating from 1765, in British Museum.

[2] *Giolla an Fhiugha*, or ' The Lad of the Ferrule ', trans. by Douglas Hyde, in *Irish Texts Society*, London, 1899.

[3] Cf. Meyer and Nutt, *Voy. of Bran*, i. 147, 228, 230, 235 ; 161.

[4] The bulk of the text comes from the *Book of Fermoy*. Cf. Stokes's trans. in *Rev. Celt.*, xiv. 59, 49, 53, &c.

a wondrous island was shown to them. A psalm-singing venerable old man, with fair, builded churches and beautiful bright altars. Beautiful green grass therein. A dew of honey on its grass. Little ever-lovely bees and fair, purple-headed birds a-chanting music therein, so that [merely] to listen to them was enough of delight.' But in another passage the Christian scribe describes Otherworld birds as souls, some of them in hell :—' " Of the land of Erin am I," quoth the bird, " and I am the soul of a woman, and I am a monkess unto thee," she saith to the elder. . . . " Come ye to another place," saith the bird, " to hearken to yon birds. The birds that ye see are the souls that come on Sunday out of hell." ' Still other islands are definitely made into Christian hells full of fire, wherein wailing and shrieking men are being mangled by the beaks and talons of birds.

But sometimes, like the legends about the Tuatha De Danann, the legends about the Otherworld were taken literally and most seriously by some early Irish-Christian saints. Professor J. Loth records a very interesting episode, how St. Malo and his teacher Brandan actually set out on an ocean voyage to find the Heaven-world of the pagan Celts :—' Saint Malo, when a youth, embarks with his teacher Brandan in a boat, in search of that mysterious country ; after some days, the waves drive him back rebuffed and discouraged upon the seashore. An angel opens his eyes : the land of eternal peace and of eternal youth is that which Christianity promises to its elect.' [1]

Not only was the Celtic Otherworld gradually changed into a Christian Heaven, or Hell, from the eighth century onward, but its divine inhabitants soon came to suffer the rationalization commonly applied to their race ; and the transcribers began to set them down as actual personages of Irish history. As we have already observed, the Tuatha De Danann were shorn of their immortality, and were given in exchange all the passions and shortcomings of men, and made subject to disease and death. This perhaps was a

---

[1] J. Loth, L'Émigration bretonne en Armorique (Paris, 1883), pp. 139–40.

natural anthropomorphic process such as is met with in all mythologies. Celtic myth and mysticism, wherein may yet be read the deepest secrets of life and death, supplied names and legends to fill out a christianized scheme of Irish chronology, which was made to begin some six thousand years ago with Adam.

A few of the pagan legends, however, met very fair treatment at the hands of poetical and patriotic Christian transcribers. Thus in *Adamnan's Vision*,[1] though the Celtic Otherworld has become ' the Land of the Saints ', its primal character is clearly discernible : to reach it a sea voyage is necessary ; and it is a land where there is no pride, falsehood, envy, disease or death, ' wherein is delight of every goodness.' In it there are singing birds, and for sustenance while there the voyagers need only to hear its music and ' sate themselves with the odour which is in the Land '.

Again, in the *Book of Leinster*, and in later MSS., there is a *dinnshenchas* of almost primal pagan purity. It alludes to *Clidna's Wave*, that of Tuag Inbir :—To Tuag, daughter of Conall, Manannan the sea-god sent a messenger, a Druid of the Tuatha De Danann in the shape of a woman. The Druid chanted a sleep spell over the girl, and while he left her on the seashore to look for a boat in which to embark for the ' Land of Everliving Women ', a wave of the flood tide came and drowned her. But the Oxford version of the same tale doubts whether the maiden was drowned, for it suggests, ' Or maybe it (the wave) was Manannan himself that was carrying her off.'[2] Thus the scribe understood that to go to Manannan's world literally meant entering a sleep or trance state, or, what is equivalent in the case of the maiden whom Manannan summoned, the passage through death from the physical body. And still, to-day, the Irish peasant believes that the ' good people ' take to their invisible world all young men or maidens who meet death ; or that

---

[1] Ed. and trans. by W. Stokes, Calcutta, 1866. This *Vision* has been erroneously ascribed to the celebrated Abbot of Iona, who died in 703; but Professor Zimmer has regarded it as a ninth-century composition; cf. *Voy. of Bran*, i. 219 ff.   [2] Cf. *Voy. of Bran*, i. 195 ff.

one under a fairy spell may go to their world for a short time, and come back to our world again.

We have frequently emphasized how truly the modern Celtic peasant in certain non-commercialized localities has kept to the faith of his pagan ancestors, while the learned Christian scribes have often departed widely from it. The story of the voyage of Fionn to the Otherworld,[1] which Campbell found living among Scotch peasants as late as the last century, adds a striking proof of this assertion. So does Michael Comyn's peasant version of Ossian in the 'Land of Youth' (as outlined above, p. 346), which, though dating from about 1749, has all the natural character of the best ancient tales, like those about Bran and Cormac. We are inclined, therefore, to attach a value even higher than we have already done to the testimony of the living Fairy-Faith which confirms in so many parallel ways, as has been shown, the Fairy-Faith of the remote past. Mr. W. B. Yeats, the Irish poet, adequately sums up this matter by saying, ' But the Irish peasant believes that the utmost he can dream was once or still is a reality by his own door. He will point to some mountain and tell you that some famous hero or beauty lived and sorrowed there, or he will tell you that Tir-na-nog, the Country of the Young, the old Celtic paradise—the Land of the Living Heart, as it used to be called—is all about him.' [2]

At the end of his long and careful study of the Celtic Otherworld, Alfred Nutt arrived at the tentative conclusion which coincides with our own, that ' The vision of a Happy Otherworld found in Irish mythic romances of the eighth and following centuries is substantially pre-Christian ', that its closest analogues are in Hellenic myth, and that with these ' it forms the most archaic Aryan presentation of the divine and happy land we possess '.[3]

[1] See J. G. Campbell, *The Fians*, pp. 260–7.
[2] *The Literary Movement in Ireland*, in *Ideals in Ireland*, ed. by Lady Gregory (London, 1901), p. 95.
[3] Cf. *Voy. of Bran*, i. 331.

SECTION II
THE RECORDED FAIRY-FAITH

CHAPTER VII

THE CELTIC DOCTRINE OF RE-BIRTH [1]

'It seems as if Ossian's was a premature return. To-day he might find comrades come back from Tir-na-nog for the uplifting of their race. Perhaps to many a young spirit standing up among us Cailte might speak as to Mongan, saying : " I was with thee, with Finn." '—A. E.

Re-birth and Otherworld—As a Christian doctrine—General historical survey—According to the Barddas MSS. ; according to ancient and modern authorities—Reincarnation of the Tuatha De Danann—King Mongan's re-birth—Etain's birth—Dermot's pre-existence—Tuan's re-birth—Re-birth among Brythons—Arthur as a reincarnate hero—Non-Celtic parallels—Re-birth among modern Celts : in Ireland ; in Scotland ; in the Isle of Man ; in Wales; in Cornwall ; in Brittany —Origin and evolution of Celtic Re-birth Doctrine.

RELATION WITH THE OTHERWORLD

HOWEVER much the conception of the Otherworld among the ancient Greeks may have differed from that among the Celts, it was to both peoples alike inseparably connected with their belief in re-birth. Alfred Nutt, who studied this intimate relation more carefully perhaps than any other Celtic folk-lorist, has said of it :—' In Greek mythology as in Irish, the conception of re-birth proves to be a dominant factor of the same religious system in which Elysium is likewise an essential feature.' Death, as many initiates have proclaimed in their mystical writings, is but a going to that Otherworld from this world, and Birth a

---

[1] General reference : *Essay upon the Irish Vision of the happy Otherworld and the Celtic Doctrine of Re-birth*, by Alfred Nutt in Kuno Meyer's *Voyage of Bran*. Chief sources : *Leabhar na h-Uidhre ; Book of Leinster ; Four Ancient Books of Wales ; Mabinogion ; Silva Gadelica ; Barddas*, a collection of Welsh manuscripts made about 1560 ; and the *Annals of the Four Masters*, compiled in the first half of the seventeenth century.

coming back again ; [1] and Buddha announced it as his mission to teach men the way to be delivered out of this eternal Circle of Existence.

HISTORICAL SURVEY OF THE RE-BIRTH DOCTRINE

Among ourselves the doctrine may seem a strange one, though among the great nations of antiquity—the Egyptians, Indians, Greeks, and Celts—it was taught in the Mysteries and Priest-Schools, and formed the corner-stone of the most important philosophical systems like those of Buddha, Pythagoras, Plato, the Neo-Platonists, and the Druids. The Alexandrian Jews, also, were familiar with the doctrine, as implied in the *Wisdom of Solomon* (viii. 19, 20), and in the writings of Philo. It was one of the teachings in the Schools of Alexandria, and thus directly shaped the thoughts of some of the early Church Fathers—for example, Tertullian of Carthage (circa A. D. 160–240), and Origen of Alexandria (circa A. D. 185–254). It is of considerable historical importance for us at this point to consider at some length if Christians in the first centuries held or were greatly influenced by the re-birth doctrine, because, as we shall presently observe, the probable influence of Christian on pagan Celtic beliefs may have been at a certain period very deep and even the most important reshaping influence.

As an examination of Origen's *De Principiis* proves, Origen himself believed in the doctrine.[2] But the theologians who created the Greek canons of the Fifth Council

---

[1] Cf. Plato, *Republic*, x ; *Phaedo* ; *Phaedrus*, &c. ; Iamblichus, *Concerning the Mysteries of Egypt, Chaldaea, Assyria* ; Plutarch, *Mysteries of Isis* (*De Iside et Osiride*).

[2] He says :—' I, for my part, suspect that the spirit was implanted in them (rational creatures, men) from without' (*De Principiis*, Book I, c. vii. 4) ; . . . ' the cause of each one's actions is a pre-existing one ; and then every one, according to his deserts, is made by God either a vessel unto honour or dishonour ' (ib., Book III, c. i. 20). ' Whence we are of opinion that, seeing the soul, as we have frequently said, is immortal and eternal, it is possible that, in the many and endless periods of duration in the immeasurable and different worlds, it may descend from the highest good to the lowest evil, or be restored from the lowest evil to the highest good ' (ib., Book III, c. i, 21) ; . . . ' every one has the reason in himself, why he has been placed in this or that rank in life ' (ib., Book III, c. v, 4).

disagreed with Origen's views, and condemned Origen for believing, among other things called by them heresies, that Jesus Christ will be reincarnated and suffer on earth a second time to save the daemons,[1] an order of spiritual beings regarded by some ancient philosophers as destined to evolve into human souls. Tertullian, contemporary with Origen, in his *De Anima* considers whether or not the doctrine of re-birth can be regarded as Christian in view of the declaration by Jesus Christ that John the Baptist was Elias (or Elijah), the old Jewish prophet, come again :—' And if ye are willing to receive it (or him), this (John the Baptist) is Elijah, which is to come. He that hath ears to hear, let him hear.'[2] Tertullian concludes, and modern Christian theologians frequently echo him (upon comparing Malachi iv. 5), that all the New Testament writers mean to convey is that John the Baptist possessed or acted in ' the spirit and power ' of Elias, but was not actually a reincarnation of Elias, since he did not possess ' the soul and body ' of Elias.[3] Had Tertullian been a mystic and not merely a theologian with a personal bias against the mystery teachings, which bias he shows throughout his *De Anima*, it is quite evident that he would have been on this doctrinal matter in agreement with Origen, who was both a mystic and a theologian,[4] and, then, probably with such an agreement of these two eminent Church Fathers on record before the time when Christian councils

[1] Cf. Bergier, *Origène*, in *Dict. de Théologie*, v. 69.

[2] *Holy Bible*, Revised Version, St. Matt. xi. 14-15 ; cf. St. Matt. xvii. 10-13, St. Mark ix. 13, St. Luke vii. 27, St. John i. 21.

[3] Tertullian's conclusion is as follows :—' These substances (" soul and body ") are, in fact, the natural property of each individual ; whilst " the spirit and power " (cf. Mal. iv. 5) are bestowed as external gifts by the grace of God, and so may be transferred to another person according to the purpose and will of the Almighty, as was anciently the case with respect to the spirit of Moses ' (cf. Num. xii. 2). —*De Anima* c. xxxv ; cf. trans. in *Ante-Nicene Christian Library* (Edinburgh, 1870), xv. 496-7.

[4] Origen says :—' But that there should be certain doctrines not made known to the multitude, which are [revealed] after the exoteric ones have been taught, is not a peculiarity of Christianity alone, but also of philosophic systems, in which certain truths are exoteric and others esoteric ' (*Origen against Celsus*, Book I, c. vii).

met to determine canonical and orthodox beliefs, the doctrine of re-birth would never have been expurgated from
Christianity.[1]

In the *Pistis Sophia*,[2] an ancient Gnostic-Christian work,
which contains what are alleged to be some of Jesus Christ's
esoteric teachings to his disciples, it is clearly stated (contrary
to Tertullian's argument, but in accord with what we may
assume Origen's view would have been) that John the
Baptist was the reincarnation of Elias.[3] The same work

---

[1] How Tertullian almost literally accepted the re-birth doctrine is shown
in his *Apology*, chapter xlviii, concerning the resurrection of the body. It
is the corrupted form of the doctrine, viz. transmigration of human souls
into animal bodies, which he therein, as well as in his *De Anima* and elsewhere, chiefly and logically combats, as Origen also combated it. He first
shows why a human soul must return into a human body in accordance
with natural analogy, every creature being after its own kind always ;
and then, because the purpose of the Resurrection is the judgement, that
the soul must return into its own body. And he concludes :—'It is surely
more worthy of belief that a man will be restored from a man, any given
person from any given person, but still a man ; so that the same kind of
soul may be reinstated in the same mode of existence, even if not into the
same outward form ' (*The Apology of Tertullian for the Christians*; cf. trans.
by T. H. Bindley, Oxford, 1890, pp. 137–9).

[2] British Museum MS. Add. 5114, vellum—a Coptic manuscript in the
dialect of Upper Egypt. Its undetermined date is placed by Woide at latest
about the end of the fourth century. It was evidently copied by one scribe
from an older manuscript, the original probably having been the *Apocalypse
of Sophia*, by Valentius, the learned Gnostic who lived in Egypt for thirty
years during the second century. See the translation of the Schwartze's
parallel Latin version of *Pistis Sophia* and its introduction, both by G. R. S.
Mead (London, 1896).

[3] The chief passages are as follows, Jesus being the speaker :—' Moreover, in the region of the soul of the rulers, destined to receive it, I found
the soul of the prophet Elias, in the aeons of the sphere, and I took him,
and receiving his soul also, I brought it to the virgin of light, and she gave
it to her receivers ; they brought it to the sphere of the rulers, and cast it
into the womb of Elizabeth. Wherefore the power of the little Iaô, who
is in the midst, and the soul of Elias the prophet, are united with the body
of John the Baptist. For this cause have ye been in doubt aforetime,
when I said unto you, " John said, I am not the Christ " ; and ye said
unto me, " It is written in the Scripture, that when the Christ shall come,
Elias will come before him, and prepare his way." And I, when ye had
said this unto me, replied unto you, " Elias verily is come, and hath prepared all things, according as it is written ; and they have done unto him
whatsoever they would." And when I perceived that ye did not understand that I had spoken concerning the soul of Elias united with John the
Baptist, I answered you openly and face to face with the words, " If ye

further expounds the doctrine of re-birth as a teaching of
Jesus Christ which applies not to particular personages only,
like Elias, but as a universal law governing the lives of all
mankind.[1]

As our discussion has made evident, during the first
centuries the re-birth doctrine was undoubtedly well known
to Alexandrian Christians. Among other early Christian
theologians and philosophers who held some form of a re-
birth doctrine, were Synesius, Bishop of Ptolemais (circa
375–414), Boethius, a Roman (circa 475–525), and Psellus, a
native of Andros (second half of ninth century). In addition
to the many Gnostic-Christian sects, the Manichaeans,
who comprised more than seventy sects connected with
the primitive Church, also promulgated the re-birth doctrine.[2] Along with the condemnation of the Gnostics and
Manichaeans as heretical, the doctrine of re-birth was likewise condemned by various ecclesiastical bodies and councils.
This was the declaration by the Council of Constantinople
in 553 :—' Whosoever shall support the mythical doctrine
of the pre-existence of the Soul, and the consequent wonderful opinion of its return, let him be anathema.' And so,
after centuries of controversy, the ancient doctrine ceased
to be regarded as Christian.[3] It is very likely, how-

will receive it, John the Baptist is Elias who, I said, was for to come " '
(*Pistis Sophia*, Book I, 12–13, Mead's translation).

[1] ' The Saviour answered and said unto his disciples :—" Preach ye
unto the whole world, saying unto men, ' Strive together that ye may
receive the mysteries of light in this time of stress, and enter into the
kingdom of light. Put not off from day to day, and from cycle to cycle,
in the belief that ye will succeed in obtaining the mysteries when ye return
to the world in another cycle ' " ' (*Pistis Sophia*, Book II, 317, Mead's
translation).

[2] Cf. Bergier, *Manichéisme*, in *Dict. de Théol.*, iv. 211–13.

[3] The *Refutation of Irenaeus*, until quite recently, has been the chief
source of much of our knowledge concerning Gnosticism. It was written
during the second century at Lyons, by Irenaeus, a bishop of Gaul, far
from any direct contact with the still flourishing Gnosticism. But now
with the discovery of genuine manuscripts of Gnostic works : (1) the
Askew Codex, vellum, British Museum, London, containing the *Pistis
Sophia* (see above, p. 361 n.) and extracts from the *Books of the Saviour*;
(2) the *Bruce Codex* (two MSS.), papyrus, Bodleian Library, Oxford, containing the fragmentary *Book of the Great Logos*, an unknown treatise, and

ever, as will be shown in due order, that a few of the early
Celtic missionaries, always famous for their Celtic inde-
pendence even in questions touching Christian theology and
government, did not feel themselves bound by the decisions
of continental Church Councils with respect to this particular
doctrine.

During the mediaeval period in Europe, the re-birth
doctrine continued to live on in secret among many of the
alchemists and mystical philosophers, and among such

fragments ; and (3) the *Akhmīm Codex* (discovered in 1896), papyrus,
Egyptian Museum, Berlin, containing *The Gospel of Mary* (or *Apocryphon
of John*), *The Wisdom of Jesus Christ*, and *The Acts of Peter*, we are able
to check from original sources the Fathers in many of their writings and
canons concerning Gnostic ' heresies '; and find that Irenaeus, the last
refuge of Christian haeresiologists, has so condensed and paraphrased his
sources that we cannot depend upon him at all for a consistent exposition
of Gnostic doctrines, which with more or less prejudice he is trying to
refute. It is true that the age of these manuscripts has not been satisfactorily determined; in fact most of them have not yet been carefully
studied. Very probably, however, as appears to be the case with the
Pistis Sophia, they have been copied from manuscripts which were contemporary with or earlier than the time of Irenaeus, and hence may be
regarded as good authority in determining Gnostic teachings. (Cf. all of
above note with G. R. S. Mead, *Fragments of a Faith Forgotten*, London,
1900, pp. 147, 151–3.)

Many unprejudiced scholars are now unwilling to admit the rulings of
the Church Councils which determined what was orthodox and what
heretical doctrines among the Gnostic-Christians, because many of their
dogmatic decisions were based upon the unscholarly *Refutation of Irenaeus*
and upon other equally unreliable evidence. The data which have
accumulated in the hands of scholars about early Christian thought and
Gnosticism are now much more complete and trustworthy than the similar
data were upon which the Council of Constantinople in 553 based its
decision with respect to the doctrine of re-birth; and the truth coming to be
recognized seems to be that the Gnostics rather than the Church Fathers,
who adopted from them what doctrines they liked, condemning those
they did not like, should henceforth be regarded as the first Christian
theologians, and mystics. If this view of the very difficult and complex
matter be accepted, then modern Christianity itself ought to be allowed to
resume what thus appears to have been its original position—so long
obscured by the well-meaning, but, nevertheless, ill-advised ecclesiastical
councils—as the synthesizer of pagan religions and philosophies. Some
such view has been accepted by many eminent Christian theologians since
Origen : i. e. the Cambridge Platonist, Henry More, openly advocated the
re-birth doctrine in the seventeenth century ; and in later times it has been
preached from Christian pulpits by such men as Henry Ward Beecher and
Phillips Brooks.

Druids as survived religious persecution ; and it has come down from that period to this through Orders like the Rosicrucian Order—an Order which seems to have had an unbroken existence from the Middle Ages or earlier— and likewise through the unbroken traditions of modern Druidism. In our own times there is what may be called a renaissance of the ancient doctrine in Europe and America —especially in England, Germany, France, and the United States—through various philosophical or religious societies ; some of them founding their teachings and literature on the ancient and mediaeval mystical philosophers, while others stand as the representatives in the West of the mystical schools of modern India, which, like modern Druidism, claim to have existed from what we call pre-historic times.[1] To-day in the Roman Church eminent theologians have called the doctrine of Purgatory the Christian counterpart of the philosophical doctrine of re-birth ; [2] and the real significance of this opinion will appear in our later study of St. Patrick's Purgatory which, as we hold, is connected more or less definitely with the pagan-Irish doctrines of the underworld of the *Sidhe*-folk and spirits, as

---

[1] See A. Bertrand, *La Religion des Gaulois, les Druides et le Druidisme* (Paris, 1897) ; H. Jennings, *The Rosicrucians* (London, 1887) ; the Work of Paracelsus ; H. Cornelius Agrippa, *De Occulta Philosophia* (Paris, 1567); H. P. Blavatsky's *Isis Unveiled*, and the *Secret Doctrine* (London, 1888); and *Hermetic Works*, by Anna Kingsford and E. Maitland (London, 1885).

[2] Cf. Bergier, *Purgatoire*, in *Dict. de Théol.*, v. 409. A Celt, a professed faithful and fervent adherent of the Church of Rome, whom I met in the Morbihan where he now lives, told me that he believes thoroughly in the doctrine of re-birth, and that it is according to his opinion the proper and logical interpretation of the doctrine of Purgatory; and he added that there are priests in his Church who have told him that their personal interpretation of the purgatorial doctrine is the same. Thus some Roman Catholics do not deny the re-birth doctrine. And such conversations as this with Catholic Celts in Ireland and Brittany lead me to believe that to a larger extent than has been suspected the old Celtic Doctrine of Re-birth may have been one of the chief foundations for the modern Roman Catholic Doctrine of Purgatory, whose origin is not clearly indicated in any theological works. For us this probability is important as well as interesting, and especially so when we remember the profound influence which the Celtic St. Patrick's Purgatory certainly exerted on the Church during the Middle Ages when the doctrine of Purgatory was taking definite shape (see our chapter x).

well as shades of the dead, and with the Celtic-Druidic Doctrine of Reincarnation.

Scientifically speaking, as shown in the Welsh Triads of Bardism, the ancient Celtic Doctrine of Re-birth represented for the priestly and bardic initiates an exposition of the complete cycle of human evolution ; that is to say, it included what we now call Darwinism—which explains only the purely physical evolution of the body which man inhabits as an inheritance from the brute kingdom—and also besides Darwinism, a comprehensive theory of man's own evolution as a spiritual being both apart from and in a physical body, on his road to the perfection which comes from knowing completely the earth-plane of existence. And in time, judging from the rapid advance of the present age, our own science through psychical research may work back to the old mystery teachings and declare them scientific. (See chap. xii.)

ACCORDING TO THE BARDDAS MSS.

With this preliminary survey of the subject we may now proceed to show how in the Celtic scheme of evolution the Otherworld with all its gods, fairies, and invisible beings, and this world with all its visible beings, form the two poles of life or conscious existence. Let us begin with purely philosophical conceptions, going first to the Welsh *Barddas*,[1] where it is said ' There are three circles of existence : the circle of Ceugant (the circle of Infinity), where there is neither animate nor inanimate save God, and God only can traverse it ; the circle of Abred (the circle of Re-birth), where the dead is stronger than the living, and where every

---

[1] *Barddas* (Llandovery, 1862) is 'a collection (by Iolo Morganwg, a Bard) of original documents, illustrative of the theology, wisdom, and usage of the Bardo-Druidic System of the Isle of Britain '. The original manuscripts are said to have been in the possession of Llywelyn Sion, a Bard of Glamorgan, about 1560. *Barddas* shows considerable Christian influence, yet in its essential teachings is sufficiently distinct. Though of late composition, *Barddas* seems to represent the traditional bardic doctrines as they had been handed down orally for an unknown period of time, it having been forbidden in earlier times to commit such doctrines to writing. We are well aware also of the adverse criticisms passed upon these documents ; but since no one questions their Celtic origin—whether it be ancient or more modern—we are content to use them.

principal existence is derived from the dead, and man has traversed it ; and the circle of Gwynvyd (the circle of the white, i. e. the circle of Perfection), where the living is stronger than the dead, and where every principal existence is derived from the living and life, that is, from God, and man shall traverse it ; nor will man attain to perfect knowledge, until he shall have fully traversed the circle of Gwynvyd, for no absolute knowledge can be obtained but by the experience of the senses, from having borne and suffered every condition and incident '.[1] . . . ' The three stabilities of knowledge : to have traversed every state of life ; to remember every state and its incidents ; and to be able to traverse every state, as one would wish, for the sake of experience and judgement ; and this will be obtained in the circle of Gwynvyd.' [2]

Thus *Barddas* expounds the complete Bardic scheme of evolution as one in which the monad or soul, as a knowledge of physical existence is gradually unfolded to it, passes through every phase of material embodiment before it enters the human kingdom, where, for the first time exercising freewill in a physical body, it becomes responsible for all its acts. The Bardic doctrine as otherwise stated is ' that the soul commenced its course in the lowest water-animalcule, and passed at death to other bodies of a superior order, successively, and in regular gradation, until it entered that of man. Humanity is a state of liberty, where man can attach himself to either good or evil, as he pleases '.[3] Once in the human kingdom the soul begins a second period of growth altogether different from that preceding—a period of growth toward divinity ; and with this, in our study, we are chiefly concerned. It seems clear that the circle of Gwynvyd finds its parallel in the Nirvana of Buddhism, being, like it, a state of absolute knowledge and felicity in which man becomes a divine being, a veritable god.[4] We

---

[1] *Barddas*, i, 189–91. [2] *Barddas*, i, 177.
[3] Preface to *Barddas*, xlii.
[4] One of the greatest errors formerly made by European Sanskrit scholars and published broadcast throughout the West, so that now it is popularly accepted there as true, is that Nirvana, the goal of Indian philosophy and

see in all this the intimate relation which there was thought
to be between what we call the state of life and the state of
death, between the world of men and the world of gods,
fairies, demons, spirits, and shades.   Our next step must
be to show, first, what some other authorities have had
to say about this relation, and then, second, and fundamentally, that gods or fairy-folk like the *Sidhe* or Tuatha De
Danann could come to this world not only as we have been
seeing them come as fairy women, fairy men, and gods, at
will visible or invisible to mortals, but also through submitting to human birth.

ACCORDING TO ANCIENT AND MODERN AUTHORITIES

First, therefore, for opinions ; and we may go to the
ancients and then to the moderns.   Here are a few from
Julius Caesar :—' In particular they (the Druids) wish to
inculcate this idea, that souls do not die, but pass from one
body to another.' [1]   ' The Gauls declare that they have all
sprung from their father Dis (or Pluto), and this they say
was delivered to them by the Druids.' [1]   And the testimony
of Caesar is confirmed by Diodorus Siculus,[2] and by Pomponius Mela.[3]   Lucan, in the *Pharsalia*,[4] addressing the
Druids on their doctrine of re-birth says :—' If you know
what you sing, death is the centre of a long life.'   And again
in the same passage he observes :—' Happy the folk upon

religion, means annihilation.   It does mean annihilation (evolutionary
transmutation of lower into higher), but only of all those forces or elements
which constitute man as an animal.   The error arose from interpreting
exoterically instead of esoterically, and was a natural result of that system
of western scholarship which sees and often cares only to examine external
aspects.   Native Indian scholars who have advised us in this difficult
problem prefer to translate *Nirvana* as ' Self-realization.', i. e. a state of
supernormal consciousness (to be acquired through the evolution of the
individual), as much superior to the normal human consciousness as the
normal human consciousness is superior to the consciousness existing in
the brute kingdom.

[1] *De Bel. Gal.*, lib. vi. 14. 5 ; vi. 18. 1.   [2] Book V, 31. 4.
[3] *De Situ Orbis*, iii. c. 2 : ' One point alone of the Druids' teaching has
become generally known among the common people (in order that they
should be braver in war), that souls are eternal and there is a second life
among the shades.'   [4] i. 449–62.

whom the Bear looks down, happy in this error, whom of fears the greatest moves not, the dread of death. Hence their warrior's heart hurls them against the steel, hence their ready welcome of death, and the thought that it were a coward's part to grudge a life sure of its return.'[1] Dr. Douglas Hyde, in his *Literary History of Ireland* (p. 95), speaking for the Irish people, says of the re-birth doctrine :—
'. . . the idea of re-birth which forms part of half a dozen existing Irish sagas, was perfectly familiar to the Irish Gael. . . .' According to another modern Celtic authority, D'Arbois de Jubainville, two chief Celtic doctrines or beliefs were the return of the ghosts of the dead and the re-birth of the same individuality in a new human body here on this planet.[2]

REINCARNATION OF THE TUATHA DE DANANN

We proceed now directly to show that there was also a belief, probably widespread, among the ancient Irish that divine personages, national heroes who are members of the Tuatha De Danann or *Sidhe* race, and great men, can be reincarnated, that is to say, can descend to this plane of existence and be as mortals more than once. This aspect of the Celtic Doctrine of Re-birth has been clearly set forth by the publications of such eminent Celtic folk-lorists as Alfred Nutt and Miss Eleanor Hull. Miss Hull, in her study of *Old Irish Tabus, or Gesa*,[3] referring to the Cuchulainn Cycle of Irish literature and mythology, writes thus :—' There is no doubt that all the chief personages of this cycle were regarded as the direct descendants, or it would be more correct to say, as avatars or reincarnations of the early gods. Not only are their pedigrees traced up to the Tuatha Dé Danann, but there are indications in the birth-stories of nearly all the principal personages that they are looked upon simply as divine beings reborn on the human plane of

---

[1] Lucan, i. 457–8 ; i. 458–62.
[2] Cf. *Le Cycle Myth. Irl.*, pp. 345, 347 ff.
[3] *Folk-Lore*, xii. 64, &c. ; also cf. Eleanor Hull, *The Cuchullin Saga in Irish Literature* (London, 1898), Intro., p. 23, &c.

life. These indications are mysterious, and most of the tales which deal with them show signs of having been altered, perhaps intentionally, by the Christian transcribers. The doctrine of re-birth was naturally not one acceptable to them. . . . The goddess Etain becomes the mortal wife of a king of Ireland. . . . Conchobhar, moreover, is spoken of as a terrestrial god ;[1] and Dechtire, his sister, and the mother of Cúchulainn, is called a goddess.[2] In the case of Cúchulainn himself, it is distinctly noted that he is the avatar of Lugh lamhfada (long-hand), the sun-deity [3] of the earliest cycle. Lugh appears to Dechtire, the mother of Cúchulainn, and tells her that he himself is her little child, i. e. that the child is a reincarnation of himself ; and Cúchulainn, when inquired of as to his birth, points proudly to his descent from Lugh. When, too, it is proposed to find a wife for the hero, the reason assigned is, that they knew " that his re-birth would be of himself " (i. e. that only from himself could another such as he have origin).'[4] We have in this last a clue to the popular Irish belief regarding the re-birth of beings of a god-like nature. D'Arbois de Jubainville has shown,[5] also, that the grandfather of Cuchulainn, son of Sualtaim, was from the country of the *Sidhe*, and so was Ethné Ingubé, the sister of Sualtaim. And Dechtire, the mother of Cuchulainn, was the daughter of the Druid Cathba and the brother of King Conchobhar. Thus the ancestry of the great hero of the Red Branch Knights of Ulster is both royal and divine. And Conall Cernach, Cuchulainn's comrade and avenger, apparently from a tale in the *Cóir Anmann* (Fitness of Names), composed probably during the twelfth century, was also a reincarnated Tuatha De Danann hero.[6]

---

[1] What is probably the oldest form of a tale concerning Conchobhar's birth makes Conchobhar 'the son of a god who incarnated himself in the same way as did Lug and Etain' (cf. *Voy. of Bran*, ii. 73).

[2] See *Leabhar na h-Uidhre*, 101[b]; and *Book of Leinster*, 123[b] :—' Cúchulainn mc dea dechtiri.'

[3] We have already mentioned the belief that gods having their abode in the sun could leave it to assume bodies here on earth and become culture heroes and great teachers (see p. 309).

[4] From *Wooing of Emer* in *Leabhar na h-Uidhre* ; cf. *Voy. of Bran*, ii. 97.

[5] *L'Épopée celt. en Irl.*, p. 11.　　　[6] Cf. *Voy. of Bran*, ii. p. 74 ff.

Practically all the extant manuscripts dealing with the ancient literature and mythology of the Gaels were written by Christian scribes or else copied by them from older manuscripts, so that, as Miss Hull points out, what few Irish re-birth stories have come down to us—and they are probably but remnants of an extensive re-birth literature like that of India—have been more or less altered. Yet to these scholarly scribes of the early monastic schools, who kept alive the sacred fire of learning while their own country was being plundered by foreign invaders and the rest of mediaeval Europe plunged in warfare, the world owes a debt of gratitude ; for to their efforts alone, in spite of a re-shaping of matter naturally to be expected, is due almost everything recorded on parchments concerning pagan Ireland.

The Re-birth Story Concerning King Mongan

We have preserved to us a remarkable re-birth story in which the characters are known to be historical.[1] It concerns a quarrel between the king of Ulster, Mongan, son of Fiachna—who, according to the *Annals of Ireland by the Four Masters* (i. 245), was killed in A. D. 620 by Arthur, son of Bicor—and Forgoll, the poet of Mongan.[2] The dispute between them was as to the place of the death of Fothad Airgdech, a king of Ireland who was killed by Cailte, one of the warriors of Find, in a battle whose date is fixed by the *Four Masters* in A. D. 285.[3] Forgoll pretended that Fothad

---

[1] In the *Leabhar na h-Uidhre*, 133ᵃ-134ᵇ ; cf. *Le Cycle Myth. Irl.*, pp. 336-43 ; cf. *Voy. of Bran*, i. 49-52 ; cf. O'Curry, *Manners and Customs*, iii. 175.

[2] Cf. Stokes's ed. *Annals of Tigernach, Third Frag.* in *Rev. Celt.* xvii. 178. In the piece called *Tucait baile Mongáin* in the *Leabhar na h-Uidhre*, p. 134, col. 2, ' Mongan is seen living with his wife the year of the death of Ciaran mac int Shair, and of Tuathal Mael-Garb, that is to say in 544,' following the *Chronicum Scotorum*, Hennessy's ed., pp. 48-9. As D'Arbois de Jubainville adds, the Irish chronicles of this epoch are only approximate in their dates. Thus, while the *Four Masters* (i. 243) makes the death of Mongan A. D. 620, the *Annals of Ulster* makes it A. D. 625, the *Chronicum Scotorum* A. D. 625, the *Annals of Clonmacnoise*, A. D. 624, and *Egerton MS.* 1782 A. D. 615 (cf. *Voy. of Bran*, i. 137-9).

[3] J. O'Donovan, *Annals of Ireland by the Four Masters* (Dublin, 1856), i. 121.

had been killed at Duffry, in Leinster, and Mongan asserted
that it was on the river Larne (anciently Ollarba) in County
Antrim.   Enraged at being contradicted, even though it
were by the king, Forgoll threatened Mongan with terrible
incantations ; and it was agreed that unless Mongan proved
his assertion within three days, his queen should pass under
the control of Forgoll.   Mongan, however, had spoken truly
and with certain secret knowledge, and felt sure of winning.

When the third day was almost expired and Forgoll had
presented himself ready to claim the wager, there was heard
coming in the distance the one whom Mongan awaited.   It
was Cailte himself, come from the Otherworld to bear testimony to the truthfulness of the king and to confound the
audacious presumptions of the poet Forgoll.   It was evening
when he reached the palace.   The king Mongan was seated
on his throne, and the queen at his right full of fear
about the outcome, and in front stood the poet Forgoll
claiming the wager.   No one knew the strange warrior as
he entered the court, save the king.

Cailte, when fully informed of the quarrel and the wager,
quickly announced so that all heard him distinctly, ' The
poet has lied ! '   ' You will regret those words,' replied the
poet.   ' What you say does not well become you,' responded Cailte in turn, ' for I will prove what I say.'   And
straightway Cailte revealed this strange secret : that he
had been one of the companions in arms under the great
warrior Find, who was also his teacher, and that Mongan,
the king before whom he spoke, was the reincarnation of
Find :—

' We were with thee,' said Cailte, addressing the king.
' We were with Find.'   ' Know, however,' replied Mongan,
' that you do wrong in revealing a secret.'   But the warrior
continued : ' We were therefore with Find.   We came from
Scotland.   We encountered Fothad Airgdech near here, on
the shores of the Ollarba.   We gave him furious battle.
I cast my spear at him in such a manner that it passed
through his body, and the iron point, detaching itself from
the staff, became fixed in the earth on the other side of

Fothad. Behold here [in my hand] the shaft of that spear.
There will be found the bare rock from the top of which
I let fly my weapon. There will be found a little further
to the east the iron point sunken in the earth. There will
be found again a little further, always to the east, the tomb
of Fothad Airgdech. A coffin of stone covers his body ; his
two bracelets of silver, his two arm-rings, and his neck-
torque of silver are in the coffin. Above the tomb rises
a pillar-stone, and on the upper extremity of that stone
which is planted in the earth one may read an inscription
in ogam : *Here reposes Fothad Airgdech ; he was fighting
against Find when Cailte slew him.*'

And to the consternation of Forgoll, what this warrior
who came from the Otherworld declared was true, for
there were found the place indicated by him, the rock, the
spear-head, the pillar-stone, the inscription, the coffin of
stone, the body in it, and the jewellery. Thus Mongan gained
the wager ; and the secret of his life which he alone had
known was revealed—he was Find re-born[1] ; and Cailte, his
old pupil and warrior-companion, had come from the land of
the dead to aid him[1] :—' It was Cailte, Find's foster-son,
that had come to them. Mongan, however, was Find,
though he would not let it be told.'[1] But not only was
Mongan an Irish king, he was also a god, the son of the
Tuatha De Danann Manannan Mac Lir : ' this Mongan is
a son of Manannan Mac Lir, though he is called Mongan,
son of Fiachna.'[2] And so it is that long after their conquest
the People of the Goddess Dana ruled their conquerors, for
they took upon themselves human bodies, being born as the
children of the kings of Mil's Sons.

There are other episodes which show very clearly the
relationship between Mongan incarnated in a human body
and his divine father Manannan. Thus, ' When Mongan
was three nights old, Manannan came for him and took him
with him to bring up in the Land of Promise, and vowed

[1] Cf. *Le Cycle Myth. Irl.*, pp. 336–43 ; O'Curry, *Manners and Customs*
iii. 175 ; *L. U.*, 133[a]–134[b] ; and *Voy. of Bran*, i. 52.

[2] *Voy. of Bran*, i. 44–5 ; from *The Conception of Mongan*.

that he would not let him back into Ireland before he were twelve years of age.'   And after Mongan has become Ulster's high king, Manannan comes to him to rouse him out of human slothfulness to a consciousness of his divine nature and mission, and of the need of action : Mongan and his wife were frittering away their time playing a game, when they beheld a dark black-tufted little cleric standing at the door-post, who said : —' "This inactivity in which thou art, O Mongan, is not an inactivity becoming a king of Ulster, not to go to avenge thy father on Fiachna the Black, son of Deman, though Dubh-Lacha may think it wrong to tell thee so. . . ." Mongan seized the kingship of Ulster, and the little cleric who had done the reason was Manannan the great and mighty.'[1]

In the ancient tale of the *Voyage of Bran*—probably composed in its present form during the eighth, possibly the seventh, century A. D.—there is another version of the Mongan Re-birth Story, which, being later in origin and composition than the *Voyage* itself, was undoubtedly clumsily inserted into the manuscript, as scholars think.[2] Therein, Mongan as the offspring of Manannan by the woman of Line-mag—quite after the theory of the Christian Incarnation—is described as ' a fair man in a body of white clay '. This and what follows in the introductory quatrain show how early Celtic doctrines correspond to or else were originated by those of the Christians. And the transcriber seeing the parallels, glossed and altered the text which he copied by introducing Christian phraseology so as to fit it in with his own idea—altogether improbable—that the references are to the coming of Jesus Christ. The references are to Manannan and to the woman of Line-mag, who by him was to be the mother of Mongan—as Mary the wife of Joseph was the mother of Jesus Christ by God the Father :—

> A noble salvation will come
> From the King who has created us,
> A white law will come over seas,
> Besides being God, He will be man.

---

[1] Meyer's version, *Voy. of Bran*, i. 73-4.   [2] Cf. *Voy. of Bran*, i. 137.

This shape, he on whom thou lookest,
Will come to thy parts ;
'Tis mine to journey to her house,
To the woman in Line-mag.

For it is Moninnan, the son of Ler,
From the chariot in the shape of a man,

.   .   .   .   .   .

He will delight the company of every fairy-knoll,
He will be the darling of every goodly land,
He will make known secrets—a course of wisdom—
In the world, without being feared.

To him is attributed the power of shape-shifting, which is
not transmigration into animal forms, but a magical power
exercised by him in a human body.

He will be throughout long ages
An hundred years in fair kingship

.   .   .   .   .

Moninnan, the son of Ler
Will be his father, his tutor.

At his death

The white host (the angels or fairies) will take him
    under a wheel (chariot) of clouds
To the gathering where there is no sorrow.[1]

The Birth of Etain of the Tuatha De Danann [2]

Another clear example of one of the Tuatha De Danann
being born as a mortal is recorded in the famous saga of
the *Wooing of Etain*. Three fragments of this story exist
in the *Book of the Dun Cow*. The first tells how Etain
Echraide, daughter of Ailill and wife of Midir (a great king
among the *Sidhe* people) was driven out of Fairyland by
the jealousy of her husband's other wife, and how after
being wafted about on the winds of this world she fell
invisibly into the drinking-cup of the wife of Etar of Inber
Cichmaine, who was an Ulster chieftain. The chieftain's
wife swallowed her ; and, in due time, gave birth to a girl :—

---

[1] *Voy. of Bran*, i. 22–8, quatrains 48–59, &c.
[2] In *L. U.* ; cf. *Le Cycle Myth. Irl.*, pp. 311–22 ; and *Voy. of Bran*, ii.
47–53.

' It was one thousand and twelve years from the first begetting of Etain by Ailill to the last begetting by Etar.'   Etain, retaining her own name, grew up thence as an Irish princess.[1]

One day an unknown man of very stately aspect suddenly appeared to Etain the princess ; and as suddenly disappeared, after he had sung to her a wonderful song designed to arouse in her the subconscious memories of her past existence among the *Sidhe* :—

> So is Etain here to-day. . . .
> Among little children is her lot. . . .
> It is she was gulped in the drink
> By Etar's wife in a heavy draught.

The scribe ends this part of the story by letting it be known that Midir has struck off the head of his other wife, Fuamnach, the cause of all Etain's trouble.

The second section of the tale introduces Etain as queen of Eochaid Airem, high king of Ireland, and the most curious and important part of it shows how she was loved by Ailill Aenguba.   Ailill, so far as blood kinship went, was the brother of Eochaid, though apparently either an incarnation of Midir or else possessed by him : Etain acceded to his love, but he was under a strange love-weakness ; and on two occasions when he attempted to advance his desires an overpowering sleep fell on him, and each time Etain met a man in Ailill's shape—as though it were his ' double '—bemoaning his weakness.   On a third occasion she asked who the man was, and he declared himself to be Midir, and besought her to return with him to the Otherworld.   But her worldly or human memory clouded her subconscious memory, and she did not recognize Midir, yet promised to go with him on gaining Eochaid's permission.   After this event, curiously enough, Ailill was healed of his strange love-malady.

In the third part of the story, Midir and Eochaid are

---

[1] In the Irish conception of re-birth there is no change of sex : Lug is re-born as a boy, in Cuchulainn ; Finn as Mongan ; Etain as a girl.   But it seems that Etain as a mortal had no consciousness of her previous divine existence, while Cuchulainn and Mongan knew their non-human origin and pre-existence.

playing games. Midir loses the first two and with them
great riches, but winning the third claims the right to place
his arms about Etain and kiss her. Eochaid asked a month's
delay. The last day of the month had passed. It was night.
Eochaid in his palace at Tara awaited the coming of his
rival, Midir ; and though all the doors of the palace had
been firmly closed for the occasion, and armed soldiers surrounded the queen, Midir like a spirit suddenly stood in the
centre of the court and claimed the wager. Then, grasping
and kissing Etain, he mounted in the air with her and very
quickly passed out through the opening of the great chimney.
In consternation, King Eochaid and his warriors hurried
without the palace ; and there, on looking up, they saw
two white swans flying over Tara, bound together by
a golden chain.[1]

THE PRE-EXISTENCE OF DERMOT

With a difficult task before him, Dermot—as was the case
with Mongan—is reminded of his pre-existence as a hero in
the Otherworld with Manannan Mac Lir and Angus Oge :—
' Now spoke Fergus Truelips, Finn's ollave, and said :
" Cowardly and punily thou shrinkest, Dermot ; for with
most potent Manannan, son of Lir, thou studiedst and wast
brought up, in the Land of Promise and in the bay-indented
coasts ; with Angus Oge, too, the Daghda's son, wast most
accurately taught ; and it is not just that now thou lackest
even a moderate portion of their skill and daring, such as
might serve to convey Finn and his party up this rock or
bastion." At these words Dermot's face grew red ; he laid
hold on Manannan's magic staves that he had, and, as once
again he redly blushed, by dint of skill in martial feats he
with a leap rose on his javelin's shafts and so gained his two

[1] Some time after this, according to one part of the tale, Eochaid stormed
Midir's fairy palace—for the purpose localized in Ireland—and won Etain
back, but the fairies cast a curse on his race for this, and Conaire, his
grandson, fell a victim to it. Such a recovering of Etain by Eochaid may
vaguely suggest a re-birth of Etain, through the power exerted by Eochaid,
who, being a king, is to be regarded in his non-human nature as one of the
Tuatha De Danann himself, like Midir his rival.

soles' breadth of the solid glebe that overhung the water's edge.'[1]

RE-BIRTH OF TUAN

Tuan, as the son of Starn, lived one hundred years as the brother of Partholon, the first man to reach Ireland ; and then, after two hundred and twenty years, was re-born as the son of Cairell. This story in its oldest form is preserved in the *Book of the Dun Cow*, and seems to have been composed during the late ninth or early tenth century.[2]

---

[1] Cf. *The Gilla decair*, in *Silva Gadelica*, pp. 300–3.

[2] Cf. *Voy. of Bran*, ii. 76 ff.   The Christian scribe's version fills up the space between Tuan's death and re-birth by making him pass eighty years as a stag, twenty as a wild boar, one hundred as an eagle, and twenty as a salmon (ib., p. 79).   In this particular example, the uninitiated scribe (evidently having failed to grasp an important aspect of the re-birth doctrine as this was esoterically explained in the Mysteries, namely, that between death and re-birth, while the conscious Ego is resident in the Otherworld, the physical atoms of the discarded human body may transmigrate through various plant and animal bodies) appears to set forth as Celtic an erroneous doctrine of the transmigration of the conscious Ego itself (see p. 513 n.).   In other texts, for example in the song which Amairgen (considered the Gaelic equivalent or even original of the Brythonic Taliessin) sang as he, with the conquering Sons of Mil, set foot on Ireland, there are similar transformations, attributed to certain heroes like Taliessin (see the *Mabinogion*) and Tuan mac Cairill during their disembodied states after death and until re-birth.   But these transformations seem to echo poetically, and often rationally, a very mystical Celtic pantheism, in which Man, regarded as having evolved upwards through all forms and conditions of existence, is at one with all creation :—

> I am the wind which blows o'er the sea ;
> I am the wave of the deep ;
> I am the bull of seven battles ;
> I am the eagle on the rock ;
> I am a tear of the sun ;
> I am the fairest of plants ;
> I am a boar for courage ;
> I am a salmon in the water ;
> I am a lake in the plain ;
> I am the world of knowledge ;
> I am the head of the battle-dealing spear ;
> I am the god who fashions fire in the head ;
> Who spreads light in the gathering on the mountain?
> Who foretells the ages of the moon ?
> Who teaches the spot where the sun rests ?

And Amairgen also says:—'I am,' [Taliessin] 'I have been' (*Book of Invasions;* cf. *Voy. of Bran*, ii. 91–2 ; cf. Rhŷs, *Hib. Lect.*, p. 549 ; cf. Skene, *Four Ancient Books*, i. 276 ff.).

In later times, especially among non-bardic poets, there has been a

RE-BIRTH AMONG THE BRYTHONS

Such then are the re-birth stories of the Gaels. Among the Brythons the same ancient doctrine prevailed, though we have fewer clear records of it. Of the Brythonic Re-birth Doctrine as philosophically expounded in *Barddas*, mention has already been made.

In the ancient Welsh story about Taliessin, Gwion after many transformations, magical in their nature, is re-born as that great poet of Wales, his mother being a goddess, Caridwen, who dwells beneath the waters of Lake Tegid. In its present mystical form this tale cannot be traced further than the end of the sixteenth century, though the transformation incidents are presupposed in the *Book of Taliessin*, a thirteenth-century manuscript.[1] Besides being the re-birth of Gwion, Taliessin may be regarded as a bardic initiate high in degree, who is possessed of all magical and druidical powers.[1] He made a voyage to the Otherworld, Caer Sidi ; and this seems to indicate some close connexion between ancient rites of initiation and his occult knowledge of all things.[2] Like the Irish re-birth and Otherworld tales,

similar tendency to misinterpret this primitive mystical Celtic pantheism into the corrupt form of the re-birth doctrine, namely transmigration of the human soul into animal bodies. Dr. Douglas Hyde has sent to me the following evidence :—' I have a poem, consisting of nearly one hundred stanzas, about a pig who ate an Irish manuscript, and who by eating it recovered human speech for twenty-four hours and gave his master an account of his previous embodiments. He had been a right-hand man of Cromwell, a weaver in France, a subject of the Grand Signor, &c. The poem might be about one hundred or one hundred and fifty years old.' It is probable that the poet who composed this poem intended to add a touch of modern Irish humour by making use of the pig. We should, nevertheless, bear in mind that the pig (or, as is more commonly the rule, the wild boar) holds a very curious and prominent position in the ancient mythology of Ireland, and of Wales as well. It was regarded as a magical animal (cf. p. 451 n.) ; and, apparently, was also a Druid symbol, whose meaning we have lost. Possibly the poet may have been aware of this. If so, he does not necessarily imply transmigration of the human soul into animal bodies ; but is merely employing symbolism.

[1] See *Taliessin* in the *Mabinogion*, and the *Book of Taliessin* in Skene's *Four Ancient Books*, i. 523 ff. ; cf. Nutt, *Voy. of Bran*, ii. 84, and Rhŷs, *Hib. Lect.*, pp. 548, 551.

[2] Cf. Rhŷs, *Hib. Lect.*, pp. 548-50.

it also suggests the relation between the world of death or Faerie and the world of human embodiment.

From his harrying of Hades, the Brythonic Gwydion secured the Head of Hades' Cauldron of Regeneration or Re-birth ; and when corpses of slain warriors are thrown into it they arise next day as excellent as ever, except that they are unable to speak ; which circumstance may be equal to saying that the ordinary uninitiated man when re-born is unable to speak of his previous incarnation, because he has no memory of it. This Cauldron of Re-birth, like so many objects mentioned in the ancient bardic literature, is evidently a mystic symbol : it suggests the same correspondences, as propounded in the modern *Barddas*, between the dead and the living, between death and re-birth ; and Gwydion having been a great culture hero of Wales probably promulgated a doctrine of re-birth, and hence is described as being able to resuscitate the dead.[1]

King Arthur as a Reincarnated Hero

Judging from substantial evidence set forth above in chapter v, the most famous of all Welsh heroes, Arthur, equally with Cuchulainn his Irish counterpart, can safely be considered both as a god apart from the human plane of existence, and thus like the Tuatha De Danann or Fairy-Folk, and also like a great national hero and king (such as Mongan was) incarnated in a physical body. The taking of Arthur to Avalon by his life-guardian, the Lady of the Lake, and by his own sister, and by two other fairy women who live in that Otherworld of Sacred Apple-Groves, is sufficient in itself, we believe, to prove him of a descent more divine than that of ordinary men. And the belief in his return from that Otherworld—a return so confidently looked for by the Brythonic peoples—seems to be a belief (whether recognized as such or not) that the Great Hero will be reincarnated as a Messiah destined to set them free. In Avalon, Arthur lives now, and ' It is from there that the Britons of England and of France have for a long time

[1] Cf. Rhŷs, *Hib. Lect.*, p. 259 ; and *Arth. Leg.*, p. 252.

awaited his coming '.[1] And Malory expressing the sentiment in his age writes [2] :—' Yet some men say in many parts
of England that King Arthur is not dead, but had by the
will of our Lord Jesu into another place ; and men say that
he shall come again, and he shall win the holy cross. I will
not say it shall be so, but rather I will say, here in this world
he changed his life.' If we consider Arthur's passing and
expected return, as many do, in a purely mythological aspect,
we must think of him for the time as a sun-god, and yet
even then cannot escape altogether from the re-birth idea ;
for, as a study of ancient Egyptian mythology shows, there
is still the same set of relations.[3] There are the sun-symbols
always made use of to set forth the doctrine of re-birth,
be it Egyptian, Indian, Mexican, or Celtic :—the death of
a mortal like the passing of Arthur is represented by the
sun-set on the horizon between the visible world here and
the invisible world beyond the Western Ocean, and the
re-birth is the sunrise of a new day.

Non-Celtic Parallels

As a non-Celtic parallel to what has preceded concerning
the Otherworld of the Celts and their Doctrine of Re-birth,
we offer the second of the *Stories of the High-priests of
Memphis*, as published by Mr. F. L. Griffith from ancient
manuscripts.[4] It is a history of Si-Osiri (the son of Osiris),
whose father was Setme Khamuas. This wonderful divine
son when still a child took his human father on a journey
to see Amenti, the Otherworld of the Dead ; and when
twelve years of age he was wiser than the wisest of the scribes
and unequalled in magic. At this period in his life there
arrived in Egypt an Ethiopian magician who came with the

---

[1] Loth, *Les Mabinogion, Kulhwch et Olwen*, p. 187 n.

[2] *Le Morte D'Arthur*, Book XXI, c. vii.

[3] See works on Egyptian mythology and religion, by Maspero; also
Lenormant, *Chaldean Magic*, p. 84, &c.

[4] F. L. Griffith, *Stories of the High-priests of Memphis* (Oxford, 1900),
c. iii. The text of this story is written on the back of two Greek documents,
bearing the date of the seventh year of the Emperor Claudius (A. D. 46–7),
not before published.

object of humbling the kingdom ; but Si-Osiri read what was in the unopened letter of the stranger, and knew that its bearer was the reincarnation of ' Hor the son of the Negress ', the most formidable of the three Ethiopian magicians who fifteen hundred years before had waged war with the magicians of Egypt. At that time the Egyptian Hor, the son of Pa-neshe, had defeated the great magician of Ethiopia in the final struggle between White and Black Magic which took place in the presence of the Pharaoh.[1] And ' Hor the son of the Negress ' had agreed not to return to Egypt again for fifteen hundred years. But now the time was elapsed, and, unmasking the character of the messenger, Si-Osiri destroyed him with magical fire. After this, Si-Osiri revealed himself as the reincarnation of Hor the son of Pa-neshe, and declared that Osiris had permitted him to return to earth to destroy the powerful hereditary enemy of Egypt. When the revelation was made, Si-Osiri ' passed away as a shade ', going back again, even as the Celtic Arthur, into the realm invisible from which he came.

As in ancient Ireland, where many kings or great heroes were regarded as direct incarnations or reincarnations of gods or divine beings from the Otherworld, so in Egypt the Pharaohs were thought to be gods in human bodies, sent by Osiris to rule the Children of the Sun.[2]   In Mexico and Peru there was a similar belief.[3]   In the Indian *Mahâbhârata*, Râma and Krishna are at once gods and men.[4]   The celebrated philosophical poem known as the *Bhagavadgîtâ* also asserts Krishna's descent from the gods ; and the same view is again enforced and extended in the *Hari-vansa* and especially in the *Bhâgavata Purâna*.[4]   The Indian *Laws of Manu* say that ' even an infant king must not be despised from an idea that he is a mere mortal ; for he is a great

[1] It is interesting to compare with this episode the episodes of how the magic of St. Patrick prevailed over the magic of the Druids when the old and the new religions met in warfare on the Hill of Tara, in the presence of the high king of Ireland and his court.

[2] E. A. Wallis Budge, *The Gods of the Egyptians* (London, 1904), p. 3.

[3] Prescott, *Conquest of Mexico* and *Conquest of Peru*.

[4] W. Crooke, *The Legends of Krishna*, in *Folk-Lore*, xi. 2–3 ff.

deity in human form '.[1] In ancient Greece it was a common
opinion that Zeus was reincarnated from age to age in the
great national heroes. ' Alexander the Great was regarded
not merely as the son of Zeus, but as Zeus himself.' And
other great Greeks were regarded as gods while living on
earth, like Lycurgus the Spartan law-giver, who after his
death was worshipped as one of the divine ones.[2]

Among the great philosophers, the ancient doctrine of re-
birth was a personal conviction: Buddha related very many
of his previous reincarnations, according to the *Gâtakamâlâ*;
Pythagoras is said to have gone to the temple of Here and
recognized there an ancient shield which he had carried in
a previous life when he was Euphorbus, a Homeric hero.[3]
From what Plato, in his *Meno*, quoted from an old poet,
it seems very probable that there may be some sort of
relationship between legends mentioning the Rites of Proserpine, like the legend of Aeneas in Virgil, and certain of the
Irish Otherworld and Re-birth legends among the Gaels, as
we have already suggested :—' For from whomsoever Perse-
phone hath accepted the atonement of ancient woe, their
souls she sendeth up once more to the upper sun in the
ninth year. From these grow up glorious kings and men of
swift strength, and men surpassing in poetical skill ; and
for all future time they are called holy heroes among men.'
Among modern philosophers and poets in Europe and
America the same ideas find their echo : Wordsworth in
his *Ode to Immortality* definitely inculcates pre-existence ;
Emerson in his *Threnody*, and Tennyson in his *De Profundis*,
seem committed to the re-birth doctrine, and Walt Whitman
in his *Leaves of Grass* without doubt accepted it as true.
Certain German philosophers, too, appear to hold views
in harmony with what is also the Celtic Doctrine of
Re-birth, e.g. Schopenhauer, in *The World as Will and
Idea*, J. G. Fichte, in *The Destiny of Man*, and Herder, in

---

[1] *Laws of Manu*, vii. 8, trans. by G. Bühler.
[2] A. B. Cook, *European Sky-God*, in *Folk-Lore*, xv. 301-4.
[3] Cf. Lucian, *Somn.*, 17, &c. See Tylor, *Prim. Cult.*,[4] ii. 13 ; also Tertullian, *De Anima*, c. xxviii, where Pythagoras is described as having
previously been Aethalides, and Euphorbus, and the fisherman Pyrrhus.

Dialogues on Metempsychosis. The Emperor of Japan is still the Divine Child of the Sun, the head of the *Order of the Rising Sun*, and is always regarded by his subjects as the incarnation of a great being. The Great Lama of Thibet is believed to reincarnate immediately after death.[1] William II of Germany seems to echo, perhaps unconsciously, the same doctrine when he claims to be ruling by divine right.[2]

That the Celtic Doctrine of Re-birth is a direct and complete confirmation of the Psychological Theory of the nature and origin of the belief in fairies is self-evident. Could it be shown to be scientifically plausible in itself, as well-educated Celts consider it to be—and much evidence to be derived from a study of states of consciousness, e. g. dreams, somnambulism, trance, crystal-gazing, changed personality, subconsciousness, and so forth, indicates that it might be shown to be so—it would effectively prove the theory. Fairies would then be beings of the Otherworld who can enter the human plane of life by submitting to the natural process of birth in a physical body, and would correspond to the *Alcheringa* ancestors of the Arunta. In chapter xii following, such a proof of the theory is attempted.

RE-BIRTH AMONG MODERN CELTS

One of the chief objects of this chapter is to show that the Re-birth Doctrine of the Celts, like most beliefs bound up with the Fairy-Faith, still survives ; thus further proving that Celtic tradition is an unbroken thing from times prehistoric until to-day. We shall therefore proceed to bring forward the following original material, collected by ourselves, as evidence on this point :—

In Ireland

In Ireland I found two districts where the Re-birth Doctrine has not been wholly forgotten. The first one is in

---

[1] Cf. Huc, *Souvenirs d'un voyage dans la Tartarie et le Thibet*, i. 279 ff.

[2] The doctrine of kingly rule by divine right was substituted after the conversion of the Roman Empire for the very ancient belief that the emperor was a god incarnate (not necessarily reincarnate) ; and the same christianized aspect of a pre-Christian doctrine stands behind the English kingship at the present day.

the country round Knock Ma, near Tuam. After Mrs. ——
had told me about fairies, I led up to the subject of re-birth,
and the most valuable of all my Irish finds concerning the
belief was the result. For this woman of Belclare told me
that it was believed by many of the old people, when she
was a girl living a few miles west of Knock Ma, that they
had lived on this earth before as men and women ; but, she
added, ' You could hardly get them to talk about their
belief. It was a sort of secret which they who held it discussed freely only among themselves.' They believed, too,
that disease and misfortune in old age come as a penalty for
sins committed in a former life.[1] This expiatory or purgatorial aspect of the Re-birth Doctrine seems to have been
more widespread than the doctrine in its bare outlines ; for
the Belclare woman in speaking of it was able to recall from
memories of forty-five or fifty years ago what was then
a popular story about a disease-worn man and an eel-
fisherman :—

The diseased man as he watches the eel-fisherman taking
up his baskets, contrasts his own wretched physical condition with the vigour and good health of the latter, and
attributes the misfortune which is upon himself to bad
actions in a life prior to the one he is then living. And here
is the unhappy man's lamentation :—

> Fliuch, fuar atâ mo leabaidh ;
> Atâ fearthâinn agus geur-ghaoith ;
> Atâim ag îoc na h-uaille,
> A's tusa ag faire do chliaibhîn.

> (Wet, cold is my bed ;
> There is rain and sharp wind ;
> I am paying for pride,
> And you watching your [eel-]basket.)

[1] A curious parallel to this Irish doctrine that through re-birth one suffers
for the sins committed in a previous earth-life is found in the Christian
scriptures, where in asking Jesus about a man born blind, ' Rabbi, who did
sin, this man, or his parents, that he should be born blind ? ' the disciple
exhibits what must have been a popular Jewish belief in re-birth quite like
the Celtic one. See St. John ix. 1-2. Though the Rabbis admitted the
possibility of ante-natal sin in thought, this passage seems to point un-
mistakably to a Jewish re-birth doctrine.

The teller of the story insisted on giving me these verses in Irish, for she said they have much less meaning in English, and I took them down ; and to verify them and the story in which they find a place, I went to the cottage a second time.   There is no doubt, therefore, that the legend is a genuine echo of the religion of pre-Christian Ireland, in which reincarnation appears to have been clearly inculcated and was probably the common belief.

I once asked Steven Ruan, the Galway piper, if he had ever heard of such a thing as people being born more than once here on this earth, seeing that I was seeking for traces of the old Irish Doctrine of Re-birth.   The answer he gave me was this :—' I have often heard it said that people born and dead come into this world again.   I have heard the old people say that we have lived on this earth before ; and I have often met old men and women who believed they had lived before. The idea passed from one old person to another, and was a common belief, though you do not hear much about it now.'

A highly educated Irishman now living in California tells me of his own knowledge that there was a popular and sincere belief among many of the Irish people throughout Ireland that Charles Parnell, their great champion in modern times, was the reincarnation of one of the old Gaelic heroes. This shows how the ancient doctrine is still practically applied.   There is also an opinion held by certain very prominent Irishmen now living in Ireland, with whom I have been privileged to discuss the re-birth doctrine, that both Patrick and Columba are likewise to be regarded as ancient Gaelic heroes, who were reincarnated to work for the uplifting of the Gael.[1]

---

[1] It is interesting to note in connexion with these two complementary ideas what has been written by Mr. Standish O'Grady concerning strange phenomena witnessed at the time of Charles Parnell's funeral :—' While his followers were committing Charles Parnell's remains to the earth, the sky was bright with strange lights and flames.   Only a coincidence possibly ; and yet persons not superstitious have maintained that there is some mysterious sympathy between the human soul and the elements. . . . Those strange flames recalled to my memory what is told of similar pheno- mena said to have been witnessed when tidings of the death of the great

A legend concerning Lough Gur, County Limerick, indicates that the sleeping-hero type of tale is a curious aspect of an ancient re-birth doctrine. In such tales, heroes and their warrior companions are held under enchantment, awaiting the mystic hour to strike for them to issue forth and free their native land from the rule of the Saxon. Usually they are so held within a mysterious cavern, as is the case of Arthur and his men, according to differently localized Welsh stories ; or they are in the depths of magic hills and mountains like most Irish heroes. The heroes under enchantment with their companions are to be considered as resident in the Otherworld, and their return to human action as a return to the human plane of life. The Lough Gur legend is about Garret Fitzgerald, the Earl of Desmond, who rebelled against Queen Elizabeth. Modern folk-tradition regards him as the guardian deity of the Lough, and as dwelling in an enchanted palace situated beneath its waters. As Count John de Salis, whose ancestral home is the Lough Gur estate, assures me, the peasants of the region declare themselves convinced that the earl once in seven years appears riding across the lake surface on a phantom white horse shod with shoes of silver ; and they believe that when the horse's silver shoes are worn out the enchantment will end. Then, like Arthur when his stay in Avalon ends, Garret Fitzgerald will return to the world of human life again to lead the Irish hosts to victory.[1]

In Scotland

Dr. Alexander Carmichael, author of *Carmina Gadelica*, who as a folk-lorist has examined modern peasant beliefs throughout the Highlands and Islands more thoroughly than any other living Scotsman, informs me that apparently there was at one time in the Highlands a definite belief in the ancient Celtic Rebirth Doctrine, because he has found traces of it there, though these traces were only in the vaguest and barest outline.

Christian Saint, Columba, overran the north-west of Europe, as perhaps truer than I had imagined.'—*Ireland : Her Story*, pp. 211–12.

[1] Cf. M. Lenihan, *Limerick ; its History and Antiquities* (Dublin, 1866), p. 725.

In the Isle of Man

Mr. William Cashen, keeper of Peel Castle, reported as follows with respect to a re-birth doctrine in the Isle of Man : —' Here in the Island among old Manx people I have heard it said, but only in a joking way, that we will come back to this earth again after some thousands of years. The idea wasn't very popular nor often discussed, and there is no belief in it now to my knowledge. It seems to have come down from the Druids.'

This is Mr. William Oates' testimony, given at Ballasalla :—' Some held a belief in the coming back (re-birth) of spirits. I can't explain it. A certain Manxman I knew used to talk about the transmigration of spirits ; but I shall not give his name, since many of his family still live here on the Island.'

Mr. Thomas Kelley, of Glen Meay, had no clear idea about the ancient Celtic Doctrine of Re-birth, though he said :— ' My grandfather had a notion that he would be back here again at the Resurrection to claim his land.' This undoubtedly shows how the Christian doctrine of the Resurrection and the Celtic one of Re-birth may have blended, both being based on the common idea of a physical post-existence.

In Wales

In the Pentre Evan country where I discovered such rich folk-lore, I found my chief witness from there not unfamiliar with the ancient Celtic belief in Re-birth. One day I asked her if she had ever heard the old folk say that they had lived before on this earth as men and women. Somewhat surprised at the question, for to answer it would reveal half-secret thoughts of which, as it proved, not even her own nephew or niece had knowledge, she hesitated a moment, and, then, looking at me intently, said with great earnestness, ' Yes ; and I often believe myself that I have lived before.' And because of the unusual question, which seemed to reveal on my part familiarity with the belief, she added, ' And I think you must be of the same opinion as to yourself.' She explained then that the belief was a rare one now, and held by only a few of the oldest of her old acquaintances in that region, and they seldom talk about it to their children for fear of being laughed at.

Mr. J. Ceredig Davies, the well-known folk-lorist of Llanilar, near Aberystwyth, speaking of the Welsh Re-birth Doctrine, said he remembers, while in Patagonia, having discussed Druidism with a friend there, the late John Jones, originally of Bala, North Wales, and hearing him remark, ' Indeed, I have a half-belief that I have been in this world before.'

Mr. Jones, our witness from Pontrhydfendigaid, offers testimony of the highest value concerning Druidism and the doctrine of re-birth in Central Wales, as follows :— ' Taliessin believed in re-birth, and he was the first to interpret the Druidic laws. He believed that from age to age he had been in many human bodies. He believed that he possessed the same soul as Enoch and Eli, that he had been a judge sitting on the case of Jesus Christ—" I was a judge at the Crucifixion," he is reported as saying—and that he had been a prisoner in bonds at the Court of Cynfelyn, not far from Aberystwyth, for a year and a day. Two hundred years ago, belief in re-birth was common. Many still held it when I was a boy. And even yet here in this region some people are imbued with the ancient faith of the Druids, and firmly believe that the spirit migrates from one body to another. It is said, too, that a pregnant woman is able to determine what kind of a child she will give birth to.' [1]

Mr. Jones's use of the phrase ' migrate from one body to another ' led us to suspect that it might refer to transmigration, i. e. re-birth into animal bodies, which Dr. Tylor in

[1] I take this to mean, somewhat as in the similar case of Dechtire, the mother of Cuchulainn (see p. 369, above), that the kind of soul or character which will be reincarnated in the child is determined by the psychic prenatal conditions which a mother consciously or unconsciously may set up. If this interpretation, as it seems to be, is correct, we have in this Welsh belief a surprising comprehension of scientific laws on the part of the ancient Welsh Druids—from whom the doctrine comes—which equals, and surpasses in its subtlety, the latest discoveries of our own psychological embryology, criminology, and so-called laws of heredity.

Primitive Culture[4] (ii. 6–11, 17, &c.) shows is a distorted or corrupted interpretation of what he calls the reasonable and straightforward doctrine of re-birth into human bodies only. But when we questioned Mr. Jones further about the matter he said :—' The belief I refer to is re-birth into human bodies. I have heard of witches being able to change their own body into the body of an animal or demon, but I never heard of men transmigrating into the bodies of animals. Some people have said that the Druids taught transmigration of this sort, but I do not think they did— though Welsh poets seem to have made use of such a doctrine for the sake of poetry.'

In order to gain evidence concerning the Re-birth Doctrine as concrete as possible from so important a witness as Mr. Jones, we asked him further if he could recall the names of one or two of his old acquaintances who believed in it; and he said :—' One old character named Thomas Williams, a dyer by trade, nearly believed in it, and Shôn Evan Rolant firmly believed in it. Rolant was the owner of Old Abbey Farm on the Cross-Wood Estate, and originally was a well-to-do and respectable farmer, but in consequence of mortgages on the estate he lost his property. After being dispossessed and badly treated, he used to recite the one hundred and ninth Psalm, to bring curses upon those who worked against him in the dispossession process ; and it was thought that he succeeded in bringing curses upon them.'

The Rev. T. M. Morgan, Vicar of Newchurch parish, near Carmarthen, who has already offered valuable evidence concerning the *Tylwyth Teg* (see pp. 149–51), contributes additional material about the Doctrine of Re-birth in South Wales :— ' My father said there used to be expressed in Cardiganshire before his time, a belief in re-birth. This was in accord with Druidism, namely, that all human beings formerly existed on the moon, the world of middle light, and the queen of heaven; that those who there lived a righteous life were thence born on the sun, and thence onward to the highest heaven; and that those whose moon life had been unrighteous were born on this earth of suffering and sin. Through right-living on earth souls are able to return to the moon, and then evolve to the sun and highest heaven ; or, through wrong living on earth, souls are born in the third condition, which is one of utter darkness and of still greater suffering and sin than our world offers. But even from this lowest condition souls can work upwards to the highest glory if they strive successfully against evil. The Goddess of Heaven or Mother of all human beings was known as *Brenhines-y-nef.* I am unable to tell if she is the moon itself or lived in the moon. On the other hand, the sun was considered the father of all human beings. According to the old belief, every new moon brings the souls who were unfit to be born on the sun, to deposit them here on our earth. Sometimes there are more souls seeking embodiment on earth than there are infant bodies to contain them. Hence souls fight among themselves to occupy a body. Occasionally one soul tries to drive out from a body the soul already in possession of it, in order to possess it for itself. In consequence of such struggling of soul against soul, men in this world manifest madness and tear themselves. Whenever such a condition showed itself, the person exhibiting it was called a *Lloerig* or " one who is moon-torn "—*Lloer* meaning moon, and *rhigo* to notch or tear ; and in the English word *lunatic*, meaning " moon-struck ", we have a similar idea.' [1]

Mr. David Williams, J.P., of Carmarthen, who has already told us much about Welsh fairies (see pp. 151–3), offers equally valuable information about the ' Three Circles of Existence ' and the Druidic scheme of soul-evolution, as follows :—' According to the Druids, there are three Circles through which souls must pass. The first is *Cylch y Ceugant*, the second *Cylch Abred*, the third *Cylch y Gwynfyd*. The name of each circle refers to a special kind of spiritual training, and if in reaching the second circle you do not gain its perfection by completing all its provisions [probably in due

---

[1] The reader is referred to the Rev. T. M. Morgan's latest publication, *The History and Antiquities of the Parish of Newchurch, Carmarthenshire* Carmarthen, 1910), pp. 155–6.

order and time], you must begin again in Circle One ; but if you reach the perfection of Circle Two you go on to Circle Three. In Circle One, which is unlocated, the soul has no condition of bodily existence as in Circle Two. The second Circle appears to be a state something like the one we are in now—a mixture of good and evil. The third Circle is a state of perfection and blessedness. In it the soul's environments correspond to all its wishes and desires, and there is contact with God.' At this point I asked if there was loss of individuality in Circle Three, and Mr. Williams replied :—' No, there is not loss of individuality.' Hence, as we suggest, *Cylch y Gwynfyd* is the Druidic parallel to the Nirvana of Indian metaphysics—being like it, a state of perfect and unlimited self-consciousness which man never knows in earth-life. And, finally, Mr. Williams said in relation to re-birth :—' About the years 1780–1820 there lived an old bard in Glamorganshire who was actually a Druid, though he professed to be a Christian as well, and he believed fully in re-birth. His common name was Edward Williams (Iolo Morganwg) ; and he [with Owen Jones and William O. Pughe] edited the famous *Archaiology of Wales*.'

In Cornwall

Mr. Henry Maddern, F.I.A.S., our very important witness from Penzance, testifies as follows concerning a re-birth doctrine in Cornwall :—' Belief in reincarnation was very common among the old Cornish peoples. For example, it was believed when an incantation had been pronounced in the proper way at the Newlyn Tolcarne, that the Troll who inhabited it could embody the person who called him up in any state in which that person had existed during a former age. You had only to name the age or period, and you could live your past life therein over again. My nurse, Betty Grancan, and an old miner named William Edwards, both believed in re-birth, and told me about it. I have heard them relate stories to one another to the effect that a person can go back into the memory of past lives. They said that the sex always remains the same from life to life.

I have never heard of any belief in transmigration of humans into animals, but in human re-birth only.' [1]

In Brittany

In chapter ii, p. 216, M. Z. Le Rouzic, keeper of the Miln Museum at Carnac, says that there is now among his Breton countrymen round Carnac a general and profound belief that spirits incarnate as men and women; and he has told me that this belief exists also in other regions of the Morbihan. And I myself found there in this Carnac country of which M. Le Rouzic speaks, that the doctrine of the reincarnation of ancestors, which, as he agrees, is the same thing as the incarnation of spirits, is quite common, though as a rule only talked about among the Bretons themselves.

M. Le Rouzic restated the belief as he knows it round Carnac, as follows :—' It is incontestable that the belief in the reincarnation of spirits is general in our country; and it is believed that the spirits embodied now are the spirits of the people of former times.'

After Louis Guézel, of the village of St. Columban, a mile from Carnac, had related to me certain legends of the dead, I asked him if he had ever heard that the dead may be born again as men and women here on this earth. Contrary to my expectations, the question caused no surprise whatever ; and I was at once given the impression that the ancient Celtic Doctrine of Re-birth is a thoroughly familiar one to him and to many Bretons about the Carnac district. As we conversed about the doctrine, he said emphatically, ' C'est la vérité' (It is the truth); and in illustration told the following anecdotes :—' A woman in a cemetery one evening saw the spirits of many dead children begging of her life, and reincarnation. A son of my son resembles my grandfather, especially in his mental traits and general character, and the family believe that this son is my grandfather reincarnated.' (Recorded at St. Columban, Brittany, August 1909.)

[1] I found, however, that the original re-birth doctrine has been either misinterpreted or else corrupted—after Dr. Tylor's theory—into transmigration into animal bodies among certain Cornish miners in the St. Just region.

Professor Anatole Le Braz, in a letter-preface to *Carnac, Légendes, Traditions, Coutumes et Contes du Pays* (Nantes, 1909), by M. Z. Le Rouzic, makes this poetical reference to his friend, its author, and thereby admirably echoes the ancient Breton Doctrine of Re-birth :—' You, your eyes, your ears are elsewhere : you are a seer and a hearer of the lower regions ; you perceive the floating images and you discern the hollow sounds of the people of the manes ; you live, literally, among them. What am I saying ? Under the form and appearance of a man of to-day, you are in reality one of them, ascended to the day and reincarnated.' Again, speaking of the Alignements of Menec, Professor Le Braz adds concerning his friend :—' You have been one of the priest-builders who worked at its erection ; you have officiated among its myriads of columns, presided amid the pomp of great funerals in its cyclopean caverns, sprinkled its sepulchral mounds, shaped like tents, with the blood of oxen and of heifers now dear to St. Cornely. And this also you confess to me yourself : these unfathomable epochs remain for you actual and present.'

Origin and Evolution of the Celtic Doctrine of Re-birth

In considering briefly what non-Celtic doctrines could conceivably have shaped the Celtic Doctrine of Re-birth, two chief streams of influence are open to examination. One stream has its source in re-birth doctrines like those set forth by Orphic, Pythagorean, Platonic, and similar orientally-derived philosophies ; while the other arises out of primitive Christianity, wherein, as literary and historical evidence suggests, re-birth may have been an equally important doctrine ; or, at all events, there was a decided tendency, later condemned as heretical, to synthesize the Alexandrian philosophy and the Jewish (which to some extent influenced the Alexandrian) with early Church doctrines. This tendency is clearly shown by Origen, and by Clemens Alexandrinus, another eminent Father.

We have a better check on the second stream than on the

first, because Christianity has a later and more definite
origin than any of the orientally-derived philosophies.
Some of the Druids, chiefly of Scotland and Wales, who are
known to have held the re-birth doctrine before conversion,
and probably after conversion, as was the case with a modern
Druid, an editor of the *Archaiology of Wales* (see p. 391,
above), accepted the New Faith as a purer form of
Druidism and Jesus Christ as the Greatest of Druids. This
ready and full acceptance would most likely not have been
possible had their cardinal re-birth doctrine been thereby
condemned. It would seem, therefore, that a primitive
Christian re-birth doctrine may have been openly held by
certain of the early Celtic missionaries. These latter, during
the centuries when Ireland was the university for all Europe,
had good opportunities for knowing much about the earliest
traditions of Christianity, and they, with their own half-
pagan instincts, would have given approval to such a doctrine without consulting Rome, just as Church Fathers like
Tertullian condemned it on their own personal authority and
Origen believed it. Further, if we hold in mind that the
doctrine of the Incarnation even now inculcates that the Son
pre-existed and united Himself with a human soul in the
act of conception, and that it may originally and by some
Irish saints have been thought of as applying to all mankind
in a more humble and less divine way, we seem to see in the
Mongan re-birth story, which Christian transcribers have
glossed, evidently with such ideas in mind, a proof that on this
doctrinal point Christian and Celtic beliefs coalesced.[1] But

[1] The primitive character of the Incarnation doctrine is clear : Origen,
in refuting a Jewish accusation against Christians, apparently the natural
outgrowth of deep-seated hatred and religious prejudice on the part of the
Jews, that Jesus Christ was born through the adultery of the Virgin with
a certain soldier named Panthera, argues 'that every soul, for certain
mysterious reasons (I speak now according to the opinions of Pythagoras,
and Plato, and Empedocles, whom Celsus frequently names), is introduced into a body, and introduced according to its deserts and former
actions '. And, according to Origen's argument, to assign to Jesus Christ
a birth more disgraceful than any other is absurd, because 'He who sends
souls down into the bodies of men' would not have thus 'degraded Him
who was to dare such mighty acts, and to teach so many men, and to
reform so many from the mass of wickedness in the world '. And Origen

the Christian beliefs did not originate the Celtic, for scholars have shown that the germ of the Mongan re-birth story, as well as that of the Cuchulainn re-birth episode, is pre-Christian, and that the Etain birth-story dates from a time when Irish myth and history were entirely free from Christian influence.[1] The same original pagan character is shown in the re-birth episodes existing in Brythonic literature.[2] And, finally, from the testimony of several ancient authorities, e.g. Julius Caesar, Diodorus Siculus, Pomponius Mela, and Lucan, who wrote, respectively, about 50 B.C., 40 B.C., A.D. 44, and A.D. 60 to 65, that the Celts already held the re-birth doctrine, it is certain that any possible influence from the Christian stream instead of originating the Celtic Doctrine of Re-birth could merely have modified it.

The question remaining, Would the classical or oriental doctrines of re-birth have originated or fundamentally shaped the Celtic re-birth doctrine? is a very difficult one. At present it cannot be answered with certainty either negatively or positively. We may suppose, however, as we did in the case of the parallel Christian re-birth doctrine, a possible contact and amalgamation, brought about in various ways, e.g. through Oriental merchants like the Phoenicians, and travellers who visited Britain in pre-Christian times, but chiefly through the continental Celts, who had direct knowledge of Greek and Roman culture, meeting their insular brethren beyond the Channel and

adds :—' It is probable, therefore, that this soul also which conferred more benefit by its residence in the flesh than that of many men (to avoid prejudice, I do not say "all"), stood in need of a body not only superior to others, but invested with all excellence' (*Origen against Celsus*, Book I, c. xxxii).

It is interesting to compare with Origen's theology the following passage from the *Pistis Sophia*, wherein Jesus in the alleged esoteric discourse to his disciples refers to the pre-existence of their souls :—' I took them from the hands of the twelve saviours of the treasure of light, according to the command of the first mystery. These powers, therefore, I cast into the wombs of your mothers, when I came into the world, and they are those which are in your bodies this day' (*Pistis Sophia*, i. 11, Mead's translation).

[1] Cf. Nutt, *Voy. of Bran*, ii. 27 ff., 45 ff., 54 ff., 98–102.

[2] Cf. ib., p. 105.

Irish Sea. All such ancient contacts push the problem further and further back in time; and our easiest and safest course is to state—as we may of the similar problem of the origin of the Celtic Otherworld belief—that available facts of comparative religion, philosophy, and myth, indicate clearly a prehistoric epoch when there was a common ancestral stock for the Mediterranean and pan-Celtic cultures. This may have had its beginnings in the Danube country, or in North Europe, as many authorities in ethnology now hold, or, as others are beginning to hold, in the lost Atlantis—the most probable home of the dark pre-Celtic peoples of Ireland, Isle of Man, Scotland, Britain, Southern and Western Europe, and North Africa, who with the Aryans are the joint ancestors of the modern Celts. Both branches of this common Celtic ancestral stock held the re-birth doctrine. And at least from their Aryan ancestors it seems to have been inherited by the Celts of history. To attempt a hypothetical proof that this race or that race, Egyptian, Phoenician, Greek, or Celtic, as the case may be, is alone the originator of this or any other particular belief is as useless and as absurd as to attempt proof that the Gael has no racial affinity with the Brython. One of the greatest services now being performed by scientific inquiry into human problems is the demonstration of the unreasonableness of assuming artificial social barriers separating race from race, religion from religion, and institution from institution, and the declaration that the unity and the brotherhood of man is a fact inherent in man's own nature, and not a sentimental ideal. But there is specialization and differentiation everywhere in nature; and while Celtic traditions and beliefs are not fundamentally unlike those found in every age, race, and cultural stage, the treatment of this common stock of prehistoric lore and mystical religion is in some respects unique, and hence Celtic. Beyond this statement we cannot go.

SECTION III

THE CULT OF GODS, SPIRITS, FAIRIES, AND THE DEAD

CHAPTER VIII

THE TESTIMONY OF ARCHAEOLOGY [1]

' As he spoke, he paused before a great mound grown over with trees, and around it silver clear in the moonlight were immense stones piled, the remains of an original circle, and there was a dark, low, narrow entrance leading therein. " This was my palace. In days past many a one plucked here the purple flower of magic and the fruit of the tree of life . . ." And even as he spoke, a light began to glow and to pervade the cave, and to obliterate the stone walls and the antique hieroglyphics engraven thereon, and to melt the earthen floor into itself like a fiery sun suddenly uprisen within the world, and there was everywhere a wandering ecstasy of sound : light and sound were one ; light had a voice, and the music hung glittering in the air . . . " I am Aengus ; men call me the Young. I am the sunlight in the heart, the moonlight in the mind ; I am the light at the end of every dream, the voice for ever calling to come away ; I am desire beyond joy or tears. Come with me, come with me : I will make you immortal ; for my palace opens into the Gardens of the Sun, and there are the fire-fountains which quench the heart's desire in rapture." '—A. E.

Inadequacy of Pygmy Theory—According to the theories concerning divine images and fetishes, gods, daemons, and ancestral spirits haunt megaliths —Megaliths are religious and funereal, as shown chiefly by *Cenn Cruaich*, Stonehenge, Guernsey menhirs, monuments in Brittany, by the circular fairy dance as an ancient initiatory sun-dance, by Breton earthworks, archaeological excavations generally, and by present-day worship at Indian dolmens—New Grange and Celtic Mysteries : evidence of manuscripts; evidence of tradition—The Aengus Cult—New Grange compared with Great Pyramid : both have astronomical arrangement and same internal plan—Why they open to the sunrise—Initiations in both—Great Pyramid as model for Celtic tumuli—Gavrinis and New Grange as spirit-temples.

In this chapter we propose to deal with the popular belief among Celtic peoples that tumuli, dolmens, menhirs, and in fact most megalithic monuments, prehistoric or historic,

[1] In this chapter, largely the result of my own special research and observations in Celtic archaeology, I wish to acknowledge the very valuable suggestions offered to me by Professor J. Loth, both in his lectures and personally.

are either the abodes or else the favourite haunts of various
orders of fairies—of pixies in Cornwall, of *corrigans* in
Brittany, of little spirits like pygmies, of spirits like mortals
in stature, of goblins, of demons, and of ghosts. Interesting
attempts have been made to explain this folk-belief by means
of the Pygmy Theory of Fairies ; and this folk-belief appears
to be almost the chief one upon which the theory depends.[1]
As was pointed out in the Introduction (p. xxiii), possibly
one of the many threads interwoven into the complex fabric
of the Fairy-Faith round an original psychical pattern may
have been bequeathed by a folk-memory of some unknown,
perhaps pygmy, races, who may have inhabited underground
places like those in certain tumuli. But even though the
Pygmy Theory were altogether accepted by us the problem
we are to consider would still be an unsolved one ; for how
explain by the Pygmy Theory why the folk-memory should
always run in psychical channels, and not alone in Celtic
lands, but throughout Europe, and even in Australia,
America, Africa, and India.

Archaeological researches have now made it clear that
many of the great tumuli covering dolmens or subterranean
chambers, like that of Mont St. Michel (at Carnac) for
example, were religious and funereal in their purposes from
the first ; and therefore the Pygmy Theory is far from a
satisfactory or adequate explanation. To us the inquiry is
similar to an investigation into the reasons why ghosts
should haunt a house, whereas the supporters of the Pygmy
Theory forget the ghosts and tell all about the people who
may or who may never have lived in the haunted house, and
who built it. The megaliths, in the plain language of the
folk-belief, are haunted by fairies, pixies, *corrigans*, ghosts,
and various sorts of invisible beings. Like the Psychical
Research Society, we believe there may be, or actually are,
invisible beings like ghosts, and so propose to conduct our
investigations from that point of view.[2]

---

[1] See David MacRitchie, *Fians, Fairies, and Picts ;* also his *Testimony of Tradition.*

[2] Myers, in the *Survival of the Human Personality* (ii. 55–6), shows that 'the

Menhirs, Dolmens, Cromlechs, and Tumuli

To begin with, we shall concern ourselves with menhirs, dolmens, cromlechs, and certain kinds of tumuli—such as are found at Carnac, round which *corrigans* hold their nightly revels, and where ghost-like forms are sometimes seen in the moonlight, or even when there is no moon. M. Paul Sébillot in *Le Folk-lore de France*[1] has very adequately described the numerous folk-traditions and customs connected with all such monuments, and it remains for us to deal especially with the psychical aspects of these traditions and customs.

The learned Canon Mahé in his *Essai sur les antiquités du département du Morbihan* (p. 258), a work of rare merit, published at Vannes in 1825, holds that not only were the majestic Alignements of Carnac used as temples for religious rites, but that the stones themselves of which the Alignements are formed were venerated as the abodes of gods.[2]

---

departed spirit, long after death, seems pre-occupied with the spot where his bones are laid '. Among contemporary uncultured races there exists a theory parallel to this one arrived at through careful scientific research, namely, that ghosts haunt graves and monuments connected with the dead : according to the Australian Arunta the ' double ' hovers near its body until the body is reduced to dust, the spirit or soul of the deceased having separated from this ' double ' or ghost at the time of death or soon afterwards (Spenser and Gillen, *Nat. Tribes of Cent. Aust.*).

[1] See *Les Grottes*, t. i; *Les Menhirs, Les Dolmens, Les Tumulus*, and *Cultes et observances mégalithiques*, t. iv.

[2] On April 17, 1909, at Carnac, in a natural fissure in the body of the finest menhir at the head of the Alignement of Kermario, I found quite by chance, while making a very careful examination of the geological structure of the menhir, a Roman Catholic coin (or medal) of St. Peter. The place in the menhir where this coin was discovered is on the south side about fifteen inches above the surface of the ground.   The menhir is very tall and smoothly rounded, and there is no possible way for the coin to have fallen into the fissure by accident.   Nor is there any probability that the coin was placed there without a serious purpose ; and it is an object such as only an adult would possess. An examination of the link remaining on the coin, which no doubt formerly connected it with a necklace or string of prayer-beads, shows that it has been purposely opened so as to free it at the time it was deposited in the stone. Had the coin been accidentally torn away from a chain or string of prayer-beads the link would have presented a different sort of opening. But it would be altogether unreasonable to suppose that by any sort of chance the coin could have reached the

And quoting Porphyry, Iamblichus, Proclus, Hermes, and others, he shows that the ancients believed that gods and daemons, attracted by sacrifice and worship to stone images and other inanimate objects, overshadowed them or even took up their abode in them. This position of Canon Mahé is confirmed by a comparative study of Celtic and non-Celtic traditions respecting the theory of what has been erroneously called 'idol-worship'. All evidence goes to show that idols so called, are simply images used as media for the manifestation of ghosts, spirits, and gods: the ancients, like contemporary primitive races, do not seem ever to have actually worshipped such images, but simply to have supplicated by prayer and sacrifice the indwelling deity.[1] The ancient Egyptians, for example, conceived the *Ka* or personality as a thing separable from the person or body, and hence 'the statue of a human being represented and embodied a human *Ka*'. Likewise a statue of a god was the dwelling-place of a divine *Ka*, attracted to it by certain mystical formulae at the time of dedication.[2] Though there might be many statues of the same god no two were alike; each was animated by an independent 'double' which the rites of consecration had elicited from the god. These statues, being thus animated by a 'double', manifested their will—as Greek and Roman statues are reported to have done—either by speaking, or by rhythmic movements. The divine virtue residing in the images of the gods was thought to be a sort of fluid, analogous to what we call the magnetic fluid, the aura, &c. It could be transmitted

place where I found it. I showed the coin to M. Z. Le Rouzic, of the Carnac Museum, and he considers it, as I do, as evidence or proof of a cult rendered to stones here in Brittany. The coin must have been secretly placed in the menhir by some pious peasant as a direct *ex voto* for some favour received or demanded. The coin is somewhat discoloured, and has probably been some years in the stone, though it cannot be very old. And the offering of a coin to the spirit residing in a menhir is parallel to throwing coins, pins, or other objects into sacred fountains, which, as we know, is an undisputed practice.

[1] Cf. A. C. Kruijt, *Het Animisme in den Indischen Archipel*; quoted in Crawley's *Idea of the Soul*, p. 133.

[2] Cf. Weidemann, *Ancient Egyptian Doct. Immortality*, p. 21.

by the imposition of hands and by magic passes, on the nape of the neck or along the dorsal spine of a patient ; [1] and no doubt extraordinary curative properties were attributed to it.

Dr. Tylor has brought together examples from all parts of the globe of so-called fetishism, which is veneration paid to natural living objects such as trees, fish, animals, as well as to inanimate objects of almost every conceivable description, including stones, because of the spirit believed to be inherent or resident in the particular object ; and he shows that idols originally were fetishes, which in time came to be shaped according to the form of the spirit or god supposed to possess them.[2] Mr. R. R. Marett, the originator of the pre-animistic theory, believes that originally fetishes were regarded as gods themselves, and that gradually they came to be regarded as the dwellings of gods.[3] Certain well-defined Celtic traditions entirely fit in with this theory :—e. g. Canon Mahé writes, ' In accordance with this strange theory they (the Celts) could believe that rocks, set in motion by spirits which animated them, sometimes went to drink at rivers, as is said of the Peulvan at Noyal-Pontivy ' (Morbihan) ;[4] and I have found a parallel belief at Rollright, Oxfordshire, England, where it is said of the King Stone, an ancient menhir, and, according to some folk-traditions, a human being transformed, that it goes down the hill on Christmas Eve to drink at the river. In the famous menhir or pillar-stone on Tara to this day, we have another curious example like the moving statues in Egypt and the Celtic stones which move ; for in the *Book of Lismore* the wonderful properties of the *Lia Fáil*, the ' Stone of Destiny ', are enumerated, and it is said that ever when Ireland's monarch stepped upon it the stone would cry out under him, but that if any other person stepped upon it, there was only silence.[5]

---

[1] Cf. Mahé, *Essai*.   [2] Tylor, *Prim. Cult.*, ii. 143 ff., 169, 172.
[3] Marett, *The Threshold of Religion*, c. i.   [4] Mahé, *Essai*, p. 230.
[5] A famous controversy exists as to whether the Coronation Stone now in Westminster Abbey is the *Lia Fáil*, or whether the pillar-stone still at Tara is the *Lia Fáil*. See article by E. S. Hartland in *Folk-Lore*, xiv. 28–60.

In the *Tripartite Life of St. Patrick* it is said that Ireland's chief idol was at Mag Slecht, and by name ' Cenn Cruaich, covered with gold and silver, and twelve other idols [1] [were] about it, covered with brass '. When Patrick tried to place his crosier on the top of Cenn Cruaich, the idol ' bowed west-ward to turn on its right side, for its face was from the South, to wit, Tara. . . . And the earth swallowed the twelve other images as far as their heads, and they are thus in sign of the miracle, and he cursed the demon, and banished him to hell '.[2] Sir John Rhŷs points out that *Cenn Cruaich* means ' Head or Chief of the Mound ', and that the story of its inclined position suggests to us an ancient and gradually falling menhir planted on the summit of a tumulus or hill surrounded by twelve lesser pillar stones, all thirteen—itself a sacred number—regarded as the abodes of gods or else as gods themselves ; and these gods are referred to as the demon exorcized from the place by Patrick. The central menhir or Cenn Cruaich probably represents the Solar God, and the twelve menhirs surrounding this probably represent the twelve months of the year.[3] In the *Colloquy* it is said that Patrick went his way ' to sow faith and piety, to banish devils and wizards out of Ireland ; to raise up saints and righteous, to erect crosses, station-stones, and altars ; also to overthrow idols and goblin images, and the whole art of sorcery '.[4] Welsh tradition says that St. David split the capstone of the Maen Ketti Cromlech (dolmen) [5] in Gower,

---

[1] These ' idols ' probably were not true images, but simply unshaped stone pillars planted on end in the earth ; and ought, therefore, more properly to be designated fetishes.

[2] Stokes, in *Rev. Celt.*, i. 260 ; Rhŷs, *Hib. Lect.*, pp. 200–1.

[3] Very much first-class evidence suggests that the menhir was regarded by the primitive Celts both as an abode of a god or as a seat of divine power, and as a phallic symbol (cf. Jubainville, *Le culte des menhirs dans le monde celtique*, in *Rev. Celt.*, xxvii. 313). As a phallic symbol, the menhir must have been inseparably related to a Celtic sun-cult ; because among all ancient peoples where phallic worship has prevailed, the sun has been venerated as the supreme masculine force in external nature from which all life proceeds, while the phallus has been venerated as the corresponding force in human nature.   [4] *Silva Gadelica*, ii. 137.

[5] Professor J. Loth says :—' *Étymologiquement, le mot est composé de* CROM, *courbe, arque, formant creux, convexe, et de* LLECH, *pierre plate* ' (*Rev. Celt.*,

in order to prove to the people that there was nothing divine in it.[1]

According to Geoffrey of Monmouth, Merlin constructed Stonehenge by magically transporting from Ireland the ' Choir of the Giants ', apparently an ancient Irish circle of stones.[2] The rational explanation of this myth seems to be that the stones of Stonehenge, not belonging to the native rocks of South England, as geologists well know, were probably transported from some distant part of Britain and set up on Salisbury Plain, because of some magical properties supposed to have been possessed by them ; and most likely ' the stones were regarded as divine or as seats of divine power '.[3] And further (thereby admitting the sacred purpose of the group), Sir John Rhŷs sees no objection to identifying Stonehenge with the famous temple of Apollo in the island of the Hyperboreans, referred to in the journal of Pytheas' travels.[4] According to Sir John Rhŷs's interpretation of this journal, ' the kings of the city containing the temple and the overseers of the latter were the Boreads, who took up the government in succession, according to their tribes. The citizens gave themselves up to music, harping and chanting in honour of the Sun-god, who was every nineteenth year wont himself to appear about the time of the vernal equinox, and to go on harping and dancing in the sky until the rising of the Pleiades.' [4]

Two menhirs, roughly hewn to simulate the human form, are yet to be found in Guernsey, Channel Islands, and formerly there was a similar menhir in the Breton village of Baud, Morbihan. One of the Guernsey figures was dug up in 1878 under the chancel of the Câtel Church, and then placed in the churchyard, so that in this instance it seems

xv. 223, *Dolmen, Leach-Derch, Peulvan, Menhir, Cromlech*). In Cornwall, Wales, and Ireland, instead of the peculiarly Breton word *dolmen* (composed of *dol* [for *tol=tavl*], meaning *table*, and of *men* [Middle Breton *maen*], meaning *stone*) the word *cromlech* is used. *Cromlech* is the Welsh equivalent for the Breton *dolmen*, but Breton archaeologists use *cromlech* to describe a circle formed by menhirs.

[1] Rhŷs, *Hib. Lect.*, pp. 193–4.
[2] Ib., p. 192 ; from Sans-Marte's edition, pp. 108–9, 361.   [3] Ib., p. 193.
[4] Ib., pp. 194–5 ; cf. *Bibliotheca* of Diodorus Siculus, ii. c. 47.

highly probable that the Christian Church was built on the site of a sacred pagan shrine where a cult of stones once existed. The second stone figure (a female), now standing as a gate-post in the churchyard of St. Martin's parish, seems also to mark a spot where a pre-Christian sanctuary was christianized. The country-people of the district, up to the middle of the last century, considered it lucky to make floral and even food offerings to this stone ; but in 1860 the churchwarden to destroy its sanctity had it broken in two, though now it has been restored.[1] A like stone image was the famous ' Vénus de Quinipilly ', near Baud, Morbihan. At its base was a stone trough, wherein until late into the seventeenth century the sick were cured by contact with the image, and young men and maidens were wont to bathe to secure love and long life.[1]

Canon Mahé recorded in 1825 that the folk-belief located ghosts and spirits of the dead round megalithic monuments, more especially those known to have been used for tombs, because the Celts thought them haunted by ancestral spirits ;[2] and what was true in 1825 is true now, for there is still in Brittany the association of ancestral spirits, *corrigans*, and other spirit-like tribes with tumuli, dolmens, menhirs, and cromlechs, and, as we have shown in chapter ii, a very living faith in the *Légende de la Mort*. In describing some curious dolmens and cromlechs (stone circles) on the summit of a mountain called the *Clech* or *Mané er kloch*, ' Mountain of the bell,' at Mendon, Arrondissement de Lorient, Morbihan, the same author gives it as his opinion, based on folk-traditions, that the cromlechs, like others in Brittany, were places in which the ancient Bretons practised necromancy and invoked the spirits of their ancestors, to whom they attributed great power. He then records a very valuable and interesting tradition concerning these monuments, which seems to indicate clearly a close relationship between the *Poulpiquets* (another name for *corrigans*), thought of as spirits by the peasants, and the magical rites

---

[1] Edith F. Carey, *Channel Island Folklore* (Guernsey, 1909).
[2] Mahé, *Essai*, p. 198.

conducted in the circles to invoke spirits or daemons :—' The people call the stones which are found there the rocks of the *Hoséguéannets* or *Guerrionets* (who are the same as the *Poulpiquets*) ; and they declare that at fixed seasons they are in the habit of coming there to celebrate their mysteries, which would prove that the race of these dwarfs is not yet extinct, as I believed.' [1]

When we hear how *corrigans* dance the national Breton *ronde* or *ridée*, at or in such cromlechs (themselves, like the dance, circular in form), which with other ancient stone monuments and earthworks are still believed to be the favourite haunts of these and kindred spirit-tribes, we seem to see, in the light of what Canon Mahé records, a psychical folk-memory about a goblin race who are now thought of as frequenting the very places where anciently such spirits are said to have been invoked by pagan priests for the purposes of divination. Further, it appears that at these sacred centres, as the quoted tradition indicates, in pre-historic times Brythonic initiations took place, like those still flourishing among a few surviving American Indian tribes (who also dance the circular initiation dance), and among other primitive peoples, as we shall more adequately show in the chapter on St. Patrick's Purgatory. The Breton dance is, therefore, most likely the memorial of an ancient initiation dance, religious in character, and, probably, in honour of the sun, being circular in the same way that cromlechs dedicated to a sun-cult are circular. Stonehenge, the most highly developed type of the cromlech, was un-doubtedly a sun-temple ; and the dance anciently held in it, as described by Pytheas, in honour of the god Apollo, was no doubt circular like the Breton national dance, and, presumably, initiatory.[2] Through a natural anthropo-

---

[1] Mahé, *Essai*, pp. 287–9.

[2] The place for holding a *gorsedd* for modern Welsh initiations, under the authority of which the Eisteddfod is conducted, must also be within a circle of stones, ' face to face with the sun and the eye of light, as there is no power to hold a *gorsedd* under cover or at night, but only where and as long as the sun is visible in the heavens' (Rhŷs, *Hib. Lect.*, pp. 208–9 ; from *Iolo* MSS., p. 50).

morphic process, this circular initiation dance has come to
be attributed to *corrigans* in Brittany, to pixies in Cornwall
and in England, and to fairies in these and other Celtic
countries. The idea of fairy tribes in such a special relation
may result from a folk-memory of the actual initiators
who, as masked men, represented spirits ; and, if this be
a plausible view, then fairies may be compared to the
initiators of contemporary initiation ceremonies among
primitive peoples and, following Dr. Gilbert Murray's theory,
to the Greek satyrs also.[1]

A circular dance like the Breton one still survives among
the peasantry in the Channel Islands, at least in Guernsey,
Alderney, and Sark, being celebrated at weddings, but the
revolution is now around a person instead of a stone, and
to this person obeisance is paid. This tends to confirm our
opinion that the dance is the survival of an ancient sun-
dance, the central figure being typical of the sun deity
himself, or Apollo ; and if we design this dance thus ⊙,
we have the astronomical emblem still used in all our calen-
dars to represent the sun, one which in itself preserves
a vast mass of forgotten lore. Formerly in Guernsey, the
sites of principal dolmens (or cromlechs) and pillar-stones
were visited in sacred procession, and round certain of them
the whole body of pilgrims ' solemnly revolved three times
from east to west '—as the sun moves.[2]

Again, according to Canon Mahé,[3] the bases and lower
parts of the sides of four singular barrows at Coët-bihan
blend in such a way as to form an enclosed court, and one
of the barrows has been pierced as though for a passage-
way into this court. And he holds that it is more than
probable that these ancient earthworks when first they were
raised, and others like them in various Celtic lands, witnessed
many mystic and religious rites and sacred tribal assemblies. The supposition that the Coët-bihan earthworks

---

[1] Recently before the Oxford Anthropological Society, Dr. Murray argued
that the satyrs of Greek drama may originally have been masked initiators
in Greek initiations. (Cf. *The Oxford Magazine*, February 3, 1910, p. 173.)
[2] Edith F. Carey, op. cit.   [3] Mahé, *Essai*, pp. 126–9.

were originally dedicated to pagan religious usages is very
much strengthened by the fact that in very early times a
Christian chapel was erected near them.[1] Mont St.
Michel at Carnac is another example of a pagan tumulus dedicated
to a Christian saint ; and, as Sir John Rhŷs says, the
Archangel Michael appears in more places than one in Celtic
lands as the supplanter of the dark powers.[2] Not only
were tumuli thus transferred by re-dedication from pagan
gods to Christian saints, but dolmens and menhirs as well.
Thus, for example, at Plouharnel-Carnac (Morbihan) there
is a menhir surmounted by a Christian cross, just as at
Dol (Ille-et-Vilaine) a wooden crucifix surmounts the great
menhir, and at Carnac there is a dolmen likewise christianized by a stone cross-mounted on the table-stone. Again,
M. J. Déchelette in his *Manuel d'Archéologie Préhistorique,
Celtique et Gallo-Romaine* (p. 380) describes a dolmen at
Plouaret (Côtes-du-Nord) converted into a chapel dedicated
to the Seven Saints, and another dolmen at Saint-Germain-
de-Confolens (Charente) likewise transformed into a place of
worship. Miss Edith F. Carey thus explains the dolmens
in the Channel Islands :—' All our old traditions prove our
dolmens to have been the general rendezvous of our insular
sorcerers. In sixteenth and seventeenth century manuscripts
I have found these dolmens described as " altars of the gods
of the sea ". . . . One of our ancient dolmens retains its
ancient name of De Hus, and a fifteenth-century " Perchage "
of Fief de Léree tells us that a now destroyed dolmen on
our western coast was dedicated to the same god, for Heus
or Hesus was the War-God of ancient Gaul.'[3] The same
writer describes excavations made at De Hus by Mr. Lukis,
and that he found in a side chamber there two kneeling
skeletons, one facing the north, the other the south. He
considered them to have been of young persons probably
interred alive as a funeral or propitiatory sacrifice to some
tribal chief, or else to a presiding deity of the dolmen. Beside a tomb of the early bronze age at the bottom of a large

---

[1] Mahé, *Essai*, pp. 126–9.   [2] Rhŷs, *Arth. Leg.*, p. 339.
[3] Edith F. Carey, op. cit.

tumulus near Mammarlöf, in Skåne, Dr. Oscar Montelius, the famous archaeologist of Sweden, discovered a circular stone altar on which reposed charcoal and the remains of a burnt animal offering, which undoubtedly was made to the dead.[1] Schliemann made a parallel discovery in an ancient tomb at Mycenae, Greece.[2] Curiously, in India to-day the Dravidian tribes, a pygmy-like aboriginal race, worship at the ancient dolmens in their forests and mountains, whether as at tombs and hence to ancestral spirits or to gods is not always clear ; but the latter form of worship is probably more common, since Mr. Walhouse once observed one of their medicine-men performing a propitiatory service to the agricultural or earth deities. The medicine-man passed the night in solitude sitting ' on the capstone of a dolmen with heels and hams drawn together and chin on knee '—evidently thus to await the advent of the Sun-god.[3]

All the above illustrations, mostly Celtic ones, tend to prove that menhirs, certain tumuli and earthworks, cromlechs, and dolmens were originally connected with religious usages, chiefly with a cult of gods and fairy-like beings, and, though less commonly, with the dead. We pass now to a special consideration of chambered tumuli, to show that the same apparently holds true of them.

[1] Montelius' *Les Temps préhistoriques en Suède*, par S. Reinach, p. 126. (Paris, 1895).

[2] H. Schliemann, *Mycenae* (London, 1878), p. 213.

[3] Walhouse, in *Journ. Anthrop. Inst.*, vii. 21. These Dravidians are slightly taller than the pure Negritos, their probable ancestors ; and Indian tradition considers them to be the builders of the Indian dolmens, just as Celtic tradition considers fairies and *corrigans* (often described as dark or even black-skinned dwarfs) to be the builders of dolmens and megaliths among the Celts. Apparently, in such folk-traditions, which correctly or incorrectly regard fairies, *corrigans*, or Dravidians as the builders of ancient stone monuments, there has been preserved a folk-memory of early races of men who may have been Negritos (pygmy blacks). These races, through a natural anthropomorphic process, came to be identified with the spirits of the dead and with other spiritual beings to whom the monuments were dedicated and at which they were worshipped. Here, again, the Pygmy Theory is seen at its true relative value : it is subordinate to the fundamental animism of the Fairy-Faith.

New Grange and Celtic Mysteries

Though, as Professor J. Loth and other eminent archaeologists hold, all tumuli containing chambers, and all *allées couvertes* of dolmens, should be considered as designedly funereal
in their purposes, nevertheless certain of the greater ones, like
New Grange and Gavrinis may also properly be considered
as places for rendering worship or even sacrifice to the dead,
and, perhaps, as places for religious pilgrimages and sacred
rites. This, too, seems to be the opinion of M. J. Déchelette in his work on Celtic and Gallo-Roman archaeology,
as he traces from the earliest prehistoric times in Europe
the evolution of the cult of the dead according to the evidence
furnished by the ancient megalithic monuments.[1]

To begin with, let us take as a type for our study the most
famous of all so-called Celtic tumuli, that of New Grange, on
the River Boyne in Ireland.[2]   In Irish literature New Grange
is constantly associated with the Tuatha De Danann as one
of their palaces, as our fourth chapter points out. Throughout
our second section generally, the testimony indicates that the
essential nature of these fairy-folk is subjective or spiritual.
These two facts at the outset are very important and fundamental, because we expect to show even more clearly than
we have just done in the case of menhirs, dolmens, cromlechs,
and smaller tumuli, that the folk-belief under consideration
is at bottom a psychical one, which has grown up out of
a folk-memory of the time when, as has just been said, Celtic
or pre-Celtic tumuli were used for interments, and probably
certain ones among them as places for the celebration of
pagan mysteries.

Mr. George Coffey, the eminent archaeologist in charge of
the archaeological collections of the Royal Irish Academy,
quotes from ancient Irish records in the *Leabhar na h-Uidhre*
and other manuscripts to show that the early traditions

---

[1] J. Déchelette, *Manuel d'Archéologie préhistorique* (Paris, 1908), i. 468,
302, 308, 311, 576, 610, &c.
[2] This famous chambered tumulus ' measures nearly 700 feet in circum-
ference, or about 225 feet in diameter, and between 40 and 50 feet in height '
(G. Coffey, in *Rl. Ir. Acad. Trans.* [Dublin, 1892], xxx. 68).

refer to the Boyne country as the burial-place of the kings of Tara, and that sometimes they seem to associate *Brugh-na-Boyne* with the tumuli on the Boyne,[1] but, no exact identification being possible, it cannot be said with certainty whether any one of the three great Boyne tumuli is meant. Even though it could be shown conclusively that some mighty hero or king had actually been entombed in New Grange, as is likely, in the earth behind the chamber, under the chamber's floor, or even within the chamber, still, as we have already pointed out, most of the great Irish heroes and kings were in popular belief literally gods incarnate, and, therefore (as commonly among all ancient peoples, civilized and non-civilized, who held the same doctrine), the tomb of such a divine personage came to be regarded as the actual dwelling of the once incarnate god, even though his bones were long turned to dust.   The *Book of Ballymote* strengthens this suggestion : in one of its ancient Irish poems, by MacNia, son of Oenna, preceded by this mystical dedication, ' Ye Poets of Bregia, of truth, not false,' the wonders of the Palace of the Boyne, the Hall of the great god Daghda, supreme king and oracle of the Tuatha de Danann, are thus celebrated :—

> Behold the *Sidh* before your eyes,
> It is manifest to you that it is a king's mansion,
> Which was built by the firm Daghda ;
> It was a wonder, a court, an admirable hill.[2]

It seems clear enough, from the old Irish manuscripts referred to by Mr. Coffey,[3] that the Boyne country near Tara was the sacred and religious centre of ancient Ireland, and was used by the Irish in very much the same way as Memphis

---

[1] G. Coffey, in *Rl. Ir. Acad. Trans.*, xxx. 73–92.

[2] Fol. 190 b ; trans. O'Curry, *Lectures*, p. 505.

[3] Mr. Coffey quotes from the *Senchus-na-Relec*, in *L.U.*, this significant passage :—' The nobles of the Tuatha De Danann were used to bury at Brugh (i. e. the Dagda with his three sons ; also Lugaidh, and Oe, and Ollam, and Ogma, and Etan the Poetess, and Corpre, the son of Etan) ' (G. Coffey, op. cit., xxx. 77).   The manuscript, however, being late and directly under Christian influence, echoes but imperfectly very ancient Celtic tradition : the immortal god-race are therein rationalized by the transcribers, and made subject to death.

and other places on the sacred Nile were used by the ancient Egyptians, both as a royal cemetery and as a place for the celebration of pagan mysteries. It is known that most of the Mysteries of Antiquity were psychic in their nature, having to do with the neophyte's entrance into Hades or the invisible world while out of the physical body, or else with direct communication with gods, spirits, and shades of the dead, while in the physical body ; and such mysteries were performed in darkened chambers from which all light was excluded. These chambers were often carved out of solid rock, as can be seen in the Rock Temples of India ; and when mountain caves or natural caverns were not available, artificial ones were used (see chapter x).

The places, like Tara and Memphis, where the great men and kings of the nations of antiquity were entombed, being the most sacred, were very often, on that account, also the places dedicated to the most magnificent temples and to the Mysteries, or among less advanced nations to the worship of the dead. On every side of sacred Stonehenge, Salisbury Plain is dotted with the burial mounds of unknown heroes and chieftains of ancient Britain ; while in modern times, even though the Mysteries are long forgotten, Westminster Abbey, at the centre of the planet's capital, has, in turn, become the hallowed Hall of the Mighty Dead for the vast British Empire. In view of all these facts, after a careful examination of the famous New Grange tumulus itself, and a study of the references to it in old Irish literature, we are firmly of the opinion that one cannot be far wrong in describing it as a spirit-temple in which were celebrated ancient Celtic or pre-Celtic Mysteries at the time when neophytes, including those of royal blood, were initiated ; and as such it is directly related to a cult of the Tuatha De Danann or Fairy-Folk, of spirits, and of the dead. Nor are we alone in this opinion. Mr. Coffey himself, we believe, is inclined to favour it ; and Mr. W. C. Borlase, author of *The Dolmens of Ireland*, who is quite committed to it, says that it is not necessary, as some do, to consider New Grange as an ancient abode of mortal men, for ' the spirits of the dead, the fairies,

the *Sidhe*, might have had their *brugh*, or palace, as well '.[1]
And he points out that in the old Irish manuscripts we
have proof that it was supposed to be thus· used. This·
proof is found in the *Agallamh na Senórach* or ' Colloquy
with the Ancients' by St. Patrick, from the *Book of
Lismore*, a fifteenth-century manuscript copied from older
manuscripts and now translated by Standish H. O'Grady :—
The three sons of the King of Ireland, by name Ruidhe,
Fiacha, and Eochaid, leaving their nurse's and guardian's
house, went to *fert na ndruadh*, i. e. ' grave of the wizards ',
north-west of Tara, to ask· of their father a country,
a domain ; but he refused their request, and then they
formed a project to gain lands and riches by fasting on the
tuatha dé Danann at the *brugh* upon the Boyne : ' " Lands
therefore I will not bestow on you, but win lands for yourself." Thereupon they with the ready rising of one man
rose and took their way to the green of the *brugh* upon the
Boyne where, none other being in their company, they sat
them down. Ruidhe said : " What is your plan to-night ? "
His brothers rejoined : " Our project is to fast on the *tuatha
dé Danann*, aiming thus to win from them good fortune in
the shape of a country, of a domain, of lands, and to have
vast riches." Nor had they been long there when they
marked a cheery-looking young man of a pacific demeanour
that came towards them. He salutes the king of Ireland's
sons ; they answer him after the same manner. " Young
man, whence art thou ? whence comest thou ? " " Out of
yonder *brugh* chequered with the many lights hard by you
here." " What name wearest thou ? " " I am the Daghda's
son Bodhb Derg ; and to the *tuatha dé Danann* it was revealed
that ye would come to fast here to-night, for lands and for
great fortune." ' Then with Bodhb Derg, the three sons of
Ireland's king entered into the *brugh*, and the *tuatha dé
Danann* went into council, and Midhir Yellow-mane son of
the Daghda who presided said : ' Those yonder accommodate
now with three wives, since from wives it is that either fortune
or misfortune is derived.' And from their marriages with

---

[1] W. C. Borlase, *Dolmens of Ireland* (London, 1897), ii. 346 n.

the three daughters of Midhir they derived all their wishes—territories and wealth in the greatest abundance. ' For three days with their nights they abode in the *sídh*.' ' Angus told them to carry away out of *fidh omna*, i. e. "Oakwood," three apple-trees : one in full bloom, another shedding the blossom, and another covered with ripe fruit. Then they repaired to the *dún*, where they abode for three times fifty years, and until those kings disappeared ; for in virtue of marriage alliance they returned again to the *tuatha dé Danann*, and from that time forth have remained there.' [1]

Mr. Borlase, commenting on this passage, suggests its importance in proving to us that during the Middle Ages there existed a tradition, thus committed to writing from older manuscripts or from oral sources, regarding ' the nature of the rites performed in pagan times at those places, which were held sacred to the heathen mysteries '.[2] The passage evidently describes a cult of royal or famous ancestral spirits identified with the god-race of Tuatha De Danann, who, as we know, being reborn as mortals, ruled Ireland. These ancestral spirits were to be approached by a pilgrimage made to their abode, the spirit-haunted tumulus, and a residence in it of three days and three nights during which period there was to be an unbroken fast. Sacrifices were doubtless offered to the gods, or spirit-ancestors ; and while they were ' fasted upon ', they were expected to appear and grant the pilgrim's prayer and to speak with him. All this indicates that the existence of invisible beings was taken for granted, probably through the knowledge gained by initiation.

The *Echtra Nerai* or the 'Adventures of Nera' (see this study, p. 287), contains a description like the one above, of how a mortal named Nera went into the *Sidhe*-palace at Cruachan ; and it is said that he went not only into the cave (*uamh*) but into the *síd* of the cave. The term *uamh* or cave, according to Mr. Borlase, indicates the whole of the interior vaulted chamber, while the *síd* of that vaulted chamber or *uamh* is intended to refer to ' the *sanctum sanctorum*, or

---

[1] As translated in the *Silva Gadelica*, ii. 109–11.
[2] Borlase, op. cit., ii. 346–7 n.

penetralia of the spirit-temple, upon entering into which the
mortal came face to face with the royal occupants, and there
doubtless he lay fasting, or offering his sacrifices, at the
periods prescribed '.[1]   The word *brugh* refers simply to the
appearance of a tumulus, or souterrain beneath a fort or
rath, and   means,   therefore,   mansion   or   dwelling-place.[2]
And Mr. Borlase adds :—' I feel but little doubt that in the
inner chamber at New Grange, with its three recesses and
its basin, we have this *síd of the cave*, and the place where
the pilgrims fasted—a situation and a practice precisely
similar to those which, under Christian auspices, were continued at such places as the Leaba Mologa in Cork, the
original Patrick's Purgatory in Lough Derg, and elsewhere.
The practice of lying in stone troughs was a feature of the
Christian pilgrimages in Ireland.   Sometimes such troughs
had served the previous purpose of stone coffins.   It is just
possible that the shallow basins in the cells at Lough Crew,
New Grange, and Dowth may, like the stone beds or troughs
of the saints,[3] have been occupied by the pilgrims engaged
in their devotions.   If so, however, they must have sat in
them in Eastern fashion.' [2]

Again, in the popular tale called *The Pursuit of Diarmuid
and Grainnè*,[4] Aengus, the son of the Dagda, one of the
Tuatha De Danann, is called Aengus-an-Bhrogha, and connected with the *Brugh-na-Boinne*.   In the tale Finn says,
' Let us leave this tulach, for fear that Aengus-an-Bhrogha
and the Tuatha-De-Danann might catch us ; and though we
have no part in the slaying of Diarmuid, he would none the
more readily believe us.'   Aengus is evidently an invisible
being with great power over mortals.   This is clear in what
follows : he transports Diarmuid's body to the *Brugh-na-
Boinne*, saying, ' Since I cannot restore him to life, I will
send a soul into him, so that he may talk to me each day.'
Thus, as the presiding deity of the *brugh*, Aengus the Tuatha

---

[1] Borlase, op. cit., ii. 346–7 n.   [2] Ib., ii. 347 n.
[3] A good example of a saint's stone bed can be seen now at Glendalough,
the stone bed of St. Kevin, high above a rocky shore of the lake.
[4] Coffey, op. cit., xxx. 73–4, from R. I. A. MS., by Michael O'Longan,
dated 1810, p. 10, and translated by Douglas Hyde.

De Danann could reanimate dead bodies ' and cause them to speak to devotees, we may suppose oracularly.'[1] In the *Bruighion Chaorthainn* or ' Fort of the Rowan Tree ', a Fenian tale, a poet put Finn under taboo to understand these verses :—

> I saw a house in the country
> Out of which no hostages are given to a king,
> Fire burns it not, harrying spoils it not.

And Finn made reply :—' I understand that verse, for that is the Brugh of the Boyne that you have seen (perhaps, as we suggest, during an initiation), namely, the house of Aengus Og of the Brugh, and it cannot be burned or harried as long as Aengus (a god) shall live.' As Mr. Borlase observes, to say that ' no hostages are given to a king ' out of· the *Brugh* is probably another way of saying that the dead pay no taxes, or that being a holy place, the *Brugh* was exempt.[2] This last evidence is from oral tradition, and rather late in being placed on record ; but it is not on that account less trustworthy, and may be much more so than the older manuscripts. Until quite modern times the folk-lore of the Boyne country still echoed similar traditions about unknown mystic rites, following what O'Donovan has recorded; for he has said that Aenghus-an-Bhrogha was considered the presiding fairy of the Boyne till quite within recent times; and that his name was still familiar to the old inhabitants of Meath who were then fast forgetting their traditions with the Irish language.[3] And this tradition brings us to consider what was apparently an Aengus Cult among the ancient Celtic peoples.

THE AENGUS CULT

Euhemeristic tradition came to represent the Great God Dagda and his sons as buried in a tumulus, probably New Grange, and then called it, as I found it called to-day, a fairy mound, a name given also to Gavrinis, its Breton parallel. The older and clearer tradition relates how Aengus

---

[1] Coffey, op. cit., xxv. 73–4, from R. I. A. MS. by Michael O'Longan, dated 1810, p. 10, and trans. by Douglas Hyde.
[2] Borlase, op. cit., ii. 347 n.   [3] O'Donovan, *Four Masters*, i. 22 n.

gained possession of the *Brugh* of the Boyne, and says nothing about it as a cemetery, but rather describes it as ' an admirable place, more accurately speaking, as an admirable land, a term which betrays the usual identification of the fairy mound with the nether world to which it formed the entrance '.[1] The myth placing Dagda at the head of the departed makes him ' a Goidelic Cronus ruling over an Elysium with which a sepulchral mound was associated '.[1] The displacement of Dagda by his son makes ' Mac Oc (Aengus), who should have been the youthful Zeus of the Goidelic world, rejoicing in the translucent expanse of the heavens as his crystal bower ', a king of the dead.[1]

In Dun Aengus, the strange cyclopean circular structure, and hence most likely sun-temple, on Aranmore, we have another example of the localization of the Aengus myth. This fact leads us to believe, after due archaeological examination, that amid the stronghold of Dun Aengus, with its tiers of amphitheatre-like seats and the native rock at its centre, apparently squared to form a platform or stage, were anciently celebrated pagan mysteries comparable to those of the Greeks and less cultured peoples, and initiations into an Aengus Cult such as seems to have once flourished at New Grange. At Dun Aengus, however, the mystic assemblies and rites, conducted in such a sun-temple, so secure and so strongly fortified against intrusion, no doubt represented a somewhat different mystical school, and probably one very much older than at New Grange. In the same manner, each of the other circular but less important cyclopean structures on Aranmore and elsewhere in west Ireland may have been structures for closely related sun-cults. To our mind, and we have carefully and at leisure examined most of these cyclopean structures on Aranmore, it seems altogether fanciful to consider them as having been *originally* and *primarily* intended as places of refuge—*dúns* or forts. Yet, because the ancient Celts never separated civil and religious functions, such probable sun-temples could have been as frequently used for non-religious tribal assemblies

---

[1] Rhŷs, *Hib. Lect.*, pp. 148–50.

as for initiation ceremonies ; and nothing makes it impossible for them to have been in times of need also places for refuge against enemies. We are led to this view with respect to Dun Aengus in particular, because the Aengus of Aranmore is known as Aengus, son of Umór, and is associated with the mystic people called the Fir Bolg ; and, yet, as Sir John Rhŷs thinks, this Aengus, son of Umór, and Aengus, son of Dagda, are two aspects of a single god, a Celtic Zeus.[1] O'Curry's statements about Dun Aengus seem to confirm all this ; and there seems to have been a tale, now lost, about the ' Destruction of *Dún Oengusa* ' (in modern Irish *Dún Aonghuis*), the Fortress of Aengus.[1]

This sun-cult, represented in Ireland by the Aengus Cult, can be traced further : Sir John Rhŷs regards Stonehenge— a sun-temple also circular like the Irish *dúns* and Breton cromlechs—as a temple to the Celtic Zeus, in Irish mythology typified by Aengus, and in Welsh by Merlin :—' What sort of a temple could have been more appropriate for the primary god of light and of the luminous heavens than a spacious, open-air enclosure of a circular form like Stonehenge ? '[2] In Welsh myth, Math ab Mathonwy, called also ' Math the Ancient ', was the greatest magician of ancient Wales, and his relation as teacher to Gwydion ab Dôn, the great Welsh Culture Hero, leads Sir John Rhŷs to consider him the Brythonic Zeus, though Merlin shares with him in this distinction ;[3] and since the Gaelic counterpart of Math is Aengus, a close study of Math might finally show a cult in his honour in Wales as we have found in Ireland an Aengus Cult.[4] We may, therefore, with more or less exact-

---

[1] Cf. O'Curry, *Manners and Customs*, ii. 122 ; iii. 5, 74, 122 ; Rhŷs, *Hib. Lect.*, pp. 150, 150 n. ; Jubainville, *Essai d'un Catalogue*, p. 244.

[2] Rhŷs, *Hib. Lect.*, p. 194.

[3] Math ab Mathonwy's Irish counterpart is Math mac Umóir, the magician (*Book of Leinster*, f. 9ᵇ ; cf. Rhŷs, *Trans. Third Inter. Cong. Hist. Religions*, Oxford, 1908, ii. 211).

[4] Rhŷs, ib., pp. 225–6; cf. R. B. *Mabinogion*, p. 60; *Triads*, i. 32, ii. 20, iii. 90. A fortified hill-top now known as Pen y Gaer, or ' Hill of the Fortress ', on the western side of the Conway, on a mountain within sight of the railway station of Tal y Cafn, Carnarvonshire, is regarded by Sir John Rhŷs as the site of a long-forgotten cult of Math the Ancient. (Rhŷs, ib., p. 225).

ness, equate the Aengus Cult as we see it in Irish myth connected chiefly with Dun Aengus and New Grange, with the unknown cult practised at Stonehenge, and this in turn with other Brythonic or pre-Brythonic sun-cults and initiations practised at Carnac, the great Celtic Jerusalem in Brittany, and at Gavrinis. All this will be more clearly seen after we have set forth what seems a definite and most striking parallel to New Grange, both as a monument erected by man and, as we maintain, as a place for religious mysteries—the greatest structure ever raised by human effort, the Great Pyramid.

New Grange and the Great Pyramid compared

Caliph Al Mamoun in A. D. 820, by a forced passage, was the first in modern times to enter the Great Pyramid, and he found nowhere a mummy or any indications that the structure had ever been used as a tomb for the dead. The King's Chamber, so named by us moderns, proved to be a keen disappointment for its first violator, for in it there was neither gold nor silver nor anything at all worth carrying away. The magnificent chamber contained nothing save an empty stone chest without a lid. Archaeologists in Egypt and archaeologists in Ireland face the same unsolved problem, namely, the purpose of the empty stone chest without inscriptions and quite unlike a mummy tomb, and of the stone basin in New Grange.[1] Certain Egyptologists have supposed that some royal personage must have been buried in the curious granite coffer, though there can be only their supposition to support them, for they have absolutely no proof that such is true, while there is strong circumstantial evidence to show that such is not true. Sir Gardner Wilkinson in his well-known publications has already suggested that the stone chest as well as the Great Pyramid itself were never intended to hold a corpse ; and

---

[1] This stone basin, now in the centre of the inner chamber, seems originally to have stood in the east recess, the largest and most richly inscribed. It is 4 feet long, 3 feet 6 inches across, and 1 foot thick. (Coffey, op. cit., xxx. 14, 21).

it is generally admitted by Egyptologists that no sarcophagus intended for a mummy has ever been found so high up in the body of a pyramid as this empty stone chest, except in the Second Pyramid. Incontestable evidence in support of the highly probable theory that the Great Pyramid was not intended for an actual tomb can be drawn from two important facts :—(1) ' the coffer has certain remarkable cubic proportions which show a care and design beyond what could be expected in any burial-coffer '—according to the high authority of Dr. Flinders Petrie ; (2) the chamber containing the coffer and the upper passage-ways have ventilating channels not known in any other Pyramid, so that apparently there must have been need of frequent entrance into the chamber by living men, as would be the case if used, as we hold, for initiation ceremonies.[1]

It is well known that very many of the megalithic monuments of the New Grange type scattered over Europe, especially from the Carnac centre of Brittany to the Tara-Boyne centre of Ireland, have one thing in common, an astronomical arrangement like the Great Pyramid, and an entrance facing one of the points of the solstices, usually either the winter solstice, which is common, or the summer solstice.[2] The puzzle has always been to discover the exact arrangement of the Great Pyramid by locating its main entrance. A Californian, Mr. Louis P. McCarty, in his recent (1907) work entitled *The Great Pyramid Jeezeh*, suggests with the most logical and reasonable arguments that the builders of the Pyramid have placed its main entrance in an undiscovered passage-way beneath the Great Sphinx, now half-buried in the shifting desert sands. If it can be shown that the Sphinx is the real portal, and many things tend to

---

[1] Cf. W. M. Flinders Petrie, *The Pyramids and Temples of Gizeh* (London, 1883), p. 201.

[2] All of the chief megaliths of this type, together with the chief alignements, which I have personally inspected—with the aid of a compass—in Ireland, Scotland, Isle of Man, Wales, Cornwall, and Brittany, are definitely aligned east and west. It cannot be said, however, that *all* megalithic monuments throughout Celtic countries show definite orientation (see Déchelette's *Manuel d'Archéologie*).

indicate that it is, the Great Pyramid is built on the same plan as New Grange, that is to say, it opens to the south-east, and like New Grange contains a narrow passage-way leading to a central chamber. South-easterly from the centre of the Pyramid lies the Sphinx, 5,380 feet away, a distance equal to 'just five times the distance of the " diagonal socket length " of the Great Pyramid from the centre of the Subterranean Chamber, under the Pyramid, to the supposed entrance under the Sphinx'[1]—a distance quite in keeping with the mighty proportions of the wonderful structure. And what is important, several eminent archaeologists have worked out the same conclusion, and have been seeking to connect the two monuments by making excavations in the Queen's Chamber, where it is supposed there exists a tunnel to the Sphinx. In all this we should bear in mind that the present entrance to the Pyramid is the forced one made by the treasure-seeking Caliph.

This very probable astronomical parallelism between the great Egyptian monument and the Irish one would establish their common religious, or, in a mystic sense, their funereal significance. In the preceding chapter we have set forth what symbolical relation the sun, its rising and setting, and its death at the winter equinox, were anciently supposed to hold to the doctrines of human death and re-birth. Jubainville, regarding the sun among the Celts in its symbolical relation to death, wrote, ' In Celtic belief, the dead go to live beyond the Ocean, to the south-west, there where the sun sets during the greater part of the year.'[2] This, too, as M. Maspero shows, was an Egyptian belief;[3] while, as equally among the Celts, the east, especially the south-east, where, after the winter solstice, the sun seems to be re-born or to rise out of the underworld of Hades into which it goes when it dies, is symbolical of the reverse—Life, Resurrection, and Re-birth. In this last Celtic-Egyptian belief, we maintain, may be found the reason why the chief megalithic monu-

---

[1] L. P. McCarty, *The Great Pyramid Jeezeh* (San Francisco, 1907), p. 402.

[2] Jubainville, *Le Cycle Myth. Irl.*, p. 28.

[3] Maspero, *Les Contes populaires de l'Égypte Ancienne*,' p. 74 n.

ments (dolmens, tumuli, and alignements), in Celtic countries and elsewhere, have their directions east and west, and why those like New Grange and Gavrinis open to the sunrise.

Greek temples also opened to the sunrise, and on the divine image within fell the first rays of the beautiful god Apollo.[1] In the great Peruvian sun-temple at Cuzco, a splendid disk of pure gold faced the east, and, reflecting the first rays of the rising sun, illuminated the whole sanctuary.[2] The cave-temple of the Florida Red Men opened eastward, and within its entrance on festival days stood the priest at dawn watching for the first ray of the sun, as a sign to begin the chant and offering.[3] The East Indian performs the ablution at dawn in the sacred Ganges, and stands facing the east meditating, as Brahma appears in all the wondrous glory of a tropical sunrise.[4] And in the same Aryan land there is an opposite worship : the dreaded Thugs, worshippers of devils and of Kali the death-goddess, in their most diabolical rites face the west and the sunset, symbols of death.[5] How Christianity was shaped by paganism is nowhere clearer than in the orientation of great cathedral churches (almost without exception in England), for all of the more famous ones have their altars eastward ; and Roman Catholics in prayer in their church services, and Anglicans in repeating the Creed, turn to the east, as the Hindu does. St. Augustine says :—' When we stand at prayer, we turn to the east, where the heaven arises, not as though God were only there, and had forsaken all other parts of the world, but to admonish our mind to turn to a more excellent nature, that is, to the Lord.'[6] Though the Jews came to be utterly opposed to sun-worship in their later history, they were sun-worshippers at first, as their temples opening eastward testify. This was the vision of

[1] Tylor, *Prim. Cult.*,[4] ii. 426.
[2] W. H. Prescott, *Conquest of Peru*, i, c. 3.
[3] Rochefort, *Iles Antilles*, p. 365 ; cf. Tylor, *P.C.*,[4] ii. 424.
[4] Colebrooke, *Essays*, vols. i, iv, v ; cf. Tylor, *P.C.*,[4] 425.
[5] *Illus. Hist. and Pract. of Thugs* (London, 1837), p. 46 ; cf. Tylor, *P.C.*,[4] ii. 425.
[6] Augustin. *de Serm. Dom. in Monte*, ii. 5 ; cf. Tylor, *P.C.*,[4] ii. 427–8.

Ezekiel :—'And, behold, at the door of the temple of Jehovah, between the porch and the Altar, were about five and twenty men, with their backs toward the temple of Jehovah, and their faces toward the east, and they worshipped the sun toward the east.' [1]

All this illustrates the once world-wide religion of our race ; and shows that sun-cults and sun-symbols are derived from a universal doctrine regarding the two states of existence— the one in Hades or the invisible lower world where the Sun-god goes at night, and the other in what we call the visible realm which the Sun-god visits daily.[2] The relation between life and death—symbolically figured in this fundamental conception forming the background of every sun-cult—is the foundation of all ancient mysteries. Thus we should expect the correspondences which we believe do exist between New Grange and the Great Pyramid. Both alike, in our opinion, were the greatest places in the respective countries for the celebration of the Mysteries. High up in the body of the Great Pyramid, after he had performed the long underground journey, typical of the journey of Osiris or the Sun to the Otherworld or the World of the Dead, we may suppose (knowing what we do of the Ancient Mysteries and their shadows in modern Masonic initiations [3]) that the royal or priestly neophyte laid himself in that strange stone coffin without a lid, for a certain period of time—probably for three days and three nights. Then, the initiation being complete, he arose from the mystic death to a real resurrection, a true child of Osiris. In New Grange we may suppose that the royal or priestly neophyte, while he ' fasted on the Tuatha De Danann for three days with their nights ', sat in that strange stone basin after the manner of the Orient.[4]

---

[1] Ezek. viii. 16. The popular opinion that Christians face the east in prayer, or have altars eastward because Jerusalem is eastward, does not fit in with facts.

[2] Cf. Lenormant, *Chaldean Magic*, p. 88 ; also Tylor, *Prim. Cult.*,[4] ii. 48–9.

[3] Though not a Mason, the writer draws his knowledge from Masons of the highest rank, and from published works by Masons like Mr. Carty's *The Great Pyramid Jeezeh.* [4] Cf. Borlase, *Dolmens of Ireland*, ii. 347 n.

The Great Pyramid seems to be the most ancient of the Egyptian pyramids, and undoubtedly was the model for all the smaller ones, which ' always betray profound ignorance of their noble model's chiefest internal features, as well as of all its niceties of angle and cosmic harmonies of linear measurement '.[1]   Dr. Flinders Petrie says :—' The Great Pyramid at Gizeh (of Khufu, fourth dynasty) unquestionably takes the lead, in accuracy and in beauty of work, as well as in size.   Not only is the fine work of it in the pavement, casing, King's and Queen's chambers quite unexcelled ; but the general character of the core masonry is better than that of any other pyramid in its solidity and regularity.'[2] And of the stone coffers he says :—' Taking most of its dimensions at their maximum, they agree closely with the same theory as that which is applicable to the chambers ; for when squared they are all even multiples of a square fifth of a cubit. . . . There is no other theory applicable to every lineal dimension of the coffer ; but having found the π proportion in the form of the Pyramid, and in the King's Chamber, there is some ground for supposing that it was intended also in the coffer, on just one-fifth the scale of the chamber.'[2]   And here is apparent the important fact we wish to emphasize ; the Great Pyramid does not seem to have been intended primarily, if at all, for the entombment of dead bodies or mummies while ' the numerous quasi-copies ' were ' for sepulchral purposes '[3] without doubt.   There appears to have been at first a clear understanding of the esoteric usage of the Great Pyramid as a place for the mystic burial of Initiates, and then in the course of national decadence the exoteric interpretation of this usage, the interpretation now popular with Egyptologists, led to the erection of smaller pyramids for purposes of actual burial.   And may we not see in such pyramid-like tumuli as those of Mont St. Michel, Gavrinis, and New Grange copies of these

---

[1] C. Piazzi Smyth, *Our Inheritance in the Great Pyramid* (London, 1890).

[2] Flinders Petrie, *The Pyramids and Temples of Gizeh*, pp. 169, 222.

[3] C. Piazzi Smyth, op. cit.

smaller funeral pyramids ; [1] or, if not direct copies, at least
the result of a similar religious decadence from the unknown
centuries since the Great Pyramid was erected by the Divine
Kings of prehistoric Egypt as a silent witness for all ages
that Great Men, Initiates, have understood Universal Law,
and have solved the greatest of all human problems, the
problem of Life and Death ?

GAVRINIS AND NEW GRANGE COMPARED

In conclusion, and in support of the arguments already
advanced, I offer a few observations of my own, made at
Gavrinis itself, the most famous tumulus in Continental
Europe.   After a very careful examination of the interior
and exterior of the tumulus, an examination extending over
more than twelve hours, I am convinced that its curious
rock-carvings and those in New Grange are by the same race
of people, whoever that race may have been ; and that there
is sufficient evidence in its construction to show that, like
New Grange, it was quite as religious as funereal in its nature
and use.   The facts which bear out this view are the following.   First, there are three strange cavities cut into the body
of the stone on the south side of the inner chamber, communicating interiorly with one another, and large enough to
admit human hands ; if used as places in which to offer
sacrifice to the dead or fairies, small objects could have been
placed in them.   In the oldest extant authentic records of them
which I have found it is said of their probable purpose :—
' Some people look on them as a double noose intended to
strangle the [animal] victims which the priest sacrificed ; for
others they are two rings behind which the hands of the
betrothed met each other to be married.' [2]   Their purpose
is certainly difficult enough to decipher, perhaps is undecipherable ; but one thing about them is certain, namely,
that a close examination round their exterior edges and

---

[1] In 1770, when New Grange apparently was not covered with a growth
of trees as now, Governor Pownall visited it and described it as like a
pyramid in general outline : ' The pyramid in its present state ' is ' but
a ruin of what it was ' (Coffey, op. cit., xxx. 13).

[2] Le Dr. G. de C., *Locmariaquer et Gavr'inis* (Vannes, 1876), p. 18.

within them also shows the rock-surface worn smooth as
though by ages of handling and touching ; and it is incontestable that this wearing of the rock-surface by human
hands could not have taken place had the inner chamber
been sealed up and used solely as a tomb. We suggest here,
as Sir James Fergusson in his *Rude Stone Monuments* (p. 366)
has suggested, that the inner chamber of Gavrinis was
probably a place for the celebration of religious rites : he
advances the opinion that the strange cavities were used to
contain holy oil or holy water. There is this second curious
fact connected with the tumulus of Gavrinis.   On entering
it—and it opens like New Grange to the sunrise, being
oriented 43° 60″ to the south-east [1]—one finds placed across
the floor of the narrow passage-way as slightly inclined steps
rising to the inner chamber three or four stones. Two of
them, now very prominent, form veritable stumbling-blocks,
and the one at the threshold of the inner chamber is carved
quite like the lintel stone above the entrance at New Grange.[2]
From what we know of ancient mystic cults, there was
a darkened chamber approached by a narrow passage-way
so low that the neophyte must stoop in traversing it to show
symbolically his humility ; and as symbolic of his progress
to the Chamber of Death, the *Sanctum Sanctorum* of the
spirit-temple, there were steps, often purposely placed as
stumbling-blocks. The Great Pyramid, evidently, conforms
to this mystical plan ; and strikes one, therefore, all the
more forcibly as the most remarkable structure for initiatory
ceremonies ever constructed on our planet. Thus, Dr. Flinders
Petrie says :—' But we are met then by an extraordinary
idea, that all access to the King's chamber after its comple-

---

[1] According to Le Dr. G. de C., op. cit., p. 18.

[2] Mr. Coffey says of similar details in Irish tumuli :—' In the construction
of such chambers it is usual to find a sort of sill or low stone placed across
the entrance into the main chamber, and at the openings into the smaller
chambers or recesses ; such stones also occur laid at intervals across the
bottom of the passages. This forms a marked feature in the construction
at Dowth, and in the cairns on the Loughcrew Hills, but is wholly absent
at New Grange ' (op. cit., xxx. 15). New Grange, however, has suffered
more or less from vandalism, and originally may have contained similar
stone sills.

tion must have been by climbing over the plug-blocks, as they lay in the gallery, or by walking up the ramps on either side of them. Yet, as the blocks cannot physically have been lying in any other place before they were let down we are shut up to this view.' [1] And as Egyptian tombs represented the mansions of the dead,[2] just so Celtic or pre-Celtic spirit-temples and place for initiations were always connected with the Underworld of the Dead ; and save for such symbolical arrangements as we see in Gavrinis, and New Grange also, they were undistinguishable from tombs used for interments only.

It seems to us most reasonable to suppose that if, as the old Irish manuscripts show, there were spirit-temples or places for pagan funeral rites, or rites of initiation, in Ireland, constructed like other tumuli which were used only as tombs for the dead (because the ancient cult was one of ancestor worship and worship of gods like the Tuatha De Danann, and spirits), then there must have been others in Brittany also, where we find the same system of rock-inscriptions. Further, in view of all the definite provable relations between Gavrinis and New Grange, we are strongly inclined to regard them both as having the same origin and purpose, Gavrinis being for Armorica what New Grange was for Ireland, the royal or principal spirit-temple.

---

[1] Flinders Petrie, *The Pyramids and Temples of Gizeh*, p. 216.

[2] Maspero, op. cit., p. 69 n., &c. The world-wide anthropomorphic tendency to construct tombs for the gods and for the dead after the plan of earthly dwellings is as evident in the excavations at Mycenae as in ancient Egypt and in Celtic lands.

SECTION III
THE CULT OF GODS, SPIRITS, FAIRIES, AND THE DEAD

CHAPTER IX

THE TESTIMONY OF PAGANISM

'The cult of forests, of fountains, and of stones is to be explained by that primitive naturalism which all the Church Councils held in Brittany united to proscribe.'—ERNEST RENAN.

Edicts against pagan cults—Cult of Sacred Waters and its absorption by Christianity—Celtic Water Divinities—Druidic influence on Fairy-Faith—Cult of Sacred Trees—Cult of Fairies, Spirits, and the Dead—Feasts of the Dead—Conclusion.

THE evidence of paganism in support of our Psychological Theory concerning the Fairy-Faith is so vast that we cannot do more than point to portions of it—especially such portions as are most Celtic in their nature. Perhaps most of us will think first of all about the ancient cults rendered to fountains, rivers, lakes, trees, and, as we have seen (pp. 399 ff.), to stones. There can be no reasonable doubt that these cults were very flourishing when Christianity came to Europe, for kings, popes, and church councils issued edict after edict condemning them.[1] The second Council of Arles, held about 452, issued the following canon :—' If in the territory of a bishop, infidels light torches, or venerate trees, fountains, or stones, and he neglects to abolish this usage, he must know that he is guilty of sacrilege. If the director of the act itself, on being admonished, refuses to correct it, he is to be excluded from communion.' [1] The Council of Tours, in 567, thus expressed itself :—' We implore the pastors to expel from the Church all those whom they may see performing before certain stones things which have no relation with

[1] Cf. Bruns, *Canones apostolorum et conciliorum saeculorum*, ii. 133.

the ceremonies of the Church, and also those who observe the customs of the Gentiles.' [1] King Canute in England and Charlemagne in Europe conducted a most vigorous campaign against all these pagan worships. This is Charlemagne's edict :—' With respect to trees, stones, and fountains, where certain foolish people light torches or practise other super-stitions, we earnestly ordain that that most evil custom detestable to God, wherever it be found, should be removed and destroyed.' [2]

The result of these edicts was a curious one. It was too much to expect the eradication of the old cults after their age-long existence, and so one by one they were absorbed by the new religion. In a sacred tree or grove, over a holy well or fountain, on the shore of a lake or river, there was placed an image of the Virgin or of some saint, and uncon-sciously the transformation was made, as the simple-hearted country-folk beheld in the brilliant images new and more glorious dwelling-places for the spirits they and their fathers had so long venerated.

THE CULT OF SACRED WATERS

In Brittany, perhaps better than in other Celtic countries to-day, one can readily discern this evolution from paganism to Christianity. Thus, for example, in the Morbihan there is the fountain of St. Anne d'Auray, round which centres Brittany's most important Pardon ; a fountain near Vannes is dedicated to St. Peter ; at Carnac there is the far-famed fountain of St. Cornely with its niche containing an image of Carnac's patron saint, and not far from it, on the roadside leading to Carnac Plage, an enclosed well dedicated to the Holy Virgin; and, less than a mile away, the beautiful fountain of St. Columba. Near Ploermel, Canton of Ploer-mel (Morbihan), there is the fountain of Recourrance or St. Laurent, in which sailors perform divinations to know the

---

[1] Cf. F. Maassen, *Concilia aevi merovingici*, p. 133.
[2] Cf. Boretius, *Capitularia regum Francorum*, i. 59 ; for each of the above references cf. Jubainville, *Le culte des menhirs dans le monde celtique*, in *Rev. Celt.*, xxvii. 317.

future state of the weather by casting on its waters a morsel
of bread. If the bread floats, it is a sure sign of fair weather,
but if it sinks, of weather so bad that no one should take
risks by going out in the fishing-boats. In some wells, pins
are dropped by lovers. If the pins float, the water-spirits
show favourable auspices, but if the pins sink, the maiden
is unhappy, and will hesitate in accepting the proposal of
marriage. Long after their conversion, the inhabitants of
Concoret (Arrondissement de Ploermel, Morbihan) paid divine
honours to the fountain of Baranton in the druidical forest
of Brocéliande, so famous in the Breton legends of Arthur
and Merlin :—' For a long time the inhabitants of Concoret . . .
in place of addressing themselves to God or to his Saints in
their maladies, sought the remedy in the fountain of Baranton, either by praying to it, after the manner of the Gauls,
or by drinking of its waters.'[1]   In the month of August
1835, when there was an unusual drought in the land, all
the inhabitants of Concoret formed in a great procession
with banners and crucifix at their head, and with chants
and ringing of church bells marched to this same fountain
of Baranton and prayed for rain.[2] This curious bit of history
was also reported to me in July 1909 by a peasant who lives
near the fountain, and who heard it from his parents ; and
he added that the foot of the crucifix was planted in the
water to aid the rain-making. We have here an interesting
combination of paganism and Christianity.

Gregory of Tours says that the country-folk of Gévaudan
rendered divine honours to a certain lake, and as offerings
cast on its waters linen, wool, cheese, bees'-wax, bread, and
other things ;[3] and Mahé adds that gold was sometimes
offered,[3] quite after the manner of the ancient Peruvians,
who cast gold and silver of great value into the waters of
sacred Lake Titicaca, high up in the Andes. To absorb into
Christianity the worship paid to the lake near Gévaudan, the
bishop ordered a church to be built on its shore, and to
the people he said :—' My children, there is nothing divine in

---

[1] Cf. Mahé, *Essai*, p. 427.   [2] See Villemarqué *sur Bretagne*.
[3] Cf. Mahé, *Essai*, p. 326 ; quoted from *De Glor. Conf.*, c. 2.

this lake : defile not your souls by these vain ceremonies ; but recognize rather the true God.'[1] The offerings to the lake-spirits then ceased, and were made instead on the altar of the church. As Canon Mahé so consistently sets forth, other similar means were used to absorb the pagan cults of sacred waters :—'Other pastors employed a similar device to absorb the cult of fountains into Christianity ; they consecrated them to God under the invocation of certain saints ; giving the saints' names to them and placing in them the saints' images, so that the weak and simple-hearted Christians who might come to them, struck by these names and by these images, should grow accustomed to addressing their prayers to God and to his saints, in place of honouring the fountains themselves, as they had been accustomed to do. This is the reason why there are seen in the stonework of so many fountains, niches and little statues of saints who have given their names to these springs.'[2]

Procopius reports that the Franks, even after having accepted Christianity, remained attached to their ancient cults, sacrificing to the River Po women and children of the Goths, and casting the bodies into its waters to the spirits of the waters.[2] Well-worship in the Isle of Man, not yet quite extinct, was no doubt once very general. As A. W. Moore has shown, the sacred wells in the Isle of Man were visited and offerings made to them to secure immunity from witches and fairies, to cure maladies, to raise a wind, and for various kinds of divination.[3] And no doubt the offerings of rags on bushes over sacred wells, and the casting of pins, coins, buttons, pebbles, and other small objects into their waters, a common practice yet in Ireland and Wales, as in non-Celtic countries, are to be referred to as survivals of a time when regular sacrifices were offered in divination, or in seeking cures from maladies, and equally from obsessing demons who were thought to cause the maladies. In the prologue to Chrétien's *Conte du*

---

[1] Cf. Mahé, *Essai*, p. 326; quoted from *De Glor. Conf.*, c. 2.
[2] Cf. Mahé, *Essai*, p. 326; quoted from *Goth.*, lib. ii.
[3] A. W. Moore, in *Folk-Lore*, v. 212–29.

Graal there is an account, seemingly very ancient, of how dishonour to the divinities of wells and springs brought destruction on the rich land of Logres. The damsels who abode in these watery places fed travellers with nourishing food until King Amangons wronged one of them by carrying off her golden cup. His men followed his evil example, so that the springs dried up, the grass withered, and the land became waste.[1]

According to Mr. Borlase, ' it was by passing under the waters of a well that the *Sidh*, that is, the abode of the spirits called *Sidhe*, in the tumulus or natural hill, as the case might be, was reached.' [2] And it is evident from this that the well-spirits were even identified in Ireland with the Tuatha De Danann or Fairy-Folk. I am reminded of a walk I was privileged to take with Mr. William B. Yeats on Lady Gregory's estate at Coole Park, near Gort (County Galway) ; for Mr. Yeats led me to the haunts of the water-spirits of the region, along a strange river which flows underground for some distance and then comes out to the light again in its weird course, and to a dark, deep pool hidden in the forest. According to tradition, the river is the abode of water-fairies ; and in the shaded forest-pool, whose depth is very great, live a spirit-race like the Greek nymphs. More than one mortal while looking into this pool has felt a sudden and powerful impulse to plunge in, for the fairies were then casting their magic spell over him that they might take him to live in their under-water palace for ever.

One of the most beautiful passages in *The Tripartite Life of Patrick* describes the holy man at the holy well called Cliabach :—' Thereafter Patrick went at sunrise to the well, namely Cliabach on the sides of Cruachan. The clerics sat down by the well. Two daughters of Loegaire son of Niall went early to the well to wash their hands, as was a custom of theirs, namely, Ethne the Fair, and Fedelm the Ruddy. The maidens found beside the well the assembly of the clerics in white garments, with their books before them. And they

---

[1] Cf. Rhŷs, *Arthurian Legend*, p. 247.
[2] Borlase, *Dolmens of Ireland*, iii. 729.

wondered at the shape of the clerics, and thought that they
were men of the elves or apparitions. They asked tidings of
Patrick : " Whence are ye, and whence have ye come ?
Are ye of the elves or of the gods ? " And Patrick said to
them : " It were better for you to believe in God than to
inquire about our race." Said the girl who was elder : " Who
is your god ? and where is he ? Is he in heaven, or in earth,
or under earth, or on earth ? Is he in seas or in streams, or
in mountains or in glens ? Hath he sons and daughters ?
Is there gold and silver, is there abundance of every good
thing in his kingdom ? Tell us about him, how he is seen,
how he is loved, how he is found ? if he is in youth, or if he
is in age ? if he is ever-living ; if he is beautiful ? if many
have fostered his son ? if his daughters are dear and beautiful
to the men of the world ? " ' [1]

And in another place it is recorded that ' Patrick went to
the well of Findmag. Slán is its name. They told Patrick
that the heathen honoured the well as if it were a god.' [2] And
of the same well it is said, ' that the magi, i. e. wizards or
Druids, used to reverence the well Slán and " offer gifts to it
as if it were a god." ' [2] As Whitley Stokes pointed out, this
is the only passage connecting the Druids with well-worship ;
and it is very important, because it establishes the relation
between the Druids as magicians and their control of spirits
like fairies.[2] As shown here, and as seems evident in
Columba's relation with Druids and exorcism in Adamnan's
Life of St. Columba,[3] the early Celtic peoples undoubtedly drew
many of their fairy-traditions from a memory of druidic rites
of divination. Perhaps the most beautiful description of
a holy well and a description illustrative of such divination
is that of Ireland's most mystical well, Connla's Well :—
' Sinend, daughter of Lodan Lucharglan, son of Ler, out of
Tír Tairngire (" Land of Promise, Fairyland "), went to
Connla's Well which is under sea, to behold it. That is
a well at which are the hazels and inspirations (?) of wisdom,

---

[1] Stokes, *Tripartite Life of Patrick*, pp. 99-101.
[2] Ib., text, pp. 123, 323, and Intro., p. 159.
[3] Book II, 69-70 ; see our study, p. 267.

that is, the hazels of the science of poetry, and in the same hour their fruit, and their blossom and their foliage break forth, and these fall on the well in the same shower, which raises on the water a royal surge of purple.   Then the [sacred] salmon chew the fruit, and the juice of the nuts is apparent on their purple bellies.   And seven streams of wisdom spring forth and turn there again.'[1]

To these cults of sacred waters numerous non-Celtic parallels could easily be offered, but they seem unnecessary with Celtic evidence so clear.   And this evidence which is already set forth shows that the origin of worship paid to sacred wells, fountains, lakes, or rivers, is to be found in the religious practices of the Celts before they became christianized.   They believed that certain orders of spirits, often called fairies, and to be identified with them, inhabited, or as was the case with Sinend, who came from the Other-world, visited these places, and must be appeased or approached through sacrifice by mortals seeking their favours. Canon Mahé puts the matter thus :—' The Celts recognized a supreme God, the principle of all things ; but they rendered religious worship to the genii or secondary deities who, according to them, united themselves to different objects in nature and made them divine by such union.   Among the objects were rivers, the sea, lakes and fountains.'[2]

THE CULT OF SACRED TREES

The things said of sacred waters can also be said of sacred trees among the Celts ; and, in the case of sacred trees, more may be added about the Druids and their relation to the Fairy-Faith, for it is well known that the Druids held the oak and its mistletoe in great religious veneration, and it is generally thought that most of the famous Druid schools were in the midst of sacred oak-groves or forests.   Pliny has recorded that ' the Druids, for so they call their magicians, have nothing which they hold more sacred than the mistletoe [3]

---

[1] Rennes *Dinnshenchas*, Stokes's trans. in *Rev. Celt.*, xv. 457.
[2] Cf. Mahé, *Essai*, p. 323.
[3] The Celts may have viewed the mistletoe on the sacred oak as the seat

and the tree on which it grows, provided only it be an oak
(*robur*). But apart from that, they select groves of oak,
and they perform no sacred rite without leaves from that
tree, so that the Druids may be regarded as even deriving
from it their name interpreted as Greek '[1] (a disputed point
among modern philologists). Likewise of the Druids,
Maximus Tyrius states that the image of their chief god,
considered by him to correspond to Zeus, was a lofty oak
tree ; [2] and Strabo says that the principal place of assembly
for the Galatians, a Celtic people of Asia Minor, was the
Sacred Oak-grove.[3]

Just as the cult of fountains was absorbed by Christianity,
so was the cult of trees. Concerning this, Canon Mahé
writes :—' One sees sometimes, in the country and in
gardens, trees wherein, by trimming and bending together
the branches, have been formed niches of verdure, in which
have been placed crosses or images of certain saints. This
usage is not confined to the Morbihan. Our Lady of the
Oak, in Anjou, and Our Lady of the Oak, near Orthe, in
Maine, are places famous for pilgrimage. In this last
province, says a historian, " One sees at various cross-roads
the most beautiful rustic oaks decorated with figures of
saints. There are seen there, in five or six villages, chapels
of oaks, with whole trunks of that tree enshrined in the wall,
beside the altar. Such among others is that famous chapel

of the tree's life, because in the winter sleep of the leafless oak the mistletoe
still maintains its own foliage and fruit, and like the heart of a sleeper
continues pulsing with vitality. The mistletoe thus being regarded as the
heart-centre of the divine spirit in the oak-tree was cut with a golden
sickle by the arch-druid clad in pure white robes, amid great religious
solemnity, and became a vicarious sacrifice or atonement for the worshippers of the tree god. (Cf. Frazer, *G. B.*,[2] iii. 447 ff.)

[1] Pliny, *Nat. Hist.*, xvi. 95 ; cf. Rhŷs, *Hib. Lect.*, p. 218.

[2] *Dissert.*, viii ; cf. Rhŷs, ib., p. 219.

[3] Meineke's ed., xii. 5, 1 ; cf. Rhŷs, ib., p. 219. The oak-tree is pre-
eminently the holy tree of Europe. Not only Celts, but Slavs, worshipped
amid its groves. To the Germans it was their chief god ; the ancient
Italians honoured it above all other trees ; the original image of Jupiter
on the Capitol at Rome seems to have been a natural oak-tree. So at
Dodona, Zeus was worshipped as immanent in a sacred oak. Cf. Frazer,
G. B.,[2] iii. 346 ff.

of Our Lady of the Oak, near the forge of Orthe, whose celebrity attracts daily, from five to six leagues about, a very great gathering of people." '[1]

Saint Martin, according to Canon Mahé, tried to destroy a sacred pine-tree in the diocese of Tours by telling the people there was nothing divine in it. The people agreed to let it be cut down on condition that the saint should receive its great trunk on his head as it fell ; and the tree was not cut down.[1] Saint Germain caused a great scandal at Auxerre by hanging from the limbs of a sacred tree the heads of wild animals which he had killed while hunting.[1] Saint Gregory the Great wrote to Brunehaut exhorting him to abolish among his subjects the offering of animals' heads to certain trees.[2]

In Ireland fairy trees are common yet ; though throughout Celtdom sacred trees, naturally of short duration, are almost forgotten. In Brittany, the Forest of Brocéliande still enjoys something of the old veneration, but more out of sentiment than by actual worship. A curious survival of an ancient Celtic tree-cult exists in Carmarthen, Wales, where there is still carefully preserved and held upright in a firm casing of cement the decaying trunk of an old oak-tree called Merlin's Oak ; and local prophecy declares on Merlin's authority that when the tree falls Carmarthen will fall with it. Perhaps through an unconscious desire on the part of some patriotic citizens of averting the calamity by inducing the tree-spirit to transfer its abode, or else by otherwise hoodwinking the tree-spirit into forgetting that Merlin's Oak is dead, a vigorous and now flourishing young oak has been planted so directly beside it that its foliage embraces it. And in many parts of modern England, the Jack-in-the-Green, a man entirely hidden in a covering of green foliage who dances through the streets on May Day, may be another example of a very ancient tree (or else agricultural) cult of Celtic origin.

[1] Cf. Mahé, *Essai*, pp. 333-4 ; quotation from *Hist. du Maine*, i. 17.
[2] Cf. Mahé, *Essai*, p. 334 ; quoted from *Lib.* VII, *indict.* i, *epist.* 5.

THE CULT OF FAIRIES, SPIRITS, AND THE DEAD

There was also, as we already know, more or less of direct worship offered to fairies like the Tuatha De Danann ; and sacrifice was made to them even as now, when the Irish or Scotch peasant pours a libation of milk to the ' good people ' or to the fairy queen who presides over the flocks. In *Fiacc's Hymn* [1] it is said, ' On Ireland's folk lay darkness : the tribes worshipped elves : They believed not the true godhead of the true Trinity.' And there is a reliable legend concerning Columbkille which shows that this old cult of elves was not forgotten among the early Irish Christians, though they changed the original good reputation of these invisible beings to one of evil. It is said that Columbkille's first attempts to erect a church or monastery on Iona were rendered vain by the influence of some evil spirit or else of demons ; for as fast as a wall was raised it fell down. Then it was revealed to the saint that the walls could not stand until a human victim should be buried alive under the foundations. And the lot fell on Oran, Columbkille's companion, who accordingly became a sacrifice to appease the evil spirit, fairies, or demons of the place where the building was to be raised.[2]

As an illustration of what the ancient practice of such sacrifice to place-spirits, or to gods, must have been like in Wales, we offer the following curious legend concerning the conception of Myrddin (Merlin), as told by our witness from Pontrhydfendigaid, Mr. John Jones (see p. 147) :—' When building the Castle of Gwrtheyrn, near Carmarthen, as much as was built by day fell down at night. So a council of the *Dynion Hysbys* or "Wise Men" was called, and they decided that the blood of a fatherless boy had to be used in mixing the mortar if the wall was to stand. Search was thereupon made for a fatherless boy (cf. p. 351), and throughout all the kingdom no such boy could be found. But one day two boys were quarrelling, and one of them in defying

[1] Stokes, *Tripartite Life*, p. 409.
[2] Cf. Wood-Martin, *Traces of the Older Faiths in Ireland*, i. 305.

the other wanted to know what a fatherless boy like him had to say to him. An officer of the king, overhearing the quarrel, seized the boy thus tauntingly addressed as the one so long looked for. The circumstances were made known to the king, and the boy was taken to him. "Who is your father?" asked the king. "My mother never told me," the boy replied. Then the boy's mother was sent for, and the king asked her who the father of the boy was, and she replied: "I do not know; for I have never known a man. Yet, one night, it seemed to me that a man noble and majestic in appearance slept with me, and I awoke to find that I had been in a dream. But when I grew pregnant afterwards, and this wonderful boy whom you now see was delivered, I considered that a divine being or an angel had visited me in that dream, and therefore I called his child Myrddin the Magician, for such I believe my son to be." When the mother had thus spoken, the king announced to the court and wise men, "Here is the fatherless boy. Take his blood and use it in mixing the mortar. The walling will not hold without it." At this, Myrddin taunted the king and wise men, and said they were no better than a pack of idiots. "The reason the walling falls down," Myrddin went on to say, "is because you have tried to raise it on a rock which covers two large sea-serpents. Whenever the wall is raised over them its weight presses on their backs and makes them uneasy. Then during the night they upheave their backs to relieve themselves of the pressure, and thus shake the walling to a fall." ' The story ends here, but presumably Merlin's statements were found to be true; and Merlin was not sacrificed, for, as we know, he became the great magician of Arthur's court.

There are two hills in the Highlands of Aberdeenshire where travellers had to propitiate the banshee by placing barley-meal cakes near a well on each hill; and if the traveller neglected the offering, death or some dire calamity was sure to follow.[1] It is quite certain that the banshee is almost always thought of as the spirit of a dead ancestor presiding

---

[1] W. Gregor, *Notes on Beltane Cakes*, in *Folk-Lore*, vi. 5.

over a family, though here it appears more like the tutelary deity of the hills. But sacrifice being thus made, according to the folk-belief, to a banshee, shows, like so many other examples where there is a confusion between divinities or fairies and the souls of the dead, that ancestral worship must be held to play a very important part in the complex Fairy-Faith as a whole. A few non-Celtic parallels determine this at once. Thus, exactly as to fairies here, milk is offered to the souls of saints in the Panjab, India, as a means of propitiating them.[1] M. A. Lefèvre shows that the Roman Lares, so frequently compared to house-haunting fairies, are in reality quite like the Gaelic banshee ; that originally they were nothing more than the unattached souls of the dead, akin to Manes ; that time and custom made distinctions between them ; that in the common language Lares and Manes had synonymous dwellings ; and that, finally, the idea of death was little by little divorced from the worship of the Lares, so that they became guardians of the family and protectors of life.[2] On all the tombs of their dead the Romans inscribed these names : *Manes, inferi, silentes*,[3] the last of which, meaning *the silent ones*, is equivalent to the term ' People of Peace ' given to the fairy-folk of Scotland.[4] Nor were the Roman Lares always thought of as inhabiting dwellings. Many were supposed to live in the fields, in the streets of cities, at cross-roads, quite like certain orders of fairies and demons ; and in each place these ancestral spirits had their chapels and received offerings of fruit, flowers, and of foliage. If neglected they became spiteful, and were then known as Lemures.

All these examples tend to show what the reviewer of Curtin's *Tales of the Fairies and of the Ghost World* states, that ' The attributes of a ghost—that is to say, the spirit of a dead man—are indistinguishable from those of a fairy. And it is well known how world-wide is the worship of the dead and the offering of food to them, among uncivilized

---

[1] Temple, *Legends of the Panjab*, in *Folk-Lore*, x. 406.
[2] Lefèvre, *Le Culte des Morts chez les Latins*, in *Rev. Trad. Pop.*, ix. 195–209.   [3] See *Folk-Lore*, vi. 192.
[4] The term ' People of Peace ' seems, however, to have originated from confounding *sid*, ' fairy abode,' and *sid*, ' peace.'

tribes like those of Africa, Australia, and America, as well as among such great nations as China, Corea, India, and Japan ; and in ancient times it was universal among the masses of the people in Egypt, Greece, and Rome.

CELTIC AND NON-CELTIC FEASTS OF THE DEAD

Samain, as we already know, was the great Celtic feast of the dead when offerings or sacrifice of various kinds were made to ancestral spirits, and to the Tuatha De Danann and the spirit-hosts under their control ; and *Beltene*, or the first of May, was another day anciently dedicated to fêtes in honour of the dead and fairies. Chapter ii has shown us how November Eve, the modern *Samain*, and like it, All Saints Eve or *La Toussaint*, are regarded among the Celtic peoples now ; and the history of *La Toussaint* seems to indicate that Christianity, as in the case of the cult of trees and fountains, absorbed certain Celtic cults of the dead which centred around the pagan *Samain* feast of the dead, and even adopted the date of *Samain* (see p. 453).

Among the ancient Egyptians, so much like the ancient Celts in their innate spirituality and clear conceptions of the invisible world, we find a parallel feast which fell on the seventeenth *Athyr* of the year. This day was directly dependent upon the progress of the sun ; and, as we have throughout emphasized, the ancient symbolism connected with the yearly movements of the Great God of Light and Life cannot be divorced from the ancient doctrines of life and death. To the pre-Christian Celts, the First of November, or the Festival of *Samain*, which marked the end of summer and the commencement of winter, was symbolical of death.[1] *Samain* thus corresponds with the Egyptian fête of the dead, for the seventeenth *Athyr* of the year marks the day on which Sîtou (the god of darkness) killed in the midst of a banquet his brother Osiris (the god of light, the sun), and which was therefore thought of as the season when the old sun was dying of his wounds. It was a time when the power of good was on the decline, so that all nature, turning

[1] Cf. *Le Cycle Myth. Irl.*, p. 102.

against man, was abandoned to the divinities of darkness, the inhabitants of the Realms of the Dead. On this anniversary of the death of Osiris, an Egyptian would undertake no new enterprise : should he go down to the Nile, a crocodile would attack him as the crocodile sent by Sîtou had attacked Osiris, and even as the Darkness was attacking the Light to devour it ; [1] should he set out on a journey, he would part from his home and family never to return. His only course was to remain locked in his house, and there await in fear and inaction the passing of the night, until Osiris, returning from death, and reborn to a new existence, should rise triumphant over the forces of Darkness and Evil.[2] It is clear that this last part of the Egyptian belief is quite like the Celtic conception of *Samain* as we have seen Ailill and Medb celebrating that festival in their palace at Cruachan.

There is a great resemblance between the christianized Feast of *Samain*, when the dead return to visit their friends and to be entertained, for example as in Brittany, and the beautiful festivals formerly held in the Sînto temples of Japan. Thus at Nikko thousands of lanterns were lighted, 'each one representing the spirit of an ancestor,' and there was masquerading and revelry for the entertainment of the visiting spirits.[3] It shows how much religions are alike.

Each year the Roman peoples dedicated two days (February 21-2) to the honouring of the Dead. On the first day, called the *Feralia*, all Romans were supposed to remain within their own homes. The sanctuaries of all the

---

[1] The crocodile as the mystic symbol of Sîtou provides one key to unlock the mysteries of what eminent Egyptologists have erroneously called animal worship, erroneously because they have interpreted literally what can only be interpreted symbolically. The crocodile is called the ' son of Sîtou ' in the *Papyrus magique*, Harris, pl. vi, ll. 8-9 (cf. Maspero, *Les Contes populaires de l'Égypte Ancienne*,[2] Intro., p. 56); and as the waters seem to swallow the sun as it sinks below the horizon, so the crocodile, as Sîtou representing the waters, swallows the Children of Osiris, as the Egyptians called themselves. On the other hand, Osiris is typified by the white bull, in many nations the sun emblem, white being the emblem of purity and light, while the powers of the bull represent the masculinity of the sun, which impregnates all nature, always thought of as feminine, with life germs.   [2] Cf. Maspero, op. cit., Intro., p. 49.

[3] Cf. Borlase, *Dolmens of Ireland*, iii. 854.

gods were closed and all ceremony suspended. The only sacrifices made at such a time were to the dead, and to the gods of the dead in the underworld ; and all manes were appeased by food-offerings of meats and cakes. The second day was called *Cara Cognatio* and was a time of family reunions and feasting. Of it Ovid has said (*Fasti*, ii. 619), ' After the visit to the tombs and to the ancestors who are no longer [among us], it is pleasant to turn towards the living ; after the loss of so many, it is pleasant to behold those who remain of our blood and to reckon up the generations of our descendants.' And the Greeks also had their feasts for the dead.[1]

CONCLUSION

The fact of ancient Celtic cults of stones, waters, trees, and fairies still existing under cover of Christianity directly sustains the Psychological Theory ; and the persistence of the ancient Celtic cult of the dead, as illustrated in the survival of *Samain* in its modern forms, and perhaps best seen now among the Bretons, goes far to sustain the opinion of Ernest Renan, who declared in his admirable *Essais* that of all peoples the Celts, as the Romans also recorded, have most precise ideas about death. Thus it is that the Celts at this moment are the most spiritually conscious of western nations. To think of them as materialists is impossible. Since the time of Patrick and Columba the Gaels have been the missionaries of Europe ; and, as Caesar asserts, the Druids were the ancient teachers of the Gauls, no less than of all Britain. And the mysteries of life and death are the key-note of all things really Celtic, even of the great literature of Arthur, Cuchulainn, and Finn, now stirring the intellectual world.

[1] Cf. Lefèvre, *Rev. Trad. Pop.*, ix. 195–209.

SECTION III
THE CULT OF GODS, SPIRITS, FAIRIES, AND THE DEAD

CHAPTER X

THE TESTIMONY OF CHRISTIANITY

' The Purgatory of St. Patrick became the framework of another series of tales, embodying the Celtic ideas concerning the other life and its different states. Perhaps the profoundest instinct of the Celtic peoples is their desire to penetrate the unknown. With the sea before them, they wish to know what is to be found beyond it ; they dream of the Promised Land. In the face of the unknown that lies beyond the tomb, they dream of that great journey which the pen of Dante has celebrated.'—ERNEST RENAN.

Lough Derg a sacred lake originally—Purgatorial rites as christianized survivals of ancient Celtic rites—Purgatory as Fairyland—Purgatorial rites parallel to pagan initiation ceremonies—The Death and Resurrection Rite—Breton Pardons compared—Relation to Aengus Cult and Celtic cave-temples—Origin of Purgatorial doctrine pre-Christian—Celtic and Roman feasts of dead shaped Christian ones—Fundamental unity of Mythologies, Religions, and the Fairy-Faith.

THE best evidence offered by Christianity with direct bearing on the Fairy-Faith comes from what may be designated survivals of transformed paganism within the Church itself. Various pagan cults, which also came to be more or less christianized, have been considered under Paganism ; and in this chapter we propose to examine the famous Purgatory of St. Patrick and the Christian rites in honour of the dead.

ST. PATRICK'S PURGATORY

In the south of County Donegal, in Ireland, amid treeless mountains and moorlands, lies Lough Derg or the Red Lake, containing an island which has long been famous throughout Christendom as the site of St. Patrick's Purgatory. Even to-day more than in the Middle Ages it is the goal of thousands of pious pilgrims who repair thither to be purified of the accumulated sins of a lifetime. In this age of commercialism the picture is an interesting and a happy one, no matter what the changing voices of the many may have to say about it. The following weird legends, which during the autumn of 1909 I found surviving among the Lough Derg peasantry, explain how the lough received its present name, and seem to indicate that long before Patrick's time the lough was already considered a strange and mysterious place, apparently an Otherworld preserve. The first legend, based on two complementary versions, one from James Ryan, of Tamlach Townland, who is seventy-five years old, the other from Arthur Monaghan, a younger man, who lives about three miles from James Ryan, is as follows :—' In his flight from County Armagh, Finn Mac Coul took his mother on his shoulder, holding her by the legs, but so rapidly did he travel that on reaching the shores of the lake nothing remained of his mother save the two legs, and these he threw down there. Some time later, the Fenians, while searching for Finn, passed the same spot on the lake-shore, and Cinen Moul (?), who was of their number, upon seeing the shin-bones of Finn's mother and a worm in one, said : " If that worm could get water enough it would come to something great." " I'll give it water enough," said another of the followers, and at that he flung it into the lake (later called Finn Mac Coul's lake).[1] Immediately the worm turned into an enormous water-monster. This water-monster it was that St. Patrick had to fight and kill ; and, as the struggle went on, the lake ran red with the blood of the water-monster, and so the lake came to be called Loch Derg (Red Lake).' The second legend, composed of folk-opinions, was related by Patrick Monaghan, the caretaker of the Purgatory, as he was rowing me to Saints' Island—the site of the original

[1] J. G. Campbell collected in Scotland two versions of a parallel episode, but concerning Loch Lurgan. In both versions the flight begins by Fionn's foster-mother carrying Fionn, and in both, when she is tired, Fionn carries her and runs so fast that when the loch is reached only her shanks are left. These he throws out on the loch, and hence its name Loch Lurgan, ' Lake of the Shanks.' (*The Fians*, pp. 18–19).

purgatorial cave ; and this legend is even more important
for us than the preceding one :—' I have always been hearing
it said that into this lough St. Patrick drove all the serpents
from Ireland, and that with them he had here his final
battle, gaining complete victory. The old men and women
in this neighbourhood used to believe that Lough Derg was
the last stronghold of the Druids in Ireland ; and from what
I have heard them say, I think the old legend means that
this is where St. Patrick ended his fight with the Druids, and
that the serpents represent the Druids or paganism.'

These and similar legends, together with what we know
about the purgatorial rites, lead us to believe that in pre-
Christian times Finn Mac Coul's Lake, later called Lough
Derg, was venerated as sacred, and that the cave which
then undoubtedly existed on Saints' Island was used as
a centre for the celebration of pagan mysteries similar in
character to those supposed to have been celebrated in
New Grange. Evidently, in the ordeals and ceremonies of
the modern Christian Purgatory of St. Patrick, we see the
survivals of such pagan initiatory rites. Just as the cults of
stones, trees, fountains, lakes, and waters were absorbed
by the new religion, so, it would seem, were all cults rendered
in prehistoric times to Finn Mac Coul's Lake and within the
island cave. Though the present location of the Purgatory
is not the original place of the old Celtic cults, there having
been a transfer from Saints' Island to Station Island, the
present place of pilgrimage, where instead of the cave there
is the ' Prison Chapel ', the practices, though naturally much
modified and corrupted, retain their primitive outlines.
Patrick in his time ordered the observance of the following
ceremonies by all penitents before their entrance into the
original cave on Saints' Island ;[1] and for a long time they were
strictly carried out :—' The visitor must first go to the bishop
of the diocese, declare to him that he came of his own free

---

[1] During the seventeenth century, the English government, acting
through its Dublin representatives, ordered this original Cave or Purgatory to be demolished ; and with the temporary suppression of the
ceremonies which resulted and the consequent abandonment of the island,
the Cave, which may have been filled up, has been lost.

will, and request of him permission to make the pilgrimage. The bishop warned him against venturing any further in his design, and represented to him the perils of his undertaking ; but if the pilgrim still remained steadfast in his purpose, he gave him a recommendatory letter to the prior of the island. The prior again tried to dissuade him from his design by the same arguments that had been previously urged by the bishop. If, however, the pilgrim still remained steadfast, he was taken into the church to spend there fifteen days in fasting and praying. After this the mass was celebrated, the holy communion administered to him and holy water sprinkled over him, and he was led in procession with reading of litanies to the entrance of the purgatory, where a third attempt was made to dissuade him from entering. If he still persisted, the prior allowed him to enter the cave, after he had received the benediction of the priests, and, in entering, he commended himself to their prayers, and made the sign of the cross on his forehead with his own hand. The prior then made fast the door, and opened it not again till the next morning, when, if the penitent were there, he was taken out and led with great joy to the church, and, after fifteen days' watching and praying, was dismissed. If he was not found when the door was opened, it was understood that he had perished in his pilgrimage through purgatory ; the door was closed again, and he was never afterwards mentioned '.

An enormous mass of literary and historical material was recorded during the mediaeval period, in various European vernaculars and in Latin, concerning St. Patrick's Purgatory ; and all of it testifies to the widespread influence of the rites which already then as now attracted thousands of pilgrims from all parts of Christendom. In the poem of *Owayne Miles*,[1] which forms part of this material, we find a poetical description of the purgatorial initiatory rites quite comparable to Virgil's account of Aeneas on his initiatory journey to Hades. The poem records how Sir Owain was locked in the cave, and how, after a short time, he began to penetrate its depths. He had but little light, and this

---

[1] Thomas Wright, *St. Patrick's Purgatory* (London, 1844), pp. 67–8.

by degrees disappeared, leaving him in total darkness. Then a strange twilight appeared. He went on to a hall and there met fifteen men clad in white and with heads shaven after the manner of ecclesiastics. One of them told Owain what things he would have to suffer in his pilgrimage, how unclean spirits would attack him, and by what means he could withstand them. Then the fifteen men left the knight alone, and soon all sorts of demons and ghosts and spirits surrounded him, and he was led on from one torture and trial to another by different companies of fiends. (In the original Latin legend there were four fields of punishment.) Finally Owain came to a magic bridge which appeared safe and wide, but when he reached the middle of it all the fiends and demons and unclean spirits raised so horrible a yell that he almost fell into the chasm below. He, however, reached the other shore, and the power of the devils ceased. Before him was a celestial city, and the perfumed air which was wafted from it was so ravishing that he forgot all his pains and sorrows. A procession came to Owain and, welcoming him, led him into the paradise where Adam and Eve dwelt before they had eaten the apple. Food was offered to the knight, and when he had eaten of it he had no desire to return to earth, but he was told that it was necessary to live out his natural life in the world and to leave his flesh and bones behind him before beginning the heavenly existence. So he began his return journey to the cave's entrance by a short and pleasant way. He again passed the fifteen men clad in white, who revealed what things the future had in store for him ; and reaching the door safely, waited there till morning. Then he was taken out, congratulated, and invited to remain with the priests for fifteen days.[1]

Here we have clearly enough many of the essential features of the underworld : there is the mystic bridge which when crossed guarantees the traveller against evil spirits, just as in Ireland a peasant believes himself safe when fairies are pursuing him if he can only cross a bridge or stream. The celestial city is both like the Christian Heaven and the *Sidhe*

---

[1] Wright, op. cit., p. 69.

world. The eating of angel food by Owain has an effect
quite like that of eating food in Fairyland ; but Owain, by
Christian influence, is sent back on earth to die ' that death
which the King of Heaven and Earth hath ordained,' as
Patrick said of the prince whom he saved from the *Sidhe*-folk.[1]

A curious story, in which King Arthur himself is made to
visit St. Patrick's Purgatory, published during the sixteenth
century by a learned Frenchman, Stephanus Forcatulus,
shows how real a relation there is between Purgatory and
the Greek or Roman Hades. Arthur, it is said, leaving the
light behind him, descended into the cave by a rough and
steep road. ' For they say that this cave is an entrance to
the shades, or at least to purgatory, where poor sinners may
get their offences washed out, and return again rejoicing to
the light of day.' But Forcatulus adds that ' I have learnt
from certain serious commentaries of Merlin, that Gawain,
his master of horse, called Arthur back, and dissuaded him
from examining further the horrid cave in which was heard
the sound of falling water which emitted a sulphureous smell,
and of voices lamenting as it were for the loss of their
bodies '.[2]

Purgatorial and Initiatory Rites

Judging from the above data and from the great mass of
similar data available, the religious rites connected with
St. Patrick's Purgatory are to be anthropologically inter-

---

[1] In the face of all the legends told of pilgrims who have been in Patrick's
Purgatory, it seems that either through religious frenzy like that produced
in Protestant revivals, or else through some strange influence due to the
cave itself after the preliminary disciplines, some of the pilgrims have had
most unusual psychic experiences. Those who have experienced fasting
and a rigorous life for a prescribed period affirm that there results a changed
condition, physical, mental, and spiritual, so that it is very probable that
the Christian pilgrims to the Purgatory, like the pagan pilgrims who ' fasted
on ' the Tuatha De Danann in New Grange, were in good condition to
receive impressions of a psychical nature such as the Society for Psychical
Research is beginning to believe are by no means rare to people susceptible
to them. Neophytes seeking initiation among the ancients had to undergo
even more rigorous preparations than these ; for they were expected while
entranced to leave their physical bodies and in reality enter the purgatorial
state, as we shall presently have occasion to point out.

[2] Wright, *St. Patrick's Purgatory*, pp. 62 ff.

preted in the light of what is known about ancient and modern initiatory ceremonies, similarly conducted. As has already been stated, the original Purgatory which was in a cave on Saints' Island is to-day typified by ' Prison Chapel ' on Station Island ; and in this ' Prison Chapel ', as formerly in the cave, pilgrims, after having fasted and performed the necessary preparatory penances, are required to pass the night. Among the Greeks, neophytes seeking initiation, after similar preparation, entered the cave-shrine recently discovered at Eleusis, the site of the Great Mysteries, and therein, in the *sanctum sanctorum*, entered into communion with the god and goddess of the lower world;[1] whereas in the original Purgatory Sir Owain and Arthur are described as having come into contact with the Hades-world and its beings. In the state cult at Acharaca, Greece, there was another cavern-temple in which initiations were conducted.[1] The oracle of Zeus Trophonius was situated in a subterranean chamber, into which, after various preparatory rites, including the invocation of Agamedes, neophytes descended to receive in a very mysterious manner the divine revelations which were afterwards interpreted for them. So awe-inspiring were the descent into the cave and the sights therein seen that it was popularly believed that no one who visited the cave ever smiled again ; and persons of grave and serious aspect were proverbially said to have been in the cave of Trophonius.[2]

The worship of Mithras, the Persian god of created light and all earthly wisdom, who in time became identified with the sun, was conducted in natural and artificial caves found in every part of the Roman Empire where his cult flourished until superseded by Christianity ; and in these caves very elaborate initiations of seven degrees were carried out. The cave itself signified the lower world, into which during the ordeals of initiation the neophyte was supposed to enter while out of the physical body, that the soul might be purged

---

[1] L. R. Farnell, *Cults of the Greek States* (Oxford, 1907), iii. 126–98, &c.

[2] Cf. Athenaeus, 614 A ; Aristoph., *Nubes*, 508 ; and Harper's *Dict. Class. Lit. and Antiq.*, p. 1615.

by many trials.[1] In Mexico the cavern of Chalchatongo led to the plains of paradise, evidently through initiations; and Mictlan, a subterranean temple, similarly led to the Aztec land of the dead.[2]

Among the most widespread and characteristic features of contemporary primitive races we find highly developed mysteries (puberty institutions) of the same essential character as these ancient mysteries. They are to uncivilized youth what the Greek Mysteries were to Greek youth, and what colleges and universities are to the youth of Europe and America, though perhaps more successful than these last as places of moral and religious instruction. These mysteries vary from tribe to tribe, though in almost all of them there is what corresponds to the Death Rite in Freemasonry; that is to say, there is either a symbolical presentation of death in a sacred drama—as there was among the Greeks in their complete initiatory rites—or a state of actual trance imposed upon each neophyte by the priestly initiators. The *sanctum sanctorum* of these primitive mysteries is sometimes in a natural or artificial cavern (as was the rule with respect to the Ancient Mysteries and St. Patrick's Purgatory on Saints' Island); sometimes in a structure specially prepared to exclude the light; or else the neophytes are symbolically or literally buried in an underground place to be resurrected greatly purified and strengthened.[3] And the mystic purification at the sea-shore and spiritual re-birth sought in the cave at Eleusis by the highly cultured Athenians and their fellow Greeks, or among other cultured and uncultured ancient and modern peoples through some corresponding initiation ceremony, find their parallel in the purification and spiritual re-birth still sought in the Christian Purgatory, now 'Prison Chapel', and in the lake waters, amid the solitude of sacred Lough Derg, Ireland, by thousands of earnest pilgrims from all parts of the world.[4]

---

[1] Cf. O. Seyffert, *Dict. Class. Antiquities*, trans. (London, 1895), *Mithras*.
[2] Brasseur, *Mexique*, iii. 20, &c.; Tylor, *P. C.*,[4] ii. 45.
[3] Cf. Hutton Webster, *Primitive Secret Societies* (New York, 1908), p. 38, and *passim*.
[4] In the ancient Greek world the annual celebration of the Mysteries

There is a correspondence between this conclusion and
what was said about the initiatory aspects of the Aengus
Cult ; and should we try to connect the Purgatory with
some particular sun-cult of a character parallel to that
of the Aengus Cult we should probably have to name Lug,
the great Irish sun-god, because of the significant fact
that the purgatorial rites on Station Island come to an end

drew great concourses of people from all regions round the Mediterranean ;
to the modern Breton world the chief religious Pardons are annual events
of such supreme importance that, after preparing plenty of food for the
pilgrimage, the whole family of a pious peasant of Lower Brittany will desert
farm and work dressed in their beautiful and best costumes for one of these
Pardons, the most picturesque, the most inspiring, and the highest folk-
festivals still preserved by the Roman Church ; while to Roman Catholics
in all countries a pilgrimage to Lough Derg is the sacred event of a lifetime.
    In the Breton Pardons, as in the purgatorial rites, we seem to see the
survivals of very ancient Celtic Mysteries strikingly like the Mysteries of
Eleusis. The greatest of the Pardons, the Pardon of St. Anne d'Auray,
will serve as a basis for comparison ; and while in some respects it has had
a recent and definitely historical origin (or revival), this origin seems on
the evidence of archaeology to have been a restoration, an expansion, and
chiefly a Christianization of prehistoric rites then already partly fallen
into decay. Such rites remained latent in the folk-memory, and were
originally celebrated in honour of the sacred fountain, and probably also of
Isis and the child, whose terra-cotta image was ploughed up in a neighbouring field by the famous peasant Nicolas, and naturally regarded by him
and all who saw it as of St. Anne and the Holy Child. Thus, in the Pardon
of St. Anne d'Auray, which extends over three days, there is a torch-light
procession at night under ecclesiastical sanction ; as in the Ceres Mysteries,
wherein the neophytes with torches kindled sought all night long for
Proserpine. There are purification rites, not especially under ecclesiastical
sanction, at the holy fountain now dedicated to St. Anne, like the purification rites of the Eleusinian worshippers at the sea-shore and their visit
to a holy well. There are mystery plays, recently instituted, as in Greek
initiation ceremonies ; sacred processions, led by priests, bearing the image
of St. Anne and other images, comparable to Greek sacred processions
in which the god Iacchos was borne on the way to Eleusis. The all-night
services in the dimly-lighted church of St. Anne, with the special masses in
honour of the Christian saints and for the dead, are parallel to the midnight
ceremonies of the Greeks in their caves of initiation and to the libations to
the gods and to the spirits of the departed at Greek initiations. Finally,
in the Greek mysteries there seems to have been some sort of expository
sermon or exhortation to the assembled neophytes quite comparable to
the special appeal made to the faithful Catholics assembled in the magnificent church of St. Anne d'Auray by the bishops and high ecclesiastics of
Brittany. (For these Classical parallels compare Farnell, *Cults of the Greek
States*, iii, *passim*.)

on the Festival of the Assumption of the Blessed Virgin, the 15th of August, a date which apparently coincides sufficiently to represent, as it probably does, the ancient August Lugnasadh, the 1st of August, a day sacred to the sun-god Lug, as the name indicates.[1]

If we are to class together the original Purgatory, New Grange, Gavrinis, and other Celtic underground places, as centres of the highest religious practices in the past, we should expect to discover that many similar structures or natural caverns existed in pagan Ireland, as indeed we find they did. Thus in different Irish manuscripts various caves are mentioned,[2] and most of them, so far as they can be localized, are traditionally places of supernatural marvels, and often (as in the case of the last one enumerated, the Cave of Cruachan) are directly related to the under-world.[3] Another of these caves is described as being under a church, which circumstance suggests that the church was dedicated over an underground place originally sacred to pagan worship, and, as we may safely assume, to pagan mysteries.

The curious custom among early Irish Christians, of retiring for a time to a cave, seems to show the lasting into historical times of the pagan cave-ritual now surviving at Lough Derg only. The custom seems to have been common among the saints of Britain and of Scotland;[4] and in Stokes's *Tripartite Life of Patrick* (p. 242) there is a very significant reference to it. In the *Mabinogion* story of *Kulhwch and Olwen* there seems to be another traditional echo of the times when caves were used for religious rites or worship, in the author's reference to the cave of the witch Orddu as being ' on the confines of Hell '. A cave was thus popularly sup-

---

[1] Cf. Rhŷs, *Hib. Lect.*, p. 411, &c.

[2] O'Curry, *Lectures*, pp. 586–7.

[3] There is this very significant legend on record about the Cave of Cruachan :—' Magh Mucrime, now, pigs of magic came out of the cave of Cruachain, and that is Ireland's gate of Hell.' And ' Out of it, also, came the Red Birds that withered up everything in Erin that their breath would touch, till the Ulstermen slew them with their slings.' (*B. of Leinster*, p. 288 a ; Stokes's trans., in *Rev. Celt.*, xiii. 449 ; cf. *Silva Gadelica*, ii. 353.)

[4] Forbes, *Lives of S. Ninian and S. Kentigern* (Edinburgh, 1874), pp. 285, 345.

posed to lead to Hades or an underworld of fairies, demons, and spirits ; again just as in St. Patrick's Purgatory. Purely Celtic instances of this kind might be greatly multiplied.

PAGAN ORIGIN OF PURGATORIAL DOCTRINE

The metrical romance of *Orfeo and Herodys* in Ritson's *Collection of Metrical Romances* [1] illustrates how in Britain (and Britain—even England—is more Celtic than Saxon) the Grecian Hell or Hades was looked on as identical with the Celtic Fairyland. This is quite unusual ; and for us is highly significant. It shows that in Britain, at the time the romance was written, there was no essential difference between the underworld of fairies and the underworld of shades. Pluto's realm and the realm where fairy kings and fairy queens held high revelry were the same. The difference is this : Hades was an Egyptian and in turn a Greek conception, while Fairyland was a Celtic conception ; they differ as the imagination at work on a philosophical doctrine differs among the three peoples, and not otherwise. And, as Wright has shown, the origin of Purgatory in the Roman Church is very obscure. As to the location of Purgatory, Roman theology confesses it has nothing certain to say.[2] The natural conclusion, as we suggested in our study of Re-birth, would seem to be that the Irish doctrine of the Otherworld in all its aspects, but especially as the underground world of the *Sidhe* or fairy-folk, was combined with the pagan Graeco-Roman doctrine of Hades in St. Patrick's Purgatory, and hence gave rise to the modern Christian doctrine of Purgatory.

CHRISTIAN RITES IN HONOUR OF THE DEPARTED

We may now readily pass from an examination of world-wide rites concerned with death and re-birth, which are based on an ancient sun-cult, to an examination of their shadows in the theology of Christianity, where they are commonly known as the rites in honour of the departed. It seems to

---

[1] Cf. Wright, *St. Patrick's Purgatory*, pp. 81-2.
[2] Cf. Godescard, *Vies des Saints*, xi. 24 ; also Bergier, *Dict. de Théol.*, v. 405.

be clear at the outset that the Christian Fête in Commemoration of the Dead, according to its history, is an adaptation from paganism; and with so many Irish ecclesiastics, or else their disciples, educated in the Celtic monasteries of Britain and Ireland, having influence in the Church during the early centuries, there is a strong probability that the Feast of *Samain* had something to do with shaping the modern feast, as we have suggested in the preceding chapter; for both feasts originally fell on the first of November. Roman Catholic writers record that it was St. Odilon, Abbot of Cluny, who instituted in 998 in all his congregations the Fête in Commemoration of the Dead, and fixed its anniversary on the first of November; and that this fête was quickly adopted by all the churches of the East.[1] To-day in the Roman Church both the first and second of November are holy days devoted to those who have passed out of this life. The first day, the Fête of All the Saints (*La Toussaint*), is said to have originated thus: the Roman Pantheon— Pantheon meaning the residence of all the gods—was dedicated to Jupiter the Avenger, and when Christianity triumphed the pagan images were overthrown, and there was thereupon originally established, in place of the cult of all the gods, the Fête of all the Saints.[2] Why *La Toussaint* should have become a feast of the dead would be difficult to say unless we admit the ancient Celtic feast of the dead as having amalgamated with it. This we believe is what took place; for if the Fête in Commemoration of the Dead was, as some authorities hold, established by St. Odilon to fall on the first of November, in direct accord with *Samain* or Halloween, then at some later period it was displaced by *La Toussaint*, for now it is celebrated on the second of November.

Likewise prayers and masses for the dead, which annually

---

[1] Cf. Godescard, *Vies des Saints*, xi. 32. But there is some disagreement in this matter of dates: Petrus Damianus, *Vita S. Odilonis*, in the Bollandist *Acta Sanctorum*, January 1, records a legend of how the Abbot Odilon decreed that November 2, the day after All Saints' Day, should be set apart for services for the departed (cf. Tylor, *Prim. Cult.*,⁴ ii. 37 n.).

[2] Cf. Godescard, *Vies des Saints*, xi. 1 n.

receive emphasis on the first two days of November, seem to have had their origin in pre-Christian cults. According to Mosheim, in his *Histoire ecclésiastique*,[1] the usage of celebrating the Sacrament at the tombs of martyrs and at funerals was introduced during the fourth century; and from this usage the masses for the saints and for the dead originated in the eighth century. Prior to the fourth century we find the newly converted Christians in all parts of Celtic Europe, and in many countries non-Celtic, still rendering a cult to ancestral spirits, making food offerings at the tombs of heroes, and strictly observing the very ancient November feast, or its equivalent, in honour of the dead and fairies. Then, very gradually, in the course of four centuries, the character of the Christian cults and feasts of the saints and of the dead seems to have been determined. The following citation will serve to illustrate the nature of Irish Christian rites in honour of the dead :—In the *Lebar Brecc*[2] we read : ' There is nothing which one does on behalf of the soul of him who has died that doth not help it, both prayer on knees, and abstinence, and singing requiems, and frequent blessings. Sons are bound to do penance for their deceased parents. A full year, now, was Maedóc of Ferns, with his whole community, on water and bread, after loosing from hell the soul of Brandub son of Echaid.'

According to St. Augustine, the souls of the dead are solaced by the piety of their living friends when this expresses itself through sacrifice made by the Church ; [3] St. Ephrem commanded his friends not to forget him after death, but to give proofs of their charity in offering for the repose of his soul alms, prayers, and sacrifices, especially on the thirtieth day ; [3] Constantine the Great wished to be interred under the Church of the Apostles in order that his soul might be benefited by the prayers offered to the saints, by the mystic sacrifice, and by the holy communion.[3] Such prayers and

---

[1] Part II, sec. 4 ; c. 4, par. 8 ; cf. Bergier, *Dict. de Théol.*, iv. 322.
[2] P. 11ᵃ, l. 19 ; in Stokes's *Tripartite Life*, Intro., p. 194.
[3] *Enchiridion*, chap. cx ; *Testament of St. Ephrem* (ed. Vatican), ii. 230, 236 ; Euseb., *de Vita Constant.*, liv. iv, c. lx. 556, c. lxx. 562 ; cf. Godescard, *Vies des Saints*, xi. 30–1.

sacrifices for the dead were offered by the Church sometimes during thirty and even forty days, those offered on the third, the seventh, and the thirtieth days being the most solemn.[1] The history of the venerable Bede, the letters of St. Boniface, and of St. Lul prove that even in the ancient Anglican church prayers were offered up for the souls of the dead ; [2] and a council of bishops held at Canterbury in 816 ordered that immediately after the death of a bishop there shall be made for him prayers and alms.[2]   At Oxford, in 1437, All Souls College was founded, chiefly as a place in which to offer prayers on behalf of the souls of all those who were killed in the French wars of the fifteenth century.

CONCLUSION

As seems to be evident from this and the two preceding chapters, all these fêtes, rites, or observances of Christianity have a relation more or less direct to paganism, and thus to ancient Celtic cults and sacrifice offered to the dead, to spirits, and to the Tuatha De Danann or Fairies. And the same set of ideas which operated among the Celts to create their Fairy-Mythology—ideas arising out of a belief in or knowledge of the one universal Realm of Spirit and its various orders of invisible inhabitants—gave the Egyptians, the Indians, the Greeks, the Romans, the Teutons, the Mexicans, the Peruvians, and all nations their respective mythologies and religions ; and we moderns are literally ' the heirs of all the ages '.

[1] St. Ambroise, *de Obitu Theodosii*, ii. 1197 ; cf. Godescard, *Vies des Saints*, xi. 31 n.

[2] Cf. Godescard, *Vies des Saints*, xi. 31-2.

SECTION IV

MODERN SCIENCE AND THE FAIRY FAITH; AND CONCLUSIONS [1]

CHAPTER XI

SCIENCE AND FAIRIES

'Puzzling and weird occurrences have been vouched for among all nations and in every age. It is possible to relegate a good many asserted occurrences to the domain of superstition, but it is not possible thus to eliminate all.'—SIR OLIVER LODGE.

Method of Examination : Exoteric and Esoteric Aspects—The X-quantity —Scientific Attitudes toward the Animistic Hypothesis : Materialistic Theory ; Pathological Theory ; Delusion and Imposture Theory— Problems of Consciousness : Dreams ; Supernormal Lapse of Time— Psychical Research and Fairies : Myers's Researches—Present Position of Psychical Research—Psychical Research and Anthropology in relation to Fairy-Faith, according to a special contribution from Mr. Andrew Lang—Final Testing of the X-quantity—Conclusion : the Celtic belief in Fairies and in Fairyland is scientific.

METHOD OF EXAMINATION

THE promise made in the Introduction to examine the Why of the belief in fairies must now be fulfilled by calling in the aid of modern science. To adduce parallels when studying a religion or a mythology is worth doing, in order to show the fundamental bond which unites all systems of belief in things called spiritual ; but it is more important to try to understand why there should be such parallels and such a unifying principle behind them. Perhaps there has

[1] I am indebted to Mr. William McDougall, M.A., Wilde Reader in Mental Philosophy in the University of Oxford, for having read through and criticized the first draft of this section ; and while he is in no way responsible for the views set forth herein, nevertheless his suggestions for the improvement of their scientific framework have been of very great value. I must also express my obligation to him for having suggested through his Oxford lectures a good share of the important material interwoven into chapter xii touching the vitalistic view of evolution.

been too much of a tendency among students of folk-lore, and of anthropology as a whole, to be content to do no more than to discover that the Eskimos in Greenland hold a belief in spirits parallel to a belief in spirits held in Central Africa, or that the Greek Pantheon (and possibly the Celtic one as well) consists of goddesses which are apparently pre-Aryan and of gods which are apparently Aryan. We, too, have drawn many parallels between the Celtic Fairy-Faith and the various fairy-faiths throughout the world ; but now we should attempt to find out why there are animistic beliefs at all.

This chapter, then, will confine itself to a scientific examination of the more popular or, as it may be called, the exoteric aspect of the Fairy-Faith, which has come to us directly from the masses of the Celtic peoples. The following chapter, which is corollary to the present one, will deal especially with the mystical aspect or, as this may be called by contrast, the esoteric aspect of the same belief, which, in turn, has come to us from learned mystics and seers, who form, in proportion, but a very small minority of the modern Celts. Each of these complementary aspects of the Celtic religion undoubtedly has its origin in the remotest antiquity. This is probably more readily seen with respect to the former than to the latter. The latter has been esoteric always, and in our opinion shows an unbroken tradition (if only a very incomplete one) from druidic times ; and it depends less upon written records, because the Druids had none, than upon oral transmission from age to age. Both aspects of the Fairy-Faith have in modern times absorbed many ideas from non-Celtic systems of religion and mystical thought. As Mr. Jenner has suggested in his Introduction for Cornwall, and as certain details in chapter ii clearly indicate, systems of modern theosophy have had a marked influence in this respect ; but it is impossible for us to-day to say what parts of the Fairy-Faith are purely Celtic and what are not so, because comparative studies prove that mysticism is fundamentally the same in all ages and among all peoples. It is psychologically true, also, that there must always exist some sort of affinity between two sets of thought in order for them to coalesce. Hence, if modern mysticism (derived from Oriental or other sources) has, as we believe, affected Celtic mysticism as handed down from the dim druidic ages, it is merely because the two occupy a common psychical territory. We must therefore be content to examine scientifically the Fairy-Faith as it now presents itself.

The analysis of evidence in chapter iii indicates clearly that there is in the exoteric part of the modern Celtic belief in fairies considerable degeneration from what must have been in pagan times a widespread and highly developed animistic creed. In the esoteric part of it there will be observed, instead of such degeneracy, a surprisingly elaborate system of the most subtle speculation, which parallels that of East Indian systems of metaphysics. If the belief be looked at in this comprehensive manner, it seems to be clear that to some extent at least, as has been pointed out already (pp. 99, 257), the Fairy-Faith in its purest form originated amongst the most highly educated and scientific Celts of ancient times rather than among their unlearned fellows. The two aspects of the belief form an harmonious whole as they will be presented in this Section IV. Chapter xi depends mostly upon the evidence set forth in chapter ii. Chapter xii depends mostly upon the evidence set forth in chapter vii.

In chapter iii we examined anthropologically the modern; and (both there and in parts of chapters following) the historical and ancient belief in fairies in Celtic countries, and found it to be in essence animistic. Folk-imagination, social psychology, anthropomorphism generally, adequately explained by far the greater mass of the evidence presented; but the animistic background of the belief in question presented problems which the strictly anthropological sciences are unable to solve. The point has now been reached when these problems must be presented to physiology and to psychology for solution. If they can be completely solved by purely rational and physical data, then the Fairy-Faith as a whole will have to be cast aside as worthless in the eyes of science.

In our generation, however, such a casting aside is not to be the fate of the folk-religion of the Celts : the following phenomena recorded in chapter ii and elsewhere throughout our study, and designated as the x- or unknown quantity of the Fairy-Faith, cannot at the present time be satisfactorily explained by science : (1) Collective hallucinations and veridical hallucinations ; (2) objects moving without contact ; (3) raps and noises called ' supernatural ' ; (4) telepathy ; (5) seership and visions ; (6) dream and trance states manifesting supernormal knowledge ; (7) ' mediumship ' or ' spirit-possession '. Independently of our own Celtic data in their support, the first class of phenomena are supported by an enormous mass of good data scientifically collected ; the second and third class are less well supported ; telepathy is almost generally accepted as now being established ; the last three classes are hypothetically accepted by many authorities in pathology, psychology, and psychical research.

SCIENTIFIC ATTITUDES TOWARDS THE ANIMISTIC HYPOTHESIS

Assertions similar to ours, that phenomena like these are incapable of being explained away by any known laws of orthodox science, have helped to bring about a marked division in the ranks of scientific workers. On one hand there are those scientists who deny the existence of anything not capable of being mathematically tested, weighed, dissected, or otherwise analysed in laboratories ; on the other hand, there are their colleagues who, often in spite of previous bias toward materialism, have arrived at a personal conviction that an animistic view of man is more in harmony with their scientific experience than any other. Both schools include men eminent in all branches of biological sciences.

Midway between these contending schools are the psychophysicists who maintain that man is a twofold being composed of a psychical and physical part. Some of them are inclined to favour animism, others are unwilling to regard the psychical part of man as separable from the physical part. So the world of science is divided.

Under such chaotic conditions of science it is our right to accept one view or another, or to reject all views and use scientific data independently. There can be no final court of appeal in matters where opinion is thus divided, save the experience of coming generations. We are therefore content to state our own position and leave it to the future for rejection or acceptance, as the case may be. To attempt a critical examination of the thousand and one theories occupying the modern arena of scientific controversy about the essential nature of man is altogether beyond the scope of this work. We must, nevertheless, blaze a rough footpath through the jungle of scientific theories, and, at the outset, put on record our opposition to that school of scientific workers who deny to man a supersensuous constitution. Their theory, if carried out to its logical conclusion, is now essentially no different from Feuerbach's theory at a time when science was far less developed than it is to-day. He held that ' the object of sense, or the sensuous, alone is really true, and therefore truth, reality, and the sensible are one '.[1] To say that we know reality through sensual perception is an error, as all schools of scientists must nowadays admit. Nature is for ever illuding the senses ; she masquerades in disguise until science tears away her mask. We must always adjust the senses to the world itself : where there are only vibrations in ether, man sees light ; and in atmospheric vibrations he hears sound. We only know things through the way in which our senses react upon them. We sum up the world-problem by saying : ' consciousness does not exhaust its object, the world.'[1] Perceptibility and reality thus not being coincident, man and the universe remain an unsolved problem, despite the noisy shoutings of the materialist in his hermetically sealed and light-excluding case called sensual perceptions. Science admits that all her explanations of the universe are mere products of human understanding and perceptions by the physical senses : the

[1] Cf. C. Du Prel, *Philosophy of Mysticism* (London, 1889), i. 7, 11.

universe of science is wholly a universe of phenomena, and behind phenomena, as no scientist would dare deny, there must be the noumena, the ultimate causes of all things, as to which science as yet offers no comprehensive hypothesis, much less an answer. To consider the materialistic hypothesis as adequate to account for the residuum or x-quantity of the Fairy-Faith would not even be reasonable, and, incontestably, would not be scientific.

When scientists holding to the non-animistic view of life are driven from their now for the most part abandoned fortress built by German scientists of the last century, of whom Feuerbach was a type, they, in opposing the animists, occupy a more modernly equipped fortress called the Pathological Theory. This theory is that ' mediumship', telepathy, hallucinations, or the voluntary and involuntary exercise of any so-called ' psychical ' faculties on the part of men and women, with the resulting phenomena, can be explained as due to abnormal and hence—according to its point of view—diseased states of the human organism, or to some derangement of bodily functions, leading to delusions resembling those of insanity, which by a sort of hypnosis telepathically induced may even affect researchers and lead them into erroneous conclusions. All scientists are in agreement with the Pathological Theory in so far as it rejects as unworthy of serious consideration all apparitions and abnormal phenomena save those observed by sane and healthy percipients under ordinary conditions. And, accordingly, whenever there can be shown in our percipients a diseased mental or psychical state, we must eliminate their testimony without argument. But since we have endeavoured to present no testimony from Celtic percipients who are not physically and psychically normal, the Pathological Theory at best can affect the x-quantity merely hypothetically.

The following admission in regard to visual and auditory hallucinations is here worth noting as coming from so thorough an exponent of materialistic psychology as M. Théodule Ribot :—' There must exist anatomical and physiological causes which would solve the problem, but unfor-

tunately they are hidden from us.' Of these hidden causes,
which he thinks create all psychical states of mind or consciousness called by him ' disease of personality ', M. Ribot
says :—' Our ignorance of the causes stops us short. The
psychologist is here like the physician who has to deal with
a disease in which he can make out only the symptoms.
What physiological influences are they which thus alter the
general tone of the organism, consequently of the coenaes-
thesis, consequently too of the memory ? Is it some condition
of the vascular system ? Or some inhibitory action, some
arrest of function ? We cannot say.' [1] And after six years
of most careful experimentation, M. Charles Richet, Professor of Physiology in the Faculty of Medicine in Paris,
reached this conclusion :—' There exists in certain persons at
certain moments a faculty of acquiring knowledge which
has no *rapport* with our normal faculties of that kind.' [2] We
seem to have here the last words of science touching the
Pathological Theory.

When driven from their pathological stronghold, and they
maintain that they have not been driven from it, the non-
animists always find a safe way to cover their retreat by
setting up the charge that all psychical phenomena are
fraudulent or else due to delusion on the part of observers.
In reply, psychical researchers readily admit that there is
a large percentage of mere trickery, delusion, and imposture
in observed ' spirit ' phenomena ; some of which is deliberate
on the part of the ' medium ' and some of which is apparently
not consciously induced. Nevertheless, such investigators are
not at all willing to say that there is nothing more than this.
The Delusion and Imposture Theory will account for a very
respectable proportion of these phenomena, but not for all
of them, and theoretically we shall admit its application to
the parallel phenomena attributed to fairies ; though it must
be acknowledged that ' fairy ' phenomena are for the most
part spontaneously exhibited rather than as in ' Spiritualism '

---

[1] T. Ribot, *The Diseases of Personality* ; cf. J. L. Nevius, *Demon Possession* (London, 1897), pp. 234-5.
[2] *Proc. S. P. R.* (London), v. 167 ; cf. A. Lang, *Making of Religion*, p. 64.

set up through holding *séances*. Further, there are comparatively few ' charmers ' or ' wise men '—the fairy ' mediums ' among the Celts—who ever make money out of their ability to deal with the ' good people', or *Tylwyth Teg* ; whence the margin of encouragement for fraudulent production of ' fairy ' phenomena is extremely limited when compared with ' Spiritualism '.

After twenty-five years of experimentation, more or less continuous, with ' mediums ', during which every conceivable test for the detection of fraud on their part was applied, William James put his conclusions on record in these words :— ' When imposture has been checked off as far as possible, when chance coincidence has been allowed for, when opportunities for normal knowledge on the part of the subject have been noted, and skill in " fishing " and following clues unwittingly furnished by the voice or face of bystanders have been counted in, those who have the fullest acquaintance with the phenomena admit that in good mediums *there is a residuum of knowledge displayed* [italics are James's own] that can only be called supernormal : the medium taps some source of information not open to ordinary people.'[1]   Mr. Andrew Lang, one of the bravest of psychical researchers in England, not only would agree with William James in this, but, having carefully examined the Delusion and Imposture Theory from the more commanding point of view of an anthropologist, would go further and include classical spiritualistic phenomena as well as those existing among contemporary uncultured races. He says :—' Meanwhile, the extraordinary similarity of savage and classical spiritualistic rites, with the corresponding similarity of alleged modern phenomena, raises problems which it is more easy to state than to solve. For example, such occurrences as " rappings ", as the movement of untouched objects, as the lights of the *séance* room, are all easily feigned. But that ignorant modern knaves should feign precisely the same raps, lights, and movements as the most remote and un-

---

[1] W. James, *Confidences of a ' Psychical Researcher'*, in *American Magazine* (October 1909).

sophisticated barbarians, and as the educated Platonists of
the fourth century after Christ, and that many of the other
phenomena should be identical in each case, is certainly
noteworthy.'[1] Evidently, then, there is a large proportion
of psychical and 'fairy' phenomena which remain unexplained even after the Delusion and Imposture Theory has
been applied to such phenomena, and in all such cases we
must look further for a scientific explanation.

PROBLEMS OF CONSCIOUSNESS

Our chief investigations will at first be directed more
especially to the problems common both to psychology and
to psychical research, namely, dream and trance states,
hallucinations, and possessions, in order to show what
bearings, if any, they have in the eyes of science upon
parallel phenomena said to be due to fairies, and set forth
in chapter ii and anthropologically examined in chapter iii.

Dreams

The popular opinion that dreams are nonsense is quite
overthrown by definite psychological facts. When during
sleep our sensory organs are exposed to external irritants
the impressions physically produced are transmitted to the
brain by the nervous system and react in dreams as they
would in the waking state, except that the reactions in the
two states of consciousness—the dream state and the waking
state—differ in proportion as the two states differ; but in
both the Ego is the real percipient.[2] Such stimuli as arise
from after-theatre dinners, wine-parties, and so forth, produce a well-known type of dreams ; and the same stimuli
at the same period of time would produce an equal effect,
though an altered one, to suit the altered psycho-physical

---

[1] A. Lang, *Cock Lane and Common Sense* (London, 1896), p. 35.

[2] According to Professor Freud, the well-known neurologist of Vienna,
external stimuli are not admitted to the dream-consciousness in the same
manner that they would be admitted to the waking-consciousness, but
they are disguised and altered in particular ways (cf. S. Freud, *Die Traumdeutung*, 2nd ed., Vienna, 1909 ; and S. Ferenczi, *The Psychological Analysis
of Dreams*, in *Amer. Journ. Psych.*, April 1910, No. 2, xxi. 318, &c.).

conditions, if the waking state were active rather than the dream state, just as would all dreams which arise from pathological disturbances in disease, or abnormal physiological functions. This is evident from dreams of a morbid and sensual type, which directly affect the physical organism and its functions as parallel waking-states would. In all such dreams of the lower order, animal and purely physical tendencies, which are directly due to the state of the body, act very freely : an imperfectly balanced, temporarily deranged, or diseased organism must correspondingly respond to its driving forces. And it is clear from comparative study of phenomena that these lower kinds of dream states express only the lower or animal consciousness, which in most individuals is the predominant or only consciousness even in the waking life ; and not the higher consciousness of the Ego or subconsciousness which may be expressed in somnambulism, for ' in somnambulism there awakes an inner, second Ego ',[1] which is the Subliminal Self of Myers. Dr. G. F. Stout urges against Myers's theory of the Subliminal Self that ' the usual incoherence of dreams is an objection to regarding them as manifestations of a stream of thought equal or superior in systematic complexity and continuity to that of the waking self ',[2] which objection Myers also observed. But if we regard all dreams which are of the lower order as being due to the imperfect response of the body to its driving forces because of various bad physical conditions in the body, and recognize that these driving forces depend ultimately on the subconsciousness, the difficulty seems to be met by observing that under such conditions there is no real mergence of the normal consciousness into the subconsciousness. Hence ordinary dreams are within the ordinary spectrum of consciousness ; but extra-ordinary dreams pass beyond the ordinary spectrum into the truly supernormal state of consciousness.

[1] Du Prel, op. cit., i. 135.
[2] G. F. Stout, *Mr. F. W. Myers on ' Human Personality and its Survival of Bodily Death '*, in *Hibbert Journal*, ii, No. 1 (London, October 1903), p. 56.

As all this indicates, dreams are of many classes : those of the lowest type, which we have explained as due to bad physiological conditions in the animal-man ; those which are readily explainable as distorted reflections of waking actions, often based on some stray thought or suggestion of the day and then comparable to post-hypnotic suggestions. Other dreams are demonstrably entirely outside the range of ordinary mental or physical disturbances, actions, reflections, or suggestions of the waking life, and seem thus ' to have a wider purview, and to indicate that the record of external events which is kept within us is far fuller than we know '.[1] In some dreams there is reasoning as well as memory, and mathematicians have been known to solve problems in sleep : an American inventor known to the writer's mother asserted that he had dreamt out the details of a certain ice-manu- facturing process which proved successful when tested ; through self-suggestion set up in the waking state, R. L. Stevenson, upon entering the dream state, secured details for his imaginary romances.[2] Dr. Stout himself, in criticizing Myers's ' Subliminal Self ', admits that ' in some very rare instances, a man has achieved, while dreaming, intellectual performances equalling or perhaps surpassing the best of which he was capable in waking life ';[3] and there are many authentic cases of dream experiences which cannot possibly be explained as revivals of facts fallen out of the range of the ordinary memory or consciousness. We seem to be led to some hypothesis like this : in dreaming there is mental activity which in the waking state is either functionless or else below the psycho-physical threshold of sensibility ; because much that is subconscious in the non-dream state is in the dream state fully conscious. And we probably do not remember one quarter of our dreams : they belong to a mainly different order of consciousness.

Professor Freud's view of dreams coincides pretty generally

[1] F. W. H. Myers, *Human Personality and its Survival of Bodily Death* (London, 1903), i. 131.

[2] R. L. Stevenson, *Across the Plains*, chapter on Dreams.

[3] Stout, op. cit., p. 54.

with this view. He holds that the subconsciousness is the storehouse out of which dream contents are drawn and acted upon by the dream mind. Very much distortion of the subconscious material takes place in the process, due to what he calls the ' endopsychic censor '. In the waking state this censor is always on the alert to keep out of consciousness all subconscious processes or deposits, but in sleep the censor is less alert, and allows some subconscious content to escape over into the ordinary consciousness. The result is a dream distorted out of all recognition of its origin. Such a dream seems to occupy a position midway between what we have classed as the lowest or animal-mind dream and the highest or subliminal dream. It possibly shows an harmonious psycho-physical condition of the dream life, whereas the lowest type of dream shows the preponderance of the physical or animal, and the highest type of dream shows the preponderance of the psychical elements in man. Further, it may be designated as the normal dream, and the other two types respectively as the physically abnormal and the psychically abnormal.

Professor Freud detects other marked processes in the dream state, all of which help to illustrate the part of the Fairy-Faith dependent upon dreaming experiences. (1) There is condensation of details frequently in a proportion so great as one for ten and one for twenty ; (2) displacement of details, or ' a transvaluation of all values ' ; (3) much dramatization ; (4) regression, a retrograde movement of abstract mental processes toward their primary conceptions ; and (5) secondary elaboration, an attempt to rationalize all dream-material.[1] Also, Professor Freud discovered from his analysis of thousands of dreams that the subconsciousness makes use of a sort of symbolism :—' This symbolism in part varies with the individual, but in part is of a typical nature, and seems to be identical with the symbolism which we suppose to lie behind our myths and legends. It is not impossible that these latter creations of the people may find

---

[1] Freud, op. cit. ; Ferenczi, op. cit. ; E. Jones, *Freud's Theory of Dreams*, in *Amer. Journ. Psych.*, April 1910, No. 2, xxi. 283–308.

their explanation from the study of dreams.'[1] Such processes, taken as a whole, show that man possesses a twofold consciousness, the ordinary consciousness and the subconsciousness. And we have every reason to believe that subconscious activities go on continually, in waking and in sleeping.

By experiments on his own perfectly healthy children, Wienholt proved that there are natural forces existing whose stimulations are never perceived in waking life : he made passes over the face and neck of his son with an iron key at the distance of half an inch without touching him, whereupon the boy began to rub those parts and manifested uneasiness. Wienholt likewise experimented on his other children with lead, zinc, gold, and other metals, and in most cases the children ' averted the parts so treated, rubbed them, or drew the clothes over them '.[2] Therefore, in sleep the consciousness perceives objects without physical contact ; and this not inconceivably might suggest, inversely, that in sleep the human consciousness can affect objects without physical contact, as it is said fairies and the dead can, and in the way psychical researchers know that objects can be affected.

We have on record an account of a most remarkable dream quite the same in character as dreams wherein certain Celts believe they have met the dead or fairies. Professor Hilprecht had a broken Assyrian cylinder in cuneiform which he could not decipher ; but in a dream an Assyrian priest in ancient garb appeared to him and deciphered the inscription. Of this dream Myers observed :—' We seem to have reached the utmost intensity of sleep faculty within the limits of our ordinary spectrum.'[3]

We may sum up the results of our examination of dreams by saying that scientific analysis of the dream life *in its higher ranges* proves that our Ego is not wholly embraced in self-consciousness, that the Ego exceeds the self-con-

---

[1] Freud, *The Origin and Development of Psychoanalysis*, in *Amer. Journ. Psych.*, April 1910, No. 2, xxi. 203.

[2] Du Prel, op. cit., i. 33.   [3] Myers, op. cit., i. 134.

sciousness. Instead of a continuity of consciousness which
constitutes self-consciousness we have parallel states of con
sciousness for the one subject, the Ego. Our study of the
Celtic theory of re-birth, in the following chapter, will further
explain this subtle aspect of the dream psychology.

When such a conclusion is applied to the Fairy-Faith, the
various dream-like or trance-like states during which ancient
and contemporary Celts testify to having been in Fairyland are seen to be scientifically plausible. In this aspect
then, Fairyland, stripped of all its literary and imaginative
glamour and of its social psychology, in the eyes of science
resolves itself into a reality, because it is one of the states of
consciousness co-ordinate with the ordinary consciousness.
This statement will be confirmed by a brief examination of
what is called ' supernatural lapse of time ', and which is
invariably connected with Fairyland.

' Supernatural ' Lapse of Time

It has already been made clear that in the dream or
somnambulic state there are invariably modifications of time
and space relations ; and these give rise to what has been
termed the ' supernatural lapse of time '. Two conditions
are possible : either a few minutes of waking-state time
equal long periods in the non-waking state ; or else, as is
usually the case in the Fairy-Faith, the reverse is true.

The first condition, which we shall examine first, occasionally appears in the Fairy-Faith through such a statement as
this :—' Sometimes one may thus go to Faerie for an hour
or two ' (p. 39). Similarly, as physicians well know, patients
under narcotics will experience events extending over long
periods of time within a few minutes of normal time. De
Quincey, the famous opium-eater, records dreams of ten to
sixty years' supernatural duration, and some quite beyond
all limits of the waking experience. Fechner records a case
of a woman who was nearly drowned and then resuscitated
after two minutes of unconsciousness, and who in that time
lived over again all her past life.[1] Another even more remark-

[1] Fechner, *Zentralblatt für Anthropologie*, p. 774 ; cf. Du Prel, op. cit., i. 92.

able case than this last concerns Admiral Beaufort, who,
having fallen into the water, was unconscious also for two
minutes, and yet he says that not only during that short
space of time did he travel over every incident of his life
with the details of ' every minute and collateral feature ', but
that there crowded into his imagination ' many trifling events
which had long been forgotten '.[1]

We shall now present examples to illustrate the second
condition. Höhne was in an unbroken magnetic sleep from
the first of January to the tenth of May, and when he came
out of it he was overcome with surprise to see that spring
had arrived, he having lain down—as he believed—only the
day before.[2] Had Höhne been an Irishman, he might very
reasonably have explained the situation by saying that he
had been with the fairies for what seemed only a night.
The Seeress of Prevorst, in a similar sleep, passed through
a period of six years and five months, and then awoke as
from a one-night sleep with no memory of what she did
during that time ; but some time afterwards memory of the
period came to her so completely that she recalled all its
details.[3] Old people, and some young people too, among
the Celts, who go to Fairyland for varying periods of time,
sometimes extending over weeks (as in a case I knew in
West Ireland), have just such dreams or trance-states as
this. Another example follows :—Chardel, in fleeing from the
Revolution, took ship from Brittany and was obliged to
induce somnambulism on his wife in order to overcome her
horror of the sea. When the couple landed in America and
Chardel awakened his wife, she had no recollection whatever
of the Atlantic voyage, and believed herself still in Brittany.[4]

Both Helmholtz and Fechner show [5] that the functions
of the nervous system are associated with a definite time-
measure, so it follows that consciousness in an organic body
like man's depends upon the nervous system ; but, as these

[1] Haddock, *Somnolism and Psychism*, p. 213 ; cf. Du Prel, op. cit., i. 93.
[2] Perty, *Mystische Erscheinungen*, i. 305 ; cf. Du Prel, op. cit., ii. 63.
[3] Kerner, *Seherin v. Prevorst*, p. 196 ; cf. Du Prel, op. cit., ii. 65.
[4] Chardel, *Essai de Psychologie*, p. 344 ; cf. Du Prel, op. cit., ii. 64.
[5] Cf. Du Prel, op. cit., i. 88–9.

examples and similar ones in the Fairy-Faith show, certain conscious states exist independently of the human nerves, and they therefore set up a strong presumption that complete consciousness can exist independently of the physical nerve-apparatus. And in proceeding to submit this presumption of a supersensuous consciousness to the further test of science we shall at the same time be testing the statements made by wholly reliable seer-witnesses, like the Irish mystic and seer (p. 65), that not only can men and women enter Fairyland during trance-states for a brief period, but that at death they can enter it for an unlimited period. Further, what is for our study the most important of all statements will likewise be tested, namely, that in Fairyland there are conscious non-human entities like the *Sidhe* races.

PSYCHICAL RESEARCH AND FAIRIES

Our present task, then, is to extend the examination beyond incarnate consciousness into the realm of the new psychology or physical research, where, as a working hypothesis, it is assumed that there is discarnate consciousness, which by the Celtic peoples is believed to exist and to exhibit itself in various individual aspects as fairies.

As to what science demands as proof of the survival of human consciousness after death, there has been no clear consensus of opinion. To prove merely the existence of ' ghosts ' would not do ; it is necessary to show by a series of proofs (1) that discarnate intelligences exist, (2) that they possess complete and persistent personal energy wholly within themselves, (3) that they are the actual unit of consciousness and memory known to have manifested itself on this plane of existence through particular incarnate personalities now deceased. Various psychical researchers assert that they have already reached these proofs and are convinced, often in spite of their initial scientific attitude of antagonism toward all psychic phenomena, of the survival of the human consciousness after the death of the human body ; and we shall proceed to present the testimony of some of them.

In chapter vii, concerning *Phantasms of the Dead*, forming part of Frederick W. H. Myers's *Human Personality and its Survival of Bodily Death*, and in the two chapters which follow, on *Motor Automatism*, and on *Trance, Possession, and Ecstasy*, all the necessary proofs above noted have been adduced ; and the author was thereby one of the very first psychical researchers to have recorded before the world his conversion from the non-animistic hypothesis to the ancient belief that Man is immortal ; for he admits his conviction that the human consciousness does incontestably survive the decay of the physical body. Types of some of these well-attested and proved cases offered as evidence by Myers may be briefly summarized as follows :—Repeated apparitions indicating intimate acquaintance with some post-mortem fact like the place of burial ; single apparitions with knowledge of the affairs of surviving friends, or of the impending death of a survivor, or of spirits of persons dead after the apparition's decease ; cases where professed spirits manifest knowledge of their earth-life, as of some secret compact made with survivors ; cases of apparitional appearances near a corpse or a grave ; occasional cases of the appearance of the dead to several persons collectively.[1] Under motor automatism, some of the most striking phenomena tending toward proof are cases where automatic writing has announced a death unknown to the persons present; knowledge communicated in a *séance*, not known to any person present, but afterwards proved to have been possessed by the deceased ; automatic writing by a child in language unknown to her.

In chapter ix trance or possession is defined by Myers, in the same list of proofs, as ' a development of Motor Automatism resulting at last in a substitution of personality '; and this harmonizes with the theory of the control of a living organism by discarnate spirits, and is supported by an overwhelming mass of scientific experiment. Telepathy suggests the possibility of communication between the living and the living and between the living and the dead, and, we

[1] Myers, op. cit., chapter vi.

may add, between the dead and the dead—as in Fairyland— without the consideration of space or time as known in the lower ranges of mental action ; and that the communication does not depend upon vibrations from a material brain-mass. Telepathy in these first two aspects has been likewise accepted as a scientific fact by workers in psychical research like Sir William Crookes, Sir Oliver Lodge, William James, and by many others.   All such phenomena as these, now being so carefully investigated and weighed by men thoroughly trained in science, are, so to speak, the proto-plasmic background of all religions, philosophies, or systems of mystical thought yet evolved on this planet ; and in all essentials they confirm the x-quantity presented in the evidence of the Fairy-Faith.

Dr. G. F. Stout, an able representative of the school of non-converts to the theories in psychology propounded by Myers and by psychical research, states his position thus :— ' But, at least, my doubt is not dogmatic denial, and I agree with Mr. Myers that there is no sufficient reason for being peculiarly sceptical concerning communications from departed spirits.   I also agree with him that the alleged cases of such communication cannot be with any approach to probability explained away as mere instances of telepathy.' [1]   In addition, Dr. Stout says :—' The conception which has been really useful to him is that of telepathy.   Given that com-munication takes place between individual minds unmedi-ated by ordinary physical conditions, we may regard intercourse with departed spirits as a special case of the same kind of process.   And clairvoyance, precognition, &c., may perhaps be referred to telepathic communication either with departed spirits or with other intelligences superior to the human.' [1]   In this last phrase, ' intelligences superior to the human ', Dr. Stout assumes our own position, that hypo-thetically there is good reason for thinking that discarnate non-human intelligences—such as the Irish call the *Sidhe*— may exist and communicate with, or influence in some unknown way, the living, as during ' mediumship ' and in ' seership '.

[1] Stout, op. cit., pp. 64, 61-2.

Mr. Andrew Lang points out, in his reply to Dr. Stout's criticism, that the only legitimate scientific resource for overthrowing Myers's position, since the evidence is ' mathematically incapable of explanation by chance coincidence ', is to say that several people are deliberate forgers and liars. And he adds :—' To myself (but only to myself and a small circle) the evidence is irrefragable, from our lifetime knowledge of the percipient.' [1] But the animistic position does not by any means depend upon the evidence presented by Myers, no matter how incontestably reliable it is. We have only to examine the voluminous publications of the *Society for Psychical Research* (London) to realize this, and especially the *Report on the Census of Hallucinations of Modern Spiritualism*, by Professor Sidgwick's Committee (*P. S. P. R.*, London).

PSYCHICAL RESEARCH AND ANTHROPOLOGY IN RELATION TO THE FAIRY-FAITH

According to a special contribution from Mr. Andrew Lang.

Mr. Andrew Lang, who has done a special service to science by showing that psychical research is inseparably related to anthropology, has favoured us with a statement of his own position toward this relationship and has made it directly applicable to the Fairy-Faith. In a general way, but not in some important details (as indicated in our annotations) we agree with Mr. Lang's position, which he states as follows :—

Mr. Evans Wentz has asked me to define my position towards psychical research in relation to anthropology. I have done so in my book, *The Making of Religion*. The alleged abnormal or supernormal occurrences which psychical research examines are, for the most part, ' universally human,' and, whether they happen or do not happen, whether they are the results of malobservation, or of fraud, or are merely mythical, as *human* they cannot be wisely neglected by anthropology.

[1] Lang, *Mr. Myers's Theory of ' The Subliminal Self '*, in *Hibbert Journal*, ii, No. 3 (April 1904), p. 530.

The fairy-folk, under many names, in many tongues, are everywhere objects of human belief, in Central Australia, in New Zealand, in the isles of the Pacific, as in the British Isles, Lowland or Highland, Celtic in the main, or English in the main, I conceive the various beings, fairies, brownies, *Iruntarinia, Djinns*, or what you will, *to be purely mythical*. I am incapable of believing that they are actual entities, who carry off men and women ; steal and hide objects (especially as the *Iruntarinia* do) ; love or hate, persecute or kiss human beings ; practise music, vocal and instrumental ; and in short ' play the pliskies ' with which they are universally credited by the identical workings of the human fancy. They tend to shade away, on one side, into the denizens of the House of Hades—phantasms of the dead. The belief in such phantasms may be partially based on experience, whether hallucinatory or otherwise and inexplicably produced.[1]

As far as psychical research studies report of these phantasms it approaches the realm of ' the Fairy Queen Proserpine '. As far as such research examines the historical or contemporary stories of the *Poltergeist*, it touches on fairies :

[1] The peculiar and often unique characteristics of the fairy-folk of any given fairy-faith, as we have pointed out in chapter iii (pp. 233, 282), are to be regarded as being merely anthropomorphically coloured reflections of the social life or environment of the particular ethnic group who hold the particular fairy-faith ; and, as Mr. Lang here suggests, when they are stripped of these superficial characteristics, which are due to such social psychology, they become ghosts of the dead or other spiritual beings.

Our own researches lead us to the conviction that behind the purely mythical aspect of these fairy-faiths there exists a substantial substratum of real phenomena not yet satisfactorily explained by science ; that such phenomena have been in the past and are at the present time the chief source of the belief in fairies, that they are the foundation underlying all fairy mythologies. We need only refer to the following phenomena observed among Celtic and other peoples, and attributed by them to ' fairy ' or ' spirit ' agency : (1) music which competent percipients believe to be of non-human origin, and hence by the Celts called ' fairy ' music, whether this be vocal or instrumental in sound ; (2) the movement of objects without known cause ; (3) rappings and other noises called ' supernatural ' (cf. pp. 81 n., 481-4, 488 ; also pp. 47, 57, 61, 67, 71, 72, 74, 88, 94, 98, 101, 120, 124, 125, 131, 132, 134, 139, 148, 156, 172, 181, 187, 213, 218, 220, &c.).

because the Irish, for example, attribute to the agency of fairies the modern *Poltergeist* phenomena, whether these, in each case, be fraudulent or, up to now, be unexplained.

There are not more than two or three alleged visions of the traditional fairies in the annals of psychical research ; and I have met with but few sane and educated persons who profess to have seen phantoms at all resembling the traditional fairy ; while phantasms supposed to be of the dead, the dying, and the absent are frequently reported. On the whole, psychical research has very little concern with the fairy-belief in its typical forms, and if the researcher did find modern cases of fairy visions alleged by sane and educated percipients, he would be apt to explain them by suggestion acting on the subconscious self.[1]

1 MARLOES ROAD, LONDON, W.
  September 26, 1910.

---

[1] It is our hope that this book will help to lessen the marked deficiency of recorded testimony concerning ' fairy ' beings and ' fairy ' phenomena observed by reliable percipients. We have endeavoured to demonstrate that genuine ' fairy ' phenomena and genuine ' spirit ' phenomena are in most cases identical. Hence we believe that if ' spirit ' phenomena are worthy of the attention of science, equally so are ' fairy ' phenomena. The fairy-belief *in its typical* or *conventional aspects* (apart from the animism which we discovered at the base of the belief) is, as was pointed out in our anthropological examination of the evidence (pp. 281–2), due to a very complex social psychology. In this chapter we have eliminated all social psychology, as not being the essential factor in the Fairy-Faith. Therefore, from our point of view, Mr. Lang's implied explanation of the typical fairy-visions, that they are due to ' suggestion acting on the subconscious self ', does not apply to the rarer kind of fairy visions which form part of our x-quantity (see pp. 60–6, 83–4, &c.). If it does, then it also applies to all non-Celtic visions of spirits, in ancient and in modern times ; and the animistic hypothesis now accepted by most psychical researchers, namely, that discarnate intelligences exist independent of the percipient, must be set aside in favour of the non-animistic hypothesis. If, on the other hand, it be admitted that ' fairy ' phenomena are, as we maintain, essentially the same as ' spirit ' phenomena, then the belief in fairies ceases to be purely mythical, and ' fairy ' visions by a Celtic seer who is physically and psychically sound do not seem to arise from that seer's suggestion acting on his own subconsciousness ; but certain types of ' fairy ' visions undoubtedly do arise from suggestion, *coming from a ' fairy ' or other intelligence*, acting on the conscious or subconscious content of the percipient's mind (cf. pp. 484–7).

Concerning phantasms of the dead into which, as above pointed out, the fairy-folk tend to shade away, Mr. Lang has elsewhere said :—' On the whole, if the evidence is worth anything, there are real objective ghosts, and there are also telepathic hallucinations : so that the scientific attitude is to believe in both, if in either.' [1] And he shows that while anthropologists have explained all animistic beliefs as the results of primitive men's philosophizing ' on life, death, sleep, dreams, trances, shadows, the phenomena of epilepsy, and the illusions of starvation ', ' normal phenomena, psychological and psychical, might suggest most of the animistic beliefs.' [1] In *The Making of Religion*, Mr. Lang has expanded this anthropological argument so as to make it even more fully embrace psychical research.

If we apply the brilliant results of Mr. Lang's investigations to our own, it is apparent that the background of the Fairy-Faith, like that of all religions, is animistic, as we have argued in chapter iii ; that it must have grown up in ancient times into its traditional form out of a pre-Celtic followed by a pre-Christian Celtic religion ; these latter due, in turn; to actual psychical experiences, such as hallucinations, visions of different sorts, clairvoyance, ' mediumship ', and magical knowledge on the part of Druid priests and, probably, to some extent, on the part of the common people as well ; and, finally, that the living Fairy-Faith depends not so much upon ancient traditions, oral and recorded, as upon recent and contemporary psychical experiences, vouched for by many ' seers ' and other percipients among our witnesses, and now placed on record by us in chapter ii and elsewhere throughout this study.

THE PRESENT POSITION OF PSYCHICAL RESEARCH

Sir William Crookes, the well-known English authority in physical science, was almost the first scientist to become seriously interested in psychics, and in Part III of *Notes of an Enquiry into the Phenomena called Spiritual, during the Years* 1870–1873 (London), boldly affirms :—' It will be

---

[1] Lang, *Cock Lane and Common Sense*, pp. 208, 35.

seen that the facts are of the most astounding character, and seem utterly irreconcilable with all known theories of modern science. Having satisfied myself of their *truth*, it would be moral cowardice to withhold my testimony because my previous publications were ridiculed by critics and others.' And this conclusion reached forty years ago has not been reversed, but has been confirmed by one after another of learned scientists on both sides of the Atlantic.

In 1908, Sir Oliver Lodge, Principal of the University of Birmingham, and at present one of the best known of scientists concerned with the study of spiritual phenomena, stated his position thus :—' On the whole, I am of those who, though they would like to see further and still stronger and more continued proofs, are of opinion that a good case has been made out, and that as the best working hypothesis at the present time it is legitimate to grant that lucid moments of intercourse with deceased persons may in the best cases supervene. . . . The boundary between the two states —the known and the unknown—is still substantial, but it is wearing thin in places ; and like excavators engaged in boring a tunnel from opposite ends, amid the roar of water and other noises, we are beginning to hear now and again the strokes of the pickaxes of our comrades on the other side.'[1] In 1909, Sir Oliver Lodge published *The Survival of Man*, in which, after a careful exposition, covering over three hundred pages, of the definite results of much scientific experimentation by the best scientists of Europe and America, in such psychical phenomena as Telepathy or Thought Transference, Telepathy and Clairvoyance, Automatism and Lucidity, the following tentative conclusion is reached :—' The first thing we learn, perhaps the only thing we clearly learn in the first instance, is *continuity*. There is no such sudden break in the conditions of existence as may have been anticipated ; and no break at all in the continuous and conscious identity of genuine character and personality.'[1] And his personal conviction is that ' Intelli-

[1] Sir Oliver Lodge, *Psychical Research*, in *Harper's Mag.*, August 1908 (New York and London).

gent co-operation between other than embodied human
minds than our own . . . has become possible '.[1]

William James, who was one of the chief psychical
researchers in the United States, published his conclusions
in October 1909 ; and of psychical phenomena he wrote :—
' As to there being such real natural types of phenomena
ignored by orthodox science, I am not baffled at all, for I am
fully convinced of it.' Of ' mediumship ', he postulated the
very interesting theory of a universally diffused ' soul-stuff ',
which elsewhere (p. 254) we have referred to as the scientific
equivalent to the Polynesian *Mana* : ' My own dramatic
sense tends instinctively to picture the situation as an inter-
action between slumbering faculties in the automatist's mind
and a cosmic environment of *other consciousness* of some sort
which is able to work upon them. If there were in the universe a lot of diffuse soul-stuff, unable of itself to get into
consistent personal form, or to take permanent possession
of an organism, yet always craving to do so, it might get its
head into the air, parasitically, so to speak, by profiting by
weak spots in the armour of human minds, and slipping in
and stirring up there the sleeping tendencies to personate.'
Expanding this theory into a ' pan-psychic ' view of the
universe and assuming a ' mother-sea ' of consciousness,
a bank upon which we all draw, James asked these questions
about it, which educated Celtic seers ask themselves about
the *Sidhe* or Fairy-World and its also collective consciousness
or life : ' What is its own structure ? What is its inner
topography ? . . . What are the conditions of individuation
or insulation in this mother-sea ? To what tracts, to what
active systems functioning separately in it, do personalities
correspond ? Are individual " spirits " constituted there ?
How numerous, and of how many hierarchic orders may
these then be ? How permanent ? How transient ? And
how confluent with one another may they become ? '[2] We
should ask the reader to compare this scientific attitude with
the almost identical attitude taken up with respect to the

---

[1] Sir Oliver Lodge, *The Survival of Man* (London, 1909), p. 339.
[2] James, op. cit., pp. 587–9.

Sidhe Races and the constitution of their world and life by the Irish mystic and seer (pp. 60 ff.).

M. Camille Flammarion, the well-known French astro- nomer, is another of the pioneer psychical researchers ; and in his psychic studies, entitled, as translated in an English edition, *The Unknown*, recently announced these definite conclusions :—' (1) *The soul exists as a real entity independent of the body.* (2) *It is endowed with faculties still unknown to science.* (3) *It is able to act at a distance, without the inter- vention of the senses.*' And in his *Mysterious Psychic Forces* (Boston, 1907, pp. 452–3), he says :—' The conclusions of the present work concord with those of the former (*The Unknown*). . . . I may sum up the whole matter with the single statement that there exists in nature, in myriad activity, a *psychic element* the essential nature of which is still hidden from us.'

The Final Testing of the X-quantity

This chapter can now be brought to its logical conclusion by directly applying the results so far attained to our still vigorous x-quantity or residuum gathered out of the Fairy- Faith. We have, although hurriedly, blazed a rough pathway through the necessary parts of the jungle of scientific theories, and have arrived at a very considerable clearing made by the pioneers, the psychical researchers. We seem, in fact, to have arrived at a point in our long investigations where we can postulate scientifically, on the showing of the data of psychical research, the existence of such invisible intelli- gences as gods, genii, daemons, all kinds of true fairies, and disembodied men. It is not necessary to produce here, in addi- tion to what already has been set forth, the very voluminous detailed evidence of psychical research as to the existence of such intelligences. The general statement may be made that there are hundreds of carefully proven cases of pheno- mena or apparitions precisely like many of those which the Celtic peoples attribute to fairies.[1]

---

[1] Readers are referred to such authoritative works as the *Phantasms of the Living* (London, 1886), by Gurney, Myers, and Podmore ; to the

Various explanations or theories are offered by our men of science as to what these invisible intelligences are, for none of our scientists would say that the dead alone are responsible, even in a majority of cases, for the observed phenomena and apparitions, but rather such beings as we call daemons, fairies, and elementals. M. Camille Flammarion says :—' The greater part of the phenomena observed—noises, movement of tables, confusions, disturbances, raps, replies to questions asked—are really childish, puerile, vulgar, often ridiculous, and rather resemble the pranks of mischievous boys than serious bona-fide actions. It is impossible not to notice this. Why should the souls of the dead amuse themselves in this way ? The supposition seems almost absurd.' [1] There could be no better description of the pranks which house-haunting fairies like brownies and Robin Goodfellows and elementals enjoy than this ; and to suppose that the dead perform such mischievous and playful acts is, in truth, absurd. M. Flammarion also says :— ' Two inescapable hypotheses present themselves. Either it is we who produce these phenomena ' (and this is not reasonable) ' or it is spirits. But mark this well : these spirits are not necessarily the souls of the dead ; for other kinds of spiritual beings may exist, and space may be full of them without our ever knowing anything about it, except under unusual circumstances. *Do we not find in the different ancient literatures, demons, angels, gnomes, goblins, sprites, spectres, elementals, &c. ? Perhaps these legends are not without some foundation in fact.*' [1]

On ' the phenomena of percussive and allied sound '— such as fairies and the dead are said to produce—Sir William Crookes made this report :—' The intelligence governing the phenomena is sometimes manifestly below that of the medium. It is frequently in direct opposition to the wishes

Report on the Census of Hallucinations of Modern Spiritualism, by Professor Sidgwick's Committee ; to the *Naturalisation of the Supernatural* (New York and London, 1908), by F. Podmore ; to the *Survival of the Human Personality*, by F. W. H. Myers ; and other like works, all of which originate from the *Proceedings of the Society for Psychical Research* (London).

[1] C. Flammarion, *Mysterious Psychic Forces*, pp. 441, 431.

of the medium. . . . The intelligence is sometimes of such a character as to lead to the belief that it does not emanate from any person present.'[1] In the case of the ' medium ' Mr. Home, Sir William Crookes used mechanical tests and proved to his own satisfaction that physical objects moved without Mr. Home or any other person being in contact with them,[2] in the way that fairies are believed to move objects. These phenomena parallel remarkable ancient and modern examples of the same nature : e. g. in the affair at Cideville, France, brought before a magistrate, there is sworn evidence by reputable witnesses that pillows and coverlets floated away from a bed in which two children were asleep, and that furniture in the house moved without contact.[3] Mrs. Margaret Quinn, originally of Mullingar, but now of Howth, gave this remarkable testimony :—' When I was a little girl, I lived with my mother in West Meath, near Mullingar. A *fort* was at the back of our house, and mother used to hear music playing round our house all night, and she has seen *them* (the *good people*). It often happened there at home that we would have clothes out on the line and they would float off like a balloon at a time when there would not be a bit of wind and in daylight. My mother would come out and say, " God bless *them* (the *good people*). *They* will bring them back." And then the clothes would slowly come floating back to the line.' And in our chapter ii there is other testimony concerning objects moved without contact with human beings, either through the agency of fairies or of the dead. After due investigation of such and various other phenomena, Sir William Crookes, among other theories to explain them, gives this theory :—' *The actions of a separate order of beings, living on this earth, but invisible and immaterial to us. Able, however, occasionally to manifest their presence.*

---

[1] Sir Wm. Crookes, *Notes of an Enquiry into Phenomena called Spiritual*, *during the years* 1870–73 (London), Part III, p. 87.

[2] See *Quart. Journ. Science* (July 1871).

[3] Cf. Lang, *Cock Lane and Common Sense*, p. 281 ; and for other cases of objects moved without contact see ib., pp. 50, 52, 53, 58, 122 ff. See also F. Podmore's article on *Poltergeists*, in *Proceedings S.P.R.*, xii. 45–115 ; and his *Naturalisation of the Supernatural*, chapter vii.

Known in almost all countries and ages as demons (not neces-sarily bad), gnomes, fairies, kobolds, elves, goblins, Puck, &c.' [1]
Here we seem to have what ought to be, by this stage of our study, proof of the Psychological Theory of the nature and origin of the Fairy-Faith.

Let us now draw a few of the direct parallels thus suggested. Consider first how a fairy is said to appear, how it is described, and how it vanishes, and then compare the facts stated in the following case of a phantom reported by Sir William Crookes [2] :—' In the dusk of the evening ' (just the time when fairies are most easily seen) ' during a *séance* with Mr. Home at my house, the curtains of a window about eight feet from Mr. Home were seen to move. A dark, shadowy, semi-transparent form, like that of a man, was then seen by all present standing near the window, waving the curtain with his hand. As we looked, the form faded away and the curtain ceased to move.' The following—Mr. Home as in the former case being the ' medium '—is a still more striking instance :—' A phantom form came from a corner of the room, took an accordion in its hand, and then glided about the room playing the instrument. The form was visible to all present for many minutes, Mr. Home also being seen at the same time. On its coming rather close to a lady who was sitting apart from the rest of the company, she gave a slight cry, upon which it vanished.' Compare the follow-ing types of observed phenomena by the same authority with what our Welsh witness from the Pentre Evan country said about death-candles (p. 155) :—' I have seen a lumi-nous cloud floating upwards to a picture.' Or, ' I have more than once had a solid self-luminous body placed in my hand by a hand which did not belong to any person in the room. In the light I have seen a luminous cloud hover over a heliotrope on a side-table, break a sprig off, and carry the sprig to a lady ; and on some occasions I have seen a similar luminous cloud visibly condense to the form of a hand and carry small objects about.' Similar lights, parallel to the death lights or death tokens observed by Celtic percipients

---

[1] Sir Wm. Crookes, op. cit., Part III, p. 100.   [2] Ib., p. 94.

in Wales and in Brittany, and to what in Ireland are called the
'lights' of the 'good people' or 'gentry'—all of which phenomena are traceable to no material causes as yet discovered
—are reported by Iamblichus and others of his school.[1]
And such lights are among phenomena best attested by
modern psychical researchers. Supernormally produced
music, said to have been produced by daemons, which is
parallel to that called by several of our own percipients
'fairy' music, was also known to the Neo-Platonists ; [1] and
in the scientific investigations to which Mr. Home was sub-
jected, musical sounds were heard which could not be
attributed to any known agency. In haunted houses, as
psychical research discovers, the rustling of dresses, movements of objects, and sounds, often occur spontaneously
without and with the occurrence of apparitions ; [1] and these
phenomena are parallel to certain ones which we have had
cited by Celtic percipients as due to fairies. Mr. Lang, too,
has set forth clearly the probability of real ' haunts ' or
spirits possessing particular places—just as fairies are said
to possess particular localities or buildings in Celtic lands.

The Report on the Census of Hallucination by Professor
Sidgwick's Committee has furnished data sufficiently good
to convince many scientists that phantoms (comparable in
a way with Irish banshees and the Breton *Ankou*) do appear
to the living directly before a death as though announcing it.[2]

[1] Lang, *Cock Lane and Common Sense*, pp. 60, 81, 139, &c.

[2] Using as a basis the data of Professor Sidgwick's Committee and the
results earlier obtained by Gurney, Myers, and Podmore (see *Phantasms
of the Living*), Mr. William McDougall shows concisely the probability of
an apparition appearing within twelve hours of the death of the individual
whom it represents. He says :—' . . . of all recognized apparitions of living
persons, only one in 19,000 may be expected to be a death-coincidence of
this sort. But the census shows that of 1,300 recognized apparitions
of living persons 30 are death-coincidences, and that is equivalent to
440 in 19,000. Hence, of recognized hallucinations, those coincident with
death are 440 times more numerous than we should expect, if no causal
relation obtained.' And Mr. McDougall concludes : ' . . . since good
evidence of telepathic communication has been experimentally obtained,
the least improbable explanation of these death-apparitions is that the
dying person exerts upon his distant friend some telepathic influence
which generates an hallucinatory perception of himself ' (*Hallucinations*,
in *Ency. Brit.*, 11th ed., xii. 863).

According to other equally reliable data, sometimes a phantasmal voice—like certain ' fairy ' voices—has given news of a death.[1] Myers and others have studied and recorded many cases of the dead appearing, as the Celtic dead appear when they have been *taken* to Fairyland.[1]

In *Phantasms of the Living*, by Gurney, Myers, and Podmore, the explanation of apparitions which are coincident with a death as being generated by a telepathic influence exerted upon the percipient by the dying friend, suggests the most rational interpretation of certain parallel kinds of apparitions, of the dead or of fairies, who, as in these last examples, appear dressed in garments. It is that all such apparitional appearances, coincident with a death or not, are equally due to a telepathic force exerted by an agency independent of the percipient. This outside force acts as a stimulus upon the nervous apparatus of the person to whom it is thus transmitted, and causes him to project out of some part of his own consciousness (which part may have passed over into the subconsciousness) a visualized image already impressed there. The image has natural affinity or correspondence with the outside stimulus which arouses it.

Such an hypothesis curiously agrees in part with the one put forth by our seer-witness, the Irish mystic (p. 60 ff.). He would probably agree as to the visualization process in most types of ordinary apparitions. In addition, he holds that Nature herself has a memory : there is some indefinable psychic element in the earth's atmosphere upon which all human and physical actions or phenomena are photographed or impressed. These records in Nature's mind correspond to mental impressions in us. Under certain inexplicable conditions, normal persons who are not seers may observe Nature's mental records like pictures cast upon a screen— often like moving pictures. Seers can always see them if they wish ; and uncritical seers frequently mistake these phantom records or pictures existing on the psychical envelope of the planet for actual events now occurring, and

[1] Myers, op. cit., ii. 65, 45 ff., 49 ff., &c.

for actual beings—fairies of various kinds and the dead. A recent book entitled *An Adventure*, by Elizabeth Morison and Frances Lamont (pseudonyms), adequately illustrates what we mean by such phantom pictures. During the year 1901 these two cultured ladies saw at *le petit Trianon* of Marie Antoinette records in the mind of Nature of past historical events dating from about 1789. Of this there seems not to be the slightest doubt. The fairy boat-race on Lough Gur, as described by Count John de Salis (p. 80), and the procession seen on Tara Hill of fairies ' like soldiers of ancient Ireland in review ' (p. 33), probably illustrate the same kind of phenomena (cf. pp. 55–7, 68, 74, 123, 126, &c.).

But in visions by natural seers, following again the theory of our Irish seer-witness, there is present not only an outside force (as seems to be the case when ordinary apparitions are seen) but also a veridical being with a form and life of its own in a world of its own. Such a real entity is as distinct from a picture in the memory of Nature as a living person is distinct from the mental picture which his friend holds and projects as a visualized image when responding to a telepathic stimulus sent by him. The natural seer, not being obliged to see with his normal sense of vision, need not use the normal method (namely, visualization) of responding to the outside telepathic stimulus, and so does not see the ordinary apparitional ghost or fairy. He exercises ' second-sight ' or ecstatic vision, and while so doing is in the same plane of consciousness and under the same conditions of perception as the intelligence which projects upon him the stimulus inducing automatically such ' second-sight ' or ecstatic vision. Therefore, if the intelligence has a form and nature of its own, the seer and not the non-seer will perceive them in their own world while his consciousness is temporarily functioning there and out of the normal plane of mental action. In other words, in the normal plane the non-seer reacts normally upon the same stimulus upon which the seer reacts abnormally. The former percipient sees a non-real apparition, a visualized image out of his own experience ; the latter claims to see a real being. The real being exists normally under conditions which are abnormal to the non-seer, but which to the seer become normal. The visualization of the non-seer is a makeshift, a psycho-physical reaction to a purely psychical stimulus.

It is mathematically possible to conceive fourth-dimensional beings, and if they exist it would be impossible in a third-dimensional plane to see them as they really are. Hence the ordinary apparition is non-real as a form, whereas the beings, which wholly sane and reliable seers claim to see when exercising seership of the highest kind, may be as real to themselves and to the seers as human beings are to us here in this third-dimensional world when we exercise normal vision.

Concerning actual demon-possession, which among spiritualists and psychical researchers would be called spirit phenomena through ' mediums ', and which, as we have elsewhere pointed out (pp .249 ff.), offers the most rational explanation for the changeling belief and related Celtic beliefs about fairies, Dr. J. L. Nevius, in his *Demon Possession*, offers very important scientific data relating to China.   Dr. F. F. Ellinwood, who like that authority studied strange psychical phenomena in the interior districts of the Shantung Province (China) for many years, says in an introductory note to that work :—' Antecedently to any knowledge of the New Testament ' (so full of cases of demon-possession) ' the people of North China believed fully in the possession of the minds and bodies of men by evil spirits. . . .   It has always been understood that the personality of the evil spirit usurped, or for the time being supplanted, that of the unwilling victim, and acted through his organs and faculties. Physical suffering and sometimes violent paroxysms attended the presence and active influence of the spirit.'   In the face of so many cases of such phenomena observed in China by the same authorities, Dr. Ellinwood adds, as Dr. Nevius's conclusion, that ' no theory has been advanced which so well accords with the facts as the simple and unquestioning conclusion so universally held by the Christians of Shantung, viz. that evil spirits do in many instances possess or control the mind and will of human beings '. Hypnotism shows how one strong and magnetic human will can control the mind and will of its subject ; the scientific results attained by the Society for Psychical Research in its study of spiritualism show a disembodied will or intelligence controlling and using the body of a living human being ; and Dr. Nevius writes :—' Now may not demon-possession be only a different, a more advanced form of hypnotism ? ' Criminal records of Europe and America show many examples of condemned criminals who confessed in all sincerity that some invisible or outside influence led them against their better judgement to commit crime ; and very often in such examples the past lives of the condemned are so good as to set up a strong probability in favour of their belief in possession. And altogether in accord with the evidence of modern medium-ship, as well as that of mediumship among the ancients, Dr. Nevius says of Chinese demon-possession:—'When normal consciousness is restored after one of these attacks, the sub-ject is entirely ignorant of everything which has passed during that state. The most striking characteristic of those cases is that the subject evidences another personality, and the normal personality for the time being is partially or wholly dormant. The new personality presents traits of character utterly different from those which really belong to the subject in his normal state, and this change of character is, with rare exceptions, in the direction of moral obliquity and impurity. Many persons while " demon-possessed " give evidence of knowledge which cannot be accounted for in ordinary ways. . . . They sometimes converse in foreign languages of which in their normal states they are entirely ignorant. There are often heard, in connexion with " demon possessions ", rappings and noises in places where no physical cause for them can be found ; and tables, chairs, crockery, and the like are moved about without, so far as can be discerned, any application of physical force, exactly as we are told is the case among spiritualists.' [1]

---

[1] Nevius, *Demon Possession*, Introduction, pp. iv, vii ; pp. 240-2, 144-5.
In accordance with all such phenomena, psychical researchers have logically

CONCLUSION

Our investigations (and far more exhaustive ones than ours touching similar psychical phenomena) show, when applied to the residuum or x-quantity, these chief results : (1) The Materialistic and the Delusion and Imposture Theories can be dismissed as not affecting it. (2) Authorities do not agree in their opinions as to the pathological and psychological processes with which we are directly concerned ; they are quite uncertain how to explain the human brain in all its more subtle functions, or the sympathetic nervous system and nervous states generally, in relation especially to human consciousness under various abnormal but not diseased conditions of the organism ; and they do not propose any conclusions as final, but only as very weakly tentative, though some of these are in favour of a psycho-physical view of man in which there is a close approach to the present more advanced position of psychical research. (3) Psychical research has furnished proof sufficient to convince such first-class scientists as Sir William Crookes, Sir Oliver Lodge, William James, M. Camille Flammarion, and others, that states of consciousness exist in nature outside of, though probably connected with, the consciousness of incarnate called spirits manifesting themselves through the body of a living person possessing spirits. And as in the case of Chinese demon-possession, the phenomena of mediumship often result in the moral derangement, insanity, or even suicide on the part of 'mediums' who so unwisely exhibit it without special preparation or no preparation at all, and too often in complete ignorance of a possible gradual undermining of their psychic life, will-power, and even physical health. All of this seems to offer direct and certain evidence to sustain Christians and non-Christians in their condemnation of all forms of necromancy or calling up of spirits. The following statement will make our position towards mediumship of the most common kind clear :

In Druidism, for one example, disciples for training in magical sciences are said to have spent twenty years in severe study and special psychical training before deemed fit to be called Druids and thus to control daemons, ghosts, or all invisible entities capable of possessing living men and women. And even now in India and elsewhere there is reported to be still the same ancient course of severe disciplinary training for candidates seeking magical powers. But in modern Spiritualism conditions are altogether different in most cases. and 'mediums' instead of controlling with an iron will, as a magician does, spirits which become manifest in *séances*, surrender entirely their will-power and whole personality to them.

human beings, and that these intelligences can produce effects on matter and on the psychical constitution of man; and some of these scientists consider certain of such intelligences to be discarnate men and women. (4) Scientific proof has been adduced that there are genuine hallucinations—like those relating to fairies—of human-like forms, seen by single percipients, or collectively; and such collective hallucinations are incapable of being explained away, which is equally true of apparitions seen by a single percipient to move physical objects. (5) Many of the foremost psychical researchers, including those named above, accept ' mediumship ' or spirit-possession as the best working hypothesis to explain automatism. (6) In the accepted theory of telepathy we have support for assuming that, like hypnosis, it is a psychical process, and can be carried on either by two embodied spirits or human beings, or by a disembodied spirit and one still incarnate. Myers's theories, including that of the Subliminal Self, embody all the preceding ones and agree in details with them. (7) The results taken together harmonize with those attained in our study of psychical phenomena attributed by the Celtic peoples to fairies ; and, if they be accepted, older psychological and pathological theories must be thoroughly revised in many cases, or else cast aside as worthless. Finally, since we have demonstrated that the background of the Fairy-Faith, and hence the residuum or x-quantity of it, is like the background of all religious and mystical beliefs, being animistic, and like them has grown up in ancient times out of definite psychical phenomena identical in character with those now studied by science, and is kept alive by an unbroken succession of ' seers ' and percipients, we have a clear right to set up under scientific authority these tentative conclusions : (1) Fairyland exists as a supernormal state of consciousness into which men and women may enter temporarily in dreams, trances, or in various ecstatic conditions ; or for an indefinite period at death. (2) Fairies exist, because in all essentials they appear to be the same as the intelligent forces now recognized by psychical researchers, be they thus collective units of consciousness like what William James has called ' soul-stuff ', or more individual units, like veridical apparitions. (3) Our examination of living children said to have been changed by fairies shows (see pp. 250–1) (a) that many changelings are so called merely because of some bodily deformity or because of some abnormal mental or pathological characteristics capable of an ordinary rational explanation, (b) but that other changelings who exhibit a change of personality, such as is recognized by psychologists, are in many cases best explained on the Demon-Possession Theory, which is a well-established scientific hypothesis.

Therefore, since the residuum or x-quantity of the Fairy-Faith, the folk-religion of the Celtic peoples, cannot be explained away by any known scientific laws, it must for the present stand, and the Psychological Theory of the Nature and Origin of the Belief in Fairies in Celtic Countries is to be considered as hypothetically established in the eyes of Science. Hence we must cease to look upon the term *fairy* as being always a synonym for something fanciful, non-real, absurd. We must also cease to think of the Fairy-Faith as being no more than a fabric of groundless beliefs. In short, the ordinary non-Celtic mind must readjust itself to a new set of phenomena which through ignorance on its part it has been content to disregard, and to treat with ridicule and contempt as so much outworn ' superstition '.

SECTION IV
MODERN SCIENCE AND THE FAIRY-FAITH; AND CONCLUSIONS

CHAPTER XII

THE CELTIC DOCTRINE OF RE-BIRTH
AND OTHERWORLD SCIENTIFICALLY EXAMINED

' If all things which partook of life were to die, and after they were dead
remained in the form of death, and did not come to life again, all would
at last die, and nothing would be alive—what other result could there
be ? '—SOCRATES, as reported by Plato.

'The soul, if immortal, existed before our birth. What is incorruptible
must be ungenerable.'—HUME.

' If there be no reasons to suppose that we have existed before that period
at which our existence apparently commences, then there are no grounds
for supposing that we shall continue to exist after our existence has apparently ceased.'—SHELLEY.

The extension of the terms Fairy and Fairyland—The real man as an invisible
  force acting through a body-conductor—A psychical organ essential
  for memory—Pre-existence a scientific necessity—The vitalistic view
  of evolution—Old theory of heredity disproved—Embryology supports
  re-birth doctrine—Psycho-physical evolution—Memory of previous existences in subconsciousness—Examples—Dream psychology furnishes
  clearest illustrations—No post-existence without pre-existence—
  Resurrection as re-birth—The Circle of Life—The mystical corollary—
  Conclusion : the Celtic Doctrine of Re-birth and Otherworld is
  essentially scientific.

IN the esoteric Fairy-Faith, the terms Fairy and Fairyland
attain their broadest meaning. To the Celtic mystic, the
universe is divisible into two interpenetrating parts or aspects :
the visible in which we are now, and the invisible which is
Fairyland or the Otherworld ; and a fairy is an intelligent
being, either embodied as a member of the human race or
else resident in the Otherworld. The latter class includes
many distinct hierarchies and lower orders. Some, like the
highest of the Tuatha De Danann, who are the same in
character as the gods of the Greeks and Hindoos, are super-

human ; others are the souls of the dead ; while many are subhuman and have never been embodied in gross physical bodies. These last include daemons (incorrectly regarded by Christian and other theologies as being in all cases evil, and called demons) ; and other like spirits, such as those which Dr. Tylor, in *Primitive Culture*, has designated nature spirits (leprechauns, pixies, knockers, *corrigans*, *lutins*, *little folk*, elves generally, and their counterparts in all non-Celtic Fairy-Faiths), which are the elementals of mediaeval mystics.

In the preceding chapter chiefly the lower species of fairies were under consideration, but now the higher orders (including human souls embodied and disembodied), in their relation toward one another, are to be considered inde-pendently. It becomes necessary, then, to present here a view of life and death not yet scientifically orthodox.

The Celt in all ages of his long history, like the ancient Greek thinkers with whom his ancestors were contemporary, has always been inclined, unlike modern scientists, to seek an explanation for the phenomena of evolutionary life by postulating a noumenal world of causes as the background of the phenomenal world of effects. To-day, the rapid march of scientific pioneers, chiefly those in psychical research, is bringing our own cold and exact science very close to that indefinable boundary which separates the two worlds ; and for that reason alone a presentation of the Celtic theory of the causes operating to produce death and birth will be, at least by way of suggestion, of some value.

Facts of common everyday knowledge are apt to lose their significance through too great familiarity. A fact of this character is that when each child is born it must awaken into life. Often it is not known whether the newly-born babe is dead or alive until it stretches forth its arms and breathes or cries. And this phenomenon of our first awakening and entry upon the visible plane of life and conscious action seems to corroborate what the early Celt who thoughtfully observed it held to be true, and what the Celt of to-day holds to be true : that the material substance composing the body of man is merely a means of expression for life, a conductor for an unknown force which exhibits volition and individual consciousness; just as material substance in a condition called inanimate is a conductor for another unknown force called electricity, which does not exhibit any volition or consciousness. Destroy the human body, and there is no manifestation of its life force; destroy a wire, and there is no manifestation of electric light : the human body seems to be merely incidental in the history of the individual consciousness, as a wire is incidental to electric light.

But is this consciousness of man which we call life simply a phenomenon of matter non-existent without a physical means of expression, or does it—like electricity after the wire is destroyed—continue to exist in an unmanifested state when the human body is cold and motionless in death ? And in the case of a child born dead has this consciousness found some organic imperfection in the newly-constructed infant body which made its manifestation impossible ? A few thoughts to aid in answering these questions will probably suggest themselves if we briefly consider the great difference between a human body in life and a human body in death. In life, there is the highly organized, delicately adjusted, perfectly balanced human body responding to the will of an invisible power ; and it is admitted by all schools of philosophers, moralists, and scientists that this invisible power—whatever it may be—is the real man.

This invisible power, beginning its manifestation through a microscopic bit of germ-plasm, gradually builds for itself a more and more complex physical habitation, until, after the short space of nine months, it claims membership among the ranks of men. During the many years of its sojourn on our planet, it renews its habitation many times. Every atom it began with in childhood is discarded and replaced by a new one long before the age of manhood is reached, and yet upon reaching manhood the invisible power remembers what it did in a child's frame. This indicates that memory or consciousness as a psychical process does not depend essentially upon a material brain nor upon a certain grouping of ever-changing brain-substance ; for if it did, apparently it would slowly and imperceptibly undergo change as completely as the whole physical body and brain. This physiological process furnishes sufficient data to allow us to postulate that there is a psychical organ of memory behind the physical sense-consciousness, and that such an organ in itself is, at least during a human-life period, unchanging in its composition. Without such an organ, the process of memory when more fully analysed (in a way we cannot here attempt) is inexplicable.[1]

The simplest hypothesis is to conceive that organ as the one connected with the subconsciousness or super-sense-consciousness, by means of which the invisible power or rememberer is able to remember and to impress its memory upon the temporary and continually unstable physical brain. In the process of memory there must be first of all a thing to be remembered; second, a record of that thing to be remembered; and third, something to remember that thing. The thing remembered is the result of a conscious experience, the record of it the result of its impress at the time it was experienced, but the rememberer is neither.

That invisible power, which we have called the real man, animates the body, it places food in it as fuel to produce animal heat, animal vitality and force, and tries to keep it in good working order as long as possible. If the body is imperfect at birth or becomes so later, that invisible power is forced to act through it imperfectly; if the brain is diseased, there is insanity, if undeveloped, idiocy; and when the body ceases to respond either perfectly or imperfectly, the invisible power must surrender it entirely, and there is what we call death.

Now what is this invisible power or force which has entirely vanished, leaving the physical body and brain cold and motionless? Let us see if there is an answer. Chemical analysis proves that the visible parts of the body of man are merely transformed gases; but in a complete analysis of a living body such as man's there are certain elements to

---

[1] Cf. Sigmund Freud, *The Origin and Development of Psychoanalysis*, in *Amer. Journ. Psych.*, xxi, No. 2 (April 1910).

be considered which are always invisible.[1] Thus at death there is instantly a cessation of all bodily consciousness— of all willing, thinking, movement. The power which has made the body conscious, and which cannot be compared to any known form of matter, is entirely gone. But there is left in the body a moment after its departure everything which we know to be material—the animal heat, the animal magnetism, the animal vitality. When these are gone, the body is cold and stiff, and in no essential way unlike any other mass of inert matter. If heat be applied to the body, or magnetism, or vital forces, there is nothing in it to retain them any more than there would be in a stone. The real man is gone. Then the body begins to disintegrate. The law of the conservation of energy and the indestructibility of matter makes it certain that in the process of death nothing has been lost, certainly nothing material. The animal heat has gone off somewhere in the atmosphere or in some other matter ; the animal magnetism and vitality are momentarily lost sight of, but soon they will be attached to other organic beings such as plants or animals to begin a new cycle of embodiment. The physical constituents of the body will go to their appropriate places, into the air as gases, into the water as fluids, into the earth as salts and minerals, and in a short time may form the parts of a flower, or fruit, or animal. But where or what is the willing, the thinking, the remembering, the directing force which once controlled all these and held them together in unity ? Ultra-violet rays are invisible, but they show their existence through their chemical action ; similarly a soul or Ego may exist invisibly and show its existence through the vital and physical unity manifested by a living human being. As we have already seen in the preceding chapter, there are a number of the first men of science who feel that when

[1] The fact that all matter is capable of assuming a gaseous or invisible state furnishes good scientific reasons for postulating the actual existence of intelligent beings possessed of an invisible yet physical body. There may well be on and about our planet many distinct invisible organic life-forms undiscovered by zoologists. To deny such a possibility would be unscientific.

all the data of the latest scientific discoveries in the realm of psychology and of psychical research are impartially examined there is no escape from some such hypothesis as the ancient hypothesis of a soul.

If we accept the soul hypothesis, as it seems we must, and regard a soul as an indestructible unit of invisible power possessing consciousness and volition, and normally able to exist independently of a human body, then it becomes a logical and a scientific necessity to postulate its pre-existence, because as such a unit it is indestructible, in accordance with the law of the conservation of energy and indestructibility of matter. We speak here not of the ordinary soul or human personal consciousness, but of that Ego which Celtic mystics conceive as the permanent principle (though probably itself relative to some still higher power) behind the personality—which, in turn, they believe is a temporary combination wholly dependent upon the Ego. Accordingly, it is scientifically possible for such a soul as a homogeneous unit of force or conscious energy to pass from one mass of matter or physical body to another without disintegration, diminution, or loss of its own identity. It is scientifically certain, also, from experiments performed to test the power of resistance to decomposition exhibited by the force which we call life in an organic body, that such a force is capable of outwearing many physical embodiments.[1] Recent demonstrations tend to show that the heredity hypothesis cannot be held to account fully for such widely varied character or soul individuality as may be exhibited by members of one family. We must therefore account for mental, moral, and certainly psychical inequalities among our race by some other hypothesis; and no hypothesis is more scientific, more in line with known physiological and psychical processes, or more in accord with the law of evolution, than that of re-birth.

[1] Cf. *Communication adressée au Dr J. Dupré*, p. 382 of an essay on *La Métempsycose basée sur les Principes de la Biologie et du Magnétisme physiologique*, in *Le Hasard* (Paris, 1909), by P. C. Revel. Cases of regeneration among the aged are known, and these show how the subliminal life-forces try to renew the physical body when it is worn out (cf. Revel, ib., p. 372).

The theory of the mechanical transmission of acquired characteristics in a purely physical manner through the germ-plasm is no longer tenable when all the data of physiology and psychology are admitted. A vitalistic view of evolution is rapidly developing in the scientific world, and the weight of evidence is decidedly in favour of regarding all evolutionary processes, reaching from the lowest to the highest organisms, as illustrating a gradual unfolding in the sensuous world of a pre-existing psychical power through an ever-increasing complexity of specialized structures, this complexity being brought about by natural selection. Such a view is also strongly supported if not confirmed by the general scientific belief that spontaneous generation of life is and always has been impossible on our planet or on any planet : there must have been life before its physical manifestation or its physical evolution began.

We may regard this psychical power as like a vast reservoir of consciousness ever trying to force itself through matter, the walls of the reservoir. Through the microscopic body of an amoeba there has percolated a very minute drop from the reservoir. As evolution advances, the walls of the reservoir become more and more porous, and little by little the drop increases to a tiny rivulet. Through the higher animals, the tiny rivulet flows as a brook. Through man as he is, the brook flows as a deep and broad river. Throughout the completely evolved man of the far distant future, the deep and broad river will have overflowed all its banks, it will have inundated and completely overwhelmed the animal-human nature of the individual through whom it flows, as the whole volume of the vast reservoir pours itself out. The ordinary consciousness of man will then have been transmuted into the subconsciousness, of which it had always been a pale reflection. In other words, if the theory of the mechanical transmission of acquired characteristics has failed, as seems to be the case, then we must assume that there is, as the bearer of all gains made from generation to generation, some sort of psychical or vitalistic principle. This, making use of the germ-plasm merely as a physical

basis for its manifestation, begins to build up a body suited
to its further evolutionary needs.

The brilliant discoveries of Dr. Jacques Loeb and of
M. Yves Delage have demolished absolutely the old idea
that each organ and each tissue contained in embryo in the
normal egg-germ must develop in a particular and co-
ordinate way into a normal organism and after the parental
type : it is possible to make a head grow where there ought
to be feet ; and at Zürich, Standfuss, solely through changing
the temperature of his laboratory, was able to obtain from
the same species of butterfly forms which were tropical and
forms which were arctic.[1] All this helps to establish the
hypothesis, which amounts to certainty, that the conforma-
tion of a physical body, or even the kind of species to be born,
is directly determined by physical environment and not by
heredity, and that the chief factor to consider in organisms
is the life animating the body. Physical environment affects
only the physical organism ; it does not affect the invisible
and unknown life-principle resident within the physical
organism.

The process of fertilization is a physical process. As such
it is simply initiatory to embryonic evolution which also is
physical. Once the proper physical conditions are set up by
the parents, life pursues its marvellous progress in the womb
of the human mother, from the amoeba-like initial embryo
to man. That is to say, parents set in motion the laws
governing the reproduction of physical bodies. They create
such conditions as enable the invisible life-force to begin its
physical manifestation.[2] In the two fused germs from the

[1] Cf. Revel, op. cit., p. 295 ff.

[2] If scientists discover, as they probably will in time, what they call
the secret of life, they will not have discovered the secret of life at all.
What they will have discovered will be the physical conditions under which
life manifests itself. In other words, science will most likely soon be able
to set up artificially in a laboratory such physical conditions as exist in
nature naturally, and by means of which life is able to manifest itself
through matter. Life will still be as great a mystery as it is to-day ; though
short-sighted materialists are certain to announce to an eager world that
the final problem of the universe has been solved and that life is merely
the resultant of a subtle chemical compound.

parents resides the physical inheritance of the offspring, to be outwardly shaped by environment ; but the physical inheritance is a thing distinct from the psychical part of the living being, just as much as the dead human body is a thing apart from the life which has left it. Though the old heredity theory is overthrown by late discoveries, the question as to what life is in human bodies under all possible environmental conditions remains unsolved ; and so do the questions why there should be sports in nature, which among man are called geniuses, and why every human being has a distinct and highly developed individual character, essentially unlike that of his immediate ancestors.

Embryology proves conclusively that the human embryo retraces in its growth the evolution of lower life-forms. At first consisting of two single cells fused into one, it is like the amoeba. By cell-division it grows and progresses step by step through each lower realm of being until it comes to be a water-creature with gills ; and science teaches that all organic life on this planet once dwelt in the seas. It grows progressively out of the water-world stage of organic life into the world of air-breathing creatures. Nature at last achieves her highest product, and a human being is born out of the Womb of Time. The initial microscopic bit of germ-plasm is endowed with power of motion, thought, and human consciousness, with dominion over all the lower kingdoms through which by right of ancient conquests it passed in the brief period of nine months. On every side the problem of life is full of poetry and wonder ; it is the greatest mystery.

Not only can we thus study the age-long evolution of the physical man, but we have recently acquired sufficient scientific data to lay foundations for a study of the evolution of the psychical man. Thus, for example, instincts seem to be nothing more than habits which through unknown periods of time have become so ingrained in the constitution of man, and of all animals, that now they have become second nature and usually are exercised without the need of reasoning processes. The influence from innate sensuous experiences rises into consciousness as the life of every normal child and youth unfolds itself; and these experiences in their full expansion, when the age of maturity has been reached, constitute in their unity what we call character, which, in one sense, may be defined as the sum total of instincts of every kind. From such a point of view, the psychical or invisible power in man is merely a bundle of acquired habits which make use of the bodily organism in order to express themselves—in the same way, as we have pointed out, that electrical forces manifest their presence through a conductor. If these habits be good, we call their possessor a good man; if evil, we call him an evil man.

The theory of Charles Darwin suggests that all evolutionary progress is directed to the acquirement of newer and ever higher instincts. And if this process be the true one, that is to say, if all instincts, which in their finer distinctions mark off species from species in all animal kingdoms, be as Darwin thought—and as is to-day more clearly evident—the result of a long and gradual evolution through experience in a sensuous realm of existence, then it would seem to follow that there must be some kind of a monad (probably a non-sensuous one) to which such acquired instincts can attach themselves. Such a monad, too, must have been a percipient and hence a recorder of such ever-accumulating experiences throughout an inconceivably long chain of lives, and it of itself must, while so perceiving and recording, not be subject to the transitoriness of the sensuous realm wherein it gathers together these instincts, which in their unified expression form its personality or human character.

In harmony with the vitalistic view of evolution, which implies a pre-existent psychical power continually striving to express itself completely through matter, yet normally able to exist independently of a physical means of expression, we should regard such high mental processes as judgement, reasoning, analysis and synthesis, and spatial perception, along with memory, as resultants of very great experience in a sensuous world, on which in our present psycho-physical constitution such processes appear to have direct bearing. In other words, for man to be able to exercise such high mental processes there is need to postulate incalculable ages of specialization in the nervous apparatus, and in psycho-physical adjustment, of a kind which has thus enabled the psychical power to express itself to such a supreme degree in the realm of mind and matter. The same vitalistic argu-ment is applicable to the lower mental processes and to the instinctual powers in man, because we cannot at any time, in viewing the complete evolution of man as a twofold being composed of a physical and a psychical part, force aside Fechner's conviction that the problem is a psycho-physical one. A study of sexual instincts in children seems to confirm this.[1]

Such a psychical and vitalistic hypothesis is, as we have seen, strongly supported by embryology; and embryology proves conclusively the need of long ages of physical evolu-tion for the development of each tissue and highly specialized organ in the human body. Certain French and German and other scientists of the vitalistic school have demonstrated physiologically the need of a pre-existent power as the unifying principle which attracts and compels material atoms to group themselves into the pattern of the human body [2]— or, as we may add, of any organic body. Psychical researchers at the outset of their science seem apparently to have demonstrated psychologically the post-existence of the personal consciousness-unity; and it is very likely when further progress has been made in psychics that there will arise a logical need to postulate, in addition to the personal consciousness-unity, a hypothetical pre-existent soul-monad as the unifying principle which attracts and compels psy-chical atoms of experience (if such an expression may be

[1] Professor Freud, after long and careful study, arrived at the following conclusion :—'The child has his sexual impulse and activities from the beginning, he brings them with him into the world, and from these the so-called normal sexuality of adults emerges by a significant development through manifold stages.' And Dr. Sanford Bell, in an earlier writing entitled *A Preliminary Study of the Emotions of Love between the Sexes* (see *Amer. Journ. Psych.*, 1902), came to a similar conclusion (cf. Freud, op. cit., pp. 207–8).

[2] Cf. Hans Driesch, *The Science and Philosophy of the Organism* (London, 1908); and Henri Bergson, *L'Évolution créatrice* (Paris, 1908).

used) to group themselves into the personal consciousness-unity which appears to survive the death of the gross physical body—for a long or short time, as future research may show.[1] Such a soul-monad, to follow the view held by Celtic mystics, led by acquired instincts which were transmitted to it through the personality (held by the Celtic esoteric doctrine to be a temporary combination), apparently weaves out of matter the body-unit adapted to its further evolution, in a way analogous to that in which a silkworm is led by acquired instincts to weave a cocoon. This body-unit is twofold : (1) the visible body derived from the visible elements of matter ; and (2) the invisible or ghost-body derived from the invisible or ethereal elements of matter.

Strictly speaking, for the Celtic mystic this soul-monad is something upon which the personal consciousness depends for its psychical unity in precisely the same way as the physical body depends upon the personal consciousness for its physical unity. The Celtic mystic holds that just as the body-unity falls back again into its primal elements of matter, so the personal consciousness-unity (apparently able to survive in the ghost-body for a long period after its separation from the grosser physical envelope or human body) also in due time is discarded by the soul-monad or individuality, and then falls back into its primal psychical constituents. In other words, the Celtic Esoteric Doctrine of Re-birth correctly interpreted does not conceive personal immortality,

[1] This Celtic view of non-personal immortality completely fits in with all the voluminous data of psychical research : after forty years of scientific research into psychics there are no proofs yet adduced that the human personality as a self-sufficient unit of consciousness survives indefinitely the death of its body. Granted that it does survive as a ghost for an undetermined period, generally to be counted in years, during which time it seems to be gradually fading out or disintegrating, there is no reliable evidence anywhere to show that a personality *as such* has manifested through a ' medium ' or otherwise after an interval of one thousand years, or even of five hundred years. We have, in fact, no knowledge of the survival of a human personality one hundred years after, and probably there are no good examples of such a survival twenty-five years after the death of the body. Such an eminent psychical researcher as William James recognized this drift of the data of psychics, and when he died he held the conviction that there is no personal immortality (see p. 505 n. following).

but it conceives a greater kind of immortality—the immortality of the unknown principle which gives unity to each temporary personality it makes use of, and which we prefer to designate as the individuality, the impersonator. And this individuality is the bearer of all evolutionary gains made in each temporary personality through which it reflects itself : it is the permanent evolving principle.

Perhaps an analogy drawn from nature will make the Celtic position clearer : we may say that the personality occupies a position between the human body and the soul-monad, just as the moon occupies a position between the earth and the sun. Personal consciousness is to the human body what the moonlight is to the earth, merely a pale reflection from a third thing, the soul-monad or individuality, which is the ultimate source of both sets of unities, the material or body-unity in its twofold aspect and the psychical or personal consciousness-unity. Each personality is temporary, while the individuality, like the sun in relation to the earth and moon, is capable of at least a relative immortality : the sun's light, as science holds, existed before there was any moon to reflect it on to the earth, and may continue to exist when both the moon and earth are disintegrated. The essential nature of the sun's energy or life remains unknown to science ; so does the essential nature of the energy or life manifesting itself as the individuality. Though all such analogies are more or less weak, this one adequately fits in with the theories concerning the Celtic Esoteric Doctrine of Re-birth which the most learned of contemporary Celts, chiefly mystics, have favoured us with ; and it is our rare privilege to put these theories on record for whatever they may be worth. The best hypothesis is always the one which best explains all available data, and, to our mind, when very minutely examined, in a way which (chiefly for reasons of space) cannot be attempted here, this Celtic hypothesis concerning the nature and destiny of man is the best hitherto adduced.[1]

---

[1] Though not inclined toward the vitalistic view of human evolution, M. Th. Ribot very closely approaches the Celtic view of the Ego (or

Objectors to the Re-birth Doctrine as held by the Celts and other peoples anciently and now, naturally ask why, if

individuality) as being the principle which gives unity to different personalities, but he does not have in mind personalities in the sense implied by the Celtic Esoteric Doctrine of Re-birth :—' The Ego subjectively considered consists of a sum of conscious states' (comparable to personalities). . . . ' In brief, the Ego may be considered in two ways : either in its actual form, and then it is the sum of existing conscious states ; or, in its continuity with the past, and then it is formed by the memory according to the process outlined above. It would seem, according to this view, that the identity of the Ego depended entirely upon the memory. But such a conception is only partial. Beneath the unstable compound phenomenon in all its protean phases of growth, degeneration, and reproduction, there is a something that remains : and this something is the undefined consciousness, the product of all the vital processes, constituting bodily perception and what is expressed in one word—the *cœnæsthesis.*' (*The Diseases of Memory,* pp. 107–8).

William James, the greatest psychologist of our epoch, after a long and faithful life consecrated to the search after a true understanding of human consciousness, finally arrived at substantially the same conviction as Fechner did, that there is no personal immortality, but that the personality ' is but a temporary and partial separation and circumscription of a part of a larger whole, into which it is reabsorbed at death ' (W. McDougall, *In Memory of William James,* in *Proc. S. P. R.,* Part LXII, vol. xxv, p. 28). He thus virtually accepted the mystic's view that the personality after the death of the body is absorbed into a higher power, which, to our mind, is comparable with the Ego conceived as the unifying principle behind personalities. In one of his last writings, James explained his belief in such a manner as to make it coincide at certain points with the view held by modern Celtic mystics which has been presented above ; the difference being that, unlike these mystics, James was not prepared to say (though he raised the question) whether or not behind the 'mother-sea' of consciousness there is, as Fechner believed, a hierarchy of consciousnesses (themselves subordinate to still higher consciousnesses, and comparable with so many Egos or Individualities) which send out emanations as temporary human personalities. The organic psychical forms (if we may use such an expression) of such temporary human personalities would have to be regarded from James's point of view as being built up out of the psychical elements constituting the ' mother-sea ' of consciousness, just as the human body is built up out of the physical elements in the realm of matter :— ' Out of my experience, such as it is (and it is limited enough) one fixed conclusion dogmatically emerges, and that is this, that we with our lives are like islands in the sea, or like trees in the forest. The maple and the pine may whisper to each other with their leaves, and Conanicut and Newport hear each other's foghorns. But the trees also commingle their roots in the darkness underground, and the islands also hang together through the ocean's bottom. Just so there is a continuum of cosmic consciousness, against which our individuality ' (used as synonymous with personality and not in our distinct sense) ' builds but accidental fences, and into which

we have lived before here on earth in physical bodies, we do not remember it. But the shallowness and unscientific nature of this question is at once apparent to psychologists who know that there exists in man a subconscious mind which in the great mass of people is almost totally dormant. ' The subconscious self,' wrote William James, ' is nowadays a well-accredited psychological entity. . . . Apart from all religious considerations, there is actually and literally more life in our total soul than we are at any time aware of.' And he added :—' It thus is " scientific " to interpret all otherwise unaccountable invasive alternations of consciousness as results of the tension of subliminal memories reaching a bursting point.' [1] Intuition, which all men have experienced, would seem to be the result of a momentary contact by the physical brain with its psychical counterpart—the subconscious self, the individuality as distinguished from the personality.

Certain observed psychological processes in ordinary men and women, who never really know that they have a subconsciousness or Transcendental Self, prove that it exists even for them, and any part of man which exists and functions of itself can be developed so as to be consciously perceived. This is incontestable. Let us point out a few of these observed and recorded psychological processes. There may be an unsolved problem in the mind, or inability to recall a certain name or fact, and then a sudden, unex-

our several minds plunge as into a mother-sea or reservoir. Our " normal " consciousness ' (the personality as we distinguish it from the Ego or individuality) ' is circumscribed for adaptation to our external earthly environment, but the fence is weak in spots, and fitful influences from beyond break in, showing the otherwise unverifiable common connexion. Not only psychic research, but metaphysical philosophy and speculative biology are led in their own ways to look with favour on some such " panpsychic " view of the universe as this.' (W. James, *The Confidences of a Psychical Researcher*, in *The American Magazine*, October 1909). Again, James wrote :—' The drift of all the evidence we have seems to me to sweep us very strongly towards the belief in some form of superhuman life with which we may, unknown to ourselves, be co-conscious.' (*A Pluralistic Universe*, New York, 1909, p. 309.)

W. James, *Varieties of Religious Experience* (London, 1902), pp. 511, 236 n.

pected intuitional solving of the problem and an instantaneous recollecting of the desired facts, at a time when the ordinary mind may be entirely absorbed in altogether foreign thoughts. Again, many persons through accident or disease have lost their memory to such an extent as to require complete re-education, and then in time, gradually or instantaneously, as the case may be, have completely recovered it.[1] And we noticed in our study of supernatural lapse of time (p. 469) that at the moment of accidental loss of consciousness, as in drowning for example, all forgotten details of life are instantaneously reproduced in a complete panorama. These psychological processes support what we have said above with respect to a psychical organ being behind the sense-consciousness, and seem thus to prove that the subconscious mind is the place for recording permanently all experiences.[2] Under hypnosis, a subject may be requested to perform a certain act, let us say 11,999 minutes after the moment of making the request. When the hypnotic condition is removed, the subject has no personal consciousness of the suggestion, but, as different experiments have proved conclusively, he invariably performs the act exactly at the expiration of the 11,999 minutes without knowing why he does so. This proves that there is a subconsciousness in man which can take full cognizance of such a suggestion, which can keep count of the passing of time and then cause the unconscious personality to act in response to its will.[3] Again, in extreme old age people who have come to have an imperfect memory or none at all in their normal consciousness, under abnormal conditions (which seemingly are due to a temporary influx of a latent psychical power into the physical body and brain, or else to an awakening of a dormant force within the physical body and brain themselves) often regain, for a time, complete and clear memory of their childhood. This proves that the memory is somewhere still

[1] M. Th. Ribot, in *Diseases of Memory* (London, 1882), pp. 82–98 ff., gives numerous examples of such loss and recovery of memory.

[2] Cf. Freud, op. cit., pp. 192, 204–5, &c.

[3] Cf. A. Moll, *Hypnotism* (London, 1890), pp. 141 ff., 126.

perfect, and that it does not reside in the consciousness of the age-exhausted physical brain and memory. Albert Moll, in his treatise on hypnotism, says that events in the normal life which have dropped out of memory can be remembered in hypnosis :—' An English officer in Africa was hypnotized by Hansen, and suddenly began to speak a strange language. This turned out to be Welsh, which he had learnt as a child, but had forgotten.' [1] And even memory of acts done in hypnotic somnambulism can be awakened in the normal state.[2] Furthermore, through psycho-analysis, as Professor Freud has shown, forgotten dreams and dreams which were never complete in the ordinary consciousness can be recovered in their entirety out of the subconsciousness.[3] How many of us can recall without some mental stimulus certain acts performed ten years ago ? A good deal of our present life is no longer vivid, much of it is forgotten, and in old age many of the memories of youth and of mature life will be subconscious. If this brain, whose total existence is comprised between birth and death, cannot remember in a normal way all its own experiences, how could it be expected to know anything at all of hypothetical past lives where there were various physical brains long ago disintegrated—unless the hypothetically ever-existing transcendental individuality, whose consciousness is the subconsciousness, be made by some unusual psychical stimuli to transmit its memory of the past lives to each new brain it creates ? In other words, to have memory of pre-existent conditions there must be continuity of association with present conditions. If such continuity exists, it exists in the subconsciousness. And if it exists therein, then in order to recall in the present personal or ordinary consciousness, which began at birth, memory of an anterior state of consciousness, it would be necessary to hold impressed upon the present physical brain and body a clear and unremittent consciousness of the sub-

---

[1] Cf. A. Moll, *Hypnotism* (London, 1890), pp. 141 ff., 126.

Cf. Freud, op. cit., p. 192.

[3] Freud, *Die Traumdeutung*, 2nd ed. (Vienna, 1906) ; cf. S. Ferenczi, *The Psychological Analysis of Dreams*, in *Amer. Journ. Psych.* (April 1910), xxi, No. 2, p. 326.

consciousness. In relation to our personal consciousness, apparently our greatest powers lie in the subconsciousness which is sleeping and in embryo, awaiting to be born into the consciousness of this world through the slow process of evolutionary gestation. In the case of a Buddha, who on good historical authority is said to have been able to recall all past existences from the lowest to the highest, this evolutionary process seems to have reached completion.[1]

Under ordinary conditions, individuals have been known to see a place which they have never seen before, or to do a thing which they have never done before in this life nor in any conscious dream-state, and yet feel that they have seen the place before and done the thing before. M. Th. Ribot, in his *Diseases of Memory* (chapter iv), has brought together many cases of this kind. Some are undoubtedly explicable as forgotten experiences of the present life. Others, to our mind, strongly support the theory of pre-existent experiences preserved in memory in the subconsciousness.

Under chloroform, or other anaesthetics, patients often recover for the time being forgotten facts of experience, and sometimes appear to make momentary contact with their subconsciousness and to exhibit therein another personality. In certain well-defined types of double personality, which are not the kind due to demon-possession nor to spirit-possession as in 'mediumship', there are two memories, 'each complete and absolutely independent of the other.'[2] And in similar cases, where the subject exhibits alternately numerous personalities, we see the individuality, that is to say the subconscious man, exhibiting, as a dramatist might, various characters or personalities of probable past existences

---

[1] A similar state of high development is to be assumed for a great Celtic hero like Arthur, who were he to be re-born would (as is said to have been the case with King Mongan, the reincarnation of Finn) bring with him memory of his past: unlike the consciousness of the normal man, the consciousness of one of the Divine Ones is normally the subconsciousness, the consciousness of the individuality; and not the personal consciousness, which, like the personality, is non-permanent *in itself*. This further illustrates the Celtic theory of non-personal immortality.

[2] Ribot, op. cit., p. 100 ff.

according as each is most active at the moment. Similarly, crystal-gazing sometimes seems not only to revive lost memories of this life, but also to call up subconscious memories of some unknown state of consciousness which may be from a previous life.[1]

M. Ribot has made it clear from his careful study of numerous cases of amnesia (loss of memory) that ' recollections return in an inverse order to that in which they disappear '. For example, a celebrated Russian astronomer lost all memory save that of his childhood, and in recovering it there appeared first the recollections of youth, then those of middle age, then the experiences of later years, and, finally, the most recent events. Many even more marked examples of the law of regression in amnesia are given by M. Ribot. We conclude from them that all strange and apparently long-forgotten facts of experience arising in consciousness out of the subconsciousness, as in the different cases which have been cited above, would necessarily be those which have been the longest lost to memory; and hence if they cannot be attached to this present life then they can only be derived from a former life, because every primary detail of memory must always originate from an experience at some past period

---

[1] Cf. Lang, *Cock Lane and Common Sense*, pp. 217 ff. *Blackwood's Magazine*, cxxix (January 1881), contains a remarkable account of a child who remembered previous lives. Lord Lindsay, in his *Letters* (ed. of 1847, p. 351), refers to a feeling when he beheld the river Kadisha descending from Lebanon, of having in a previous life seen the same scene. Dickens in his *Pictures from Italy* testifies to a parallel experience. E. D. Walker, in his interesting work on *Reincarnation* (pp. 42–5) has brought together many other well-attested cases of people who likewise have thought they could remember fragments of a former state of conscious existence. In his diary, under date of February 17, 1828, Sir Walter Scott wrote as follows :—
' I cannot, I am sure, tell if it is worth marking down, that yesterday, at dinner-time, I was strangely haunted by what I would call the sense of pre-existence, viz. a confused idea that nothing then passed was said for the first time.' Lockhart, *Life of Scott* (first ed.), vii. 114. Bulwer Lytton in *Godolphin* (chapter xv), and Edgar Allen Poe in *Eureka*, record similar experiences. Mr. H. Fielding Hall, in *The Soul of a People* [4] (London, 1902), pp. 290–308, reports several very remarkable cases of responsible natives of Burma who stated that they could recall former lives passed by them as men and women. Mr. Hall has carefully investigated these cases, and gives us the impression that they are worthy of scientific consideration.

of time. M. Ribot himself, in his conclusion to *The Diseases of Memory*, makes this significant observation with respect to the law of regression in amnesia :—' This law of regression provides us with an explanation for extraordinary revivification of certain recollections when the mind turns backward to conditions of existence that had apparently disappeared for ever.'

In dreams there is a great wealth of latent memory ; sometimes memory of the present waking life, but often not capable, apparently, of being attached to it, nor explicable as due to the soul wandering from the body during sleep : the hypothesis of re-birth seems to be the only adequate one here. Certain dreams suggest that man possesses innate memories extending backwards to prehistoric times (cf. p. 5 above). This fits in with Professor Freud's theory in his *Die Traumdeutung*, that ' the dream is nothing else than the concealed fulfilment of a repressed wish.' Some dreams are ' in the form of frightful, cruel, horrible scenes, which seem frightful to us, but in a certain depth of the unconscious satisfy wishes which, in the " prehistoric " ages of our own mental development, were actually recognized as desires.'[1] This also supports our vitalistic view of the evolution of human instincts. Again, in somnambulism there is a much more exalted memory, and clear cases are on record of facts being then consciously present which cannot be accounted for save through the same hypothesis.[2]

If we keep in mind the psychology of the dream state, we

---

[1] Cf. Ferenczi, op. cit., p. 316, &c. Professor Freud's theory of dreams supports entirely, but does not imply our hypothesis that some (and probably many) abnormal dreams of a rare kind, whether good or bad in tendency, may be due to the latent content of subconsciousness, out of which they undoubtedly arise, having been collected and carried over from a previous state of consciousness parallel to our present one. In respect to our present life Professor Freud holds, as a result of psycho-analysis of thousands of dream subjects, that the latent content of every dream in the adult is directly dependent upon mental processes which frequently reach back to the earliest childhood ; and he gives detailed cases in illustration. In other words, there is always a latent dream-material behind the conscious dream-content, and probably a part of it was innate in the child at birth, and hence, according to our view, was pre-existent. (Cf. Ernest Jones, *Freud's Theory of Dreams*, in *Amer. Journ. Psych.*, April 1910, xxi, No. 2, pp. 301 ff.)

[2] Cf. Du Prel, *Philosophy of Mysticism*, ii. 25 ff., 34 ff.

shall probably get the clearest intellectual theory as to why, if pre-existence be true, we do not remember various previous states of existence. In our present state of consciousness we may enter a dream state, in that dream state by dreaming we enter a second dream state, and theoretically, though not by common experience, there may be no limit to super-imposed dream states, each one in itself a state of consciousness distinct from the waking consciousness. Accordingly, if, as Wordsworth put it, ' our birth is but a sleep and a forgetting ' of another state of consciousness, and death the abrupt ending of that sleep of dreams and a waking up, or if the direct opposite be true, and death is the entrance to a sleep and dream state of consciousness, it becomes very clear how difficult it would be for us here now either to recall what we may have dreamt or have actually done in another state of conscious existence corresponding to our present one. The subtle thinkers of modern India, who completely accept the doctrine of re-birth as a universal law, have summed up this abstruse aspect of the dream psychology as follows :—
' The first or spiritual state was ecstasy ; from ecstasy it (the Ego) forgot itself into deep sleep ; from deep sleep it awoke out of unconsciousness, but still within itself, into the internal world of dreams ; from dreaming it passed finally into the thoroughly waking state, and the outer world of sense.' [1] But our own psychologists are not yet far enough advanced to accept this ; much more work in psychical research must first be done before it will be possible for them to announce to the West that pre-existence is a necessary condition for post-existence which they now hypothetically accept. If for the present our standpoint be that of our own psycho-logists, we may then think of the human consciousness as a spectrum whose central parts alone are visible to us. Beyond at either end lies an unseen and to us unknown region, awaiting its explorer from the West. ' Each one of us is in reality an abiding psychical entity far more extensive than he knows—an individuality which can never express itself completely through any corporeal manifestation. The

The Dream of Ravan, in *Dublin Univ. Mag.,* xliii. 468.

Self manifests through the organism ; but there is always some part of the Self unmanifested ; and always, as it seems, some power of organic expression in abeyance or reserve.'[1] William James stated the position thus :—' The B. region ' (another name for the region of subconsciousness), ' then; is obviously the larger part of each of us, for it is the abode of everything that is latent, and the reservoir of everything that passes unrecorded and unobserved.'[2]

Men of science see no way of accepting the doctrine of the resurrection of the physical body as at present interpreted by Christian theology ; but the late Professor Th. Henri Martin, Dean of the Faculty of Letters of the University of Rennes, has suggested in his *La Vie future* that the doctrine may be the exoteric interpretation of a long-forgotten esoteric truth ; namely, that the soul may be resurrected in a new physical body, and this is scientifically possible.[3]

The ancient scientists called Life a Circle. In the upper half of this Circle, or here on the visible plane, we know that in the physiological history of man and of all living things there

[1] Myers, in *Proc. S. P. R.*, vii. 305.

[2] James, *Varieties of Religious Experience*, p. 483.

[3] The esoteric teaching in many of the mystic schools of antiquity was that the atoms of each human body transmigrate through all lower forms of life during the long period supposed to intervene between death and re-birth of the individuality. This doctrine seems to be one of the main sources of the corruption which crept into the ancient re-birth doctrines and transformed many of them into doctrines of transmigration of the human soul into animal and plant bodies ; and some unscrupulous priest-hoods openly taught such corrupted doctrines as a means of making the ignorant populace submissive to ecclesiastical rule, the theological theory expounded by such priesthoods being that the evil-doer, but not the keeper of the letter of the canonical law, is condemned to expiate his sins through birth in brute bodies. The pure form of the mystic doctrine was that after the lapse of the long period of disembodiment the individuality reconstructs its human body anew by drawing to itself the identical atoms which constituted its previous human body—these atoms, and not the individuality, having transmigrated through all the lower kingdoms. Such an esoteric doctrine probably lies behind the exoteric Egyptian teaching that the human soul after the death of its body passes through all plant and animal bodies during a period of three thousand years, after which it returns to human embodiment. Some scholars have held that the exoteric interpretation of this theory and its consequent literal interpretation as a transmigration doctrine led the Egyptians to mummify the bodies of their dead. Cf. Lucretius, *De Rerum Natura*, Book III, ll. 843–61 ; and Herodotus, Book II, on Egypt.

is first the embryonic or prenatal state, then birth; and as life, like a sun, rises in its new-born power toward the zenith, there is childhood, youth, and maturity; and then, as it passes the zenith on its way to the horizon, there is decline, old age, and, finally, death ; and as a scientific possibility we have in the lower half of the Circle, in Hades or the Otherworld of the Celts and of all peoples, corresponding processes between death and a hypothetical but logically necessary re-birth.[1]

The logical corollary to the re-birth doctrine, and an integral part of the Celtic esoteric theory of evolution, is that there have been human races like the present human race who in past aeons of time have evolved completely out of the human plane of conscious existence into the divine plane of conscious existence. Hence the gods are beings which once were men, and the actual race of men will in time become gods. Man now stands related to the divine and invisible world in precisely the same manner that the brute stands related to the human race. To the gods, man is a being in a lower kingdom of evolution. According to the complete Celtic belief, the gods can and do enter the human world for the specific purposes of teaching men how to advance most rapidly toward the higher kingdom. In other words, all the Great Teachers, e. g. Jesus, Buddha, Zoroaster, and many others, in different ages and among various races, whose teachings are extant, are, according to a belief yet held by educated and mystical Celts, divine beings who in inconceivably past ages were men but who are now gods, able at will to incarnate into our world, in order to emphasize the need which exists in nature, by virtue of the working of evolutionary laws (to which they themselves are still subject), for man to look forward, and so strive to reach divinity rather than to look backward in evolution and thereby fall into mere animalism. The stating of this mystical corollary makes the exposition of the Fairy-Faith complete, at least in outline.

[1] Cf. Dr. L. S. Fugairon's *La Survivance de l'âme, ou la Mort et la Renaissance chez les êtres vivants ; études de physiologie et d'embryologie philosophiques* (Paris, 1907) ; cf. Revel, *Le Hasard*, p. 457.

As shown by the Barddas MSS. in our chapter vii, the Celtic Doctrine of Re-birth is the scientific extension of Darwin's law as corrected,[1] that alone through traversing the Circle of Life man reaches that destined perfection which natural analogies, life's processes as exhibited by living things, and evolution, suggest, and from which at present man is so far removed. There seems to emerge this postulate : the world is the object of normal consciousness, the Ego or Soul-Monad the object of subconsciousness ; and the subconsciousness cannot be realized in the world until through the normal consciousness of man the Ego is able to function completely, and so endow man with full self-consciousness in matter, which endowment seems to be the goal of all planetary evolution.

We conclude that the Otherworld of the Celts and their Doctrine of Re-birth accord thoroughly in their essentials with modern science ; and, accordingly, with other essential elements in the complete Celtic Fairy-Faith which we have in the preceding chapter found to be equally scientific, establish our Psychological Theory of the Nature and Origin of that Fairy-Faith upon a logical and solid foundation ; and we now submit this study to the judgement of our readers. With more complete evidence in the future, both from folk-lore and from science, there will be, we trust, a better vindication of the Theory, and perhaps finally there will come about its transformation into what it but seems to us to be now—a Fact.

Some beliefs which a century ago were regarded as absurdities are now regarded as fundamentally scientific. In the same way, what in this generation is heretical alike to the Christian theologian and to the man of science may in coming generations be accepted as orthodox.

[1] Darwin never considered or attempted to suggest what it is that of itself really evolves, for it cannot be the physical body which only *grows* from immaturity to maturity and then dissolves. Darwin thus overlooked the essential factor in his whole doctrine ; while the Druids and other ancients, wiser than we have been willing to admit, seem not only to have anticipated Darwin by thousands of years, but also to have quite surpassed him in setting up their doctrine of re-birth, which explains both the physical and psychical evolution of man.

INDEX

A CATALOG OF SELECTED DOVER
BOOKS IN ALL FIELDS OF INTEREST

100 BEST-LOVED POEMS, Edited by Philip Smith. "The Passionate Shepherd to His Love," "Shall I compare thee to a summer's day?" "Death, be not proud," "The Raven," "The Road Not Taken," plus works by Blake, Wordsworth, Byron, Shelley, Keats, many others. 96pp. 5 3/16 x 8 1/4.   0-486-28553-7

100 SMALL HOUSES OF THE THIRTIES, Brown-Blodgett Company. Exterior photographs and floor plans for 100 charming structures. Illustrations of models accompanied by descriptions of interiors, color schemes, closet space, and other amenities. 200 illustrations. 112pp. 8 3/8 x 11.   0-486-44131-8

1000 TURN-OF-THE-CENTURY HOUSES: With Illustrations and Floor Plans, Herbert C. Chivers. Reproduced from a rare edition, this showcase of homes ranges from cottages and bungalows to sprawling mansions. Each house is meticulously illustrated and accompanied by complete floor plans. 256pp. 9 3/8 x 12 1/4.

0-486-45596-3

101 GREAT AMERICAN POEMS, Edited by The American Poetry & Literacy Project. Rich treasury of verse from the 19th and 20th centuries includes works by Edgar Allan Poe, Robert Frost, Walt Whitman, Langston Hughes, Emily Dickinson, T. S. Eliot, other notables. 96pp. 5 3/16 x 8 1/4.   0-486-40158-8

101 GREAT SAMURAI PRINTS, Utagawa Kuniyoshi. Kuniyoshi was a master of the warrior woodblock print — and these 18th-century illustrations represent the pinnacle of his craft. Full-color portraits of renowned Japanese samurais pulse with movement, passion, and remarkably fine detail. 112pp. 8 3/8 x 11.   0-486-46523-3

ABC OF BALLET, Janet Grosser. Clearly worded, abundantly illustrated little guide defines basic ballet-related terms: arabesque, battement, pas de chat, relevé, sissonne, many others. Pronunciation guide included. Excellent primer. 48pp. 4 3/16 x 5 3/4.

0-486-40871-X

ACCESSORIES OF DRESS: An Illustrated Encyclopedia, Katherine Lester and Bess Viola Oerke. Illustrations of hats, veils, wigs, cravats, shawls, shoes, gloves, and other accessories enhance an engaging commentary that reveals the humor and charm of the many-sided story of accessorized apparel. 644 figures and 59 plates. 608pp. 6 1/8 x 9 1/4.

0-486-43378-1

ADVENTURES OF HUCKLEBERRY FINN, Mark Twain. Join Huck and Jim as their boyhood adventures along the Mississippi River lead them into a world of excitement, danger, and self-discovery. Humorous narrative, lyrical descriptions of the Mississippi valley, and memorable characters. 224pp. 5 3/16 x 8 1/4.   0-486-28061-6

ALICE STARMORE'S BOOK OF FAIR ISLE KNITTING, Alice Starmore. A noted designer from the region of Scotland's Fair Isle explores the history and techniques of this distinctive, stranded-color knitting style and provides copious illustrated instructions for 14 original knitwear designs. 208pp. 8 3/8 x 10 7/8.   0-486-47218-3

Browse over 9,000 books at www.doverpublications.com

ALICE'S ADVENTURES IN WONDERLAND, Lewis Carroll. Beloved classic about a little girl lost in a topsy-turvy land and her encounters with the White Rabbit, March Hare, Mad Hatter, Cheshire Cat, and other delightfully improbable characters. 42 illustrations by Sir John Tenniel. 96pp. 5³⁄₁₆ x 8¼.   0-486-27543-4

AMERICA'S LIGHTHOUSES: An Illustrated History, Francis Ross Holland. Profusely illustrated fact-filled survey of American lighthouses since 1716. Over 200 stations — East, Gulf, and West coasts, Great Lakes, Hawaii, Alaska, Puerto Rico, the Virgin Islands, and the Mississippi and St. Lawrence Rivers. 240pp. 8 x 10¾.
    0-486-25576-X

AN ENCYCLOPEDIA OF THE VIOLIN, Alberto Bachmann. Translated by Frederick H. Martens. Introduction by Eugene Ysaye. First published in 1925, this renowned reference remains unsurpassed as a source of essential information, from construction and evolution to repertoire and technique. Includes a glossary and 73 illustrations. 496pp. 6½ x 9¼.   0-486-46618-3

ANIMALS: 1,419 Copyright-Free Illustrations of Mammals, Birds, Fish, Insects, etc., Selected by Jim Harter. Selected for its visual impact and ease of use, this outstanding collection of wood engravings presents over 1,000 species of animals in extremely lifelike poses. Includes mammals, birds, reptiles, amphibians, fish, insects, and other invertebrates. 284pp. 9 x 12.   0-486-23766-4

THE ANNALS, Tacitus. Translated by Alfred John Church and William Jackson Brodribb. This vital chronicle of Imperial Rome, written by the era's great historian, spans A.D. 14-68 and paints incisive psychological portraits of major figures, from Tiberius to Nero. 416pp. 5³⁄₁₆ x 8¼.   0-486-45236-0

ANTIGONE, Sophocles. Filled with passionate speeches and sensitive probing of moral and philosophical issues, this powerful and often-performed Greek drama reveals the grim fate that befalls the children of Oedipus. Footnotes. 64pp. 5³⁄₁₆ x 8 ¼.   0-486-27804-2

ART DECO DECORATIVE PATTERNS IN FULL COLOR, Christian Stoll. Reprinted from a rare 1910 portfolio, 160 sensuous and exotic images depict a breathtaking array of florals, geometrics, and abstracts — all elegant in their stark simplicity. 64pp. 8⅜ x 11.   0-486-44862-2

THE ARTHUR RACKHAM TREASURY: 86 Full-Color Illustrations, Arthur Rackham. Selected and Edited by Jeff A. Menges. A stunning treasury of 86 full-page plates span the famed English artist's career, from *Rip Van Winkle* (1905) to masterworks such as *Undine, A Midsummer Night's Dream,* and *Wind in the Willows* (1939). 96pp. 8⅜ x 11.
    0-486-44685-9

THE AUTHENTIC GILBERT & SULLIVAN SONGBOOK, W. S. Gilbert and A. S. Sullivan. The most comprehensive collection available, this songbook includes selections from every one of Gilbert and Sullivan's light operas. Ninety-two numbers are presented uncut and unedited, and in their original keys. 410pp. 9 x 12.
    0-486-23482-7

THE AWAKENING, Kate Chopin. First published in 1899, this controversial novel of a New Orleans wife's search for love outside a stifling marriage shocked readers. Today, it remains a first-rate narrative with superb characterization. New introductory Note. 128pp. 5³⁄₁₆ x 8¼.   0-486-27786-0

BASIC DRAWING, Louis Priscilla. Beginning with perspective, this commonsense manual progresses to the figure in movement, light and shade, anatomy, drapery, composition, trees and landscape, and outdoor sketching. Black-and-white illustrations throughout. 128pp. 8⅜ x 11.   0-486-45815-6

Browse over 9,000 books at www.doverpublications.com

THE BATTLES THAT CHANGED HISTORY, Fletcher Pratt. Historian profiles 16 crucial conflicts, ancient to modern, that changed the course of Western civilization. Gripping accounts of battles led by Alexander the Great, Joan of Arc, Ulysses S. Grant, other commanders. 27 maps. 352pp. 5⅜ x 8½.   0-486-41129-X.

BEETHOVEN'S LETTERS, Ludwig van Beethoven. Edited by Dr. A. C. Kalischer. Features 457 letters to fellow musicians, friends, greats, patrons, and literary men. Reveals musical thoughts, quirks of personality, insights, and daily events. Includes 15 plates. 410pp. 5⅜ x 8½.   0-486-22769-3

BERNICE BOBS HER HAIR AND OTHER STORIES, F. Scott Fitzgerald. This brilliant anthology includes 6 of Fitzgerald's most popular stories: "The Diamond as Big as the Ritz," the title tale, "The Offshore Pirate," "The Ice Palace," "The Jelly Bean," and "May Day." 176pp. 5⅜ x 8½.   0-486-47049-0

BESLER'S BOOK OF FLOWERS AND PLANTS: 73 Full-Color Plates from Hortus Eystettensis, 1613, Basilius Besler. Here is a selection of magnificent plates from the *Hortus Eystettensis*, which vividly illustrated and identified the plants, flowers, and trees that thrived in the legendary German garden at Eichstätt. 80pp. 8⅜ x 11.
0-486-46005-3

THE BOOK OF KELLS, Edited by Blanche Cirker. Painstakingly reproduced from a rare facsimile edition, this volume contains full-page decorations, portraits, illustrations, plus a sampling of textual leaves with exquisite calligraphy and ornamentation. 32 full-color illustrations. 32pp. 9⅜ x 12¼.   0-486-24345-1

THE BOOK OF THE CROSSBOW: With an Additional Section on Catapults and Other Siege Engines, Ralph Payne-Gallwey. Fascinating study traces history and use of crossbow as military and sporting weapon, from Middle Ages to modern times. Also covers related weapons: balistas, catapults, Turkish bows, more. Over 240 illustrations. 400pp. 7¼ x 10⅛.   0-486-28720-3

THE BUNGALOW BOOK: Floor Plans and Photos of 112 Houses, 1910, Henry L. Wilson. Here are 112 of the most popular and economic blueprints of the early 20th century — plus an illustration or photograph of each completed house. A wonderful time capsule that still offers a wealth of valuable insights. 160pp. 8⅜ x 11.
0-486-45104-6

THE CALL OF THE WILD, Jack London. A classic novel of adventure, drawn from London's own experiences as a Klondike adventurer, relating the story of a heroic dog caught in the brutal life of the Alaska Gold Rush. Note. 64pp. 5³⁄₁₆ x 8¼.
0-486-26472-6

CANDIDE, Voltaire. Edited by Francois-Marie Arouet. One of the world's great satires since its first publication in 1759. Witty, caustic skewering of romance, science, philosophy, religion, government — nearly all human ideals and institutions. 112pp. 5³⁄₁₆ x 8¼.   0-486-26689-3

CELEBRATED IN THEIR TIME: Photographic Portraits from the George Grantham Bain Collection, Edited by Amy Pastan. With an Introduction by Michael Carlebach. Remarkable portrait gallery features 112 rare images of Albert Einstein, Charlie Chaplin, the Wright Brothers, Henry Ford, and other luminaries from the worlds of politics, art, entertainment, and industry. 128pp. 8⅜ x 11.   0-486-46754-6

CHARIOTS FOR APOLLO: The NASA History of Manned Lunar Spacecraft to 1969, Courtney G. Brooks, James M. Grimwood, and Loyd S. Swenson, Jr. This illustrated history by a trio of experts is the definitive reference on the Apollo spacecraft and lunar modules. It traces the vehicles' design, development, and operation in space. More than 100 photographs and illustrations. 576pp. 6¾ x 9¼. 0-486-46756-2

THE METAMORPHOSIS AND OTHER STORIES, Franz Kafka. Excellent new English translations of title story (considered by many critics Kafka's most perfect work), plus "The Judgment," "In the Penal Colony," "A Country Doctor," and "A Report to an Academy." Note. 96pp. 5³⁄₁₆ x 8¼. 0-486-29030-1

MICROSCOPIC ART FORMS FROM THE PLANT WORLD, R. Anheisser. From undulating curves to complex geometrics, a world of fascinating images abound in this classic, illustrated survey of microscopic plants. Features 400 detailed illustrations of nature's minute but magnificent handiwork. The accompanying CD-ROM includes all of the images in the book. 128pp. 9 x 9. 0-486-46013-4

A MIDSUMMER NIGHT'S DREAM, William Shakespeare. Among the most popular of Shakespeare's comedies, this enchanting play humorously celebrates the vagaries of love as it focuses upon the intertwined romances of several pairs of lovers. Explanatory footnotes. 80pp. 5³⁄₁₆ x 8¼. 0-486-27067-X

THE MONEY CHANGERS, Upton Sinclair. Originally published in 1908, this cautionary novel from the author of *The Jungle* explores corruption within the American system as a group of power brokers joins forces for personal gain, triggering a crash on Wall Street. 192pp. 5⅜ x 8½. 0-486-46917-4

THE MOST POPULAR HOMES OF THE TWENTIES, William A. Radford. With a New Introduction by Daniel D. Reiff. Based on a rare 1925 catalog, this architectural showcase features floor plans, construction details, and photos of 26 homes, plus articles on entrances, porches, garages, and more. 250 illustrations, 21 color plates. 176pp. 8⅜ x 11. 0-486-47028-8

MY 66 YEARS IN THE BIG LEAGUES, Connie Mack. With a New Introduction by Rich Westcott. A Founding Father of modern baseball, Mack holds the record for most wins — and losses — by a major league manager. Enhanced by 70 photographs, his warmhearted autobiography is populated by many legends of the game. 288pp. 5⅜ x 8½. 0-486-47184-5

NARRATIVE OF THE LIFE OF FREDERICK DOUGLASS, Frederick Douglass. Douglass's graphic depictions of slavery, harrowing escape to freedom, and life as a newspaper editor, eloquent orator, and impassioned abolitionist. 96pp. 5³⁄₁₆ x 8¼. 0-486-28499-9

THE NIGHTLESS CITY: Geisha and Courtesan Life in Old Tokyo, J. E. de Becker. This unsurpassed study from 100 years ago ventured into Tokyo's red-light district to survey geisha and courtesan life and offer meticulous descriptions of training, dress, social hierarchy, and erotic practices. 49 black-and-white illustrations; 2 maps. 496pp. 5⅜ x 8½. 0-486-45563-7

THE ODYSSEY, Homer. Excellent prose translation of ancient epic recounts adventures of the homeward-bound Odysseus. Fantastic cast of gods, giants, cannibals, sirens, other supernatural creatures — true classic of Western literature. 256pp. 5³⁄₁₆ x 8¼. 0-486-40654-7

OEDIPUS REX, Sophocles. Landmark of Western drama concerns the catastrophe that ensues when King Oedipus discovers he has inadvertently killed his father and married his mother. Masterly construction, dramatic irony. Explanatory footnotes. 64pp. 5³⁄₁₆ x 8¼. 0-486-26877-2

ONCE UPON A TIME: The Way America Was, Eric Sloane. Nostalgic text and drawings brim with gentle philosophies and descriptions of how we used to live — self-sufficiently — on the land, in homes, and among the things built by hand. 44 line illustrations. 64pp. 8⅜ x 11. 0-486-44411-2